W9-BAX-824

UNDERSTANDING POPULATION CHANGE

CHARLES B. NAM
Florida State University

F.E. Peacock Publishers, Inc.
Itasca, Illinois

Library of Congress Catalog Card No. 93-71269
ISBN 0-87581-377-1
Printed in the United States of America
Printing: 10 9 8 7 6 5 4 3 2 1
Year: 98 97 96 95 94

Contents

PART TWO

Dynamics of Population Change 127

Figures

Tables

Preface

Teaching never came easy to me. In my childhood years, I was regarded as quiet and shy and a better listener than a speaker. Those characteristics stayed with me as I moved through secondary school, Army life, and college. When I entered the world of full-time work, becoming a federal civil service employee suited me just fine. It did not require me to speak often, yet I could accomplish things in other ways. But the work of a government bureaucrat did not satisfy me intellectually. I preferred a research career that would allow me to advance my own ideas, and that led me to become a professor in a university. Being a professor meant that I could do my own research, but it also meant teaching students.

With no real preparation for teaching and my "quiet and shy" reputation, I became a teacher under fire. For nearly three decades now, my teaching has probably improved modestly; but I am still not entirely comfortable in the classroom. My voice is not a pleasing one, anxiety and nervousness accompany me to every class, and I still lack the showmanship flair that marks a first-rate instructor.

However, many years ago I realized that "teaching" does not necessarily involve face-to-face contact. That was when becoming a textbook writer first appealed to me. *Population and Society; A Textbook of Readings* (Houghton Mifflin, 1968)—a collection of the writings of others edited by me with substantial chapter introductions—was my first effort. Those chapter introductions were later expanded into a full textbook called *Population: The Dynamics of Demographic Change* (Houghton Mifflin, 1976), co-authored with a former student, Susan O. Gustavus. A subsequent version of that book, *Population: A Basic Orientation* (Prentice-Hall, 1984) was produced by me and my co-author, then and now Susan G. Philliber. I also wrote *Our Population: The Changing Face of America* (Walker, 1988) as part of a Think Series for secondary school students.

The present book is intended to be my last attempt to teach through writing. Although I have taken on the task alone, a number of people have contributed to it in various ways. I am indebted to Ted Peacock for encouraging me to undertake the book and letting me try a somewhat different approach to presenting the study of population change. Richard G. Rogers, Avery Guest, Robert H. Freymeyer, and Marjorie Tallant Nam read the manuscript and offered suggestions for modification, most of which I gratefully accepted.

In addition, useful ideas were given to me by my former students, Louis G. Pol and Robert A. Hummer. I am especially grateful to my editor, Bob Cunningham, who took what I thought was a reasonably good text and used his editorial pencil to make the language flow more smoothly and to give the book a great deal more polish. I wish also to acknowledge the fine design of Jeanne Calabrese as well as the skillful work of the production editor, Kim Vander Steen. For better or worse, however, I must assume the prime responsibility for what you will read within these covers.

Most of you who make your way through this volume will never have met me. The course in which this book is being used will have an instructor who adds to the contents and interprets what I have written. Yet if this book has any impact on you at all, if you feel as though you have learned from it, you might think of me as one of your teachers whose voice was heard through the written page, and I will think of you as my students.

Charles B. Nam

Introduction

There are some things in life that are relatively invisible and whose influence is so subtle that we hardly notice their effects, except perhaps in retrospect. For example, we may not notice that our fingernails have been growing until we scratch someone else or ourselves, or one of the nails gets broken. Or, while we are aware that we are part of a family, we may not be very sensitive to the reality that the family can provide social, economic, and emotional support until a crisis emerges. It is usually at times of crisis that we become aware of the fact that such potential support has existed all the time. If we need someone to talk to about a problem, or need a helping hand with regard to money, or maybe need a shoulder to cry on or someone to embrace, more often than not the person we turn to is a family member.

Population change falls into the category of such somewhat invisible and often subtle processes that go on continuously. But we only pay attention to them when they visibly impact the world we live in. Moreover, the impacts occur at so many levels of our experience and in so many forms that we frequently are not very conscious of them.

Understanding population change means becoming aware of all of the means through which demographic shifts take place and learning about their determinants and consequences. These demographic shifts involve births and deaths and changes of residence, urban and rural transformations, as well as changing population characteristics, such as getting older and marrying or divorcing.

Becoming aware of population change does not mean concentrating on population dynamics through every waking minute, but it does mean sensitizing ourselves to the ways in which the various population processes take place. It also involves understanding how these processes assume different forms under varying circumstances, so that we can be conscious of, and deal with, them when the occasion arises.

When we think about this matter, we discover that population change is indeed quite pervasive. In its myriad forms, it has global, national, regional, community, organizational, associational, household, familial, and individual repercussions. It touches us in all contexts and at all times. It is our phantom social force, generally not conspicuous in its influence but there nevertheless.

At the global level, demographic changes result in higher or lower population densities on the Earth, demands made on natural resources, challenges to the natural environment, pretexts for war, grounds for overtures to peace, evolving needs for food and other forms of sustenance, modified governmental forms and relationships, new monetary and fiscal policies, and many other consequences.

Within nations, because of population changes, frontiers are opened and closed, businesses and industries are established or relocated, social services are provided, transportation networks are extended to various parts of the country, urban centers become focal points for entertainment activities, and transformations in small towns take place.

Because of demographic shifts, states and communities expand or consolidate school systems, attract commercial centers, provide housing for the elderly or the young or working-age couples, reinforce their planning agencies, upgrade traffic patterns, build civic centers, further bureaucratize their governments, and engage in numerous other actions, all in response to population movements that affect the numbers, locations, and characteristics of the residents (and often the visitors).

Organizations and associations respond to population changes by estimating their target groups, assessing their personnel needs, marketing their products or services, strategically locating their offices, and establishing linkages with other groups having related interests.

Because of population dynamics, households and families adapt to the changing community environment, alter their life cycles, modify their daily time schedules, take account of their new kinship relations, and adjust to consumption expectations.

Individuals are not immune to demographic forces. They take account of population change in planning for their own children, guarding their health, and seeking a satisfying locale in which to live, as well as experiencing phases of their personal lives that are new, such as having great-grandchildren or great-grandparents or living without a spouse or alone.

Because population change is so pervasive, understanding it means examining it in great detail and in its many contexts. But doing this does not mean that the subject is inevitably a boring one, enmeshed in voluminous statistics, plastered with charts and graphs, and discussed using extensive technical jargon that is hard to decipher. On the contrary, although statistics, graphs and charts, and technical terms will find their way into our presentation as it does in those of other population specialists, we will basically offer you a narrative.

Talking about great details and many contexts means that we have numerous stories to tell. They are concerned with eons of time as well as yesterday, today, and tomorrow. They deal with rich nations and poor ones. They encompass people in all walks of life. They include tragedies and successes. They involve things that are known, as well as imponderables.

These stories about population change are like those we hear about and read about on many different subjects in our daily lives. In fact, while this book attempts to integrate and attach further meaning to these stories, you will recognize many of them as stories with which you are already familiar. Maybe you had forgotten them or you knew about them but did not realize their significance at the time. Some of them were passed down from earlier generations or told to you by friends; some you heard about on the radio, records, or audiocassettes; still others you saw in other books, magazines, and newspapers, or on television.

In this book, the stories are embedded in the continuing saga of time-immemorial, worldwide population change. Let us tell you about the settings, the plots, and the cast of characters, as we present them in this volume.

The complete tale of this book has four parts. Part One is concerned with Fundamentals of Population Change. Here we tell about what makes populations get larger or smaller, how populations have changed over history, the ways in which people have thought about population over the centuries, and what it takes to acquire population information. In Part Two, the plot thickens as we discover the contributions of births, deaths, and residential movements to population change. More important, we identify why some people live longer than others, why some couples have more babies than other couples, and why moving to other places is more likely for some persons than others. Not least of all, we show how these factors are related to where we find concentrations of people and where there are relatively few, as well as how old or young is the population. Part Three then addresses the issue of what this all means for the way we live—what constitutes our families and our households, our educational statuses and opportunities, our work and economic welfare, how we are governed, and our religious activities—what sociologists call our social institutional behavior. Finally, in Part Four we look at the matter of *who* influences population change and *how* those influences take place. These concerns get to the core of debates around the world on whether it is advisable to intervene in hastening or slowing population change, and through what mechanisms these processes should operate.

What can we say about the benefits to you once you have finished the saga presented here? Well, a few of you might actually decide to go on to study this subject area further, by continuing to higher levels of education or by seeking employment in an organization that deals with population matters. That would be fine because it is a topic that needs more attention and there is a demand for persons with that kind of background. But most of you will not be headed in that direction. If you fall into this latter category, however, this book should open vistas for you by giving you greater insight into the dynamics of population change that will help you to attach meaning to other events and processes that happen in your life, that will enable you to inform others about knowledge that you possess that they do not have but should have, and that will permit you to understand better some of the things to which you are exposed through the printed or broadcast media—what you read in newspapers, magazines, or books; what you see on television or in the movies, and hear about on radio or from speakers. It is unlikely that this book will radically change your life, but it may broaden it in ways that make it somewhat more satisfying. If that is the case, then our mission is accomplished.

PART ONE
Fundamentals of Population Change

To write or tell a tale, there should be some sort of structure that holds the tale together. It is akin to examining the human body. It is difficult to imagine bodily organs, flesh, skin, and hair as a totality without also recognizing that a skeleton exists that is the foundation for them.

The skeleton for our tale includes a number of parts that we consider fundamentals of population change. That is, before we can delve into the full aspects of our subject, we must discuss the basic points about population change that give us a firm orientation to the proper way of interpreting our findings.

In this part of the book, the fundamentals of population change incorporate four chapters dealing with the nature of population change itself; the forms of population change, which we label *transitions* and *cycles;* some critical theoretical and conceptual population perspectives that help us form a view of *how* to think about population change and its elements; and a primer about population knowledge and population data.

In the first of these chapters, we introduce basic concepts about population trends and their dynamics and give historical illustrations. We search for the early development of populations and get some notion of how fast or slow they have been growing over time, and even how large (or small) they might eventually get. The chapter also reflects on population change from different viewpoints—what we call the *macro* and *micro* views. How different the Earth appears when we look at it from our backyards, or from the top of a tall building, or from a commercial airliner, or from a rocket in space! Our ideas about population change can also vary, depending on different perspectives.

The second chapter is concerned with the patterns of change in population. How have trends appeared over the long course of history? Have they differed from one country to another? Have they varied from one part of a country to another? Do the basic components of population change—mortality, fertility, and mobility—affect population change in fixed ways, or are their effects modified under different circumstances? Are short-term effects similar to long-term effects? The answers to these questions let us understand what determines the pace of population change.

The third of the chapters allows us to step back from the more factual aspects of population change to contemplate how the great thinkers of the past and present perceive the subject. We meet philosophers and scientists and politicians, people who were highly regarded by many but criticized by others. Involved are simple ideas and complex ones. We try to show that ideas of the distant past sometimes retain their validity but that modern thinkers are leading us to frame our thinking about population change in ways that will undoubtedly result in more substantial gains in knowledge and understanding.

The fourth chapter covers the nature of the demographic knowledge we have gained so far (the specific parts of it to be elaborated on later in the book). Of particular importance in this chapter is learning (a) *where* we obtain our population information (some sources may surprise you), (b) the relative *accuracy* of the information gathered, and (c) how to be cautious about accepting population *measures* that we read about. Even good data can be transformed into misleading indicators of a population phenomenon. For example, if the country's rate of unemployment is reported to have dropped two-tenths of a percent from one month to the next, is that a sign of an improving work force situation? The answer may be yes or it may be no, depending on additional information.

By the time you finish this first part of the book, you should be exceptionally well prepared to hear the stories about the dynamics of population change and get more out of them. That is, you will be a little bit more sophisticated about the subject and feel more confident about your ability to master it. You may even challenge your friends in a game of population facts or in a profound discussion of the role of population change in world history.

1. The Nature of Population Change

Before we can talk about population change, we need to be sure that we comprehend the basic concept itself. When we say "population," we mean *human population.* There are populations of spiders, camels, bluejays, and even inanimate objects, but we are not concerned with them here. Our focus is on human populations.

But if we go back to the early epochs of time, we have some trouble deciding what species should be regarded as "human." If you believe that Adam was the first human, that would be a starting point for counting people. If you accept the discoveries of archaeologists, paleontologists, and cultural anthropologists, you might argue that some form of human being began to evolve several million years ago. If you consider the evidence of some who have compared fossil findings with genetic evaluation of DNA in ancient remains, you may reach the conclusion that the modern form of humans (what are called *Homo sapiens*) emerged no more than 100,000 or so years ago (Stringer, 1990). It would then follow that we should date population change from that time. Of course, that is not an easy task because there were not any official census takers a hundred thousand years ago and records about people for a long time afterward were very spotty and unreliable. But we do have some indications about how many humans were living in prehistory.

Let us think, however, about still another dimension of populations, namely, that they can be seen as static or dynamic. In reality, populations are always dynamic, always changing. Since you started reading this paragraph, babies were being born, people were dying, and some folks were moving into new residences in all parts of the world.

When we take a census or a survey, we capture a population at a point in time. By the time a census or survey is complete, the information is already outdated. That does not mean it is no longer useful. On the contrary, we can then report what the static demographic situation was at that particular time.

The analogy can be made to a snapshot versus a movie. A photograph of you shows what you looked like when the picture was taken. By the time the photo was developed, you were already older. Maybe some of your features even changed, if you were in an auto accident and were injured or if you subsequently dyed your hair a different color. Years later, you can tell someone that this was the way you looked when you were x years old or just before your auto accident. We do the same in population studies. We might say that this was what the population was like just before the war took place or before the birth rate zoomed up. The dynamic aspect enters when we look at a time series of censuses or surveys or have a continuous population registration.

Another matter we have to think about is that a population is made up of individual people and, as a population changes, its size may increase, decrease, or remain the same. So we can talk about the population of Thailand, for instance, and think of it as getting larger over a twenty-year time period by a certain number of additional people being there; whereas, the fact is that there will be many more different people in the population at the beginning and end of the period because some people were added to the population and some were subtracted from it, but there was a net gain of people. It has to do with the population dynamics generated by the *basic components of population change*. We might say that people come and people go but populations remain.

POPULATION GROWTH, STABILITY, AND DECLINE

The mass media keep us informed about overall population change. Most of us know that the world's population has passed the 5 billion mark and will reach 6 billion before the end of this century. And we have a sense that a long way back in time there were very few people on Earth, and that the number continued to grow until it reached the point where it is now.

In fact, there is still some controversy about the early pattern of population change. We can present a better picture of it for the last few hundred years than for the several hundred years before that and certainly than for tens of thousands or hundreds of thousands or millions of years ago.

Some demographers (e.g., Durand, 1967) have portrayed population in the long sweep of history (at least since 8000 B.C.) as growing linearly until a few centuries ago. That is, they saw population as always gaining in size, sometimes slowly and sometimes more rapidly but always increasing in approximately a straight line. Others (United Nations, 1973) have determined that "the secular trend of man's increase ... was interrupted by periods of decline and at other times quickened its pace." Deevey (1960) used archaeological evidence to estimate three different surges of population growth that were linked, respectively, with the revolution that brought toolmaking perhaps hundreds of thousands of years ago, the agricultural revolution that began about ten thousand years ago, and the Industrial Revolution that started in about the eighteenth century. In the first instance, hunting and gathering provided a basis for populations spreading to new lands. In the second instance, the development of crops in specific locations was coupled with construction of more permanent habitats that protected people from environmental hazards. In the third instance, growing national economies gave an opportunity for some countries to improve levels of living and increase survival prospects.

FIGURE 1.1 World Population Growth through History

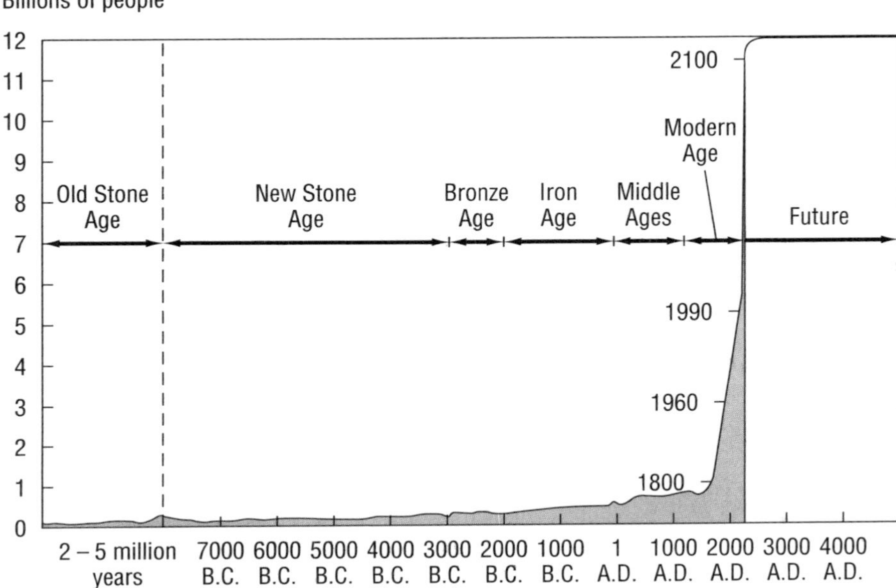

Source: Joseph A. McFalls, Jr. 1991. "Population: A Lively Introduction." *Population Bulletin* 46:2, 32.

It would be anyone's guess as to how many humans roamed the Earth hundreds or tens of thousands of years ago. We might speculate that, by about 4000 B.C., the number of people on the globe may well have reached 80 or so million. At the time of the birth of Christ, it is believed that the figure stood between 270 and 330 million. By 1500 A.D., probably 440 to 540 million people dotted the sphere and the pace of demographic growth was augmented (Nam and Philliber, 1984).

We can say with some assurance that the world's population took all of human history up to the beginning of the nineteenth century to reach 1 billion (see Figure 1.1), and that it hit 2 billion only 130 years later (about 1930), 3 billion only thirty years after that (about 1960), 4 billion only fifteen years beyond then (about 1975), and 5 billion in just twelve more years (about 1987). That signifies that the last couple of centuries were marked by especially rapid population growth, and that what many call the world's *population explosion* has been most evident in "our time" (since World War II).

Since demographers think that they now know enough about patterns of population change to say what will happen to it from now on, they predict that its rate of growth will slow down progressively and that it will stabilize at less than 13 billion sometime more than a hundred years from now (World Bank, 1990).

TABLE 1.1 Trends in Average Annual Rate of Population Increase for the World and Major Areas: 1750–1800 to 1950–1981

AREA	YEAR 1750–1800	1800–1850	1850–1900	1900–1950	1950–1981
WORLD TOTAL	0.4	0.5	0.5	0.8	1.9
ASIA (Exclusive of former U.S.S.R.)	0.5	0.5	0.3	0.8	2.0
China (mainland)	1.0	0.6	0.0	0.5	1.8
India, Bangladesh, and Pakistan	0.1	0.3	0.4	0.8	2.2
Japan	0.0	0.1	0.7	1.3	1.1
Indonesia	0.2	1.2	1.2	1.2	2.1
Remainder of Asia (Exclusive of former U.S.S.R.)	0.1	0.5	0.7	1.3	2.5
AFRICA	0.0	0.1	0.4	1.0	2.5
North Africa	0.2	0.5	1.2	1.4	2.5
Remainder of Africa	0.0	0.0	0.2	0.9	2.6
EUROPE (Exclusive of former U.S.S.R.)	0.4	0.6	0.7	0.6	0.7
FORMER U.S.S.R.	0.6	0.6	1.1	0.6	1.3
AMERICA	1.1	1.5	1.8	1.5	2.0
North America	2.5	2.7	2.3	1.4	1.4
Middle and South America	0.8	0.9	1.3	1.6	2.6
OCEANIA	0.0	0.0	0.0	1.6	1.8

Source: John Durand. "The Modern Expansion of World Population." *Proceedings of the American Philosophical Society*, Philadelphia, June 1967, p. 137; and data derived from Population Reference Bureau, *1981 World Population Data Sheet.*

Many parts of the world did not experience the Industrial Revolution, which took place largely in Europe, so that the time when the different regions and nations accelerated their population growth occurred at varying points in history. Table 1.1 presents data on rates of population growth from 1750 to 1981 that demonstrate that pattern. The world's growth rate reached a peak after 1950. Europe's most rapid growth occurred before 1750. (Reliable data for other parts of the world are not available for that period; hence the table begins with 1750). Since then, the rate of increase for Europe has been moderate to low. For North America, a substantial increase probably began before 1750 but was sustained at high levels until the late nineteenth century. Japan seemed to have peaked in the early twentieth century, whereas the rest of Asia

TABLE 1.2 Population Growth Rates for the World, Continents, and Selected Countries: 1985–1990

(The five-year population growth rate is the increase in population during a year divided by the population at the beginning of the year, averaged over the five years, and multiplied by 100.)

Region/Country	Rate	Region/Country	Rate
WORLD TOTAL	1.7		
ASIA	1.9	AFRICA	3.0
Japan	0.4	South Africa	2.2
China	1.4	Egypt	2.4
Israel	1.7	Ethiopia	2.7
Indonesia	1.9	Ghana	3.1
India	2.1	Nigeria	3.3
Bangladesh	2.7	Uganda	3.7
Iraq	3.5	Libya	3.7
Saudi Arabia	4.0	EUROPE	0.2
LATIN AMERICA	2.1	Hungary	0.2
Cuba	1.0	Italy	0.0
Jamaica	1.2	Sweden	0.2
Haiti	2.0	United Kingdom	0.2
Colombia	2.0	France	0.3
Brazil	2.1	FORMER U.S.S.R.	0.8
Mexico	2.2	NORTH AMERICA	0.8
Costa Rica	2.6	United States	0.8
Paraguay	2.9	Canada	0.9
Nicaragua	3.4		
OCEANIA	1.5		
Guam	0.9		
Australia	1.3		
Papua New Guinea	2.3		

Source: United Nations World Population Chart, 1990.

and the other less-developed regions of the world (Latin America and Africa) grew most rapidly after 1950.

The picture of relative population growth in Table 1.2 shows the contemporary situation (for the 1985–1990 period) for regions and selected countries of the world. Some dramatic changes have taken place in recent times. The world's population growth rate has been slowing down. Asia as a whole has not changed much, but there have been significant declines for some countries

FIGURE 1.2 Population Gain and Loss in U.S. Counties: 1980–1990

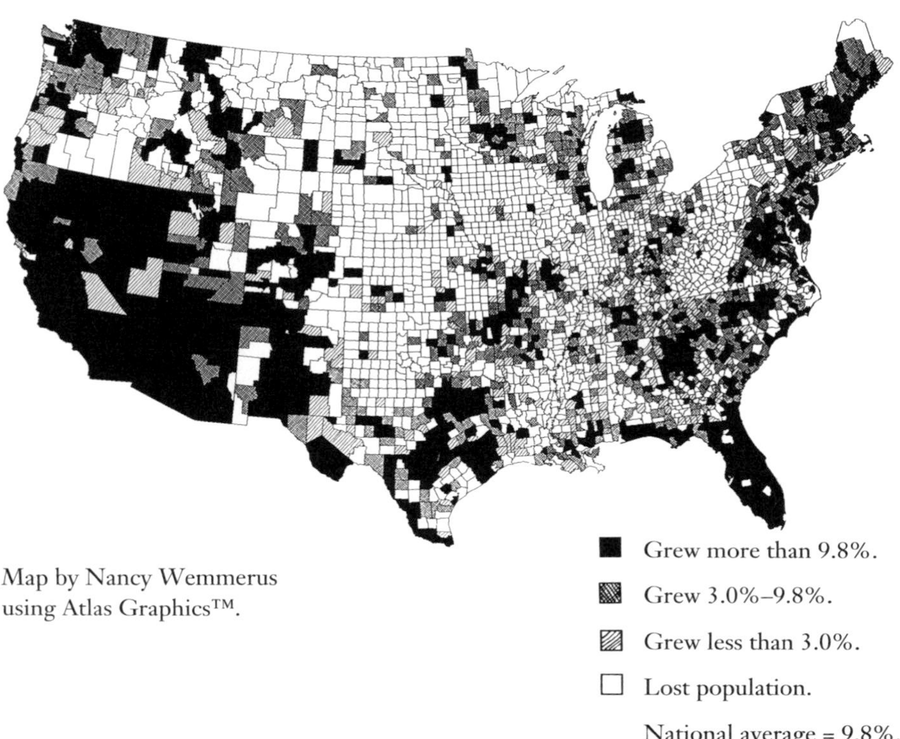

Map by Nancy Wemmerus using Atlas Graphics™.

Source: Population Reference Bureau, "People Patterns," *Population Today* 19 (1991): 5, 10.

(Japan, China, and Indonesia) and continued high growth rates for most of the remainder of Asia, especially the Middle East. Africa's population has increased its rate of growth significantly, with levels in many countries substantially above the world average. In Latin America, Cuba has led the way to reduction of growth rates, but many nations of the region continue to grow at high rates. In Europe, stability or near-stability of population size is common and some population declines have been experienced (e.g., Hungary). The United States and Canada have shared with the former U.S.S.R. a moderate population growth rate, while Oceania has had a somewhat higher level.

These variations in rates of population change among nations are matched by variations among areas within most of the countries. In the former Soviet Union, growth rates are much higher in the ethnic republics than in the Russian Republic that was the seat of national government. In the United States, the moderate rate of population growth for the whole nation masks the considerable differences that are found when counties are the units of analysis and 1980–1990 changes are recorded. Figure 1.2 shows that sharp growth characterized the Sun Belt and a number of other areas throughout the country, whereas some counties grew at a less rapid rate and a vast number of counties (largely those that are rural) actually lost population.

So when we think about population change, we must think about population growth, population stability, and population decline as possible change scenarios. These alternatives may appear as variations over time in particular geographic locations, or they may be seen as differences observed among geographic units at the same point in time.

ELEMENTS OF POPULATION CHANGE

Up to now, we have been talking about population change in terms of people as units, although we did suggest that population change involved additions and subtractions of people. Let us pursue that notion in several ways. First, we will discuss the concept of the "balancing equation" of demographic change and present a graphic picture of how it is the net effect of the *basic components of population change* that establishes the population balance at the end of a period of time. Second, we will illustrate this phenomenon by simply describing how the U.S. population change from 1950 to 1990 was created by a balance of the basic components. Third, our attention will be turned to how the basic components of population change determine not only the size of a population but also some of the essential characteristics of the people involved. In each case, we will be merely introducing the topics; later in the book, we will expand on them to place them even more directly in familiar territory.

The *balancing equation* is simply an account of the basic components of population change in a formula format. The equation below tells us that population change, as measured by the difference in population at two points in time, is equal to a balance of three basic demographic components—fertility (or births), mortality (or deaths), and mobility (or changes in where people live).

Population at Time 2 – Population at Time 1 =
Fertility – Mortality +/– Mobility

The part of the equation before the equals sign could be a population increase if population were greater at the second point; it could be a population decrease if population were smaller at the second point in time; or it could be zero if the populations were the same at the two points in time.

Fertility is always a plus factor, in that babies always add to the population. Mortality is always a minus factor, in that deaths always subtract from a population. But mobility can work in both directions, some people moving into the area being studied and some people moving out of the area. If more people move in than move out, mobility is a plus factor; if more people move out than move in, mobility is a minus factor.

Put them all together and you have a balancing equation. The net result of the pluses and minuses determine how much population change has taken place and in what direction. Another way to consider this phenomenon is to imagine a container with inlets and outlets as follows:

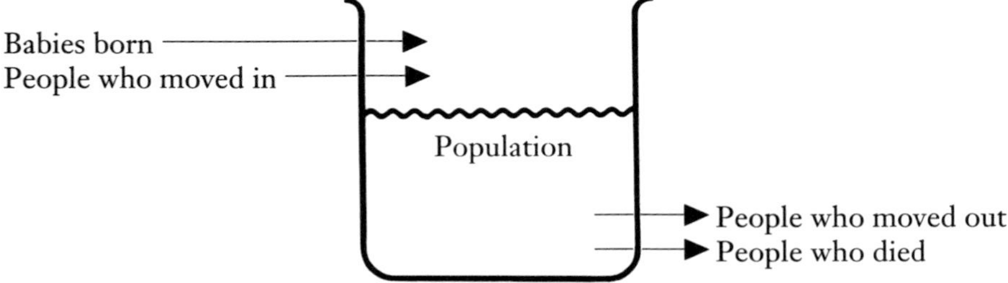

The level of the container's contents (people in an area) will be a consequence of the balance of births, deaths, and people moving in and out of the area during the period of time covered. The basic components of population change are the only sources through which the population of an area can change. And the two plus factors and two minus factors can occur in various combinations and amounts in different places and times.

If we think about population change for a political unit (such as a city) instead of a fixed land unit, then one more factor can enter the equation—boundaries of the unit changing. If a city expands its boundaries (through annexation of territory), it is likely to be adding people from the new location who are other than births or persons who moved in. If that city reduces its boundaries (by ceding territory to another political unit), then it is apt to be losing people from the area who are other than deaths or people who moved out. Hence, it would make a difference if the population change was for a fixed area of space or a place that can change its boundaries.

Examine the approximate change factors for the United States during the period 1950 to 1990:

U.S. population, 1950	151 million
+ babies born between 1950 and 1990	150 million
– people who died between 1950 and 1990	76 million
+ people who moved into the United States, 1950–1990	30 million
– people who moved out of the United States, 1950–1990	8 million
+ people on land added to the United States, 1950–1990	1.5 million
– people on land ceded by the United States, 1950–1990	0 million
U.S. population, 1990	248.5 million

Some simple comparisons reveal the dynamics of population change just in terms of these essential elements. The population growth from 151 to 248.5 million meant an increase of 97.5 million persons. But if we sum the various plus and minus factors, we find that the 97.5 million increase was the result of 181.5 million persons being added to the population (births + those who moved in + residents of Alaska and Hawaii, which joined the United States in 1959) and 84 million being subtracted from the population (deaths + those who left the country). To broaden the picture, we can say that the result took 265.5 million demographic shifts (181.5 million additions and 84 million subtractions) that balanced out to a growth of 97.5 million.

The complexity of population change can be indicated by pointing out that every area or political unit has its own balance of demographic components. Moreover, since people have different characteristics, the composition of the population based on age, sex, race and ethnicity, and social and economic variables, can shift meaningfully as the balancing equation takes on different forms for each category of person in the population. That is, the balance of plus and minus factors may not be the same for 20-year-old Hispanic women with a high level of education and 55-year-old white men with a low level of education. Since births are not relevant to the accounting of these categories, the rate at which each category changes its size depends on the balance of deaths, in-mobility, and out-mobility for each group.

Population change is thus reducible to changes in the basic demographic elements. Therefore, we need to understand the basic demographic elements themselves. In the remainder of this section, we will focus on mortality, fertility, mobility, and population composition as ingredients of population change. They too, like population change in general, can be viewed as having static and dynamic aspects. Although each of them may be seen as demographic events or statuses (a birth, a death, a movement, an age status), each is best examined as the outcome of a process that may have gone on for some time and which resulted in the event or status. In later chapters, these basic elements of population change will be dealt with more fully, but at this point we want to familiarize you with their essence.

Mortality Processes

Pick up the daily newspaper and turn to the obituary page. Here local governmental officials have provided information about the persons who died during the previous day or two. Typically, we are given descriptions about the time, place, and circumstance of death, the decedent's past occupation and affiliations, the surviving family, and funeral and burial arrangements. Perhaps we know the person but, in any event, it is a personalized account of death. We can imagine some of the social settings of life and then death. We might think about our own family members and acquaintances who have passed on, or we might consider the implications of the story for the survival of others and ourselves.

If the obituary is of an infant, it generally elicits feelings of sorrow; for that of someone in the prime of life, it saddens to think of a person who did not live a longer life; for an older person, there may be expressions of regret but also the idea that a full life was lived. Personalized reports of death bring out strong emotions in most of us.

Contrast that phenomenon with a media announcement that 750 people were killed in an earthquake in a far-off place, or that a large number of persons died in the sinking of a ship, or that a war took a toll of thousands killed in action. We are not apt to be so moved, because the people involved were anonymous to us and, while death is never pleasant, the happenings do not really affect us.

Consider further an official report of mortality statistics of the United States for 1988. The records show that 2,167,999 people died that year. Of these, 38,910 were infants (less than 1 year old), and more than a third of those had not survived the first month of life. Three hundred and thirty mothers had died from causes related to childbearing. Of persons at least 20 years old, 117,889 died that year without seeing their 40th birthday. Of all who died, 49,078 were victims of motor vehicle accidents, 30,407 were suicides, 16,602 succumbed to AIDS (HIV infection), 10,917 died directly from drug-induced causes, 473 perished from appendicitis, and 85 were victims of syphilis (National Center for Health Statistics, 1990a). We might feel revulsion at seeing some of these data, but they are statistics, the facts of death. Maybe we can rejoice in knowing that some of the numbers mentioned were smaller than those reported in an earlier year, and be concerned that some were larger than estimated for previous dates. But we are not likely to get emotional about the data.

Demographers who examine such statistics and analyze them are not unconcerned with the personal tragedies involved. But their orientation is to understand them—their trends and their determinants. The better we can understand them, the easier it will be to come up with solutions for lessening their occurrence.

How do we achieve understanding? First, we must recognize the importance of being very specific about concepts and data. If we talk about deaths due to AIDS, are we including all deaths in which AIDS was a complicating factor or just those in which the disease was believed to be the underlying cause? Is the statistical information about AIDS reliable? How many people who had AIDS at the time of death were not so identified by medical examination? These and related issues will be discussed more fully in later chapters.

Second, it is necessary to realize that death to an individual is the outcome of a process that may have had roots in the far past or may be explained largely by recent events. An infant's death is probably related to a host of factors, some having to do with the way the mother was raised by her parents and the kind of nutrition she got when she was a child. Such conditions would help to understand why a particular infant may have been born with low birth weight and be subject to a high risk of death. On the other hand, the death of a child who was regarded as perfectly healthy but darted out into the street in front of a truck to recover a ball would seem to have a more immediate explanation. Maybe it was merely chance, or perhaps it could be interpreted in terms of the social situation that allowed the child to play in a hazardous environment. Take the case of an 80-year-old woman who had suffered from osteoporosis (decalcification of the bone structure). She became so fragile that she had a bad fall that led to a fatal brain hemorrhage. Many women in that stage of life have similar experiences. What is involved that gives us the reasons why the death occurred at that age of that cause? We can imagine many different factors—some that come under the heading of biological conditions that the persons inherited or acquired, some that we can call social background variables that have origins in both the family and in the community and society, and some factors that we cannot specify and, for lack of a better term, we call chance.

Most demographic studies of mortality are based on analysis of official statistics or carefully designed sample surveys. The interest in understanding a particular mortality phenomenon (such as changes in the infant mortality level or group differences in the incidence of adult cancer deaths) requires conceptualizing the various factors that might be involved and the nature of their interrelationships, and then trying to accumulate data that are appropriate for that analysis. Often we find that some of the information we need is not available. In that case, we might do the analysis without including that particular information or we may consider alternative indicators (what are called *proxy variables*) for the absent data.

An overriding finding of demographic research on mortality is that death, like life, is very complex. In most societies, people are increasing their chances of living a long life. But there are significant differences in life expectancy according to the characteristics of persons and where they reside. Moreover, the factors that contribute to the risks of death at a given age are multitudinous—among them are biological inheritance (e.g., genetic makeup, physical features, cognitive abilities), socioeconomic means (e.g., income and wealth, education, work status, occupations engaged in, home environments), environmental qualities (e.g., purity of the air and water, availability of natural resources), individual behaviors (e.g., smoking, diet, drinking, exercise, rest), community provisions (e.g., health care arrangements, accessibility to medical facilities and personnel), and cultural practices (e.g., beliefs about the ability of humans to control their destiny, the relative emphasis on health and survival, uses of traditional and modern medicine).

Over the course of time and among various categories of people, these several factors have become more or less important. By integrating our knowledge about the many variables that can influence the chances of death, its timing, and its nature, we can achieve a higher level of understanding of the determinants and, with that in place, we can propose ways by which lives could be longer (and possibly healthier as well).

Fertility Processes

The female body is programmed to be the carrier of fetuses that will have an opportunity to become human babies once they mature. Of course, the creation of fetuses is dependent on the chance meeting of a viable sperm from a male and a receptive ovum from a female under circumstances that sustain and nurture the union to the point of producing a fetus. Hence, the process that leads up to the prospects of a baby being born is biological in essence. At the same time, there are personal and social actions that precipitate having sexual intercourse, so that it takes a combination of biological and social factors to initiate the fertility process.

Once the "seeds" of fetal development have been sown, other biological, personal, and social forces determine the survival of the fetus over a span of months and its prospective evolvement into a human birth.

At times in the past, demographers regarded the biological aspects of this total process as outside their domain and left them to the consideration of biologists. The demographers' task was believed to be to deal with the social aspects and, sometimes more narrowly, with the purely demographic elements. Today, the perspective of demographers is to extend their interdisciplinary orientation and to examine phenomena such as the fertility process by taking account of biological, psychological, social, and other dimensions of the population process.

Having once been babies ourselves, and realizing that everyone we have ever known or have ever seen—our parents, brothers and sisters, other relatives, friends, sports and entertainment figures, and others—were also babies at one time, makes us sensitive to the birth process. We are also aware that births are almost essential for a nation or society to survive, so we take it for granted that producing babies is a way of life. There are only questions of when and how many, but these two considerations are crucial to the nature of population change of a nation or society.

In your own experience, you no doubt have become aware of various intricacies of the fertility process that may have elicited joy or sorrow or surprise. We delight in giving baby presents (even when we can hardly afford them), we are saddened when an acquaintance who had looked forward to having a child is the victim of a miscarriage, and we are puzzled when a newborn baby appears to lack physical features of either parent.

Being one of three children in an era when parents with that number were thought to be having a small family, our household wondered why some of our neighbors were having many more babies. Not yet being a demographer, I was more concerned with whether one of the neighbor's children was my age and would likely be a playmate than I was with trying to understand the reasons my parents had three children and the neighbors had more.

Have you sometimes wondered why a woman who was married for several years had no children? Was it by choice or unavoidable? If the latter, what steps might have been taken to have a pregnancy? Was the reason inactive sperm of the husband, fallopian tube complications of the wife, inadequate knowledge about the time in the female menstrual cycle when sexual intercourse has the greatest chance to result in a fusion of a viable sperm and ovum, or a combination of some of these factors?

Secondary schools today are having to deal with the situation of early teenagers who have become pregnant (usually involuntarily). Should they be permitted to remain in school and continue their education? Should they be placed in a special school where they do not suffer the stigma of being a pregnant teenager? Are they better off leaving school, at least until the baby is born or the pregnancy no longer exists? If the fetus is brought to term, what are its prospects of a successful life and what are the consequences for the mother? These are frequent dilemmas in some places and rare occurrences in others. Why?

These kinds of fertility-related events are in our world of experience. In the impersonal sphere, fertility matters can also be a topic of conversation or a matter of conjecture. Why are large families no longer fashionable in most societies? Why are they still acceptable in some societies? What set of conditions led to a "baby boom" in a number of Western countries after World War II? Why did that *baby boom* end and why was it followed by what some call a *baby bust* (a significant decline in the national fertility level)? To what extent do people with certain social or personal characteristics have more or fewer births than others? These are some of the concerns of population analysts.

Official statistics for 1988 chronicle the tale of U.S. fertility. There were 3,909,510 babies born that year (in the following year the number would reach 4 million for the first time since 1964!). The birth rate (births in relation to population) for young teenagers increased 6 percent over the previous year and was then higher than at any time since the 1970s. Women at ages 30 to 34 also increased their birth rate, which had risen 41 percent from 1975 to that point. Even women 40 to 44, though not having many children, were having more of them (National Center for Health Statistics, 1990b). Could these data be reconciled with a picture of low and stable fertility in the United States?

The official reports also showed that birthdays were more likely to take place in July, August, or September than in other months of the year. Moreover, the babies were more apt to be born during the week than on weekends or holidays. In addition, there was a sharper increase in multiple births (twins, triplets, etc.) than in single births. Are there good explanations for these phenomena?

The account also reveals that 1,005,299 babies were born to unmarried mothers in 1988. In 1980, there were 665,747. How many of those mothers would get married shortly after the birth? To what extent is the rise in fertility to unmarried women the result of changing marriage patterns? These are kinds of questions that demographers try to answer.

In carrying out research, analysts will make certain that as many variables as might be involved are examined (if data permit) and that attention will be given to all steps in the fertility process. This will entail acquiring information about previous pregnancies and births the woman had, the length of time that has expired since the last birth, fertility control measures used, personal and social attributes of the parents, the health status of the mother (and father too) at both earlier and recent points in time, the dietary practices of the mother, the pattern of doctor visits for prenatal care, the length of the pregnancy, and various other bits of information.

Mobility Processes

When the components of mortality and fertility are examined jointly (without the effect of mobility), demographers refer to their balance as *natural change.* If fertility exceeds mortality, there is *natural increase;* if mortality exceeds fertility, there is *natural decrease.* Of course, there is nothing unnatural about mobility, except that it is basically not a result of biological processes, as are fertility and mortality.

We have already indicated the necessity of incorporating mobility into the balancing equation of population change. The only case where it would seem not to be relevant would be in accounting for population change on Earth. Here, natural change would seem to explain it all. If some Martians have really crept into our planet, we will have underestimated the population data. On the other hand, if they returned to Mars and took some of our earthlings with them, net migration would be relevant. However, until such time as space travel becomes more than a temporary sojourn out of the Earth's gravitational pull, world population change is a function of the balance of births and deaths.

For any geographic area or political unit on Earth, it is important to gauge net mobility (and sometimes the streams of mobility in different directions, the balance of which makes up net mobility) in measuring population change.

Although we will say more later about the concept of mobility, we should point out now that it is imperative that the criteria for mobility be specified. In these days of frequent movement of people and multiple residences for many, when is a person a mover (demographically) and when not? As with other concepts, there are certain conventions in this respect but they are not consistent from country to country. In the United States, when a census is taken, it is intended that a person be counted at least once but only once and in the location where the person "usually resides." Then, whether or not the person is considered to be mobile is based on a change in the usual residence over some specified period of time.

Mobility is generally differentiated according to boundaries crossed (movement within a county or province, within a country, or across national boundaries), direction of movement, and time span involved (since birth, during the past five years, or during the previous year). Rules of residence come into play, such that someone who has left home to take a temporary job elsewhere is not regarded as a mover so long as the residence the person left is still considered the usual residence.

In some countries (e.g., Indonesia), although the concept of usual residence in censuses and surveys may be about the same, there are alternative concepts for movers who are commuters or visitors for a day or two; who are seasonal residents in another location; who return to the place where they were born; who stay for a while in a workplace but return after some time to their main residence; and who surrender one residence and become firmly based in another one (Mantra, 1981). In other countries that adopt a procedure that places people where they are at the time of the census rather than at a usual residence, the measurement of mobility assumes a different form.

In our own experience, we know of persons (maybe ourselves) who have moved frequently and of others who have remained all or most of their lives in the same place; we know of those who moved but stayed in the community (who refer to the "old place" and the "new place") and of others who went a long distance to relocate and whom we never or hardly ever see again. We also know of people who moved but did so as a family unit in contrast to those whose movement was related to family dissolution (maybe because of a divorce or a death or a child's departure for college or one family member's entry into a new job).

Official statistics indicate that, in the twelve-month period from March 1986 to March 1987, 42,551,000 persons in the United States (or nearly a fifth of the population) changed residences. More than half (27,196,000) stayed in the same county. In the same time span, 8,762,000 left the county but remained in the state; 6,593,000 left the state but not the region; and 3,546,000 went to a different region (U.S. Bureau of the Census, 1989).

What is interesting is that these numbers have changed very little year after year. What is different is that the people involved are mostly not the same from one year to the next. What are the explanations for this steadiness of mobility patterns? What are the factors that led some persons to move and others to stay?

The data also show that net migration is typically a small amount compared to the counterstreams that generated it. For example, 2,686,000 moved from nonmetropolitan to metropolitan areas while 1,754,000 moved from metropolitan to nonmetropolitan areas. So it took over 4 million moves to create a net migration into metropolitan areas of slightly less than a million. Clearly, mobility has its own balancing equation, as well as being part of the larger population change balancing equation.

Other types of mobility exchanges are notable. In the 1986–87 twelve-month span, the central cities of metropolitan areas lost 1,040,000 more residents than they gained from the suburbs and nonmetropolitan locations. On the other hand, the suburbs had a net gain of 1,972,000 residents from the central cities and outside metropolitan areas. So, of the three geographic categories mentioned, suburbs were the greatest gainers.

Still, not all movements were between such areas. As many as 10,606,000 persons moved from one central city to another. Fully 11,948,000 people shifted from one suburb to another. Even 6,920,000 residents of nonmetropolitan areas moved but to other nonmetropolitan areas.

If we were able to specify the particular origins and destinations of all these moves and plot lines for them on a U.S. map, we would observe a configuration that resembled a plate of spaghetti. This should lead us to think of the factors that prompt some people to select one destination over another. It should also make us ask why there are people who move from place A to place B at the same time that others are moving from place B to place A. Are there easy explanations for residential "musical chairs"? Do we have the concepts and the data that allow us to unravel the mystery?

These questions are dealt with in demographic research. One approach that is often used is to analyze the characteristics of those who move (to and from various locations) and those who do not. How selective are such variables as age, sex, race and ethnicity, educational level, work status and occupation, income level, and the like? To the extent that there are differences by categories of these variables, we can infer the importance of these effects. But certainly we need to delve into the reasons for moving with greater precision. We should identify all steps in the mobility process, including mobility histories (the more that people have moved in the past, the more they are likely to move in the future); the nature of cultural values and attitudes about moving; the knowledge that people have about the pros and cons of living in different places; and the content of discussions with family, friends, and others that might lead up to a decision whether or not to move.

Population Distribution and Composition Dynamics

The foregoing sections have stressed the role of mortality, fertility, and mobility in accounting for overall population change—whether increase, decrease, or stability. The same three components are involved in two other dimensions of population, namely, how it is distributed over land areas and how the population is composed of persons with different ages, sexes, race/ethnicity traits, and other characteristics.

Changes in the distribution of population seem to be highly linked to mobility patterns, as the previous discussion suggests, and in fact they are. But mobility is not the whole story. Fertility and mortality also make contributions, and sometimes those contributions are substantial.

Consider two halves of a country. Let us call them East and West. Suppose that a census showed that each of them contained half of the country's population. Ten years later, another census is taken and the East is discovered to have 60 percent of the people with 40 percent in the West. What changed the proportions in each half of the country? Mobility most probably was an influence in several ways. There may have been a net gain by the East as a result of the balance of West to East and East to West movements. Also, people coming into the country may have gone disproportionately to the East. It is possible, however, that more immigrants to the country went to the West but that the exchanges between the two regions more than offset the greater gain through immigration by the West. Or the reverse scenario may have occurred. It is even conceivable that the West benefited more from net mobility than did the East, even though the East increased its share of the national population. An even more extreme possibility is that there was heavy movement away from the country but that the West lost more than did the East, leaving the East with a larger share of the remaining population. In any event, you can see how various mobility sequences could be involved in the population redistribution.

Wait, you say, how could the East increase its proportion of the population if the West benefited most through mobility patterns? That is where fertility and mortality would come in. If those residing in the East had higher levels of fertility or lower levels of mortality, or both, or even net natural increase, then the East would have gained through the balance of births and deaths. Further, if that balance more than compensated for the relative gain of the West through mobility, then population change overall would be greater in the East. You can imagine even other combinations of basic demographic processes that would result in a gain for the East that would raise its percentage of the country's population.

Multiply the number of areas under consideration—states or provinces or counties or neighborhoods or residential streets—and you have a sense of how the basic population components establish a balancing equation for each area and how the relative balance of all of the areas determines the extent of population shifts among the areas.

Similarly, changes in population composition are due to the balance of the basic components. Take the case of the age structure of a population. If two successive censuses showed that there were higher percentages of people at older ages (say, 65 and over) by the later date, whereas there were smaller percentages of those at young ages (say, under 15), we might agree that the population is getting "older." But which of the basic components contributed to that change in age composition, and in what ways?

If fertility increased during the period between the censuses, that would add to the young population and give it greater weight; if fertility decreased in that time span, then it would lower the weight of the young ages. If mortality decreased during the period, we would need to know at what ages the deaths were relatively greatest. If the reduction was primarily in infant and childhood mortality, that would have the effect of benefiting the young ages (in the same way that increased fertility would do so). If the reduction was disproportionately at the older ages, leading to greater survival of the elderly, that would have the effect of increasing the proportion of older persons in the population. With regard to mobility, if the area is a country, then how selective the age pattern of movement into and out of the country was is relevant. If immigrants were mostly older persons, that would help age the population; if they were disproportionately at younger ages, that segment of the population would be strengthened.

But we come back to the balance of all of these factors. All three demographic processes are usually working simultaneously. Therefore, there will be many possible combinations of effects of basic components—plus or minus and of varying amounts—and the net result of the combination that takes place will determine the changing age composition.

Combinations of the same three basic components explain how the racial composition or ethnic composition or makeup of the population according to

BOX 1.1 A Macro Perspective on Population

Bangladesh is a country we read about and see on television news reports frequently because of the great hardships inflicted on many of its people due to severe weather and food shortages. Bangladesh is also among those developing areas of the world that have a relatively high level of childbearing which contributes to a higher-than-average population growth rate. One rural section of Bangladesh called Matlab has been the focus for an intensive project designed to monitor demographic change in the area. A Cholera Research Laboratory was established there in the early 1960s and a Demographic Surveillance System put in place in 1966. Since that time, a series of censuses and village population registrations have provided a rich source of data that can tell us what population changes have been occurring there and some of the factors involved. (Matlab is probably atypical of the areas of Bangladesh in that some special interventions with regard to health and fertility control have been made there.)

Menken and Phillips (1990) analyzed population changes in the Matlab area from 1967 to 1987 using the aggregate data that were available. They observed that the length of life expected was generally low for residents and lower for females than for males, contrary to what is found for most countries of the world. This resulted from the fact that the higher death rates for females in infancy (after the first month of life) and during childbearing ages more than compensated for the higher death rates of males at older ages. Programs to reduce deaths due to measles have had some success whereas programs dealing with diarrheal problems have not had much impact. Infectious and parasitic diseases, along with famine, take a heavy toll of the population.

education or occupation or some other characteristic undergoes change. In the case of race or any other trait that is unchangeable, the three components alone will account for alterations in the composition of a population based on that trait. In the case of characteristics that are changeable, however, an additional factor is the possibility that the characteristic of the person may itself change.

For example, the percentage of American Indians in the population of the United States increased during the 1980–1990 decade, so we would expect that the balance of births, deaths, and net immigration for American Indians was greater than the same balance for non-Indians. (This assumes that both Indians and non-Indians reported themselves correctly in the census.) On the other hand, the percentage of college graduates in the population increased during the same time period, but that could be due not only to the balancing equations of basic components of population for college graduates and nongraduates but also to the fact that some persons who were not college graduates in 1980 became college graduates by 1990. A look at the mix of these several factors

continued

Even apart from family planning, fertility in the region is below the maximum biologically feasible. Contributing factors are extensive breast-feeding of babies, which reduces the potential for conception and thus extends the interval between births, and the occurrence of famines, which makes it even less likely that harvested food can be given to babies in place of breast-feeding. Famine may also affect the health of both men and women and inhibit sexual intercourse as well as the probability of conceiving. Fertility levels, in general, have been influenced by family planning efforts but are also kept high by traditional cultural practices regarding reproduction and low socioeconomic levels, which have been universally associated with higher birth rates.

Over the time span studied, out-migration has exceeded in-migration in Matlab. (A six-month absence defines migration there.) Women are more likely than men to move out of the area because of the cultural practice of brides' going to the husband's place of residence. But men at older ages are more likely to move when work opportunities outside the region beckon them.

Although births typically exceed deaths, net out-migration partly compensates for the natural increase and population growth is normally at a rate that hovers around 2 percent. Thus, the authors have described a developing country area, whose patterns of population change are found in similar rural areas throughout the Third World. Later in this book, we will try to discover the more detailed factors that lead to high population growth in such areas, as well as what modifications might lower the growth rate.

would tell us which ones were most responsible for the increasing percentage of college graduates.

THE MACRO VIEW

A perusal of demographic publications over a long period of time will show that the perspective on population taken by demographers (and most other social scientists) has been primarily one of looking at the "big picture." We call this the *macro view*.

Macro (short for macroscopic) means large units or elements. In population studies it means focusing attention on large geographic areas, such as the world, countries, or large cities, and collecting our data through censuses or general surveys or other large-scale data-collection mechanisms. It can also mean that the phenomena we are studying are conceptualized and/or measured in broad terms, such as an infant mortality rate or a crude birth rate, or net migration between California and Ohio. A further meaning is that our attempts at explanation of the phenomenon are based on general variables that describe broad categories of the population (such as family income). The essence of macro studies is that the units of analysis are typically large and the people for whom the data were assembled are treated impersonally, grouped together according to a few indicators but stripped of their personality. There is nothing wrong with macro research. It provides answers to questions that only require a "big picture" perspective. Often, that is sufficient for our purposes. The census and survey statistics already presented fit the category in that some useful information was conveyed without having to be very specific about the people involved (see Box 1.1 for a particular example of a macro study).

Macro studies can range far and wide. In some respects, they seem to be less interesting because they are less personalized. But in many areas of application, that demographic research is best which provides needed answers to critical questions. For the government of Bangladesh and the nations that offer aid to that country, it is perhaps more important to know the big picture than to reflect on particular individuals or groups of human interest whose situations may not be representative. Regional and economic planners in Italy would likely be better served by information about general migration tendencies than about migration patterns of particular people, although the latter may be of great interest to those people and others concerned with their welfare.

THE MICRO VIEW

Looking at population data more intensively can sometimes be done within a macro perspective. We can always specify greater and greater details of the aggregate statistics that enable us to pinpoint patterns more accurately and add information about our subject matter. At some point, however, aggregated statistical data will be insufficient for delving into explanations about the phenomena we are studying.

When we feel it necessary to get more focused on demographic behaviors, we often turn to a *micro approach*. Micro (short for microscopic) research can mean several things in population studies. It can mean that we are studying small geographic areas or small groups, couples, or individuals, and often employing intensive interview, survey, or observational techniques. It can also mean that the phenomena we are studying are conceptualized and/or measured in specific terms, such as having a particular cultural trait, or as being classified in a given category of a variable or set of variables (e.g., teenage female from low-income background with a history of sexual promiscuity). Still another meaning is that our method of explaining the phenomenon of interest is in terms of particular factors (sometimes those that are not obtainable from census, surveys, and other large-scale data sets). Hence, micro studies are typically based on small units of analysis. Although those involved are perceived as persons in their entirety, not just lifeless statistics, they retain their anonymity in research (that is, the information they provide is held confidential). Micro research is especially helpful when

BOX 1.2 A Micro Perspective on Population

Religious and caste differences in fertility have been observed in India for some time. Mahadevan (1986) believed that "several deep-rooted cultural and social factors relevant in the Indian context" could help to elaborate the differentials and he conducted a micro study. He chose as a study site a village named Ramapuram in Andhra Pradesh State in South India. By using a combination of study methods—gathering of historical and current information about the village's social institutions, in-depth interviewing of fifty families with varying religious and caste characteristics over a one-year period during which six rounds of interviews were obtained, and collecting daily time allocation of activities of one family from each of the three major religious-caste groups—a vast amount of important information was assembled.

The higher fertility of Muslims in the area is supported by several factors, among which are belief that family planning will lead one to hell; belief in childbearing to be up to God; emphasis on extended kinship; and greater value attached to sons. Caste Hindus have lesser fertility than Muslims, and Harijans (traditionally the Untouchables) have still lower fertility. In the country as a whole, the Harijans are observed to have higher fertility. The particular group of them in this area, however, are better educated than their counterparts elsewhere, even though they have less prestigious occupations and lower incomes than the neighboring Muslims and caste Hindus. The Harijan women engaged in a long duration of breast-feeding. The caste Hindu women were more apt to be users of family planning than the other groups. Along with a variety of other social differences among the groups, the net effect of the specific practices determined their relative fertility levels. No one factor alone could explain the differences in fertility, and some of the factors would not have been discovered directly in a macro study.

probing inquiries are necessary to get at aspects of the phenomena studied that cannot be reached by macro research. However, one should think of macro and micro research as being not only compatible but complementary. Either can stand on its own, but understanding can be enhanced if both are used to explore a research question (see Box 1.2 for an example of a micro study).

Chapter Highlights

1. Human populations can be studied in both static and dynamic perspectives. The static perspective enables us to view populations as they can be described at a point in time. The dynamic perspective lets us see populations as they change over time.

2. Population change can mean population increase, decrease, or stability. All three have characterized populations in different locations at different times.
3. While our knowledge about the early history of population change is limited by available information, we know that the rapid growth of population has been a modern phenomenon with a peak world growth rate attained during the middle of this century.
4. Despite a continuing increase in world population growth, there are some countries with stable or declining populations, and simultaneous demographic growth, decline, and stability exists among areas within most countries of the world.
5. All population change takes place through the basic components of change—mortality, fertility, and mobility. The balancing equation of population change shows the net effect of the plus and minus contributions of each component.
6. The balance of fertility and mortality is referred to as natural change—natural increase if births exceed deaths and natural decrease if deaths exceed births.
7. Since mobility can be either in or out of an area, it has its own form of balance—net in-mobility if movement in exceeds movement out, and net out-mobility if the reverse.
8. Each of the components can be examined as the outcome of a process through which numerous factors influence the probability of the demographic event's occurring. These factors may be biological, psychological, or social in nature.
9. The dynamics of population distribution and composition are also determined by the balancing equation of components. The relative size of any geographic area is a function of how its balance compares with that of other areas. Likewise, the relative size of any age, sex, or race/ethnic category is also a function of how its balance compares with that of other categories of the variable.
10. Population can be studied from both macro and micro perspectives. The macro perspective uses general levels of concepts, measurement, and data to arrive at broad generalizations about the phenomena we are studying. The micro perspective uses more specific levels of concepts, measurement, and data to reach more focused generalizations.

Discussion Questions

1. We are told that early estimates of population size are based on knowledge derived by archaeologists, paleontologists, and cultural anthropologists. What do each of these specialists do, and what techniques did they probably use to estimate the population in those early periods?

2. Looking at the map in Figure 1.2, and considering what you have already learned about population change, what might explain the fact that so many counties in the United States had a population decrease during the 1980–90 decade?
3. Think about your own community (city, town, county, or other place). What do you think a balancing equation would look like for the 1980–90 period in that area? Do you think it has changed since 1990?
4. Select a demographic topic that you feel would best be studied using a macro approach, and identify some of the factors you would include in trying to explain that phenomenon.
5. Select a demographic topic that you feel would best be studied using a micro approach, and identify some of the factors you would include in trying to explain that phenomenon.

Suggested Readings

U.S. Bureau of the Census. *Current Population Reports*, especially Series P-20 and P-23. These reports can be found in most college and university libraries. In addition to statistics about current population trends, they provide analysis of such topics as marriage and family patterns, education, and the social progress of women and minority groups.

Population Reference Bureau Reports. The bureau is a private organization that specializes in communicating population information within the United States and around the world. Check with your library for such publications of theirs as *Population Bulletin*, which goes into depth on particular topics, and *Population Today*, a newsmonthly.

American Demographics. Published by Dow Jones & Company, it presents original short articles of general population interest, much of it oriented to the business community.

United Nations *Population Bulletin*. Whereas the items already mentioned are written in a nontechnical style, the reports in this series have a stronger professional orientation and take an international point of view.

Various professional journals in the population field include *Demography*, *Population Studies*, *Population and Development Review*, *Population Research and Policy Review*, and *Social Biology*. Peruse the latest issues in your library.

References

Deevey, Edward S., Jr. 1960. "The Human Population." *Scientific American* 203: 195–204.

Durand, John D. 1967. "The Modern Expansion of World Population." *Proceedings of the American Philosophical Society*, 111:3, 136–159.

Mahadevan, K. 1986. "Determinants of Religious and Caste Differentials in Fertility: A

Village Study." In K. Mahadevan, ed., *Fertility and Mortality: Theory, Methodology, and Empirical Issues*, pp. 100–22. New Delhi: Sage.

Mantra, I.B. 1981. *Population Movement in Central Java.* Yogyakarta, Indonesia: Gadjah Mada University Press.

Menken, Jane, and James F. Phillips. 1990. "Population Change in a Rural Area of Bangladesh, 1967–87." *Annals of the American Academy of Political and Social Science* 510: 87–101.

Nam, Charles B., and Susan Gustavus Philliber. 1984. *Population: A Basic Orientation.* Englewood Cliffs, N.J.: Prentice-Hall.

National Center for Health Statistics. 1990a. "Advance Report of Final Mortality Statistics, 1988." *Monthly Vital Statistics Report* 39:7, suppl.

———. 1990b. "Advance Report of Final Natality Statistics, 1988." *Monthly Vital Statistics Report* 39:4, suppl.

Stringer, Christopher B. 1990. "The Emergence of Modern Humans." *Scientific American* 263:6, 98–104.

United Nations. 1973. *The Determinants and Consequences of Population Trends.* Vol. 1. New York: United Nations.

U.S. Bureau of the Census. 1989. *Current Population Reports*, Series P-20, no. 430, "Geographic Mobility: March 1986 to March 1987."

World Bank. 1990. *World Development Report.* New York: Oxford University Press.

2. Population Transitions and Cycles

The previous chapter acquainted you with some essential elements of understanding population change. Such change, we pointed out, is the result of the net balance of changes in mortality, fertility, and mobility for the geographic area in question. Even the categories of characteristics of the population undergo change as a result of the balance of these basic components for one category as compared with another. This fundamental way of looking at population change will give us a lever, in later chapters, for uncovering some of the complexities of demographic explanation.

Before we proceed to that step, however, we want to continue with other fundamentals of population change. In this chapter, our emphasis will be on what we call *population transitions and cycles.* We have already talked about the course of population over time. Now we need to decide whether there is any regularity to that course. Does population change follow any predictable path? If so, is that path followed by all societies, or are there variations or exceptions? How do the basic components of population change contribute to conformity and deviation in these patterns? How can we best differentiate long-term from shorter-term variations in population, mortality, fertility, and mobility changes? What have been some of the more interesting developments in these respects?

Our intrusion into this arena will let us witness the slow march of population during some periods of time and the explosive nature of population change at other times. We will also become cognizant of the devastating toll of "great mortalities"; the unexpected baby dearths, baby booms, and baby busts; and the mass migrations of history.

With regard to *transitions*, which basically refer to major shifts from one level of demographic indicators to another, we need to know how to identify them, including when they begin and when they end. With regard to *cycles*, our interest will be drawn to similar concerns of knowing when they start and finish. But since cycles are generally of shorter duration than transitions, there is also the question of when a change in mortality or fertility or mobility is merely a small deviation from a transitional trend and when it is profound enough to be regarded as a distinct phenomenon with a character of its own.

Population understanding involves both description and explanation. Our discussion here will remain at the descriptive level. We need to first comprehend what we are trying to explain before we can explain it. Once we further spell out the "plot," our aim will then be to unravel the mystery by attaching significance to various factors that precede, accompany, or intervene in the processes of concern.

LONG-TERM DEMOGRAPHIC TRANSITIONS

Although Deevey proposed that the long span of population change (over perhaps a million or so years) included at least three separate surges of population growth, the lack of adequate data to definitively establish the first two of those surges keeps them in the realm of informed speculation. Even if we agreed that the evidence was strong enough to mark those surges of population, we would be at a loss to elaborate what the forces were that produced them.

The third population surge mentioned by Deevey is, however, largely beyond the realm of informed speculation and within the field of modern knowledge. To go back a few hundred years most certainly tests our ability to recreate history, but historians have provided insight into the ways people lived through the Industrial Revolution and beyond.

In fact, the period of time during which the modern surge of population took place was one that saw the creation of new or improved systems of information that helped historians as well as demographers to chronicle events as they occurred. These systems included more extensive registering of critical life events in the community (a task that the Church had begun in the medieval period); the advent of statistical reporting systems (an adjunct of the expansion of governmental bureaucratic activity); and the rise of a publications industry (that made available to a wide audience the perceptions of contemporaries about conditions of the times).

These kinds of knowledge sources have enabled us to document many of the goings-on of the past, at least in a general way and often in fairly specific ways. Based on these sources, we can tell about the demographic transitions that took place in Europe. Subsequent transitions have occurred in other parts of the world in more recent periods when it has been even more possible to describe their features.

To tell the story of demographic transitions well, we have to relate how the concept itself evolved and the way in which the transitions for different societies have run their course or, as in the case of many still developing nations, are running their course.

The Concept of a Demographic Transition

Ideas typically precede the names given to them. The idea that populations grow at different rates and that the balance of births and deaths contributes to those rates was bandied about for a long stretch of time. But in 1798 a famous work entitled *An Essay on Population* by English economist Thomas R. Malthus (1914) caught the public's attention. Malthus' thesis was that (1) the rapid growth of population would outstrip the resources needed to provide for it; and (2) this growth was due to the excess of births over deaths.

As we will indicate in the next chapter, Malthus' thesis is sometimes given the status of a theory. Whether this is justifiable or not, his thesis included descriptions of changes in population (as well as in fertility and mortality) in various countries of the world. This concept gave rise to the basic notion that substantial population growth was indeed occurring on the European continent and elsewhere in the world; moreover, this growth was due to the basic population components. Malthus saw the limits of resources as restricting the growth of population primarily through the suffering of people and a consequent rise in the death rate. Although he did not formulate the demographic transition as we now know it, his writings gave impetus to that idea.

Thompson (1929) made a first approach to the transition idea when he tried to generalize the experience of European countries by defining three groups of nations according to the levels of their birth and death rates: those where neither births nor deaths are controlled but some signs of mortality control seem imminent; those with declining birth and death rates for some categories of the population, but with mortality falling more rapidly than fertility; and those with steadily declining birth and death rates, but with the former declining more rapidly. In his later work, Thompson broadened the coverage of countries included under this classification by adding those of other developed countries and developing areas.

Later, Landry (1934) identified three main stages of population change: the primitive, the intermediate, and the modern. Under the primitive regime, fertility is not restricted by economic factors and mortality fluctuates around the level of the birth rate, so that population balance between the two is basically achieved. Landry's discussion of the intermediate stage is somewhat vague, but in the modern phase fertility is brought down to more nearly equate with mortality.

Notestein (1947) attempted to give more form to the stages of population change by placing them in the context of forces of modernization. He also renamed the three stages: high-growth potential, transitional, and incipient decline. The term *demographic transition* seems to have emerged here.

Davis (1945), a colleague of Notestein, wrote about the "world demographic transition" and enlarged on the economic and social mechanisms that generated it by specifying behavioral changes that accompanied rising industrialization and urbanization. In addition, he tried to envisage the post–World War II changes that would affect the course of the transition, especially the spread of literacy and declining reliance on agriculture.

Blacker (1947), also writing in terms of stages of change or differences among countries, perceived five stages of demographic evolution: a high stationary stage with high birth and death rates, an early expanding stage with high birth rates and decreasing mortality, a late expanding stage with falling

BOX 2.1 The Process of the Demographic Transition

"...an agrarian peasant economy (characterized by a high degree of self-sufficiency within each community and each family, by relatively slow change in technique, and by the relatively unimportant role of market exchange) typically has high average death rates. Moreover, these death rates usually fluctuate in consequence of variations in crops, the varying incidence of epidemics, etc. In such an economy birth rates are nearly stable at a high level. Death rates are high as a consequence of poor diets, primitive sanitation, and the absence of effective preventive and curative medical practices. High birth rates result from social beliefs and customs that necessarily grow up if a high death-rate community is to continue in existence. These beliefs and customs are reinforced by the economic advantages to a peasant family of large numbers of births. The burden of child care rests primarily on the women in a peasant society, and the place of women is typically a subordinate one. The costs of educating children are minimal because of the low level of education given. Children contribute at an early age to agrarian production and are the traditional source of security in the old age of parents. The prevalent high death rates, especially in infancy, imply that such security can be attained only when many children are born....

"The reduction in death rates may be ascribed partly to greater regularity in food supplies, to the establishment of greater law and order, and to other fairly direct consequences of economic change. Other factors contributing to the decline—improvements in sanitation, the development of vaccines and other means of preventive medicine, and great and rapid strides in the treatment of disease—can themselves be considered as somewhat indirect consequences of economic change....

"The changing structure of production, with a declining importance of the family as a production unit, with the growth of impersonal systems for the allocation of jobs, and with the development of economic roles for women outside of the home, tends to increase the possibility of economic mobility that can better be achieved with small families, and tends to decrease the economic advantages of a large family."

birth rates but more rapidly decreasing death rates, a low stationary stage with low birth rates and low death rates, and a declining stage with deaths exceeding births.

In their classic study of population growth and economic development in low-income countries, Coale and Hoover (1958) gave an eloquent statement about the process of the demographic transition (see Box 2.1).

The Coale-Hoover statement neatly sums up the traditional view of the demographic transition. Although looked at from solely a macro perspective and explained largely in economic terms, it identifies the key elements of the

FIGURE 2.1 Classical Demographic Transition

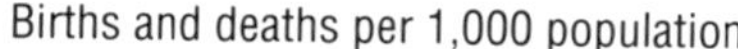

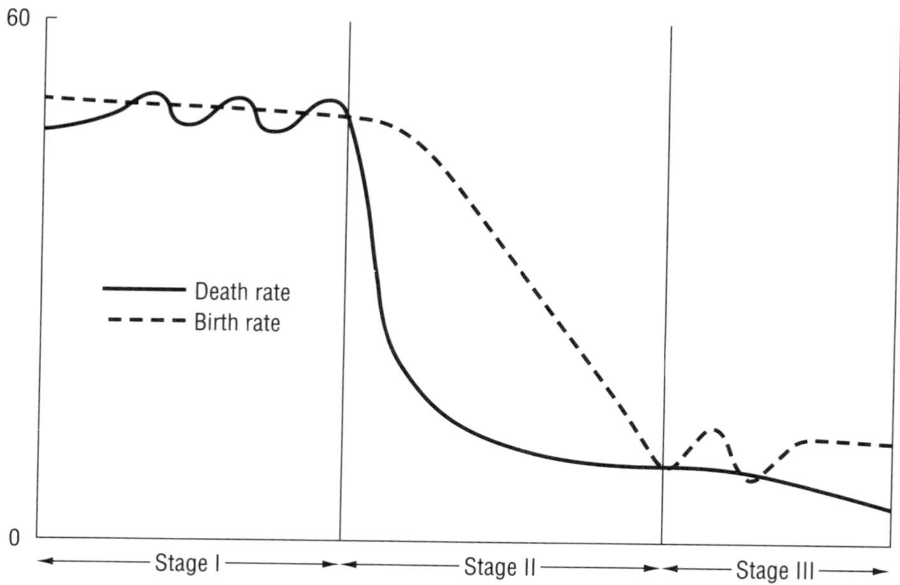

Source: Charles B. Nam and Susan G. Philliber, *Population: A Basic Orientation*, 2nd ed. (Englewood Cliffs, N.J.: Prentice-Hall, 1984).

transitional process as it occurred in the nations of the West over a span of a century and one half.

The lines in Figure 2.1 depict the trends of birth and death rates as the traditional description of the transition makes them out to be. However, as historians began to uncover new bits of information about demographic processes in Europe and as students of population considered the implications of those findings for the description of the transition, it became clear that the transition was neither so regular nor identical from one European country to another. So, even as a description of what happened demographically in Europe from the eighteenth century onward, it had its limitations.

Under the transition idea, mortality would fluctuate during the formative years of a society and would begin its sustained downward course when heroic efforts were made to control certain diseases. Once the transition of mortality from high to low levels was achieved, it is assumed that the death rate would remain at a low point. Fertility, on the other hand, would be maintained at a high level past the point when mortality decline was substantial, and it would eventually begin its transition from high to low levels as a result of social and economic forces.

Critics of the demographic transition notion over the past few decades have pointed to particular shortcomings of the basic assumptions. Some amendments became necessary and some problematic issues arose, simply in terms of the form of the transition itself. The matter of what sets of factors produced the transition or initiated various stages of demographic history introduced other points of controversy, which we will discuss later.

One amendment to the classic transition framework relates to the behavior of fertility during the period when mortality starts its sustained decline. The birth rate is seen as not being very much affected, at least until sometime later when a reduced infant death rate might convince couples that they did not have to bear as many children to guarantee that a desired number would survive to adulthood. Contrary to what the classic notion suggested, new research showed that in many countries of Europe, when mortality started down the level of fertility had actually gone up! Factors that probably accounted for that development were more universal marriage and a more fecund group of women (owing to health improvements associated with lower mortality) who could bear more children (Petersen, 1960). In still other nations of Europe, fertility trends were downward at an earlier point in time than expected. This was especially true in Austria-Hungary (Demeny, 1968) and in France, whose demographic regime was quite different from the other European countries.

Another amendment to the transition framework has to do with the role of migration, the third component of demographic change. The classic statement disregarded the importance of that factor in ushering in a rise in a country's population growth. It was assumed that the gap between births and deaths alone would account for substantial population increase. But Davis (1963) discussed the part that out-migration played in Ireland and other countries to temper the mortality and fertility transitions. Friedlander (1969) showed how rural-to-urban migration within countries was also a potent force in shaping the demographic patterns during the early stages of the transition. To leave migration out of the transition framework is thus both conceptually unsound and empirically fallacious. Zelinsky (1971) has outlined the stages of change in mobility patterns as countries go through phases of social and economic development (see Chapter 7). This serves as a complement to the classic demographic transition based on mortality and fertility.

It would be fair to say at this point that the experience of European countries in moving through the demographic transition was not at all a common one, and that there were both unique sets of circumstances and differential patterns of timing that characterized them.

The classic framework also left unanswered some questions that we will subsequently deal with to fully comprehend the transition idea. One has to do with the relative importance of economic growth and social and cultural change in bringing about the transition itself (Caldwell, 1976). Another has to do with the point when relatively low mortality and fertility were reached. When was the transition in fact complete? A third issue is the ability to generalize the European experience, in terms of its common elements, to other parts of the world. Can we expect developing nations to follow the course of developed countries? In particular, will the timing of the stages and the length of the transitional phase itself be reproduced?

Despite these amendments and problematic issues, there is some support for the idea that, over some span of time, every society should undergo a change from high death and birth rates to low death and birth rates and that, in interaction with mobility forces, a significant amount of population growth will occur. The usefulness of employing the transition framework is that it does capture the way that major alterations of the basic components of population change can produce significant increases in population. Moreover, it enables us to compare and contrast various countries in terms of the way in which development takes place. To use the phrase of Vance (1952), the demographic transition can provide demography with "a binder for its diverse and particularized findings."

To trace the transitional process as it emerged in some Western countries, and as it has been emerging in some of the Third World countries, the following discussion provides examples of each. (A type of transition that is related to the demographic transition is the so-called *epidemiologic transition*. This will be discussed in Chapter 5 on mortality.)

Transitions of Now-Developed Nations

The area of *northern and western Europe* was the seat of demographic transitions as they were originally described. The Industrial Revolution that started in Great Britain and moved across the continent brought about social and economic changes. In turn, these changes contributed to the rise of cities and helped to initiate modern views of life.

Prior to the Industrial Revolution, Britain was typical of the areas described by Coale and Hoover as heavily rural and quite traditional in social behavior. It encompassed England and Wales and Scotland as of 1707 but extended its empire to far-flung parts of the world. The number of people on the island was not very large and not growing very rapidly. A high birth rate was compensated for by a high infant death rate, and disease also took a heavy toll of children and adults. Moreover, the natural increase that existed was muted by movements of British to occupied areas around the globe.

The Industrial Revolution of the 1700s changed all that. Sustained declines in death rates followed later by persistent decreases in birth rates occurred in Great Britain, and the same pattern took place in other countries of northern and western Europe.

Existing data do not permit us to define the patterns very sharply, but we can conclude that the growing gap between births and deaths led to significant natural increase in all of the countries of the region. The patterns were not identical, however. In France, fertility declines appeared to have started earlier than in Britain. In Ireland, migration to other countries slowed the rate of population growth (actually producing a population reduction).

Once begun, the transition continued largely unabated until death rates had assumed a fairly low level and birth rates came down to nearly meet the death rates. At that point, population growth was slowing and the third stage of the classic transition was being reached.

Today, these countries of northern and western Europe are characterized by very low fertility. The birth rate (at one time 50 or more per thousand population) stands between 12 and 15, and the average number of children born to women who complete their reproductive span (once 8 or more) ranges from 1.5 to 2.1, an interval demographers would call "at or below replacement level." The average mortality has also gotten quite low. Death rates (at one time 25 or more per thousand) hover between 9 and 12, and the average lifetime expected for people of the area (once as low as 30 or so years) was between 74 and 78 in 1992.

The demographic transition has also run its course in areas of *southern and eastern Europe*, which started the process at a later time. In fact, Italy and Spain have recently acquired even lower fertility than northern and western European countries, and mortality has reached extremely low levels there (Perez and Livi-Bacci, 1992).

Van de Kaa (1987) has spoken of "Europe's Second Demographic Transition," one answer to what happens to a transition once it has been accomplished. For him, that new transition was begun when fertility fell from about replacement level to a level well below replacement and stabilized there. The significance of that turn of events is the implication it has for population change. With mortality also about stable, the countries involved face imminent population decline unless they open their borders to immigrants. But immigration brings in people who challenge the prevailing cultural patterns, and resistance to such movements has developed in most European countries. Furthermore, the second demographic transition is characterized, according to van de Kaa, by meaningful changes in popular attitudes toward life. Emphasis is placed on individualism and postmaterialism (the greater importance of personal relationships and self-reliance, suspicion of technological innovation, environmental concerns, and less value on luxury goods).

Some of the governments have reacted with policies to reverse the new demographic trends. For example, Germany (one of the countries which has already experienced some population decrease) introduced rewards to couples who have more children in an effort to bring fertility back above replacement level. Such policies have to overcome the new popular attitudes. Arguments often focus on the nation's future, its role as an economic power and its ability to serve an aging population (Heilig et al., 1990).

While the first transitions were completed in Europe, they have also taken place in other parts of the world by now. The trend in the population of the *United States* is not unrelated to that of Europe. The first non-Indian settlements were those of Europeans and increases in the number of inhabitants came from immigration from several European nations. The people who arrived in the new continent in the seventeenth and eighteenth centuries continued their practices of high fertility, and the risks to life were no less, and perhaps greater, than in Europe at the time.

When the first U.S. census was taken in 1790, there were just under 4 million persons in the country. Demographically, the nation was similar to those of the least developed countries today. The birth rate stood above 50 per 1,000 (equivalent to an average number of children born to women of about 8). The mortality level was exceedingly high and life expectancy stood at no better than 35 years. Despite substantial numbers of deaths, natural increase alone accounted for a 30 percent rise in population per decade (Taeuber and Taeuber, 1971).

By 1790, however, there were already signs of economic development that carried from the European continent, and death rates had begun their decline in response to it. A significant amount of natural increase would continue for some time. Moreover, this was a nation of sustained immigration, so a substantial impetus to population growth was achieved.

The forces that produced the major transition in Europe also operated in the United States. By the early 1800s, fertility was well on its way downward; the decline persisted throughout the nineteenth century and into the twentieth century. By 1930, it reached a level that began to alarm many in the country in the same way that Europeans experiencing the second demographic transition are concerned. After a short-term rise in fertility in the following era, fertility in the United States resumed its low level until the present.

But the birth rate in the United States today is still higher than in most European countries and natural increase is, therefore, not as low as in Britain, Germany, and Italy. On top of that, both legal immigration and illegal immigration to the United States are substantial enough to keep population growth at a moderate level.

One can still speculate about whether a second demographic transition will occur in the United States. Some of the social and psychological factors that are observed in Europe to keep fertility below the replacement level seem to be present in the United States as well; marriage and living patterns have been altered, and the population is aging. On the other hand, the United States has a more heterogeneous population and rates of reproduction are more variable in such a population. In addition, if in-migration flows continue, both those coming to the United States and their progeny can sustain population growth.

While other demographic transitions have now been completed outside of Europe and the United States, these have occurred mainly in areas regarded as within the Western cultural sphere. Only Japan from outside that sphere can be said to have run the transitional course before 1960. A few other Asian nations have essentially completed it by now. These are all countries that we can call newly developed ones. But have their demographic transitions followed the Western pattern? Both negative and positive responses would be appropriate.

The transition of Japan was not quite the same as those of Western countries. It was achieved in a shorter period of time and relied heavily on the use of abortion to control fertility. Yet industrialization and urbanization were undoubtedly moving forces in effecting the changed attitudes of the people and the consequent control of mortality and fertility. Hong Kong and Singapore are essentially city-states, so they did not require transformations of rural populations to modern forms of behavior to complete their transitions.

One can make the argument that each national demographic transition that takes place from now on will be like the classic one in terms of bringing mortality and fertility from high to low levels but different in the sense that each society may have a unique combination of factors that produces it and a varying time period during which it occurs.

Transitions of Third World Nations

Throughout the Third World, countries are at different points of the classic demographic transition. The idea that the transition is a process that can be arbitrarily divided into any number of stages (three or five or whatever) but is basically a continuum was suggested some time ago (e.g., Hatt et al., 1955). The notion of continuum in transition has acquired more credence.

Tanaka (1989) used indicators of fertility, mortality, and urbanization to mark the progressive evolution toward transition completion in Asia. On that basis, he found that Japan, Hong Kong, and Singapore had completed it; Cyprus, Israel, Korea, and China were approaching completion, the latter two being three-fourths of the way there; Sri Lanka, Malaysia, and Thailand led the Philippines and Indonesia, all of which were more than half way there; India, Iran, and Iraq were about at the halfway mark; Pakistan, Nepal, Bangladesh, Bhutan, Jordan, Syria, and Saudi Arabia lagged far behind India, Iran, and Iraq; and other Asian countries were dispersed mostly at the lower end, with Yemen and Afghanistan being less than one-fourth of the way into the transition.

Variations also exist in Latin America. But, although the region as a whole can be said to be less advanced than Asia with respect to the transition, none of its countries are found to be at the point of Yemen or Afghanistan. Excepting some of the Caribbean islands, no area of Latin America has yet achieved the relative low balance of births and death rates seen in Europe, the United States, and a few parts of Asia. Cuba, Costa Rica, and Chile have attained the low infant mortality and high life expectancies of the West, but their levels of fertility are still elevated above those of Western countries. Most of the nations of the region have reduced their death and birth rates but are only perhaps two-thirds of the way toward completing the transition.

Africa also shows great variations among countries in its pace of change through the demographic transition, but overall it remains a continent with great population growth potential. In most countries of the region, mortality levels have not yet begun their sustained downward course. Fertility not only remains high, but has even increased in several of the countries in recent years. In a few places, there are signs of fertility reduction but not enough to convince analysts that it will continue downward in the short run. (However, see discussion of this topic in Chapter 6.)

In what ways is Africa (especially the sub-Saharan part that covers most of the continent) unique in practices that keep the transition from evolving? According to Tabah (1990), education is not well advanced; disease and disaster take a heavy toll of infants and children; long breast-feeding practices have been largely abandoned; marriage is already near universal and ages at marriage remain quite low; and the long-term problem of sterility resulting from widespread venereal diseases is being dealt with more effectively. These are in stark contrast with the situation in Asia. A more intensive examination of transitional states in a few of the Asian and African countries would, therefore, be instructive. We have chosen China, Indonesia, and some of the African countries as examples.

China has become the demographic wonder of the world in at least two respects. First, it was the initial country to reach 1 billion in population size, about one-fifth of the world's people. The population of this ancient nation fluctuated between 60 and 100 million prior to 1650. From the late seventeenth century to the mid-nineteenth century, it grew to 413 million. No significant growth occurred from then until the mid-twentieth century when disease control, agricultural advances, and improved health and medical services reduced the death rate appreciably without impacting the birth rate. The population grew steadily for the next few decades, passing the 1 billion mark by 1981 (Tien, 1983).

The second wonder has been China's ability to curtail its fertility level in a very short period of time and thus limit its rate of population growth. It did this by instituting a one-child-per-couple policy and enforcing it fairly strictly. Beginning about 1980, couples throughout the country had to pledge that they would not have more than one child (unless given authorization by the government). This contractual relationship was supported with rewards for those who abided by the rule and penalties for those who violated it. (Some issues regarding maintenance of this policy are discussed later in this book.)

The reduction in Chinese fertility was unparalleled. Yet, as successful as the fertility program may have been, it did not bring the end of the demographic transition to China. Births still exceed deaths by a significant amount and, with migration being a negligible factor for China, population growth continues for the country but at a slower rate (Tien et al., 1992).

An important distinction in the way that China and other countries of the Asian region are moving through the transition is that they are doing it without the kind of industrialization that characterized Western nations when their transitions were evolving. Indonesia, which was described as being more than halfway through the transition, is a case in point. Although it has several large cities and has begun to get involved in industrial development, it has a large rural population and remains traditional in many of its cultural practices and behaviors. The reduction in infant and child mortality has been slower than among its neighbors, but it is continuing downward. More significantly from a demographic point of view, its fertility has declined sharply from about six children per woman going through the reproductive period in about the 1960s to just over three by 1985. This was not done by employing the authoritarian fertility control approach of China, but rather through an aggressive but educational approach of convincing Indonesians to adopt family planning and link it to other aspects of family life and in the context of some meaningful socioeconomic changes in the society (Hull and Hatmadji, 1990).

Indonesia's lower population growth rate, compared with two decades ago, may be a bit misleading because mortality is still relatively high. Thus, the narrowing gap between births and deaths may be due as much to slow mortality decline as to rapid fertility reduction. The population growth rate could get larger if greater success at reducing the death rate takes place while fertility declines more slowly.

A number of African nations have started into the transition and others are still at a pretransition stage. Kenya is an example of the former in that it has lowered its infant mortality rate to a level not much different from some Southeast Asian countries and life expectancy at birth stood at about 63 in 1990. This significant movement in the mortality transition was not matched by the beginning of a fertility transition until very recently. In fact, by the mid-1980s Kenya had the highest recorded fertility level in the world (over 8 children per woman going through the reproductive period). This situation existed despite the fact that a family planning program had existed in the country for some time. Kenyan men would not be involved in fertility control and Kenyan women were not motivated enough to participate in the program in any significant numbers. Kenya's population growth rate exceeded 4 percent per year, equivalent to a doubling of the population every 16 or so years. Kenya has now begun to reduce its fertility level to the extent that Kenyan women now average fewer than 7 children, a reflection of the fact that socioeconomic changes and consequent altered attitudes toward fertility are having a greater effect on childbearing (Robinson, 1992).

While some gains have been made in mortality reduction in the vast majority of African countries, infant mortality rates are disturbingly high in most of them, and life expectancy at birth has not surpassed 50 years in a considerable number. The prospects are that mortality will eventually decline faster than fertility in these areas, and that population growth rates will thereby rise before any declines can be witnessed.

In short, there exists around the world the whole spectrum of stages (or points on the continuum) of the demographic transition. Allowing for variations in timing of mortality and fertility declines, it is reasonable to assume that all countries will eventually achieve low levels of those two population components. Some may resort to migration to modify patterns of population change. It is not inconceivable, however, that a few countries may reach population balance first by an increase in death rates that meet the level of birth rates.

SHORTER-TERM POPULATION CYCLES

The significance of the demographic transition and its variants is that it is essentially long-term. In some countries, it took over a century for it to run its course. It is clear that the transition is being effected in now-developing countries in much shorter periods of time. For areas just entering into the transition, the length of time for vital rates to coalesce at a low level may take several decades or a somewhat shorter period. In any event, demographic transitions occur over a fairly long span of time.

Of course, minor fluctuations exist at many points along the transition. When birth and death rates change over time, they are not likely to do so in a smooth fashion. In some years, the rates of births and deaths may respond to particular events in such a way that they depart from the trend lines that underlie their long-term changes. Chance alone would account for some variations from trends. The same can be said of mobility patterns, to the extent that they alter the course of transitions.

There is, however, a form of variation in fertility, mortality, and mobility changes that falls between the longer-term transitions and minor fluctuations that are seen to occur throughout the transitional period. We are calling these variations *population cycles* (or just plain *cycles*).

Cycles usually imply repetitive events, but they may also be thought of as departures from a normal state of affairs, with a return to the normal state after some period of time, that do not necessarily occur regularly. Economists refer to several types of cycles of economic change. One is the so-called *business cycle*, which was believed to take place with some regularity in all industrialized countries since at least the early nineteenth century. But of these, Samuelson (1970) wrote:

> No two business cycles are quite the same. Yet they have much in common. Though not identical twins, they are recognizable as belonging to the same family. No exact formula, such as might apply to the motions of the moon or of a simple pendulum, can be used to predict the timing of future (or past) business cycles. Rather, in their rough appearance and irregularities, business cycles more closely resemble the fluctuations of disease epidemics, of the weather, or of a child's temperature (p. 235).

It is in this sense that we speak of population cycles. To give it more specificity, however, think of such cycles as involving changes in mortality, fertility, or mobility that are of a shorter period than transitions but are of such magnitude that they have a significant impact on population size or structure.

Population cycles, like mortality, fertility, or mobility transitions, must have a defined beginning and ending. But population cycles, unlike transitions, have very little predictability. Once started, we may anticipate their continuation for a while; but we are usually unable to mark the point when they will cease to exist and a more normal situation will resume.

The Concept of Population Cycles

Having defined population cycles, let us give them a bit more substance by showing how they have previously been used in demographic discussions and then further specifying their characteristics as used here and giving examples of them in history.

Pearl (1930) wrote about growth cycles that applied to a wide variety of forms of living organisms. He demonstrated that among fruitflies, chickens, yeast plants, and humans, growth of their numbers over time takes the form of an *S-shaped curve* (sometimes called a *logistic curve*). The growth typically starts off slowly, then takes place more rapidly, later slowing down, and then reaching some level above which it ceases to grow. Pearl saw this type of growth as a natural phenomenon. It was not unreasonable to expect populations in various locations to undergo growth in this fashion. Moreover, he identified these growth curves as constituting *cycles*.

The logistic growth principle had actually been applied to population change by Verhulst as early as 1845 and was referred to by others during the late nineteenth and early twentieth centuries. What Pearl had done was extend the application to other types of organisms and show that it was a natural phenomenon.

The growth curve of human population described by Pearl as a population cycle was interpreted as being due to high fertility restrained by space limitations and a rising death rate. In this sense it supported the expectations of Malthus.

One demographer interested in population growth cycles was Cowgill (1949). Not being satisfied with discussions by Pearl and earlier writers, he sketched out four different logical combinations of birth and death rate trends that would result in the population growth rate logistic curve.

One was the cycle we associate with the demographic transition, a consequence of initially high birth and death rates with death rates declining before birth rates and the two eventually reaching a common low level. Indeed, this would produce a logistic growth curve.

A similar curve would also be generated, surmised Cowgill, if birth rates remained at a high level indefinitely while death rates first declined substantially and then increased enough to recover to their initial level. He did not refer to the time during which this might take place, but it would result in an S-shaped growth curve.

A third possibility was one in which just the obverse took place. If a death rate maintained its level indefinitely while the birth rate rose substantially and then declined again to meet the death rate, a logistic pattern of growth would have evolved.

The fourth logical combination assumed initially low birth and death rates with a rising birth rate followed by an increasing death rate, the two meeting at a higher level.

Cowgill identified the first cycle mentioned as essentially the one that describes the classic demographic transition, the second and third as cycles that can be found in the history of populations, and the fourth as one that has not been observed in reality. His main point, however, was that demographic growth can be engineered by different combinations of mortality and fertility trends and that not all population growth cycles can be said to emanate from identical causes.

Cowgill's use of the term *cycles* was restricted to periods of population growth (and their mechanics). He was not concerned with the time periods during which growth took place. In addition, he did not specify what magnitudes of fertility and mortality changes needed to be involved for a cycle of growth to be identified.

The manner in which the term *population cycle* is employed in this book serves to analytically separate three types of changes in population components. Transitions are the long-term sweeps in population components that can affect the course of population change; minor fluctuations in the components can cause ripples in population trends but their impacts are not fundamental. In contrast, *population cycles are changes in population components that are shorter in time than transitions and longer in time than minor fluctuations and also of such magnitude that they have a significant impact on population size or structure.*

Although the records may not always permit identification of minor fluctuations and cycles of population components before a demographic transition was begun, there is evidence for some of them and others can be hypothesized. In countries that are yet to complete the transition, we can still see the minor fluctuations and cycles in population components that have already occurred. If we examine the course of the demographic transition in countries that have completed it, we can observe the transition itself, as well as the minor fluctuations and the cycles that have transpired. Unless population growth transitions of Cowgill's fourth type are to be realized in now-developed nations, we can look forward to a continuation of minor fluctuations and cycles in population components for an indefinite period in such countries.

To illustrate population cycles as they have occurred in history, the following sections give examples of cycles of mortality, fertility, and mobility. The length of time and the magnitude of these cycles vary but, in each case, the combination of the two produced a significant consequence for the population size and/or structure of the group involved.

Mortality Cycles

Before any modern demographic transition took place, a high level of mortality was variable. Sometimes it declined or rose for short periods of time; at other times it was of great or little magnitude. The principal causes of death during the pretransition era were infectious and parasitic diseases and natural disasters, the latter often affecting the ability to grow food crops and harvest them. A high death rate among infants and children was commonplace, and adults could not expect to survive for very long before being subject themselves to the threats that took the lives of their young ones.

Even though survival was a dim prospect in the normal state of affairs, there were occasions when devastating events made typical mortality seem providential. Some diseases of the period were widespread, and their severity was often disastrous. Without the means to combat these scourges, tremendous numbers of people could be victims.

The bubonic plague was one such disease. It was known since ancient times and is still around today. Plague is transmitted to human beings chiefly by fleas from infected rats. Since rats were often transported by ships and trains and followed armies in their field battles, the plague was subject to export from one area to another. One form of it was called the pneumonic plague because it had the characteristics of a virulent pneumonia, and it could be passed from human to human. People in an area who had not experienced the disease before were particularly vulnerable to its effects.

In the mid-1300s, a form of the plague called the *Black Death* reached Europe. It was so-called because it led to spots of blood that turned black under the skin. It attacked the body's lymph glands and generally proved fatal (Smith, 1972).

The Black Death was believed to have killed some 24 million people, about one-fourth of the European population, between about 1346 and 1361. The disease halted trade between nations, suspended wars, and transformed the pattern of farming, all because of the changing availability of labor for these pursuits (Cartwright, 1972).

After it had spent its course in a few years, the Black Death receded and the European people were again subject only to the continual dangers of persistent diseases and disasters that were "normally" experienced. A high birth rate contributed to a revitalization of the population of the several countries of the continent and there were intermittent periods of population gain.

Uncontrollable diseases were not the only sources of mortality cycles in history. Wars and other forms of conflict have had their impacts as well. Often, the number of deaths resulting from these combats were insufficient to upset the normal processes of demographic change. The heavy bombings of Hamburg, Germany, during World War II demolished 48 percent of the city's dwellings and killed 3 percent of the civilian population (Ikle, 1951), creating a mortality cycle. Other war-torn areas, however, suffered much less. Yet in some instances, wars have produced profound mortal consequences, as in the case of the atomic bombings of Hiroshima and Nagasaki in Japan at the end of World War II. Deaths were due not only to the direct effects of the bombs but also from radiation effects that lingered for some time afterward. In each case, these cities had been experiencing the significant mortality declines before the war that is characteristic of the transition.

An even more telling mortality cycle occurred during the World War II period. While linked to the war, it could be considered independent of the war. This had to do with the fate of the European Jews. As a people, they had their own demographic transition prior to the rise of Hitler as a political power in Germany. Although their normal death rates were not as low as those found by populations at the end of the transition, they were generally favorable. Their birth rates were not very high, so that population growth for them stood at a moderate level. Although heavily committed to being Europeans, many of them had emigrated from the Soviet Union and other areas, where they had been victims of persecution in earlier years, to other eastern and western European nations. The largest number resided in Poland, but substantial numbers also remained in Ukraine and Russia. Still others lived in Germany, Hungary, and Romania.

The tale of Hitler's rise to power and his special targeting of Jews as scapegoats is well known. His "final solution" to the problem of dealing with the Jews—their transport to concentration camps and their annihilation—has also been described in many accounts. But what impact did these deeds have on the European Jews as a population? Of the nearly 9 million Jews scattered across Europe at the beginning of World War II (some having escaped the continent before then), almost 6 million were annihilated by the end of the war. This included about 90 percent of the Jews who had resided in Poland, the Baltic countries, Germany, and Austria (Dawidowicz, 1975). Mortality cycles of this magnitude are rare in modern history.

Not all mortality cycles are of past history. We seem to be involved today in the emergence of a relatively new threat to life that endangers large numbers of people in several parts of the world. Reference is to the spread of HIV (human immunodeficiency virus) and the AIDS (acquired immunodeficiency syndrome) condition it creates.

The disease was not identified until about 1980, but its transmission has been accelerated to the point where it poses one of the most serious international health and survival risks to populations for some time. In both the United States, where the mortality level was already low, and several African countries, where mortality was still at high levels, the death rate from AIDS is growing rapidly. Expectations are for the death rate to increase, even if the spread of the disease is curtailed, because of the substantial number of people who are already infected.

The areas of the world where AIDS is most widespread are precisely those areas with inadequate data-reporting systems, so it is likely that the incidence of HIV and AIDS is currently underestimated. There is also the problem of labeling deaths as due to AIDS. Since this illness destroys the body's ability to defend against other diseases, a person suffering from AIDS is a candidate for acquiring other illnesses. In the United States as well as in sub-Saharan Africa, there has been a rise in tuberculosis accompanying the increase of AIDS. When persons with the two diseases die, some may be classified as having died from one of the causes and some from the other.

Bongaarts (1988) developed a computer simulation model to estimate the incidence and prevalence of HIV and AIDS and its future course, and he applied the model to a Central African population. By the year 2000, mortality was estimated to be about double the level that would have prevailed in the absence of the epidemic. How many unexpected diseases of the future will create such mortality cycles?

Fertility Cycles

Departures from normal transitional states can also appear in the case of fertility. Once the trend in the birth rate for the United States had started downward in about 1800, the decline seemed to be fairly smooth until the early 1900s.

When the Great Depression of the late 1920s and early 1930s shocked the economy of the nation, demographers observed a lowering of the birth rate to a point that was not expected. Some argue that this was a low fertility cycle because its effect on slowing the population growth rate was significant.

The lessened childbearing (dubbed by some the *baby dearth*) was of great concern to many in the country who feared an imminent population decline. In a sense, it was a forerunner to the demographic situation faced by some European countries today, except that the U.S. population was not yet aging rapidly and mortality decline had not yet reached its expected low point. Nevertheless, this development led to the first major study of social and psychological factors affecting fertility (the so-called Indianapolis Study begun in 1940). The hope was to gain knowledge that could lead to a public policy to induce a higher level of fertility.

Before the results of the study could be digested, much less interpreted, World War II intervened and societal conditions changed. By 1946, the birth rate had turned back up and continued sharply upward until it reached a peak in 1957. It was not until 1964 that the *baby boom* was pronounced as ended. By that time, a generation of babies had been born that greatly outnumbered the generations before and after it. It is estimated that perhaps 20 million "excess" births took place, or one-fourth more than would have occurred without the baby boom. Analysts are still trying to complete the explanations for the U.S. baby boom phenomenon. At the same time, they are trying to understand why fertility levels subsequently were lowered (the *baby bust*) and remained low. (We will return to these issues in Chapter 6 on fertility processes.)

Other countries of the developed world have had their baby booms and baby busts. For example, Germany's fertility trends mirrored those of the United States to a considerable extent. It, too, experienced such a sharp decline in the birth rate by the late 1920s that the nation was concerned about a falling population level. It, too, participated in the baby boom of the World War II era (although its fertility rise started earlier than in the United States, was interrupted during the conflict itself, and did not reach quite as high a level as in the United States).

However, with the political separation of West and East Germany after the war, the fertility patterns of the two areas diverged. In West Germany, the birth rate continued its decline until the mid-1980s. In East Germany, the baby bust lasted only until the early 1970s, at which time there was a recovery in the birth rate. In fact, by 1980 East German women averaged half a child more than West German women. In the late 1980s, the two fertility patterns began to converge in the opposite way; the East German fertility level had been reduced to the low point reached in the early 1970s while the West German fertility level rose again to nearly meet that of East Germany (Heilig et al., 1990). It was almost as if national reunification were anticipated! In any event, these several departures from the normal fertility trend constituted fertility cycles, both because of their length of time and their magnitudes. Are there good explanations for these cycles? Demographers believe that most of the explanation can be accounted for (see Chapter 6).

We conclude this subsection with an additional illustration of fertility cycles. We have already mentioned that the time period for cycles may vary, but the magnitude of impact must be sufficient to affect population size or structure in a meaningful way. The baby boom and baby bust were fertility cycles occurring over a span of ten or more years in different countries. Some fertility cycles can, however, occur over a much shorter span of time.

A classic example of the short cycle with a strong impact is the fertility change that occurred in Romania in the late 1960s. To put it more correctly, the country experienced a startling change in fertility in one year, but the fertility cycle itself lasted for several years.

Following World War II, Romania had a fertility level higher than that of other eastern European countries. The government, intent on seeing the level decline, made abortion on request available to the public starting in 1957. This had the effect of reducing the birth rate so that by 1966 it was not only lower than that of the other eastern European countries but stood at a mere 14 births per thousand population. In effect, abortion had become a major means of fertility control.

The government's reaction to the decline was decidedly unfavorable because population growth would be severely limited. As a consequence, in October 1966 the legal use of abortion was restricted to certain conditions, such as risk to the woman's life, rape, and risk to the fetus. The birth rate responded by increasing to 27 per thousand in 1967, a virtual doubling in one year! The sudden policy changes had left the general public unprepared to regulate childbearing according to their own wishes. Although couples subsequently substituted other forms of fertility control for abortion, and thereby reinstituted a more normal family planning situation, the birth rate declined but did not return to the level of the early 1960s until the early 1980s. In that range of time, it is estimated that the number of Romanian babies who were born exceeded what would have been "normal" by one-fourth (Berelson, 1979).

Mobility Cycles

Population cycles involving movements of people can occur within countries (internal migration or mobility) or between countries (international migration). There are many examples of each of these, but we will give just four.

Few episodes of international migration have captured the fancy of historical writers of fact and fiction more than the large streams of migrants from Ireland during the nineteenth century. At the beginning of that century, the periodic failure of potato crops (the main Irish food staple) and recurring epidemics affected survival prospects, especially for agricultural laborers. By the early 1800s, the combined threat to life was unbearable enough for a large segment of the citizens. The family and economic systems offered little hope, and the Irish sought refuge in other places. With a population size of about 5.5 million in 1821, an annual average outflow of 30,000 persons during the next few decades would not seem to be very great, but many fewer had left before and the pace was picking up. The famine of 1845–48 that followed the worst potato crop resulted in an average out-migration from the country of about 150,000 per year. Large outward flows continued for some time after the famine ended. Between 1845 and 1870, at least 3 million people left the country; between 1871 and 1891, an additional 1 million were gone. A significant number went across the sea to Britain, but the major movement was to the United States, where the urban areas beckoned. By the end of the nineteenth century, about 40 percent of all living Irish-born resided outside of Ireland. From a peak population of 6.5 million in 1841, the number of people in Ireland was less than half of that by 1901. In fact, population did not stabilize until the 1920s. Although natural increase contributed to a rise in the population after that, by 1961 there were still fewer people in Ireland than in 1777! The key element of demographic change for the country was the emigration cycle of the mid-1800s (Kennedy, 1973; O'Sullivan and Winsberg, 1990; Nam and Philliber, 1984).

Many countries regard themselves as being "a nation of immigrants." If one goes far enough back in time, all societies have been nations of immigrants. If we restrict determination of that status by referring only to the modern period, then at least Australia, New Zealand, Israel, and the United States would have a claim to the status.

Allowing for the fact that Indians (Native Americans) had already migrated into the area now called the United States before Europeans arrived in sizable numbers, it is still the case that subsequent immigration of non-Indians has contributed substantially to the size of the U.S. population since the country's beginnings. Yet the flows were relatively minor in some years and relatively major in others.

The mobility transition (as described by Zelinsky) does not have the same consistent directional pattern as do the mortality and fertility transitions. Hence, there may be more instances where we would label deviations as mobility cycles rather than part of the mobility transition. But again, we are thinking of deviations from the trend of mobility that is shorter-term and of such considerable magnitude that it has a special impact on the population.

A particularly good illustration with regard to immigration to the United States is the arrivals during the period 1905–14. Prior to that time, the flows had frequently been large but never reached 1 million a year. Immigration exceeded 1 million for the first time in 1905, and did so in six of the ten years starting at that time. Even in the four years when there were fewer than 1 million a year, the annual number of immigrants was more than three-fourths of a million. The total number of arrivals during the ten-year span was over 9 million. In 1915, with World War I in progress, the immigrant flow dropped off sharply. It never again came close to reaching 1 million in a year.

BOX 2.2 A Brazilian Migration Cycle

Brazil is a country whose population historically has been concentrated on its eastern coast. The capital city for many years was Rio de Janiero. Along with São Paulo and Porto Alegre in the southeast coastal zone, it has been among the world's faster-growing cities. For many decades, however, it was the hope of Brazilian political leaders to develop the largely uninhabited interior of the nation. The frontier was there to be developed. But residents of the large cities were not attracted to the area. Finally, in 1960, without the benefit of progressive growth on the frontier, a new city was established six hundred miles inland and designated the capital to replace Rio. Although farmers had lived in the general area for some time, the city (called Brasilia) was carved out of the wilderness, complete with modern governmental structures and a superhighway from the coastal area to facilitate transportation. The expectation was that vast numbers would be attracted there. While this assumption was not realized, Brasilia and the highway together may have drawn 150,000 to 275,000 migrants, some to staff offices of government, others to supplement the agricultural labor force, and still others to occupy service villages along the highway (Cardozo, 1972; Katzman, 1977).

This migration cycle involved more than just a sharp increase in numbers. Throughout most of the nineteenth century, the persons coming to the United States were largely from northern and western Europe. By the end of the century, and especially during the 1905–1914 period, southern and eastern Europeans dominated the arrivals. The changing national character of the movement led to social and political reactions that had a profound effect not only on social relationships but on later immigration policy as well. (We will deal with that effect in Chapter 7.)

Internal migration within a transition framework takes many forms, but some of the more patterned movements are mobility toward the frontiers, urbanization, and migration from regions of lesser to regions of greater attractiveness. From time to time, mobility cycles occur that do not conform to these patterns, as in the case of Brazil (see Box 2.2).

Mobility cycles can be consequences of natural disasters or those caused by humans. The immense dust storms in the Great Plains region of the United States during the 1930s made farming nearly impossible and led many families to move westward to seek better opportunities. John Steinbeck's *Grapes of Wrath* (1939) gives a fictional account of an extended family that heads for California under those circumstances and their plight. Wars have displaced populations, some of whom eventually return to the area. Hurricanes, floods, and tornadoes have produced similar effects.

In the contemporary world, a growing peril has been the possibility of nuclear accidents. The disaster that took place in the Chernobyl nuclear power station in the former Soviet Union in 1986 had severe repercussions for the health and survival of people in a large portion of the country and, because of the spread of radioactive material by air, in neighboring countries as well.

One of the critical controversies surrounding the disaster was the issue of how serious a threat was the radioactivity posed to residents of Chernobyl and nearby areas and the advisability of evacuating people from the region. Because of disagreements among officials about the threat, evacuations were at first delayed. At greatest risk were the 50,000 or so residents of Prypyat, a city about three kilometers from the nuclear plant. But there were also sixty-eight other population points in the danger zone.

After evacuations had taken place, the official count of those who were displaced stood between 116,000 and 135,000. These figures apparently ignored the children evacuated from larger cities in the region; this raised the total to something more like 500,000. Within a year of the tragedy, some of the villages in the area were "decontaminated," and people were returned to their residences or replacements for them. But Prypyat and a number of other locations remained largely uninhabited except for temporary workers. Ultimately, a sizable number of people can be said to have been permanently displaced by the disaster and many others were migrants who may have come back to the region, likely to a different residence than they had before (Marples, 1988).

OVERVIEW OF TRANSITIONS AND CYCLES

The picture that emerges from an examination of historical descriptions of population changes shows a great deal of variability superimposed on a relatively common foundation. The basic demographic transition (and its accompanying mortality, fertility, and mobility transitions) differs from country to country, but these differences are largely in timing. Their fundamental aspects are not greatly different from place to place. It is also the case that these transitions typically incorporate numerous minor fluctuations over time that are overlayed on a transitional trend line. The transitions are predictable within limits, whereas the minor fluctuations and the population cycles that occur periodically are usually not very predictable, either in terms of their starting and ending times or their magnitudes.

The number of permutations and combinations of the cycles themselves are extensive. Cycles of mortality, fertility, and mobility can take place simultaneously, or overlap, or be quite independent of each other. Moreover, they may be experienced before the onset of a transition, during one or another phase of a transition, or after the transition has essentially spent itself.

It is not surprising, therefore, that every country seems to have a unique historical description of its population change. What is perhaps surprising is that there are sufficient common elements to population transitions and cycles that they are found, in retrospect, to repeat themselves from one area to another with a fair amount of regularity.

Chapter Highlights

1. Changes in population size and in its basic components (mortality, fertility, and mobility) take place over time in three forms—long-term transitions, short-term cycles, and minor fluctuations.
2. The so-called demographic transition is a description of how basic population changes have taken place over a long span of time in now-developed countries, and are expected to take place over a substantial period of time in countries still undergoing development.
3. In the classic statement of the demographic transition, high birth and death rates are eventually brought down to low levels. Because the death rate declines earlier and faster than the birth rate, however, a significant amount of population growth occurs during the process.
4. There are several limitations to the original transition framework. It did not incorporate the mobility component (which was later done); population growth during the initiation of the transition in some Western countries was later discovered to be due to some rise in fertility as well as to a downturn in mortality; and the framework left unspecified what happens to the trend in the components after the transition is complete.
5. It is clear that the period of time it takes to go through the transition varies from one nation to another, and the particular pattern of the transition components can differ among countries.
6. The demographic transition is ordinarily not a smooth one, since minor fluctuations in mortality, fertility, and mobility are apt to occur as a result of unique factors. But these fluctuations do not have significant effects on changes in population size or structure.
7. Population cycles are changes in population components that are shorter in time than transitions and longer in time than minor fluctuations, and also of such magnitude that they have a significant impact on population size or structure.
8. Population cycles can take place before, during, or after a transition. Consequently, significant population changes can occur even apart from a population transition.
9. The complexity in the pace of population change is reflected in the fact that transitions, cycles, and minor fluctuations can occur simultaneously, for overlapping periods of time or for nonoverlapping periods.

Discussion Questions

1. Looking at the country as a whole, how different from the classic form has the demographic transition been, and why?
2. What are examples of minor fluctuations in population change (or its components) that can occur during the course of the demographic transition?
3. The chapter gives examples of mortality cycles. What other mortality examples can you think of?
4. A few illustrations of fertility cycles are given. Can you identify some additional fertility illustrations?
5. Mobility cycles can be related to either internal or international mobility. In addition to the examples given in the chapter, can you come up with other examples of each type of mobility cycle?
6. Why do we say that "significant population changes can occur even apart from a demographic transition"?

Suggested Readings

Chesnais, Jean-Claude. 1983. "Patterns of Demographic Transition." In Parviz Khalatbari, ed., *Demographic Transition*, pp. 105–113. Berlin: Akademie-Verlag. A quantitative review of the dimensions of changes in demographic transitions around the world that shows their great variability.

Teitelbaun, Michael S. 1975. "Relevance of Demographic Transition Theory for Developing Countries." *Science* 188: 420–25. A thoughtful consideration of the factors that make demographic transitions in developing nations different from what had earlier transpired in now-developed nations.

Zelinsky, Wilbur. 1971. "The Hypothesis of the Mobility Transition." *Geographical Review* 61: 219–49. Zelinsky not only gives the mobility counterpart to the classical demographic transition but also discusses alternative forms of mobility within the framework.

Cartwright, Frederick F. 1972. *Disease and History*. New York: Thomas Y. Crowell. Already cited in the discussion on the Black Death, Cartwright also deals with other disease epidemics that produced mortality cycles in earlier periods of time.

Easterlin, Richard A. 1968. "The American Baby Boom in Historical Perspective." In *Population, Labor Force, and Long Swings in Economic Growth*, pp. 77–110. New York: National Bureau of Economic Research. An attempt by a noted economist-demographer to link the baby boom to economic cycles.

References

Berelson, B. 1979. "Romania's 1966 Anti-Abortion Decree: The Demographic Experience of the First Decade." *Population Studies* 33:2, 209–22.

Blacker, C.P. 1947. "Stages in Population Growth." *Eugenics Review* 39:88–102.

Bongaarts, John. 1988. "Modeling the Spread of HIV and the Demographic Impact of AIDS in Africa." *Center for Policy Studies, Working Papers*, no. 140. New York: Population Council.

Caldwell, John C. 1976. "Toward a Restatement of Demographic Transition Theory." *Population and Development Review* 2: 3/4, 321–66.

Cardozo, Manoel. 1972. Brazil. In *The World Book Encyclopedia*, Chicago: Field Enterprises.

Cartwright, Frederick F. 1972. *Disease and History*. New York: Thomas Y. Crowell.

Coale, Ansley J., and Edgar M. Hoover. 1958. *Population Growth and Economic Development in Low-Income Countries*. Princeton, N.J.: Princeton University Press.

Cowgill, Donald Olen. 1949. "The Theory of Population Growth Cycles." *American Journal of Sociology* 55:2, 163–70.

Davis, Kingsley. 1945. "The World Demographic Transition." *Annals of the American Academy of Political and Social Sciences* 237: 1–11.

———. 1963. "The Theory of Change and Response in Modern Demographic History." *Population Index* 29:4, 345–66.

Dawidowicz, Lucy S. 1975. *The War against the Jews, 1933–1945*. New York: Holt, Rinehart & Winston.

Demeny, Paul. 1968. "Early Fertility Decline in Austria-Hungary." *Daedalus* 97:2, 502–22.

Friedlander, Dov. 1969. "Demographic Responses and Population Change." *Demography* 6:4, 359–81.

Hatt, Paul K., Nellie L. Farr, and E. Weinstein. 1955. "Types of Population Balance." *American Sciological Review* 20, 14–21.

Heilig, Gerhard, Thomas Buttner, and Wolfgang Lutz. 1990. "Germany's Population: Turbulent Past, Uncertain Future." *Population Bulletin* 45:4,1–46.

Hull, Terence H., and Sri Harijati Hatmadji. 1990. *Regional Fertility Differentials in Indonesia: Causes and Trends*. Working Papers in Demography, no. 22. Canberra: Australian National University.

Ikle, Fred Charles. 1951. "Effect of War Destruction upon the Ecology of Cities." *Social Forces* 29:4, 383–91.

Katzman, Martin T. 1977. *Cities and Frontiers in Brazil*. Cambridge, Mass.: Harvard University Press.

Kennedy, Robert E., Jr. 1973. *The Irish: Emigration, Marriage and Fertility*. Berkeley, Calif.: University of California Press.

Landry, Adolphe. 1934. "*La Révolution demographique: Etudes et essais sur les problèmes de la population*. Paris: Sirey.

Malthus, T. R. 1914. *An Essay on Population*. London: J.M. Dent. Everyman's Library Edition, no. 692.

Marples, David R. 1988. *The Social Impact of the Chernobyl Disaster*. London: Macmillan.

Nam, Charles B., and Susan Gustavus Philliber. 1984. *Population: A Basic Orientation*. Englewood Cliffs, N.J.: Prentice-Hall.

Notestein, Frank W. 1945. Population—The Long View. In Theodore W. Schultz, ed., *Food for the World*, pp. 36–57. Chicago: University of Chicago Press.

O'Sullivan, Patrick M., and Morton D. Winsberg. 1990. Ireland. In William J. Serow, Charles B. Nam, David F. Sly, and Robert H. Weller, eds. *Handbook on International Migration*, pp. 115–29. Westport, Conn.: Greenwood Press.

Pearl, Raymond. 1930. *The Biology of Population Growth*. New York: Alfred A. Knopf.

Perez, Margarita Delgado, and Massimo Livi-Bacci. 1992. "Fertility in Italy and Spain: The Lowest in the World." *Family Planning Perspectives* 24:4, 162–71.

Petersen, William. 1960. "The Demographic Transition in the Netherlands." *American Sociological Review* 25:3, 334–47.

Robinson, Warren C. 1992. "Kenya Enters the Fertility Transition." *Population Studies* 46:3, 445–57.

Samuelson, Paul A. 1970. *Economics*. 8th ed. New York: McGraw-Hill.

Smith, Austin Edward. 1972. "Bubonic Plague." In *The World Book Encyclopedia*, vol. 2, p. 545. Chicago: Field Enterprises.

Steinbeck, John. 1939. *The Grapes of Wrath*. New York: Sun Dial Press.

Tabah, Leon. 1990. "From One Demographic Transition to Another." *Population Bulletin of the United Nations*, no. 28.

Taeuber, Irene B., and Conrad Taeuber, 1971. *People of the United States in the 20th Century*. Washington, D.C.: Government Printing Office.

Tanaka, Tatsuo. 1989. *Demographic Transition and Development in Asian Countries*. Tokyo: Asian Population and Development Association.

Thompson, Warren S. 1929. "Population." *American Journal of Sociology* 34, 959–75.

Tien, H. Yuan. 1983. "China: Demographic Billionaire." *Population Bulletin* (a publication of the Population Reference Bureau) 38:2, 3–42.

———, Zhang Tianlu, Ping Yu, Li Jingneng, and Liang Zhongtang. 1992. "China's Demographic Dilemmas." *Population Bulletin* (a publication of the Population Reference Bureau) 47:1, 1–44.

van de Kaa, Dirk J. 1987. "Europe's Second Demographic Transition." *Population Bulletin* (a publication of the Population Reference Bureau) 42:1, 1–57.

Vance, Rupert B. 1952. "Is Theory for Demographers?" *Social Forces* 31, 9–13.

Zelinsky, Wilbur. 1971. "The Hypothesis of the Mobility Transition." *Geographical Review* 61: 219–49.

3. Approaches to Understanding Population Change

When we are asked if we understand something, our response will usually be conditioned by our perception of what there is to know about the topic and how much of that we think we are expected to know. For instance, if we are questioned about our understanding of the game of baseball, we might encompass within that level of comprehension the basic rules of the game; the strategies that managers, coaches, and players use to try to win; the contributions observers of the game make to it; the impact of weather and playing field conditions; and the actual performance of teams and players at present and in the past.

If we have a thorough knowledge of all these things, then we are approaching complete understanding of the game of baseball. If we know about the basic rules of the game and maybe are familiar with the names and performances of most of the participants, but are not very sophisticated about strategies used to win, then the "experts" might say that we have only a general understanding of the game. If we do not even comprehend the basic rules of the game, despite the fact that we are aware that Babe Ruth and Nolan Ryan have been celebrated baseball players, that would put us in the category of the "uninformed."

We could also differentiate people not only by their comprehension of dimensions of the game but also by the depth of their understanding of each dimension. The experts know about nuances of strategies that others, who are generally well schooled about the game, do not know.

So there are levels and degrees of understanding of different phenomena. The level and degree of understanding one possesses are related to certain benefits that can be derived. You do not have to be an expert to enjoy watching a baseball game, but you should be an expert if you are a participant or your occupation is writing a baseball column for the newspaper.

Turning to population change, how much understanding of that topic must there be for you as students of the subject to benefit from it? One possible answer is as much as it takes to perform well on tests or earn a particular grade in the course using this book. A more general answer would be as much as it takes for you to appreciate how population change takes place, and what are its determinants and consequences, so that you can use that knowledge to enhance your life satisfactions (which might mean, for example, qualifying for a job or gaining insights into your own personal and family life).

If we survey the records of history, we find that approaches to understanding population change have evolved considerably over time. What you can be told in this book reflects substantially more kinds and amounts of knowledge about population processes than was known a few decades ago and an enormously greater range of knowledge than existed a few hundred years ago.

The approaches used to acquire that knowledge have taken on different forms as well. In the following sections, you will become acquainted with philosophical and ideological perspectives on population that were exceedingly common in earlier times but are still around today. You will also learn about both simple and complex analytical approaches to understanding population change.

The purpose of this coverage is to make you familiar with the way knowledge about population has been conceptualized and the kinds of factors that have been taken into consideration. Like the game of baseball, the study of population has its rules (of inquiry), its principal players (those who have done research and/or have written about it), and its strategies (the ways population scholars have attempted to derive knowledge about population change).

The study of population (*demography*) is basically a social science. That means that the manner in which knowledge about the subject is developed follows certain rules of inquiry. Often we are told that science involves dealing with natural problems, like those studied in physics, chemistry, biology, geology, and other such fields. So many people think that science only relates to certain kinds of subject matter. On the contrary, science can relate to a broad range of subject matter, including the *social sciences.* Science depends on methods of inquiry that help us to gather evidence and test ideas. It is an approach to gaining knowledge through employment of methods of study that are reliable, valid, and reproducible. Studies using such an approach (and there are many alternative approaches for studying any particular topic) can be regarded as scientific. Reports that do not follow the canons of science are not scientific. Not everything written about the *natural sciences* by natural scientists is scientific. If a physicist offers an opinion that nuclear power is the best energy source for the world for the next several decades, that may or may not be based on scientific evidence.

It is also true that some writings by social scientists are scientific and others are not. The determination of whether some report on population is scientific or not depends on whether the rules of scientific inquiry have been followed. In this chapter, we will look at attempts to understand population change in terms of their scientific and nonscientific content. Our position is that attempts that are scientific give us a better basis for understanding the phenomenon we are trying to learn about.

PHILOSOPHICAL AND IDEOLOGICAL APPROACHES

Population is a topic that has been spoken about and written about since the earliest recorded history. Population change, and its components, were always concerns of people whose lives were intertwined with it. Having more or fewer residents of an area, dying at a young or old age and under what circumstances, bearing many or few children, remaining in one location or moving to other locations—these have always been matters that people have talked and written about because they are essential aspects of societal, communal, and family life. This has been true throughout history.

Before the canons of science as we know them today were developed, people had ideas about population matters. In general, these ideas were expressed in terms of philosophical or ideological orientations. We are regarding a *philosophical point of view* as one rooted in the religious or ethical beliefs of a group of people. It is an integral part of the group's culture and is derived from the acceptance of a deity or of the primacy of nature or of the power of supernatural forces. We are defining an *ideological point of view* as one based on a particular set of values held by an individual or group. It can emanate from the philosophy of life that guides an individual, but that philosophy is tempered by associations and experiences that the individual has had. Thus, two people may share the same religious or natural philosophy but have somewhat different views about the appropriateness of abortion or the desirability of tightening immigration laws because of varying ideological perspectives. Since we have a tendency to think of sets of compatible values as clustering in an ideological orientation, we sometimes label sets of values, such as when we refer to political liberals and conservatives.

What makes philosophy and ideology so important in trying to understand population change is that everyone of us, scientists and nonscientists alike, think in terms of the philosophies and ideologies to which we have become attached and that orient our thought processes. Max Weber, a noted sociologist who himself wrote as both a scientist and nonscientist, cautioned social scientists about the need for guarding against having their own values influence their analysis and interpretation of scientific data.

The scientists' own values cannot be divorced from their thinking processes (they are much too ingrained in their consciousness for that to happen), but scientists can be aware of their own values and try to separate them from their analysis. Nonscientists, and even scientists who speak out on issues beyond the scientific realm, draw on their philosophical and ideological backgrounds and perspectives. That is why, say, two nuclear scientists who comprehend equally well the scientific aspects of constructing and detonating a nuclear bomb can differ greatly about the wisdom of using it in warfare. Their understanding of nuclear science is *value-neutral*, or generally separated from value considerations, whereas their views on using nuclear power in wartime differ because of the varying philosophical and/or ideological perspectives that the two scientists bring to bear in deciding about an ethical matter.

Wisdom of the Ages

Ancient religious doctrine was typically oriented to increasing population size. The writers of such doctrines called attention to the insufficient numbers of people for warfare and security and, because of short life expectancy at the time, for maintaining the family and kinship lines.

The admonition to "increase and multiply" is found not only in the Old Testament of the Hebrews but in the religions of practically every ancient nation (Stangeland, 1966). In early India, a common prayer was that a marriage might be blessed by numerous offspring. According to Confucius (the ancient Chinese philosopher), a son failed in his first duty if he did not beget children to perpetuate his name and family. But Confucius was also mindful of the negative aspects of too much population growth. Such growth, he wrote, may reduce output per worker, depress levels of living for the masses and engender strife (United Nations, 1973). So, while the ancients saw the necessity of having larger numbers of people, they could also anticipate some detrimental societal effects if the numbers got too large.

The ideal of achieving an "optimum population size," which is implied in the Confucian expression, was a focus of the classical Greek doctrines. The Greek philosophers, living in a period when urban centers were emerging, formulated their ideas about the desirable city-state. The primacy of government efficiency was stressed, and the numbers and distribution of people were critical elements of that condition.

However, because frequent wars took a heavy toll of the population, Spartans compelled their citizens to marry and Spartan fathers who had three or four sons were publicly rewarded. Even in Athens, where population increase was not championed so much, there were laws against celibacy as well as customs promoting the fruitfulness of marriage. But during periods of extended peace, later marriages were often recommended as a means of reducing childbearing, and excess population was sent off to develop new colonies (Stangeland, 1966).

The idea of an "optimum" population was central to the writings of Plato (427–347 B.C.) and Aristotle (384–322 B.C.). In his ideal city-state, Plato proposed a particular form of population distribution (see Box 3.1).

Aristotle was less enamored than Plato of a communistic organization of the ideal city-state, but he too was aware of the need to have an optimum population size "sufficient for a good life in the political community." His concern about too large numbers of people is addressed in the statement that "experience shows that a very populous city can rarely, if ever, be well governed; since all cities which have a reputation for good government have a limit of population" (Aristotle, 1943).

BOX 3.1 Plato's Ideal Population Distribution

Plato believed that the city should lie at the center of the territory, and that the land should be divided into twelve parts, varying in size according to the quality of the soil. Because he considered 5,040 landholders as the right number for the area (the number being easily divisible for different functions), he would divide the area into 10,080 half-allotments so that each landholder could have two houses, one nearer the center of the state and the other nearer the border.

So that the number of households might remain constant, Plato (1960) proposed:

> Let him who has a lot assigned him ever leave after him one son, of his own preference, to be his heir in that household...; as for other children, when a man has more than one, let him give the females in marriage as a law yet to be enjoined shall direct; the males let him distribute among citizens who have a lack of offspring, to be their sons, and that preferably by friendly agreement.

Since he realized that all of these proposals might not work out precisely if fertility were too high or if proper arrangements for allocating children could not be made, he further suggested that the magistrates should employ the best devices to keep the number of households at 5,040 and no more. According to Plato:

> [There should be] shifts for checking propagation when its course is too facile, and, on the other side,...ways of fostering and encouraging numerous births which affect the young by marks of honour and dishonour and admonition conveyed in warning speeches by their seniors,...[or] if mated love should cause an excessive glut of population,...we can send out colonies of such persons as we deem convenient with love and friendship on both sides.

In the Roman period an expansive view of the state led to an emphasis on having larger populations. The laws of Augustus (Emperor from 27 B.C. to A.D. 14) put special stress on the advantages of marriage and childbearing. Early Christian writers also emphasized the need for population growth and were wary of possible depopulation due to the great losses of life from disease and natural disasters. A sustained high birth rate seemed to be a necessity.

As Christianity spread, the moral persuasion of Church authors was to honor celibacy, continence, and virginity (all symbolized by the great Church figures). Yet high mortality in that period still gave rise to the need for high fertility, as seen by political regimes. These perspectives were maintained for a number of centuries.

Views during Later Periods

Many persons wrote on population topics from the end of the early Christian period until the time of the Renaissance and Reformation (fourteenth to sixteenth centuries), but few of their comments are remembered today. In the main, population growth was still regarded as a goal to be achieved.

The rise of cities and states, the expansion of commerce and trade, and what some call the "new intellectual awakening" during the fourteenth century later brought forth writers who were sensitive to population conditions. The fourteenth-century Arab philospher Ibn-Khaldun (1950), whose writings were not translated into English until the modern period, was known outside Europe as a scholar who discussed the structure of society and social processes. He wrote about the mutual links between population size and prosperity and the impact of urban air pollution on the death rate. This was a rare example in the premodern era of population thinking that went beyond philosophical and ideological views.

On the European continent, intellectual debate revolved around the factors affecting the economy and politics of nations. Foreign trade and manufacturing were seen as the prime tools for economic gain and the acquisition of political power. Population growth occupied an important place in the scheme for creating markets and staffing armies.

Mercantilist writers in general stressed the advantages of a large and growing population and favored policies aimed at stimulating population growth, including measures to encourage marriage and large families, to improve public health, to check emigration to other countries, and to promote immigration especially of skilled workers. Although some writers of the time alluded to a variety of factors affecting population growth, such as plagues, wars, climate, infecundity, vice, abortion, delay of marriage, mortality, the effects of emigration to colonies, and of immigration, they did not attempt a systematic explanation of population changes and their causes (United Nations, 1973).

Throughout the period, speculation about causes and consequences of population change were superimposed upon policy statements about the desirability of population growth, these flowing from philosophical and ideological positions of the era.

Prior to Malthus in the late eighteenth century and beyond, those who had something to say about population were considered to be optimists or pessimists. The *optimistic point of view* was that a large and growing population was the source of national strength and security and of power and wealth. Morever, population growth, it was reasoned, promoted the efficiency of production and stimulated economic progress. The earth's resources were not regarded as limited, and plentifulness meant that everyone could enjoy the benefits of a good life and no one should lack welfare.

The *pessimistic point of view* was that a population too large in relation to its means of subsistence was immediately or ultimately harmful. Special emphasis was put on the high reproductive levels of the poor and their unwillingness to limit their childbearing, with consequent pressure on the general economy (Hutchinson, 1967).

Optimistic and pessimistic views of population size and growth continue to characterize the major distinctions in population thought based on philosophies and ideologies of life. These perceptions of the consequences of demographic change are generally intertwined with concerns about other aspects of societal and communal conditions. As a result, the major camps of thinking about population right up to the present appear to have taken on the tone of optimism or pessimism. Of course, there are variations in the optimistic or pessimistic outlooks.

Contemporary Views

Although modern population study has been essentially based on what we call the "scientific" perspective, philosophy and ideology still play a significant part in framing questions we ask about population change and in arriving at answers to them.

Hodgson (1991) has made the case that the Population Association of America (the U.S. national organization of demographers), was founded on the basis of certain ideological concerns about dominant social problems in the early 1900s. These include eugenics (the quality of population and its implications for the future population structure); the national composition of immigration; and birth control. At times, all these preoccupations have been integrated into a common ideological concern (Wattenberg, 1987). However, while population study in the United States may have received its impetus from such concerns, the field of demography as a whole and the professional organization that guides the field have increasingly emphasized the need for using reliable and valid methods of examining population issues.

Yet ideological positions based on religious perspectives and concern about environmental preservation have become critical orientations in thinking about, and interpreting, population matters today, in addition to those that carry over from earlier periods.

Religious doctrine often provides guidance for thinking about population, especially in relation to the fertility component. At the same time, it has been increasingly the case that many people who are otherwise devoted to their religion have not abided by its stipulations in matters related to population. It is also true that all major religious groups are divided by levels of orthodoxy and reform so that different religious messages may come to members of the same group.

Campbell (1960) tells us that Christian doctrine regarding deliberate family limitation was clear-cut and unambiguous for centuries. The middle of the twentieth century, he says, has, however, "been remarkable for an almost complete reversal of traditional doctrine on birth control by the Protestant Churches, and serious modifications by the Roman Catholic Church." Starting with the Anglican Church, a considerable liberalization of positions on marriage and fertility control practices has taken place. Although there are significant differences among the Protestant denominations concerning these matters even today, their views have departed greatly from those held in the nineteenth century.

The modifications by the Roman Catholic Church, mentioned by Campbell, are summed up by Noonan (1986):

> That intercourse must only be for a procreative purpose, that intercourse in menstruation is mortal sin, that intercourse in pregnancy is forbidden, that intercourse has a natural position—all these were once common opinions of the theologians and are so no more.

Noonan points out that recent popes and the Second Vatican Council have placed the locus of responsibility for the number of children in the decision of the married couple, but they have also continued to insist that contraception (other than as a result of the natural rhythm method), sterilization, and abortion are contrary to Church teaching.

Other religions provide guidelines for their followers concerning fertility control and other aspects of population change. Often, the interpretation of the Scriptures as they bear on these issues will differ from one subgroup to another. The overriding point, nevertheless, is that religion has long been a philosophical source of attitudes and behaviors relative to demographic concerns, and continues to be so in today's world. Feelings of optimism or pessimism about population change may have something to do with the nature and extent to which religions might have changed their historical positions.

Philosophical and ideological orientations toward population, and especially fertility control, are also rooted in ethical concerns about the economic welfare of nations and the disadvantaged classes of societies. The notion that social and economic reforms are needed to benefit the underclasses is frequently combined with programs to assist low-income couples to restrict their fertility. The family planning movement (to be discussed more fully later in this book) is based on a view of population growth in the world, in less-developed countries, and among lower classes in developed countries that is essentially pessimistic in character.

We can likewise ascribe this pessimistic orientation to those who advocate greater attention to protecting the natural environment. Brown (1991) is representative in stating the following belief:

> Ecologists looking at biological indicators...see rising human demand, driven by population growth and rising affluence, surpassing the carrying capacity of local forests, grasslands, and soils in country after country. They see sustainable yield thresholds of the economy's natural support systems being breached throughout the Third World. And as a result, they see the natural resource base diminishing as population growth is expanding.

Some with different ideologies have come to different conclusions about the environmental crises resulting from population change. Repetto (1987), writing from a more optimistic perspective that assumes both that science will deal adequately with resource needs and that people will control their fertility in time to prevent population-resource imbalances, affirms:

> There is no reason to conclude that substantial, sustainable improvements in living conditions for all the world's people are beyond reach and no reason to neglect opportunities to promote that goal by adopting policies to bring the two sides of the equation into balance, so that sustainable population numbers will be balanced with sustainable resource supplies and environmental quality.

These opposite views are not based on radically different estimates of present population and resource amounts, but they are related to expectations about what future trends in the two areas will be. The future is determined as much by pessimistic or optimistic perceptions as by information on what the course of population and resource trends might reasonably be. Even estimates of the present population and resource situation can be a consequence of those opposite views (see Box 3.2).

We know that philosophical and ideological perspectives orient the policies and programs of governments in many spheres. Political actions based on alternative outlooks have indeed affected policies and programs concerning population matters in the United States. Some presidential administrations (both Democratic and Republican) gave encouragement to fiscal support for population control measures in the United States and overseas. In the period 1980–92, administration positions were reversed. A leading population consultant to those administrations offered the optimistic ideology that shaped national political decisions on population issues:

> The standard of living has risen along with the size of the world's population since the beginning of recorded time. And with increases in income and population have come less severe shortages, lower costs, and an increased availability of resources, including a cleaner environment and greater access to natural recreation areas. And there is no convincing economic reason why these trends toward a better life, and toward lower prices for raw materials (including food and energy) should not continue indefinitely (Simon, 1981, p. 345).

This consultant also recognizes that his view and that of many others can differ because of philosophical or ideological orientation:

> Science alone does not, and cannot, tell us whether any population size is too large or too small, or whether the growth rate is too fast or too slow. Science can sometimes give citizens and policy makers a better understanding of the consequences of one or another decision about population; sadly, however, too often scientific work on this subject has instead only misinformed people and confused them. Social and personal decisions about childbearing, immigration, and death inevitably hinge upon values as well as upon probable consequences. And there is necessarily a moral dimension to these decisions over and beyond whatever insights science may yield (Simon, 1971, p. 344).

The understanding of population change was limited throughout past history. To a great extent, pronouncements about perceived or desired population

BOX 3.2 Pessimism, Optimism, and Population Projections

An example of how views of the present can be colored by ideology relates to the publication of varying projections of population size for the world and major countries by a number of different organizations. Most such organizations rely on credible statistical sources, such as the United Nations or U.S. Bureau of the Census, for their base data. But uncertainty about the levels of factors that affected population trends in the then recent past leads those agencies to suggest a range of alternative current population sizes according to variations in recent fertility and mortality (and sometimes mobility). It is then up to the organization publishing the estimates to either present all of the alternatives or select one of them.

Several years ago, two organizations (The Environmental Fund and the U.S. State Department's Agency for International Development known as AID) published data sheets for public information showing significantly different numbers about the current size of world and national populations. The numbers from The Environmental Fund were on the high side and those from AID on the low side. United Nations (UN) estimates for the same point in time were in between. What happened was that The Environmental Fund, whose ideology included concern about large populations in the world, chose the UN high series of estimates, whereas AID, which was engaged in an extensive birth control campaign, was content to choose the UN low series that suggested the success of their program. In each case, the organization showed numbers derived from certain assumptions about future population trends. (Neither organization highlighted those assumptions.) There was no trickery or dishonesty in their presentations. It was just that The Environmental Fund presented the pessimistic view about what population size was like at the time, while AID presented the optimistic view. (In Chapter 4 we will give greater consideration to issues about data collection and presentation.)

conditions were a function of the philosophies or ideologies of the pronouncers and not a consequence of reasoned study of population processes. Moving through time, there was a greater development of the scientific approach to understanding population change, but to a greater or lesser degree the science has been conducted or interpreted from the vantage point of certain value positions.

THEORETICAL AND CONCEPTUAL APPROACHES

Philosophy and ideology can sensitize us to critical matters of population change that we need to address, but they can also lead us astray in our effort to find the fundamental truth about the determinants and consequences of population change. That is why scientists, in general, have developed research approaches that attempt to minimize bias in studying phenomena of interest. There are many possible forms of bias leading to distorted results, but one of them relates to bias in identifying the relevant factors to be studied and their interrelationships.

One way of reducing the chances that this latter type of bias will distort conclusions is to make clear what factors are being considered in conducting a study. Accordingly, scientists adopt what are called *theoretical frameworks* for doing their research. Regrettably, the term *theory* has come to have several meanings, some of which are not pertinent to basic scientific study. We sometimes refer to theory when we mean a hunch or speculation. In most sciences, the term *hypothesis* refers to an informed hunch or speculation that can be tested for its accuracy. We also talk about a theory when we think about a body of partly confirmed knowledge in a particular area. For example, Einstein's theory of relativity has to do with a framework relating various phenomena in the universe that is logical and has, up until now, met several tests of some of its aspects. Theories in this sense can be modified when tests of their elements are not met, or they can be discarded in favor of other theories that seem to have more merit at the time.

There is a third sense in which the term *theory* can be used—that is, as any rigorous, systematic approach to developing knowledge about an area of study. Here, theory comes to mean an approach maximizing the chances of developing reliable and valid knowledge of a topic.

Theory in this sense is the general approach used to accumulate useful knowledge in an area. What must accompany it is a well-defined set of interrelated factors that we wish to develop understandings about. This supposes that we can stipulate the factor whose condition or change we wish to understand (the *dependent variable*, in research parlance), all of the potential factors that might "explain" it (*independent variables*) or be used to qualify it (*control variables*), and a *conceptual framework* used to interrelate all of these in a logical fashion. In this context, understanding population change means reaching some conclusions about factors important within a conceptual framework and the nature of their importance. (This means the strength of each factor in relation to the population phenomenon and the manner in which each factor is linked to other factors and to the population phenomenon.)

All attempts to introduce understandings of population change involve conceptual frameworks, either explicitly or implicity. Those who expound particular conceptual approaches are not always explicit about their assumptions concerning what factors are involved. In addition, some "theorists" do not successfully account for their philosophical or ideological biases. Hence, it is often difficult to deduce whether the conclusions reached are based on sound reasoning and reliable, valid analysis.

The following discussion distinguishes several classical conceptual approaches from those we might regard as contemporary. Specific attention is given to the classical approaches of Malthus and of Marx, because of the extent to which they are referred to in the population literature. Among contemporary approaches, there is a wide range that encompasses different levels of analysis, different methodologies, and different degrees of complexity.

Knowing what constitutes an appropriate conceptual framework is essential for someone conducting population research, but it is also useful for someone trying to comprehend reports of the research. Being a critical reader is a necessary part of understanding population change.

Classical Approaches

If philosophy and ideology dominated population thinking for generations, then theoretical and conceptual approaches have been increasingly central in more recent periods. And just as philosophy and ideology remain influences in today's thinking about population, so did theoretical reasoning find its way into thinking of the past.

While some may quibble about who presented the first truly scientific theory about population change, the credit for it is generally given to *Thomas R. Malthus*, whose work was first discussed in Chapter 2. In the last half of the eighteenth century, a number of writers reacted to mercantilist notions of population and economic matters and suggested factors contributing to a troublesome rate of population growth. The arguments were put forward by a number of "pessimists" opposed by social reformers who took a more "optimistic" point of view, and the debate took place mainly on the European continent, where laws to alleviate the plight of the poor had been proposed (United Nations, 1973).

It was in this context that Malthus wrote the first edition of his essay on the principle of population. Later editions of the work were significant modifications of the first one, incorporating new knowledge, altered perspectives, and responses to his critics (Malthus, 1914).

What gave Malthus' treatise the status of theory was the careful and thorough way he crafted his analysis of population change. Dupaquier (1983) alludes to Malthus' concentrating on "how a demographic system works," affirming that Malthus "devised a model and a general explanation, and this led him to lay the foundations of the sociology of population."

What Malthus is best known for are his basic assumptions, his generalizations about the growth tendencies of population and subsistence, and the checks to population growth. His first essay began with the assumptions that "food is necessary to the existence of man" and that "the passion between the sexes is necessary and will remain nearly in its present state." He argued that man could increase his subsistence only in arithmetical progression, whereas his numbers tended to increase in geometrical progression. Moreover, the history of humanity demonstrated, he said, that population always tended toward the limit set by subsistence and was contained within that limit by the operation of "positive and preventive checks" (United Nations, 1973).

As stated in later editions of the essay, the preventive check arises from reasoning "about distant consequences" and leads to prevention or delay of marriage. Positive checks included every cause "which in any degree contributes to shorten the natural duration of human life." These incorporate "all unwholesome occupations, severe labour and exposure to the seasons, extreme poverty, bad nursing of children, great towns, excesses of all kinds, the whole train of common diseases and epidemics, wars, plagues, and famine." All these checks were resolvable into moral restraint (the restraint from marriage), vice, and misery (Nam and Philliber, 1984). Essentially, moral restraint (the preventive check) deals with factors affecting fertility, while vice and misery (the positive checks) deal with factors affecting mortality. Mobility is discussed but does not receive a critical place in the framework.

Davis (1955) took the position that, while "Malthus' theories are not now and never were empirically valid,...they nevertheless were theoretically significant and, as a consequence, they hold a secure place in intellectual history." The lack of validity, he claims, arises mainly from the confusion of moral evaluation with scientific analysis within Malthus' conceptual framework. Most fundamentally, according to Davis, Malthus' religious inhibitions (he was an Anglican clergyman) prevented him from considering contraception as a potentially important preventive check to population growth. As a consequence, positive checks (or mortality) became the driving force in population limitation.

Wrigley (1983) calls attention to the fact that Malthus was writing in the context of his times, and the analysis he framed about the relationship between population, economy, and society depended heavily on the fact that fluctuations in fertility in his day were "almost solely a function of changes in the timing and incidence of marriage since age-specific marital fertility rates varied only trivially."

Von Tunzelmann (1986) concludes that Malthus had indeed developed a sound theoretical framework that was basically a systems model with interrelated parts, and that he was primarily concerned with the behavior of that system when out of equilibrium—that is, when its long-run properties were disturbed.

Van de Walle (1983) imagines how Malthus would feel about his essay if he were to return to earth today and observe population conditions around the world. What would surprise him the most? According to van de Walle, three historical developments would be seen as contradicting Malthus' theory: (1) The population of the world is much greater than he ever thought possible; the positive checks have not limited the growth of population; (2) the passion between the sexes has abated, or at least, the preventive check in its contraceptive form prevails in a substantial portion of the world; and (3) an enormous increase in subsistence has taken place, beyond anything imaginable, resulting in large improvements in the standard of living.

In the first instance, says van de Walle, Malthus believed strongly in the equilibrium notion (indicated by von Tunzelmann). Hence, he would not have expected the system to get so out of balance that population growth would be enormous. Basically, he underestimated the long-term mortality decline while fertility decline was delayed.

In the second instance, while passion between the sexes may not have been reduced, and marriage remains a vibrant social institution, social change in the forms of urbanization and modernization have led many to question the benefits of large family size. Voluntary fertility control has become desirable as a means of realizing improved levels of living. At the same time, sexual relations do not automatically lead to pregnancy, not even for the lower classes.

In the third instance, Malthus did not perceive the potential of the industrial and technological revolutions in increasing the yields of agriculture, exploiting the natural resources, and introducing substitutes to conventional forms of subsistence in order to raise living standards.

But these stated limitations on Malthus' earlier thinking do not make Malthusianism irrelevant. In the vast rural regions of the world, especially in developing nations, population growth and resource restrictions do present themselves in a Malthusian framework. Malthus' essay was derived in an era of rural societies, and his theory still has applicability in such places.

Perhaps a more important aspect of Malthus' essay was that he presented a discussion of population change that included, for the first time, a systematic account of the basic components of its dynamics. One can fault him for not expressing the relationship of the components precisely enough or for not taking into account enough of the extraneous factors that influence the behavior of the components. But one cannot deny that he laid the groundwork for demographic theorizing that even today is the benchmark against which other theoretical ideas are measured.

Flew (1957) summarizes Malthus' basic contributions to population theory, as follows:

(1) "...Malthus introduced no new concept and embodied no factual discovery in his theory. What he did was to bring together one or two familiar facts of life, make an unfortunately precise and general supposition about a limit on the expansion of food production, and try to deduce the necessary consequences of these facts....";

(2) "...the master question which stimulates and guides Malthus' population studies is negative: he is asking why and how something does *not* happen. This question is generated by his fundamental law of population, which states the rate at which population increases, *when unchecked*....";

(3) "...this conceptual framework was originally built as a practical theory, designed as a guide to political and social action (or inaction)....It should therefore not surprise us that these ideas are more suited for the rough and ready understanding of broad trends and for guiding the wide lines of general policy than for assisting in detailed demographic analysis."

The writings of Malthus on population were clearly prepared as a response to the social reformists of his time, who sought to find ways of improving the lot of deprived categories of people. Malthus made clear in the first edition of his essay that his main objective in drafting the piece was to answer the arguments of the social reformers, and he couched his principle in that context:

> This natural inequality of the two powers of population and of production in the earth, and that great law of our nature which must constantly keep their effects equal, form the great difficulty that to me appears insurmountable in the way to the perfectibility of society (Malthus, 1914).

In later editions of the essay, explaining population change became more paramount and the political arguments were clearly separated. Yet the latter has continued to be the basis for most of the post-Malthusian reactions to the essay. To be sure, these political debates are founded in disagreements about historical economic changes. It is for this reason that *Karl Marx* became a principal antagonist of Malthus' ideas.

Karl Marx lived during the heart of the nineteenth century, when the writings of Malthus were still controversial and heavily debated. Along with his collaborator, Friedrich Engels, Marx developed ideas about the economic history of societies that were at great variance with those of Malthus, among others. In many of his writings, Marx referred particularly to the works of Malthus and often used them as targets.

While much of Marx' contentions were directed at issues of economics, population concerns did not go unnoticed. But in the case of Marx and Engels, the dispute was not so much with the data Malthus had assembled as with his structuring of a contest between the growth of population and the growth of sustenance. For Marx and Engels, the pressure of population was really against the "means of employment" rather than against the means of subsistence. In the Marxian scheme of things, there was denial that "the law of population is the same at all times and at all places." It was argued that "every stage of development has its own law of population."

In a capitalist society, argued Marx, "it is capitalistic accumulation itself that constantly produces, and produces in the direct ratio of its own energy and extent, a relatively redundant population of labourers, i.e., a population of greater extent than suffices for the average needs of the self-expansion of capital, and therefore a surplus-population" (Meek, 1953, p. 27).

Marx contended that a fallacy in Malthus' thinking was that he assumed a "law of diminishing returns," in which each added interval of labor and capital will not produce a corresponding interval of product on a fixed amount of land. Engels clarified this issue by arguing that land may indeed be fixed but the rest of the equation should be stated differently:

> But the labour power to be employed on this area increases together with the population; and even if we assume that the increase of output associated with the increase of labour is not always proportionate to the latter, there still remains a third element—which the economists, however, never consider as important—namely, science, the progress of which is just as limitless and at least as rapid as that of population (Meek, 1953, p. 30).

In that passage Marx and Engels offer themselves as optimists as against Malthus' pessimism. It is also the case that Marx adopts a different conceptual framework from that of Malthus. The Marxian framework emphasizes forms of labor and capital and the means and mode of production, with population an extraneous and determined element. The Malthusian framework stresses the variables of subsistence, population, and checks on population, with relatively fixed notions about the nature of the economic enterprise.

We do not do justice to the population writings of either Malthus or Marx. Both wrote considerably about specifics of the demographic system. What is important for our present purpose, however, is to indicate that each had constructed a theoretical framework dealing with population factors (Malthus much more explicitly than did Marx). The discussions of both thinkers, however, were heavily colored by their ideological positions. Moreover, as with any historical theory, both had not anticipated some of the social changes yet to occur.

But just as Malthus is seen by many today as relevant for understanding population change, so is Marx viewed by many others as having grasped some of the essential variables affecting the welfare of people and nations. Stripped of its political ramifications, Marxian thought has been incorporated in modified form into the economic and social systems of a number of nations. Democratic socialism recognizes social class differences and makes provision for the welfare of the less fortunate.

At the same time, major Communist countries that have traditionally depended on Marxian ideas have not differed very much in their approach to population change from the approach taken in countries regarded as capitalist. An examination of past Soviet journals on population shows that contemporary approaches to analysis of demographic dynamics were shared with those found in journals of the United States and western Europe, even if the Soviets paid lip service to Marxian theory.

Similarly, an English-language book on Chinese population printed in Beijing reveals an accommodation of Marxist theory to the realities of the modern period. Quoting Engels: "If communist society should one day be compelled to regulate the production of human beings, as it regulates the production of goods, then it and it alone will be able to do this without difficulty." It goes on to point out:

> In China today, it is possible not only for individual families to practise planned birth control, but for society as a whole to exercise planned regulation over population reproduction in line with the needs of the developing social productive forces (Zheng, 1981).

Thus, whereas population was once considered by Communist regimes as an automatic consequence of societal organization, today planning population change is seen as an appropriate and necessary aspect of government intervention. In this sense we are observing a coming together of broad theoretical orientations relating to demographic change.

Throughout the nineteenth and early twentieth centuries, the discussions of population ideas were heavily oriented to debating the arguments of Malthus and of Marx. From time to time, however, a number of theorists introduced a conceptual framework that attempted to explain population change in terms of variables other than those advanced by the two intellectual giants. We need to mention a few of these thinkers because of their influence on later population formulations.

Some of these theories incorporated biological variables. Spencer (1852) developed a theory of biological evolution which introduced a self-regulating principle of population growth. He regarded the power to maintain life and the power to propagate as antagonistic to each other; the former power varied directly while the latter varied inversely with the development of the nervous system. If the power to maintain life was low, survival of the population required high fertility. But high fertility led to population pressure which increased nervous tension. As nervous systems became enlarged, the power to maintain life increased while the power to reproduce diminished (United Nations, 1973).

Biology also played a role in the formulation of Gini (1930), who advanced the idea that populations go through cycles of change as a result of fluctuations in fecundity (the biological ability to conceive). Fecundity increases lead to population growth which, in time, is counterbalanced by the deterioration of germinal cells. Selective immigration may provide for a new infusion of fecundity into the population (United Nations, 1973).

Dumont (1890) developed a more sociological theory of population change that attributed reductions in family size to the ambition to improve one's position in society. Using the analogy of water rising under the force of capillarity in thin tubes, he termed his concept the *principle of social capillarity.*

A more economically based theoretical orientation is referred to as the *optimum population theory.* Plato and Aristotle both discussed population optima, but less from a theoretical perspective than from a value position. Sidgwick (1883) observed that the productivity of labor tended to diminish as the ratio of laborers to land increased after a certain degree of density had been reached. The optimum was the point of maximum return per head.

If we recognize an optimum population size, then overpopulation and underpopulation are relevant concepts. But there has never been agreement on the exact criterion for determining the optimum. Indicators used by various theorists include per capita income, productivity, economic welfare, level of living, real income, and employment.

None of the grand population theories of the post-Malthusian era have had the appeal of Malthusian or Marxian thought. All of those theories were not only simplistic in their approach to understanding population change; they also were highly deterministic in focusing on one or two variables which the author saw as of crucial importance.

Contemporary Approaches

As we move into the modern period of population analysis, we will note that conceptual approaches have been more attuned to the kinds of data available as well as to the range of variables that belong in any theoretical equation. This is because demographic research now demands empirical testing of propositions about population change that go well beyond the approaches of Malthus and Marx.

To get a sense of the variations in newer theoretical approaches, we will divide our discussion between theoretical foci, descriptive analyses, typologies, and explanatory models.

By *theoretical foci* we mean both the level at which the substantive interest is focused and the disciplinary orientation given to it. *Levels of substantive interest* include the micro and macro perspectives referred to earlier. Some analysts have also identified a middle (or medial) level. If we want to understand population change, or some facet of it, at an aggregate level (that is, in terms of anonymous collectivities of people), then a macro theoretical perspective is called for. On the other hand, if we desire understanding at a small-group or individual level, then a micro theoretical perspective is in order. There are times when comprehending population change means focusing attention on intermediate groups or structures. In such situations, a medial theoretical approach would be appropriate. This latter situation would be relevant when, for example, we are interested in the part that neighborhood religious organizations play in shaping residents' ideas about desired family size or the acceptable forms of birth control. Sociological, economic, and psychological perspectives dominate among the disciplinary orientations, but others are occasionally introduced.

Four macro perspectives are frequently used in attempts to theorize about population change. One is an *ecological approach* based on the idea of organisms adapting biologically to their environment. The unit of ecological analysis is the human population located in a particular area. Major conceptual categories in this framework are technology, social organization, and natural environment. Studies employing an ecological framework are typically interested in broad relationships among these categories although one or more of the categories may be further specified (for instance, different elements of the natural environment). The ecological perspective emphasizes the relative balance among parts so that equilibrium is a critical concern. Malthusian theory seems to have a strong ecological orientation in this sense.

Another macro approach is termed *sociocultural* because the type of social and cultural system in an area is seen as shaping demographic processes. Anthropologists frequently adopt this approach in studying population since it enables them to focus on their critical interest in culture and emphasize larger systemic changes. But researchers from any discipline can find this perspective useful if they are interested in the "big picture" and want to identify the effects of broad-gauged variables. The theoretical orientation of Marx might be placed within this framework. Research on how values of a society determine where newly married couples will locate their residence would find this theoretical approach compatible.

A third macro approach that has achieved great popularity is the one identified as *modernization*. As societies modernize, they increase division of labor, introduce specialization, differentiate the functions of social institutions, and transform traditional ways of doing things into newer modes. Through the process of modernization, societies and communities have adapted to living conditions in ways that have changed ideas about population size and structure.

Still a fourth macro approach is one that we can refer to as *institutional*. We can link transformations of particular societal institutions (economic, educational, religious, and political) to population changes by stressing the institutional forms and mechanisms that create demographic processes. For example, a study could be concerned with how a changing economic system alters the provisions for better health maintenance and longer life expectancy.

At the micro level, the theoretical focus is on the family, a couple, an individual, or some other small group. A great deal of emphasis is likely to be placed on the *decision-making processes* related to population phenomena and factors associated with them. Why do persons prefer to have a certain number of children? Which forms of family planning are used and which rejected? What social, psychological, and economic variables affect the decisions made in determining population-related behavior? How important are the personal characteristics of the parties involved, their power relationships, their knowledge of relevant information, the modes of communication between them?

The medial approaches include frameworks that attempt to bridge the macro and micro approaches. What happens at the micro level is certainly affected by occurrences at the macro level. In turn, macro relationships are determined ultimately by what behaviors occur at the micro level. Yet the two levels seem to be so far apart that it is difficult to relate them. This raises the notion that there are connectives that take still other forms. For instance, cultural changes in a society result in new or modified norms of behavior that guide individual actions. Thus the *normative perspective* is a medial approach that helps to provide a linkage between the macro and micro relationships. Some studies focus attention on these medial forces.

Another medial approach involves *socialization processes*. Here the emphasis is placed on the mechanisms through which norms are inculcated into an individual's or small group's mental view. The use of socialization frameworks usually includes identification of who does the socializing and what is the nature of the process.

These theoretical foci are heuristic devices—that is, devices focusing attention on certain substantive interests and disciplinary orientation—for researchers and guides for readers that serve to structure the kinds of analysis to be done and discussed. The main point is that they define the frame of reference within which they can identify critical variables and study hypothetical relationships. A deterministic or biased focus is likely to exclude important elements of an analysis and give the appearance that what is included is all that is relevant. Theoretical foci give us one more stage of movement toward understanding phenomena.

Modern demographers were long regarded as being atheoretical because their research typically took the form of *descriptive analyses* that told about the distributions of variables and the simple relationships of two variables without any apparent theoretical underpinnings. These often assumed the guise of lower-order generalizations. Ravenstein's work late in the last century is an example (see Box 3.3).

It is clear, however, that descriptive analyses or simple relational analyses imply some kind of theoretical association. Throughout the second half of the twentieth century, population researchers have relied heavily on studies of demographic *differentials* to express such associations. If we compare persons with different educational attainments in terms of their propensity to migrate and find distinct differences by level of education, then is it not reasonable to conclude that education is a determinant of the probability of migrating? Perhaps, but one would want to know other things about that type of relationship before being certain that a causal connection exists between education and migration. Do other variables intervene in the relationship? Can a third variable explain both educational and migratory levels? And what is it about education, as it is measured, that is the explanation (if, indeed, educational attainment can "explain" migration)? Is the variable too broad to enable us to achieve real understanding?

Many of the well-known studies of population are based on analysis of differentials. Kitagawa and Hauser (1973) conducted a mammoth study of U.S. mortality patterns as they were related to socioeconomic differences, especially variations by education and income. In reporting the research, they indicated that the "importance of socioeconomic differentials in mortality is that they point to the possibilities of reducing mortality through the betterment of socioeconomic conditions in the population." And they went on to show interest in "the extent to which differences in socioeconomic status are *responsible* [italics mine] for differences in mortality and [this relationship] indicates the gains that might be achieved in life expectancy if socioeconomic conditions are improved.

In a similar vein, Rindfuss and Sweet (1977) prepared a thorough account of fertility trends and differentials in the U.S., based on the 1960 and 1970 Censuses. They tell us: "Social differences—whether they be educational, residential, religious, or racial differences—have consistently been found to be strong *determinants* [italics mine] of fertility behavior." They also caution that "emphasis throughout the monograph will be on investigating *what* has been occurring; as such the study should sharpen the focus of the question of *why* recent fertility trends have occurred the way they have. Although we will occasionally speculate about why certain trends have occurred, an explanation for all of the patterns found is clearly beyond the scope of the present study."

Many publications in the demographic field today are concerned with population differentials. These descriptive analyses do provide information on a

BOX 3.3 Ravenstein's Laws of Migration

Ravenstein (1885, 1889) stated what he observed to be *laws of migration.* Based on empirical findings from studies of developed nations, he concluded:

1. The great body of migrants move only a short distance.
2. People tend to move in the direction of great centers of commerce and industry.
3. Rural residents near a city tend to move into the city while persons living in more remote places take their places.
4. Each main current of migration produces a compensating countercurrent.
5. The natives of towns are less migratory than those of the rural parts of the country.
6. Females are more migratory than males.
7. Migration from rural to urban, and from urban to rural, areas generally proceeds by stages.

You may recognize some of these statements as unsupportable at the present time. Of course, times change and relationships can undergo change, as did those described by Malthus and Marx. Beyond that, Ravenstein may have overgeneralized his findings because he did not take account of the variability that existed among different groups or the varying conditions under which many of these relationships occurred.

Even if they were not always made explicit, there were some underlying theoretical notions about the forces that affected migrations. In later years, researchers tried to be more specific about those relationships and either added related variables or examined the simple relationships within categories of other (control) variables. (Chapter 7 will discuss some of those relationships.)

limited number of variables associated with the population topic of interest. We can often hypothesize linkages between variables based on such analyses, but the conceptual frameworks that underlie these studies are incomplete. True understanding must await fuller analyses that consider a broader set of relevant variables looked at in their interrelationships.

What might be considered a step beyond descriptive or differential analysis involves the construction of *typologies.* Here the aim is to develop combinations or clusters of variables that can be labeled to indicate an underlying concept that is broader than the single variables analyzed in the study of differentials.

The stages of the demographic transition constitute one form of typology used in population study. Although we have argued that it is more reasonable to treat that transition as a continuum, most analysts have continued to refer to specified stages. The traditional classification of three transition stages (graphed in Figure 2.1) refers to a typology based on combinations of mortality and fertility trends and associated societal changes. Each stage constitutes a different set of circumstances that form a particular construct. In thinking about any stage, we can envisage a situation that encompasses a number of variables. From a theoretical point of view, our thinking becomes more complex and we can see connections between several factors. The fact that some writers chose to specify more than three demographic transition stages is an indication that they perceived one or more of the three stages as not being homogeneous enough. Consequently, they elected to create four or more stages that had meaningful distinctions among them.

In Chapter 5 we will allude to the *epidemiologic transition*, which is analagous to the demographic transition and deals with changing patterns of cause of death as societies undergo change. The traditional typology makes mention of stages that are clusters of kinds of diseases and accidents. The use of cause-of-death stages in this formulation enables researchers to deal with what medical causes led to death in different eras; limitation to three stages provides an economical classification system.

An attempt by Petersen (1958) to attach theoretical importance to variations in migration forms led him to establish a *general typology of migration*. Revising a similar approach by Fairchild (1925), Petersen used criteria of what forces brought about the migration and whether the movement was designed to retain a way of life or introduce a new mode of life. Resulting types of migration include primitive (resulting from an ecological push to change the relationship between people and nature); forced (deriving from a governmental policy affecting the relationship between people and the state which leaves the migrant no alternative); impelled (also deriving from a governmental policy affecting the relationship between people and the state, but which grants the person some option as to whether to leave); free (based on the individual's will or aspiration, which may involve relatively small groups); and mass (in which the aspirations of large groups of people produce social momentum that generates migration from an area).

The typology offered by Petersen can be criticized from a number of angles, but its main contribution is in identifying several types of movement that we are familiar with and which make us think about combinations of specific factors that can result in demographic behaviors.

A similar theoretical function is performed by using typological constructs for geographic areas. A basic distinction between rural and urban areas was made to denote fundamentally different ways of life that characterized residential locations. As urban areas became more differentiated, the typology was expanded in various ways to indicate the disparate urban forms in which people resided. Because population distribution and redistribution patterns have been altered significantly in recent decades, analysts have developed new typologies to express the essential characteristics of these types and, thereby, have given more relevant meaning to distributional differences. For example, at one time the concept of a *metropolitan area* may have had a fairly unitary meaning. However, as more and more urban areas have met the criteria for metropolitan designation, we need to make distinctions among metropolitan types. Such typological elaboration assists in theoretical formulation by calling attention to significant characteristics that generate population dynamics. It also requires us to think about the combination of forces that produce demographic change.

Descriptive analysis and typology formation do not often carry us to the point where we can achieve substantial understanding of population change. As Willigan and Lynch (1982) indicate, they rarely prove to be general enough to incorporate all of the salient variables required to produce completely satisfying causal explanations.

Demographic research has been building toward more complete population understanding by the development of *explanatory models*. The ideal approach here is to construct a conceptual framework that encompasses as many of the relevant variables as are theoretically significant and to establish the nature of linkages among those variables. The latter can be done either deductively or inductively. A deductive strategy hypothesizes the nature of the linkages and then tests these hypotheses with empirical data. If any hypotheses are not supported, then alternative hypotheses can be proposed and revised empirical analysis done to test the new hypotheses. An inductive strategy uses the conceptual framework as a basis for undertaking empirical studies involving variables related in the framework in order to arrive at established linkages among variables. This approach is thus more exploratory and is often used when little knowledge about the associations among variables exists.

Constructing a conceptual framework requires us to make a thorough review of past studies dealing with the subject matter. The conceptual framework should build on the body of knowledge that already exists (a principal function of theory). Variables can be included in a framework if it seems logical to do so, even if past studies have not considered them. The purpose here might be to add to the possible explanatory power of the model and thus fill in gaps in explanation.

The explanatory model approach to theoretical development, if properly done, forces us to carefully consider what are the important variables involved in explaining a population phenomenon and the nature of their association. Descriptive analysis and typological formation do not necessitate such a comprehensive examination. Of course, one can find many different kinds of explanatory models in demographic research, and some appear to be more exhaustive than others.

One type of model is concerned with the internal structure of populations and how it changes. In our earlier discussion, we demonstrated how the three basic components of population change—*mortality*, *fertility*, and *mobility*—together determine the rate and nature of population change as well as *age composition* of the population. The interrelationships of those four variables have been shown to be highly predictable in a population in which the basic components have remained at a constant level. Some very elegant mathematical

BOX 3.4 Intermediate Variables Affecting Fertility

Davis and Blake posited that there were three necessary steps in the process of reproduction—intercourse, conception, and gestation and parturition. They asked themselves what were the mechanisms chanelling reproduction in each of these categories. Based on a thorough review of what had been written before, they arrived at the following *intermediate variables:*

I. Factors Affecting Exposure to Intercourse
   A. Those governing the formation and dissolution of unions in the reproductive period.
      1. Age of entry into sexual unions.
      2. Permanent celibacy: proportion of women never entering sexual unions.
      3. Amount of reproductive period spent after or between unions.
         a. When unions are broken by divorce, separation, or desertion.
         b. When unions are broken by death of husband.
   B. Those governing the exposure to intercourse within unions.
      4. Voluntary abstinence.
      5. Involuntary abstinence (from impotence, illness, unavoidable but temporary separations).
      6. Coital frequency (excluding periods of abstinence).

II. Factors Affecting Exposure to Conception
      7. Fecundity or infecundity, as affected by involuntary causes.
      8. Use or nonuse of contraception.
         a. By mechanical and chemical means.

formulations can be expressed to describe the characteristics of populations in such a condition (Lotka and Sharpe, 1911). (We will present simplified notions of these characteristics in Chapter 8.)

Those demographers who are especially concerned with the internal structure of populations have built mathematical models that specify the workings of that internal structure (United Nations, 1983). In nations where population data are limited or faulty, if some of the data are reasonably accurate (fertility or mortality or age distribution, for example), then the other variables can be estimated using the known relationships among them. In this way, the theoretical models of the internal structure of populations provide a basis for acquiring useful data that are lacking.

Other explanatory models in population study deal more with the impact of external factors on population phenomena. These cover the range of theoretical foci mentioned before as well as the scope of population topics. At this

continued

b. By other means.
9. Fecundity or infecundity, as affected by voluntary causes (sterilization, subincision, medical treatment, etc.).

III. Factors Affecting Gestation and Successful Parturition
10. Fetal mortality from involuntary causes.
11. Fetal mortality from voluntary causes.

They then elaborated each of these intermediate variables and gave historical examples of them as they related to reproduction. Generalizing to the initial concern, they determined that "pre-industrial societies have high fertility-value for those variables farthest removed from the actual moment of parturition and which, therefore, imply an overall outlook favorable to fertility." Moreover, "A key to the position of the industrial societies lies in the fact that, as compared to pre-industrial cultures, they have achieved their lower reproduction, not by acquiring low fertility-values for *all* the intermediate variables, but by singling out particular ones as the means to that result. They took those means of reducing fertility which involved the least institutional organization and re-organization and which involved the least human cost."

This formulation of institutional factors affecting fertility has been a prime framework for researchers because of its insights into the mechanisms producing reproductive change. Others have extended the theory by relating social factors to it (e.g., Freedman, 1963) and by giving it greater specificity and a quantitative form (e.g., Bongaarts, 1976).

point, we will give examples of such explanatory model approaches along with indications of some of the theoretical thinking of the researchers who developed them. In subsequent chapters, we will refer to them again in the context of the substantive topics.

Davis and Blake (1956) were impressed with the fact that the fertility levels of underdeveloped areas were different from those of developed nations and also varied among each other. The several societies were known to have different social organizations, yet some of them had similar fertility levels. The researchers wondered about the institutional mechanisms that produced the differences as well as similarities in reproductive performance. What were the factors through which cultural influences determined fertility levels? (See Box 3.4.)

When we proceed to develop more complete understandings of fertility changes (as we will see in Chapter 6), other theoretical orientations will be introduced. Some are tied to issues relating to family planning access and use and others to such matters as reasons for alternative patterns of family size and child spacing. Some, like the Davis-Blake approach, take a macro position; others are more oriented to medial or micro levels of understanding.

Nam and Eberstein were interested in the reasons why infant mortality levels in a place like Florida were so different for whites, blacks, and Hispanic groups. Most analyses up to the time had been fairly simplistic in terms of focusing on a few related variables. They decided to study the problem in as broad a context as possible. For them, this meant considering infant mortality as the possible outcome of a temporal process impacted by many different variables.

The researchers drew partly on a formulation by Mosley and Chen (1984) that had dealt with child survival in developing countries and had tried to bridge across biological and social factors. Nam and Eberstein designed a conceptual framework that took account of (a) factors existing prior to a conception (social background of mother); (b) factors close to, or just after, the time of birth (e.g., prenatal care, mother's earlier conception and fertility experiences, and birth weight); and (c) factors related to the death of those who did not survive the first year of life (age at death and medical causes of death).

The research strategy was to find out which factors differentiated the infant mortality process for the various race and ethnic groups. From a theoretical standpoint, the aim was to derive a model that could specify the most critical factors and how they were interrelated to each other and to the risk of infant death, in a combined medial and micro approach.

Some of the findings of this study will be reported in Chapter 5; however, we should remark on the fact, known to all analysts of population, that a conceptual framework based on logic and past studies cannot necessarily be tested in its entirety because of limitations on the availability of data that encompass all the theoretical variables simultaneously or because of inadequacies of present statistical and computer techniques. For example, in this research information on the mother's smoking and drug use was not available. Conceptually, there is reason to believe that these are relevant variables related to possible infant mortality. As a consequence, the study produced findings that tested the broad theoretical formulation to only a limited degree, if even in a more comprehensive way than had previously been the case (Nam et al., 1989; Eberstein et al., 1990).

One final illustration of an explanatory model involving factors external to population phenomena relates to migration decision making. DeJong and Fawcett (1981) realized that, while there were many macro studies addressing the determinants of migration, few studies examined such determinants at the micro level. We needed to know more about why some people moved and why others with the same apparent characteristics did not. Furthermore, while motivations to move (in the broad sense) were generally seen as mainly based on economic considerations, it seemed logical that individuals and families had multiple motives to move or not that spanned a range of social and psychological as well as economic factors.

FIGURE 3.1 **A Value-Expectancy-Based Model of Migration Decision-Making Behavior**

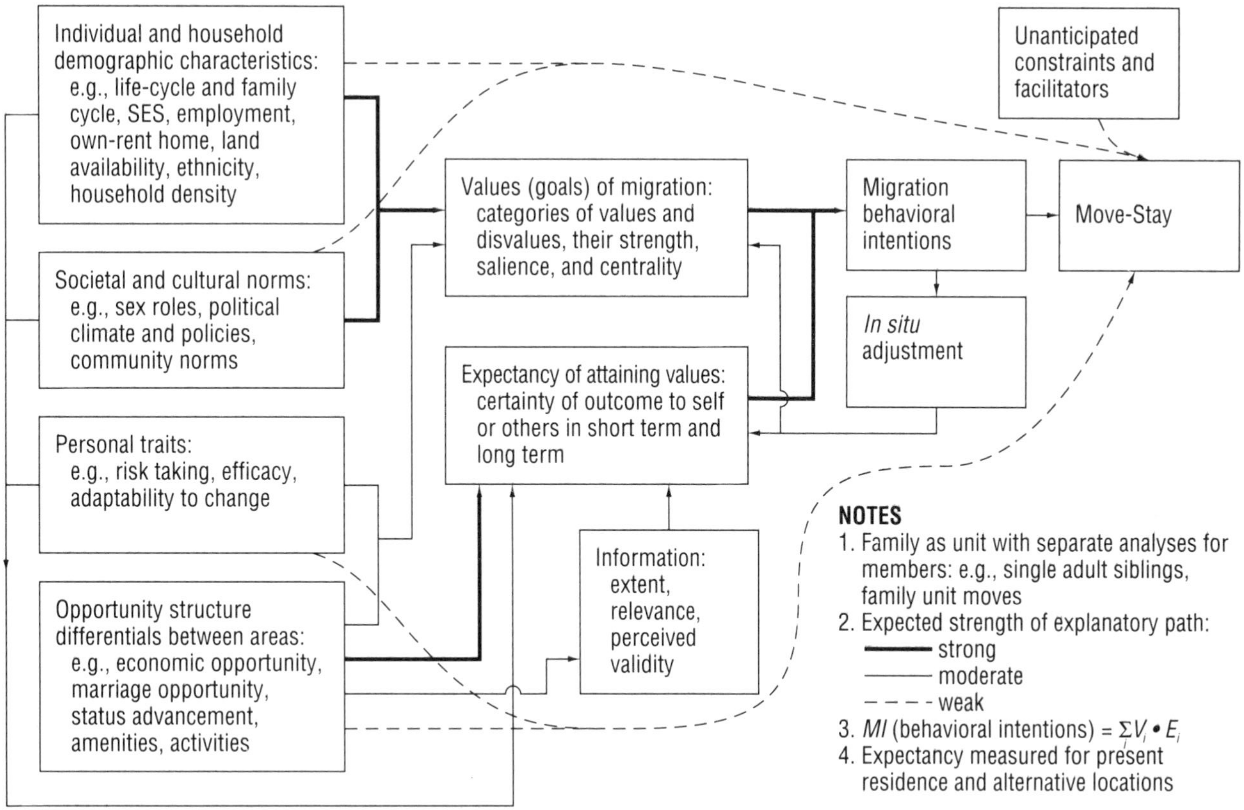

NOTES

1. Family as unit with separate analyses for members: e.g., single adult siblings, family unit moves
2. Expected strength of explanatory path:
   - ▬▬ strong
   - —— moderate
   - – – – weak
3. *MI* (behavioral intentions) = $\sum_i V_i \bullet E_i$
4. Expectancy measured for present residence and alternative locations

Source: See Gordon F. DeJong and James T. Fawcett (1981).

The approach taken by DeJong and Fawcett was to apply an existing social-psychological micro behavior model to migration. That model was based on the idea that the strength of a tendency to act in a certain way depends on the *expectancy* that the act will be followed by a given consequence (or goal) and the *value* of that consequence or goal to the individual (Crawford, 1973). Adopting a set of seven values and goals related to migration (wealth, status, comfort, stimulation, autonomy, affiliation, and morality) and hypothesizing various macro, medial, and micro factors that might be associated with these consequences and goals, the researchers sketched out a causal diagram. They assumed that data could be collected which would identify how each person stressed particular values and their expectancy about each of them (see Figure 3.1).

This model and many other contemporary explanatory models in the population field go far beyond earlier theoretical formulations in developing strong conceptual frameworks that come as close as possible to reality and in including relevant variables. Such models can lead us to a greater understanding of the forces that bring about population change.

Chapter Highlights

1. Approaches to understanding population change have included those based on philosophical and ideological ideas as well as those founded on theoretical and conceptual orientations.
2. Philosophical and ideological views dominated the population thinking of writers from early religious periods through the historical Greek, Roman, Renaissance, and Reformation eras up to the modern period.
3. Writers of the early periods as well as later scholars are regarded as either optimists or pessimists, on the basis of how they view the advantages and disadvantages of population growth and the human ability to support increased population.
4. Scientifically based theories of population are attempts to derive reliable and valid knowledge about population phenomena through systematic research strategies.
5. Such strategies involve explanatory models that specify the population topic of interest, identify all the relevant variables, and develop a conceptual framework indicating how these variables are related to each other and to the topic of interest. Studies can then be done to reinforce or modify the suggested conceptual framework.
6. The population theory approaches of Malthus and Marx represent attempts at scientific study of population that were, nevertheless, strongly affected by their respective philosophical and ideological orientations.
7. Malthus believed that population grew up to the limit set by available subsistence and was contained within that limit by various positive and preven-

tive checks, principally those of factors leading to mortality. His critics have pointed to his failure to recognize the importance of fertility control and to anticipate developments raising levels of subsistence.

8. Marx and his frequent coauthor Engels were critical of Malthus' views on population because their historical analysis of societal change led them to argue that the pressure of population was against the means of employment rather than against the means of subsistence, and that surplus population could only exist in a capitalist society.
9. In the contemporary period, theoretical approaches have assumed various forms focused on different disciplinary orientations and different levels of analysis (macro, medial, and micro).
10. There has also been an evolving set of analytical approaches that range from more descriptive analyses with a limited number of potentially explanatory variables to typologies that try to cluster factors into meaningful conceptual configurations, to more sophisticated explanatory models that attempt to maximize the number and relationships of variables in an effort to represent reality. These explanatory models include those concerned with the internal structure of population change as well as those which emphasize the connections between external variables and their effects on population phenomena.

Discussion Questions

1. What do you regard as the contributions that historical philosophical and ideological thinking about population change have made to societies? Are they the same as or different from the contributions that today's philosophical and ideological thinking about population change make?
2. What are the advantages of a scientific approach in trying to understand population change?
3. What were the critical factors that differentiated the positions of Malthus and Marx on the issue of the advantages and disadvantages of population growth?
4. Choose one population phenomenon you would like to understand better. What would be some good examples of analysis you could do using the descriptive approach to advancing theory?
5. Select another population phenomenon of importance. Discuss the kind of explanatory conceptual framework you might design and indicate what variables would be included and how they might be interrelated with each other and with the population phenomenon.
6. What might be some reasons that we can never achieve complete understanding of a population phenomenon?

Suggested Readings

Wood, John Cunningham. 1986. *Thomas Robert Malthus: Critical Assessments.* 4 vols. London: Croom Helm. Malthus has generated many reactions—some favorable and others unfavorable—among a wide array of publication outlets for almost two centuries. These volumes provide broad coverage of such writings by others and help to reassess Malthus' essay in a more complete way.

Keyfitz, Nathan. 1977. *Applied Mathematical Demography.* New York: Springer Publishing Co. For the more technically sophisticated reader, the author demonstrates how theory of the internal structure of population can be applied to answer some commonly asked questions about population change and its effects.

United Nations. 1973. *The Determinants and Consequences of Population Trends.* Vol. 1, New York: United Nations. Chapter 2 of this book gives a complete survey of population theory from ancient times up to the middle of the twentieth century.

References

Aristotle. 1943. *Politics.* Translated by Benjamin Jowett. Modern Library. New York: Random House.

Bongaarts, John. 1976. "Intermediate Fertility Variables and Marital Fertility Rates." *Population Studies* 30:2, 227–41.

Brown, Lester R. 1991. "The New World Order." In *State of the World, 1991*, pp. 3–20. New York: W. W. Norton.

Campbell, Flann. 1960. "Birth Control and the Christian Churches." *Population Studies* 14:2, 131–47.

Crawford, Thomas. 1973. "Beliefs about Birth Control: A Consistency Theory Analysis." *Representative Research in Social Psychology* 4: 53–65.

Davis, Kingsley. 1955. "Malthus and the Theory of Population." In Paul F. Lazarsfeld and Morris Rosenberg, eds., *The Language of Social Research*, pp. 540–53. Glencoe, Ill.: Free Press.

———, and Judith Blake. 1956. "Social Structure and Fertility: An Analytic Framework." *Economic Development and Cultural Change* 4, 211–35.

DeJong, Gordon F., and James T. Fawcett. 1981. "Motivations for Migration: An Assessment and a Value-Expectancy Research Model." In Gordon F. DeJong and Robert W. Gardner, eds., *Migration Decision Making; Multidisciplinary Approaches to Microlevel Studies in Developed and Developing Countries*, pp. 13–50. New York: Pergammon Press.

Dumont, Arsène. 1890. *Dépopulation et civilisation; étude demographique.* Paris: Lecrosnier et Babe.

Dupaquier, Jacques. 1983. Preface to J. Dupaquier, A. Fauve-Chamoux, and E.

Grebenik, eds., *Malthus Past and Present.* London: Academic Press.

Eberstein, Isaac W., Charles B. Nam, and Robert A. Hummer. 1990. Infant Mortality by Cause of Death: Main and Interaction Effects. *Demography* 27:3, 413–30.

Fairchild, Henry Pratt. 1925. *Immigration: A World Movement and Its American Significance.* New York: Macmillan.

Flew, A. 1957. "The Structure of Malthus' Population Theory." *Australian Journal of Philosophy* 35: 1–20.

Freedman, Ronald. 1963. "Norms for Family Size in Underdeveloped Areas." *Proceedings of the Royal Society* 159, 220–34.

Gini, Corrado et al. 1930. *Population.* Chicago: University of Chicago Press.

Hodgson, Dennis. 1991. "Ideological Origins of the Population Association of America." *Population and Development Review* 17:1, 1–34.

Hutchinson, E.P. 1967. *The Population Debate: The Development of Conflicting Theories up to 1900.* Boston: Houghton Mifflin.

Khaldun, Ibn. 1950. *An Arab Philosophy of History: Selections from the Prolegomena of Ibn Khaldun.* Translated by Charles Issawi. London: John Murray.

Kitagawa, Evelyn M., and Philip M. Hauser. 1973. *Differential Mortality in the United States: A Study in Socioeconomic Epidemiology.* Cambridge, Mass.: Harvard University Press.

Lotka, Alfred J., and F.R. Sharpe. 1911. "A Problem in Age Distribution." *Philosophical Magazine* 21:124, 435–38.

Malthus, T.R. 1914. *An Essay on Population.* London: J.M. Dent. Everyman's Library Edition, no. 692.

Meek, Ronald L. 1953. *Marx and Engels on Malthus.* London: Lawrence and Wishart.

Repetto, Robert. 1987. "Population, Resources, Environment: An Uncertain Future." *Population Bulletin* 42:2. A publication of the Population Reference Bureau.

Nam, Charles B., Isaac W. Eberstein, Larry Deeb, and E. Walter Terrie. 1989. "Infant Mortality by Cause: A Comparison of Underlying and Multiple Cause Designations." *European Journal of Population* 5, 45–70.

———, and Susan Gustavus Philliber. 1984. *Population: A Basic Orientation.* Englewood Cliffs, N.J.: Prentice-Hall.

Noonan, John T., Jr. 1986. *Contraception: A History of Its Treatment by the Catholic Theologians and Canonists.* Cambridge, Mass.: Harvard University Press.

Petersen, William. 1958. "A General Typology of Migration." *American Sociological Review* 23:3, 256–66.

Plato. 1960. *Laws.* Translated by A.E. Taylor. Everyman's Library. New York: E.P. Dutton Co.

Ravenstein, E.G. 1885. The Laws of Migration. *Journal of the Royal Statistical Society* 48, 167–235.

———. 1889. "The Laws of Migration." *Journal of the Royal Statistical Society* 52, 241–305.

Mosley, W. Henry, and Lincoln C. Chen. 1984. "An Analytical Framework for the Study of Child Survival in Developing Countries." In W. Henry Mosley and Lincoln C. Chen, eds., *Child Survival: Strategies for Research*, pp. 25–45. A supplement to vol. 10 of *Population and Development Review*.

Rindfuss, Ronald R., and James A. Sweet. 1977. *Postwar Fertility Trends and Differentials in the United States*. New York: Academic Press.

Sidgwick, Henry. 1883. *The Principles of Political Economy*. London: Macmillan.

Simon, Julian L. 1981. *The Ultimate Resource*. New York: Pharos Books.

Spencer, Herbert. 1852. Theory of Population. *Westminster Review* (April).

Stangeland, Charles Emil. 1966. *Pre-Malthusian Doctrines of Population: A Study in the History of Economic Theory*. New York: Augustus M. Kelley.

United Nations. 1973. *The Determinants and Consequences of Population Trends*. Vol. 1. New York: United Nations.

———. 1983. *Manual X: Indirect Techniques for Demographic Estimation*. New York: United Nations.

van de Walle, E. 1983. "Malthus Today." In J. Dupquier, A. Fauve-Chamoux, and E. Grebinik, eds., *Malthus Past and Present*, pp. 233–45. London: Academic Press.

von Tunzelmann, G. N. 1986. "Malthus' Total Population System: A Dynamic Reinterpretation." In David Coleman and Roger Schofield, eds., *The State of Population Theory: Forward from Malthus*, pp. 65–95. London: Basil Blackwell.

Wattenberg, Ben J. 1987. *The Birth Dearth*. New York: Pharos Books.

Willigan, J. Dennis, and Katherine A. Lynch. 1982. *Sources and Methods of Historical Demography*. New York: Academic Press.

Wood, John Cunningham. 1986. *Thomas Robert Malthus: Critical Assessments*. 4 vols. London: Croom Helm.

Wrigley, E. A. 1983. "Malthus' Model of a Pre-Industrial Economy." In J. Dupaquier, A. Fauve-Chamoux, and E. Grebenik, eds., *Malthus Past and Present*, pp. 111–24. London: Academic Press.

Zheng, Liu. 1981. "Population Planning and Demographic Theory." In Liu Zheng, Song Jian, and others, *China's Population: Problems & Prospects*, pp. 1–24. Beijing: New World Press.

4. Population Knowledge and Population Data

Our discussion of the fundamentals of population change up to this point has covered the nature of population change in very general terms, including how population change has evolved with regard to what we called transitions and cycles as well as types of conceptual thinking that have provided the frameworks for understanding various population phenomena.

Implicit in these previous chapters have been the assumptions that, first, we already have a clear notion of what it is about population that we want to understand and, second, we can acquire the relevant and accurate information necessary to achieve such understanding. These assumptions need to be examined carefully because it is often the case that either we are not sure precisely what we need to know, or we are uncertain about the form in which we need to know it, or we are not well informed about where to find the information.

In this chapter we will explore these issues. Attention will first be given to "what we want to know," and this will be followed up by an examination of "where we get the data." Then we'll consider *general measurement issues.* This latter section will include a discussion of some of the general problems often faced in using data and how demographers customarily deal with them.

Table 4.1 presents an outline of the broad types of population data which are topics of general interest (which we will look at in some detail in later chapters), as well as the broad categories of population data sources. Potentially, every data source can be the location for information on each of the topics of interest. In fact, some data sources are more useful than others for acquiring certain kinds of data, as we will point out. In addition, population research increasingly involves the merging of data from different sources to maximize the sorts of information that can be made available. We will discuss how this is done in this chapter.

WHAT WE WANT TO KNOW

Throughout documented history, there has been interest in the numbers of people, their locations, and their personal and family characteristics. Holy Scriptures that tell about past centuries inform us that citizens were counted in

TABLE 4.1 Population Topics and Population Data Sources

POPULATION TOPICS	POPULATION DATA SOURCES
Population size	Censuses
Mortality and morbidity	Surveys
Fertility and contraception	Registrations
Mobility and migration	Civil or vital
Local mobility	Other public records
Internal migration	Private records
International migration	Merged records
Population distribution	Population registers
Population density	Other linked records
Geographic distribution	Estimates
Urbanization	
Population composition	
Age and sex	
Race and ethnicity	
Population characteristics	
Education	
Economic status	
Marital and family status	
Living patterns	

censuses and registrations as a means of determining who should be taxed and who was eligible for military service. Officials of past eras frequently referred to these goals to justify the task of collecting information on an area's population.

In today's world, population data are of interest for a much wider array of uses. For every segment of government, for every private sector organization—in fact, wherever people as a group or aggregate are subjects of inquiry or the basis for actions—there is a demand for demographic information of some kind, and the range of information requested is extensive.

The topics in Table 4.1 cover a broad spectrum of items of information about populations. We have referred to them already in previous chapters. However, these are only general topics and there are specific categories within each of them. Moreover, the topics themselves do not signify *what* it is we want to know about the subject.

For example, let us consider fertility and contraception. Since fertility is a component of population change, we might want to know the extent to which it contributes to population change at different times among different groups in different geographic areas. To understand the fertility process better, our interest might focus on the following subjects: the ages at which pregnancy and childbearing take place; the marital statuses of women when they become pregnant and the kind of family and other support systems they have; the women's previous reproductive history and especially any complications that took place; the sexes of the children already born; whether each pregnancy and childbirth were wanted or desired by the woman and man involved; the extent to which the woman received medical and other prenatal care; her dietary practices; her use of tobacco and drugs before and throughout the pregnancy; the spacing intervals between children; and many other factors.

Regarding contraception prior to a pregnancy, we might try to learn how accessible it was, what techniques were used, how often they changed, how regularly they were used, what side effects there were, what advice was received about their use from doctors and others, and various other factors.

The particular items of information we need will relate to the questions asked about the topic. When academic researchers are attempting to do studies that will build on existing theory about a topic, the kinds of information to be acquired may be extensive and informational detail needed can be elaborate. If the information is required for an official purpose, for the need of a private sector, for a media presentation, or for personal interest, the kinds and detail of data will probably not be the same.

What then are more specific illustrations of data needs that each of these user groups have? Because governments are such prime users of population information, we will first address that demand. Then we will discuss the various other uses typically made of population data.

Governmental Uses

Every country in the world collects information on its population, and every national government specifies uses to which the data should be put. In addition, regional, state or provincial, and local governments are consumers of population data. These various governmental units depend on censuses, surveys, civil or vital registrations, and various record systems on a systematic basis for many of their needs. Moreover, they frequently turn to such information for special needs that are not part of regular operations.

The kinds of uses to which governments put population data are so vast that it would take one or more volumes of books of this size to chart them. To show some of the range of uses, we will summarize those by one government (the United States) based on one directive (congressional legislation) and utilizing one data source (the census). These mandated uses of the data do not include uses of the U.S. census by the Congress that are not based on legislative requirements. Similarly, they do not include census uses by executive agencies of the government.

Laws passed by the U.S. Congress specify the particular types of information required to determine the numbers of people who qualify for participation in certain programs or who are eligible for various kinds of benefits or who are the subjects of diagnostic or evaluative research. The law indicates, directly or by implication, which items of census information are involved in the determination.

As of 1987, census information was stipulated by sex (gender) in 11 laws, by age in 20 laws, by relationship to household members in 14 laws, by race in 39 laws, by Hispanic origin in 22 laws, by other ancestries in 14 laws, by language in 12 laws, by birthplace or citizenship in 11 laws, by marital status in 6 laws, by children ever born in 5 laws, by migration status in 7 laws, by employment status in 24 laws, by veteran status in 8 laws, by occupation and/or industry of work in 18 laws, by place of work or journey to work in 31 laws, by education in 15 laws, by income in 20 laws, by disability status in 13 laws, as well as by housing characteristics in a large number of laws (U.S. Bureau of the Census, 1990a).

What are the legislative topics for the twenty needs for age data? They include funding to states for postsecondary education, funding to states for student loans, funding to states for community college expansion, funding for adult basic education, education grant eligibility for handicapped persons, funding for state vocational education, evaluation of state vocational education programs, career education incentive programs, transportation for the elderly and handicapped persons, research on needs and abilities of older persons, vocational rehabilitation, work activities of the handicapped, vital and health statistics, bilingual requirements for voting rights, voter registration, work-study programs, juvenile justice and delinquency prevention, and prevention of age discrimination (two laws).

What are the legislative topics for the twenty needs for income data? They include insured loans for rural development, education programs for low-income children, mortgage subsidy bonds programs, job training programs, revenue sharing, housing assistance for low-income families, rehabilitation of privately owned property for residential use, housing needs of the handicapped, loans to farm owners for dwelling repairs, rural housing rental assistance, supplemental food programs for low-income infants and children, work-study programs, legal assistance for those who cannot afford it, elderly social service programs, community development block grants, grants to cities and counties for economic recovery, financial assistance for persons with developmental disabilities, weatherization assistance for low-income persons, grants to states for home energy assistance for low-income persons, and social services under the Head Start program.

Operational activities of federal agencies depend on a wide range of census data. The U.S. Postal Service must know where people live so that it can develop appropriate delivery routes and assign deliverers according to the population size of each area. Because the Department of Agriculture has to plan for advising and assisting farmers, their numbers and whereabouts are crucial. The armed forces need to keep track of where potential recruits are located. The Department of Justice has to set up federal court systems and staff them according to demographic needs. The Social Security Administration must monitor the population it serves based on knowing the location of the people who need its services. These are just a few examples of nonlegislative federal governmental uses of census data alone.

Multiply these by similar uses by states, counties, cities, and local governments in their own areas. Further multiply them by uses of other kinds of population data—surveys, registrations, and calculated estimates—and the number of demographic data applications by governmental groups is legion.

Nongovernmental Uses

Although the U.S. federal demographic data sources are justified mainly in terms of governmental needs, there are numerous applications of census data by businesses, industry, and private agencies and organizations. Hence, the private sector is highly dependent on such information.

In the business world, the larger companies have hired demographic specialists as staff members. Major newspapers and magazines regularly assign reporters to write about changing population conditions and to highlight the population data sources (such as the census and vital registration). Hardly a day goes by without the mention of some aspect of population in nightly news coverage on radio and television. The private sector is highly sensitive to the importance of demographic information for its operations and planning.

Courses on population analysis, in addition to those in the social sciences, now occupy niches in the academic curricula of business schools and colleges, and even textbooks for that application have been written (Pol, 1987). Courses have also been offered, and books on population written, for schools of urban and regional planning (Myers, 1992) and schools of public health and medicine (Pol and Thomas, 1992). The U.S. Bureau of the Census (1989) itself suggests what items of census data might be useful to private groups that have decisions to make about their activities (see Box 4.1).

Pol (1987) describes several specific cases of business applications of demographic data. They include Levi Strauss' awareness of shifts in women's occupations and introducing a new career line of clothing for professional women; Dow Jones segmenting social-demographic markets to improve sales of their *Wall Street Journal* publication; Time Inc. relying on household and family demography to better plan direct mail solicitations for its magazines; Associated Dry Goods basing the selection of new retail sites on identification of areas with high percentages of middle- and upper-middle-class clientele; the Credit Union National Association altering its market strategy based on demographic projections showing that nearly half of credit union membership growth in the late 1970s and early 1980s was due to shifts in the age structure; Boston Edison drawing on demographic information to plan for physical plant expansion; General Motors Corporation developing a demographic profile of its active and inactive employees in order to gauge the nature of their health benefit pro-

BOX 4.1 Census Data for the Private Sector

ACTIVITY	RELATED DATA FROM THE CENSUS
Selecting the best location for a store	Household composition, age, income, education, occupation, autos, rent/value, tenure, shelter costs
Planning a job training program	Age, education, unemployment, work experience, language, marital status
Estimating need for home health care and support services	Household composition, age, marital status, income, language, tenure, disability, telephone, plumbing, kitchen facilities
Assessing the need for a reverse mortgage program	Household composition, age, marital status, income, tenure, value of home, shelter costs
Selecting merchandise lines of the right price level for a store	Household composition, income, age, tenure, value/rent, shelter costs
Setting fund-raising goals, by neighborhood, for house-to-house canvassers for a charity	Household composition, income, age, education, tenure, value/rent, year moved into residence

grams; and various life insurance companies taking account of changing survival patterns and socioeconomic trends to reassess the way they identify people requiring insurance.

One of the most successful periodicals in the business community is *American Demographics*, which interprets research reports in academic and professional sources for business use and catalogs the places where economic planners can find data and advice on relating population and socioeconomic changes to their needs. The suppliers of this information are a growing number of market research and computer data generation companies that act as intermediaries among the basic data producers (the Census Bureau, vital statistics agencies, and the like) and commercial interests.

Other nongovernmental users of demographic data include the mass media, which are communicators to the general public. If people learn about population change today, some of it might come through the educational system for younger persons but more of it will likely be discovered for all age groups through television, radio, and the popular press (magazines and newspapers).

A substantial group of nongovernmental population data users are researchers who try to interpret demographic data for both enhancing population theory and providing findings that can be used by other groups in a practical way. The journal *Population Index* canvasses research books, monographs, and periodicals in all languages in all parts of the world and gives its readers an annotated bibliography in English on a quarterly basis. Its annotations indicate the vast amount of population data that are analyzed by research specialists.

We have alluded to the range of uses of population information by governmental and nongovernmental agencies and organizations. Specific reference was given to symptomatic uses of a few types. It is clear that population knowledge is required by a broad spectrum of people and groups who rely on basic data sources for that knowledge. What, then, can we say about those sources? What are the principal ones, and how does the information they produce reach the interested users?

Where We Get the Data

Looking back at Table 4.1, we can see the several sources of today's population data. Some sources have long histories as data-gathering mechanisms; others are more recent in their development. Computer-age technology is creating even newer forms of information acquisition.

The list includes censuses (traditional sources which have been undergoing change over time), surveys (the scientific ones which evolved from the establishment of sampling theory), registrations (which are based on record-keeping of governments and of private organizations on almost every imaginable topic), merged records (the sets of procedures for joining sources of data to maximize available information), and estimates (calculations of data when censuses, surveys, registrations, and other records are lacking or insufficient).

The term *demography* (in its French form, *démographie*) was first attributed to Achille Guillard (1855) in a book written in France on the subject. However, the concepts of demographic data and analysis go back to the works of John Graunt (1662), who studied records of burials and christenings in London in the early and mid-seventeenth century in an effort to make inferences about the risks of mortality at the time.

It has been said that "Graunt approached his material in a critical spirit and carried out an ingenious and painstaking investigation of its significance. He aimed at a precise statement of the grounds for each inference and presented his basic data in detail" (Lorimer, 1959). Graunt's work was performed in an era when statistical records were increasingly used to describe the conditions of states. This general development took on the name *political arithmetic*, and a book by that title was written soon after by William Petty (1690). This volume is acknowledged as the forerunner of the broader discipline of statistics.

The evolution of censuses, surveys, registrations, and estimations can be marked from that period. The course of each of these data-collection methods was quite different, however. Censuses became the foundation of population information throughout the world, and only recently has their indispensability been challenged. The scientific basis for the conduct of surveys was formed, and that mechanism has assumed a great importance in recent years. Registrations continue to be valuable sources of information, as they were in Graunt's day, but they are now used in more innovative ways. Estimations remain a required data source because of the lagged development of the other sources and the pressing need to have population statistics for critical decision making. The facility with which these various sources can be combined is probably a key to some of the more creative research in progress. We will deal with each of these data bases in turn.

Censuses

Censuses are familiar to most people since they are taken in nearly all parts of the world and are administered by countries, including nearly all of the population of the globe. Even if individuals have not themselves been interviewed by census takers or completed census forms, they are generally aware that census information about them was obtained from adult members of their households or from neighbors (Nam and Philliber, 1984).

The United Nations Department of International Economic and Social Affairs prescribes standards for the taking of a census of population (and housing as well). It defines a population census as "the total process of collecting, compiling, evaluating, analysing and publishing or otherwise disseminating demographic, economic and social data pertaining, at a specified time, to all persons in a country or in a well-delimited part of a country" (United Nations, 1980).

It goes on to specify four essential features of such a census:

1. *Individual enumeration*—that each individual and each living quarters are enumerated separately and that their characteristics are separately recorded;
2. *Universality* within a defined territory—that the census should include every person present and/or residing within its scope, depending upon the type of population count required;
3. *Simultaneity*—that each person and each living quarters should be enumerated as nearly as possible in respect of the same well-defined point of time and the data collected should refer to a well-defined reference period; and
4. *Defined periodicity*—censuses should be taken at regular intervals so that comparable information is made available in a fixed sequence.... It is recommended that a national census be taken at least every ten years.

To facilitate comparisons of countries, it is further suggested that censuses be taken in the years ending in zero or as near to those years as possible (United Nations, 1980).

Like most standards, these are generally adhered to by the many countries of the world, but there are variations. Sometimes decisions are affected by cultural practices. The cost of taking a census may be so prohibitive that some countries are not able to meet all the standards. Geographic or climatic conditions may dictate census features peculiar to a particular country or part of a country.

The principal advantages of *individual enumeration* are that census results can be tabulated with the individual as a unit of analysis and that characteristics of the individual can be cross-tabulated. Most of the information we usually want from a census relates to summaries for individuals, and cross-tabulations permit us to discover how different traits of an individual (e.g., age, race, and education) are related to each other.

From the first U.S. census in 1790 through the one in 1840, enumeration was done on a household or housing unit basis. That is, the numbers of persons in certain demographic categories were given for each household alongside the name of the head of the household. Individual characteristics were not specified. Thus, it was established that John Jones' household had, for instance, 15 residents, of whom 5 were free white males, 7 were free white females, and 5 were slaves. The age distribution of the residents was also given. In those early censuses, it was considered important to associate the household's population composition with the name of the household head. In fact, the publications of the 1790 Census report the data in that way. One can find Thomas Jefferson in Virginia and learn about how many males and females of different ages, as well as slaves, were part of his household. (Confidentiality of information was not an issue in those days.)

The matter of *universality* is often a confusing one in census taking. The population of a country may, at a point in time, include persons who may not be regarded, or regard themselves, as permanent residents of that country. A well-conducted census will count everyone and then decide who should not be included in the totals. The UN standards are just that, of course, and any country is free to set its own rules about who should and should not be included in the count and in the totals. For example, some include foreigners, others do not.

The question of where people should be counted is also an issue of universality. If people have more than one residence, at which one should they be placed? If someone is attending college, is that person to be counted back home or at college? If an individual is on a vacation at an out-of-town place when the census is taken, where should the census count him or her? Each census has established rules of residence for that purpose. In the United States at present, those with more than one residence get counted where they spend the greater part of the year. College students are included in the communities where they live while they go to college. Vacationers are enumerated where they usually live. These kinds of rules are based on legal decisions after much consideration of the alternatives. The impact of the rules can be great, as in the case of college towns that are credited with many more people under the current residence rule for college students than they would have with a different rule.

BOX 4.2 Steps in U.S. Census Taking

These steps generally include:

1. Legal basis for the census: The U.S. census was the first one ever stipulated by a country in its Constitution (Article I, Section 2). A continuing legal basis is provided by Congress for each census period, which gives the census director authority to plan and organize the enumeration, subject to the final approval of the Congress and President.
2. Budget and cost control, and census calendar: Like any other organization or household, the Census Bureau receives allocations within which it must operate. Censuses can be very costly, so it is essential that the available funding be spent wisely. A calendar insures that timely progress will be achieved in carrying out the census.
3. Administrative organization and consultation: Usually a census requires a large number of staff members for a short period of time and a smaller staff for the remaining period. Trying to hire competent staff for short periods can often be a difficult proposition and sometimes plays havoc with the quality of a census. As good as the census personnel might be, expert advice is necessary both to make sure the census is done as correctly as possible and to ascertain what uses of the census are paramount.
4. Area identification and mapping: A feature of a census is the ability to learn about the population in all geographic areas, however small. Census planning must include designation of such areas. (We will elaborate on them in Chapter 8.) Preparation of maps for all enumeration areas serves the purposes of assisting those who are collecting the data as well as those who are responsible for tabulating the statistics for different areas.

These rules of residence are necessary in a census based on de jure or usual residence concept of inclusion. In some countries, censuses are taken on a de facto basis, which means that people are counted wherever they are at the time of the census. Each country must decide which basis is better for itself, according to which meets the country's data needs more efficiently.

Censuses are not taken in a day, although de facto censuses can usually be taken more quickly than de jure censuses. It is not uncommon for a census enumeration to continue for months. The issue of simultaneity thus becomes critical. If one part of a state were to be enumerated in April of a year and another part in June of that year, combining the two parts would not produce a count with a common time reference. People move between locations, and both double counting and undercounting would be possible outcomes. As a consequence, censuses have a reference date that is the time point for counting people. In the United States, the date is April 1. Even if some individuals are not

continued

5. Questionnaire development and tabulation design: The previous census is usually a starting point for what is to be included on a census form but new questions, or variations on old questions and/or response categories, are suggested for each census. If some of these innovations have apparent merit, they must be field-tested and justified for inclusion.

   Many censuses use two questionnaire forms—a short form with a limited number of questions for most respondents and a long form with the same and additional questions for a sample of the population. (The long form for the 1990 U.S. Census is shown in Figure 4.1.) It is desirable to determine what tabulations will eventually be made at the same time as the questionnaires are being devised in order to guarantee that the necessary data will be available in the proper form.

6. Conducting the census and processing the data: Before the census is actually taken, all living quarters must be identified (whether occupied or vacant). Traditionally, enumerations have been conducted with interviewers (census takers) who go from door to door to get information. The most recent censuses have involved mailings of forms to living quarters and self-enumeration and mailback of forms to central census offices. Follow-up interviews are conducted by phone or in person, when needed.

Processing the data involves coding, editing, and classifying the responses and putting them into tabulation format (computer tapes or disks). Tabulations of the U.S. census are published, but copies of computer tapes for samples (without identifying information for individuals) are made available to researchers and others who may want to prepare their own unique analyses.

enumerated until June, the question is where they would have been counted on April 1. In this way, all the statistics compiled from the census can refer to a particular point in time.

The Census Bureau in the United States strives to count everyone. To enumerate the homeless in the 1990 Census, an S-night (street and shelter night) was designated, when census takers canvassed shelters, flophouses, bus stations, and all-night movie theaters from 6 p.m. until midnight. From 2 to 4 a.m. people were interviewed in congregating places near the streets. The resulting count of the homeless may have been deficient, but the special procedures used led to counting many persons who would otherwise have been missed in the census.

Defined periodicity is also variable, but the UN standard has brought about a high degree of consistency. A majority of countries take a census in the decennial years, those ending in 0. For some, that is their only census; for others, additional censuses are taken in intermediate years (e.g., in years ending in 5). A number of countries that traditionally took censuses in years ending in 1 or 9 have continued that practice in order to maintain continuity with the past (e.g., Canada and India).

Most of us learn about a census from a time just before it is taken (and some publicity encouraging cooperation surrounds it) to a time soon after it is taken and the main results are presented—a span of maybe two years. However, a census operation covers a much longer time. Planning for the 1990 Census of the United States began before the 1980 Census was completed. The reason is that there are many steps that must be taken before a good census is ready to be executed (see Box 4.2).

Because censuses are the bases for meeting many crucial needs of people, they are not without controversy. The issue of most concern in the United States has been completeness of the enumeration for the country as a whole and for specific geographic areas and population categories.

Postenumeration studies reveal that there was a net undercount of 1.6 percent in the 1990 U.S. Census, slightly higher than was estimated for 1980 and somewhat lower than for the several preceding censuses. However, the net undercount was much higher for males than females and substantially higher for blacks than whites and others. Five percent of black males were undercounted in 1990, and possibly double that percent were missed among black males at young adult ages. Therefore, uses made of the reported data can result in misleading findings, in particular with regard to comparisons of groups differentially covered (West and Fein, 1990). Throughout U.S. census history, no attempt has been made to adjust the reported data for known undercounting.

One might ask why this knowledge about undercounting is not used to arrive at better data. The principal reason has been that estimated levels of undercounting have been made for the country as a whole and comparable estimates have not been made for geographic areas. In recent years, however, census methodologists have designed procedures for improved estimates of missed persons that could be used to adjust the data. Even among the technicians, there is no agreement on the improvement that would result from making adjustments. Wolter (1991) has argued that the "corrected counts should be closer than uncorrected counts to the true population, both in absolute terms and, more critically, in the distribution of the population across states and other areas." Freedman (1991), on the other hand, concluded, "There is little hard evidence to show that current adjustment methodologies would improve the accuracy of the census, and much can go wrong." Freedman's comment refers to the possibility of adjustments based on national or regional patterns of undercounting leading to improvement in counts of some small areas and greater error introduced in others. A decision was ultimately made by the Secretary of Commerce, under whose command the Bureau of the Census is officially located, to refrain from adjusting the data that the government reports. (See Chapter 14 for further discussion of public policy implications.)

FIGURE 4.1 Official 1990 U.S. Census Form

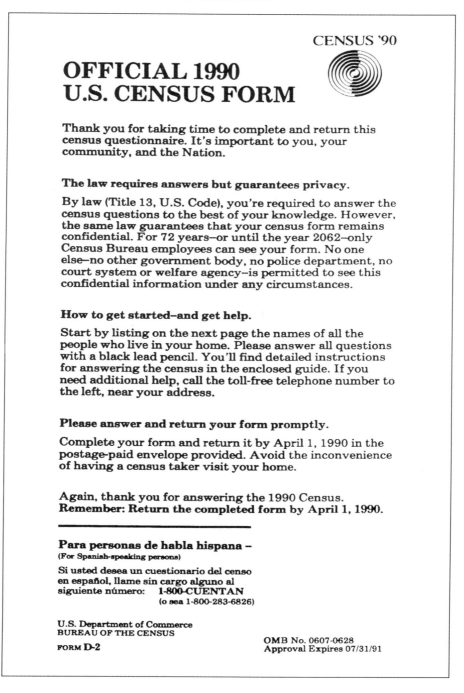

CENSUS '90

OFFICIAL 1990 U.S. CENSUS FORM

Thank you for taking time to complete and return this census questionnaire. It's important to you, your community, and the Nation.

The law requires answers but guarantees privacy.

By law (Title 13, U.S. Code), you're required to answer the census questions to the best of your knowledge. However, the same law guarantees that your census form remains confidential. For 72 years–or until the year 2062–only Census Bureau employees can see your form. No one else–no other government body, no police department, no court system or welfare agency–is permitted to see this confidential information under any circumstances.

How to get started–and get help.

Start by listing on the next page the names of all the people who live in your home. Please answer all questions with a black lead pencil. You'll find detailed instructions for answering the census in the enclosed guide. If you need additional help, call the toll-free telephone number to the left, near your address.

Please answer and return your form promptly.

Complete your form and return it by April 1, 1990 in the postage-paid envelope provided. Avoid the inconvenience of having a census taker visit your home.

Again, thank you for answering the 1990 Census.
Remember: Return the completed form by April 1, 1990.

Para personas de habla hispana –
(For Spanish-speaking persons)

Si usted desea un cuestionario del censo en español, llame sin cargo alguno al siguiente número: **1-800-CUENTAN**
(o sea 1-800-283-6826)

U.S. Department of Commerce
BUREAU OF THE CENSUS

FORM D-2

OMB No. 0607-0628
Approval Expires 07/31/91

FIGURE 4.1 *continued*

Page 1

The 1990 census must count every person at his or her "usual residence." This means the place where the person lives and sleeps most of the time.

1a. List on the numbered lines below the name of each person living here on Sunday, April 1, including all persons staying here who have no other home. If EVERYONE at this address is staying here temporarily and usually lives somewhere else, follow the instructions given in question 1b below.

Include	Do NOT include
• Everyone who usually lives here such as family members, housemates and roommates, foster children, roomers, boarders, and live-in employees	• Persons who usually live somewhere else
• Persons who are temporarily away on a business trip, on vacation, or in a general hospital	• Persons who are away in an institution such as a prison, mental hospital, or a nursing home
• College students who stay here while attending college	• College students who live somewhere else while attending college
• Persons in the Armed Forces who live here	• Persons in the Armed Forces who live somewhere else
• Newborn babies still in the hospital	
• Children in boarding schools below the college level	
• Persons who stay here most of the week while working even if they have a home somewhere else	• Persons who stay somewhere else most of the the week while working
• Persons with no other home who are staying here on April 1	

Print last name, first name, and middle initial for each person. Begin on line 1 with the household member (or one of the household members) in whose name this house or apartment is owned, being bought, or rented. If there is no such person, start on line 1 with any adult household member.

	LAST	FIRST	INITIAL		LAST	FIRST	INITIAL
1				7			
2				8			
3				9			
4				10			
5				11			
6				12			

1b. If EVERYONE is staying here only temporarily and usually lives somewhere else, list the name of each person on the numbered lines above, fill this circle → ○ and print their usual address below. DO NOT PRINT THE ADDRESS LISTED ON THE FRONT COVER.

House number	Street or road/Rural route and box number	Apartment number
City	State	ZIP Code
County or foreign country	Names of nearest intersecting streets or roads	

NOW PLEASE OPEN THE FLAP TO PAGE 2 AND ANSWER ALL QUESTIONS FOR THE FIRST 7 PEOPLE LISTED. USE A BLACK LEAD PENCIL ONLY.

FIGURE 4.1 *continued*

Page 2

PLEASE ALSO ANSWER HOUSING QUESTIONS ON PAGE 3 →

	PERSON 1	PERSON 2
Please fill one column → **for each person listed in Question 1a on page 1.**	Last name First name Middle initial	Last name First name Middle initial
2. How is this person related to PERSON 1? Fill ONE circle for each person. If **Other relative** of person in column 1, fill circle and print exact relationship, such as mother-in-law, grandparent, son-in-law, niece, cousin, and so on.	START in this column with the household member (or one of the members) in whose name the home is owned, being bought, or rented. If there is no such person, start in this column with any adult household member.	If a RELATIVE of Person 1: ○ Husband/wife ○ Brother/sister ○ Natural-born or adopted son/daughter ○ Father/mother ○ Grandchild ○ Other relative ○ Stepson/stepdaughter If NOT RELATED to Person 1: ○ Roomer, boarder, or foster child ○ Unmarried partner ○ Housemate, roommate ○ Other nonrelative
3. Sex Fill ONE circle for each person.	○ Male ○ Female	○ Male ○ Female
4. Race Fill ONE circle for the race that the person considers himself/herself to be. If **Indian (Amer.)**, print the name of the enrolled or principal tribe. → If **Other Asian or Pacific Islander (API)**, print one group, for example: Hmong, Fijian, Laotian, Thai, Tongan, Pakistani, Cambodian, and so on. → If **Other race**, print race. →	○ White ○ Black or Negro ○ Indian (Amer.) (Print the name of the enrolled or principal tribe.) ○ Eskimo ○ Aleut Asian or Pacific Islander (API) ○ Chinese ○ Japanese ○ Filipino ○ Asian Indian ○ Hawaiian ○ Samoan ○ Korean ○ Guamanian ○ Vietnamese ○ Other API ○ Other race (Print race)	○ White ○ Black or Negro ○ Indian (Amer.) (Print the name of the enrolled or principal tribe.) ○ Eskimo ○ Aleut Asian or Pacific Islander (API) ○ Chinese ○ Japanese ○ Filipino ○ Asian Indian ○ Hawaiian ○ Samoan ○ Korean ○ Guamanian ○ Vietnamese ○ Other API ○ Other race (Print race)
5. Age and year of birth **a.** Print each person's age at last birthday. Fill in the matching circle below each box. **b.** Print each person's year of birth and fill the matching circle below each box.	a. Age 0 ○ 0 ○ 0 ○ 1 ○ 1 ○ 1 ○ 2 ○ 2 ○ 3 ○ 3 ○ 4 ○ 4 ○ 5 ○ 5 ○ 6 ○ 6 ○ 7 ○ 7 ○ 8 ○ 8 ○ 9 ○ 9 ○ b. Year of birth 1 1 ● 8 ○ 0 ○ 0 ○ 9 ○ 1 ○ 1 ○ 2 ○ 2 ○ 3 ○ 3 ○ 4 ○ 4 ○ 5 ○ 5 ○ 6 ○ 6 ○ 7 ○ 7 ○ 8 ○ 8 ○ 9 ○ 9 ○	a. Age 0 ○ 0 ○ 0 ○ 1 ○ 1 ○ 1 ○ 2 ○ 2 ○ 3 ○ 3 ○ 4 ○ 4 ○ 5 ○ 5 ○ 6 ○ 6 ○ 7 ○ 7 ○ 8 ○ 8 ○ 9 ○ 9 ○ b. Year of birth 1 1 ● 8 ○ 0 ○ 0 ○ 9 ○ 1 ○ 1 ○ 2 ○ 2 ○ 3 ○ 3 ○ 4 ○ 4 ○ 5 ○ 5 ○ 6 ○ 6 ○ 7 ○ 7 ○ 8 ○ 8 ○ 9 ○ 9 ○
6. Marital status Fill ONE circle for each person.	○ Now married ○ Separated ○ Widowed ○ Never married ○ Divorced	○ Now married ○ Separated ○ Widowed ○ Never married ○ Divorced
7. Is this person of Spanish/Hispanic origin? Fill ONE circle for each person. If **Yes, other Spanish/Hispanic**, print one group. →	○ No (not Spanish/Hispanic) ○ Yes, Mexican, Mexican-Am., Chicano ○ Yes, Puerto Rican ○ Yes, Cuban ○ Yes, other Spanish/Hispanic (Print one group, for example: Argentinean, Colombian, Dominican, Nicaraguan, Salvadoran, Spaniard, and so on.)	○ No (not Spanish/Hispanic) ○ Yes, Mexican, Mexican-Am., Chicano ○ Yes, Puerto Rican ○ Yes, Cuban ○ Yes, other Spanish/Hispanic (Print one group, for example: Argentinean, Colombian, Dominican, Nicaraguan, Salvadoran, Spaniard, and so on.)
FOR CENSUS USE →	○ ○	○ ○

FIGURE 4.1 *continued*

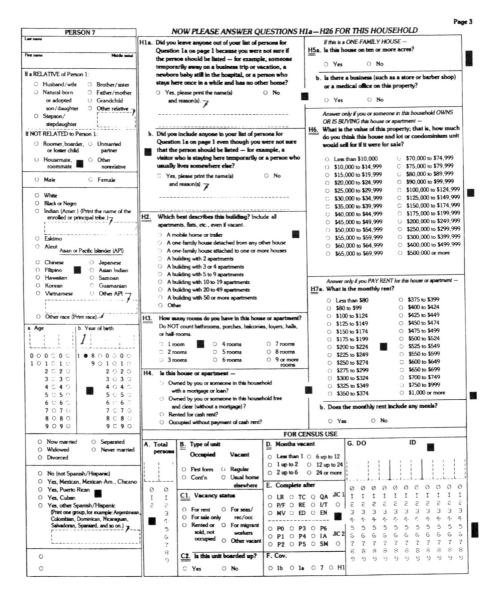

Page 3

PERSON 7

Last name

First name — Middle initial

If a RELATIVE of Person 1:
- ○ Husband/wife
- ○ Brother/sister
- ○ Natural-born or adopted son/daughter
- ○ Father/mother
- ○ Grandchild
- ○ Other relative
- ○ Stepson/stepdaughter

If NOT RELATED to Person 1:
- ○ Roomer, boarder, or foster child
- ○ Unmarried partner
- ○ Housemate, roommate
- ○ Other nonrelative

- ○ Male
- ○ Female

- ○ White
- ○ Black or Negro
- ○ Indian (Amer.) (Print the name of the enrolled or principal tribe.)
- ○ Eskimo
- ○ Aleut

Asian or Pacific Islander (API)
- ○ Chinese
- ○ Japanese
- ○ Filipino
- ○ Asian Indian
- ○ Hawaiian
- ○ Samoan
- ○ Korean
- ○ Guamanian
- ○ Vietnamese
- ○ Other API
- ○ Other race (Print race)

a. Age — b. Year of birth

0 ○ 0 ○ 0 ○	1 ● 8 ○ 0 ○ 0 ○
1 ○ 1 ○ 1 ○	9 ○ 1 ○ 1 ○
2 ○ 2 ○	2 ○ 2 ○
3 ○ 3 ○	3 ○ 3 ○
4 ○ 4 ○	4 ○ 4 ○
5 ○ 5 ○	5 ○ 5 ○
6 ○ 6 ○	6 ○ 6 ○
7 ○ 7 ○	7 ○ 7 ○
8 ○ 8 ○	8 ○ 8 ○
9 ○ 9 ○	9 ○ 9 ○

- ○ Now married
- ○ Separated
- ○ Widowed
- ○ Never married
- ○ Divorced

- ○ No (not Spanish/Hispanic)
- ○ Yes, Mexican, Mexican-Am., Chicano
- ○ Yes, Puerto Rican
- ○ Yes, Cuban
- ○ Yes, other Spanish/Hispanic (Print one group, for example: Argentinean, Colombian, Dominican, Nicaraguan, Salvadoran, Spaniard, and so on.)

○

○

NOW PLEASE ANSWER QUESTIONS H1a–H26 FOR THIS HOUSEHOLD

H1a. Did you leave anyone out of your list of persons for Question 1a on page 1 because you were not sure if the person should be listed — for example, someone temporarily away on a business trip or vacation, a newborn baby still in the hospital, or a person who stays here once in a while and has no other home?
- ○ Yes, please print the name(s) and reason(s).
- ○ No

b. Did you include anyone in your list of persons for Question 1a on page 1 even though you were not sure that the person should be listed — for example, a visitor who is staying here temporarily or a person who usually lives somewhere else?
- ○ Yes, please print the name(s) and reason(s).
- ○ No

H2. Which best describes this building? Include all apartments, flats, etc., even if vacant.
- ○ A mobile home or trailer
- ○ A one-family house detached from any other house
- ○ A one-family house attached to one or more houses
- ○ A building with 2 apartments
- ○ A building with 3 or 4 apartments
- ○ A building with 5 to 9 apartments
- ○ A building with 10 to 19 apartments
- ○ A building with 20 to 49 apartments
- ○ A building with 50 or more apartments
- ○ Other

H3. How many rooms do you have in this house or apartment? Do NOT count bathrooms, porches, balconies, foyers, halls, or half-rooms.
- ○ 1 room
- ○ 2 rooms
- ○ 3 rooms
- ○ 4 rooms
- ○ 5 rooms
- ○ 6 rooms
- ○ 7 rooms
- ○ 8 rooms
- ○ 9 or more rooms

H4. Is this house or apartment —
- ○ Owned by you or someone in this household with a mortgage or loan?
- ○ Owned by you or someone in this household free and clear (without a mortgage)?
- ○ Rented for cash rent?
- ○ Occupied without payment of cash rent?

If this is a ONE-FAMILY HOUSE —

H5a. Is this house on ten or more acres?
- ○ Yes
- ○ No

b. Is there a business (such as a store or barber shop) or a medical office on this property?
- ○ Yes
- ○ No

Answer only if you or someone in this household OWNS OR IS BUYING this house or apartment —

H6. What is the value of this property; that is, how much do you think this house and lot or condominium unit would sell for if it were for sale?
- ○ Less than $10,000
- ○ $10,000 to $14,999
- ○ $15,000 to $19,999
- ○ $20,000 to $24,999
- ○ $25,000 to $29,999
- ○ $30,000 to $34,999
- ○ $35,000 to $39,999
- ○ $40,000 to $44,999
- ○ $45,000 to $49,999
- ○ $50,000 to $54,999
- ○ $55,000 to $59,999
- ○ $60,000 to $64,999
- ○ $65,000 to $69,999
- ○ $70,000 to $74,999
- ○ $75,000 to $79,999
- ○ $80,000 to $89,999
- ○ $90,000 to $99,999
- ○ $100,000 to $124,999
- ○ $125,000 to $149,999
- ○ $150,000 to $174,999
- ○ $175,000 to $199,999
- ○ $200,000 to $249,999
- ○ $250,000 to $299,999
- ○ $300,000 to $399,999
- ○ $400,000 to $499,999
- ○ $500,000 or more

Answer only if you PAY RENT for this house or apartment —

H7a. What is the monthly rent?
- ○ Less than $80
- ○ $80 to $99
- ○ $100 to $124
- ○ $125 to $149
- ○ $150 to $174
- ○ $175 to $199
- ○ $200 to $224
- ○ $225 to $249
- ○ $250 to $274
- ○ $275 to $299
- ○ $300 to $324
- ○ $325 to $349
- ○ $350 to $374
- ○ $375 to $399
- ○ $400 to $424
- ○ $425 to $449
- ○ $450 to $474
- ○ $475 to $499
- ○ $500 to $524
- ○ $525 to $549
- ○ $550 to $599
- ○ $600 to $649
- ○ $650 to $699
- ○ $700 to $749
- ○ $750 to $999
- ○ $1,000 or more

b. Does the monthly rent include any meals?
- ○ Yes
- ○ No

FOR CENSUS USE

A. Total persons

0 0 / 1 1 / 2 2 / 3 / 4 / 5 / 6 / 7 / 8 / 9

B. Type of unit

Occupied
- ○ First form
- ○ Cont'n

Vacant
- ○ Regular
- ○ Usual home elsewhere

C1. Vacancy status
- ○ For rent
- ○ For sale only
- ○ Rented or sold, not occupied
- ○ For seas/rec/occ
- ○ For migrant workers
- ○ Other vacant

C2. Is this unit boarded up?
- ○ Yes
- ○ No

D. Months vacant
- ○ Less than 1
- ○ 1 up to 2
- ○ 2 up to 6
- ○ 6 up to 12
- ○ 12 up to 24
- ○ 24 or more

E. Complete after

○ LR ○ TC ○ QA JIC 1 ○
○ P/F ○ RE ○ I/T
○ MV ○ ED ○ EN

○ P0 ○ P3 ○ P6
○ P1 ○ P4 ○ IA JIC 2 ○
○ P2 ○ P5 ○ SM

F. Cov.

○ 1b ○ 1a ○ 7 ○ H1

G. DO — **ID**

0	0	0	0	0	0	0	0	0	0	0
1	1	1	1	1	1	1	1	1	1	1
2	2	2	2	2	2	2	2	2	2	2
3	3	3	3	3	3	3	3	3	3	3
4	4	4	4	4	4	4	4	4	4	4
5	5	5	5	5	5	5	5	5	5	5
6	6	6	6	6	6	6	6	6	6	6
7	7	7	7	7	7	7	7	7	7	7
8	8	8	8	8	8	8	8	8	8	8
9	9	9	9	9	9	9	9	9	9	9

FIGURE 4.1 *continued*

Page 4

PLEASE ALSO ANSWER THESE

H8. When did the person listed in column 1 on page 2 move into this house or apartment?

- O 1989 or 1990
- O 1985 to 1988
- O 1980 to 1984
- O 1970 to 1979
- O 1960 to 1969
- O 1959 or earlier

H9. How many bedrooms do you have; that is, how many bedrooms would you list if this house or apartment were on the market for sale or rent?

- O No bedroom
- O 1 bedroom
- O 2 bedrooms
- O 3 bedrooms
- O 4 bedrooms
- O 5 or more bedrooms

H10. Do you have COMPLETE plumbing facilities in this house or apartment; that is, 1) hot and cold piped water, 2) a flush toilet, and 3) a bathtub or shower?

- O Yes, have all three facilities
- O No

H11. Do you have COMPLETE kitchen facilities; that is, 1) a sink with piped water, 2) a range or cookstove, and 3) a refrigerator?

- O Yes
- O No

H12. Do you have a telephone in this house or apartment?

- O Yes
- O No

H13. How many automobiles, vans, and trucks of one-ton capacity or less are kept at home for use by members of your household?

- O None
- O 1
- O 2
- O 3
- O 4
- O 5
- O 6
- O 7 or more

H14. Which FUEL is used MOST for heating this house or apartment?

- O Gas: from underground pipes serving the neighborhood
- O Gas: bottled, tank, or LP
- O Electricity
- O Fuel oil, kerosene, etc.
- O Coal or coke
- O Wood
- O Solar energy
- O Other fuel
- O No fuel used

H15. Do you get water from —

- O A public system such as a city water department, or private company?
- O An individual drilled well?
- O An individual dug well?
- O Some other source such as a spring, creek, river, cistern, etc.?

H16. Is this building connected to a public sewer?

- O Yes, connected to public sewer
- O No, connected to septic tank or cesspool
- O No, use other means

H17. About when was this building first built?

- O 1989 or 1990
- O 1985 to 1988
- O 1980 to 1984
- O 1970 to 1979
- O 1960 to 1969
- O 1950 to 1959
- O 1940 to 1949
- O 1939 or earlier
- O Don't know

H18. Is this house or apartment part of a condominium?

- O Yes
- O No

If you live in an apartment building, skip to H20.

H19a. Is this house on less than 1 acre?

- O Yes — *Skip to H20*
- O No

b. In 1989, what were the actual sales of all agricultural products from this property?

- O None
- O $1 to $999
- O $1,000 to $2,499
- O $2,500 to $4,999
- O $5,000 to $9,999
- O $10,000 or more

H20. What are the yearly costs of utilities and fuels for this house or apartment?
If you have lived here less than 1 year, estimate the yearly cost.

a. Electricity

$ ______ .00
Yearly cost — Dollars

OR

- O Included in rent or in condominium fee
- O No charge or electricity not used

b. Gas

$ ______ .00
Yearly cost — Dollars

OR

- O Included in rent or in condominium fee
- O No charge or gas not used

c. Water

$ ______ .00
Yearly cost — Dollars

OR

- O Included in rent or in condominium fee
- O No charge

d. Oil, coal, kerosene, wood, etc.

$ ______ .00
Yearly cost — Dollars

OR

- O Included in rent or in condominium fee
- O No charge or these fuels not used

FIGURE 4.1 *continued*

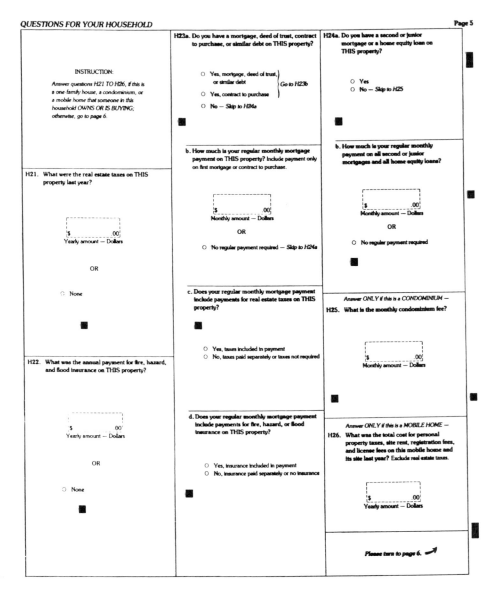

QUESTIONS FOR YOUR HOUSEHOLD Page 5

INSTRUCTION:

Answer questions H21 TO H26, if this is a one-family house, a condominium, or a mobile home that someone in this household OWNS OR IS BUYING; otherwise, go to page 6.

H21. What were the real estate taxes on THIS property last year?

$ .00
Yearly amount — Dollars

OR

○ None

H22. What was the annual payment for fire, hazard, and flood insurance on THIS property?

$ .00
Yearly amount — Dollars

OR

○ None

H23a. Do you have a mortgage, deed of trust, contract to purchase, or similar debt on THIS property?

○ Yes, mortgage, deed of trust, or similar debt } *Go to H23b*
○ Yes, contract to purchase } *Go to H23b*
○ No — *Skip to H24a*

b. How much is your regular monthly mortgage payment on THIS property? Include payment only on first mortgage or contract to purchase.

$ .00
Monthly amount — Dollars

OR

○ No regular payment required — *Skip to H24a*

c. Does your regular monthly mortgage payment include payments for real estate taxes on THIS property?

○ Yes, taxes included in payment
○ No, taxes paid separately or taxes not required

d. Does your regular monthly mortgage payment include payments for fire, hazard, or flood insurance on THIS property?

○ Yes, insurance included in payment
○ No, insurance paid separately or no insurance

H24a. Do you have a second or junior mortgage or a home equity loan on THIS property?

○ Yes
○ No — *Skip to H25*

b. How much is your regular monthly payment on all second or junior mortgages and all home equity loans?

$ .00
Monthly amount — Dollars

OR

○ No regular payment required

Answer ONLY if this is a CONDOMINIUM —

H25. What is the monthly condominium fee?

$ .00
Monthly amount — Dollars

Answer ONLY if this is a MOBILE HOME —

H26. What was the total cost for personal property taxes, site rent, registration fees, and license fees on this mobile home and its site last year? Exclude real estate taxes.

$ .00
Yearly amount — Dollars

Please turn to page 6.

FIGURE 4.1 *continued*

Page 6

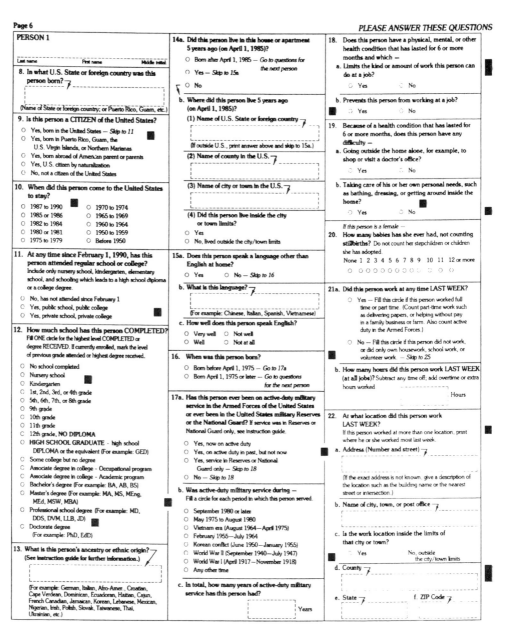

PLEASE ANSWER THESE QUESTIONS

PERSON 1

Last name First name Middle initial

8. In what U.S. State or foreign country was this person born?

(Name of State or foreign country; or Puerto Rico, Guam, etc.)

9. Is this person a CITIZEN of the United States?

- ○ Yes, born in the United States — *Skip to 11*
- ○ Yes, born in Puerto Rico, Guam, the U.S. Virgin Islands, or Northern Marianas
- ○ Yes, born abroad of American parent or parents
- ○ Yes, U.S. citizen by naturalization
- ○ No, not a citizen of the United States

10. When did this person come to the United States to stay?

- ○ 1987 to 1990
- ○ 1985 or 1986
- ○ 1982 to 1984
- ○ 1980 or 1981
- ○ 1975 to 1979
- ○ 1970 to 1974
- ○ 1965 to 1969
- ○ 1960 to 1964
- ○ 1950 to 1959
- ○ Before 1950

11. At any time since February 1, 1990, has this person attended regular school or college? Include only nursery school, kindergarten, elementary school, and schooling which leads to a high school diploma or a college degree.

- ○ No, has not attended since February 1
- ○ Yes, public school, public college
- ○ Yes, private school, private college

12. How much school has this person COMPLETED? Fill ONE circle for the highest level COMPLETED or degree RECEIVED. If currently enrolled, mark the level of previous grade attended or highest degree received.

- ○ No school completed
- ○ Nursery school
- ○ Kindergarten
- ○ 1st, 2nd, 3rd, or 4th grade
- ○ 5th, 6th, 7th, or 8th grade
- ○ 9th grade
- ○ 10th grade
- ○ 11th grade
- ○ 12th grade, NO DIPLOMA
- ○ HIGH SCHOOL GRADUATE - high school DIPLOMA or the equivalent (For example: GED)
- ○ Some college but no degree
- ○ Associate degree in college - Occupational program
- ○ Associate degree in college - Academic program
- ○ Bachelor's degree (For example: BA, AB, BS)
- ○ Master's degree (For example: MA, MS, MEng, MEd, MSW, MBA)
- ○ Professional school degree (For example: MD, DDS, DVM, LLB, JD)
- ○ Doctorate degree (For example: PhD, EdD)

13. What is this person's ancestry or ethnic origin? (See instruction guide for further information.)

(For example: German, Italian, Afro-Amer., Croatian, Cape Verdean, Dominican, Ecuadoran, Haitian, Cajun, French Canadian, Jamaican, Korean, Lebanese, Mexican, Nigerian, Irish, Polish, Slovak, Taiwanese, Thai, Ukrainian, etc.)

14a. Did this person live in this house or apartment 5 years ago (on April 1, 1985)?

- ○ Born after April 1, 1985 — *Go to questions for the next person*
- ○ Yes — *Skip to 15a*
- ○ No

b. Where did this person live 5 years ago (on April 1, 1985)?

(1) Name of U.S. State or foreign country

(If outside U.S., print answer above and skip to 15a.)

(2) Name of county in the U.S.

(3) Name of city or town in the U.S.

(4) Did this person live inside the city or town limits?

- ○ Yes
- ○ No, lived outside the city/town limits

15a. Does this person speak a language other than English at home?

- ○ Yes
- ○ No — *Skip to 16*

b. What is this language?

(For example: Chinese, Italian, Spanish, Vietnamese)

c. How well does this person speak English?

- ○ Very well
- ○ Well
- ○ Not well
- ○ Not at all

16. When was this person born?

- ○ Born before April 1, 1975 — *Go to 17a*
- ○ Born April 1, 1975 or later — *Go to questions for the next person*

17a. Has this person ever been on active-duty military service in the Armed Forces of the United States or ever been in the United States military Reserves or the National Guard? If service was in Reserves or National Guard only, see instruction guide.

- ○ Yes, now on active duty
- ○ Yes, on active duty in past, but not now
- ○ Yes, service in Reserves or National Guard only — *Skip to 18*
- ○ No — *Skip to 18*

b. Was active-duty military service during — Fill a circle for each period in which this person served.

- ○ September 1980 or later
- ○ May 1975 to August 1980
- ○ Vietnam era (August 1964—April 1975)
- ○ February 1955—July 1964
- ○ Korean conflict (June 1950—January 1955)
- ○ World War II (September 1940—July 1947)
- ○ World War I (April 1917—November 1918)
- ○ Any other time

c. In total, how many years of active-duty military service has this person had?

Years

18. Does this person have a physical, mental, or other health condition that has lasted for 6 or more months and which —

a. Limits the kind or amount of work this person can do at a job?

- ○ Yes
- ○ No

b. Prevents this person from working at a job?

- ○ Yes
- ○ No

19. Because of a health condition that has lasted for 6 or more months, does this person have any difficulty —

a. Going outside the home alone, for example, to shop or visit a doctor's office?

- ○ Yes
- ○ No

b. Taking care of his or her own personal needs, such as bathing, dressing, or getting around inside the home?

- ○ Yes
- ○ No

If this person is a female —

20. How many babies has she ever had, not counting stillbirths? Do not count her stepchildren or children she has adopted.

None	1	2	3	4	5	6	7	8	9	10	11	12 or more
○	○	○	○	○	○	○	○	○	○	○	○	○

21a. Did this person work at any time LAST WEEK?

- ○ Yes — Fill this circle if this person worked full time or part time. (Count part-time work such as delivering papers, or helping without pay in a family business or farm. Also count active duty in the Armed Forces.)
- ○ No — Fill this circle if this person did not work, or did only own housework, school work, or volunteer work. — *Skip to 25*

b. How many hours did this person work LAST WEEK (at all jobs)? Subtract any time off; add overtime or extra hours worked.

Hours

22. At what location did this person work LAST WEEK?

If this person worked at more than one location, print where he or she worked most last week.

a. Address (Number and street)

(If the exact address is not known, give a description of the location such as the building name or the nearest street or intersection.)

b. Name of city, town, or post office

c. Is the work location inside the limits of that city or town?

- ○ Yes
- ○ No, outside the city/town limits

d. County

e. State

f. ZIP Code

FIGURE 4.1 *continued*

FOR PERSON 1 ON PAGE 2 — Page 7

23a. How did this person usually get to work LAST WEEK? If this person usually used more than one method of transportation during the trip, fill the circle of the one used for most of the distance.

- ○ Car, truck, or van
- ○ Bus or trolley bus
- ○ Streetcar or trolley car
- ○ Subway or elevated
- ○ Railroad
- ○ Ferryboat
- ○ Taxicab
- ○ Motorcycle
- ○ Bicycle
- ○ Walked
- ○ Worked at home — *Skip to 28*
- ○ Other method

If "car, truck, or van" is marked in 23a, go to 23b. Otherwise, skip to 24a.

b. How many people, including this person, usually rode to work in the car, truck, or van LAST WEEK?

- ○ Drove alone
- ○ 2 people
- ○ 3 people
- ○ 4 people
- ○ 5 people
- ○ 6 people
- ○ 7 to 9 people
- ○ 10 or more people

24a. What time did this person usually leave home to go to work LAST WEEK?

[ ] ○ a.m. ○ p.m.

b. How many minutes did it usually take this person to get from home to work LAST WEEK?

[ ] Minutes — *Skip to 28*

25. Was this person TEMPORARILY absent or on layoff from a job or business LAST WEEK?

- ○ Yes, on layoff
- ○ Yes, on vacation, temporary illness, labor dispute, etc.
- ○ No

26a. Has this person been looking for work during the last 4 weeks?

- ○ Yes
- ○ No — *Skip to 27*

b. Could this person have taken a job LAST WEEK if one had been offered?

- ○ No, already has a job
- ○ No, temporarily ill
- ○ No, other reasons (in school, etc.)
- ○ Yes, could have taken a job

27. When did this person last work, even for a few days?

- ○ 1990
- ○ 1989
- ○ 1988
- ○ 1985 to 1987
  } Go to 28
- ○ 1980 to 1984
- ○ 1979 or earlier
- ○ Never worked
  } *Skip to 32*

28-30. CURRENT OR MOST RECENT JOB ACTIVITY. Describe clearly this person's chief job activity or business last week. If this person had more than one job, describe the one at which this person worked the most hours. If this person had no job or business last week, give information for his/her last job or business since 1985.

28. Industry or Employer

a. For whom did this person work? If now on active duty in the Armed Forces, fill this circle → ○ and print the branch of the Armed Forces.

[ ]
(Name of company, business, or other employer)

b. What kind of business or industry was this? Describe the activity at location where employed.

[ ]
(For example: hospital, newspaper publishing, mail order house, auto engine manufacturing, retail bakery)

c. Is this mainly — Fill ONE circle

- ○ Manufacturing
- ○ Wholesale trade
- ○ Retail trade
- ○ Other (agriculture, construction, service, government, etc.)

29. Occupation

a. What kind of work was this person doing?

[ ]
(For example: registered nurse, personnel manager, supervisor of order department, gasoline engine assembler, cake icer)

b. What were this person's most important activities or duties?

[ ]
(For example: patient care, directing hiring policies, supervising order clerks, assembling engines, icing cakes)

30. Was this person — Fill ONE circle

- ○ Employee of a PRIVATE FOR PROFIT company or business or of an individual, for wages, salary, or commissions
- ○ Employee of a PRIVATE NOT-FOR-PROFIT, tax-exempt, or charitable organization
- ○ Local GOVERNMENT employee (city, county, etc.)
- ○ State GOVERNMENT employee
- ○ Federal GOVERNMENT employee
- ○ SELF-EMPLOYED in own NOT INCORPORATED business, professional practice, or farm
- ○ SELF-EMPLOYED in own INCORPORATED business, professional practice, or farm
- ○ Working WITHOUT PAY in family business or farm

31a. Last year (1989), did this person work, even for a few days, at a paid job or in a business or farm?

- ○ Yes
- ○ No — *Skip to 32*

b. How many weeks did this person work in 1989? Count paid vacation, paid sick leave, and military service.

[ ] Weeks

c. During the weeks WORKED in 1989, how many hours did this person usually work each week?

[ ] Hours

32. INCOME IN 1989 —
Fill the "Yes" circle below for each income source received during 1989. Otherwise, fill the "No" circle.
If "Yes," enter the total amount received during 1989.
For income received jointly, see instruction guide.
If exact amount is not known, please give best estimate.
If net income was a loss, write "Loss" above the dollar amount.

a. Wages, salary, commissions, bonuses, or tips from all jobs — Report amount before deductions for taxes, bonds, dues, or other items.

○ Yes → $ .00 ○ No
Annual amount — Dollars

b. Self-employment income from own nonfarm business, including proprietorship and partnership — Report NET income after business expenses.

○ Yes → $ .00 ○ No
Annual amount — Dollars

c. Farm self-employment income — Report NET income after operating expenses. Include earnings as a tenant farmer or sharecropper.

○ Yes → $ .00 ○ No
Annual amount — Dollars

d. Interest, dividends, net rental income or royalty income, or income from estates and trusts — Report even small amounts credited to an account.

○ Yes → $ .00 ○ No
Annual amount — Dollars

e. Social Security or Railroad Retirement

○ Yes → $ .00 ○ No
Annual amount — Dollars

f. Supplemental Security Income (SSI), Aid to Families with Dependent Children (AFDC), or other public assistance or public welfare payments.

○ Yes → $ .00 ○ No
Annual amount — Dollars

g. Retirement, survivor, or disability pensions — Do NOT include Social Security.

○ Yes → $ .00 ○ No
Annual amount — Dollars

h. Any other sources of income received regularly such as Veterans' (VA) payments, unemployment compensation, child support, or alimony — Do NOT include lump-sum payments such as money from an inheritance or the sale of a home.

○ Yes → $ .00 ○ No
Annual amount — Dollars

33. What was this person's total income in 1989? Add entries in questions 32a through 32h; subtract any losses. If total amount was a loss, write "Loss" above amount.

○ None OR $ .00
Annual amount — Dollars

Please turn the page and answer questions for Person 2 listed on page 1. If this is the last person listed in question 1a on page 1, go to the back of the form.

Pitcairn Island may be the only place in the world that can claim a complete census count. It had a population of fifty-five in 1985. Pitcairn islanders are descended from the mutinous crew of the British ship *Bounty* (about which a famous movie was made) (Population Reference Bureau, 1988).

Surveys

While the principle of a census is that it attempts to produce a complete enumeration of a population, the principle of a survey is that highly reliable data can be obtained by securing similar information from a well-designed sample of a population.

Using samples to generalize to larger populations has been done for a good many years, but not all samples lead to statistics representative of a target group. Some sample results can be extraordinarily misleading if the sample is chosen in a biased manner or the sample size is insufficient. There have been instances in social science research where poor samples produced erroneous findings. More often, poor samples are used in surveys performed by persons who are not skilled in their use or who are downright dishonest.

Good sampling procedures are founded on rules of statistical probability that permit a researcher to determine the appropriate size and nature of a sample and to estimate the chances that information derived from the sample survey corresponds to the true data. This applies whether the survey is conducted by a national government, a marketing research firm, or the staff of a newspaper.

As indicated earlier, sampling is involved in censuses. Because of the burden placed on respondents and the added costs of asking a large number of questions of everyone in a population, it has become commonplace for censuses to include a limited number of questions for everyone and a greater number for some fraction of the population. Census sample information can always be adjusted to the total enumeration results of which it is part.

Sample surveys, on the other hand, are usually taken at times when complete counts of the population are not available (other than census periods). Hence, the samples cannot be linked to enumerated populations. This is why surveys basically produce data in the form of proportions, percentages, and rates (e.g., the unemployment rate, percentage of high school dropouts, average family income, and the like).

Sample surveys that collect population data cover a broad range of types. Foremost are the regular and special surveys conducted by national governments. In the United States, these include the monthly Current Population Survey and the continuous National Health Survey, and occasional surveys aimed at special topics or follow-ups on existing surveys in order to extend information. Many countries around the world conduct such regular and special surveys.

In recent years there have been such cooperative efforts among nations in survey taking that common survey designs are used to acquire data from many different parts of the world at about the same time. Excellent examples of this approach are the World Fertility Survey and the Demographic and Health Surveys.

Governments do not provide all the necessary survey data for demographic analysis; hence, nongovernmental groups fill in the gaps in many instances. Research agencies, some publicly and some privately supported, have been responsible for major survey operations. Examples are the Monterrey Mobility Study and the Family Growth in Metropolitan America Study.

Still other surveys are taken by private polling organizations, such as Gallup, Roper, and Yankelovich, by market research companies, and by newspapers, television stations, and other independent groups. The quality of these surveys varies from excellent to awful, and one must be cautious in accepting the findings without adequate information about how the survey was done. In many cases, knowing how the survey was done will convince you that it is not worth paying attention to.

Well-done sample surveys have several advantages, compared to censuses. They are less costly. They can be taken more quickly. They can produce data for years when censuses are not taken. They can include items not appropriate for censuses, such as attitudinal questions or residential histories.

The United Nations (1971) has also devised standards for sample surveys in the demographic field. Because of the great variation in types of surveys, some of which are not covered in the UN report, a brief review of the surveys cited will give us an idea of some of their features.

Perhaps the best-known survey, although maybe not by its title, is the Current Population Survey (CPS) conducted by the U.S. Bureau of the Census. Started in the 1940s in response to a need for better current data on the working force, it is the major national source for information on the labor force and its employment and unemployment components. Using an area probability sample, questions are asked about the (civilian noninstitutionalized) residents of over 70,000 occupied housing units each month. Parts of the sample are rotated so that certain fractions of the sample units reappear for several months and some every year to provide stability in month-to-month and year-to-year estimates. The results of the sample inquiries are weighted by independent estimates of the population within demographic categories as a means of indicating the national numbers involved in each type of response. From time to time, questions other than those concerning the labor force are added to the survey. Items on education and income are included once a year, and even special topics such as smoking behavior are occasionally part of the inquiry. Since the U.S. census is taken only once every ten years, the CPS is used to monitor changes in many of the topics during the intercensal years. Several series of publications give CPS findings (e.g., LeClere and Dahmann, 1990).

Because of its highly respected sample design, several other major surveys build on the CPS design and the data are collected by the Census Bureau. One such example is the National Health Interview Survey (NHIS), started in 1957, which is the principal source of information on health in the United States.

From this survey one can learn about U.S. national patterns of the incidence of acute illness and injuries, the prevalence of chronic conditions and impairments, the extent of disability, the utilization of health care services, and other health-related topics. Results are published in various topical series of *Vital and Health Statistics* (Chyba and Washington, 1990).

Many other surveys, most of them much smaller in size than the CPS and NHIS, are conducted by federal, state, and local governmental agencies. Some of these attempt to "follow up" on earlier basic surveys by collecting supplemental information that can enlarge the scope of data available for analysis.

The idea of fielding a great number of national surveys at about the same time and using common designs and questionnaires was intended to produce broad regional or worldwide statistics on certain topics. Such surveys were deemed exceedingly ambitious when first proposed. We have now seen two fairly successful efforts of this type. The World Fertility Survey (WFS) was actually a group of surveys conducted in 42 developing and 20 developed countries of the world during the period 1974–82 with support from a number of national and international agencies and a battery of consultants to assist the various countries in achieving comparable surveys. The WFS resulted in a vast compendium of knowledge about fertility trends and differentials and associated factors for a sizable segment of the world's population (Gille, 1984).

A similar program under the title of Demographic and Health Surveys (DHS) has been underway since the mid-1980s, with second rounds of the surveys continuing in the early 1990s. These national surveys encompass questions on both fertility and family planning as well as health and mortality. Again, expert consultants are maintained to advise on study design and on the tabulation of results. However, the bulk of the operations and the analyses are conducted by staffs of the countries involved (see, e.g., Lesetedi et al., 1989).

There are times when surveys seem to be the appropriate data-collection instrument for certain information, but government surveys do not provide the needed data. In such instances, those engaging in a study may design the study themselves or engage a private survey-taking organization. Balan et al. (1973) were interested in learning about "how and why men move geographically and occupationally within the context of a developing society." Through interuniversity cooperation of the Universidad de Nuevo León and the University of Texas, a survey was set up and administered in the metropolitan area of Monterrey, Mexico. The authors and their associates were well trained in the technical aspects of survey design and analysis and did not have to depend on governmental or other expert sources.

In the case of the Family Growth in Metropolitan America Study (Westoff et al., 1961), because of the large scope of the survey that was devised to collect the data, researchers employed National Analysts, Inc., a private survey organization, to design the sample, construct and pretest questionnaires, do the interviewing, and process the data.

This cursory review cannot indicate the great variety of types and designs of surveys. Excellent summaries of the thinking that has gone into many different migration surveys throughout the world can be found in Goldstein and Goldstein (1981) and Findley (1982).

The surveys that most of us are familiar with are those done for economic marketing purposes or to sample opinion on political or other social issues. Experts in the field are well aware that there are both good and bad surveys and polls, and that the public can easily be misled by exciting findings from bad inquiries (Bradburn and Sudman, 1988). Others of us are either unaware of the limitations of some surveys or are too casual about trying to find out if the survey or poll is a good one or not and whether the cited findings are justified.

The long-time polls of Gallup, Roper, and Yankelovich, among others, are based on strong sample designs and good survey procedures, and findings from them can generally be trusted, with due attention to sampling variability (also true of the CPS and the NHIS). Data from such surveys have been used effectively by demographers to analyze important population matters (see Blake, 1974).

Many less well-known surveys or polls are highly suspect, but they still get the public's attention. When producers of a household product tell you that their brand is preferred by twice as many users as competitors' brands, do you try to find out how they arrived at that ratio and whether it is credible? When a newspaper conducts a "survey" of readers by printing a response form in the paper, or a television station asks people to call a 900 exchange telephone number to register their opinions on an issue, do you accept the results of those inquiries uncritically? Do you know if the respondents are a representative sample of the target population and if they understand the nuances of the typically simple question being asked? Reports on many demographic topics are based on inadequate surveys and polls and need to be evaluated carefully before we can use their results.

Registrations

Censuses and surveys both involve collecting data describing sets of conditions as of the point in time when the census or survey is taken—the age, sex, and race of people; their past fertility and migration patterns; their living quarters; their attitudes toward sterilization and abortion; their occupations and income; and the like. They are forms of stocktaking. The information is about the statuses of people that may have been entered into at any time in the past.

Registrations, on the other hand, have to do with recording events as they occur or statuses as they are acquired at the time of occurrence or acquisition, not at some later time. Under this heading are several types of registrations or record-keeping. One is called civil or vital registration. Another set relates to other forms of public recordings. A third is concerned with various private records. Examples of these are given below.

Civil or vital registration is defined as "the process by which facts regarding individual civil or vital events are recorded by governmental agency as official records. Vital events may be defined as live births, deaths, fetal deaths (stillbirths), marriages, divorces, adoptions, legitimations, recognitions, annulments, and separations; in short, all the events which have to do with an individual's entrance into or departure from life, together with the changes in civil status which may occur during his lifetime" (Linder and Moriyama, 1985).

The United Nations (1973) also sets standards for vital records systems and statistics. It attaches first priority to births, deaths, marriages, and divorces, among the several kinds of data obtained through this mechanism. Unlike censuses, civil or vital registration is not nearly universal around the world. In fact, most developing countries lack such systems or have them only in major cities. Even if they exist in such places, they are apt to be highly inadequate. Civil and vital registrations are generally complete in developed countries, and thus provide a unique and valuable source of data that supplement censuses and surveys in those areas.

The vital registration system in the United States, like that in other developed nations, is based on a reporting network. The National Center for Health Statistics recommends the forms to be used and the procedures to be followed in collecting the data. It is the local province of each state (or other independent registration area), however, to specify the data form and procedures. The U.S. system is comprised of fifty-seven registration areas, including each state, the District of Columbia, New York City, American Samoa, Guam, Northern Mariana Islands, Puerto Rico, and the Virgin Islands (Tolson et al., 1991). While most areas conform closely to the national recommendations, some collect less information than is suggested and some collect more.

According to law, the reports of events originate with private citizens. Registration of births is the responsibility of the professional attendant at birth, generally a physician or midwife. Registration of deaths is the responsibility of the funeral director or person acting as such. An attending physician or coroner supplies the cause-of-death information. Marriages and divorces are reported first by the civil authority that sanctions these events.

The coordinator of local reports of vital events is someone so designated by the state or other area to cover specified local districts. At one time, when the population was relatively small and scattered, these persons were clerks of cities, villages, towns, and townships. Today the coordination of local reports is done at the county (or equivalent) level and the responsible person is the area's health officer, typically a medical doctor.

At periodic intervals, the area health officer summarizes the vital data for the county (or equivalent area) and transmits them to the state (or equivalent) vital registrar. That person assembles the information for the state, usually publishes some of it, and sends the data to the National Center for Health Statistics, which combines state (and other area) reports for the national picture. So when you read about the number of births or infant deaths in the United States, this information has been derived from the accumulated reports of local areas throughout the country.

Shown in Figure 4.2 is the nationally recommended birth certificate for the United States. You can see that there is much more information asked for than

FIGURE 4.2 U.S. Standard Certificate of Live Birth

TYPE/PRINT IN PERMANENT BLACK INK FOR INSTRUCTIONS SEE HANDBOOK

U.S. STANDARD
CERTIFICATE OF LIVE BIRTH

LOCAL FILE NUMBER — BIRTH NUMBER

CHILD
1. CHILD'S NAME *(First, Middle, Last)*
2. DATE OF BIRTH *(Month, Day, Year)*
3. TIME OF BIRTH — M
4. SEX
5. CITY, TOWN, OR LOCATION OF BIRTH
6. COUNTY OF BIRTH
7. PLACE OF BIRTH: ☐ Hospital ☐ Freestanding Birthing Center ☐ Clinic/Doctor's Office ☐ Residence ☐ Other *(Specify)* ____
8. FACILITY NAME *(If not institution, give street and number)*

CERTIFIER/ATTENDANT
9. I certify that this child was born alive at the place and time and on the date stated. *Signature* ▶
10. DATE SIGNED *(Month, Day, Year)*
11. ATTENDANT'S NAME AND TITLE *(If other than certifier) (Type/Print)* Name ____ ☐ M.D. ☐ D.O. ☐ C.N.M. ☐ Other Midwife ☐ Other *(Specify)* ____
12. CERTIFIER'S NAME AND TITLE *(Type/Print)* Name ____ ☐ M.D. ☐ D.O. ☐ Hospital Admin. ☐ C.N.M. ☐ Other Midwife ☐ Other *(Specify)* ____
13. ATTENDANT'S MAILING ADDRESS *(Street and Number or Rural Route Number, City or Town, State, Zip Code)*

DEATH UNDER ONE YEAR OF AGE Enter State File Number of death certificate for this child

14. REGISTRAR'S SIGNATURE ▶
15. DATE FILED BY REGISTRAR *(Month, Day, Year)*

MOTHER
16a. MOTHER'S NAME *(First, Middle, Last)*
16b. MAIDEN SURNAME
17. DATE OF BIRTH *(Month, Day, Year)*
18. BIRTHPLACE *(State or Foreign Country)*
19a. RESIDENCE—STATE
19b. COUNTY
19c. CITY, TOWN, OR LOCATION
19d. STREET AND NUMBER
19e. INSIDE CITY LIMITS? *(Yes or no)*
20. MOTHER'S MAILING ADDRESS *(If same as residence, enter Zip Code only)*

FATHER
21. FATHER'S NAME *(First, Middle, Last)*
22. DATE OF BIRTH *(Month, Day, Year)*
23. BIRTHPLACE *(State or Foreign Country)*

INFORMANT
24. I certify that the personal information provided on this certificate is correct to the best of my knowledge and belief. *Signature of Parent or Other Informant* ▶

INFORMATION FOR MEDICAL AND HEALTH USE ONLY

25. OF HISPANIC ORIGIN? (Specify No or Yes—If yes, specify Cuban, Mexican, Puerto Rican, etc.)
26. RACE—American Indian, Black, White, etc. *(Specify below)*
27. EDUCATION *(Specify only highest grade completed)* Elementary/Secondary (0-12) | College (1-4 or 5+)

MOTHER 25a. ☐ No ☐ Yes Specify: — 26a. — 27a.
FATHER 25b. ☐ No ☐ Yes Specify: — 26b. — 27b.

28. PREGNANCY HISTORY *(Complete each section)*
LIVE BIRTHS *(Do not include this child)* — OTHER TERMINATIONS *(Spontaneous and induced at any time after conception)*
28a. Now Living Number ____ ☐ None
28b. Now Dead Number ____ ☐ None
28d. Number ____ ☐ None
28c. DATE OF LAST LIVE BIRTH *(Month, Year)*
28e. DATE OF LAST OTHER TERMINATION *(Month, Year)*
29. MOTHER MARRIED? (At birth, conception, or any time between) *(Yes or no)*
30. DATE LAST NORMAL MENSES BEGAN *(Month, Day, Year)*
31. MONTH OF PREGNANCY PRENATAL CARE BEGAN—First, Second, Third, etc. *(Specify)*
32. PRENATAL VISITS—Total Number *(If none, so state)*
33. BIRTH WEIGHT *(Specify unit)*
34. CLINICAL ESTIMATE OF GESTATION *(Weeks)*
35a. PLURALITY—Single, Twin, Triplet, etc. *(Specify)*
35b. IF NOT SINGLE BIRTH—Born First, Second, Third, etc. *(Specify)*

MULTIPLE BIRTHS Enter State File Number for Mate(s) LIVE BIRTH(S)

FETAL DEATH(S)

36. APGAR SCORE: 36a. 1 Minute — 36b. 5 Minutes
37a. MOTHER TRANSFERRED PRIOR TO DELIVERY? ☐ No ☐ Yes If Yes, enter name of facility transferred from:
37b. INFANT TRANSFERRED? ☐ No ☐ Yes If Yes, enter name of facility transferred to:

38a. MEDICAL RISK FACTORS FOR THIS PREGNANCY *(Check all that apply)*
- Anemia (Hct. < 30/Hgb. < 10) .... 01 ☐
- Cardiac disease .... 02 ☐
- Acute or chronic lung disease .... 03 ☐
- Diabetes .... 04 ☐
- Genital herpes .... 05 ☐
- Hydramnios/Oligohydramnios .... 06 ☐
- Hemoglobinopathy .... 07 ☐
- Hypertension, chronic .... 08 ☐
- Hypertension, pregnancy-associated .... 09 ☐
- Eclampsia .... 10 ☐
- Incompetent cervix .... 11 ☐
- Previous infant 4000+ grams .... 12 ☐
- Previous preterm or small-for-gestational-age infant .... 13 ☐
- Renal disease .... 14 ☐
- Rh sensitization .... 15 ☐
- Uterine bleeding .... 16 ☐
- None .... 00 ☐
- Other ____ 17 ☐ *(Specify)*

38b. OTHER RISK FACTORS FOR THIS PREGNANCY *(Complete all items)*
- Tobacco use during pregnancy .... Yes ☐ No ☐
- Average number cigarettes per day ____
- Alcohol use during pregnancy .... Yes ☐ No ☐
- Average number drinks per week ____
- Weight gained during pregnancy ____ lbs.

39. OBSTETRIC PROCEDURES *(Check all that apply)*
- Amniocentesis .... 01 ☐
- Electronic fetal monitoring .... 02 ☐
- Induction of labor .... 03 ☐
- Stimulation of labor .... 04 ☐
- Tocolysis .... 05 ☐
- Ultrasound .... 06 ☐
- None .... 00 ☐
- Other ____ 07 ☐ *(Specify)*

40. COMPLICATIONS OF LABOR AND/OR DELIVERY *(Check all that apply)*
- Febrile (> 100°F. or 38°C.) .... 01 ☐
- Meconium, moderate/heavy .... 02 ☐
- Premature rupture of membrane (> 12 hours) .... 03 ☐
- Abruptio placenta .... 04 ☐
- Placenta previa .... 05 ☐
- Other excessive bleeding .... 06 ☐
- Seizures during labor .... 07 ☐
- Precipitous labor (< 3 hours) .... 08 ☐
- Prolonged labor (> 20 hours) .... 09 ☐
- Dysfunctional labor .... 10 ☐
- Breech/Malpresentation .... 11 ☐
- Cephalopelvic disproportion .... 12 ☐
- Cord prolapse .... 13 ☐
- Anesthetic complications .... 14 ☐
- Fetal distress .... 15 ☐
- None .... 00 ☐
- Other ____ 16 ☐ *(Specify)*

41. METHOD OF DELIVERY *(Check all that apply)*
- Vaginal .... 01 ☐
- Vaginal birth after previous C-section .... 02 ☐
- Primary C-section .... 03 ☐
- Repeat C-section .... 04 ☐
- Forceps .... 05 ☐
- Vacuum .... 06 ☐

42. ABNORMAL CONDITIONS OF THE NEWBORN *(Check all that apply)*
- Anemia (Hct. < 39/Hgb. < 13) .... 01 ☐
- Birth injury .... 02 ☐
- Fetal alcohol syndrome .... 03 ☐
- Hyaline membrane disease/RDS .... 04 ☐
- Meconium aspiration syndrome .... 05 ☐
- Assisted ventilation < 30 min .... 06 ☐
- Assisted ventilation ≥ 30 min .... 07 ☐
- Seizures .... 08 ☐
- None .... 00 ☐
- Other ____ 09 ☐ *(Specify)*

43. CONGENITAL ANOMALIES OF CHILD *(Check all that apply)*
- Anencephalus .... 01 ☐
- Spina bifida/Meningocele .... 02 ☐
- Hydrocephalus .... 03 ☐
- Microcephalus .... 04 ☐
- Other central nervous system anomalies *(Specify)* ____ 05 ☐
- Heart malformations .... 06 ☐
- Other circulatory/respiratory anomalies *(Specify)* ____ 07 ☐
- Rectal atresia/stenosis .... 08 ☐
- Tracheo-esophageal fistula/Esophageal atresia .... 09 ☐
- Omphalocele/Gastroschisis .... 10 ☐
- Other gastrointestinal anomalies *(Specify)* ____ 11 ☐
- Malformed genitalia .... 12 ☐
- Renal agenesis .... 13 ☐
- Other urogenital anomalies *(Specify)* ____ 14 ☐
- Cleft lip/palate .... 15 ☐
- Polydactyly/Syndactyly/Adactyly .... 16 ☐
- Club foot .... 17 ☐
- Diaphragmatic hernia .... 18 ☐
- Other musculoskeletal/integumental anomalies *(Specify)* ____ 19 ☐
- Down's syndrome .... 20 ☐
- Other chromosomal anomalies *(Specify)* ____ 21 ☐
- None .... 00 ☐
- Other ____ 22 ☐ *(Specify)*

DEPARTMENT OF HEALTH AND HUMAN SERVICES PUBLIC HEALTH SERVICE NATIONAL CENTER FOR HEALTH STATISTICS 1989 REVISION

PHS-T-002 REV. 1/89

just the occurrence of a birth. Items included are the place of birth and place of usual residence; the characteristics of the baby, the mother, and the father; medical information about the pregnancy, delivery, and any abnormalities associated with the birth; and who provided the data.

Vital certificates are used for legal, administrative, and programmatic as well as research purposes. Hence, the decision as to what should be included depends on balancing the various needs and not placing too many demands on the supplier of the information, who may be burdened already with many activities.

In many developing countries, good vital registration is lacking because of any of several factors—financial constraints (the cost of maintaining registrars at local levels is considerable), ineffective legal basis for registration, organizational problems (often because of responsibility conflicts among governmental agencies), shortage of trained staff (insufficient numbers of educated persons who could serve in this respect), public apathy, and the complexity of reporting networks and data generation even when information is collected (United Nations, 1987). Considerable attention is now being given to improving civil and vital registration in most developing countries.

Other public records exist that can be useful for some types of demographic analysis. These include social security records (especially valuable for studying older populations), military records (in the United States these records were once the main source of height and weight data), public school records (not only for educational data on the younger population but also for indirect measures of geographic mobility), internal revenue reports (within the confines of confidentiality, aggregate income data can be used), driver licenses, and many others.

Private records of various kinds can likewise be utilized for population study. Such records might include life insurance records, church or other religious records, genealogies, telephone and city directories, and many others.

Merged Records

While censuses, surveys, and registrations are all basic sources of population data that can be used individually as a basis for analysis, there are times when combinations of the several types of data gatherings result in a more powerful set of data. Two categories of merged records fall under this general heading: population registers and other linked records.

Population registers must be differentiated from civil and vital *registration*. In several countries of the world, the civil or vital registration forms are sent to a community-based population registrar who merges them with other kinds of records and thereby creates an integrated body of statistics about all persons living in the community. These population registers are continually updated. When a birth occurs in the community, a new integrated record is set up for the baby which will be added to as other civil records for that person become available and so long as the person remains in the community. Likewise, when an individual moves into the community, the population registrar of the community from which the person came will transfer the person's records to the new community. On the other hand, when a person moves out of the community, the reverse procedure takes place. When an individual dies, the integrated records for that person are removed from the register. As a consequence, at any point in time the existing population register for a community describes the population of residents, much in the same way that a census does. However, the kinds of information included in the register will be partly different from that of a census and is usually not as extensive as in a census (Verhoef and van de Kaa, 1987).

Denmark and the Netherlands are examples of countries that have population registers. The actual systems of data collection for the two are somewhat different; Denmark has a more centralized system, and the specific items in the two registers do not correspond. The cost of a population register is less than the cost of a census, and the register does meet many of the needs for which a census is taken. For these and other reasons, the government of the Netherlands chose to bypass the census scheduled to be taken in 1980 and has not taken one since.

The United Nations (1969) has provided recommendations for setting up a population register and has outlined the several statistical uses to which it can be put. These include having counts of population at any date, measuring migration (an item absent from the civil and vital registration systems), planning population censuses (where registers are not substitutes for them), evaluating census results (for the items of information appearing in both sources), and providing frames of individuals or households for survey sample selection.

Other linked records can take many forms. The study of infant mortality mentioned in Chapter 3 linked birth registrations to death records for those dying during the first year of life. Since each record has some unique items, the merged records extend the kinds of information available for analysis.

The research literature is replete with illustrations of record linkages that involve various vital certificates (as above), a vital certificate and a census, either of those data sources and a survey, or any of those three with other public or private records.

It is difficult to link records in terms of methodology. If a common identification number for an individual appears on the records to be merged, it is simpler to join the records. (Even here, we would have to assume that the ID numbers were recorded accurately.) If one or more of the records do not have an ID number or there is a restriction on making that number available, we have to undertake other procedures. In the infant mortality study mentioned above, no ID number was available to the researchers, but they were able to devise an algorithm by which several items of information common to the two records were matched and a determination was made of the probable matches. In fact, nearly all the death certificates could be linked to birth certificates in this way (without knowing the names or addresses of the persons). The researcher could then perform an aggregate analysis using the linked records, and no violation of confidentiality took place.

Estimates

In a very real sense we can regard population statistics from any source as estimates. That is, we know that there are limitations on collecting the data and that the results are not likely to be precisely correct. However, when demographers refer to *estimates*, they mean the calculation of information not directly available from the sources already mentioned; this information has to be determined indirectly by relating various kinds of known information.

As we know, censuses are taken at infrequent intervals. Yet we might want to know something about a population at different times, such as when the first census of an area was taken, or for a specific time between censuses, or since the last census was taken. We might even want to estimate the possible results of a future census. Alternatively, we might be interested in certain data collected at a time of interest to us but not included in the classifications of interest. For example, we might want to know certain data about persons of a particular ancestry between the ages of 20 and 29, even though the census may not have specified such data. How do we handle these situations? You may be reassured to learn that demographers can draw on their ingenuity to develop estimates of the needed information.

Anthropologists and archaeologists date the remains of long-deceased persons to estimate the age at death and medical causes involved for ancient periods. (There is actually an academic field called paleodemography that engages in such study.)

Most national governments and some private agencies issue regular population estimates for noncensus periods. Estimates for times not long before the first census of an area can be made with a reasonable amount of accuracy if historical knowledge of the area is available. Intercensal estimates tend to be even more accurate, because the two censuses form base points within which we can make interpolations reinforced by other related information. Estimates for periods since the last census was taken are most accurate soon after the census and get weaker as the date departs from the last census date. Projections of the population, sometimes called *future estimates*, depend on even more conjecture about what will happen in the years ahead. In each case the person doing the estimation must make certain assumptions about relevant information not already collected, and the estimates (of population size, births, deaths, or any other population factor) will then follow from the assumptions made and the formula used to do the estimation. A number of alternative procedures are used in making estimates (see Shryock, Siegel, and Associates, 1976, Chapters 22 and 23 and Appendix A of this book).

Because developing countries collect relatively little data on population or the data they collect are often inadequate, there exists a whole battery of estimation techniques geared to these places (United Nations, 1983). A fundamental aspect of these techniques is their dependence on theories of the internal structures of populations (relationships between births, deaths, migration, age structure, and population size). An example of an estimation tool that specialists in this area have devised is the model life table that describes the age-related mortality of populations at similar stages of development in locations with known data. (In Chapter 5, we will talk about life tables as assembled information about mortality from which we derive such familiar statistics as life expectancy, that is, the average number of years a person can expect to live.)

A GUIDE TO GENERAL MEASUREMENT ISSUES

Once the necessary population data have been collected or obtained from an existing publication or unpublished source, the next task for population analysis is to convert the items of interest in those data to a form most relevant for the questions that need to be answered.

We have already discussed some conceptual issues which will be addressed again in later chapters. However, assuming that we have identified meaningful variables and that the data are of good quality, our next task will be to convert the information into quantitative form or into classifications appropriate for what we want to know.

Although our task here is not to delve into concerns about statistical methodology, we should be aware of some simple considerations related to quantitative analysis. In the next few pages, we will consider five types of measurement issues which span the range of population topics to be discussed in this book. These relate to categorization of variables (how many intervals of a variable are needed); relative measures (those involved in comparisons); reliance on averages as indicators of what we want to know; incidence versus prevalance measures; and period versus cohort measures. These five kinds of measurement consideration are applicable to most, if not all, of population analysis.

Categorization is a crucial issue in analysis. How many categories of a variable you have and what they represent can make the difference between an appropriate or inappropriate answer to a research question. In determining the right number and types of categories, we must depend on the nature of the data collected (which provide flexibility in our choice of categories) and the insightfulness of the analyst (who should know what are the most meaningful categories). Of course, there are times when these two criteria for categorization cannot be satisfied because the size of the sample we are studying is too small to permit us to construct categories with sufficient numbers of cases in each category.

Let us take an example of one kind of population analysis where categorization can become an issue. Suppose that our interest is in knowing how different are patterns of population change among racial and ethnic groups in the

United States. We have then to ask ourselves which racial and ethnic groups we want to compare. One choice might be to categorize race and ethnicity into the conventional government classifications, such as black or African-American, Hispanic, Native American (Indian), Asian-American, and non-Hispanic white. This might be quite adequate for our purpose, but we must realize that some of these categories encompass subcategories that may have different patterns of population change. For instance, among Hispanics do persons with Cuban, Mexican, Puerto Rican, Carribean, and Central or South American ethnicity all have the same patterns of population change? Are these distinctions important for our analysis? If so, do we have sufficient representation of each category in our study sample to make the distinction?

Another example has to do with how much earnings from work differ by educational level of the worker. If the data on education used to analyze this question classified persons according to three categories—no education or elementary schooling, at least some secondary school, and at least some higher education—are these categories sufficient for the analysis? Probably not, because there are distinctions within these educational categories that are very important for earnings potential. A high school graduate would be expected to have much greater potential for earnings than a high school dropout. Likewise, we would expect the earnings potential of a college graduate to be higher than that of a person who attended college but did not graduate.

In these examples, and in many others that could be cited, measuring an effect is highly dependent on the number and kinds of categories we use in the analysis. Choosing the wrong number or the wrong intervals can lead us to conclusions that are not responsive to the research question.

Relative measures are of great concern in population study because, although we may focus our attention at times on one type of population (e.g., residents of New York State), very often we want to compare population data for different geographical areas or population subgroups or the same area or group at various points in time. In making comparisons, we have to compare those groups on an equal footing.

A hypothetical illustration can be used here. If our interest is in voting patterns of state A relative to those of state B and we report that state A has twice as many voters as state B, is that an indication that people in state A are more inclined to vote? Not necessarily, since we would first have to know how many persons in each state were eligible to vote. If the total population of state A was twice as large as that of state B, we might say that we would expect twice as many voters. However, not everyone in the population can vote. In order to be eligible to vote, you have to be of at least a certain age and also meet other state and national requirements. If we examine the relationship of the number who voted to the number who were eligible to vote in each state and then compare the two states, we are on firmer footing in determining the relative tendency to vote in the two areas. (Still other factors, such as the demographic and social composition of each population, would help to interpret why the states might differ even after the right kinds of comparisons are made.)

Relative measures are designed to facilitate comparisons. They involve *standardizing* quantitative data so that there are fair comparisons. Several kinds of relative measures can be used. A *ratio* is a single number that expresses the relative size of two numbers which are not necessarily related to each other. A *sex ratio* is the number of males compared to the number of females in a population (usually multiplied by 100 to make it a more manageable number). *Proportions* are a special type of ratio in which the denominator (the lower part of the fraction) includes the numerator. The *masculinity proportion* is the number of males relative to the total population. *Percentages* are a special type of proportion, one in which the ratio is multiplied by a constant, 100, so that the ratio is expressed per 100. If we multiply the foregoing example by 100, we have the percentage of males in the total population (Palmore and Gardner, 1983).

Because groups being compared can differ with regard to a number of characteristics that are not part of what we are trying to compare, relative measures often are standardized further to remove the complicating effects of those extraneous factors. In later chapters, we will give a few illustrations of such standardized measures. (Also see Appendix A.)

A more refined relative measure used in population analysis is a *rate*, which refers to the occurrence of events over a given interval of time. For example, we might indicate the number of births that occurred in Japan during 1989 relative to the number of Japanese women of childbearing age. This is called a *fertility rate*. Demographers use the term *population at risk* to refer to a denominator of a rate that includes the persons who are "at risk," that is, who could possibly be in the numerator. The most efficient rate is one in which the population at risk is correctly specified. (Some so-called rates do not meet that condition very well, yet are used in population analysis. We will indicate some of these later in the book.)

When we look at population information, we generally want to reduce the information to simple measures that can be summarized easily. Ratios, proportions, percentages, and rates often serve that purpose. When we are presented with data on a variable for a given population and want to describe how that population stands with regard to that variable, the favorite summary measure is an *average*. An average is a measure of central tendency, sometimes thought of as a typical report of that variable for the population. There are different kinds of averages, principally the mean, median, and mode, and the most often used average is the arithmetic mean (which is calculated by dividing the sum of values of repeated measurements of a variable by the number of measurements taken). For instance, a college grade-point average (GPA) is the sum of all of the numerical equivalents of letter grades received in courses by a student divided by the number of courses taken.

Averages can be very useful statistical summaries, but they can also be deceiving. This is because how typical an average is depends on the form of the distribution that underlies it. Take the case of a football player (we'll call him Sam) who, the television game reporter tells us, "averages 5.4 yards every time he runs the ball." First of all, he can't average anything *every time* he runs the ball because, by definition, an average is not based on one experience but rather on several experiences that are summarized. Second, how typical a 5.4 yard average is needs to be related to the distribution of yards gained for all of the runs Sam made. If Sam ran 10 times during the game and his gains in yardage were, sequentially, 2, 35, 8, –11 (loss), –5, 1, 3, –4, 12, and 13, then it is true that the average was 5.4 (a net of 54 yards gained divided by 10), but 5.4 is not at all a typical gain in yardage. In fact, on none of the 10 runs did Sam come close to gaining 5.4 yards. If Sam had run about 5 or 6 yards on each of his 10 tries, then the 5.4 yard average would be a fairly typical summary of his running experience.

How many times have you heard that the lifetime earnings of a college graduate are vastly higher than those of a high school graduate? Maybe that was one of the principal motivations that convinced you to go to college. The amounts typically reported in such calculations are averages for persons who have completed, respectively, college and high school. An important point is that these are not highly typical amounts because there is a great deal of variation in earnings for persons with different educational levels. Some college graduates will earn much more in their lifetimes than the average, and some will earn much less. Actually, some college graduates will eventually earn less than some high school graduates. The reason for this is that education is not the only factor that determines earnings potential. People who attain the average or higher for their category are those who very likely have more favorable values on other characteristics (which may include getting better grades in school, working harder on the job, coming from an advantaged socioeconomic background, and numerous other factors). Averages are not guarantees; they are only central tendencies. For this reason we often attach to averages some measure of dispersion of the distribution around the average so that readers can be aware of how typical the average is.

Frequently we want to study a population phenomenon in terms of its changing importance over time. Two ways of looking at the phenomenon are in terms of its *incidence* and its *prevalence.* Incidence refers to the new cases of an event or characteristic in some time period. Prevalence refers to the total number of persons who retain the incidence designation, regardless of when it was attained.

We can measure the number of marriages that occur or the marriage rate in an area during a series of years as reflecting the trend in incidence of marriage for that area. If the marriage incidence rate is declining, we might conclude that the institution of marriage is in trouble. However, if we look at the percentage of the population at ages 18 and over who are married and see how that has changed over the same time span, we might find out that the percentage is high and has not changed appreciably over time. The latter prevalence measure would suggest that the marital institution is fairly stable and robust.

Incidence and prevalence measures are used widely in studies of health and disease. We might record a decline in the number of new cases (incidence) of AIDS reported, yet find the number of people who carry the AIDS virus (prevalence) to be remaining high and still a critical problem.

The last measurement issue to be discussed here is also related to the timing factor but is most relevant in analyzing *trends* in a phenomenon. Demographers make a distinction between *period* and *cohort* measures. *Cohort* is a term used by demographers to refer to a group of people with the same initial starting point, e.g., born in the same year (a birth cohort) or married in the same year (a marriage cohort) who can be followed over time. Think about annual divorce rates (the incidence of divorces in a year relative to the number of married persons). If we analyze the trend in that rate over a period of years, we get a picture of the fluctuations in the annual probability of divorce, and the trend is a real one. If, instead of examining the relative number of married persons who get a divorce in a particular year (a period measure), we find out what proportion of persons who were married in a given year eventually got divorced, say, within ten years of their marriage (a cohort measure), we may learn something very different. The reason is that divorce is often a response to conditions strongly determined by societal events. The annual divorce rate might rise sharply in stressful times and be stable or decline somewhat during nonstressful periods. Is the fact that divorces can bunch up in particular years of more or less interest to us than the fact that people who married at certain times have more or less risk of eventually getting divorced? The analytical strategy will be the key to which type of measure is appropriate to calculate.

Chapter Highlights

1. Data used in population analysis cover a wide range of topics, including basic demographic information as well as information about the social, economic, and living circumstances of people.
2. Governments are prime users of population data because meeting legislative and regulatory targets often necessitates having meaningful population data and because governmental operations frequently involve such data as well.
3. Population data are also valuable to nongovernmental groups, such as businesses, industries, and private agencies and organizations.
4. There are five broad sources of population data: censuses, surveys, registrations, merged records, and estimates. Each of these serves certain data needs better than others.
5. Censuses are attempts at complete enumeration of a population in a given area at a certain point in time. There are universal standards for taking a census and most nations of the world adhere to such standards, but censuses still have their limitations in coverge and accuracy.
6. Surveys have some common features with censuses, but surveys are based on samples of households or persons. Consequently they cost less, are taken more frequently (especially in intercensal periods), and often explore

topics not appropriate for inclusion in censuses. Although there are standards for survey taking, the ease with which some types of surveys can be taken results in wide variations in survey quality.

7. Registrations have to do with recording events as they occur or statuses as they are acquired. The best-known are civil or vital registrations (including birth and death certification). There are also other forms of public and private records that are of population interest.
8. Merged records have increasingly been used to expand the kinds of population data available for analysis. In some countries population registers are composites of vital and other records. Advances in computer technology now permit us to merge census, survey, and general record data to include a broader range of topics in population studies.
9. If population information is not directly available from censuses, surveys, registrations, or other records, we can estimate needed data by using formulas that build on related information. Estimates can apply to the past, present, or future.
10. Using population data involves many considerations about measurement that affect the analysis and interpretation we might make of the data. Some critical measurement issues are concerned with proper categorization and classification of reported information, measures used in comparisons, the proper use of averages and indicators of dispersion, and distinctions between incidence and prevalence of events and statuses as well as between period and cohort approaches to examining trend data.

Discussion Questions

1. Inquire of your local governments (counties, cities, towns, or villages) as to the kinds of population data they depend on to conduct their activities. How similar are they to those of the national government? How different?
2. All types of population data sources rely on individuals providing information that is partly generally known and partly of a personal nature. What are the advantages and disadvantages of providing personal information for government or business use? Are the safeguards provided for confidentiality of information adequate?
3. Censuses are known to undercount populations in certain population categories more than in others. What are the advantages and disadvantages of correcting or adjusting the data after they are collected, assuming there are techniques for doing so?
4. Locate a mass media report on a survey related to population information. From the information you are given, what can you say about the quality of the survey information? Devise minimal standards for reporting survey information that would give users confidence that the survey quality is adequate.

5. Obtain a copy of your own birth certificate. Who provided the information on the certificate? Are there any questions or items on the certificate that you think could have been requested in a better way? If so, which are they and what modifications would you propose?
6. Find two examples of the use of averages that relate to population data. Evaluate those measures in terms of how typical the averages are and what factors might complicate the picture.

Suggested Readings

Bradburn, Norman M., and Seymour Sudman. 1988. *Polls & Surveys; Understanding What They Tell Us.* San Francisco: Jossey-Bass.

Miller, Delbert C. 1991. *Handbook of Research Design and Social Measurement.* 5th ed. Newbury Park, Calif.: Sage Publications. An extremely useful reference work that reviews all aspects of the research process and summarizes leading scales and indexes used in social science research.

Robey, Bryant. 1989. "Two Hundred Years and Counting: The 1990 Census." *Population Bulletin* 44:1, 1–43. This report of the Population Reference Bureau provides a popularly written account of U.S. census history, with emphasis on the latest one.

Shryock, Henry S., Jacob S. Siegel, and Associates. 1976. *The Methods and Materials of Demography.* Condensed edition by Edward Stockwell. San Diego, Calif.: Academic Press. Parts of this work need updating, but it is still the foremost reference book for the use of demographic data sources and techniques of analysis.

United Nations, 1988. *Censuses of Population and Housing in Asia and the Pacific: Towards the 1990 Round.* New York: United Nations. Discussions of the features of censuses throughout this part of the world indicate some of the variations that can be found globally.

Willigan, J. Dennis, and Katherine A. Lynch. 1982. *Sources and Methods of Historical Demography.* San Diego, Calif.: Academic Press. This valuable book on demographic methods is especially oriented to the research and understanding of historical situations.

References

Balan, Jorge, Harley L. Browning, and Elizabeth Jelin. 1973. *Men in a Developing Society: Geographic and Social Mobility in Monterrey, Mexico.* Austin, Tex.: University of Texas Press.

Blake, Judith. 1974. "Can We Believe Recent Data on Birth Expectations in the United States?" *Demography* 11:1, 25–44.

Bradburn, Norman M., and Seymour Sudman. 1988. *Polls & Surveys; Understanding What They Tell Us.* San Francisco: Jossey-Bass.

Chyba, Michele M., and Linda R. Washington. 1990. "Questionnaires from the National Health Interview Survey, 1980–84." *Vital and Health Statistics.* Series 1, no. 24. Hyattsville, Md.: U.S. Department of Health and Human Services.

Findley, Sally E. 1982. *Migration Survey Methodologies: A Review of Design Issues.* IUSSP Papers no. 20. Liège: IUSSP.

Freedman, David A. 1991. "Adjusting the 1990 Census." *Science* 252, 1233–1236.

Gille, Halvor. 1984. *World Fertility Survey; Major Findings and Implications.* Oxford: Alden Press.

Goldstein, Sidney, and Alice Goldstein. 1981. *Surveys of Migration in Developing Countries: A Methodological Review.* Papers of the East-West Population Institute, no. 71. Honolulu: East-West Center.

Graunt, John. 1662. *Natural and Political Observations Mentioned in a Following Index, and Made upon the Bills of Mortality.* London. Reprinted in 1975 by Arno Press of New York.

Guillard, Achille. 1855. *Elements de statistique humaine ou démographie comparée.* Paris: Guillaumin.

LeClere, Felicia, and Donald Dahmann. 1990. "Residents of Farms and Rural Areas, 1989." *Current Population Reports.* Series P-20, no. 446. Washington, D.C.: Government Printing Office.

Lesetedi, Lesetedinyana T., Gaboratanelwe D. Mompati, Pilate Khulumani, Gwen N. Lesetedi, and Naomi Rutenberg. 1989. *Botswana Family Health Survey II 1988.* Botswana: Central Statistics Office.

Linder, Forrest E., and Iwao M. Moriyama. 1985. Introduction in *Improving Civil Registration,* pp. 1–14. Bethesda, Md.: International Institute for Vital Registration and Statistics.

Lorimer, Frank. 1959. The Development of Demography. In Philip M. Hauser and Otis Dudley Duncan, eds., *The Study of Population; An Inventory and Appraisal,* pp. 124–79. Chicago: University of Chicago Press.

Myers, Dowell. 1992. *Analysis with Local Census Data: Portraits of Change.* San Diego, Calif.: Academic Press.

Nam, Charles B., and Susan Gustavus Philliber. 1984. *Population: A Basic Orientation.* Englewood Cliffs, N.J.: Prentice-Hall.

Palmore, James A., and Robert W. Gardner. 1983. *Measuring Mortality, Fertility, and Natural Increase: A Self-Teaching Guide to Elementary Measures.* Honolulu: East-West Population Institute.

Petty, William. 1690. *Political Arithmetik.* London.

Pol, Louis G. 1987. *Business Demography.* New York: Quorum Books.

———, and Richard Thomas. 1992. *The Demography of Health and Health Care.* New York: Plenum Publishing.

Population Reference Bureau. 1988. *Population Today* 16:4, 2.

Robey, Bryant. 1989. "Two Hundred Years and Counting: The 1990 Census." *Population Bulletin* 44:1, 1–43.

Shryock, Henry S., Jacob S. Siegel, and Associates. 1976. *The Methods and Materials of Demography.* San Diego, Calif.: Academic.

Tolson, George C., Judy M. Barnes, George A. Gay, and Julia L. Kowaleski. 1991. "The 1989 Revision of the U.S. Standard Certificates and Reports." *Vital and*

Health Statistics. Series 4, no. 28. Hyattsville, Md.: U.S. Department of Health and Human Services.

United Nations. 1969. *Methodology and Evaluation of Population Registers and Similar Systems.* New York: United Nations.

———. 1971. *Methodology of Demographic Sample Surveys.* Statistical Papers, Series M, no. 51. New York: United Nations.

———. 1973. *Principles and Recommendations for a Vital Statistics System.* New York: United Nations.

———. 1980. *Principles and Recommendations for Population and Housing Censuses.* Statistical Papers, Series M, no. 67. New York: United Nations.

———. 1983. *Manual X. Indirect Techniques for Demographic Estimation.* New York: United Nations.

———. 1987. *Status of Civil Registration and Vital Statistics in Asia and the Pacific.* Bangkok: United Nations.

———. 1988. *Censuses of Population and Housing in Asia and the Pacific: Towards the 1990 Round.* New York: United Nations.

U.S. Bureau of the Census. 1989. *Census ABC's, Applications in Business and Community.*

———. 1990a. Federal Legislative Uses of Decennial Census Data. *1990 Census of Population and Housing.* Content Determination Reports. 1990 CDR-14.

———. 1990b. *Census '90 Basics.* Washington: Bureau of the Census.

Verhoef, Rolf, and Dirk van de Kaa. 1987. Population Registers and Population Statistics. *Population Index* 53:4, 633–42.

West, Kirsten K., and David J. Fein. 1990. "Census Undercount: An Historical and Contemporary Sociological Issue." *Sociological Inquiry* 60:2, 127–41.

Westoff, Charles F., Robert G. Potter, Jr., Philip C. Sagi, and Elliot Mishler. 1961. *Family Growth in Metropolitan America.* Princeton, N.J.: Princeton University Press.

Wolter, Kirk M. 1991. "Accounting for America's Uncounted and Miscounted." *Science* 253: 12–15.

PART TWO

Dynamics of Population Change

The first part of this book was concerned with the fundamentals of population change. These related to the nature of population change itself, transitions and cycles of population change, some theoretical and conceptual perspectives on population, and the various kinds of population data and their uses.

Throughout that part we discussed the basic components of population change—in particular, the elements of mortality, fertility, mobility, distribution, and composition. But our treatment of those topics was illustrative and general since we needed this opportunity to acquaint you with how some of the important pieces of the population puzzle fit together. To use the metaphor of the Introduction and Part One of the book, there is much more of the story to tell.

In Part Two we will go back to the basic aspects of population change—mortality, fertility, mobility, distribution, and composition—and give them greater attention. Our objective in each chapter will be to focus on the critical concepts and measures of the topic and then to place the topic in historical perspective.

For each major concept, we will clarify definitions, try to comprehend the nuances of the terms involved, place the concept within the broader topic, and give illustrations. Because the study of a topic requires some type of quantification in order to get a sense of its level and degree of difference or change, we will examine alternative statistical measures of the topic and evaluate them in terms of their utility for the purposes intended. Our discussion of measurement in this part of the book is primarily restricted to narratives. Those who want formulae for calculating the several measures will find them in Appendix A, which also provides examples of their use and additional references.

The historical perspective of the topic is offered by using the demographic transition framework as a binder, and giving examples of the specified topic as it was relevant to population change over the course of the transition. We will draw examples from both the United States (and the same area before the nation was created) and various developed and developing countries.

As a consequence of this form of presentation, you should develop a good sense of each of the basic aspects of population change as a general process or set of processes rather than as just a static situation. Viewing such processes in terms of the essential changes and the myriad factors associated with them will increase your understanding of the dynamics of population change and of the elements that contribute to it.

If we accomplish that purpose, you can then be prepared to examine how population changes, in all of their manifestations, have impacts on the social institutions of societies and communities and on social behaviors of individuals. This will give us the basis for comprehending why and how the fact of demographic change is so crucial to the development of societies and communities and the forms and patterns they take.

5. Mortality Processes

Chapter 1 gave an overview of mortality as a component of population change by sketching out some important matters for examination. You were told that it is necessary to make certain that concepts are well defined and understood, and that the data used for analysis are appropriate and accurate. We also indicated that you can best understand mortality as the outcome of a process in which a host of different kinds of factors are involved.

This chapter pursues those directions by dealing with some of the critical concepts and measures of mortality and related factors and by tracing some of the key developments in mortality changes over time. Before proceeding with that task, we will first elaborate the notion that mortality should be viewed as an outcome, sometimes early and sometimes late in life, that depends on a range of variables interacting with each other in complex ways to determine the risks of survival for individuals and groups.

Throughout our lives, death always exists as a possibility. Yet we do not become sensitive to it or the probabilities involved until we are faced with a situation frequently associated with a substantial risk of death. But the makeup of the fetus and, subsequently, of the human body includes elements that are weak or strong and that change with time. In some populations these factors are similar for many individuals because of societal or community commonalities; as a result, we can describe survival tendencies for aggregates of people.

Yet as Weiss (1990) indicates, a population is composed of individuals who are heterogeneous (variable) in their susceptibility to disease and death. Hence, every population has a distribution of *frailty* (from the very weak to the very strong). This variation, he says, is made up of two essential components. The first has an underlying *genetic* basis. Fetuses already have implanted within them a genetic construct that they carry from their parents. These can incorporate both normal and defective genes. The second component has to do with *environmental exposures* (both natural and social) that can affect a person's chances of remaining in a healthy state. Total frailty, resulting from these two basic aspects, is unique for each individual. For any age group there is a distribution of relative frailty. As a cohort ages, the frailty distribution changes. Understandably, those already weak are more likely to die; but new threats to frailty from the natural and social environments also have an impact.

Because the chances of death are related to frailty conditions, it is important to know the relative health of individuals. Demographers and others use the term *morbidity* to indicate the limits to health (of both a genetic and non-genetic kind) and *disability* to indicate limitations on activities performed by persons because of physical or mental handicaps. Both morbidity and disability can influence the risks of death.

The amount of knowledge we have about mortality and disability themselves is limited. Physicians can only identify observable diseases and impairments. The idea of an *iceberg of morbidity* in which the tip is barely seen is now widely referred to, and a parallel *iceberg of disability* is now discussed in the same terms (Verbrugge, 1990). That is, physicians can only detect so much of the frailty of an individual. The individual may have feelings of other frailties not yet diagnosed by a physician. So measurement of morbidity and disability have their limits. (We will consider some of these in the section below on morbidity, disability, and risk behaviors.) Even less is known about these two phenomena as they relate to mortality.

When population researchers study mortality changes, they often restrict their analysis to more obvious associated factors. As our ability to measure morbidity and disability effects grows, the picture of the process ending in mortality will become much clearer. Still we are making good progress in moving toward that goal.

A major framework for studying child survival in developing countries (Mosley and Chen, 1984) reflects this awareness that understanding mortality change must derive from incorporating both social and biological variables and relating both morbidity and mortality. The so-called *proximate determinants* through which social and economic factors affect child survival include maternal factors (such as the mother's age and previous birth history), environmental contamination, nutrient deficiency, injury, and personal illness control.

Manton (1986) has shown how taking into account chronic morbidity and disability variables for older persons helps to produce better forecasts for survival prospects of the elderly population. The dynamic ways in which various illness states decrease or increase are not reflected well enough in the factors customarily used as forecast indicators (past mortality trends and socioeconomic shifts). We need to specify them in order to be able to determine a complete picture of mortality change.

We return, therefore, to the theme that death is best understood as the end point of a process in which many types of risks are posed to life, that the nature of these risks and their variations within populations are complex, and that we must be sensitive to these facts of life and death if we are to achieve a good degree of comprehension of mortality trends and differences.

CRITICAL CONCEPTS AND MEASURES

We begin this section with some common distinctions about mortality. Do death and mortality require definitions, or are they so well understood that definitions are not necessary? Are life span and life expectancy synonymous terms? At which points in the age cycle is mortality most critical? Keeping in mind the measurement cautions of Chapter 4, what are the best ways to measure mortality phenomena? How do we usually measure morbidity and disability? Does it make much difference as to which measure is used? Are medical causes of death simple to diagnose? What are the most significant bases for studying categorical differences in morbidity and mortality? These questions will be answered as we discuss these items and provide examples of their use. With this background, we can then explore how relevant they are to understanding the mortality transition in countries around the world.

Death and Mortality

Death is defined by the United Nations as "the permanent disappearance of all evidence of life at any time after birth has taken place (post-natal cessation of vital functions without capability of resuscitation)" (United Nations, 1973). Several aspects of this definition are extremely important for the study of population change. Because it refers to cessation of life after birth, it excludes fetal deaths occurring prior to live birth. (As we will see in the following chapter, the definition of a live birth is itself a critical definitional problem when death occurs at about the time of birth.) Also, the functions of all vital organs must cease and not return. This means that, in the case where the brain no longer functions but the heart still pumps, one cannot speak officially of a death. In some places the concept of a *brain death* has been given formal sanction in order that certain medical and legal actions can be taken. From a demographic perspective, death statistics include only those terminations of life that meet the definition given above.

Death and mortality can be distinguished by regarding the former as what can occur to an individual, whereas *mortality* is an aggregate phenomenon or the sum of deaths that occur in a population of an area over a specified period of time.

In analyzing mortality conditions, the facets typically covered are the incidence and prevalence of deaths in given areas at specified times, trends over time in mortality, the association of demographic and socioeconomic characteristics with mortality, comparisons among areas and population subgroups, and similar measures relating to morbidity (and disability).

A key factor determining the way we measure mortality is that there is a fairly universal relationship of age and dying. Figure 5.1 presents six curves which show, for each sex, the death rate according to age (age-specific death rates) for three hypothetical populations. These populations have mortality levels indicative of three points in the mortality transition. An impressive feature of the figure is the similarity in general shape of all the curves. Regardless of the level of mortality in the populations, death rates decline from infancy to the early teen ages and increase thereafter. Countries with more favorable life expectancies at birth (e_X values) have considerably lower death rates at younger ages and somewhat lower death rates at middle and older ages. Although this age pattern of mortality is common to all areas, these curves represent averages of patterns for countries at each mortality level, and there is some variation around the typical pattern. The occurrence of mortality cycles can also affect the shape of the age-mortality curve at certain points in time (see Figure 5.1).

Analysts must consider this typical age pattern of deaths in a population in adopting mortality measures (in particular when making comparisons). As a consequence, there is a range of measures going from the unrefined to the refined (adjusted for complicating factors, such as comparing populations with different age structures). Why do we bother with the unrefined measures? Because the availability of data necessary for refined measures is lacking in some countries, and unrefined measures provide at least some indication of mortality conditions.

The simplest relative mortality measure is the *crude death rate* (CDR), which is defined as the number of deaths in a year per 1,000 persons in the population. It is calculated by dividing the number of deaths occurring in a calendar year by the total population in the year (usually the size of the population at midyear), and multiplying this quotient by 1,000 to make it a number larger than a fraction.

In several countries of Africa today, where survival conditions are extremely poor, crude death rates are in the range of 20–25 per thousand. In times past the CDR in many countries was higher than that. The CDR for the United States in 1993 is at the 9 per thousand mark.

In a number of countries (including a few that are considered in a developing stage), the CDR is much *lower* than in the United States! For instance, the crude death rate for Panama is about half of what it is for the United States. This reflects the main weakness of the CDR, because its level is strongly affected by the age distribution of the population. Keeping in mind the age curve of mortality, Panama has a higher proportion of its population in the younger age categories (where the risks of death are least), whereas the United States has a higher proportion in the older age groups (where the risks of death are high).

In fact, in every age category the percentage dying in a given year is *higher* in Panama than in the United States. Yet because of the larger concentration of persons in Panama at the younger ages, the weighted combination of age-specific death rates (which is what the CDR actually is) is lower for Panama. Another way of expressing this paradox is to say that relatively more people survive to older ages in the United States, which then creates an older population whose members are more at the risk of death.

FIGURE 5.1 Models of Age-Specific Death Rates for Each Sex Corresponding to Three Different Values of Expectation of Life at Birth (Logarithmic Scale)

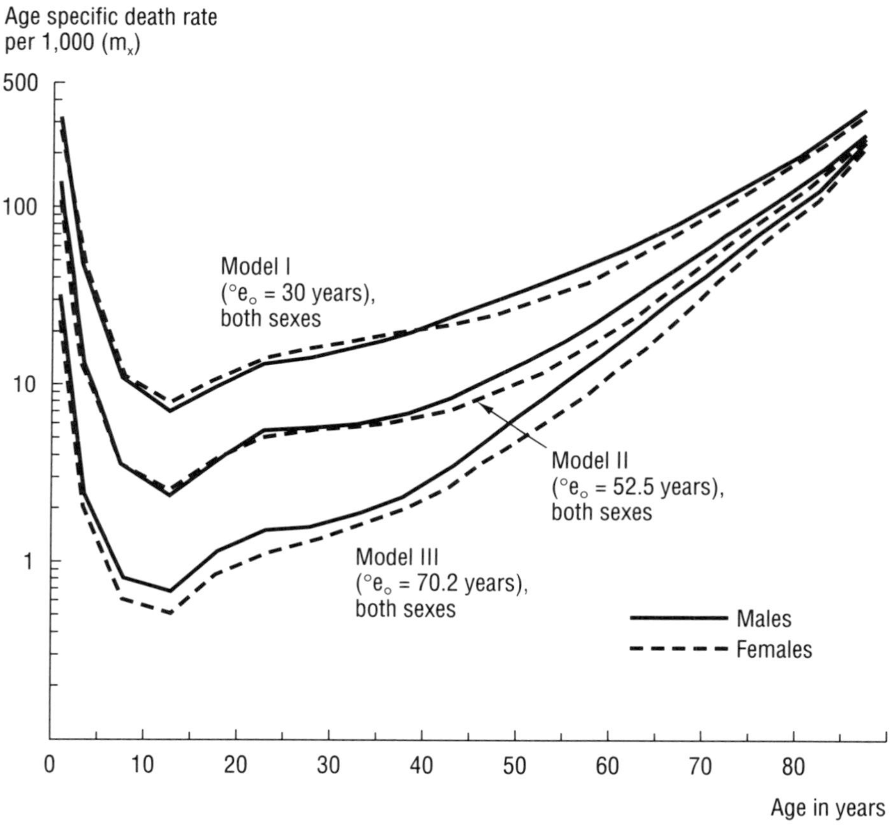

Source: United Nations, *Population Bulletin of the United Nations, no. 6–1962* (New York: United Nations, 1963), p. 52.

For the above reason, the crude death rate in states like Florida and Arizona are unusually high. Since these areas are attractive because of their favorable climates, older persons tend to move there to escape the harsher climates of many other states. But when these older persons die, they die in Florida or Arizona instead of where they came from, thus inflating the CDR for those states.

One way to escape this dilemma of the crude death rate is to analyze *age-specific death rates* separately (if the data on deaths by age are available for the population being studied). If we compare death rates age for age, we do not have the complication of varying age composition in the areas being compared.

One shortcoming of using age-specific measures is that you have a lot of comparisons to make (as many as there are age groups). To avoid this problem, demographers create what they call *age-standardized mortality* measures. That is, they pose the question: What would the CDRs of the areas being compared be like if their age compositions were alike and only the risks of death at each age remained the same? Of course, this is a hypothetical question, but it permits us to adjust for the confounding age factor and focus on the death risk itself. The advantage of age-standardized measures is that they get us back to a single indicator instead of a series of age-specific indicators (see Appendix A for an example of standardization).

Either age-specific or age-standardized mortality measures put relative mortality in proper perspective. If our interest is in assessing the facts of death at any age, these measures give the comparisons more validity. Places at an early stage of the mortality transition will almost invariably have relatively high age-specific mortality indicators, and those at a late stage of the transition will almost surely have relatively low age-specific mortality indicators.

Both crude death rates and age-specific or age-standardized death rates have one common feature. They present a picture of mortality at a point or period of time (hence, they are known as *period measures*). If the circumstances of that period are not normal, then the measures will not be typical of a broader range of time. Therefore, these indicators have to be looked at over a span of years in order to assess their typicality. (Often the agencies publishing such information will show three-year averages of period measures of mortality in order to smooth out the effects of unusual years.) On the other hand, if we really want to know how mortality varies from period to period (say, year to year), then we should use period mortality measures for each separate period (that is, year by year).

Period measures are very important when our goal is to find out what the mortality consequences were of certain events, such as a disease epidemic or an economic recession or a war that may occur primarily in a given year.

Life Span and Life Expectancy

In one sense period mortality measures represent reality. When we die, it is at a point or period of time. The mortality experience of a population can be expressed likewise at a point or period of time. But there is another way of indicating the risks of death that also represents reality.

If we pose the question about mortality prospects in terms of people's lifetimes, we can produce an answer that gives us the same kind of information as for period measures but puts it into a different form. We referred in Chapter 4 to cohort measures of population phenomena. What we are saying here is that we can look at mortality from a cohort perspective as well as a period perspective and get different views of what occurs.

The *cohort, or life cycle, perspective* leads us to ask about survival from one age we attain to another. This is the form in which we usually question our mortality chances. If a baby is born, how many years can he or she expect to live? Once I reach age 65, how many more years of life can I expect? What is the probability of a 20-year-old's surviving to age 30? We can pose many similar questions using the cohort view, which is not more valid than the period viewpoint. Rather, the cohort view enables us to ask different kinds of questions about the same basic information.

In using the cohort approach to studying mortality, two concepts are extremely relevant, namely, life span and life expectancy. In the popular media, and even unfortunately among some academic scholars, the two terms are often regarded as synonymous. In fact, they have distinct meanings that have important consequences for mortality analysis and therefore should be kept separate.

Life span refers to the maximum number of years a person can be expected to live under the most ideal circumstances. This is essentially a fixed number. Fries and Crapo (1981) cite 115 as the oldest age of the longest-lived human being and point out that it has been constant for centuries. Why, then, do we read about the sturdy mountain people in the Caucasus of the Georgian Republic who are reported to extend their lives to 150 with a yogurt-based diet? Is it not the case that Andean villagers in Ecuador have reached similar ages for a long period of time? The response to these questions is that there is no documented case of anyone in the world living beyond 115. That is, where higher numbers are cited, they are not based on acceptable evidence of a date of birth. Given the tendency for many people to exaggerate their age (see Chapter 8), reports of extreme ages are not unexpected. But they should not be taken at face value.

To say that life span is a constant is to say that there are biological limits to human survival. Life span is determined by the aging process, which is linked to the process of cell reproduction in each bodily organ. Because of recent developments in biological research on genes, some persons believe that the time will soon come when the cap on life span will be lifted or at least set at a higher limit. Others are dubious about such changes, and see genetic research as likely being successful in identifying particular genes relating to diseases and disabilities that can be altered. But these same observers do not believe that such research will be able to modify the aging process in such a way as to allow the life of body organs to continue their vitality beyond their present capacity (Hayflick, 1982).

Life expectancy is defined as the average number of years of life remaining to a group of persons reaching a certain age. We need to emphasize the word *average* because there is much variability around that average. Life expectancy, in contrast to life span, is not fixed; in fact, in most societies it increases with time. Yet in some places it can decrease for some stretches of time.

The reason that life expectancy generally increases with time is that, with development of an area, there is a tendency for a greater proportion at each age to survive to older ages. As a result, the average expectation of life rises. One can see, however, that there are limits to life expectancy. We would never assume life expectancy to reach life span for any population. Age 85 is often mentioned as an estimate of the peak that life expectancy (as the average years lived by a population) could eventually reach.

Life expectancy is a measure of survival derived from what is called a *life table*. (The construction of such a table is illustrated in Appendix A.) A life table is designed to show the survival and longevity prospects for a group of babies (conventionally 100,000) who are born at the same time and are subject to a particular pattern of age-specific death rates as they go through life. This table includes information enabling us to answer the kinds of questions posed earlier about cohort mortality.

To construct a life table, the basic data required are age-specific death rates for the population under consideration. There is a compound dilemma here. First, for those countries which lack good data on deaths and population by age, one cannot use the conventional methods to calculate a life table. Second, even when the data exist for a current period of time, ideally we would want to have the age-specific death rates for cohorts of people (because a life table is supposed to be a cohort mortality experience). But age-specific death rates are rarely available for a group of persons going through life. Moreover, for which cohorts would we want the data? Life tables are generally used to gauge future life expectancy. If the death experience relates to a cohort born in the distant past whose members have by now gone through life, is that a good indication of the future? This would not be the case when mortality has been in the process of transition. If we start with a group of babies born today and wait until they all live their lives, we could not construct a life table for a hundred years, and who among us would be around to construct it? So we compromise by using the present pattern of age-specific death rates as data input to the life table. In effect, we are assuming that current patterns will be what newborn babies will experience as they go through life. For most developed nations, this assumption is not too unreasonable; for developing countries, it is not a good assumption, because it understates progress in survival that will be made.

Model life tables (mentioned in Chapter 4) are valuable as substitutes for "real" life tables when necessary data are lacking or inaccurate. The relative predictability of age curves of mortality gives us a pretty good basis for the substitution.

Table 5.1 shows the range of life expectancy at birth for nations around the world as of about 1993. The lowest estimated life expectancy of 42 years was for Sierra Leone, which was also shared by Guinea. Since this is somewhat higher than life expectancies estimated for early historical periods, even those countries have made some progress in controlling deaths. In contrast, Japan's life expectancy stood at 79, almost twice as high.

One can observe average regional differences in the world, ranging from 54 for Africa to 76 for North America and Europe. But it is also the case that there is considerable variation among countries within the regions. There are ranges from 42 to 68 in Africa, from 54 to 79 in Asia, from 54 to 76 in Latin America, from 55 to 77 in Oceania, and from 70 to 78 in Europe.

TABLE 5.1 Life Expectancy at Birth for Selected Countries around the World: Circa 1993 (Both Sexes Combined)

REGION AND COUNTRY	LIFE EXPECTANCY AT BIRTH (YEARS)
WORLD	65
AFRICA	54
Sierra Leone	42
Senegal	48
Zaire	52
Egypt	60
Kenya	62
Libya	63
Seychelles	68
ASIA	64
Nepal	54
India	59
Saudi Arabia	66
Malaysia	71
Jordan	71
Israel	76
Japan	79
NORTH AMERICA	76
Canada	77
United States	75
LATIN AMERICA	68
Haiti	54
El Salvador	63
Colombia	71
Chile	73
Cuba	76
EUROPE	75
Hungary	70
Ireland	75
Italy	77
Sweden	78
RUSSIA	69
OCEANIA	73
Papua–New Guinea	55
Fiji	64
New Zealand	75
Australia	77

Source: Population Reference Bureau, *World Population Data Sheet* (Washington, D.C., 1993).

Morbidity, Disability, and Risk Behaviors

History tells us that humans are not immortal, and it also provides reports of age-old occurrences of disease, infirmity, and physical and mental handicap. A sweep of history reveals that the risks of these conditions have changed with time (see Box 5.1).

In considering these phenomena, we can refer to *illness* or *sickness* as individual experiences of disease or injury and *morbidity* as aggregate phenomena of the same. Hence, there is a parallel here to the comparative concepts of death and mortality. Likewise, *handicap* represents a state of an individual's physical or mental limitation whereas *disability* is the aggregate equivalent.

The historical process described by Dubos is referred to by demographers and health scientists as the *epidemiologic transition*. Epidemiology is concerned with the distribution of disease and death and with their determinants and consequences in population groups. Omran (1971) first highlighted the ways in which health and disease patterns shift over time as countries go through stages of social and economic development. Basically, "pandemics of infection are gradually displaced by degenerative and man-made diseases as the chief form of morbidity and primary cause of death." Omran saw three stages in the epidemiologic transition that paralleled stages of the mortality transition. These were the age of pestilence and famine, the age of receding pandemics, and the age of degenerative diseases and diseases of human origin.

Riley and Alter (1989) emphasize that Omran's account of the transition focuses on changes in the ages and causes of death and less on morbidity changes. They argue that the arrest of many acute conditions permitted higher proportions to survive to older ages at which point chronic degenerative diseases became the dominant causes of death. The incidence and prevalence of disease, however, took different forms. For example, they describe the history of disease in western Europe in terms of fluctuating trends and cycles and altered consequences:

> Specific diseases join and leave the profile, appearing sometimes as virgin soil epidemics with high fatality rates..., sometimes as endemic diseases occasionally taking epidemic form but rarely causing fatalities at high rates, and sometimes as endemic diseases of diminishing importance in fatality rates.

Drawing on historical morbidity data for Europe and the United States, Riley and Alter conclude that, while the risk of death declined sharply during the nineteenth century, the age-specific *incidence* of disease and injury remained approximately level and the age-specific *duration* of disease and injury increased. These findings are in keeping with other analyses showing that longer life can occur simultaneously with worsening health (e.g., Verbrugge, 1984).

The tendency to view morbidity and disability as concepts that are unidimensional and related to certain disease and physical or mental handicap states has been questioned by many (e.g., Antonovsky, 1979). Most would agree that these conditions are complex since various diseases, handicaps, pain, and activi-

BOX 5.1 Dubos on Changing Causes of Mortality

The scholar René Dubos (1987) relates:

> War, Famine, and Pestilence still commonly ride in advance of Death in most of the world today. But these time-honored allies of the pale rider are now less feared than they used to be. Men may not be happier, nor even fundamentally healthier, than their ancestors but in the Western world at least life expectancy is longer. The human mind has been freed of its obsession with death and disease caused by violence, nutritional deficiencies, or infectious fevers, and it can now return with more confidence to some of its ancient dreams of eternal youth and long life.
>
> Death, however, is now acquiring new allies that are taking the place of Famine and Pestilence. Horsemen of destruction that were rarely seen in the past are increasingly threatening the life and soul of modern man. Vascular diseases ruin his heart or brain; cancers run riot; mental diseases break his contact with the world of reason. As was the case for the great epidemics, two kinds of medical philosophy are guiding the approach to the control of these modern endemics. One is the search for drugs capable of reaching the site of the disease within the body of the patient. The other is the attempt to identify those aspects of modern life thought to be responsible for the disease problems peculiar to our times (pp. 197–98).

ty limitation can occur in combinations at different points in time. Consequently, the risks of death are variable, dependent on the seriousness and multiplicity of conditions. In addition, measures of morbidity and disability depend on the types of data collected and their reliability. Both individuals and their doctors understate the true state of ill health.

Biraben (1982) described a study by two British biologists, Scott-Williamson and Pearce, of a socially heterogeneous area of southeast London during the late 1930s. They examined 3,911 individuals from 1,206 families and found that 90 percent of them had one or more of the pathological deficiencies generally recognized by doctors at that time. But only 21 percent of the persons were aware of any deficiency, and 69 percent thought they were in perfect health.

In the 1989 U.S. National Health Interview Survey (Adams and Benson, 1990), 40 percent of a national sample of civilian noninstitutionalized adults assessed their health as "excellent," 28 percent as "very good," and 22 percent as "good"—a combined 90 percent in these three categories. Roughly 7 percent regarded their health as "fair" and under 3 percent as "poor." Yet 62 percent reported acute conditions (illnesses or injuries of less than three months duration that required physician attention or interrupted daily activity). This resulted in an average of three bed days during the year, and sizable numbers reported chronic conditions of various types.

Although medical examinations are more likely to uncover states of ill health that even the patient was unaware of, we realize that physicians are limited in their diagnosis by the technology available to them and the extent to which medical practice has enabled them to interpret signs of illness correctly. The "icebergs" of morbidity and disability thus make a proper determination of those conditions in the population very difficult.

Since our purpose here is to examine morbidity and disability as preludes to mortality, our interest in those states is related to the risks of death. The concept of medical *causes of death* (discussed in the next section) enables us to trace back from death to the medical conditions believed to lead to the end of an individual's life. Genetic and environmental hazards have long histories of contributing to those medical causes. Only in more recent years have we become sensitive to the ways that styles of life adopted by persons have made their marks on survival chances.

Increasingly, as infectious and parasitic diseases have been replaced by chronic and degenerative illnesses in developing societies, attention has turned to risk behaviors of persons that increase the chances of premature death. *Risk behaviors* are those practices of individuals that contribute to various causes of death. Seven health habits are usually measured to indicate the level of risk behaviors. These are smoking, drinking, length of sleeping, exercising, height/weight relationship, eating snacks, and eating breakfasts regularly.

According to the Alameda County study, a nine-and-one-half-year follow-up of a 1965 cohort of adults showed that poor behaviors on each of these dimensions enhanced the probability of early death. An examination of the same behaviors through the 1985 National Health Interview Study in the United States found similar results (Schoenborn, 1986). Good health habits included not currently smoking cigarettes, having had less than five alcoholic drinks during the previous two weeks, meeting the 1983 Metropolitan Life Insurance height/weight standards, exercising at a level of three or more kilocalories per kilogram per day, eating breakfast almost every day, rarely or never snacking, and sleeping either seven or eight hours a night.

Survey findings were that 33 percent of men and 28 percent of women were current smokers, 10 percent of men and over 2 percent of women drank over the standard limit, 26 percent of men and 22 percent of women were at least 20 percent over the height/weight standard, 49 percent of men and 62 percent of women were classified as sedentary (inactive physically), one-fourth of U.S. adults rarely or never ate breakfast, 40 percent of men and women ate snacks daily, and 20 percent of the respondents reported sleeping an average of six hours a night or less. Overall, more than half of the adults reported no more than four or five of the good habits, and about one-third had zero to three good habits.

Medical Causes of Death

The morbidity and disability processes that beleaguer people during their lives usually contribute to their demise when life comes to an end. Yet the determination of the medical causes of death is difficult and depends not only on the diagnostic skills of a physician but also on the susceptibility of some conditions to detection by existing methods of medical discovery.

In the United States a portion of the death certificate completed after a person dies is devoted to descriptions of the causes of death. Figure 5.2 shows the standard U.S. death certificate on which some information is recorded. *Medical cause of death* refers to the conditions certified by a physician as having contributed to the death. The form of entry of this information is a bit complicated, and the decision as to what cause of death should be identified as the critical one follows from a set of rules specified by the World Health Organization (WHO).

The physician is asked to enter the immediate or final cause (item 27), in terms of the disease or condition that just preceded death, on the first line. Prior causes that led to the immediate cause are then listed sequentially on the following lines, with the last-mentioned cause regarded as the "underlying cause." The assumption is that, if the starting point of a sequence of events is known, death can be postponed by preventing the initiating cause from operating (Israel et al., 1986). Still another line is provided for recording other significant conditions contributing to death but not resulting in the underlying cause. As a consequence of this set of information, one or more causes are identified and one of them is indicated as the underlying cause of death. Under WHO procedures, it is only this underlying cause that is included in official cause-of-death statistics.

The epidemiologic transition posited by Omran can be pictured in terms of the changing cause-of-death composition of mortality as societies go through the demographic transition. In Figure 5.3, the mix of broad categories of cause of death is shown according to levels of life expectancy at birth. When a country has an expectation of life at birth of about 40 years, infectious and parasitic diseases are seen as the underlying causes for almost half the deaths; cancers, cardiovascular diseases, and various forms of violence account for another 20 percent or so; and over 30 percent are other causes (including some fraction in which the cause cannot be diagnosed). With the rise in life expectancy at birth, infectious and parasitic causes diminish, cancers and cardiovascular diseases gradually increase their prominence as a cause, the proportion of deaths due to violence remains about constant, and other causes eventually are reduced. (Note that these cause distributions are of all deaths occurring at that period of time. The number and rate of deaths may be changing over time.)

Reasonably reliable information on medical causes of death is widely available in all developed countries and in some countries of Asia and Latin America. In other areas, ironically those with high death rates and a pressing need for good cause-of-death data, the information is sparse.

FIGURE 5.2 U.S. Standard Certificate of Death

TYPE/PRINT IN PERMANENT BLACK INK FOR INSTRUCTIONS SEE OTHER SIDE AND HANDBOOK

LOCAL FILE NUMBER

U.S. STANDARD
CERTIFICATE OF DEATH

STATE FILE NUMBER

DECEDENT

1. DECEDENT'S NAME *(First, Middle, Last)*
2. SEX
3. DATE OF DEATH *(Month, Day, Year)*
4. SOCIAL SECURITY NUMBER
5a. AGE—Last Birthday *(Years)*
5b. UNDER 1 YEAR — Months | Days
5c. UNDER 1 DAY — Hours | Minutes
6. DATE OF BIRTH *(Month, Day, Year)*
7. BIRTHPLACE *(City and State or Foreign Country)*
8. WAS DECEDENT EVER IN U.S. ARMED FORCES? *(Yes or no)*
9a. PLACE OF DEATH *(Check only one; see instructions on other side)* HOSPITAL: ☐ Inpatient ☐ ER/Outpatient ☐ DOA OTHER: ☐ Nursing Home ☐ Residence ☐ Other *(Specify)*
9b. FACILITY NAME *(If not institution, give street and number)*
9c. CITY, TOWN, OR LOCATION OF DEATH
9d. COUNTY OF DEATH
10. MARITAL STATUS—Married, Never Married, Widowed, Divorced *(Specify)*
11. SURVIVING SPOUSE *(If wife, give maiden name)*
12a. DECEDENT'S USUAL OCCUPATION *(Give kind of work done during most of working life. Do not use retired.)*
12b. KIND OF BUSINESS/INDUSTRY

SEE INSTRUCTIONS ON OTHER SIDE →

13a. RESIDENCE—STATE
13b. COUNTY
13c. CITY, TOWN, OR LOCATION
13d. STREET AND NUMBER
13e. INSIDE CITY LIMITS? *(Yes or no)*
13f. ZIP CODE
14. WAS DECEDENT OF HISPANIC ORIGIN? *(Specify No or Yes—If yes, specify Cuban, Mexican, Puerto Rican, etc.)* ☐ No ☐ Yes Specify:
15. RACE—American Indian, Black, White, etc. *(Specify)*
16. DECEDENT'S EDUCATION *(Specify only highest grade completed)* Elementary/Secondary (0-12) | College (1-4 or 5+)

PARENTS

17. FATHER'S NAME *(First, Middle, Last)*
18. MOTHER'S NAME *(First, Middle, Maiden Surname)*

INFORMANT

19a. INFORMANT'S NAME *(Type/Print)*
19b. MAILING ADDRESS *(Street and Number or Rural Route Number, City or Town, State, Zip Code)*

DISPOSITION

20a. METHOD OF DISPOSITION ☐ Burial ☐ Cremation ☐ Removal from State ☐ Donation ☐ Other *(Specify)* ______
20b. PLACE OF DISPOSITION *(Name of cemetery, crematory, or other place)*
20c. LOCATION—City or Town, State
21a. SIGNATURE OF FUNERAL SERVICE LICENSEE OR PERSON ACTING AS SUCH ▶
21b. LICENSE NUMBER *(of Licensee)*
22. NAME AND ADDRESS OF FACILITY

SEE DEFINITION ON OTHER SIDE

PRONOUNCING PHYSICIAN ONLY

Complete items 23a-c only when certifying physician is not available at time of death to certify cause of death.
23a. **To the best of my knowledge, death occurred at the time, date, and place stated.** *Signature and Title* ▶
23b. LICENSE NUMBER
23c. DATE SIGNED *(Month, Day, Year)*

ITEMS 24-26 MUST BE COMPLETED BY PERSON WHO PRONOUNCES DEATH →

24. TIME OF DEATH M
25. DATE PRONOUNCED DEAD *(Month, Day, Year)*
26. WAS CASE REFERRED TO MEDICAL EXAMINER/CORONER? *(Yes or no)*

CAUSE OF DEATH

SEE INSTRUCTIONS ON OTHER SIDE

27. **PART I.** Enter the diseases, injuries, or complications that caused the death. Do not enter the mode of dying, such as cardiac or respiratory arrest, shock, or heart failure. List only one cause on each line.

Approximate Interval Between Onset and Death

IMMEDIATE CAUSE (Final disease or condition resulting in death) → a. ______
DUE TO (OR AS A CONSEQUENCE OF):
b. ______
DUE TO (OR AS A CONSEQUENCE OF):
c. ______
DUE TO (OR AS A CONSEQUENCE OF):
d. ______

Sequentially list conditions, if any, leading to immediate cause. Enter **UNDERLYING CAUSE** (Disease or injury that initiated events resulting in death) **LAST**

PART II. Other significant conditions contributing to death but not resulting in the underlying cause given in Part I.
28a. WAS AN AUTOPSY PERFORMED? *(Yes or no)*
28b. WERE AUTOPSY FINDINGS AVAILABLE PRIOR TO COMPLETION OF CAUSE OF DEATH? *(Yes or no)*

29. MANNER OF DEATH ☐ Natural ☐ Accident ☐ Suicide ☐ Homicide ☐ Pending Investigation ☐ Could not be Determined
30a. DATE OF INJURY *(Month, Day, Year)*
30b. TIME OF INJURY M
30c. INJURY AT WORK? *(Yes or no)*
30d. DESCRIBE HOW INJURY OCCURRED
30e. PLACE OF INJURY—At home, farm, street, factory, office building, etc. *(Specify)*
30f. LOCATION (Street and Number or Rural Route Number, City or Town, State)

SEE DEFINITION ON OTHER SIDE

CERTIFIER

31a. CERTIFIER *(Check only one)*
☐ CERTIFYING PHYSICIAN *(Physician certifying cause of death when another physician has pronounced death and completed Item 23)*
To the best of my knowledge, death occurred due to the cause(s) and manner as stated.
☐ PRONOUNCING AND CERTIFYING PHYSICIAN *(Physician both pronouncing death and certifying to cause of death)*
To the best of my knowledge, death occurred at the time, date, and place, and due to the cause(s) and manner as stated.
☐ MEDICAL EXAMINER/CORONER
On the basis of examination and/or investigation, in my opinion, death occurred at the time, date, and place, and due to the cause(s) and manner as stated.
31b. SIGNATURE AND TITLE OF CERTIFIER ▶
31c. LICENSE NUMBER
31d. DATE SIGNED *(Month, Day, Year)*
32. NAME AND ADDRESS OF PERSON WHO COMPLETED CAUSE OF DEATH (ITEM 27) *(Type/Print)*

REGISTRAR

33. REGISTRAR'S SIGNATURE ▶
34. DATE FILED *(Month, Day, Year)*

NAME OF DECEDENT: ______ For use by physician or institution

DEPARTMENT OF HEALTH AND HUMAN SERVICES · PUBLIC HEALTH SERVICE · NATIONAL CENTER FOR HEALTH STATISTICS · 1989 REVISION

PHS-T-003
REV. 1/89

FIGURE 5.3 Distribution, in a Standard Population, of Deaths (All Ages and Both Sexes) by Cause-of-Death Groups for Different Levels of Expectation of Life at Birth Ranging from 40 to 76 Years

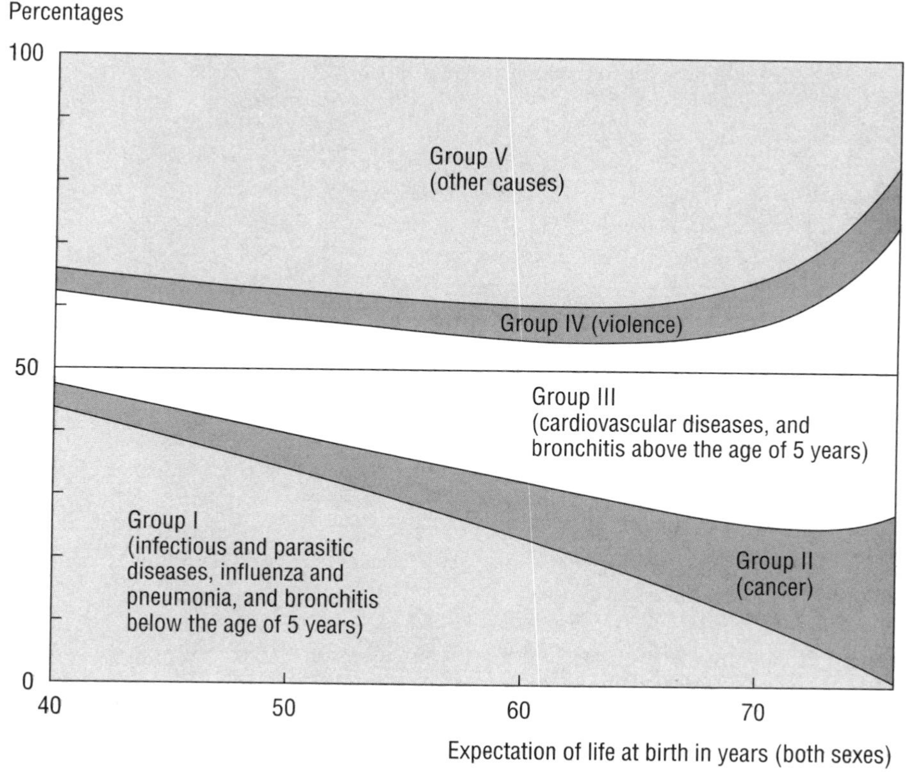

Source: United Nations, *Population Bulletin of the United Nations, no. 6–1982* (New York: United Nations, 1963), p. 110.

On occasions, surveys are conducted in the absence of death registration data to gather some useful information on causes of death. Omondi-Odhiambo and his colleagues (1990) conducted one such study as part of a larger project on morbidity and mortality in a rural area of Kenya during the late 1970s. Nonmedical interviewers were trained by physicians to recognize and record specific signs and symptoms of communicable diseases in infancy and childhood, and they also asked relatives of the deceased about their awareness of the nature of illnesses of all household members. Residents of the area were interviewed every two weeks. A medical student did follow-up interviews of a sample of the respondents to evaluate the findings and to improve the results. The information derived may not have been of high quality, but it did serve to describe the cause-of-death patterns typical of developing areas and thus confirm that health programs were needed to arrest common infectious and parasitic diseases.

Collecting data on cause of death is one thing, and putting that information into a classification system for analytical purposes is quite another. Such classifications were devised as early as the eighteenth century and improved with time as the result of a series of international conferences to periodically evaluate and modify the system. At each of these conferences, a revised International Classification of Diseases (ICD) was established (Nam, 1990). The ninth revision (ICD-9), devised in 1975, remains the current standard until the tenth revision is issued, prospectively during the middle of the 1990–2000 decade. Each revision produces changes arising out of discovery of new diseases and the regrouping of previously known causes. The ICD identifies detailed causes and then groups them at several levels.

An example of a disease that has not been separately identified in the ICD until recently but is now of epidemic proportions is AIDS. As of early 1991, WHO reported records of 340,000 cases of the disease but estimated that the true figure was closer to 1 million. Many other millions of persons were believed to be harboring the virus (HIV) that produces the autoimmune deficiency. Although the greatest concentrations of the disease are in sub-Saharan Africa, the incidence appears to be increasing sharply in other regions (Palca, 1991). Without attention to this cause in ICD-9, deaths attributed to AIDS would be classified in another category determined by a physician or other medical person to be equivalent.

Lopez (1990a) summarized cause-of-death data for countries around the world for the period around 1985. In industrialized (or developed) countries, 54 percent of the deaths were due to diseases of the circulatory system (22 percent of these from ischemic heart disease, 14 percent from strokes, and 1 percent from diabetes). Cancers accounted for 21 percent, injuries and poisonings for 7 percent, and the remainder was distributed over categories of infectious and parasitic diseases and other chronic and degenerative causes. The pattern of these causes varied by age and gender categories.

In developing countries at the same time, 45 percent of the deaths were due to various infectious and parasitic diseases (principally diarrheal diseases, acute respiratory diseases, tuberculosis, measles, whooping cough, diphtheria, and malaria), 10 percent were attributed to other infant diseases about the time of birth or to maternal deaths due to childbirth, and smaller but significant percentages were due to other diseases (including chronic and degenerative causes).

The difficulty of diagnosing and classifying causes of death is compounded by the fact that the underlying cause basis for reporting causal patterns hides the effects of other conditions present at the time of death or known to have been present at an earlier critical stage of life. Researchers have done studies showing that taking into account all of the information on causes of death that appear on the certificate leads to an expanded and sometimes different interpretation of the causal structure.

The data on all conditions listed on a death certificate are coded and accessible to researchers. Israel et al. (1986) indicate that "multiple cause data can give a more complete description of trends for chronic diseases such as diabetes, chronic respiratory diseases, hypertension, and kidney-related diseases because the underlying cause trends can be masked by the changing priority given to these causes as underlying than as nonunderlying causes of death."

Wrigley and Nam (1987) have demonstrated that patterns of differences between the sexes and races in cancer mortality are modified when cancer is examined in a multiple-cause rather than an underlying-cause framework. This is because the several forms of cancer are not always cited as underlying causes by physicians if other conditions are also listed. Similarly, a disease such as diabetes, although widespread and a basis for the emergence of other serious medical conditions, is understated in official data because one of the other conditions is typically cited as the underlying cause.

Looking at multiple causes of death in conjunction with the multiple morbidities and disabilities in a person's life, as well as various risk behaviors and personal and social background factors, enables us to see the process from birth to death as not only complex but also as involving a great variety of interactions of both a positive and negative nature. Hence, it would improve understanding to say that someone who was reported to have died of a stroke at age 41 may have lived more (or maybe fewer) years if complicating conditions had not been present.

Infant and Childhood Mortality

Because the risks of death begin at birth and, in fact, are highest at that point and for a period until the body has developed substantial resistance to various forms of disease and injury, concern about death during infancy and childhood has been great in all parts of the world, especially in developing countries.

For purposes of mortality measurement, infancy is regarded as the first year of life. An *infant death* exists when a baby born alive dies before the first birthday is reached. Thus *infant mortality* excludes deaths to fetuses which did not survive to birth. (There are separate measures of fetal mortality.)

Clearly, however, risks of death to infants are greatest at the instant after birth and decline subsequently. For this reason infant mortality is traditionally divided into components according to time of death. Such divisions may include the first weeks, hours, or minutes of survival, but the most frequently used distinctions are deaths in the first month or twenty-eight days of life (called *neonatal mortality*) and deaths in the remaining months of the first year of life (called *postneonatal mortality*). When this distinction is used, it recognizes the different pattern of causes of death in each of the periods—neonatal deaths often involving genetic and structural malformations and birth delivery complications, and postneonatal deaths being more associated with external social or environmental conditions.

Especially in developing countries, the risks of death remain relatively high through the first several years of life. Therefore, *childhood mortality* is often identified separately in these areas. Childhood is typically regarded as the period after infancy and until the age of five. Distinctions are also made within this interval. For example, mortality during the second year of life is generally referred to as *toddler mortality* and mortality during other childhood years is referred to by the years during which it occurs (e.g., under-3 mortality).

Conventionally, age-specific death rates are measured by relating deaths in the age group (in the numerator) by population in the age group (in the denominator) and multiplying by a constant to produce a number greater than one. In the case of the infant mortality rate, however, deaths to infants in a given year are related to births that occurred in that area in that year and then multiplied by a constant. This is done because births are generally better reported than population under 1 year of age (through the census). In the case of childhood mortality rates, the denominator can be either the number of births for the cohort in which that age group was born or the number who survived to the beginning of the age group of concern (these cohort measures being consistent with the life table approach).

The fact that determination of whether a fetus has been born live or dead is based on a judgment by an attending physician, nurse, or midwife has an influence on infant and childhood mortality measures (see Chapter 6 for discussion of this judgment). If there is ambiguity about whether a live birth has occurred, then it has a consequence for whether a fetal death or death to a liveborn has taken place. For this reason, analysts also calculate a measure of *perinatal mortality*, which relates deaths that occur during the last stage of pregnancy or first month of life to the births during the year. This measure indicates the incidence of death just before or just after birth. The reasoning is that very late fetal deaths occur from pretty much the same causes as do neonatal deaths.

Worldwide, the probability of dying in the first year of life stood at 71 per 1,000 births during the 1985–90 period (Table 5.2). The variation across subregions was considerable, ranging from 8 per 1,000 in northern Europe to 116 per 1,000 in eastern Africa. The levels exceeded 100 (or 1 out of 10 births) in most of Africa and in southern Asia. In addition to northern Europe, they were 10 or below (or 1 out of 100 or less) in western Europe, Australia–New Zealand, and northern America. Other data show that infant mortality rates (similar but measured slightly differently) were estimated in 1993 to be 70 in the world as a whole, but as high as 168 in Afghanistan (in southern Asia) and as low as 4 in San Marino (near Italy) (Population Reference Bureau, 1993).

The second column in Table 5.2 shows the probability of dying in the first five years of life. The world figure of 105, when compared with the level of 71 for deaths before age 1, indicates that half again as many babies die during the second, third, fourth, and fifth years of life combined as die during the first year. The probability of childhood deaths (the difference between the two figures) is highest in Africa (especially eastern, middle, and western Africa) and lowest in northern America, Europe, and parts of Oceania.

TABLE 5.2 Probability of a Newborn Baby Dying before the First and Fifth Birthdays: Regions of the World, 1985–1990 (Both Sexes Combined)

REGION AND COUNTRY	NUMBER DYING BEFORE AGE 1 (PER 1,000 BIRTHS)	NUMBER DYING BEFORE AGE 5 (PER 1,000 BIRTHS)
WORLD	71	105
AFRICA	106	167
Eastern Africa	116	191
Middle Africa	107	178
Northern Africa	86	129
Southern Africa	77	103
Western Africa	112	188
LATIN AMERICA	56	78
Caribbean	57	78
Central America	50	73
South America	58	80
NORTHERN AMERICA	10	11
ASIA	73	108
Eastern Asia	30	41
Southeastern Asia	68	96
Southern Asia	102	160
Western Asia	70	95
EUROPE	13	15
Eastern Europe	17	20
Northern Europe	8	10
Southern Europe	15	17
Western Europe	9	10
OCEANIA	26	33
Australia–New Zealand	9	10
Melanesia	52	70
Micronesia	30	36
Polynesia	26	27
FORMER USSR	24	32

Source: United Nations, *World Population Monitoring 1989* (New York: United Nations, 1990), Table 36.

Surveys have shown that as many as one-third of infant and childhood deaths in developing countries are due to four diseases—neonatal tetanus, pertussis, measles, and acute lower respiratory tract infection. Although the first three can be prevented by immunization, only a small fraction of infants and children in developing countries receive the needed vaccines. Drugs that can contain the respiratory illnesses are also lacking (Foster, 1984).

Perhaps another third of infant and childhood deaths in these areas is related to diarrheal diseases. These are largely due to contaminated food and water and to unclean environmental conditions that spawn various types of bacterial and viral agents (Black, 1984). Diarrhea leads to dehydration and renders the infant or child incapable of maintaining the proper level of fluids in the body. In fact, there are many forms of diarrhea (emanating from a variety of pathogens), and this makes coping with the disease more difficult.

Several diseases associated with animal parasites (protozoa and worms) also take a heavy toll of infants and children in less developed parts of the world. Chief among the resulting illnesses is malaria. Parasitic infections can lead to death directly (as in the case of malarial fever) or indirectly (by leading to malnutrition or undernutrition) (Bradley and Keymer, 1984).

Nutritional status is crucial to the survival prospects of these young ones (Martorell and Ho, 1984). Poor diets not only affect the workings of the bodily organs but they also weaken infants and children and make them more susceptible to different types of diseases.

The factors that differentiate the risks of infant and child deaths include socioeconomic variables, such as the education of the mother and community environmental conditions. Education and other variables shaping women's roles relate to the level and kinds of child care found in the less developed world (Ware, 1984).

In more developed countries, the higher incidence of infant mortality in some areas than others is due to several conditions as well. These include various behaviors of the mother prior to and during pregnancy, inadequate prenatal care, low birth weight, and inappropriate postnatal care.

Behaviors of potential mothers detrimental to the viability of infants born to them later include the mothers' nutritional practices, short intervals between pregnancies (which tax the capacity of a woman's body to provide for the fetus), tobacco smoking, and alcohol or other substance abuse.

Adequate *prenatal care* requires medical examination beginning within the first thirteen weeks of pregnancy and continuing regularly until delivery of the baby (Kessner, 1973). Although risks of infant death vary generally according to birth weight, it has been determined that low birth weight means less than 2,500 grams or about 5.5 pounds at delivery. Once a baby is born alive, the effects of proper nutrition, protection against diseases and injury, and "tender loving care" become critical.

Hale (1990) examined these factors for the United States and concluded that the country, which had a generally low and declining infant mortality rate, still had a rate much higher than that of some other countries because of conditions at two levels. A higher percentage of babies in the United States were of low birth weight and prenatal care was not as extensive. These, in turn, could be explained by a less adequate infant health care system and high infant mortality rates among the socially disadvantaged sectors of society for whom access to care is more limited.

No single factor alone can produce and maintain a low infant mortality level. Circumstances must be favorable for all the conditions mentioned as related to the risks of infant death. In addition, it has become clear that many of the risk factors are far more potent in their effect when they exist in combination with other risk factors. Eberstein et al. (1990) found that the probability of infant death was particularly enhanced when biological (or endogenous) risk factors were present in combination with social (or exogenous) risk factors. Moreover, the different medical causes of death were associated with varying sets of risk factors. This highlights the complexity of infant mortality.

Maternal and Adult Mortality

Once the challenges of survival are met at infant and early childhood ages, mortality reaches its lowest point in the life cycle. After later childhood, however, the risks mount again and continue to progress until old age consumes us all.

Fatal *injuries* constitute the leading causes of death during the late teens and early adulthood. Most prominent among these injuries are motor vehicle crashes (frequently resulting from the driver's being intoxicated), but violent deaths (including homicide and suicide) and other unintentional injuries (such as falls, poisonings, drownings, and burns) involve significant numbers. These causes are more predominant for males than females among teenagers and young adults.

During a woman's reproductive period (typically mid-teen ages to late forties), the childbearing process introduces mortal risks that add to the probabilities of death from other causes. *Maternal mortality* refers to deaths to women as a result of conditions associated with pregnancy and childbearing. In developing nations, where childbearing is more frequent and extends over a longer period of the reproductive ages than in developed nations, maternal mortality can be exceptionally high.

Worldwide, we estimate over 300 maternal deaths for every 100,000 births. This is about the level experienced in countries such as England, Switzerland, and the United States during the 1920s and 1930s. But maternal deaths have become much rarer in developed countries today. In northern America generally, they stand at about 10 per 100,000 births. Meanwhile, maternal mortality attains high levels in most developing areas. In South Asia reports of over 600 maternal deaths per 100,000 births are common (Kamel, 1983).

The general factor that most determines maternal mortality is delayed treatment of obstetric complications (Thaddeus and Maine, 1990). Women often delay the decision to seek care. If they do seek it, their arrival at a health facility may also be delayed; and once at a health facility, the provision of adequate care may be delayed. The long distances from residences to a health facility imposes a severe problem. The known cost of services can also be a barrier. Moreover, the poor quality of medical attention at a facility may deter a woman from going there and, once there, may involve extensive waiting for treatment as well as unqualified staff and shortages of drugs and supplies.

Women in reproductive ages, especially in developing nations, are subject to death from all causes, not just maternal ones. Kamel (1983) reports that, among women 25 to 34 years of age, less than 2 percent of deaths in the United States and Australia were from maternal causes, and that even in developing areas maternal deaths were less than one-fourth of all female deaths at those ages. In a more intensive study of Menoufia, Egypt and Bali, Indonesia, Fortney et al. (1987) found that about 23 percent of deaths to women in the reproductive ages was caused by complications of pregnancy, childbirth, and the puerperium. The remaining deaths were distributed among infectious and parasitic diseases, circulatory complications, cancers, and other more common causes of death.

Generally speaking, mortality rates climb steadily as adults age. At working ages in both developed and developing countries, the incidence of accident mortality declines and the incidence of cardiovascular and cancer mortality increases. In recent years the substantial attention given to everyday practices of good nutrition, exercise, rest, and avoidance of tobacco and alcohol has succeeded in restricting many deaths from heart and cancer causes and enabled many persons to survive to older ages.

As older ages are reached, both the prospects of death and its medical causes change. As life expectancy gets pushed up in most countries, the chances of surviving to ages 65 and over are increased. In developed countries generally in the years close to 1980, about three-fourths of the men and over four-fifths of the women survived to age 65 (Myers, 1989). For those who got to that age, the average additional number of years of life was between 12 and 15 for men and between 15 and 19 for women. Even those who attained age 85 could expect 4 to 6 more years of life.

In the case of developing countries, not only do fewer persons survive to older ages but continued survival at older ages is also lower than in developed nations. For example, in 1981 Swedish females who reached age 65 could expect 18 more years of life on the average. In contrast, Peninsular Malaysian females who attained age 65 in 1980 had an average of 14 more years of life and Indonesian females at the same age in 1976 had an average of 11 more years to live (Nam and Pagtolun-an, 1988).

The pattern of causes of death is different at the older than at the younger and middle ages, and even at older ages it is not the same between developed and developing areas. Persons who have reached older ages have often successfully combatted diseases at younger ages but are now subject to the fatal ailments of later years. Persons in areas undergoing development experience different environmental and cultural conditions from those in developed nations.

As a result, in each case the causes of death reflect the prevailing mortal risks existing when people attain old age.

Rosenberg et al. (1991) determined that the leading underlying causes of death among the elderly in the United States were heart diseases (42 percent), cancers (21 percent), and stroke (9 percent). Multiple cause-of-death analysis revealed that the chances of dying from these diseases were often influenced by other medical conditions. For instance, the presence of diabetes increased the prospect of dying from a heart disease, although this interaction was more likely to occur at younger than older adult ages.

In Japan, cardiovascular diseases were also the leading cause of death for both men and women at ages 65 and over in 1980. Likewise, cancers were the second leading cause of death. In contrast, respiratory tuberculosis and other infectious and parasitic diseases rivaled cardiovascular diseases as the main cause of death among those 65–69 in the Philippines in 1980. While heart ailments predominated at ages 70 and over, the infectious and parasitic diseases were more likely to be killers than cancers among Filipinos (Nam and Pagtolun-an, 1988).

Differential Mortality

When we compare categories of people with different characteristics in terms of their mortality chances, significant variations often appear. Some of these variations change over time while others remain fairly constant. Patterns of *differential mortality* are of interest in population analysis because they indicate inequalities in life chances that require explanation.

While many variables are used to examine patterns of differential mortality, we will discuss three here as receiving heightened attention in the research literature. They are mortality disparities by socioeconomic status, gender, and race and ethnicity. Although most of the analysis on these topics is highly descriptive in nature, there are also attempts to explain the differences and to consider what factors could alter the differentials.

The significance of *socioeconomic differentials* in mortality is that people who have fewer resources and lower social and economic standing are observed to have greater death risks and lower life expectancy. Ruzicka (1989) points to a wide range of socioeconomic variables associated with survival in infancy and early childhood. These include family income, quality of housing, household amenities, education, occupation, caste, and other traditional status ranks.

Guzman (1989) has shown that variations in infant mortality rates by social class (as measured by occupation of the household head) in three Latin American countries were maintained between 1970 and 1980 even though infant mortality was declining during that period. Classifying his occupational data into five categories, he showed that the lowest status group had an infant mortality rate twice as high as that of the highest status group.

Feldman et al. (1989) discovered, among men and women ages 55 to 84 in the United States from 1971 to 1984, not only that a lower level of education was associated with an elevated risk of death but also that reductions in mortality since 1960 were more rapid for the better-educated groups, thus widening the differentials. The medical cause of death most related to the change was heart disease. Better-educated persons were more successful at reducing their risks of death from that cause than were the less well-educated. Variations in health behaviors linked to educational level are suspected of contributing to the explanation.

Lynge (1984) also found that social inequalities in mortality patterns persisted in Europe in recent decades while overall death rates were declining. In England and Wales and in France, infant mortality was two to three times as high in families where the father had a low-status occupation as among those where the father's occupational status was high. In France and in Scandinavian countries, mortality was more than twice as high among unskilled workers as among professionals for men in the 40–55 age range.

The clear indication is that the forces that have led to a reduction in mortality overall during recent times have not been universal, and in most cases have not diminished socioeconomic disparities in survival.

Another area in which differential mortality has been studied relates to *disparities between the sexes (genders)*. It is the typical pattern that females have lower mortality than males at every age in the life cycle. The main exception is in less developed countries where the high rate of childbearing leads to excessive maternal mortality. As a result, mortality rates are often higher for women during the principal reproductive ages. In such places, when the fertility level declines and maternal mortality is lessened, the death rate for women in the reproductive age falls below that of men in comparable ages.

Lopez and Ruzicka (1983) identify three sets of factors that can be associated with sex differences in mortality. First, they list explanations dealing with biological variations between the sexes. To the extent that genetic and constitutional differences exist between males and females, these can contribute to varying mortality risks. Such factors would be especially pertinent to understanding why certain causes of death are most common in one or the other sex (e.g., deaths from complications of childbirth for women and prostate cancer for men). However, even if we examine such common causes of death as cardiovascular disease, men and women appear to be quite different with respect to heart ailments (Kolata, 1987). Women who have had children are observed to have wider coronary arteries. In studies of monkeys on a high fat diet, researchers found that the females tend to produce more high-density lipoproteins (HDL, which carries cholesterol away from blood vessels) than do the males. Hormonal composition is believed to favor women at the period in the life cycle when coronary heart disease first becomes a great risk. Yet women who have a heart attack are twice as likely as men to die within sixty days.

A second set of factors that may explain sex differentials in mortality are sociocultural in nature. Traditional practices in many societies give an advantage to one sex or the other. In fact, such practices are more often detrimental to females. Male children in developing societies are given superior health care and are fed better than are female children (Nag, 1991). On the other hand, women are more likely to be protected from hazardous activities than are men.

A third set of factors has to do with variations in life-styles. Behaviors that have distinguished males from females include practices of smoking, drinking, drug use, dietary habits, health care, and exercise regimens. Retherford (1975) estimated that half the sex difference in deaths at adult ages in the United States in 1962 could be accounted for by differences in smoking habits. In fact, three-fourths of the increase in those differences between 1910 and 1962 was attributable to smoking patterns. The later adoption of smoking by women than men in the United States may just mean that the mortal consequences of smoking (involving some time lag) will be more rapid for women than men in the years ahead. With regard to health care, women visit a doctor more frequently than men; although reporting more illnesses, women are less likely to have fatal diseases.

Still another area of differential mortality concerns *race and ethnic distinctions.* Levels of both infant and adult mortality vary among groups categorized by such distinctions. For example, infant mortality rates in the United States are twice as high for black as for white babies, at an intermediate level for American Indians and Puerto Ricans, at levels comparable to whites for those of Mexican, Cuban, Central or South American, and Filipino background, and slightly lower than for whites for Chinese and Japanese Americans. Yet no single factor explains infant mortality differentials among racial and ethnic groups. The risk factors associated with infant mortality in general do not have the same relative importance for all race/ethnic groups. For instance, when we compare infant mortality for Mexican-Americans (moderately low) and blacks (high), we find that the former actually have a higher percentage with inadequate prenatal care and lower maternal education, whereas the latter have a higher percentage of infants with low birth weight, of unmarried mothers, and of mothers who smoke. On the other hand, lower maternal education and poor measures of prenatal care are characteristic of Central and South American persons even though their infants have more favorable infant survival prospects (Eberstein, 1991).

The picture that emerges indicates a complex network of factors that account for race and ethnic variations. Keep in mind that there is variability within as well as between groups, and that we are talking about average group differences. At the same time, certain risk factors (e.g., mothers who are young, unmarried, and who smoke) are persistent across groups. Conditions providing an unsatisfactory social environment for mothers are more likely to increase the risk of infant death, and mothers who engage in medically hazardous behaviors, such as smoking, do likewise. Racial and ethnic groups more prone to experiencing these characteristics are, therefore, more apt to have higher infant mortality rates.

Race and ethnic differences in mortality extend beyond infancy. Those who survive the early years of life are subject to varying risks of death in later years. The dominant medical causes of death at these older ages have greater impact on some groups than on others. When we compare black and white adults in the United States, we note that death rates are consistently higher for blacks (except at the oldest ages); the incidence and prevalence of every major cause of death is higher for them as well. One can relate less satisfactory social conditions (lower socioeconomic levels and poorer residential environments), resulting family instabilities, and more life-threatening behaviors (poorer dietary practices and greater substance abuse along with higher probabilities of violence) for blacks than for whites to these disparities in causes of death.

Varying characteristics of race and ethnic groups linked to differing mortality chances are sometimes described as being reinforced by cultural practices of each group that either isolate one group from another or sanction certain types of risky behaviors. At the same time, other descriptions emphasize the barriers to healthier lives erected by outside forces confronting some groups more than others.

THE STAGES OF MORBIDITY AND MORTALITY

The previous discussion has highlighted the critical concepts and measures relevant to an understanding of morbidity and mortality changes and differences in human populations. We have paid some attention to these phenomena as they typically occur.

Since our examples were drawn haphazardly from a variety of geographic and temporal situations, we could not obtain any sense of continuity. But the story of morbidity and mortality change unfolds historically, as indicated from our understanding of mortality transitions and cycles. What, then, are the patterns of factors that accompany long-term and short-term statistical trends?

Dividing history into four stages—pretransition, early transition, late transition, and posttransition—we will attempt to offer an overview of the changing prospects of life and death in societies. In some cases our illustrations will be of contemporary situations; in others, we will hark back to past points in time, but we will try always to keep the perspective of the evolving transition. Intermeshed with stories of the factors that routinely influence the survival of people will be accounts of those that sometimes shock the world and drain emotions.

Pretransition Stage

Zinsser (1934) surmised that there is "a good deal of evidence that bacteria became capable of producing infections millions of years ago, and there is no reason to doubt that man from the very beginning suffered from infectious disease," and "it is certain that epidemics were prevalent thousands of years before Christ" (p. 106).

Infectious and parasitic diseases, combined with the ravages of wars, natural disasters, and limitations of food productivity, kept life expectancy low for many centuries. Early death was a major factor in crippling the efforts of royalty and military leaders to establish and maintain nation-states. While we are often introduced to the political chicanery that removed rulers of these governments, we may not be given a vivid enough sense of the impact of diseases on their turnover. In writing of the decline of the Roman Empire, Cartwright (1972) tells us, "By her contacts with distant lands and peoples, Rome opened her gates to pestilence." Plagues returned again and again and created rapid changes among both leaders and the public.

Proceeding into the Middle Ages, we discover that survival conditions were not unlike those of the Roman period. Expectation of life at birth was no more than 30 to 35 years during the entire feudal period. Very slow decreases in mortality rates were estimated, but "ravaging epidemics played havoc with populations to a degree probably unknown even to prehistoric man" (Acsadi and Nemeskeri, 1970). Combined with wars and occasional famines, epidemics often contributed to an increase in an already high level of mortality.

The inability to conquer fatal diseases carried on well into the seventeenth century and stifled the chances for any significant rise in life expectancy. The search for new lands to conquer and occupy usually meant also that disease was being spread to new areas and new populations. The celebration of Columbus' discovery of America and the related opening of new opportunities for Europeans has to be matched with the severe impact it had on the Indian people then residing in the New World.

Most Indian tribes living during the ninth through the fifteenth centuries had life expectancies not greatly different from Europeans of comparable periods. But the ailments that took a toll of Indians before Columbus' arrival did not include those most common in European countries. Indians experienced many types of parasitic, viral, and diet-related diseases and may have also been subjected to malaria, yellow fever, tuberculosis, and syphilis. But Columbus and his followers from several areas of Europe and Africa introduced smallpox, cholera, measles, diptheria, some influenzas, typhoid fever, and the plague (Thornton, 1987). The inability to cope physiologically with these new diseases served to decimate the Indians and reduce their population size greatly.

Episodes of sickness continued on the European mainland for some time. In fact, it was not until the 1740s that a sustained reduction in mortality took place, indicating the beginning of the mortality transition. Meanwhile, however, various mortality cycles ran their course and then later reappeared. Length of life was extremely uncertain.

The establishment of the American colonies provided new opportunities for Europeans, but sickness and high risks of death were still commonplace. In the late sixteenth and early seventeenth centuries, colonial life in Jamestown included a "daily roll call to ascertain how many had died, how many were sick, and how many were left to work or to guard the settlement." These reports were funneled back to the London Company in England. "Mortality, in fact, was so consistently and shockingly high that the Company dared not make the figures public." Three-fifths of the original settlers of the colony had died within less than a year. Famine and fatal diseases were implicated as causes (Cassedy, 1969).

Cotton Mather, a pastor and spiritual leader in the Massachusetts Bay Colony, was obliged to keep records during smallpox and other epidemics. Cassedy (1969) tells us, "In 1702 he [Mather] barely found time to record in his diary that several of his own children had died (of smallpox) and that his wife had succumbed to another disease after a long illness." This episode was typical in earlier periods in Asia and Africa (see Box 5.2).

These historical episodes of high mortality preceding the mortality transition have their counterparts in accounts of survival conditions in now-developing nations as they experience similar threats to life in the pretransition phase. Such nations include those where significant mortality declines took place in recent times as well as those which can be regarded as still awaiting a survival breakthrough.

The dreadful survival conditions of countries in the pretransition stage has been experienced in modern times. In the case of sub-Saharan Africa, Ewbank (1988) indicates, "Because of harsh environments, low levels of income and shortages of trained health personnel, African populations suffer from many diseases which have been brought under control or were never a problem in higher income countries."

Today, sub-Saharan Africa is undergoing some improvements in survival. While most countries in the region have exceedingly high mortality levels, declines in both infant and childhood mortality and adult mortality have occurred in some areas. Yet further declines are problematic because of the many threats to the health of the population, a condition characteristic of pretransition societies.

In whatever time period and in whatever area of the world, societies in the pretransition stage have suffered greatly from high mortality associated with infectious and parasitic diseases and unhealthful diets. There are few places in the world today where populations remain in the pretransition stage, but even movement into the early transition would not have alleviated some of the harsher conditions of life under which people suffered.

Early Transition Stage

While the first mortality transition occured in Europe, the beginning of the sustained decline in the death rate is difficult to date and the progress of reductions was uneven (Riley, 1989). We can regard the mortality transition as beginning in the seventeenth century. It produced an accelerated decline in the 1740s, which continued until the 1820s. It then leveled off until the 1870s, when it resumed its downward course until the present.

We can thus place the early transition of mortality as taking place from the early 1700s to the 1820s. Doubtlessly, the first downward surge resulted from control over some epidemic diseases. The plateau that later existed can be at-

BOX 5.2 High Mortality in Early Asia and Africa

High mortality persisted in many parts of Southeast Asia well through the nineteenth century. Short life expectancies were expected in countries like Indonesia, and even the protection of high status did not guarantee long life. Thomas Stamford Raffles, England's lieutenant-governor of Java (in Indonesia) and later founder of Singapore, spent many years in that region, where he raised a family but saw its members succumb to the ravages of disease. His first wife died in Java, and his children by his second wife suffered from fatal infant and childhood ailments. Wurtzburg (1986) quotes from Raffles' letter to a friend in 1821 as follows: "We have this morning buried our beloved Charlotte. Poor Marsden was carried to the grave not ten days before, and within the last six months we have lost our three eldest children; guess what must be our distress."

The people of Africa had lived at a subsistence level for centuries (Ransford, 1983). Thiey were continually exposed to tropical infections transmitted by mosquitos, tsetse flies, or snails. Over time, they developed immunities to these diseases, but three forces helped maintain a dreadful health environment. First, the diets of these people were highly deficient in the necessary nutrients for a healthy life. For example, insufficient protein resulted in a disease called kwashiorkor, which most affected children by producing a general swelling of the body and protrusion of the belly, together with sparseness and reddish coloring of the hair. Other diet deficiencies and inadequate supplies of food in some areas led to hunger and starvation or at least stunting (inadequate bodily growth). Second, polluted environment resulted in illnesses from parasites such as bilharzia, hook worm infection, and dysentery. Third, the European colonization of these backward nations introduced the residents to new infectious diseases, such as cholera, syphilis, gonorrhea, influenza, measles, and pneumonia.

tributed to the rise of cities, where unsuitable living conditions and overcrowding facilitated infections (Riley, 1989).

Some controversy about the effective factors in this early decline still exists. McNeill (1976) believed that populations that survived epidemics developed resistance to many infections. McKeown (1976) argued that better evidence supported a finding that greater food supplies, improved nutrition, and attendant better living standards were crucial. Kunitz (1983) elaborated McKeown's argument by specifying that:

> ...mortality continued to be high in the peripheral nations where...epidemics continued to be more frequent than in northwest Europe. These included louse-borne typhus, which was ideally suited to the conditions found in eastern Europe and the Balkans. The shift in the disease patterns was ragged and did

> not occur at precisely the same time throughout Europe. Nonetheless, the great pandemics had waned in the peripheral nations, and the major determinant of death had become the living conditions of an impoverished peasantry. In the core nations, where the quality of rural life was higher, mortality dropped to relatively low levels, while in the cities it remained high so long as poverty, crowding, hazardous working conditions, and poor sanitation continued to be common.

Not all analysts agree that human factors precipitated the mortality decline. Perrenoud (1984) summarizes the views of some that natural factors may have played a role, including climatic conditions and the minimum presence of sunspots during the time of the early mortality decline. Still the prevailing view is that the reduction of epidemics was the paramount explanation for the falling mortality levels in the first transition stage, and that economic, political, and social changes were mainly responsible.

The mortality transition proceeded in the United States at a period comparable to that in Europe. Colonial populations had very high levels of mortality, and the decline appeared in different parts of North America at different times. Malaria had been hyperendemic in the region, and smallpox and yellow fever epidemics were frequent. Dysentery was also a substantial problem (Kunitz, 1983). There is evidence that by the end of the colonial period epidemics depending on dense populations had declined as a result of changed living standards.

The improving health conditions in the United States were partly arrested because of the diseased state of many immigrants who came to America during the nineteenth century. In addition to bringing diseases with them on the journey to the New World, they usually ended up in slums of port cities, where their crowded environment generated further illnesses and often death (Cassedy, 1986).

In England and Wales, the lowered mortality continued well through the nineteenth century and into the twentieth century. But the factors that sustained the decline shifted in importance as time went on. McKeown (1976) determined that improved hygienic conditions contributed substantially to reductions in mortality from the mid-1800s. These included purification of water, efficient sewage disposal, and better food hygiene. But a more productive agriculture continued to be an important element in the mortality transition. Reductions in respiratory tuberculosis, whooping cough, measles, scarlet fever, and diphtheria all took place long before medical interventions were used. The rise of public health methods, with their attention to better environmental conditions and improved personal behaviors, reduced both the acquisition of diseases and the deaths of those who contracted them.

In the United States, from the Civil War to World War I, mortality levels sloped downward even before the public health movement took hold, but the development of public health gave impetus to the reduction (Kunitz, 1984). Moreover, the post–Civil War decline in disease was heaviest for those specific named illnesses (e.g., measles and smallpox), whereas only later did the nonspecific pneumonia-diarrhea complex come under control.

The epidemiological transition in the United States from infections to degenerative diseases and diseases of human origin during the late nineteenth century owed little to medical progress, sanitation measures, or organized health services. Rather, it was due to improvements in living standards, personal hygiene, nutrition, housing, and the recession of certain diseases, according to Omran (1977).

In New York City in 1866, tuberculosis was the leading cause of death. By 1900, pneumonia-influenza-bronchitis had surpassed it as a cause-of-death category. By 1930, heart diseases had become the leading cause, ahead of pneumonia-influenza-bronchitis; cancers had become the third-ranked cause; and tuberculosis had fallen to sixth place (Omran, 1977).

Around the globe, both the epidemiologic and mortality transitions have been evolving. In Third World countries still in the early transitional stage, some factors expedite the mortality decline and others retard it. What speeds up the decline is the ready availability of knowledge and methods for mortality reduction that took the developed part of the world many decades to create. These could be transferred without delay if donor countries or agencies would offer them and countries where they are needed would accept them. The sharp reduction in malaria in Ceylon (now Sri Lanka) after World War II through the use of pesticides to control breeding mosquitos is one example. The several programs to make available antibacterial medicines is another. But knowledge of how to cope with disease and the acquisition of material to combat it are only part of the solution. In now-developed nations, discovery of knowledge and methods of disease control went hand-in-hand with the building of a health and medical infrastructure that produced hospitals, clinics, and medical personnel sufficient to deal with most existing health problems. In Third World countries that have made their way through the early transitional phase, most of that infrastructure is lacking and the costs of erecting it for the needs of large populations are enormous.

Late Transition Stage

Sustained declines in mortality have brought now-developed nations to the point where it is reasonable to expect a baby to survive infancy and childhood and continue on to adulthood, even though that is far from a certainty and is more likely for some categories of the population than for others. Developed nations have also offered people who reach adulthood a better chance for attaining much older ages than was true of their counterparts who lived during the earlier transition period.

According to Omran (1977), different forms of the epidemiologic transition brought countries to the later stage. In Western societies, such as those of western Europe, Canada, and the United States, the transition evolved in a *classical* way, through a slow and gradual process over a long period of time in which economic development, technological innovation, the rise of sanitation and public health, and later medical contributions to curative disease took hold. In Japan and eastern European countries, the transition was more *accelerated*, with the accumulated knowledge of the Western countries being transferred to these areas, permitting declines in mortality over a shorter period of time. In Third World countries that have made substantial progress toward the later transitional stage, a *delayed* pattern has been apparent in which the widespread use of insecticides, antibiotics, and organized disease eradication programs brought about sharp declines that could not be sustained until low mortality levels were reached. The death rate in these countries leveled off until other forces could produce more fundamental changes in factors that improve health conditions.

With infectious diseases decreasingly contributing to death, especially at early ages, nations in the late mortality transition stage were more and more characterized by degenerative diseases that took their toll mainly at adult ages. Among causes of death in the United States in 1970, diseases of the heart accounted for 38 percent of deaths, cancers another 17 percent, and strokes 11 percent. Together, they totaled two-thirds of the underlying causes. A significant proportion of the remaining causes were not infectious and parasitic (e.g., accidents, diabetes, cirrhosis of the liver).

One could argue that these causes of death reflected progress in life expectancy—now one could live long enough to experience them. Lopez (1990b), assessing the statistics on death in developed countries in 1987, described them in somewhat different terms. "Viewed from the standpoint of competing risks from different causes, roughly 1 in 3 newborn infants would, on average, eventually die from all forms of heart disease....The chances of dying from cancer are about 1 in 5...and from a stroke about 1 in 7. The risks of succumbing to one of the respiratory diseases or of dying a violent death are similar, being roughly 5% in each case."

The pace of change in the later mortality transition has been similar but not exactly the same for the different countries involved. For example, in the early 1950s Japan had an infant mortality rate (51 per 1,000) roughly two and one-half times that of Sweden and twice that of the United States. By the late 1980s Japan had matched the infant mortality rate of Sweden (both at 6 per 1,000) after falling below the rate of the United States (which by 1988 had only dropped to 10 per 1,000). Similarly, in the early 1950s life expectancies at birth for Sweden, the United States, and Japan were 72, 69, and 64, respectively. By the late 1980s they stood at just under 77 for Sweden, 75 for the United States, and just over 77 for Japan (Nam and Pagtolun-an, 1988).

Japan's life expectancy at birth for males caught up to and then surpassed that of Sweden between 1972 and 1982. How was that accomplished? First of all, the greater relative reductions in mortality for Japan occurred primarily at the older ages. At the younger ages, Sweden's gain matched that of Japan. Thus one has to look to developments at the older ages to explain the overall greater improvement in life expectancy. Inspection of cause-of-death patterns offers some clues. Although the rate of cerebrovascular disease was much lower in Sweden, the rate of ischemic heart disease was much lower in Japan. Rates of lung cancer and colorectal cancer were higher in Sweden, but the rate of stomach cancer was higher in Japan. The more rapid reduction in mortality in Japan than in Sweden was due to a more favorable trend in diseases of the circulatory system, especially among those 55 and over (Yanagishita and Guralnik, 1988). Further investigation into risk behaviors of the affected populations would probably reveal which of them were most responsible. One would have to look at smoking habits, diet, exercise regimens, and other individual behaviors, as well as external environmental influences and such factors as Japan's emphasis on public health programs.

The fact is that females have led males through the later stage of the mortality transition. Life expectancy between the sexes widened considerably as mortality fell to low levels. Only a small part of the widening gap could be attributed to biological factors—the genetic, hormonal, and physical advantages that females may have that give them greater resistance to the major killer diseases. The more substantial gains for women than for men were due to social, behavioral, and cultural variables favoring women. The traditional roles of men that put greater stress on them, their greater exposure to motor vehicle and industrial hazards, and their more intense smoking habits all eventuated in earlier male deaths (Lopez and Ruzicka, 1983). Yet both men and women improved their survival prospects as the mortality transition moved to the late stage. The more fundamental changes in societies that reached that stage—rising standards of living, health promotion in its many forms, and emerging preventive as well as curative medicine—more than overcame what risks to life were still posed. Since women enjoyed the benefits of the changes more than men, this only accelerated women's life expectancies more quickly.

Clearly, such practices as reducing the intake of dietary fats and salts, avoiding obesity, exercising, sleeping and eating regularly, using alcohol moderately, and avoiding tobacco have had a major effect on life-styles in many developed countries. In developed countries where improvements in such areas were not experienced, as in eastern Europe in recent years, gains in life expectancy were slowed considerably. As a result of increases in alcohol consumption and smoking, deterioration in diets, more accidents, and growing pollution, mortality rates for men in eastern European countries leveled off or increased (Mosley and Cowley, 1991). Hence, economic development alone cannot account for the transition to low mortality levels and their maintenance.

Posttransition Stage

For populations that have already moved through the epidemiologic and mortality transitions, what lies ahead? Does low overall mortality characterized by chronic and degenerative disease largely among the elderly describe adequately the state of survival prospects? Have morbidity and mortality trends leveled off in a way that suggests no major changes in the risks of death in the future? On a number of issues sprouting from these kinds of questions, debates continue to be aired. Our attention below will be given to several of them: Are there stages beyond the traditional end of the transition? Are cause-of-death structures becoming more or less complex? Does longer life mean better health for older people? Will the role of public health in affecting survival expand or diminish? Will sex differences in mortality widen, remain the same, or narrow? How long can persons be expected to live and what can we project for future mortality?

Rogers and Hackenberg (1987) claim that the classical epidemiologic transition was based on the premise that early shifts in disease patterns were due to improved nutrition, rising standards of living, and changes in the nature of some diseases, while later shifts in disease patterns resulted from medical progress and public health programs. The story of the epidemiologic transition seems to end there. But Rogers and Hackenberg argue that, although degenerative diseases and diseases of human origin continue to dominate causes of death, they are influenced less over time by medicine and public health and more by individual behaviors and life-styles.

As a consequence, they go on to say, we have edged into a new stage of the transition characterized by interventions to deal with risky behaviors and life-styles. While public health programs may still be important, their significance lies in their ability to influence individual practices and not, as in the past, to combat disease by affecting the external environment.

Rogers and Hackenberg label this new epidemiologic transition phase the *hybristic stage* (referring to a term meaning excessive self-confidence bordering on arrogance). Living the "good life" for many means satisfying the senses. Smoking and alcohol provide release from inner tensions and portray relaxed forms of enjoyment. Eating heartily not only fills the palate with exquisite tastes but builds a substantial body. Taking drugs, engaging in sex without genital protection, and driving vehicles with abandon are thrilling. Yet they all introduce a new or expanded set of risks to life that challenge our life expectancy. These modern individual behaviors and life-styles have altered the chances of particular causes of death—lung cancer, cirrhosis of the liver, ischemic heart disease, AIDS, and auto fatalities.

Behaviors and life-styles in recent years have cast a different light on mortality risks. Manton and Myers (1987) have examined causes of death at the older ages in a cohort framework in an effort to identify the changing relative contributions of cancer, stroke, and heart disease to mortality. They also looked at the way multiple causes modify the picture. They found that stroke and heart disease, whose rates have been falling, declined more rapidly as underlying causes than they have as contributory multiple causes, suggesting that we are likely to witness an increased prevalence of multiple chronic conditions at death. At the same time, this multiple causation occurs at later ages, indicating delays in the progression of the disease processes.

One conclusion they reach is that the prevalence of major circulatory diseases is likely to rise at very advanced ages as life expectancy increases. As a consequence, we cannot expect older people in the future to live healthy lives until the time comes for them to die. Rather, there will probably be complex morbid patterns at advanced ages that describe the trials of living at older ages. Medical interventions may increasingly keep people alive to later ages, but may not succeed in coping with some diseases which have had their origins earlier in life and which handicap people without killing them immediately.

This issue of the state of health that accompanies longer life has engaged numerous students of mortality trends in recent years. Verbrugge (1984) keyed the discussion when she presented evidence that, as persons got older, morbidity increased while mortality decreased for most killer diseases (diabetes, diseases of the heart, hypertension, cerebrovascular diseases, arteriosclerosis, bronchitis/emphysema/asthma, and hernia). She went on to discover that other diseases may have increased in their incidence but are not as fatal, partly because of modern medical care that eliminates the complications of terminal infections.

Some experts, such as Fries (1987), have argued that reductions in risk factors and improvements in medical treatment will be postponed to ages closer to death; as a result, the period of morbidity in older life will be compressed into a short time span prior to death. The debate between Fries (and those who agree with him) and others who adopt the position put forth by Manton and Myers and by Verbrugge seems to center on the question of the duration and degree of disability associated with longer life (Haan et al., 1991). A number of specialists in this area (e.g., Kaplan, 1991) share the judgment of Guralnik (1991) that "a compression of morbidity may not be possible unless there is a reduction in the high rate of disability prior to death in the large segment of the future older population who will die at the oldest ages." According to these researchers, such a reduction is not likely to take place. Still others believe that additional information about morbidity patterns at older ages is needed before we can answer the question definitively (Manton and Tolley, 1991; Olshansky at al., 1991).

A related issue is the responsiveness of the public health sector in dealing with illness among the aging population. Breslow (1990) has written about the "reconstitution of public health" in order to address this and other health problems. A shift in orientation from disease control to health promotion for all segments of the population is needed, he argues.

Such a shift could provide greater equality in health conditions for sectors of the public. Racial and ethnic minorities with higher rates of morbidity and lower life expectancies would benefit from more equal treatment, both from public health and from public and private medicine and health insurance. The disparity between the sexes in health and life expectancy could also be reduced.

In fact, changes in individual behaviors and life-styles that make them more similar for different categories of people would contribute even more to parity in survival. One has only to consider that the tendency of women to smoke more and men less in recent decades, allowing for the time lag between initiation of smoking and its fatal consequences, will slow down the relative gain in longer life for women compared to that for men and may even result in some narrowing of the sex differential (Nathanson and Lopez, 1987).

Some persons have contemplated extensions of life span (the highest age to which one could possibly live) as a result of potential discoveries by geneticists of genes that control the aging process and how they can be manipulated. Although the rapid gains in molecular biological research place that prospect in the realm of possibility now, whereas it was considered in the realm of science fiction in earlier decades, it is not likely that such breakthroughs would significantly alter morbidity and mortality patterns in the near future.

Bulatao et al. (1989) have constructed a set of mortality projections for all countries through the year 2100 that is based on "reasonable, though inevitably somewhat arbitrary, assumptions." Alternative assumptions about maximum attainable life expectancy are made, but they do not include heroic assumptions about changes in life span.

Their findings show the expected further declines in infant mortality and continued rises in life expectancy for the less developed parts of the world. These are consistent with trends seen before in countries that have traversed the mortality transition. In more developed nations, a continuation of low infant mortality and a slowdown in the increase in life expectancy is anticipated. This is likewise in line with expectations from transition theory.

Like all estimates and projections, these are as reliable as the assumptions upon which they are based. The authors themselves state,

> The critical assumption in this exercise, that future trends will resemble what we know of past trends, will undoubtedly not be universally true. For instance, the spread of Human Immunodeficiency Virus infection is not reflected in the data, and therefore is not factored into the derived procedures....Other uncertainties regarding future mortality trends also exist, such as uncertainty about the ultimate limits to life expectancy.

The task of mortality researchers will be to identify facts behind the present uncertainties and factor them in so that we can become aware of future survival patterns.

Chapter Highlights

1. Every population has a distribution of frailty (from the very weak to the very strong), of morbidity (from the very healthy to the very unhealthy), and of disability (unlimited to exceedingly limited physical and/or mental handicaps). These distributions, along with human behavioral patterns and social institutional forces, create the bases for exposure of populations to the risks of death that threaten us all.
2. Death is best understood as the end point in a process in which many types of risks are posed to life. The nature of these risks and their variations within populations are exceedingly complex.
3. With regard to cessation of life, death is the term applied to individuals and mortality the term applied to aggregate populations.

4. The chances of death and mortality vary greatly over the life cycle. Risks are highest at the youngest and oldest ages and lowest for those in the age range from late childhood to early adulthood.
5. A variety of additional measures of mortality are used to indicate risks at different stages of life. Some measures are based on period or cross-sectional data, such as the crude death rate and age-specific death rates. Other measures are based on cohort or life-cycle data, such as the infant mortality rate and life expectancy (which is derived from life tables).
6. Life span refers to the maximum number of years a person can be expected to live under the most ideal circumstances, and it has remained constant for at least centuries. Life expectancy, on the other hand, has increased in most populations as death rates were reduced.
7. The epidemiologic transition describes the way in which cause-of-death patterns in populations have changed over periods of time. As countries proceed through stages of development, the predominant causes of death tend to shift from infectious and parasitic diseases to chronic and degenerative diseases.
8. Mortality transitions, from high to low levels of death, have been associated with changes in nutrition, standards of living, medical advances, and the evolution of public health programs. In nations that have completed the traditional stages of the mortality transition, risks of death are increasingly related to dangerous behaviors and life-styles.
9. Infant survival is strongly affected by prenatal care, birth weight, and postnatal care, but there are numerous other factors that intertwine with these to determine the chances of infant death.
10. At older ages, heart diseases, cancers, and stroke are the major medical causes of death, but there are numerous factors that interrelate with these to affect the chances of dying in the later years of life.
11. Mortality risks can vary among socioeconomic groups, between the sexes, and among racial and ethnic categories, but the nature of such differences can fluctuate according to stages of the mortality transition and during mortality cycles.
12. The future of mortality trends and differences is uncertain because of unknowns about the continued course of past challenges to life as well as the possible appearance of new challenges, and unknowns about the ability of humans to deal effectively with these challenges.

Discussion Questions

1. The United States is reported to have a higher infant mortality rate than most developed countries. What do you think are the reasons for the inferior position of the United States in this regard?

2. Examine the death certificate shown in this chapter (Figure 5.2). What items of information would you consider as important additions to those that are already included?
3. Some persons are optimistic that the limits on life span can be lifted and that humans can live to a much older age than has the oldest person in the world today. What would you consider to be the prospects of that happening? What would be the advantages and disadvantages of attaining extremely old ages?
4. Which human behaviors and life-styles do you regard as most threatening for human survival? Would communities and societies be better off if these behaviors and life-styles were changed radically, or are the satisfactions that people get from them too great to eliminate?
5. What would it take for mortality differentials due to socioeconomic status, sex, and race and ethnicity to disappear?
6. Mortality has been described as the aggregate manifestation of individual deaths. Compare and contrast these two concepts in terms of understanding their population significance.

Suggested Readings

Rothschild, Henry R., ed. 1981. *Biocultural Aspects of Disease.* San Diego, Calif.: Academic Press. A comprehensive exploration of the variations of disease patterns that exist among varied groups around the world.

Zinsser, Hans. 1934. *Rats, Lice, and History.* Boston: Little, Brown. A classic treatise, told in a scholarly but humorous vein, about the scourge of typhus in history and the ability of society to deal with it.

United Nations. 1982. *Levels and Trends of Mortality Since 1950.* New York: United Nations. A somewhat outdated but useful review of the trends and related factors in the various phases of the mortality transition during the latter part of the twentieth century.

Lopez, Alan D., and Lado T. Ruzicka, eds. 1983. *Sex Differentials in Mortality; Trends, Determinants, and Consequences.* Canberra: Australian National University. All you ever wanted to know about how and why males and females have different life risks and changes in them over time.

Mosley, W. Henry, and Peter Cowley. 1991. "The Challenge of World Health." *Population Bulletin* 46:4. A good account of contemporary worldwide conditions of health and mortality and the forces that shape them.

References

Acsadi, Gy., and J. Nemeskeri. 1970. *History of Human Life Span and Mortality.* Budapest: Akademiai Kiado.

Adams, Patricia F., and Veronica Benson. 1990. "Current Estimates from the National Health Interview Survey, 1989." *Vital and Health Statistics.* Series 10, no. 176. Hyattsville, Md.: National Center for Health Statistics.

Antonosky, Aaron. 1979. *Health, Stress, and Coping.* San Francisco: Josey-Bass.

Biraben, J. N. 1982. "Morbidity and the Major Processes Culminating in Death." In Samuel H. Preston, ed., *Biological and Social Aspects of Mortality and the Length of Life*, pp. 385–392. Liège: Ordina Editions.

Black, Robert E. 1984. "Diarrheal Diseases and Child Morbidity and Mortality." In W. Henry Mosley and Lincoln C. Chen, eds., *Child Survival: Strategies for Research*, pp. 141–61. *Population and Development Review.* Supplement to vol. 10.

Bradley, David J., and Anne Keymer. 1984. "Parasitic Diseases: Measurement and Mortality Impact." In W. Henry Mosley and Lincoln C. Chen, eds., *Child Survival: Strategies for Research. Population and Development Review.* Supplement to vol. 10.

Breslow, Lester. 1990. "The Future of Public Health: Prospects in the United States for the 1990's." *Annual Review of Public Health* 11: 1–28.

Bulatao, Rodolfo A., Eduard Bos, Patience W. Stephens, and My T. Vu. 1989. "Projecting Mortality for All Countries." *Working Papers, World Bank Population and Human Resources Department*, WPS 337.

Cartwright, Frederick F. 1972. *Disease and History.* New York: Thomas Y. Crowell.

Cassedy, James H. 1969. *Demography in Early America: Beginnings of the Statistical Mind, 1600–1800.* Cambridge, Mass.: Harvard University Press.

———. 1986. *Medicine and American Growth 1800–1860.* Madison, Wis.: University of Wisconsin Press.

Dubos, René. 1987. *Mirage of Health.* New Brunswick, N.J.: Rutgers University Press.

Eberstein, Isaac W. 1991. *Race/Ethnicity and Infant Mortality.* Working Paper 92–90, Center for the Study of Population, Florida State University.

———, Charles B. Nam, and Robert A. Hummer. 1990. "Infant Mortality by Cause of Death: Main and Interaction Effects." *Demography* 27:3, 413–30.

Ewbank, Douglas. 1988. Health in Africa. In Etienne van de Walle, Patrick O. Ohadike, and Mpembele D. Sala-Diakanda, eds., *The State of African Demography*, pp. 87–101. Liège: IUSSP.

Feldman, Jacob J., Diane M. Makuc, Joel C. Kleinman, and Joan Cornoni-Huntley. 1989. "National Trends in Educational Differentials in Mortality." *American Journal of Epidemiology* 129:5, 919–33.

Fortney, Judith A., Saad Gadalla, Saneya Saleh, Inne Susanti, Malcolm Potts, and Susan M. Rogers. 1987. "Causes of Death to Women of Reproductive Age in Two Developing Countries." *Population Research and Policy Review* 6:2, 137–48.

Foster, Stanley O. 1984. "Immunizable and Respiratory Diseases and Child Mortality." In W. Henry Mosley and Lincoln C. Chen, eds., *Child Survival: Strategies for Research*, pp. 119–40. *Population and Development Review.* Supplement to vol. 10.

Fries, James F. 1987. "An Introduction to the Compression of Morbidity." *Gerontologica Perspecta* 1: 5–7.

———, and Lawrence M. Crapo. 1981. *Vitality and Aging.* New York: W. H. Freeman.

Guralnik, Jack M. 1991. "Prospects for the Compression of Morbidity: The Challenge Posted by Increasing Disability in the Years Prior to Death." *Journal of Aging and Health* 3, 138–54.

Guzman, Jose Miguel. 1989. "Trends in Socio-economic Differentials in Infant Mortality in Selected Latin American Countries." In Lado Ruzicka, Guillaume Wunsch, and Penny Kane, eds., *Differential Mortality; Methodological Issues and Biosocial Factors*, pp. 131–44. Oxford: Clarendon Press.

Haan, Mary N., Dorothy P. Rice, William A. Satariano, and Joe V. Selby. 1991. Introduction. *Journal of Aging and Health* 3: 133–37.

Hale, Christiane B. 1990. "Infant Mortality: An American Tragedy." *Population Trends and Public Policy*, no. 18. A publication of the Population Reference Bureau.

Hayflick, Leonard. 1982. "Biological Aspects of Aging." In Samuel H. Preston, ed., *Biological and Social Aspects of Mortality and the Length of Life*, pp. 223–56. Liège: Ordina Editions.

Israel, Robert A., Harry M. Rosenberg, and Lester R. Curtin. 1986. "Analytical Potential for Multiple Cause-of-Death Data." *American Journal of Epidemiology* 124:2, 161–79.

Kamel, Nahid M. 1983. "Determinants and Patterns of Female Mortality Associated with Women's Reproductive Roles." In Alan D. Lopez and Lado T. Ruzicka, eds., *Sex Differentials in Mortality; Trends, Determinants, and Consequences*, pp. 179–91. Canberra: Australian National University.

Kaplan, George A. 1991. "Epidemiologic Observations on the Compression of Morbidity: Evidence from the Alameda County Study." *Journal of Aging and Health* 3, 155–71.

Kessner, David M. 1973. *Infant Death: An Analysis by Maternal Risk and Health Care*, vol. 1. Washington, D.C.: National Academy Press.

Kolata, Gina. 1987. "The New Mystery of the Female Heart." *New York Times*, November 17.

Kunitz, Stephen J. 1983. "Speculations on the European Mortality Decline." *Economic History Review* 36, 349–64.

———. 1984. "Mortality Change in America, 1620–1920." *Human Biology* 56: 559–82.

Lopez, Alan D. 1990a. "Causes of Death: An Assessment of Global Patterns of Mortality around 1985." *World Health Statistics Quarterly* 43, 91–104.

———. 1990b. "Who Dies of What? A Comparative Analysis of Mortality Conditions in Developed Countries around 1987." *World Health Statistics Quarterly* 43: 105–14.

———, and Lado T. Ruzicka. 1983. Introduction. In Alan D. Lopez and Lado T. Ruzicka, eds., *Sex Differentials in Mortality; Trends, Determinants, and Consequences*, pp. 1–5. Canberra: Australian National University.

Lynge, Elsebeth. 1984. *Socio-Economic Differences in Mortality in Europe*. Population Studies, no. 9. Strasbourg: Council of Europe.

Manton, Kenneth G. 1986. "Past and Future Life Expectancy Increases at Later Ages: Their Implications for the Linkage of Chronic Morbidity, Disability, and Mortality." *Journal of Gerontology* 41:5, 672–81.

———, and George C. Myers. 1987. "Recent Trends in Multiple-Caused Mortality, 1968 to 1982: Age and Cohort Components." *Population Research and Policy Review* 6: 161–76.

———, and H. Dennis Tolley. 1991. "Rectangularization of the Survival Curve: Implications of an Ill-Posed Question." *Journal of Aging and Health* 3: 172–93.

Martorell, Reynaldo, and Teresa J. Ho. 1984. "Malnutrition, Morbidity, and Mortality." In W. Henry Mosley and Lincoln C. Chen, eds., "Child Survival: Strategies for Research." *Population and Development Review*, pp. 49–68. Supplement to vol. 10.

McKeown, Thomas. 1976. *The Modern Rise of Population.* San Diego, Calif.: Academic.

McNeill, William H. 1976. *Plagues and People.* New York: Doubleday.

Mosley, W. Henry, and Lincoln C. Chen. 1984. "An Analytical Framework for the Study of Child Survival in Developing Countries." *Population and Development Review* 10. Supplement, pp. 25–45.

———, and Peter Cowley. 1991. "The Challenge of World Health." *Population Bulletin* 46:4.

Myers, George C. 1989. "Mortality and Health Dynamics at Older Ages." In Lado Ruzicka, Guillaume Wunsch, and Penny Kane, eds., *Differential Mortality: Methodological Issues and Biosocial Factors*, pp. 189–214. Oxford: Clarendon Press.

Nag, Moni. 1991. "Sex Preference in Bangladesh, India, and Pakistan, and Its Effects on Fertility." *The Population Council Working Papers*, no. 27.

Nam, Charles B. 1990. "Mortality Differentials from a Multiple-Cause-of-Death Perspective." In Jacques Vallin, Stan D'Souza, and Alberto Palloni, eds., *Measurement and Analysis of Mortality; New Approaches*, pp. 328–42. Oxford: Clarendon Press.

———, and Imelda G. Pagtolun-an. 1988. "Adult Mortality Patterns in Southeast Asia." *Philippine Population Journal* 4: 1–13.

Nathanson, Constance A., and Alan D. Lopez. 1987. "The Future of Sex Mortality Differentials in Industrialized Countries: A Structural Hypothesis." *Population Research and Policy Review* 6: 123–36.

Olshansky, S. Jay, Mark A. Rudberg, Bruce A. Carnes, Christine K. Cassel, and Jacob A. Brody. 1991. "Trading Off Longer Life for Worsening Health: The Expansion of Morbidity Hypothesis." *Journal of Aging and Health* 3: 194–216.

Omondi-Odhiambo, J. K. van Ginneken, and A. M. Voorhoeve. 1990. "Mortality by Cause of Death in a Rural Area of Machakos District, Kenya in 1975–78." *Journal of Biosocial Science* 22: 63–75.

Omran, Abdel R. 1971. "The Epidemiologic Transition: A Theory of the Epidemiology of Population Change." *Milbank Memorial Fund Quarterly* 49:4, 509–38.

———. 1977. "A Century of Epidemiologic Transition in the United States." *Preventive Medicine* 6: 30–51.

Palca Joseph. 1991. "The Sobering Geography of AIDS." *Science* 252: 372–73.

Perrenoud, Alfred. 1984. "Mortality Decline in Its Secular Setting." In Tommy Bengtsson, Gunnar Fridizius, and Rolf Ohlsson, eds., *Pre-Industrial Population Change: The Mortality Decline and Short-Term Population Movements*, pp. 41–69. Stockholm: Almquist and Wicksell International.

Population Reference Bureau. 1993. *World Population Data Sheet 1991.* Washington, D.C.: Population Reference Bureau.

Ransford, Oliver. 1983. *Bid the Sickness Cease: Disease in the History of Black Africa.* London: John Murray.

Retherford, Robert D. 1975. *The Changing Sex Differential in Mortality.* Westport, Conn.: Greenwood Press.

Riley, James C. 1989. *Sickness, Recovery, and Death.* Iowa City: University of Iowa Press.

———, and George Alter. 1989. "The Epidemiologic Transition and Morbidity." *Annales de démographie historique,* 199–213.

Rogers, Richard G., and Robert Hackenberg. 1987. "Extending Epidemiologic Transition Theory: A New Stage." *Social Biology* 34, 234–43.

Rosenberg, Harry M., Frances Chevarley, Eve Powell-Griner, Kenneth Kochanek, and Manning Feinleib. 1991. "Causes of Death Among the Elderly: Information from the Death Certificate." In National Center for Health Statistics, Proceedings of 1988 International Symposium on Data on Aging. *Vital and Health Statistics,* Series 5, no. 6, pp. 35–58.

Ruzicka, Lado. 1989. "Problems and Issues in the Study of Mortality Differentials." In Lado Ruzicka, Guillaume Wunsch, and Penny Kane, eds., *Differential Mortality: Methodological Issues and Biosocial Factors,* pp. 3–17. Oxford: Clarendon Press.

Schoenborn, C.A. 1986. "Health Habits of U.S. Adults: The Alameda 7 Revisited." *Public Health Reports* 101, 571–80.

Thaddeus, Sereen, and Deborah Maine. 1990. *Too Far to Walk: Maternal Mortality in Context.* New York: Columbia University, Center for Population and Family Health.

Thornton, Russell. 1987. *American Indian Holocaust and Survival: A Population History Since 1492.* Norman, Okla.: University of Oklahoma Press.

United Nations. 1963. *Population Bulletin of the United Nations, no. 6-1982.* New York: United Nations.

———. 1973. *Principles and Recommendations for a Vital Statistics System.* Statistical Papers, Series M, no. 19, Rev. 1. New York: United Nations.

———. 1990. *World Population Monitoring 1989.* New York: United Nations.

Verbrugge, Lois. 1984. "Longer Life but Worsening Health? Trends in Health and Mortality of Middle-Aged and Older Persons." *Milbank Memorial Fund Quarterly* 62: 475–519.

———. 1990. "The Iceberg of Disability." In Sidney M. Stahl, ed., *The Legacy of Longevity: Health and Health Care in Later Life,* pp. 55–75. Newbury Park, Calif.: Sage Publications.

Ware, Helen. 1984. "Effects of Maternal Education, Women's Roles, and Child Care on Mortality." In W. Henry Mosley and Lincoln C. Chen, eds., "Child Survival: Strategies for Research." *Population and Development Review,* pp. 191–214. Supplement to vol. 10.

Weiss, Kenneth W. 1990. "The Biodemography of Variations in Human Frailty." *Demography* 27:2, 185–206.

Wrigley, J. Michael, and Charles B. Nam. 1987. "Underlying vs. Multiple Causes of Death: Effects on Interpreting Cancer Mortality Differentials by Age, Sex, and Race." *Population Research and Policy Review* 6:2, 149–60.

Wurtzburg, C. E. 1986. *Raffles of the Eastern Isles.* Singapore: Oxford University Press.

Yanagashita, Machiko, and Jack M. Guralnik. 1988. "Changing Mortality Patterns That Led Life Expectancy in Japan to Surpass Sweden's: 1972–1982." *Demography* 25: 611–24.

Zinsser, Hans. 1934. *Rats, Lice, and History.* Boston: Little, Brown.

6. Fertility Processes

Just as we can best view mortality as the end result of a process incorporating a range of factors over a stretch of time, we can also see fertility as the consequence of a host of variables and conditions operating from the time even before a female has reached the age of potential childbearing until the end of the childbearing period.

Likewise, just as the prospect of mortality at any age is influenced by biological, psychological, social, and demographic characteristics, as well as by physical and social settings, so is the prospect of fertility at any age influenced by these same factors.

Therefore, any analysis of fertility levels and changes must take into account the myriad factors that relate to how a fetus is created and its viability and survival until a live birth does or does not occur. This encompasses the intentional and unintentional efforts of males and females to produce a pregnancy or not, the intentional and unintentional efforts to preserve the fetus or not, and the intentional and unintentional efforts to "bring a baby into the world." However, while we will allude to some biological and psychological aspects and briefly discuss some of the moral issues involved, our interest in these efforts will be largely restricted to the social and demographic determinants of the fertility process.

From an aggregate point of view, fertility operates through three basic channels—a population's *demand for children*, its *supply of children*, and the *costs of regulating* the supply and demand (Bulatao and Lee, 1983). Demand refers to "the family size and composition a couple would choose, abstracted from all concern with the childbearing process required to attain that outcome." Demand can relate to number, gender, and spacing of children. Supply refers to "the surviving children the couples would have if they did not regulate their fertility, or their children's survival." It depends on the biological capability of a couple producing fetuses as well as on child survival, and it is influenced by various attributes of the individuals involved and the persons and groups with whom they interact. Regulation costs refer to the consequences of facilitating or impeding the fertility process. This includes such factors as the desire to prevent a conception or birth, the difficulty of obtaining contraceptive information, distance to a family planning clinic, religious or moral attitudes, and perceived health consequences.

The more one thinks about what is involved in having (or not having) a child, the more one realizes that the process is very extensive and complex. Moreover, the set of influential factors changes with each passing stage. Although persons may have an early notion of what constitutes a proper number of children to have, the considerations involved may be quite different for the first child, the second, the third, and so on. Each sequential child changes the orientation to having another one, and the biological and social contexts that condition that orientation become altered as well.

In this chapter we will explore these several areas of influence to comprehend what produces fertility transitions and cycles and why some categories of people have different fertility patterns than others.

CRITICAL CONCEPTS AND MEASURES

The discussion above refers to a number of different ideas that relate to fertility. We will elaborate on them within a set of six general categories—first, *fertility orientations*, or the many dimensions that identify the feelings people have about having children; second, *fecundity*, the biological capability of a woman being involved in childbearing; third, *fertility*, the actual childbearing events that can be looked at as a single occurrence or summarized over a woman's reproductive span; fourth, *institutional factors*, the nonbiological background factors that influence childbearing; fifth, *control variables*, the range of contraceptive mechanisms and abortion people can use to intervene in the fertility process; and sixth, *differential fertility*, the observed differences in childbearing behavior among various categories of the population.

In dealing with all these elements, our focus will always be on how they interact with each other to produce varying levels of fertility at the several stages of the demographic transition and during fertility cycles. At the same time, we will recognize that the events of pregnancy and childbearing, and even childlessness, are human population experiences that combine with those related to mortality and geographic mobility to help shape the individual's personal world as well as the populations of larger structures (family, community, society, and globe) of which the individual is a part.

Fertility Orientations

Do you recall when you first became sensitive to the notion that a certain size family was "right"? Was it your own family's size, because what was right for your parents would be correct for you? Or did you think it would be better to have fewer or more children, because of certain experiences you had that led you to think that way? And how have your ideas about family size changed since that time?

It is common to regard childbearing as an event occurring to females who have reached an age when they can have children, which is true. It is uncom-

BOX 6.1 Orientations to Fertility

In their 1965 National Fertility Study of the United States, Ryder and Westoff (1971) included questions about four orientations to fertility—the number of children a woman intends to have, the number she expects to have, the number she would really want, and the number she considers ideal for the average American family. The way the questions were asked and how the orientations were measured provide points of controversy, but we shall just examine what kinds of relationships they found among the four views, apart from the methodological concerns. There was a high degree of association among these orientations, but there were also some important differences. Ideal fertility was least like the others because the women tended to report numbers within a narrow range of what the society considered most acceptable. Intended and expected fertility were indistinguishable as views, even though the latter would seem to represent more the number one would anticipate based on a realistic assessment of what kinds of constraints may operate in the future. Of the women who reported that they intended to have more children, 80 percent gave the same response to the questions on number intended and number desired. Of the women who did not intend to have any more children, only 44 percent responded the same way to the questions on intentions and desires. From these findings, the authors concluded that it did make a difference how a person's orientations to fertility were determined.

mon to think of childbearing as a consequence of a series of thought processes and events that have occurred to females and males over a span of time since earliest childhood, which is also true.

Beginning at some very young age, we become oriented to the number of pregnancies a female has and the number of children resulting from them, and we see these as forming the basis for a family and a sibling group. Studies of youth show that, as early as the fifth grade of school and maybe earlier, children can express their preferences for a particular size of family and describe its sex composition (Philliber and Nam, 1980). Of course, these early expressions are reflections of the limited experience with family sizes these children have had, and they are likely to be related to knowledge of their own families and the few others they have become familiar with. (Before the advent of television, these experiences were limited indeed; now, television presents views of many forms of family and household groups so that the perception of family size is enhanced.) Because sisters and brothers are real people, not just abstract numbers, there is a tendency for young people to cite their own family size of origin or something close to it as the right size. In the process of growing up, we find that there are many factors that lead us to change our views of that early family size determination, but the original view typically remains as a reference point on which our later views are based.

From youth to later ages, we all have various mental images of our own and other contributions to fertility. How can we best describe those mental images? The research conducted on this subject is widespread, and there is no consensus about the most meaningful terms (see Box 6.1) and their actual impact on the fertility process. Included are terms such as ideal, intended, desired, expected, wanted or unwanted, as well as considerations of what is normative and what are the values and costs of having children.

Over the years a variety of approaches to measuring and analyzing fertility views have been made. Some have linked desires and expectations to motivations in an effort to determine the root of the orientations. Miller and Pasta (1988) constructed a conceptual model in which motivations were prior to desires which, in turn, were prior to expectations. Looking separately at just-married women and women who had just become mothers, they discovered that positive or negative motivations to have children affected the number of children a woman desires and the number she perceives her husband to desire in both cases. Both of these orientations separately affect the number of children she expects to have. Moreover, just-married women who expect their next child sooner in time expect to have fewer, not more, children. Further, having the first child seems to change the equation. The authors conclude that, before her first child when a woman is setting her expectations about when to have a child, she may consider how many children she wants, over what period of time she wants to be involved in childbearing, and how soon she wants to begin her reproductive career. Once she has her first child, her primary consideration in subsequent timing of childbearing is how many children she expects to have eventually. (This is because the spacing of children is decided within the framework of the number expected.)

The thought processes a person has about fertility are linked not only to how many children are already born (a second, third, or later birth will alter the equations even further) but also to the feelings of the spouse or mate. Thomson, McDonald, and Bumpass (1990) reanalyzed the Princeton Fertility Survey, one of a series of fertility studies conducted during the 1940s and through the 1970s in the United States, to find out how wives' and husbands' fertility desires were interrelated in their effect on actual fertility. In general, they found that wives and husbands were equally likely to achieve their fertility desires, and couples whose desires were not the same tended to have a number of children midway between the desires of each spouse.

Are these findings for the United States applicable to the situation of developing countries? Mason and Taj (1987) discovered that there is considerable variation in the relative fertility goals of the sexes across countries and studies, that men's strong preference for sons accounts to some extent for their desire to have additional children more than women do, but that women's and men's fertility goals are generally very similar.

Fawcett (1986) describes the so-called value and cost of children perspective that places some of the factors previously mentioned in a more general framework. Motivations and choices regarding childbearing are conditioned by the following assumptions:

1. People act in anticipation of future rewards and costs;
2. Children provide important satisfactions in life, but not without cost;
3. People differ with respect to the types of satisfactions and costs important to them;
4. These differences are related to both internal psychological factors and external social and economic factors which also affect the desirability and availability of alternatives to having children;
5. The balance of satisfactions and costs of children changes over the life cycle; and
6. Choices about children versus alternatives are made by most people at some point in the life cycle, although not necessarily for every birth.

Social class, culture, and the sex of parent and child all have some bearing on the value-cost calculus, according to Fawcett, but one can reach certain general conclusions about the value-cost relationship specific to the number of children already attained. The values of having a first child strongly outweigh the costs of having it, the latter having to do more with the timing of the first child. Yet some women remain childless voluntarily because they refrain from marriage or wish to focus on their own careers. The peak of childbearing motivations seems to occur after having the first child; they are related to the perceived need for a sibling for the first child, the desire to balance the sex composition of children, and a heightened emotional benefit (provided that the experience with the first child has been rewarding). Those who expect long-term economic benefits from children are not usually deterred by short-term cost considerations, says Fawcett. Parents who choose to have only one or two children do not generally expect economic benefits from their children, are more oriented toward a psychological appreciation of childbearing, and appear to be influenced heavily by quality and convenience considerations.

Most of the studies dealing with orientations to childbearing have questioned women who have already started the process and who have had to recreate their mental states about preferences for children, at least in part, in retrospect. Most recent discussions of this phenomenon have focused on so-called wanted and unwanted fertility. Two complications are involved in determining the level of wantedness: Are those feelings the same before and after childbearing, and are the wants patterned the same way with regard to the number of children one has as well as the timing of childbearing? Bongaarts (1990a) argues that desired family size, as a measure of preferred fertility, overestimates true wanted total fertility by a substantial margin because (1) unwanted births are rationalized; (2) involuntary fertility limitation due to sterility, marital disruption, and nonmarriage is not taken into account; (3) social, economic, and health reasons may lead to voluntary decisions to stop childbearing before the desired family size is reached; and (4) delays in the timing of childbearing may affect the ultimate family size. The estimation of wanted births from direct questions about the wanted status of recent births, he further argues, also produces an overestimate because women are understandably reluctant to classify their offspring as unwanted. Instead, he proposes a measure of wantedness status that builds on a woman's interests in continuing childbearing beyond what she already has. Using this approach in an analysis of forty-eight developing countries, he concludes that a substantial proportion of births is still unwanted and that eliminating unwanted births could reduce the birth rate by 22 percent in those countries overall.

Are fertility orientations significant aspects of fertility outcomes? The mental images that form pregnancy and childbearing preferences may not be clearly understood, but there is evidence that both women and men set their sights on a preferred family size and modify that notion as conditions alter the basis for choice. Fertility orientations are related both to the use of fertility controls and to the actual fertility level attained.

In subsequent discussion we will examine actual fertility patterns, the use of controls, and the social and cultural milieu that surrounds them. However, to pursue our story of how and why births do or do not take place requires us first to pay attention to the biological constraints operating on the process of childbearing. These constraints operate both in defining what number of children couples can reasonably choose to have and in explaining in part why preferences do not necessarily result in the anticipated fertility.

Fecundity

The fertility process can be regarded as beginning when individuals give thought to what constitutes a proper family size and its characteristics. The next crucial step takes place when these same persons engage in sexual acts that have the prospect of resulting in a female's becoming pregnant.

There are many biological reasons why a pregnancy might not be a possible outcome of sexual intercourse. For a pregnancy to take place, both the female and male involved in the act must be biologically capable of contributing to reproduction. The state of being so capable is called *fecundity.* Women whose capability is completely lacking are regarded as *infecund,* and those whose capability is diminished are regarded as being in a state of *subfecundity.* Additionally, women who become pregnant are at risk of not bringing the fetus to term. *Infertility* refers to the failure to produce a child, whatever the explanations. Factors that might affect the chances of a woman's becoming pregnant or bearing a child include her age and that of her mate, the viability of the female's ovum and the male's sperm (for biological, social, and psychological reasons), and the extent to which diseases and other impairments have interfered with the reproductive process.

The reproductive ages of human females are defined generally by demographers as being in the range of 15 to 49. The age range in which human males can contribute to fertility extends to much older ages. But the beginning and ending ages fluctuate among various groups and according to some characteristics of the individual. Fecundity of females is considered as actually possible when the menstrual cycle begins (*age at menarche*). In fact, girls from well-off families in Hong Kong are reported to reach menarche at age 12.4 whereas Bundi girls from New Guinea have an average age at menarche of 18 (Menken, 1987). Both genetic and environmental influences (such as nutrition and physical activity) are involved. Blacks reach menarche earlier than whites in the United States. In both Europe and North America, age at menarche has been declining for a century and a half. Hence, exposure to pregnancy at earlier ages has been increasing.

However, the beginning age at menstruation is not a good marker for fecundity. In early adolescence, menstruation may be irregular and inability to produce ova may be so common that subfecundity is a typical state. As girls age, they achieve fuller biological maturity, even though they are subject to diminished fecundity from a variety of sources.

The upper age of fecundity is more difficult to determine. The time when a woman ceases to ovulate and menstruate (*menopause*) is a consequence of the natural aging process, but various factors lead most women to reach that stage when they are between 45 and 50 while others can become menopausal as early as 35 and as late as 55. It is often the case that physiological impairments have interfered with the reproductive capacity of women before the maximum age of fecundity is reached.

Infecundity also takes place during the main reproductive years when a woman has had a child. At the end of a pregnancy, a woman cannot conceive again until ovulation has resumed. This postpartum infecund period (*amenorrhea*) typically lasts for one and one-half to two months, somewhat longer when a woman has been breast-feeding.

The fact is that fecundity is both biologically and socially determined. Hence, the time to conception is based on several factors: (a) the probability that a particular menstrual cycle is ovulatory; (b) the length of time of the fertile period (when the ovum can be fertilized); (c) the probability that sexual intercourse coincides with the fertile period; (d) the effectiveness of the male's sperm; and (e) the probability that the pregnancy lasts long enough for a conception to be recognized (half of all fertilizations are believed not to last long enough to be identified) (Menken, 1987).

Individual fecundity can vary widely. Some women are unable to have children throughout their reproductive lives. Others are extremely fecund, giving birth to large numbers of children (the world's record is believed to be sixty-nine babies for one woman). For populations, however, it has been estimated that maximum fecundity is about fifteen children per woman. That would be the average for a group of women who engage in regular sexual intercourse from menarche to menopause without using any form of birth control. In reali-

BOX 6.2 Disease and Fecundity

Disease has by far the most devastating impact on population fecundity (McFalls and McFalls, 1984). It operates through three subfecundity variables—coital inability, conceptive failure, and pregnancy loss.

Disease causes coital inability in men through impotence (the inability to achieve and maintain an erection sufficient to accomplish successful intercourse), through difficult or painful coitus, and through genital deformities. Disease affects coital inability through coitus problems and genital deformities in women as well. Influential conditions in these areas include debilitating diseases, metabolic disorders, central nervous system diseases, cardiovascular disorders, certain forms of cancer, and venereal diseases.

With regard to conceptive failures, infections accompanied by high fever and venereal diseases can affect the quantity and quality of sperm production. They can also hinder the transport of sperm through the sperm duct and of the movement of ovarian eggs through the fallopian tubes of females.

Disease also operates to result in pregnancy loss. Those associated with blockage of the fallopian tube can prevent the development of an early fetus. Spontaneous abortions and stillbirths may result from anemia, from malaria resulting in high fever, and from pelvic inflammatory disease (McFalls and McFalls, 1984).

The specific mechanisms through which disease affects the prospects of conception and viability of the fetus are numerous and their details are beyond the scope of this analysis. Likewise, other limitations on fecundity are extensive. The main point to be made is that biological conditions create barriers to the implementation of choices of individuals with regard to fertility orientations. Moreover, social and cultural factors influencing the regulation of reproduction add to the biological forces that impinge on fertility outcomes.

ty, no population has achieved that maximum state. The Hutterites, a small religious sect located in North Central United States and adjoining Canadian provinces, are usually cited as having the highest fecundity. Shunning birth control and leading a healthy life-style, only 2 percent of Hutterite women remain childless. The average Hutterite woman goes through the reproductive period producing about ten children (far from the maximum fecundity because, even among the Hutterites, there are social influences that limit fertility). Residents of the Bas-Uele district of Zaire are often cited as being at the opposite extreme of the fecundity potential. A poverty-stricken group, they suffer from malnutrition, lack of adequate health care, multiple deleterious behaviors, and numerous disease forms. As many as 50 percent of Bas-Uele women remain childless despite cultural supports for childbearing (McFalls and McFalls, 1984).

There are many ways in which subfecundity throughout the reproductive age span may be brought about. Five major categories that have been identified are genetic factors, disease (see Box 6.2), psychopathology, nutritional deficiencies, and other environmental factors.

Nutritional and other environmental factors are social in nature and relate to the ability of society to provide proper nourishment and adequate living conditions to people. The several psychopathologies include psychic stress, psychoses, sexual deviations, alcoholism, cigarette smoking, and illicit drug use—forms of individual behavior that may hamper a person's fertility potential. Genetic factors, which were described in the previous chapter as influencing survival odds, are also characteristics of groups that predispose them to subfecundity or infecundity.

The U.S. National Center for Health Statistics has derived estimates of fecundity and infertility for the nation by asking questions in surveys designed to classify women or couples into three categories: surgically sterile (unable to have a baby because of surgery); having impaired fecundity (sterile for reasons other than surgery, or difficult or dangerous to have a baby); and fecund (no known physical problem). Our attention is directed to the category of impaired fecundity, which includes women who said that (a) it was impossible to have a baby for some reason other than a sterilization operation, such as an accident, illness, or unexplained inability to conceive; (b) it was physically difficult for them to conceive or deliver a baby, or a doctor told them never to become pregnant again because a pregnancy would pose a danger to the woman, the baby, or both; or (c) they and their spouses were continually married, did not use contraception, and did not become pregnant for thirty-six months or more. Of course, these survey responses reflect the women's beliefs about their conditions and may not always indicate the true set of circumstances (Mosher and Pratt, 1990b).

On this basis, however, 8 percent of women 15–44 in 1988 had impaired fecundity, and this varied from 5 percent for those 15–24 years old to 11 percent for those 35–44 years old. Furthermore, among women who were still childless, the percentage with impaired fecundity ranged from 4 percent among those 15–24 to 21 percent for those 35–44. For those who had already had one or more children, the comparable proportions were both about 8 percent.

Although the level of impaired fecundity is not very high in the United States, it does represent a contribution to lower fertility. In the event that such subfecundity is lowered over time (and reduced percentages were generally observed between 1982 and 1988), then fertility potential would be increased.

Couples who strive for a conception (have sexual intercourse at least a few times a week and have no known impaired fecundity) may succeed in starting the fertility process in the first month of effort or it may take as many as ten months for that to happen. Any elements of subfecundity will reduce the chances of an early conception.

For a conception to develop into a live birth, an average period of nine months transpires. While people have different views about the point in this cycle when the creation has life, and even more differ about when the fetus takes on the status of a "person," there is general consensus that development of the zygote (the joining of a woman's egg and a man's sperm to form a fertilized cell) proceeds in definable stages.

About one out of six zygotes will not survive to a later stage. Those which survive will have multiplied to twelve to sixteen cells within three days. In about one week, a blastocyst (now a flat disk within a hollow ball of several hundred cells) plants itself in the uterus wall. There is still no appearance of an animal form. In one month, three layers of the disk constitute an embryo containing the ingredients of an animal form. By two months, the fetus has emerged with arms, legs, fingers, and toes, and other elements of a human form. In succeeding months, the fetus becomes more and more human and by the end of the ninth month (sometimes before, sometimes after) it is ready for delivery as a live birth.

Fertility

Just as we had indicated in Chapter 5 that death is a familiar concept but not easy to define with certainty, so is birth a somewhat nebulous concept. *Birth*, or more directly a live birth, is described by the United Nations (1955) as "the complete expulsion or extraction from its mother of a product of conception, irrespective of the duration of pregnancy, which, after such separation, breathes or shows any other evidence of life, such as beating of the heart, pulsation of the umbilical cord, or definite movement of voluntary muscles, whether or not the umbilical cord has been cut or the placenta is attached; each product of such a birth is considered live born."

A delivery that lacks the signs of life indicated above would be classified as a stillbirth and not included in the count of live births. You will recall from the previous chapter that the judgment of whether a delivery is of a live birth affects how we measure infant mortality. An infant death can be recorded only when the baby has been born alive. If there has been a stillbirth, then it would be classified as a fetal death and not be included in either official birth or death statistics.

Although human females have a reproductive span that ranges from the ages of menarche to menopause, actual fertility is not distributed evenly over that period. For both biological and social reasons, childbearing is minimal at the ages closest to menarche and menopause. The peak is typically reached when women are in their twenties.

Figure 6.1 presents a general picture of the *age curve of fertility* within the context of the *age curve of fecundity*. The variations of both (especially of fertility) can be substantial as populations move through the fertility transition. It is quite obvious that the fertility of the average group of women does not even come close to their fecundity. Hutterite women would have an age curve of fertility higher than that of the average group of women (pictured here) but their fertility would also be far from the biological maximum.

FIGURE 6.1 Hypothetical Fecundity Model and Average Age-Specific Birth Rates in Seventy-Two Countries

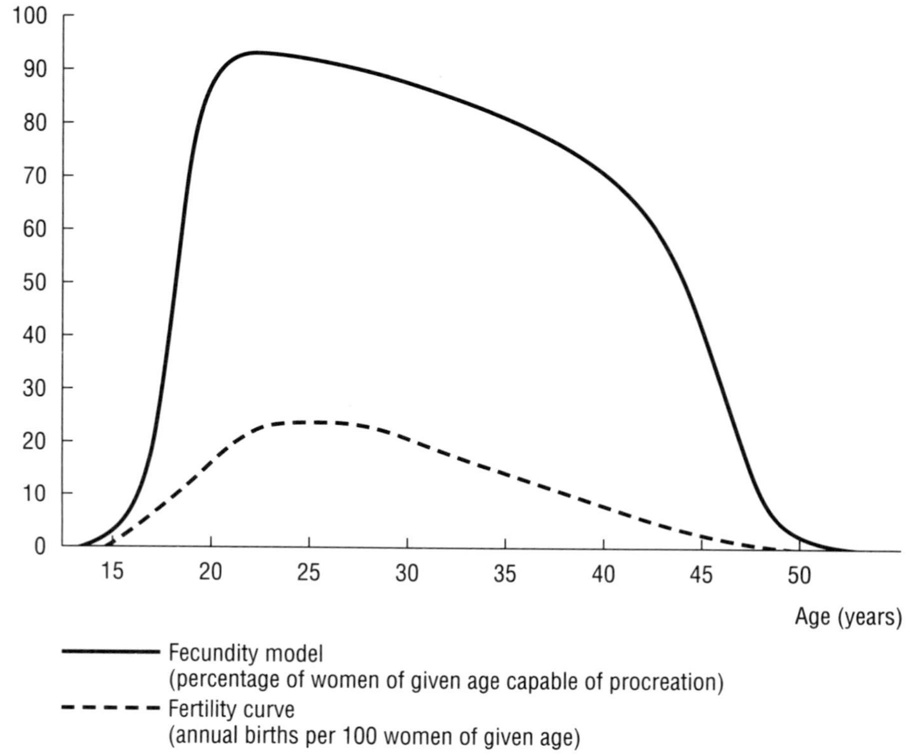

Source: *Population Bulletin of the United Nations*, no. 7, 1963, Figure 7.1, p. 101.

The ages at which women bear children is a function of their fecundity, the social and cultural situation of an area, and the fertility control practices that change over the transition. A comparison of two Asian countries, Japan and Malaysia, in 1960 and 1970 (Figure 6.2) reveal how different they can be. (These graphs are not scaled in the same way as the previous one. Rather, the attempt is to show what percentage of births are concentrated at each age of the mother at that time.) One can see that Japan's childbearing was heavily concentrated in the 25–29 age range, typical of a country with a relatively late age at marriage and low fertility level. Childbearing levels were much less at earlier and later ages. In Malaysia, on the other hand, births were distributed more broadly. Although fertility also peaked at the 25–29 age level of mothers, childbearing tended to begin earlier and continue to later reproductive ages. This is more typical of countries that have higher fertility.

FIGURE 6.2 Age Patterns of Fertility: Japan and Malaysia, 1960 and 1970

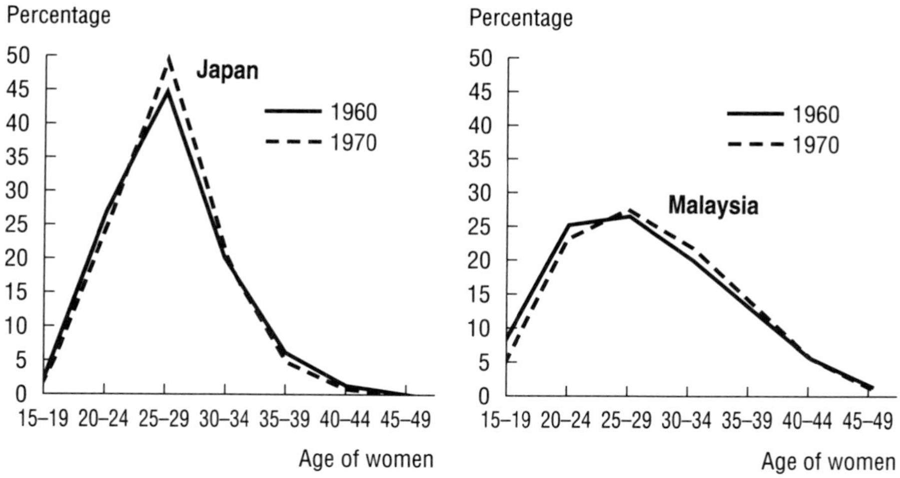

Souce: United Nations, 1977. *Levels and Trends of Fertility Throughout the World, 1950–1970.* New York, United Nations. Figure 7.

Because of these variations in the age pattern of fertility, how we measure the level of childbearing makes a difference in the conclusions we reach about fertility change over time in a given population or in comparing fertility levels of two or more populations at the same time. Measurement of childbearing is also affected by the kinds of questions about fertility we want to have answered. In this sense, there are many similarities in the alternative ways that we measure mortality and fertility.

Assuming that live births are accurately recorded in a vital registration system or survey or census, we can obtain a count of them during a particular period of time. That would provide useful information for some purposes. However, more often we will want to have a relative measure of fertility that can be compared for different populations. This entails relating the number of live births to some base population in a given time period. Considerations of the appropriate base (denominator of a rate) are even more complex than in the case of mortality. Deaths happen once to each individual at a single age. Births can happen not at all or many times to the same woman at various times in her reproductive career. Also, some women have multiple births (that is, twins or triplets or more at the same time).

Just as there is a crude death rate, so there is a *crude birth rate*, which is expressed as the number of births in a time period (usually a calendar year) divided by the total population of the area at that time (typically the middle of that year) and multiplied by a constant 1,000. Obviously, the denominator is not an appropriate *population at risk.* Females outside the reproductive ages cannot bear children, and men and women should not both get credit for the same birth. Why, then, do we have such a measure? Because sometimes we need to have some indicator of fertility and the only information available for many places is the number of births and the total population.

It is true that countries at different stages of the fertility transition have generally different crude birth rates (CBRs). In 1993, the CBR of Malawi was recorded as 53 per 1,000 population; in India, the CBR was about 31; in Thailand, it was 21; and in Japan, Greece, Spain, Germany, and Italy, it was only 10.

But the inappropriateness of the CBR denominator can create some misleading comparisons. Chile and Argentina both had CBRs of 21 in 1993, yet their age patterns of fertility were not similar. Nevertheless, the crude birth rate is a better indicator of comparative overall fertility than the crude death rate is of comparative overall mortality.

One alternative to the crude birth rate that makes the population at risk more appropriate is the *general fertility rate*, which relates the number of births to the number of women in reproductive ages and then multiples by a constant 1,000. This measure eliminates females outside the reproductive ages as well as all males from the denominator. But it requires classification by age of data on females in the population. Also, despite being a better measure than the CBR, it still suffers from the fact that the number of women distributed across the reproductive age span may not be the same for the populations being compared; for example, there may be more women at the most fertile ages in one of the populations.

We can avoid the latter pitfall by examining each *age-specific fertility* level separately. This serves to control for age differences, but it leaves us with a range of age-specific fertility measures to compare and hence is somewhat burdensome. It would be desirable to have just a single measure of fertility that is free of the age bias (that, in effect, adjusts for the varying age composition of women but still indicates the underlying level of fertility in the population).

One way to do this (as in the case of mortality) is to create *age-standardized birth rates*, in which we hypothetically ask what the fertility level would be if the populations being compared had the same age distributions of women. In reality, we then get back to a single measure of fertility (like the general fertility rate) but one which adjusts for age variations in the denominator of that rate.

One limitation of all the aforementioned measures is that the indicators emerging from our calculations are not in a form we associate with levels of childbearing. We cannot visualize a crude birth rate or age-standardized birth rate in terms of the number of children a woman has.

What we would really like to have (if the requisite data are available) are measures of fertility that tell us how many children women are having during, and at the end of, their reproductive cycle. One possibility is to ask a direct question of women in a census or survey as to the number of *children ever born* to them. We can then find out what the *cumulative fertility* was of women in any age category of a population at that point in time. Such information is frequently gathered from censuses and surveys and is analytically useful. For many areas, however, such data are lacking.

If statistics on births by age of women are available—the type that permits calculation of age-specific fertility rates—we can construct another measure that converts those data into a form that represents the average number of children a group of women have had. The measure is called a *total fertility rate* (TFR). We can calculate it by taking the current age-specific fertility rate for each age group of women in a population and multiplying it by 1,000 (and additionally by 5 if five-year age groups of women are used) and then summing them and dividing by 1,000. The total fertility rate estimates the average number of live births 1,000 women would have if they all live through their entire reproductive period and are subject to a given set of age-specific fertility rates. It is also a hypothetical measure, but it reflects the underlying fertility performance of a group of women that is real as of a point in time.

In Chapter 5 we discussed life tables and life expectancy. The total fertility rate is analogous to the latter in that it shifts the focus from a cross-sectional or period perspective to a longitudinal or cohort perspective. Although based on information for a period of time, as are conventional life tables, it transforms the data into a cohort form so that we can say what the fertility experience will be of women who go through their lives with specified childbearing patterns at each age. Of course, as age-specific fertility rates change, so will the TFR change (Palmore and Gardner, 1983).

Table 6.1 shows the variations in TFRs across the world in 1993. The highest are in Africa, most parts of which are in the pretransition or early transition phase of demographic change. Malawi, with an average number of children per woman going through the reproductive period of close to 8, shows the highest fertility level. Northern African countries vary between TFRs of 3.4 and 6.5. Parts of Asia have TFRs still in excess of 7 (Iraq, Syria, and Yemen), while other parts have TFR levels below 2 (Singapore, Hong Kong, Japan, South Korea, and Taiwan). Considerable variation also exists in Latin America, where TFRs range from 6.0 in Haiti to 1.8 in Cuba. With few exceptions, TFRs in North America, Europe, and Oceania fluctuate between 2.2 and 1.3 children. Greater variations among population subgroups may appear within countries.

The *gross reproduction rate* is comparable to the total fertility rate, except that only female births are counted in the numerator of the rate. In this way, one can gauge the extent to which women are "reproducing" themselves with girls in the next generation. A further refinement of this measure is found in the *net reproduction rate*, which doesn't assume that all women will survive through their reproductive period but that, as in fact, some will die before completing it.

Where births are neither recorded nor easily estimated, but censuses are taken which have reasonably good age data, we can obtain a rough approximation of fertility levels by calculating the ratio of children 0–4 years old to the number of women in the reproductive ages. This so-called *child-woman ratio* suffers from variations among populations in the infant and child mortality rates; hence, fertility differences are typically greater than the ratios imply.

TABLE 6.1 Total Fertility Rates for Selected Countries of the World, by Region: Circa 1993

	TFR
AFRICA	
Northern	
Algeria	4.9
Egypt	4.6
Libya	6.4
Sudan	6.5
Tunisia	3.4
Western	
Burkina Faso	7.1
Ivory Coast	7.4
Ghana	6.2
Guinea	6.1
Liberia	6.8
Mali	7.3
Nigeria	6.6
Senegal	6.3
Sierra Leone	6.5
Togo	7.1
Eastern	
Burundi	6.9
Ethiopia	7.5
Kenya	6.5
Madagascar	6.1
Malawi	7.7
Mozambique	6.5
Rwanda	6.2
Somalia	7.0
Tanzania	6.4
Uganda	7.3
Zambia	6.5
Zimbabwe	5.3
Middle	
Angola	7.2
Cameroon	5.9
Cent.Afr.Rep.	5.6
Chad	5.9
Zaire	6.7
ASIA	
Western	
Iraq	7.0
Israel	2.9
Jordan	6.0
Kuwait	4.4
Lebanon	3.7
Saudi Arabia	6.8
Syria	7.1
Turkey	3.6
Yemen	7.5
Southeast	
Cambodia	4.6
Indonesia	3.0
Laos	6.3
Malaysia	3.6
Myanmar	3.9
Philippines	4.1
Singapore	1.7
Thailand	2.4
Viet Nam	4.0
East	
China	1.9
Hong Kong	1.2
Japan	1.5
North Korea	2.5
South Korea	1.6
Taiwan	1.6
Southern	
Afghanistan	6.9
Bangladesh	4.9
India	3.9
Iran	6.6
Nepal	5.6
Pakistan	6.7
Sri Lanka	2.3
NORTH AMERICA	
Canada	1.8
United States	2.0
LATIN AMERICA	
Central	
Costa Rica	3.3
El Salvador	4.6

continued

Guatemala	5.2
Honduras	5.6
Mexico	3.4
Nicaragua	4.8
Panama	2.9
Caribbean	
Cuba	1.8
Dom. Repub.	3.3
Haiti	6.0
Jamaica	2.4
Puerto Rico	2.2
South	
Argentina	2.9
Bolivia	4.9
Brazil	2.6
Chile	2.6
Columbia	2.8
Ecuador	3.8
Paraguay	4.4
Peru	3.5
Uruguay	2.5
Venezuela	3.7
EUROPE	
Northern	
Denmark	1.7
Finland	1.8
Ireland	2.2
Norway	1.9
Sweden	2.1
United Kingdom	1.8
Western	
Austria	1.5
Belgium	1.6
France	1.8
Germany	1.4
Netherlands	1.6
Switzerland	1.6
Eastern	
Bulgaria	1.6
Czech Republic	1.8
Hungary	1.9
Poland	2.0
Romania	1.6
Southern	
Albania	3.0
Greece	1.6
Italy	1.3
Portugal	1.4
Spain	1.3
Yugoslavia	2.0
RUSSIA	1.7
OCEANIA	
Australia	1.8
New Zealand	2.2
Papua–New Guinea	5.4

Note: The total fertility rate (TFR) is the average number of children that would be born to a group of women who went through their lifetime subject to the current age-specific fertility patterns of the country.

Source: Population Reference Bureau, *1993 World Population Data Sheet.*

Also, small children are most likely to be underenumerated in a census, so that the ratio underestimates fertility for that reason. But, as with other limited measures, we can use the child-woman ratio when better ones are lacking.

As Vaupel and Goodwin (1987) have noted, the distribution of childbearing in a population is such that a small proportion of women produce a disproportionate number of children. They found that, while the cohort of U.S. women who completed their fertility in 1980 had 3.16 children on average, 36 percent of the women (those who had four or more children) accounted for 63 percent of all of the children who had been born to that cohort. In comparing groups of U.S. women born in 1868, 1906, and 1931, they found that for both the 1868 and 1931 cohorts the most prolific eighth of the women had about one-quarter of the children. For both the 1868 and 1906 cohorts, the most prolific half of the women had about five-sixths of the children.

Using the same approach, Lutz (1989) has calculated that half the children born within the past 10,000 years were born within the past 1,000 years. Furthermore, of all births occurring in that 10,000-year-span (from 8,000 B.C. to A.D. 2,000), 10 percent will have taken place since 1931 (or the last 70 years of the period). The unequal distribution of births occurs not only over long stretches of time but also within short periods of time. Within a given year, there is a *seasonality of births* related to month-of-marriage patterns, as well as variations by day of the week that can be attributed to such factors as cultural practices and the availability of hospitals and medical personnel. In Finland, births are most numerous in March and April, nine months after midsummer, with a smaller peak in September, nine months after Christmas. In Austria, the greatest number of births happen on Tuesday and the fewest on Sunday. These patterns will vary from place to place, depending on the conditioning factors.

The graph of Japanese age-specific fertility, when compared with that of Malaysia, shows that lower overall fertility has been associated with greater concentration of childbearing in the central reproductive ages, with lesser fertility at the youngest and oldest ages of reproduction. But fertility performance at these extreme ages has captured the most attention in recent years. A vast amount of research has been linked to sexual practices and pregnancy among teenagers and their fertility outcomes. Such outcomes have been complicated in recent years by threats of venereal diseases and HIV-AIDS. A growing number of studies has also focused on the fertility of women in later childbearing years, especially in countries at the end of the fertility transition. This is because many of these women had deferred having any, or more, children in their peak reproductive years and their attitudes with regard to further childbearing seemed to be changing.

Growing attention to teenage motherhood and fatherhood is related to the perception that teen parents and their offspring are highly likely to be disadvantaged socially, economically, and in terms of health in later years (Crews, 1989). Teenage parenting has, in fact, been declining in most countries. Yet the levels vary greatly among nations and are regarded as unduly high in many of them.

Teenage fertility, defined as births to women under 20, is highest in many less developed regions of Africa, Asia, and Latin America, and moderate to low in other areas. During the 1970s, 22 percent of female teenagers in Mali had a birth. Countries that exceeded 14 percent included Senegal, Liberia, Pakistan, and El Salvador. With the exception of Liberia, these countries had reduced their teen fertility by the 1980s. In countries such as Australia, Denmark, France, Israel, and South Korea, the percentage of female teenagers who gave birth in a given year during the 1970s was under 5 percent. In Japan, it was as low as one-half of 1 percent.

With respect to overall teenage fertility in the United States, the percentage giving birth annually dropped from about 6 percent in the 1970s to about 5 percent in the 1980s but rose again beginning in the late 1980s. More detailed examination of the teen pattern uncovers particular points of concern. In 1985, over 1 million teenagers became pregnant and as many as 31,000 of them were under 15. Among girls 15 to 17 years of age, 57 out of 1,000 whites and 134 out of 1,000 nonwhites became pregnant. While many of the girls resorted to abortions, substantial numbers carried their fetuses to term, resulting in birth rates at ages 15 to 17 of 24 per 1,000 for whites and 63 per 1,000 for nonwhites (Henshaw and Van Vort, 1989).

Nathanson and Kim (1989) took note of the fact that, despite the decline in U.S. adolescent fertility during the early 1980s, there was a shift toward nonmarital fertility in this group. Since the greatest concern was for girls who were not married and had babies, this discovery muted the positive aspect of overall teenage fertility decline. They went on to analyze the relative contributions to changes during the 1970s in two dimensions of adolescent fertility—the probability of a teenager's having a nonmarital live birth and the odds that a live birth to a teenager would be nonmarital. They found that the largest component of change in the rate of nonmarital births for teenagers was the increased probability of sex before marriage. Increased pregnancy rates were less important, indicating the wider effective use of contraception. The largest single component of change in the odds that a teenage birth would be nonmarital rather than marital was the delay in marriage until after sexual experience, and there was also a decreasing tendency for marriage to legitimate a birth soon after the event. These findings indicate alterations in the attitudes of teenagers toward sex and marriage, a subject we will discuss in some detail in Chapter 9.

The fertility level of U.S. women, in general, rose during the period 1976 to 1992, despite the fact that childbearing remained close to replacement level. The sharpest increases were at the older reproductive ages. In the sixteen-year time span, births per 1,000 women went up from 56 to 76 for those in the 30–34 age group and from 23 to 38 for those in the 35–39 group (Bachu, 1993). Although the numbers of births in these age categories are not large, they contribute disproportionately to the overall fertility increase. Resumed fertility for these older reproductive-age women is somewhat of a counterforce to the increased lifetime childlessness that has been observed in recent studies. As many as 16 percent of the women who reached the end of the childbearing period in 1992 in the United States had not borne a child. That percentage had only been 10 in 1976. Even though more women in their 30s were having children in 1992 than in earlier years, it was also true that the rate of childlessness was being maintained, and that 15 to 20 percent were estimated to stay childless until the end of their childbearing years. Part of this level of childlessness is involuntary (due to fecundity problems), but an increasing part is voluntary (the desire of some men and/or women not to have children) (Poston and Kramer, 1983).

Responses to questions on birth expectations indicate further that U.S. women do not anticipate changing their fertility patterns in the near future. Reports of expected births have averaged in the 2.0–2.1 range since 1977, and this is as common among younger as older women. The immediate prospect of significantly increased fertility for U.S. women is, therefore, not very great.

Institutional Factors

Childbearing does not happen within a social and cultural vacuum. Decisions made by people about their family size, when to have children, and how to affect the prospects of a conception and birth, all hinge in part on conformity to, or deviation from, the society's and community's norms and other social structural forces that influence the outcomes. We combine the several types of social and cultural effects under the caption of *institutional factors.*

Such factors typically encompass the nature of sexual unions, for example, the formation of such unions, how stable they are, their social contexts, and when and how they become dissolved. Also involved are the religious, educational, economic, and political forces in societies and communities that can facilitate or impede the fertility process.

That individuals respond to *normative influences* from others around them is a fundamental tenet of sociological study. Yet it is difficult to describe the concept of norms and even more problematic to measure it. In his essay on "Shooting an Elephant," Orwell (1950) describes an Englishman residing in South Asia who responds to the threat of a wild elephant by tracking it with his gun through a village, surrounded by the natives. Not inclined to kill the elephant but wanting only to scare it off, he finds himself pressured by the natives to do away with it. The normative expectations become too great and his own feelings about the situation get minimized.

Do norms operate in the same way to affect our fertility decisions and actions? On theoretical grounds, we can find very strong arguments in favor of that principle (Freedman, 1963). On empirical grounds, support is more tenuous. We can observe the tendency for groups of people to share family size desires and for others to shift their fertility orientations in the direction of those who are setting styles, as is the case when modernization is occurring. But we cannot easily link the normative effects to individual behaviors with data collected from surveys. Mason (1983) makes the further point that what we may perceive as norms operating specifically to affect fertility may be a reflection of other societal norms that indirectly influence fertility behaviors. Nevertheless, no one doubts that the fertility process depends on institutional forces.

Marriage, cohabitation, and family structures clearly operate to produce effects on fertility. Ryder (1983) believes that too much emphasis in fertility analysis has been given to individual factors (the micro aspect). He suggests greater recognition of the fact that the sociocultural context of reproduction (the macro aspect) is vitally important.

Despite the fact that marriage and childbearing have no necessary biological connection, most fertility occurs within marriage in virtually all societies. It then becomes crucial to determine when people get married. In the least developed countries, age at first marriage usually comes early and this serves to expose the female population to higher probabilities of becoming pregnant and having children. In developed countries, age at first marriage is more likely to be delayed, so that there is less opportunity for childbearing. In most societies the variables that contribute to determining the age at marriage are cultural prescriptions and proscriptions (which may have their origins in religious or other traditional practices), the relative attractiveness of staying single, the marriage market for persons of the opposite sex, and the resources required and the resource transfers involved in getting married (Bulatao and Lee, 1983). These marriage propensities are, in turn, influenced by demographic and other social factors, which we will examine more fully in Chapter 9 on families and households.

The emphasis on marriage as a context for fertility often ignores the fact that there are three types of sexual unions that can produce offspring—legal or religiously sanctioned marriages, consensual unions that are socially recognized and fairly stable but which have no legal standing, and more casual unions characterized by regular or irregular cohabitation. In different parts of the world, the latter two forms may constitute a significant element of all sexual unions. For example, consensual unions are common in parts of Latin America, and cohabitation has become a more popular type of union in developed countries.

According to Cherlin (1990), delayed age at marriage and the great increase in cohabitation in the United States in recent years resulted in sexual unions beginning well before marriage for many young adults, and the rising divorce rates and cohabitation among older divorced women meant that sexual unions existed outside marriage for them as well. As a consequence, the connection between marriage and sexual relations, and hence with fertility, was much weaker by 1990 than two or three decades earlier. Despite the increasing resort to abortion among unmarried women, fully one out of four births in the United States in 1987 were to women who were not then married. It was also estimated that one-fourth of the births to unmarried women were to those who were cohabiting.

Rindfuss and Parnell (1989) point out that differences in fertility of married and nonmarried women depend heavily on the socioeconomic characteristics of those involved. Among highly educated white women who had not yet had a child, the probability of having one is ten times as great among those who are married. Another factor the researchers discuss as relevant to the marriage-fertility linkage is that, while marriage may provide the sanction for having children for many women, for others marriage may take place after pregnancy or childbirth to legitimize a birth. Hence, marriage may be a potent institutional force even when it does not occur prior to sexual relations or pregnancy.

Other institutional effects on fertility may be as great or greater than marital unions (Potter, 1983). The educational attainment of women is strongly tied to fertility levels (Farooq and DeGraff, 1988; Cochrane, 1979; Caldwell, 1980). Female education can affect fertility quite directly by increasing knowledge about birth control and by creating an atmosphere that places high value on the quality of life in a family that can be improved when fewer rather than more children are produced. But it can also operate indirectly on fertility through influencing the age at marriage, increasing the capability of women to reduce the mortality of their infants and children and thus to lessen their desire for additional births, and revealing the options for women to engage in activities outside the home that compete with childbearing and the raising of children.

None of the factors have probably had such a profound effect on the fertility transition as the *changing roles of women.* The growing independence of women over time has permitted them to engage in activities outside the household; this, in turn, has reduced their time for having and raising children. Female independence meant acquiring more education, taking on roles previously reserved for men, and assuming an increasing amount of power in interpersonal relationships, both within and outside the family. In all countries, this reshaping of women's roles strongly challenged the cultural definitions of what women could and could not do, and the changes that took place typically occurred very slowly at first but more rapidly as institutions underwent modification.

Today, in developed countries and increasingly in developing countries, women's work roles have been significantly altered. In developed nations, employment rates of women have increased sharply and the gap between male and female employment patterns has been reduced appreciably (see Chapter 11 for further discussion of this point). As developing countries have improved their overall economic position, women's involvement in work activities has expanded. It has been found that the rise in the percent of women who are working in a country is associated with a decline in the fertility level of women in that country (United Nations, 1985).

All the factors mentioned so far have had the potential for interacting with each other so that their effects appear both singly and jointly. Some analysts have treated the several factors as constituting an integrated concept that is called either *modernization* or *development.* By this researchers mean changes in the institutions of a society or community that shift those institutions away from their traditional forms.

Easterlin and Crimmins (1985) sum up the reproductive effects of these changes by stating:

> With the onset of modernization, the number of children that would result from unregulated fertility gradually comes to exceed desired family size, and an incentive to limit family size emerges and grows.... Initially fertility control is probably used only for short periods and not very efficiently. However, associated with the spread of control there is a growth in both the length and efficiency of use, and eventually, the spread of control translates into fertility decline....

A major point made by the authors is that modernization, or institutional change, operates first and foremost to create motivations for lower fertility and only later do fertility control mechanisms respond to those motivations. This argument has been contested by some who believe that family planning has been the most critical factor in bringing about reductions in fertility, especially in nations recently undergoing a fertility transition.

Fertility Control

Institutional changes of some sorts have preceded sustained fertility decline in all countries and have also accompanied such decline. The prior motivation that Easterlin and Crimmins refer to can likewise be extended after fertility reduction has begun in order to provide incentives for those who have not yet become motivated. The ideal setting for reproductive change is thus one where there is an efficient family planning program that is responsive to the fertility orientations of the people and sensitive to the local social and cultural conditions.

Fertility control encompasses an array of behaviors that lead toward lowering the prospect of births. In Chapter 3, we outlined the framework of Davis and Blake (1956) that classified the several variables involved into factors affecting exposure to intercourse, exposure to conception, and gestation and successful parturition. Variables related to marriage, sexual activity, contraception, and fetal deaths were included among those factors. This broad framework allows us to examine the influences intervening between social and cultural forces and childbearing itself. Davis and Blake agreed that every society initiates and sustains fertility declines with its own mix of these factors (called *intermediate variables*).

In later years other analysts elaborated the workings of these intermediate variables (renamed *proximate variables*) and developed techniques for measuring their effects (Bongaarts, 1978; Menken, 1987). Greater attention was given to the postpartum infecund period and the contribution made by patterns of *breast-feeding*, as a result of which hormonal changes have the effect of limiting ovulation. Emphasis was also placed on the importance of *child spacing*, the time intervals between union of couples and their first child and between succeeding children that a woman has, for eventual fertility.

A sense of how much fertility controls reduce childbearing depends on a notion of what such childbearing would be in the absence of controls (what is called *natural fertility*). It is conventional to regard the Hutterite population of

North America as typifying the practice of natural fertility because its religious principles prevent the Hutterites from using contraception. Robinson (1986) has shown that Hutterite women do not marry at a very early age, have higher lactational amenhorrea than other populations, have moderate coital frequencies, and agree to sterilization late in the childbearing period when the woman's health and life may be challenged by having another child. As a result, the fertility of Hutterite women (as high as an average of ten children for those going through the reproductive period) is kept from being higher (as much as an average of fifteen children). If there are no societies that can be described as practicing natural fertility, that concept is at least a useful one for representing the biological potential of childbearing.

What forms of *birth control* (prevention of births) have been available to reduce natural fertility in populations? Some people have the impression that *contraception* (preventing conception) is a modern innovation. In fact, some form of contraception has been known since time immemorial. The "traditional" methods are cited in biblical accounts and in other early historical writings about human groups. *Celibacy* (in the sense of prolonged sexual abstention) has been common not only among the clergy but also among some in the general population. *Coitus interruptus* ("withdrawal") is not only a technique of teenagers who are lax about other methods but also widespread among societies now as in the past. It was the major form of control used in France during its fertility transition.

Many "barrier" methods likewise have a long history. The *condom* for males remains popular because of its ease of use, and it offers some protection against unwanted pregnancy as well as AIDS and sexually transmitted diseases (Liskin et al., 1990). A condom for females is now available as well. The *diaphragm*, *cervical cap*, and *spermicidal products* offer barrier alternatives for women (Population Crisis Committee, 1991).

Various hormonal techniques of contraception represent more modern innovations in birth control. Included here are *oral contraceptives* (the Pill) that are available in both a combined form and progestin-only minipill form, *injectable contraceptives* (such as Depo-Provera), and *contraceptive implants* (such as Norplant). Injectables and implants have met with some national resistance and are still not available on a worldwide basis. A high-dosage estrogen pill (called the *morning-after pill*) can be taken within a few days after sexual intercourse, but it is associated with undesirable side effects. *Intrauterine devices* (IUDs) are also modern and appear in many different forms.

"Surgical" methods of contraception, including *female sterilization* (tubectomy and tubal litigation) and *male sterilization* (vasectomy), are used by the largest numbers of people in the world. They have become increasingly widespread in recent years, but principally among persons who have already reached their intended family size (Ross, 1992). A concern about sterilization is that it has long been considered an irreversible method for both men and women, thus bringing about a certain finality to the reproductive potential of those who have sexual relations. (Its use as part of population policy in countries such as India has stirred considerable controversy.) Yet sterilization operations can be reversed under certain conditions (Church and Geller, 1990; Liskin et al., 1992).

Periodic sexual abstinence is a contemporary form of birth control that includes the calendar rhythm method (once popular among Catholics because of its sanction by the Popes but more recently receding in use because of its relatively low reliability and the need for record-keeping), as well as other techniques of calculating a "safe period" for sexual intercourse.

Contraceptive prevalence worldwide varies considerably by region and country. By 1990, roughly half of the world's couples with the woman in reproductive ages practiced some form of contraception. The vast majority of them were using modern methods (pill, condom, IUD, or sterilization). Contraceptive use was as high as 81 percent among such countries as Japan, Belgium, and France, and as low as 1 percent in Mauritania (Population Reference Bureau, 1992). Contraceptive use has been increasing in most developing countries. It is likely that under 10 percent of couples in developing nations were using contraception before the mid-1960s whereas by 1990 the level had reached about 45 percent (United Nations, 1989). Yet many countries in South Asia and sub-Saharan Africa still had low levels of contraceptive use by 1990.

In the United States, the use of contraception is spread among different methods and varies by age (see Table 6.2). In a survey taken in 1988, 30 percent of all women 15 to 44 years old were found to be sterile, most of them on the basis of surgery on them or their mates. Almost 9 percent were pregnant or seeking pregnancy. An additional 25 percent were nonusers of contraception because either they did not have intercourse or had intercourse but shunned methods of contraception. That left only 37 percent of all women in the reproductive ages who were nonsurgical contraceptors. Roughly half of those primarily used the Pill. Another 9 percent relied on condom use by the male. Smaller percentages of the women used other forms of contraception.

Age differences were significant. The younger group (15–24) was much less likely to be sterile, much more likely to be nonusers of contraception (probably because teenagers were included in the group), and more apt to be Pill users if they used any method of contraception. Those 25–34 were much more likely than the younger group to have been sterilized, much less likely to be nonusers and, among users, similarly attracted to the Pill. Sterilization accounted for 61 percent of the women at ages 35–44. They were less likely than either of the other age groups to be nonusers, but also less likely to be contraceptors. Among the 22 percent in the 35–44 age group who were contraceptors, condom and diaphragm use were more prevalent than Pill use.

The most controversial birth control methods have been *induced abortion* techniques (aspiration, dilation, and curettage) that are used primarily during the first trimester of pregnancy. Because they are not contraceptive but are used to terminate conceptions (including fetuses in their very early or predevelopment stage) many people regard abortion techniques as destroying life (or more pointedly, human life). Those who contest that view argue that human life begins at birth and that fetal life before the second trimester of pregnancy

TABLE 6.2 Percent of U.S. Women 15–44 Years of Age, by Current Contraceptive Status and Principal Method, by Age: 1988

CONTRACEPTIVE STATUS AND METHOD	TOTAL 15–44	15–24	25–34	35–44
TOTAL	100.0	100.0	100.0	100.0
STERILE	29.7	3.1	27.0	61.3
Surgically sterile	28.3	2.4	26.0	58.7
Contraceptively sterile	23.6	2.2	23.3	46.7
Female	16.6	1.6	16.6	32.5
Male	7.0	0.6	6.7	14.2
Noncontraceptively sterile	4.7	0.2	2.7	12.0
Female	4.7	0.2	2.7	11.9
Male	0.0	0.0	0.0	0.0
Nonsurgically sterile	1.4	0.7	0.9	2.7
PREGNANT OR POSTPARTUM	4.8	5.0	7.6	1.1
SEEKING PREGNANCY	3.8	2.7	5.8	2.4
OTHER NONUSER	25.0	45.7	16.7	13.5
Never had intercourse	11.5	30.0	3.6	1.6
No intercourse in 3 months	6.2	5.4	6.4	6.8
Intercourse in last 3 months	6.5	7.8	6.4	5.0
NONSURGICAL CONTRACEPTORS	36.7	43.5	43.0	21.6
Pill	18.5	29.7	21.6	3.0
IUD	1.2	0.1	1.4	2.1
Diaphragm	3.5	1.3	4.8	4.1
Condom	8.8	9.5	9.1	7.7
Foam	0.6	0.3	0.8	0.8
Periodic abstinence	1.4	0.6	1.7	1.8
Natural family planning	0.4	0.2	0.5	0.4
Withdrawal	1.3	1.5	1.9	0.6
Douche	0.1	0.0	0.0	0.2
Other methods	1.2	0.5	1.7	1.4

Source: Derived from William D. Mosher and William F. Pratt, 1990, "Contraceptive Use in the United States, 1973–88," *Advance Data from Vital and Health Statistics*, no. 182, Tables 1 and 2, National Center for Health Statistics.

has not yet assumed a truly human form. There is also a debate over the maturity of the fetus at the time of an abortion because the length of pregnancy can be measured from the first day of the last menstrual period or from the probable date of fertilization (about two weeks later) (Santee and Henshaw, 1992). The controversy about abortion is waged mainly on religious and moral grounds (Petchesky, 1990). Hardly anyone states a preference for abortion over forms of birth control used to prevent pregnancies.

The fact remains that there is a worldwide trend toward liberalization of abortion laws, with 40 percent of the world's population living in countries where induced abortion is permitted on request and an additional 25 percent living in countries where it is allowed only if the woman's life would be endangered if she kept the pregnancy through the reproductive period. It has been estimated that between 26 and 31 million legal abortions were performed in 1987 as were between 10 and 22 million illegal abortions (Henshaw, 1990). Evidence from the reanalysis of U.S. surveys suggests that levels of abortion are underreported and that their extent is even higher than official estimates show (Jones and Forrest, 1992). Despite the burgeoning contraceptive programs that make abortion less necessary, induced abortion levels remain comparatively high in areas of central and eastern Europe (David, 1992).

Sometimes related to abortion are *menses-inducing drugs* which can be administered soon after a woman's menstruation has ceased and there is medical certification of the joining of sperm with the ovum. These drugs serve to cause expulsion of the uterine contents and allow menstruation to resume. The French-produced drug RU-486, highly restricted outside France, is the first such drug that has been adequately tested (Holt et al., 1991). Groups opposed to abortion under any circumstance generally regard RU-486 as an abortifacient. Others believe that it should be considered a contraceptive.

It has frequently been commented that birth control has been mainly the responsibility of women, even though both genders are involved in the fertility process. Abstinence, withdrawal, the condom, and sterilization are methods that males can initiate. The traditional roles of the genders placed most of the burden on women in the past. In fact, a greater variety of techniques of birth control are available to women than to men. However, commensurate with the changing roles of women (and of men), there is a new emphasis on male birth control. This includes not only the existing methods but also the development of new male contraceptive techniques, such as hormonal suppression of sperm production, chemical interference with sperm production, and more easily reversible forms of vasectomy (Gallen et al., 1986).

Although knowledge about these various techniques of birth control has been disseminated by their developers and by governments interested in fertility control, a critical factor in the worldwide process of lowering fertility levels has been the international *family planning movement*, a social movement that has involved United Nations agencies, national governments, philanthropic groups, and affiliates of the International Planned Parenthood Federation (IPPF) (Donaldson and Tsui, 1990) (see Box 6.3).

Today the family planning programs of the world are flourishing. By 1983, in fact, 76 percent of the population of the Third World lived in countries with official policies and national family programs designed to reduce their popula-

BOX 6.3 Brief History of the Family Planning Movement

The movement can be traced through four general stages. In the first stage (from the late nineteenth century to the end of World War I), birth control advocates, led by Margaret Sanger in the United States and Marie C. Stopes in Britain, opened the first birth control clinics but had to fight strong opposition from those who feared that destruction of family life and promotion of promiscuity would result from the movement. Although the American Medical Association gave qualified endorsement to family planning in the 1930s, the thrust of the movement was stifled until the end of World War II when the second stage began, which continued through the 1950s. Emphasis in this stage was on disassociating the family planning movement from eugenic interests (those tied to improving the human genetic stock by controlling physical and mental traits) and linking it more to economic development and political stability. The International Planned Parenthood Federation (IPPF) took root during this time, and the United Nations oriented some of its work on social issues toward population change, including family planning. The third stage began about 1960 and lasted until the mid-1980s. At this time national governments built family planning support into their budgets for foreign aid (the U.S. Agency for International Development within the State Department was a prime example of such a functional unit). The United Nations Fund for Population Activities was created as a central agency for population matters within the UN; population centers sprang up in many of the major universities within the United States and other developed countries and many of these centers had programs focusing on fertility reduction; and the UN held a World Population Conference in Bucharest (in 1974) that proposed a World Population Plan of Action. The fourth stage has been going on since the mid-1980s and is characterized by increasing commitments from Third World leaders to family planning at the same time that developed countries (especially the United States) have shown a reluctance to support the movement further (Donaldson and Tsui, 1990).

tion growth by reducing fertility (Freedman, 1990). Yet it has been difficult to separate the fertility effects of the family planning programs from those of modernization and development. One could note that the first national family planning program was established in India in 1951 and fertility reduction in that country has not been very great. Likewise, Egypt's program was initiated in 1965 and the annual growth rate there has declined very slowly. In Pakistan, which started a family planning program in 1960, fertility has actually increased. On the other hand, in other countries with family planning programs in place, such as Taiwan, Sri Lanka, and Singapore, the demographic transition has moved along swiftly.

Efforts to estimate the impact of family planning programs on fertility more directly (Bongaarts, Mauldin, and Phillips, 1990b, Mauldin and Ross, 1991; Entwistle, 1989; Hernandez, 1984, 1989) have been complicated by the fact that many variables are changing at the same time as is family planning input, and the presence of a family planning program as well as information on the number of people using its services does not necessarily indicate to what extent effective use of the methods and material acquired gets translated into birth control at the individual level. Many family programs do not offer cafeteria-style methods and often restrict the available techniques to those acceptable to major religious and ethnic groups within the country; as a result, some people are effectively outside the range of these services.

It seems necessary to know the particulars about a society before one can render judgment about the relative contributions made by various factors to fertility decline (or increase). The reduction of the fertility level in Singapore was certainly tied to the reality that it is a city-state with no rural population, that socioeconomic change had been evident there for some time, and that the government met little resistance in adopting and implementing a vigorous family planning program. In the case of India, a lack of success in fertility reduction despite a long-standing family planning program can be traced to its large rural population, its slow socioeconomic progress, and many cultural practices that have pronatal consequences.

Hull (1986) has pointed to several social changes within Indonesia that facilitated the family planning movement there, including a political atmosphere following independence that stressed personal freedom and equality (elements of Panca Sila, the new national value system), greater mobility chances for the young, an expanded educational system, an agency of government devoted exclusively to family planning, and an agency head who has been a charismatic and devoted advocate of fertility decline in the country and who has had the President's attention.

Warwick (1988) has identified critical cultural factors facilitating family planning implementation and has shown how these were present in Indonesia but not in Kenya, where family planning programs floundered.

There are, however, different styles of effective programs. Consider the reported sharp decline in fertility in China, where government support for family planning began in 1962 but only received strong implementation in recent years. In opposition to the more educational approach of Singapore and Indonesia, the authoritarian approach of China required mechanisms for closely monitoring the behavior of Chinese couples who had pledged to adhere to the specifications of the one-child policy. A principal mechanism has been the millions of neighborhood watchers, mainly older women, some of them volunteers and others paid moderately, who combine keeping track of political dissidents and delinquents with close checks on the comings and goings of young women who already have one child. Persuasion is used to caution couples about the need to adhere to family policy, and pressure to abort and monetary fines are employed when violations of the policy occur.

Of course, in all countries social and economic change and family planning are complementary, not competitive, means for fertility control. Moreover, as Easterlin and Crimmins indicate, if the motivation is there, the people will seek the means even if they are not widely available. Family planning programs make it more likely that they will find what they seek.

Differential Fertility

When we compare categories of women with different characteristics in terms of their fertility performance, significant variations often appear. Moreover, many of these variations change with time. Patterns of *differential fertility* are of interest in demographic analysis because they reveal the different exposures of categories of people to influences on fertility demand and supply and the costs of control. They also indicate the differing contributions made to overall fertility by various groups.

The differentials we will focus on in this section will be socioeconomic, racial and ethnic, and religious. Discussions of them will be highly descriptive and will serve to indicate the disparities that do and do not occur. The varying fertility patterns of groups will also allow us to place characteristics of people within the broader frameworks that we use to understand fertility changes over time.

The general significance attached to the appearance of differential fertility is that the social and cultural milieu in which persons find themselves partly shapes their orientations to fertility and their birth control habits. Where differentials are observed, however, we must try to discover if the measured characteristics have direct effects on fertility or if they are just proxies for other variables that are directly influential.

One critical socioeconomic characteristic is the education of the woman (and of her mate as well). We have already addressed the importance of education of women as a potent force in shaping the environment that leads to fertility decline. But just how different is the fertility of women who are well educated and those who are poorly educated?

India's high fertility is associated with low levels of literacy and even lower levels of an adequate formal education. Only one in four Indian women is literate, perhaps not surprising for a highly rural country. But the proportions illiterate are even high in urban areas, although much higher in rural areas. Sheer literacy, the ability to read and write in at least one language, can permit a woman to do things that she could not do otherwise. Literate women tend to become more knowledgeable about family planning and are more likely to use contraceptive methods. They are also more likely to have interests outside their immediate family and to play social roles beyond childbearing. Their visions of the world and the prospects for their children are more realistic, and so they put emphasis on improving the quality of life for their children.

Sharma and Retherford (1990) compared the literacy rates for Indian states with the fertility rates in those areas. They discovered a high degree of inverse association. The state with the lowest female literacy level had the highest fertility rate; the state with the highest female literacy level was among those with the lowest fertility rate. Their further analysis led them to conclude that half of the association between the variables was directly due to literacy effects and half was indirect, operating through literacy's influence on a lower infant and child mortality level that lowered intended future fertility as well as through age at marriage, with literate women marrying later.

Rodriguez and Aravena (1991) reviewed the findings of a range of country studies conducted as part of the Demographic and Health Surveys (DHS). Not only was the educational factor important in all the countries, but its influence was modified as the fertility transition proceeded. In Kenya, the reduction in fertility was observed in all educational strata but was greatest among the better-educated. Fertility limitation was more pronounced among the well-educated in Morocco whereas in Thailand, where the transition was more advanced, lower-educated groups were reducing their fertility even more rapidly than the better-educated. These researchers, too, found that half of the educational effect was direct and half indirect. The direct effect alone, however, served to lower fertility by one child per woman for the average DHS country, and more in some African nations.

Recent patterns in the United States show that, among women who have reached the later stages of the reproductive period, those with the poorest educational attainment have had the highest number of children ever born, with those not completing high school averaging 2.7 children compared to 1.7 children for college graduates and 2.0 children for high school graduates (Bachu, 1993).

As evidence that the general socioeconomic background of the woman is crucial in relation to her childbearing, not just her education level, one can turn to the husband's occupation (for married women) and the family's income as more general indicators. In the United States in 1990, the average number of children who had been born to women 35 to 44 years old was slightly higher for women whose husbands were in blue-collar jobs (2.2) than for those with husbands in white-collar positions (2.0). Family income provided sharper fertility differentials. When the wife was not in the labor force, children ever born ranged from 2.8 for women in the under $10,000 family income category to 2.3 for those in the $50,000 category. If women were in the labor force, the differences were still apparent, stretching from 2.6 for the low-income group to 1.9 for the higher-income category.

Fertility has always been different for various racial and ethnic groups. Examining U.S. women 35 to 44 in 1992 who have ever been married according to race-ethnic categories (white, black, and Hispanic) and in terms of their children ever born, we find that the Hispanic category shows the highest average number of children born to them (2.5), compared to 1.9 for white women and 2.2 for black women. Among those not finishing high school, the highest children-ever-born level is 2.8 for blacks, compared to 2.6 for whites and 3.0 for Hispanics. Similar disparities exist for those who completed high school but did not go on to college. Among college graduates, the differences are small but whites have the lowest childbearing levels (1.7 as compared with 1.9 for Hispanics and 1.8 for blacks) (Bachu, 1993). Thus, while it is clear that getting better educated reduces fertility for all of the race-ethnic categories, within educational categories the race-ethnic differences persist.

Researchers have debated the extent to which the race-ethnic factor is grounded in cultural variations among the categories. The U.S. data indicate that socioeconomic factors (in this case, only education of the women is measured) account for a considerable part of the disparity among race-ethnic groups, but a part still remains unaccounted for. Actual fertility differences are a function of fertility orientations combined with fertility control. In the case of black-white comparisons in the United States, studies have shown that both fertility desires and contraceptive use are quite similar for the two groups when socioeconomic variables are controlled (O'Hare et al., 1991). This finding suggests that the independent cultural effect in this case is quite small, and that overall fertility differentials that are observed exist principally because more blacks than whites are socioeconomically disadvantaged.

Finally, we consider religious differences in fertility. These would seem to be very important because of the official stands of religious organizations over the years. One's beliefs are strong influences on fertility desires and birth control use.

Childbearing differences among religious categories of the population have been reported in studies for some time. They include higher Muslim than Christian fertility in developing areas and higher Catholic than Protestant fertility in developed countries. You may recall that, earlier in this book, attention was called to the fact that we often analyze broad categories of variables without taking note that there are variations within the broad categories. For example, Hispanic infant mortality varies significantly, depending on whether the Hispanics are Cuban, Puerto Rican, Mexican, or of other Spanish origin.

Chamie (1981) showed the same phenomenon in his study of fertility among Muslims. In Lebanon in 1971, non-Catholic Christian women had fewer children than did Catholic women, and both had lower fertility than did Muslim women. However, when the latter were separately identified by their Muslim religious affiliations, substantial differences appeared. Fertility was high for both Shia and Sunni Muslims but significantly higher for the former. The fertility level of Druze women was roughly intermediate between Catholics and non-Catholic Christians.

In the United States, Catholics traditionally have had the highest level of fertility, while childbearing levels were higher for Protestants than for Jews. During the baby boom era the traditional differences persisted. But, with continued fertility declines, the religious differentials have narrowed considerably.

Mosher et al. (1992) have conducted an in-depth study of religious variations in fertility in the United States, controlling for complicating factors, for births occuring in the 1980s. The average number of children ever born to women 15 to 44 was slightly higher for Catholics than for Protestants among Hispanics (1.6 versus 1.5). But the number was lower for Catholics than for Protestants among non-Hispanic blacks (1.4 versus 1.5) and lower for Catholics than for Protestants among non-Hispanic whites (1.1 versus 1.3). The average number of children ever born was 1.1 for Jewish women and 0.8 for those who professed no religious identification. Non-Hispanic white Protestant fertility could be further differentiated by specific denomination. Mormon women had an average of 1.8 children ever born while the figure for Methodists was 1.2. Between the two were Fundamentalist groups (1.6), Baptists (1.4), Lutherans (1.3), and other Protestants (1.2).

If these religious categories are further separated by their ethnicity (e.g., Irish Catholics versus Italian Catholics), additional distinctions in fertility levels might be made. In addition, specifying the geographic location and socioeconomic background of the categories introduces further variation. The reasons for remaining differences might lie in varying marriage patterns as well as cultural factors associated with each group.

Of great significance is the fact that, compared with earlier points in time in the United States, religious differentials have narrowed considerably. Have national norms about childbearing now become so common, and fertility control practices so similar, that fertility performance varies within a narrow range?

THE STAGES OF FERTILITY

In the previous chapter, we followed our discussion of major concepts and measures with an account of the stages of the mortality transition, using examples from different countries as they passed through comparable stages. That approach will be continued here with regard to the fertility transition. We will examine each stage in history (noting that different countries reach each stage at different times in their own area), and we will determine the common and unique aspects of their fertility processes. This review is illustrative and not comprehensive, but it should give a sense of the flow of the fertility transition as it has evolved across time and nations.

Although some persons have questioned the usefulness of the fertility transition idea for characterizing the course of fertility in recent decades, others have drawn on the framework for summarizing the picture of childbearing patterns as they have changed in time. Is there a progression of fertility declines in the less developed world that was anticipated from the experience of earlier transitions completed by now-developed nations? Have some factors affecting fertility become more prominent than before?

Freedman and Blanc (1991) reviewed the factual information amassed through various United Nations statistics and Demographic and Health Surveys around the world. Between 1965–1970 and 1980–1985, total fertility rates in Third World countries declined by 30 percent, which meant that in fifteen years those nations as a whole had moved their fertility levels about halfway toward the goal of replacement level (2.1). In the fifteen years prior to this period, there had only been a fertility reduction of about 3 percent, so that the late 1960s was a significant turning point.

Admittedly, the fertility declines were not uniform in all less developed parts of the world. Reductions of one-fourth or more were found in Latin America and East and Southeast Asia. In southern and western Asia and in the extreme northern and southern parts of Africa, declines were more modest. In other parts of Africa, they were nonexistent; in fact, some fertility increases were recorded. Moreover, what declines were noted in some countries seem to have leveled off.

The recent decreases in fertility that have taken place have been accompanied by a telescoping of a woman's childbearing period. The gap between first and last birth has been shortened considerably. Thus the fertility decline and reduction in the fraction of a woman's life that involves childbearing generally are characteristic of what took place in more developed countries in earlier time periods. The fact that nations are still diverse in their fertility levels means that fertility is at different points in the transition of different less developed countries. However, indications are that the transition is yet an ongoing process, interrupted at times but with prospects of resuming its course.

Pretransition Stage

Although data are lacking on fertility experience in the earliest of societies, there is every reason to believe that they had very high fertility. Lorimer (1954) points out that "our proto-human ancestors, without the support of kinship structures or social ideals conducive to high fertility, must have maintained a level of fertility like that found in many non-industrial societies today." He went on to say that "our proto-human ancestors, prior to the rise of culture, achieved effective reproduction...with essentially the same biological equipment and basic psychological impulses as modern man, and without institutional sanctions....This basic pattern tending toward the replacement of generations requires no ingenious interpretation in terms of cunning design or the different survival of beneficent innovations, though the basic pattern may be profoundly modified in different cultures."

As has been the case with societies in recent times, those of the past did not reproduce to the maximum biological capacity. Levels of fecundity were affected by genetic factors, malnutrition, venereal diseases, and other diseases (during a time when mortality was also high). In addition, those women who conceived had a high probability of not carrying the fetus to term. In such a context, it is perhaps surprising that a high level of fertility was reached. Yet countervailing high infant and child mortality meant that a relatively small proportion of the young would survive to create families of their own (Wood, 1990).

It would be more accurate to say, as Coale (1986) has argued, that "traditional societies developed customs that kept fertility at moderate levels, avoiding both fertility so low that negative growth would make the population shrink to zero, or so high that positive growth would lead to an overcrowded habitat...." The customs that were developed included such practices as tabus on sexual intercourse under some circumstances and breast-feeding of babies that led to spans of nonfecundity between pregnancy efforts.

In earliest America, childbearing levels were as high as in any developing country today—a crude birth rate of about 55 per 1,000, which translates into a completed childbearing pattern of about eight children (Taeuber and Taeuber, 1971). This was higher than that found in Europe at the time, where fertility had begun to decline, so that those who came to America may have been both selective of those from Europe with higher fertility and encouraged to continue that level in a country that was attempting to populate sparsely occupied land and an advancing frontier.

A social historian of the southern colonies in the United States in the eighteenth century (Spruill, 1938) describes the rationale for having high fertility in that era:

> Men and women prided themselves upon their numerous offspring, not only because of a belief that they were obeying a scriptural command to replenish the earth and a patriotic duty to add new citizens to the Empire, but also because they regarded children as a material investment, a kind of insurance against old age and misfortune.

In contemporary Africa, as in other areas of the pretransition period that have had high levels of childbearing, fertility maximization is based on the universality of marriage, limitation of sexual-exposure time lost through disruptions of unions, a strong desire for large families, and recognition of the major economic and social contributions that children can make to family welfare (Lesthaeghe, 1989).

Why haven't birth levels in most of Africa declined when those in other developing countries have started into the transition? According to Caldwell and Caldwell (1990), the countries of sub-Saharan Africa owe their continued high fertility to certain social and family patterns that have developed over millennia in response to conditions of the region. One pattern is the religious belief in the supreme importance of ancestral spirits and in the overriding need for descendants to avoid being cursed by the dead by ensuring the survival of that lineage with high fertility. Another pattern relates to the fact that the emotional and economic bonds of marriage in sub-Saharan Africa are weak, with separation rates high and polygyny widespread. Childbearing is thus largely independent of family considerations. Women may have children with several mates, and births to an unmarried woman do not have the social stigma they have had in Western countries nor do they pose an economic problem because kin will accept them. As a result of these relatively unique cultural patterns, combined with the more traditional justifications of the value of children to a less developed society, high fertility is sustained in much of sub-Saharan Africa. Yet there are now indications that some of these patterns are changing and that the fertility transition has begun in several countries of the region (Robinson, 1992; Caldwell et al., 1992).

Early Transition Stage

Many forces bring about a decline in fertility in countries that start to experience development. Economic institutions are transformed from family-based agricultural and service activities to community-organized business organizations. Such economic change produces shifts in the roles of women so that they are less related to the home and more linked to the outside world. The strength of traditional religious ties is weakened by the introduction of an element of worldliness into the belief systems of people. More of the population gets located in cities and fewer in rural areas, and the cost of raising children goes up and their economic contributions are reduced to the extent that their net economic value recedes. On balance, the motivation for continuing high levels of childbearing declines.

Family patterns were also involved in the early transition of fertility. Prior to the onset of sustained fertility decline, marriages took place at a relatively early age and little conscious fertility control was used. As motivations for having fewer children developed, age at marriage was delayed and birth regulation became more of a reality (Knodel and van de Walle, 1986).

Because innovations in fertility-reducing behavior, as in mortality-reducing behavior, typically start with the upper social strata, it was they who first deferred marrying and it was they who first employed birth control methods to lower fertility. These "social-group forerunners" of fertility decline in Europe were the aristocracies and many Jewish communities. Both of these categories were among those who first lowered their death rates. Both typically resided in urban areas. Both were comparatively economically advantaged. Marriage patterns of the two groups were not identical but delayed age at marriage was common to most of those populations that were studied. These conditions facilitated the lower fertility desires and the use of fertility control measures by these populations (Livi-Bacci, 1986).

In country after country in Europe, fertility was well on its way downward by the middle of the nineteenth century. In the United States, parallel declines occurred as industrial expansion proceeded. The birth rate in the United States was less than 50 by 1850 and fell down to 40 by 1880 (Taeuber and Taeuber, 1971). The decline started later in the southern region and still later among rural farm women (see Box 6.4).

The early fertility transition in Australia was not essentially different from that of European countries (particularly Great Britain) and the United States, but there were some unique factors (Caldwell and Ruzicka, 1978). In the third quarter of the nineteenth century, Australia's population was heavily composed of British immigrants. The immigrants had brought with them the cultural values of England and Wales, and their family form was already predominantly nucleated (parents and children without other kin). Traditional practices required that a man get into a secure occupation before he married and raised a family. Late age at marriage, which was then the practice in England and Wales, also became the norm in Australia. Although there was an elite class and

BOX 6.4 Fertility Attitudes of Nineteenth-Century U.S. Women

Indicative of the attitudes toward childbearing during a time when fertility is high but conditions are there for lowering them is a report on North Carolina farm women when the beginning of their fertility transition was imminent (Hagood, 1939):

> Undoubtedly there is ambivalence. The traditional pattern of the glory and the actual or imagined value of a large number of children pull in one direction, while the desire to avoid the suffering of childbearing, the trouble of caring for another child, and the responsibility of another mouth to be fed and body to be clothed pull in the other. An approximate balance of these forces means that the former wins out because children keep arriving when a laissez-faire policy is adopted. And yet the trend, indicated by the verbal expressions of the mothers and confirmed by quantitative birth rate data, is an increase in the response to the latter forces accompanied by a greater availability of techniques for preventing births.

privileged education was available for some, as in Britain, mass education soon became a reality. The values placed on good education for children and good employment for men elevated the cost of childraising and introduced a rationality to childbearing behavior. Since the country found itself in an economic depression beginning in the last decade of the nineteenth century, there was a further incentive to having fewer births. Thus, while Australia's fertility level was never as high as that experienced by most countries in their formative stages, the transition to low fertility began in a way similar to that seen in these other countries.

In developing countries that have recently begun to lower their fertility levels, the factors were similar although their relative importance may have been different. The crude birth rate had begun to fall in the Indian state of Kerala in the late 1950s. Many factors were at work but, in general, the decline stemmed from a favorable ecological and social setting in the area. Kerala was different from other Indian states in its religious mix and tolerance, its progressive rulers, and its slant toward egalitarianism (it was the first state to abolish the caste system). These conditions precipitated the spread of female education and the extension of primary health care centers when they had not developed in other states. Child survivorship improved and age at marriage went up which, in turn, influenced the number of children a woman wanted to have (Nayar, 1986). The conditions that initiated the transition in Kerala were slow to develop in most other Indian states.

One complicating factor in initiating a sustained fertility decline is that reductions in mortality that occur first mean not only greater survivorship of infants and children but also better health and survival of women in the reproductive period. Women are, therefore, apt to be more fecund and thus more biologically capable of having children. As a consequence, in many countries one can observe a rise in fertility before any sustained decline begins.

Late Transition Stage

Once the fertility level had broken a threshold signaling a continued decline, the forces that produced it maintained their importance until a low level of fertility was reached. However, in many developed nations, the confluence of a world war, a rapidly improving economy, changing women's roles, and other modern developments created a *baby boom* that interrupted the long-term fertility decline. As reported in Chapter 2, this fertility cycle was more than just a blip on the transition curve. It changed family structures at the time and continues to have an echo effect on all the social institutions of the societies involved.

Despite its strong impact on the society, some viewed the baby boom as a correction to the long-term fertility decline, which they saw as having dropped too precipitously in the previous period. In the United States, the baby boom that began in 1946 and peaked in 1957 essentially ended in 1964. At least, at that point the fertility level resumed its long-term transitional course and coasted down to its lowest level.

Easterlin (1973) advanced the notion (sometimes referred to as the *relative income hypothesis*) that the baby boom was one of a potential sequence of fertility cycles resulting from changes in the relative economic benefits accruing to different cohorts. He argued that it worked in this way: Survivors of small birth cohorts (as in the time of the Great Economic Depression of the late 1920s and early 1930s in the United States) would reach working ages with relatively little competition and derive economic benefit from that situation. This would cause them to believe that they could afford more children than their parents had had. The children of survivors of the Depression, in turn, would be part of a larger cohort size that felt competition in school as well as in the economy. As a result, they would desire fewer children than did their parents. The cycles would continue to reverberate, although not necessarily at the same scale of magnitude. The validity of Easterlin's notion has been tested and debated ever since although demographers have not arrived at a consensus about its validity. (We will cover some of this debate in the next section.)

In the post–baby boom era of western Europe (since the mid-1960s), fertility declined steadily and in all countries although the pace and form varied among countries (Prioux, 1990). The percentage of women eventually marrying declined and those who did so married at younger ages. The small family norm was realized with a reduction in childlessness and a corresponding decrease in the proportion of women with large families. Most important, there was widespread growth in the proportion of women with exactly two children. In fact, this was the case for almost half of the women in the cohort born in 1950.

In some of the developed countries, fertility levels dipped so low that they fell below replacement (an average of slightly above 2 children per woman). This low level resulted from an accentuation of factors that had brought fertility down generally—the postponement of marriage; an increase in nonmarital fertility, which is less prolific than marital fertility; high divorce rates; and an increase in wives working outside the home. According to Davis (1986), these forces are part of a more basic underlying explanation of below-replacement fertility, which is the incompatibility of the family as a social unit and the industrial economy. Industrialism, he argues, generates competition and mobility that place tension on family structures and interfere with their traditional reproductive processes.

Preston (1986a) analyzed the fertility trends in the United States, Canada, Australia, New Zealand, and Japan, all countries that had below-replacement fertility for at least a decade. While the English-speaking countries all experienced the causal factors cited by Davis and others, Japan followed the same fertility course despite little nonmarital childbearing, less divorce, and the use of less efficient means of contraception. Preston explains the Japanese pattern in terms of the emphasis on traditional family values, greater economic pressures than in the other countries, and the greater premium attached to education in Japan. But he concludes that Japan shared with the other nations a growing emphasis on individualism (also cited by Lutz with regard to Germany) combined with concerns about the environment and a strong economic base.

The factors cited as contributing to the late fertility transition and even below-replacement fertility make sense as causal explanations. But Keyfitz (1986) raises a more fundamental question: Why do women choose work and leisure over childbearing? This gets back to the issue of motivations and desires. His answer is that, in the modern world, parents' control of children is minimized, and that the marginal benefits of childrearing are not able to compete in attractiveness with those derived from both work and leisure. Most couples will still have two children out of a sense of duty to maintain their lineage, if not out of an obligation to replenish the population. This may seem like a crass way of viewing childbearing, but it is less crass than the econometric approach, which leaves personal tastes out when calculating the costs and benefits of having children. It is also perhaps a realistic assessment of the decisions people make when confronted with their expectations about a future life.

The foregoing discussion focused on countries that moved through the fertility transition over a fairly long period of time. Few non-Western nations have reached the late fertility transition stage, although some are clearly headed in that direction. China is an unusual example of a country that reached the late transition stage in roughly a decade without any conversion from a developing to a developed economy. It accomplished the task by a strong one-child policy. For couples to have only one child (and most of those couples come from large or intermediate-size families themselves) means much greater effort than that expended by Westerners who have two children. Chinese authorities wanted population growth reductions quickly, and their policy was designed to achieve that end. Yet social motivations do not respond so quickly, and most Chinese couples accept the policy but not its implications. Having two children does not guarantee a son, and having one child provides even less likelihood of a male child. When couples want a boy and a girl, having two children is the least they could have and reach their goals (Whyte and Gu, 1987; Feeney et al, 1989). The tensions resulting from the dilemma faced by choices, or the lack of them, produce elements of social instability in Chinese society.

Many of the less developed countries that have moved at least halfway through the fertility transition may require different approaches than those used so far in order to continue the decline to the late transitional stage. Such countries adopted or promoted among their citizens desires or motivations that aimed for lower fertility than was common at earlier times. Yet the targets set were not for very low levels of childbearing, much less replacement fertility.

Birth control practices in such places have succeeded in lowering fertility close to the "wanted" level. Improvements in extending contraceptive use would further reduce fertility to some extent. However, to bring fertility down to late transition levels, there must be a decline in the number of children wanted (Westoff et al., 1989). Some developing countries have established incentive programs for women to lower the number of children they wish to have but most governments of countries in the intermediate transition phase have not looked beyond family planning as a means of achieving desired family size.

Posttransition Stage

Fertility levels stabilized in most developed countries once replacement or just below-replacement indicators were reached. In areas where below-replacement levels were seemingly locked in, governments became sensitive to the prospect of a population decline in combination with the aging of the population. This was a development that boded poorly for countries concerned about stimulating the economy with a vibrant labor force that would depend on having younger people enter the labor market. Despite the disadvantages of importing foreign workers, governments considered immigration a more acceptable policy tool for adding to the labor force in the short run. Yet many observers believed that the long-run solution would require a reinvigorated birth rate.

When the Japanese government started telling its citizens in 1991 to bear more children, many women became incensed. Since reduced childbearing was part and parcel of the social configuration that gave women a new-found freedom, many women felt that increasing their fertility could only diminish their new status. The government reacted with promises of family subsidies and increased child-care programs, but the women were not persuaded (Weisman, 1991).

The Japanese childbearing dilemma is common to most of the world's developed nations. Fertility has reached the point of subreplacement in a vast array of countries that have completed the transition. In fact, in many of them it has fallen far below the replacement level. For example, the total fertility rate in Italy was 40 percent below replacement by 1990. What are the prospects for an increase? The transition framework offers no guidance. Hypotheses like Easterlin's suggest some cycles of fertility in the future, but we cannot predict their magnitude, and these cycles would fluctuate above and below the prevailing current level.

Westoff (1991) asks if any of the bases for earlier fertility declines are likely to reverse themselves. He answers the question by stating that incentives for childbearing, such as subsidies, could be strengthened, and restrictions on contraception and abortion could be reintroduced in many of the countries, but he thinks such measures are unlikely. On the other hand, fertility control technology could still improve, and even a higher proportion of women could become attached to the labor force than is part of it now. On balance, he thinks, there is little reason to anticipate any significant rise in fertility and believes that one could make an argument for a further decline. Ryder (1990) offers parallel interpretations and fails to detect any bases for additional baby booms in the near future.

Prioux (1990) sees additional signs of continued low fertility in the countries of western Europe. The proportion of women who ever marry continues to drop; the average age at marriage continues to increase; childlessness is becoming more common; and what births do take place get spaced out even more than before. The married couple with two children no longer seems to be the universal model.

Because Sweden has often been a precursor of demographic trends in other developed countries, some analysts have looked in that direction for imminent changes in Western fertility. Hoem (1990) looked at recent fertility trends in Sweden with a special emphasis on how the country's social policies have had an impact on the directions of childbearing practices. It was found that the basic low-fertility regime in the country had not changed measurably over the past couple of decades. However, Sweden's traditional practice of facilitating women's entry into the labor market (through expanded public day care, child benefits, parental leave provisions, and parents' rights to part-time work) has been augmented most recently by extending the period of paid parental leave to two years or more. Previously, the paid leave provision allowed Swedish women to have a child without losing the benefits that would accrue from work. The new provision allows them to have as many as two children in the allotted time for paid leave if they are spaced closely together. In fact, this change in the law has had just that effect. In this way a woman can bear two children in a short period of time with a minimal consquence for her work career. In some cases three children are born to a woman in a relatively narrow time frame without significant damage to her career. Indications are that childbearing preferences have priority over the wife's job prospects for many couples at the prevailing level of financial incentives. However, these alterations in childbearing practices have had more of an effect on the timing of fertility (and hence spacing of children) than on the ultimate family size in Sweden. At most, it has added a marginal increment to cohort fertility (that is, the number of children women will bear throughout their reproductive cycle).

The pattern of low fertility existing in the posttransition period, it seems likely, will not be radically altered in the years ahead. At the same time we must realize that almost everything we know about innovative demographic behavior we have learned in retrospect. Demographers were able to forecast neither the accelerated decline in fertility during the Great Economic Depression, nor the baby boom, nor the baby bust. Our understanding of those processes has come from analyzing these phenomena after the fact. (Likewise, we did not anticipate many important mortality developments, such as the resurgence of malaria and tuberculosis and the advent of AIDS.) Perhaps events will occur, or new behaviors arise, that will lead to increased desires or expectations about family size. It could come in the form of threats to a society, the revelation of negative consequences of popular forms of birth control, or a new-found appreciation of the traditional family as a social form.

It is also the case that advancing reproductive technologies are allowing couples to have children who were prevented from having them because of biological shortcomings. Such technologies include artificial insemination, *in vitro* fertilization, and surrogate motherhood. Although ethical, legal, and social issues involved in these new processes may hinder their further development, such means of facilitating procreation can be made available to couples who have the desire for one or more children (Isaacs and Holt, 1987). The future of fertility in the posttransition era remains an enigma.

Chapter Highlights

1. From an aggregate point of view, fertility operates through three basic channels—a population's demand for children, its supply of children, and the costs of regulating the supply and demand.
2. From an individual point of view, childbearing is a function of the person's desire and motivation for childbearing. It depends on the family and other social contexts in which people make decisions about pregnancy and childbirth as well as on the effort made to facilitate or impede pregnancy and childbirth through various control mechanisms.
3. The fertility process begins in early childhood when young people become oriented to notions about having children; it continues to the end of the reproductive period for women and to still older ages for men.
4. Fertility desires, intentions, ideals, and expectations can all change over time as conditions affecting them undergo change.
5. Fecundity is the biological capability of a female to have a pregnancy and bring it to term. Its level can vary by group and cultural situation and is al-

tered over the course of the life cycle. The age when females can first become fecund (menarche) occurs in the early teens, but it fluctuates among various groups. The age when females can no longer be fecund (menopause) also varies among groups.

6. We can define birth as the complete expulsion or extraction from its mother of a product of conception, which, after such separation, breathes or shows other evidence of life. Such signs of life include the beating of the heart, pulsation of the umbilical cord, or a definite movement of the infant's voluntary muscles, whether or not the umbilical cord has been cut or the placenta is still attached. Fetuses that do not result in a live birth are not counted as part of fertility for demographic purposes.
7. Within the span of fecundity, the actual childbearing incidence varies by age. The age pattern of fertility varies across societies and at different stages of economic development, but the greatest probability of births occurs when women are in their 20s.
8. Because many factors extraneous to the underlying pattern of childbearing influence fertility levels, the various statistical measures of fertility range from simple to complex indicators. Since most fertility occurs within marriage in all societies, consideration of when persons marry is crucial to the analysis of fertility trends. Distinction between period (current) and cohort (life cycle) fertility is also important because of the effects of timing of childbearing.
9. Although human beings have known about means of controlling conception throughout history, the range and effectiveness of contraception has increased sharply in modern times. Likewise, abortion has long been used as a method of preventing births, but religious and moral objections have often come into conflict with public acceptance of this approach.
10. In addition to variations in fertility among nations, differences in fertility occur among categories of a population based on socioeconomic, racial and ethnic, religious and other characteristics. Some of these differentials have narrowed with time while others have remained more persistent.
11. Just as mortality tends to go through a transition from high to low levels in all societies over time, so does fertility go through such a transition. The fertility transition has been less predictable than the mortality transition in many countries because many more factors appear to influence the level of fertility at any point in time.
12. Highly developed nations that have reached the end of the classical fertility transition can experience fertility cycles of considerable magnitude, such as a baby boom, but the underlying level of fertility tends to remain low because the conditions that brought the level to that point seem to be irreversible. Nevertheless, there is some uncertainty about the course of childbearing in the future in nations that have attained replacement or below-replacement fertility.

Discussion Questions

1. Discuss your remembrances of your own introduction to the meaning of family size and what your orientations were to the right number of children to have. What factors do you think were most influential in determining those orientations?
2. Visit a hospital birth clinic. Talk to physicians there about the complications of childbirth and find out how difficult or easy it is for the doctors to apply the definition of a live birth. Ask them also about the procedures used for completing a birth certificate. Report these back to the class.
3. Obtain reports on your state's birth statistics and analyze the trends in fertility in recent years. Are there indications of significant departures from past trends? How different are the patterns for different categories of the population? Tell your fellow students about the findings.
4. Contact organizations interested in various aspects of family limitation (e.g., religious leaders, planned parenthood groups, right-to-life organizations, medical groups) and discuss with them the complex issues related to moral and practical concerns about restricting or not restricting conception and childbearing. What can you say about the grounds for developing any consensus about these issues?
5. Why are many less-developed areas of the world not reducing their birth rates as rapidly as would be indicated by the traditional fertility transitional model?
6. Converse with your parents or other older persons about the small-family norm and the pressures they might have felt in adhering to it. Did they have few children or many, and why?

Suggested Readings

McFalls, Joseph A., Jr., and Marguerite Harvey McFalls. 1984. *Disease and Fertility*. San Diego, Calif.: Academic Press. An excellent review of the illnesses that can produce infecundity and subfecundity and the mechanisms through which they have an effect.

Baldwin, Wendy H., and Christine Winquist Nord. 1984. "Delayed Childbearing in the U.S.: Facts and Fiction." *Population Bulletin* 39:4; and Bouvier, Leon F., and Carol J. De Vita. 1991; and "The Baby Boom—Entering Midlife." *Population Bulletin* 46:3. Two accounts of the factors associated with the pattern of U.S. women delaying childbearing until their later reproductive ages.

Davis, Kingsley, Mikhail S. Bernstam, and Rita Ricardo-Campbell, eds. 1986. "Below Replacement Fertility in Industrial Societies: Causes, Consequences, Policies." *Population and Development Review*, vol. 12 (Supplement). A thought-provoking set of essays on the reasons fertility have come to such a low point in developed nations and why it seems to be staying there.

Demographic and Health Surveys World Conference. 1991. Columbia, Md.: IRD/Macro International. A summary of the major findings of a range of studies in different developing countries of the world. The studies attempt to assess the patterns of birth control and childbearing taking place and some of the variables linked to them.

References

Bachu, Amara. 1993. "Fertility of American Women: June 1992." *Current Population Reports*, Series P–20, no. 470 (Washington, D.C.: Bureau of the Census).

Bongaarts, John. 1978. "A Framework for Analyzing the Proximate Determinants of Fertility." *Population and Development Review* 4: 105–32.

———. 1990a. "The Measurement of Wanted Fertility." *Population and Development Review* 16:3, 487–506.

———. 1990b. "The Demographic Impacts of Family Planning Programs." *The Population Council Working Papers*, no. 17.

Bulatao, Rodolfo A., and Ronald D. Lee. 1983. *Determinants of Fertility in Developing Countries*. San Diego, Calif.: Academic Press.

Caldwell, John C. 1980. "Mass Education as a Determinant of the Timing of Fertility Decline." *Population and Development Review* 6, 225–56.

———, and Pat Caldwell. 1990. "High Fertility in Sub-Saharan Africa." *Scientific American* xx, 118–25.

———, and Lado T. Ruzicka. 1978. "The Australian Fertility Transition: An Analysis." *Population and Development Review* 4:1, 81–103.

———, I. O. Orubuloye, and Pat Caldwell. 1992. "Fertility Decline in Africa: A New Type of Transition?" *Population and Development Review* 18:2, 211–42.

Chamie, Joseph. 1981. *Religious Patterns of Fertility: Arab-Christian Differences in the Middle East.* London: Cambridge University Press.

Cherlin, Andrew. 1990. "Recent Changes in American Fertility, Marriage, and Divorce." *The Annals of the American Academy of Political and Social Science* 510: 145–54.

Church, Cathleen A., and Judith S. Geller. 1990. "Voluntary Female Sterilization: Number One and Growing." *Population Reports*, Series C, no. 10 (Baltimore: Johns Hopkins University Press).

Coale, Ansley J. 1986. "The Decline of Fertility in Europe since the Eighteenth Century as a Chapter in Human Demographic History." In Coale, Ansley J., and Susan Cotts Watkins, *The Decline of Fertility in Europe*, pp. 1–30. Princeton, N.J.: Princeton University Press.

Cochrane, Susan H. 1979. *Fertility and Education: What Do We Really Know?* Baltimore: Johns Hopkins University Press.

Crews, Kimberly A. 1989. *Teenage Parents: A Global Perspective.* Washington, D.C. Population Reference Bureau.

David, Henry P. 1992. "Abortion in Europe, 1920–91: A Public Health Perspective." *Studies in Family Planning* 23: 1–22.

Davis, Kingsley. 1986. "Low Fertility in Evolutionary Perspective." *Population and Development Review* 12 (Supplement): 48–65.

———, and Judith Blake. 1956. "Social Structure and Fertility: An Analytic Framework." *Economic Development and Cultural Change* 4: 211–35.

Donaldson, Peter J., and Amy Ong Tsui. 1990. "The International Family Planning Movement." *Population Bulletin* 45:3.

Easterlin, Richard A. 1973. "Relative Economic Status and the American Fertility Swing." In Eleanor B. Sheldon, ed., *Family Economic Behavior: Problems and Prospects*, pp. 170–223. Philadelphia: J.B. Lippincott.

———, and Eileen M. Crimmins. 1985. *The Fertility Revolution: A Supply-Demand Analysis*. Chicago: University of Chicago Press.

Entwistle, Barbara. 1989. "Measuring Components of Family Planning Effort." *Demography* 26:1, 53–76.

Farooq, Ghazi M., and Deborah S. DeGraff. 1988. *Fertility and Development: An Introduction to Theory, Empirical Research and Policy Issues*. Geneva: International Labour Office.

Fawcett, James T. 1986. "The Value and Cost of Children: Converging Theory and Research." In K. Mahadevan, ed., *Fertility and Mortality: Theory, Methodology, and Empirical Issues*, pp. 65–84. New Delhi: Sage Publications.

Feeney, Griffith, Feng Wang, Mingkun Zhou, and Baoyu Xiao. 1989. "Recent Fertility Dynamics in China: Results from the 1987 One Percent Population Survey." *Population and Development Review* 15:2, 297–322.

Freedman, Ronald. 1963. "Norms for Family Size in Underdeveloped Areas." *Proceedings of the Royal Society* 159: 220–34.

———. 1990. "Family Planning Programs in the Third World." *The Annals of the American Academy of Political and Social Science* 510: 33–43.

———, and Ann K. Blanc. 1991. "Fertility Transition: An Update." In *Demographic and Health Surveys World Conference*. Proceedings, vol. 1, pp. 5–24. Columbia, Md.: IRD/Macro International.

Gallen, Moira E., Laurie Liskin, and Neeraj Kak. 1986. "Men—New Focus for Family Planning Programs." *Population Reports*, Series 1, no. 33 (Baltimore: Johns Hopkins University).

Hagood, Margaret Jarman. 1939. *Mothers of the South: Portraiture of the White Tenant Farm Woman*. Chapel Hill, N.C.: University of North Carolina Press.

Henshaw, Stanley K. 1990. "Induced Abortion: A World Review, 1990." *Family Planning Perspectives* 22:3, 76–89.

———, and Jennifer Van Vort. 1989. "Teenage Abortion, Birth and Pregnancy Statistics: An Update." *Family Planning Perspectives* 21:2, 85–88.

Hernandez, Donald J. 1984. *Success or Failure? Family Planning Programs in the Third World*. Westport, Conn.: Greenwood Press.

———. 1989. "'Comment' on Barbara Entwistle: Measuring Components of Family Planning Effort." *Demography* 26:1, 77–80.

Hoem, Jan. 1990. "Social Policy and Recent Fertility Change in Sweden." *Population and Development Review* 16:4, 735–48.

Holt, Renee, Diane Lachman, Frederica C. Overstreet, and Elisa S. Wells. 1991. "RU 486 in Developing Countries: Questions Remain." *Outlook* 9:3, 1–6.

Hull, Terence H. 1986. "Socio-Demographic Change in Indonesia." In K. Mahadevan, ed., *Fertility and Mortality: Theory, Methodology, and Empirical Issues*, pp. 197–217. New Delhi: Sage Publications.

Isaacs, Stephen L., and Renee J. Holt. 1987. "Redefining Procreation: Facing the Issues." *Population Bulletin* 42:3.

Jones, Elise, and Jacqueline Forrest. 1992. "Underreporting of Abortion in Surveys of U.S. Women: 1976–1988." *Demography* 29:1, 113–26.

Keyfitz, Nathan. 1986. "The Family That Does Not Reproduce Itself." *Population and Development Review* 12 (Supplement), pp. 139–54.

Knodel, John, and Etienne van de Walle. 1986. "Lessons from the Past: Policy Implications of Historical Fertility Studies." In Ansley J. Coale and Susan Cotts Watkins, eds., *The Decline of Fertility in Europe*, pp. 390–419. Princeton, N.J.: Princeton University Press.

Lesthaeghe, Ron. 1989. "Production and Reproduction in Sub-Saharan Africa: An Overview of Organizing Principles." In Lesthaege, Ron J., ed., *Reproduction and Social Organization in Sub-Saharan Africa*, pp. 13–59. Berkeley, Calif.: University of California Press.

Liskin, Laurie, Chris Warton, and Richard Blackburn. 1990. "Condoms—Now More Than Ever." *Population Reports*, Series H, no. 8 (Baltimore: Johns Hopkins University).

———, Ellen Benoit, and Richard Blackburn. 1992. "Vasectomy: New Opportunities." *Population Reports*, Series D, no. 5 (Baltimore: Johns Hopkins University).

Livi-Bacci, Massimo. 1986. "Social Group Forerunners of Fertility Control in Europe." In Ansley J. Coale and Susan Cotts Watkins, eds., *The Decline of Fertility in Europe*, pp. 182–200. Princeton, N.J.: Princeton University Press.

Lorimer, Frank. 1954. *Culture and Human Fertility*. Paris: UNESCO.

Lutz, Wolfgang. 1989. *Distributional Aspects of Human Fertility*. London: Academic Press.

Mason, Karen Oppenheim. 1983. "Norms Relating to the Desire for Children." In Bulatao, Rodolfo A., and Ronald D. Lee, *Determinants of Fertility in Developing Countries*, pp. 388–428. San Diego, Calif.: Academic Press.

———, and Anju Malhotra Taj. 1987. "Differences between Women's and Men's Reproductive Goals in Developing Countries." *Population and Development Review* 13:4, 611–38.

Mauldin, W. Parker, and John A. Ross. 1991. "Family Planning Programs: Efforts and Results, 1982–89." *The Population Council Working Papers*, no. 34.

McFalls, Joseph A., Jr., and Marguerite Harvey McFalls. 1984. *Disease and Fertility*. San Diego, Calif.: Academic Press.

Menken, Jane. 1987. "Proximate Determinants of Fertility and Mortality: A Review of Recent Findings." *Sociological Forum* 2:4, 697–716.

Miller, Warren B., and David J. Pasta. 1988. "A Model of Fertility Motivation, Desires, and Expectations Early in Women's Reproductive Careers." *Social Biology* 35:3–4, 236–50.

Mosher, William D., and William F. Pratt. 1990a. "Contraceptive Use in the United States, 1973–88." *Advance Data from Vital and Health Statistics*, no. 182. Hyattsville, Md.: National Center for Health Statistics.

———, 1990b. "Fecundity and Infertility in the United States, 1965–88." *Advance Data from Vital and Health Statistics*, no. 192. Hyattsville, Md.: National Center for Health Statistics.

———, Linda B. Williams, and David P. Johnson. 1992. "Religion and Fertility in the United States: New Patterns." *Demography* 29:2, 199–214.

Nathanson, Constance A., and Young J. Kim. 1989. "Components of Change in Adolescent Fertility, 1971–1979." *Demography* 26:1, 85–98.

Nayar, P. K. B. 1986. "Factors in Fertility Decline in Kerala." In K. Mahadevan, ed., *Fertility and Mortality: Theory, Methodology, and Empirical Issues*, pp. 155–67. New Delhi: Sage Publications.

O'Hare, William P., Kelvin M. Pollard, Taynia L. Mann, and Mary M. Kent. 1991. "African Americans in the 1990's." *Population Bulletin* 46:1 (Washington, D.C.: Population Reference Bureau).

Orwell, George. 1950. *Shooting an Elephant and Other Essays.* New York: Harcourt Brace Jovanovich.

Palmore, James A., and Robert W. Gardner. 1983. *Measuring Mortality, Fertility, and Natural Increase.* Honolulu: East-West Center.

Petchesky, Rosalind Pollack. 1990. *Abortion and Woman's Choice.* Boston: Northeastern University Press.

Philliber, Susan, and Charles B. Nam, eds. 1980. "Special Issue on Population Socialization." *Population and Environment* 3:1.

Population Crisis Committee. 1991. *A Guide to Methods of Birth Control.* Washington, D.C.: Population Crisis Committee.

Population Reference Bureau. 1992. *1992 World Population Data Sheet.* Washington, D.C.: Population Reference Bureau.

Poston, Dudley L., Jr., and K. B. Kramer. 1983. "Voluntary and Involuntary Childlessness in the United States, 1955–1973." *Social Biology* 30, 290–306.

Potter, Joseph E. 1983. "Effects of Societal and Community Institutions on Fertility." In Bulatao, Rodolfo A., and Ronald D. Lee, eds., *Determinants of Fertility in Developing Countries*, pp. 627–65. San Diego, Calif.: Academic Press.

Preston, Samuel H. 1986a. "The Decline of Fertility in Non-European Industrialized Countries." *Population and Development Review* 12 (Supplement), pp. 26–47.

———. 1986b. "Changing Values and Falling Birth Rates." *Population and Development Review* 12 (Supplement), 176–95.

Prioux, France. 1990. "Fertility and Family Size in Western Europe." *Population* (English selection) 2: 141–61.

Rindfuss, Ronald R., and Allan M. Parnell, 1989. "The Varying Connection between Marital Status and Childbearing in the United States." *Population and Development Review* 15:3, 447–70.

Robinson, Warren C. 1986. "Another Look at the Hutterites and Natural Fertility." *Social Biology* 33:1–2, 65–76.

———. 1992. "Kenya Enters the Fertility Transition." *Population Studies* 46:3, 445–57.

Rodriguez, German, and Ricardo Aravena. 1991. "Socioeconomic Factors and the Transition to Low Fertility in Less Developed Countries: A Comparative Analysis." In *Demograhpic and Health Surveys World Conference*, Proceedings, vol. 1, pp. 39–72. Columbia, Md.: IRD/Macro International.

Ross, John A. 1992. "Sterilization: Past, Present, Future." *Studies in Family Planning* 23:3, 187–98.

Ryder, Norman B. 1983. "Fertility and Family Structure." *Population Bulletin of the United Nations*, no. 15. New York: United Nations.

———. 1990. "What Is Going to Happen to American Fertility?" *Population and Development Review* 16:1, 433–54.

———, and Charles F. Westoff. 1971. Chapter 2 in *Reproduction in the United States 1965*. Princeton, N.J.: Princeton University Press.

Santee, Barbara, and Stanley Henshaw. 1992. "The Abortion Debate: Measuring Gestational Age." *Family Planning Perspectives* 24:4, 172–73.

Sharma, O. P., and Robert D. Retherford. 1990. "How Female Literacy Affects Fertility: The Case of India." *Asian-Pacific Population & Policy*, no. 15 (Honolulu: East-West Population Institute).

Spruill, Julia Cherry. 1938. *Women's Life and Work in the Southern Colonies*. Chapel Hill, N.C.: University of North Carolina Press.

Taeuber, Irene B., and Conrad Taeuber. 1971. *People of the United States in the 20th Century*. Washington, D.C.: U.S. Government Printing Office.

Thomson, Elizabeth, Elaine McDonald, and Larry L. Bumpass. 1990. "Fertility Desires and Fertility: Hers, His, and Theirs." *Demography* 27:4, 579–88.

United Nations. 1955. *Principles for a Vital Statistics System*. Statistical Papers, Series M, no. 19. New York: United Nations.

———. 1985. *Women's Employment and Fertility*. Population Studies no. 96. New York: United Nations.

———. 1989. *Levels and Trends of Contraceptive Use as Assessed in 1988*. Population Studies no. 110. New York: United Nations.

Vaupel, James W., and Dianne G. Goodwin. 1987. "The Concentration of Reproduction of U.S. Women, 1917–80." *Population and Development Review* 13:4, 723–30.

Warwick, Donald P. 1988. "Culture and the Management of Family Planning Programs." *Studies in Family Planning* 19:1, 1–18.

Weisman, Steven R. 1991. "In Crowded Japan, a Bonus for Babies Angers Women." *New York Times*, February 19.

Westoff, Charles F., Lorenzo Moreno, and Noreen Goldman. 1989. "The Demographic Impact of Changes in Contraceptive Practice in Third World Populations." *Population and Development Review* 15:1, 91–106.

Whyte, Martin King, and S. Z. Gu. 1987. "Popular Response to China's Fertility Transition." *Population and Development Review*, 13:3, 471–93.

Wood, James W. 1990. "Fertility in Anthropological Populations." *Annual Review of Anthropology* 19: 211–42.

7. Mobility Processes

We have already made the point that population change is the result of the combination of three basic demographic processes—mortality, fertility, and mobility. After examining in some detail the first two of those factors, we will now turn our attention to the third one. Mobility means movement, and in a demographic context mobility means geographic movement. When we talk about moving or migrating, we usually have a sense of people picking up their belongings and transporting them somewhere else where they set up stakes again. This is, in fact, what is intended by our use of the mobility concept. However, as we have already seen with regard to other topics, simple concepts can become complex in their elaboration. In this chapter we will try to acquire an understanding of all the dimensions of mobility as a demographic process, and we will trace the evolution of mobility throughout the demographic transition of countries.

A good starting point in understanding mobility is to differentiate it from mortality and fertility as population processes. Goldscheider (1971) has identified three types of important differences. *First*, birth and death are biological events, whereas mobility is not. Through the biological process of birth, a person enters into a population; through the biological process of death, a person is removed from a population. The mobility process has no biological imperative. Moreover, there is no biological limit on the number of moves one can make in a lifetime, and moves can occur at any age for either sex. *Second*, fertility only adds to a population and mortality only subtracts from a population, but mobility simultaneously adds to one population and subtracts from another. Whenever you are going *to* someplace, you are coming *from* someplace. Where a birth came from and where a death goes to are not demographically relevant. *Third*, fertility and mortality are demographic universals. Births are necessary for a population to survive and deaths are inevitable. Mobility, on the other hand, can be nonexistent without threatening the viability of a population. In short, mobility differs more in kind from the other two processes than they do from each other. Yet all three processes are potentially critical for population change.

Our discussion of mobility will explore the many conceptual distinctions by including under this heading such diverse actions as relocating to another apartment in the same complex, moving to a second home to work on a six-month project, or immigrating to a new nation. We will make it clear that mobility can be conceptualized as a personal, decision-making process or as an aggregate social change. Furthermore, why people do or do not move is tied up in a complex set of explanatory factors, just as complexity describes the explanation of birth and death processes. Finally, although mobility was not accounted for within the framework of the demographic transition as it was first posed, it logically should have been. In fact, demographers have increasingly over time related how the forms and volume of mobility undergo change as the society goes through stages of development. We will examine these stages in the following sections.

CRITICAL CONCEPTS AND MEASURES

In a general sense all geographic mobility is meaningful; yet different forms of mobility have different meanings and some forms of mobility have more demographic import than others. How, then, can we best classify mobility into its various forms? The key to this classification lies in defining mobility in terms of three major elements: (1) Has one's *primary residence* changed?; (2) Has a *secondary residence* been established?; and (3) What kind of *geographic boundary* has been crossed in the process of moving?

You will remember that "usual residence" was an essential concept in determining where a person was located in taking a census. Since a census is intended to be a count of population in a particular area at a specified point in time, and since each individual can only be counted once, it is reasonable to count the person where he or she usually resides. But some of us have more than one residence simultaneously, and that must figure in when we think about mobility.

The fact is that some types of mobility that do not involve changes of one's primary residence can be analytically important. We are frequently on the move, but most of our movements do not result in our changing our primary residence. Such movement is called *temporary mobility*. It is what describes our daily trips, but we do not change our usual residence as a result of them. Because our daily movements relate to our statuses as students, workers, shoppers, players, visitors, and users of various services, they acquire importance despite being "temporary" in nature.

Moreover, the time element in establishing usual residence is not uniform among countries. In the United States, as soon as you establish new living quarters you are regarded as having changed your usual residence. In Indonesia, on the other hand, you must have held the new living quarters for six continuous months before a change in usual residence is recorded. This raises a question about the person who does not surrender the primary residence but acquires a secondary (or tertiary) residence. The secondary residence may be a vacation spot or the home of a relative or a place to live while working on a job that has an intermediate fixed term. Movement among such places, when the primary residence still exists, is called *circulatory mobility*.

Among those who have changed their primary residences, forms of mobility are classified according to the boundaries crossed. The United Nations recommends that each country specify a type of geographic boundary whose crossing will signify that a person has become a *migrant*. The point is that migrants should be regarded as persons who have changed their primary residence to the extent that they relocated to a different community. Persons who change their primary residence but remain within a community are called *local movers*. The significance is that migrants are intended to be those who have severed ties with the people and institutions of an area, whereas local movers have not. A major difficulty in the measurement of migration and local mobility is that there is no consistent way of describing the boundaries of communities. In the United States the county is the standard geographic unit whose boundaries are crossed by migrants but not by local movers. In other countries it may be a province or other geographic unit. Clearly, using the county boundary as a critical crossing point in distinguishing migration from local mobility is arbitrary. Because some counties are small and others are large, and because some people live in the middle of counties and others at the periphery, crossing the boundary may mean a short trip for some and a long trip for others. Correspondingly, some people may move long distances and still be local movers; others may move short distances and be migrants.

Migrants are further differentiated according to boundaries they may have crossed beyond the county (or provincial) line. An *interstate migrant* is one who has crossed a state boundary. An *interregional migrant* is one who has crossed a regional boundary. Those who have migrated but remain within a country are called *internal migrants*. An *international migrant* is one who has established a new primary residence in another country.

Because mobility means leaving one area and entering another one, every mover is labeled differently depending on the area to which the mobility is related. Those moving from one neighborhood to another within a city are called *in-movers* to the new area and *out-movers* from the old area. Persons who move across a county (or provincial) boundary but stay within a country are referred to as *in-migrants* to their new locations and *out-migrants* from their old locations. Those who change their usual residence from one country to another are called *immigrants* from the perspective of the receiving nation and *emigrants* from the point of view of the nation from which they came. We summarize these classifications in Table 7.1.

Temporary and Circulatory Mobility

Few of us spend the major part of a twenty-four-hour day situated in our usual residence. Throughout the day, we are temporary movers. Infants and small children go to day-care centers and playgrounds. Older children go to formal

TABLE 7.1 Types of Geographic Mobility

TYPES	NATURE	PERSON CALLED
Geographic mobility	All geographic moves	Mover
Temporary mobility	Moves between primary residence and daily activity (school, work, leisure site, etc.)	Temporary mover (commuter)
Circulatory mobility	Moves between primary and secondary residence (second home, home of relatives, work station, etc.)	Circulatory mover
Residential mobility	Changes in primary residence location	Residential mover
Local mobility	Relocation of residence within community	Local mover Out-mover from place of origin In-mover to place of destination
Internal migration	Relocation of residence within nation but out of community of earlier residence (intercounty, interprovince, interstate, interregional, etc.)	Internal migrant Out-migrant from place of origin In-migrant to place of destination
International migration	Relocation of residence outside of nation	International migrant Emigrant from place of origin Immigrant to a new destination

schools. Older youths may head to technical schools or college. Employed persons commute to their jobs. Volunteers make their way to their appointed stations. Others seek out shopping centers or amusement areas. Some attend religious services. Often a day is spent shuttling from one such location to another and then back home. The fact is that we are a highly mobile people in ways that do not alter our usual residences.

It is not only daily movement that makes us mobile. During the course of a year, we are apt to pay short visits to relatives in far-off places, take vacations in places where we can escape from our daily routines, make business trips, or attend conferences or conventions that keep us away from home for a few days or weeks.

When you read or hear discussion of how the family has been disrupted in modern society (a topic we will cover in Chapter 9), the emphasis is usually placed on how divorce or widowhood or small family size has changed the structure of the family. We hear or read much less about how the increase in daily and annual nonresidential mobility has meant that families appear together as a unit far less frequently than before.

Temporary mobility does not modify the population structure of an area (based on the usual residence criterion), but it does alter the whereabouts of populations at different times of the day (and month and year). During prime school and working hours, residences are depleted of many of their occupants. Conversely, office buildings or educational establishments are densely crowded during that time. Paris assumes some of the characteristics of a ghost town in August when Parisians are most likely to be taking an out-of-town vacation and most shops are closed down.

Commuting patterns—to school, work, shopping centers, and elsewhere—are the concern of road traffic planners and public transportation specialists who must provide for the commuting flows in an adequate and orderly manner. Temporary mobility thus taxes the efforts of most of us without having any impact on our usual residences.

When an individual or family has two or more residences they identify with, the one we call a *usual residence* can also be called the primary residence and other residences can be called secondary residences. There are some of us (single or married) who have our own living places but still think of "home" as where our parents or other original family members are located. There are some of us who maintain residences at more than one location, the second one possibly in an area away from the hustle and bustle of the city. There are some of us who leave our families for an intermediate period of time (perhaps several months or the better part of a year) to be employed elsewhere for that fixed period of time. In each of these cases, we may move back and forth between the primary and secondary residence. Such moves constitute circulatory moves. The secondary residence may be dropped at some point or it may eventually become the primary residence. The so-called snowbirds in the United States (people who have primary residences in colder climates and spend part of a year in locations in warmer climates) circulate between the primary and secondary residences. This pattern may continue over the lifetime, or a permanent move to the warmer climate may result from the annual experience. Men from villages in Central Java in Indonesia often journey to the major city of Jakarta or another large city to become vehicle drivers or peddlers in the informal sector to earn a living. Initially, at least, they leave their families behind but make frequent visits back home to see their spouses and children and to give them needed money. At some point they have to make a decision about whether the family should be brought to the city, or whether they should continue the circulatory mobility or make a permanent return to the village.

Residential Mobility and Migration

Measuring mobility requires us to gather information on the movement made by people between residences. The ideal kind of data for this picture would be continuing accounts of the moves that take place. Vital registration (which provides records of births and deaths) does not include recording of changes of residence. Population registers, where they exist, typically incorporate changes of residence as a means of keeping the population register for a local area up-to-date. As a consequence, mobility information becomes available from that source. However, such registers record only the one move that puts a person in or out of the population. A history of moves by persons is not ordinarily obtained. Moreover, only a primary residence is identified.

For fertility analysis, we can acquire birth histories of women from surveys to construct a cumulative fertility experience. In a similar manner, we can use surveys to obtain *residential histories* of people that can be analyzed to learn about mobility over their lifetime (Goldstein and Goldstein, 1981; Findley, 1982). In reality, very few such histories have been collected. The reason is that the average person makes numerous moves in a lifetime, and a considerable amount of survey time and questionnaire space would be required to record such information. This is especially so if the intention is not only to note each move but also to have details about specific locations. In addition, secondary residences are ordinarily not identified.

What has become the substitute for residential or mobility histories is the derivation of segments of those histories from census or survey questions that ask about residence at selected earlier points in time. For example, in the U.S. census, in addition to asking about a person's place of birth and the place of current residence, a question is included about where the person lived five years before the census date. That enables us to identify three points in the person's residential history. A truncated picture of the person's mobility can be extracted from that information. We can compare birthplace and present residence, birthplace and residence five years before the census, and residence five years before and at the time of the census. In the U.S. Current Population Survey, the intermediate question relates to residence one year before the survey rather than five years before.

These census and survey data are the principal sources of information we have about U.S. mobility and migration within the national borders, and they only approximate the mobility situation, both because not all primary residences are identified and because no secondary residences are specified. If a person is reported at different primary residences at the last two dates (five years or one year ago and currently), we know that at least one move was made but we do not know how many other times the person may have moved. If a person is reported at the same location at the two dates, we cannot be certain that he or she has not moved because the person may have moved away from the first location and then returned to it before the current date.

The cumbersome nature of aggregate mobility data makes even this limited amount of relevant information difficult to process. Consider an attempt to summarize the volume of *streams of mobility or migration* (movements of aggregates between given places). If we are interested in finding out the places in which all current (as of 1990) residents of Atlanta, Georgia, lived five years before the 1990 Census, that tabulation can be conducted readily by accessing the current data for Atlantans. However, if we want to know where all residents of Atlanta five years before the census were located at the time of the census—that is, the streams of mobility from Atlanta to other places—that would be a formidable task involving the tabulation of data for every place in the United States and beyond. (Because most countries use similar approaches to gather mobility data, the analytical problems for those countries are similar.)

Allowing for limitations of the data and drawing on the use of indirect methods of analysis, we can still derive a considerable amount of information about mobility. For instance, by employing the life table approach, Long (1988) estimated that the average American in 1982–83 was making 10 or 11 moves over a lifetime. At least 6 of those moves were within the county of residence, 2 between counties within the state, and about 2 between states. These levels of lifetime mobility were lower than during the 1966–71 period when U.S. residents were actually more mobile (almost 13 lifetime moves). Again, we must caution that these are averages and that some Americans spent all of their lives in the same house while others moved a vast number of times. Despite the fact that these calculations show that the mobility practices of persons in the United States have declined somewhat, the evidence is that people in many other countries are much less mobile. As an example, the average American has made as many moves by age 21 as a resident of Ireland makes in a lifetime.

Although countries may differ in the volume of their mobility and migration, indications are that the *age curve of mobility and migration* is fairly universal. That is, there is a systematic pattern of mobility at given ages. Figure 7.1 shows that the variations by age in the percentage of population changing residence are generally comparable for the United States, Great Britain, Japan, Ireland, and New Zealand. The greater mobility of U.S. residents is observable at all ages. The standard age pattern is one in which rates of moving are relatively high among children under age 5, drop considerably for those in their low and mid-teens, rise rapidly among persons in their early 20s, then decline first more rapidly and later more gradually with older age. This age pattern of mobility is tied to changes in critical life cycle stages (e.g., the dependency of children on parental mobility; moves after the late teenages to go to college, take a job, and get married; and leaving the old homestead after retirement).

Because mobility involves both entering and leaving an area, at any point in time we are likely to see some people entering an area at the same time as others are leaving it. This presents a corollary to the earlier statement that mobility is not necessary for a population to survive; namely, that whatever the volume of mobility it tends to be largely offsetting. Streams of mobility from place A to place B counteract each other in their effects on the population size of an area. If, for instance, 10,000 people moved from Paris to London during a

FIGURE 7.1 Percentage of Population Changing Residence in One Year, by Age, for the United States, Great Britain, Japan, Ireland, and New Zealand: 1970 or 1971

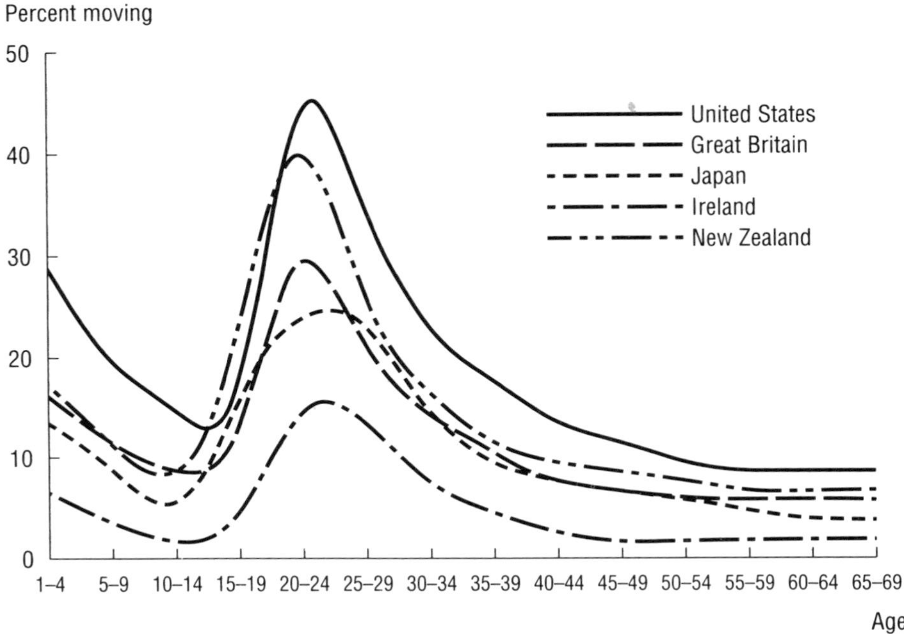

Source: Reprinted from *Migration and Residential Mobility in the United States*, by Larry Long, © 1988 the Russell Sage Foundation. Used with permission of the Russell Sage Foundation.

given year while 10,000 other people moved from London to Paris during the same year, then 20,000 persons would have moved between the two places but the number of people in Paris and London would not be affected by the exchange—they would have balanced out. Demographers refer to the sum of the individual streams from place to place as *gross mobility or migration* and the balance of numbers involved as *net mobility or migration*. If 10,000 persons had moved from Paris to London, but only 9,000 had moved from London to Paris during the same time span, then gross migration between the two places would be 19,000 and there would be a net migration of 1,000 that would be positive (or a plus) for London and negative (or a minus) for Paris. Of course, we are only referring to total numbers of people and not people with certain characteristics. The 10,000 who moved from Paris to London could have been young people and the 9,000 who moved from London to Paris could have been older people. Moreover, each of the 19,000 would be individuals with somewhat unique sets of characteristics and reasons for moving.

Mobility within countries has been studied with regard to many different types of geographic areas. Analysis might be concerned with movement in and out of neighborhoods, villages, towns, cities, counties or provinces, states, and regions. It can also track the advancement of population along frontiers of a nation or reveal shifts of people between rural and urban areas and between various other types of areas, such as metropolitan areas (see Chapter 1 for examples).

International Migration

What sets off international migration from other forms of mobility is that a country boundary has been crossed. Nations are very conscious of their borders with other countries and usually have much more severe restrictions related to crossing those borders than to crossing internal geographic boundaries. Protection of these dividing lines increases the chance of maintaining the country's security and regulating the number and types of people who enter the area. What typically holds a nation together is a common set of cultural values and a set of social institutions with governmental controls which determine civil authority. Many nations include people with varying cultural values along with a common set of social institutions. In recent years, some countries (e.g., the former Soviet Union and the former Yugoslavia) have become subdivided because of the incompatibility of groups with different cultural values. In each case, the new nations' borders are specified and relevant rules of international migration are established.

Still, movement across national borders includes several different types that have alternative implications for the nation and the movers. Within the legal framework of a country, people may enter as immigrants, refugees, parolees, and *asylees* (asylum seekers), or as visitors, temporary workers, and individuals in other nonimmigrant statuses. In addition, movement across national borders can take place outside the legal framework.

Immigrants are typically defined as people who come to settle, live, and work in a new homeland and usually, but not necessarily, to become citizens in due course (Bean, Vernez, and Keely, 1989). The United States has a long history of immigration, as reflected in our legislation (see Box 7.1). Immigrants are persons who have been given visas that permit them to acquire permanent resident status. These visas are allotted according to immigration legislation that specifies what types of people can be included and what priority they will have when the number wishing to enter exceeds the number set as a maximum for a particular year.

At present, immigrants to the United States can qualify for entry in one of four categories: (1) immediate relatives of adult U.S. citizens (spouse, children, and parents); (2) other relatives of U.S. citizens and the spouses and unmarried children of permanent residents; (3) needed workers or persons in the arts or professions, or in occupations of short supply; and (4) refugees and asylees (Bean, Vernez, and Keely, 1989). Because of numerical limitations placed on

BOX 7.1 U.S. Immigration Laws

The history of U.S. immigration legislation has incorporated times when no restrictions existed, times when quotas were set for persons who left certain countries, and times when criteria for admission was based on family linkages and/or the kind of work skills individuals had.

When the United States was formed and for a short time thereafter, immigration was free of restrictions of any kind. In 1798 an Alien Act authorized the President to send back aliens regarded as dangerous to the country. It was not until 1875 that convicts and prostitutes were barred from entering the country. In 1882 the first legislation directed toward an ethnic group was passed (the Chinese Exclusion Act). Chinese laborers had been brought in to help build the railroads and to supplement agricultural and factory workers. The relatively large number of Chinese who located in some places raised fears about a "yellow peril." This led to the congressional act, which not only banned further Chinese immigration but also eliminated the possibility of anyone with Chinese ancestry becoming a citizen of the United States. Initially a two-year embargo, the act was extended periodically until 1943, when it was repealed as a gesture of wartime friendship to Chiang Kai-shek, leader of the Nationalist Chinese government (Linford, 1973).

Additional legislation in 1882 barred idiots, lunatics, and those likely to become public charges. Two decades later the Immigration Act of 1903 excluded from immigration diseased persons, polygamists, paupers, criminals, and anarchists. As part of the Gentlemen's Agreement of 1906–07, the United States and Japan agreed that passports to the United States would only be given to family members of Japanese resident in this country.

Following several decades during which immigration numbers rose and the proportion of immigrants from southern and eastern Europe overtook the number from northern and western Europe, a Congress concerned with the rising tide of "different" immigrants passed the Quota Act of 1921. It established national origin quotas that set a limit on immigrants from any country to 3 percent of people residing in the United States in 1910 who had that national background. Because the results were not satisfying (the allowable numbers still considered too large for some of the countries), the National Origins Act of 1924 reduced the 3 percent to 2 percent and the base year from 1910 to 1890. The effect was to diminish the eligible numbers from southern and eastern European countries whose emigrants to the United States had begun to reach large numbers at the turn of the century. The Immigration and Nationality Act of 1952 maintained the national origins quotas but added some preferences for categories of people within the quotas.

It was not until the Immigration Reform Act of 1965 that the U.S. government dropped national quotas on immigration but kept a restriction on overall numbers and broadened the preferences.

entry in the second and third categories, many such applicants wait several years before receiving their immigrant visas.

Alien immigrants may apply for citizenship in the United States, usually after five years of residence, through a process called *naturalization*. Children born outside the country but who have at least one parent who is a U.S. citizen are treated as naturalized citizens (Levine, Hill, and Warren, 1985).

A *refugee*, according to the 1967 UN Protocol on Refugees, is anyone "who, owing to well-founded fear of being persecuted for reasons of race, religion, nationality, membership of a particular social group or political opinion, is outside the country of his nationality and is unable or, owing to such fear, is unwilling to avail himself of the protection of that country" (Keely, 1981). People have differed in their interpretation of what is meant by being persecuted or outside the country of one's nationality. Are those fleeing war to be considered as refugees? Are people who believe that they are denied an adequate economic level of living to be treated as refugees? In a strict sense, the definition of a refugee would exclude these persons, but in some instances admitting countries have accorded them refugee status (Keely, 1981).

Parolees are those who are allowed to enter the country temporarily under emergency conditions. Subsequently, they may be assigned a refugee status or some other status. *Asylees* (asylum seekers) are persons who are already in the country as nonimmigrants or those at a port of entry who are unable or unwilling to return to their country because of fear of persecution. These individuals are given asylum until such time as a refugee or some other status can be determined (Levine, Hill, and Warren, 1985). The world refugee population has been estimated at about 12.6 million people and is overwhelmingly located in developing countries (Keely, 1981).

Among the persons who enter the United States as nonimmigrants are *visitors*, whose visas are for temporary stays; *students*, who can be admitted if they are accepted for study in a certified educational institution; and *temporary workers*, such as those employed by international corporations. All nonimmigrants (those not entering for the purpose of acquiring permanent resident status) are assigned fixed time periods for their stay.

In many nations of the world, labor shortages are met by admitting foreign workers under controlled arrangements. Such *international labor migration* can constitute a substantial part of the total work force of a receiving country (as much as one-third in Luxembourg) and of a sending country (up to 11 percent from some Mediterranean countries) (Kols and Lewison, 1983). Labor migrants frequently are circulatory migrants in that they may be seasonal workers or intend to return to their homelands on completion of a work contract.

All the types of international movers we have identified so far are those who are documented in some way. It is obvious to us that some people enter a country without documentation or outside the legal framework of a country's international mobility policy. Such persons are referred to as *illegal or undocumented immigrants*. Entry may be by land, water, or air. Although the government of a country may station patrols at specified points of land borders, seaports, and airports, the vast majority of illegal immigrants enter at unprotected locations. In an effort to restrict illegal immigration into the United States, the Immigration Reform and Control Act of 1986 gave legal immigrant status to many undocumented immigrants, enforced the prohibition on hiring undocumented workers, and increased resources for enforcing border patrols. While we can make reasonable estimates of the number of legal immigrants, it is more difficult to gauge the number of illegal immigrants because many of them are circulatory migrants whose entrances and exits from the country are clandestine (Bean, Vernez, and Keely, 1989).

It should be kept in mind that immigration to a country has its counterpart in emigration from another country. It is also the case that some people who migrate internationally spend brief periods of time in third or fourth countries en route from their native lands to their ultimate destinations. This sometimes complicates the determination of their country of origin. Moreover, it is sometimes assumed that most immigrants remain in their country of destination. In fact, perhaps a third of all "permanent" immigrants to the United States eventually leave the country. During the peak period of U.S. immigration at the turn of the twentieth century, emigration approached or exceeded immigration in some years. Administrative records are used to record immigration, but no record-keeping is attempted for those emigrating. Our knowledge about the volume of emigrants comes from indirect estimates, a type of procedure also used to estimate illegal immigration.

Explaining Mobility and Migration

All residential movement, whether local mobility, internal migration, or international migration, can be either *involuntary* or *voluntary*. Persons may be required to move for reasons they do not choose. For instance, people have been displaced by the enemy in wars, through natural catastrophes, and by their own governments which may want to make a different use of the land on which the people live. Historically, forced mobility has included the Nazis' sending of Jews and others to concentration camps during World War II, the U.S. government's confining of Indians to reservations, Russia's dispatching of political prisoners to Siberian camps, convicted criminals' being sent off to prisons, and urban renewal's eliminating whole residential areas in depressed sections of cities in various countries.

People have been impelled to move involuntarily in other circumstances. Racial and religious persecution has driven some groups from lands where they would have preferred to live; children have moved with their families at times when remaining with their friends would have been preferable; and workers in large business organizations who liked their residential locations have been reassigned to other cities and have gone only to preserve their jobs.

Mobility that is primarily voluntary often seems to be the result of a simple decision (an unemployed person moving in order to take an available job elsewhere) whereas, in reality, it is most often the case that the decision to move or not to move may be embedded in a complex set of factors. Such factors may involve many people, may depend on the state of knowledge about opportunities and places, and may incorporate some variables both tangible and intangible. Ultimately the decision will depend on the judgments of individuals or groups about the "right thing to do under the circumstances," and such a decision may or may not be correct from someone else's perspective.

A long-time student of mobility, reviewing the myriad attempts to develop explanations of mobility, has concluded that the range of approaches taps various dimensions of the phenomenon but fails to generalize satisfactorily about the mobility process. If there is one underlying axiom that suffices to encompass all moves, it is that "subject to the limitations imposed by social, political, physical, or other barriers and the quantity and quality of available information, human beings will tend to gravitate from places having fewer advantages (however they are defined) to those having more" (Zelinsky, 1983).

If perceived relative advantages are the motivating forces for voluntary mobility, then many of the geographic distinctions conventionally used in mobility analysis (such as local mobility versus migration, provincial versus regional movement, internal versus international migration) may be arbitrary in terms of our understanding them as processes. Movement in certain directions and for given distances may hinge largely on where people see the relative advantages to be greatest (within the context of reasonable alternatives).

Shaw (1975) attempted to systematize the existing knowledge about mobility by developing a typology of the different lines of inquiry. First, he distinguished between deterministic and probablistic approaches. In the *deterministic* approach, the objective is a precise relationship between the mobility event and the explanatory variables. In the *probablistic* approach, by way of contrast, the objective is to specify a statistical relationship between dependent and independent variables that operates within certain limits or variation. Under the former are included reports of patterned differentials among population categories and the economic and social-behavorial factors that affect mobility patterns, as well as the importance of space as a mediating factor in mobility outcomes. Under the latter are various types of quantitative models which indicate the chances of moving under different circumstances. Each of the lines of inquiry seems to follow from the subject matter and/or methodological preference of the analyst.

A great deal of early research on mobility was couched in the framework of *mobility differentials*. Here, the aim was to compare mobility tendencies for different characteristics of the population and to deduce from empirical data on the subject the nature of the influence involved (much as we described the earliest attempts to generalize about factors affecting mortality and fertility). In the late nineteenth century, Ravenstein (1885, 1889) drew up what he called the *laws of migration*, which were empirical generalizations based on the existing data about then current mobility phenomena (see Chapter 3). In subsequent years, numerous studies have updated the picture of differential mobility and migration (Thomas, 1938; Shryock, 1964; Lee, 1966; Long, 1988). These studies, done mostly by sociologists, tell us the greater or lesser incidence of mobility of persons in different categories with respect to age, sex, marital status, education, occupation, and income. We are led to the conclusion that having those particular characteristics determines the extent to which we will move.

Similar inquiries by economists have focused more on employment status and wages and salaries of jobs as the factors that individuals and groups are likely to consider before making a move or not. Frequently, such decisions have been placed in an economic cost-benefit framework (Sjaastad, 1962).

These research studies of both sociological and economic differential mobility have been criticized as (a) lacking attention to myriad other factors associated with the mobility process, and (b) failing to explain the basis of moves by people who are not covered by the specified variables (for example, nonworkers, retired persons, those in institutions, and students).

Those who make reference to spatial dimensions of the mobility process emphasize the importance of the territory to be traversed in a move and of the conditions relating to space. The human ecological approach considers the roles of the environment, technology, and social organization as contexts for adaptive mobility behavior. Movement is seen as a mechanism for achieving balance or equilibrium among the several elements of the ecological phenomena.

We can find a more direct emphasis on space in the various frameworks that attribute the flows of mobility to the relative attraction of numbers of people in different places. Sometimes labeled *gravity models*, they are based on the premise that the volume of migration between two places is inversely proportional to some function of their distance and directly related to the size of their populations (Shaw, 1975; Zelinsky, 1983). Related approaches have taken account of intervening opportunities between places (Stouffer, 1960). While these orientations to mobility identify important aspects of the process, they seem to ignore many others.

Probabilistic studies are generally based on quantitative models of mobility designed to determine the chances of moving, given certain past patterns of movement. For instance, it has been found that the longer someone lives in a given location the less likely that person is to move, and that a small number of movers makes a disproportionate percentage of all moves (Shaw, 1975).

Studies employing a micro orientation have moved in the direction of incorporating a greater range of social, psychological, and behavioral variables into mobility analysis. They examine the question "Why do people move?" (see Box 7.2) and generally focus on the decision-making process and what factors are included in the decision.

Some micro studies have explored the *mobility decision-making process* in various ways. In Chapter 3 we presented a graphic model of migration behavior using a value-expectancy framework. Other models use different social, psychological, or behavioral variables as focal points, but all attempt to incorporate a wide range of other variables that condition the mobility decision-making process.

BOX 7.2 Why People Move

A direct approach uses surveys to ask people who moved what the main reasons were for the mobility. Surveys of male migrants from over a dozen largely developing countries found that between 55 and 85 percent mentioned work as the major reason for their moves. Younger male migrants are more likely to move for educational or family reasons, while older male migrants more often move to find jobs. Work and school are less important and family reasons more important for women than for men in these countries, but considerable variations exist among countries in the importance of individual reasons (Kols and Lewison, 1983).

Reasons given for moving between states in the United States by key household persons also emphasize decisions related to work. Significant percentages of those who move cite family factors and other social satisfactions (Long, 1988). Survey questions on *reasons for moving* are asked retrospectively, often some time after a move has been made. It is quite possible that respondents to such questions answer them by combining what they considered at the time the move was made with rationalizations for moving that were later given credence. The fact is that questions on reasons for moving do not permit complex answers and force respondents to overgeneralize about important factors. It is also the case that questions are never asked as to why people choose not to move when presented with an opportunity.

Trying to reproduce the mobility process itself is not an easy task because of the many intangible as well as tangible aspects that are present. Controversy surrounds even the basic issues for which decisions are made. It has long been assumed that there are two stages to such decisions, the first being whether or not to move and the second being where to locate. This assumes that individuals or groups perceive one or more dissatisfactions which might trigger a move; they then decide on its relative importance and reach a judgment about moving. Then they select a place to move to that would improve their level of satisfaction (or reduce their level of dissatisfaction).

A more general perspective would recognize that, at any point in time, persons may take stock of their welfare and initiate a decision to possibly move. Alternatively, a prospect for moving, of which they were previously not aware, may be presented to them and they must then act on this issue. Persons may reach this decision on their own or acting in concert with others. Also, the decision may be based on a minimum or maximum amount of information about the critical factors involved. Thus, there is probably no fixed pattern to the mobility decision.

DaVanzo (1976) studied why married couples move in the United States, using a national longitudinal survey, and arrived at several findings, some of which ran counter to earlier notions of factors affecting mobility. Unemployment or dissatisfaction with a job does push a family to move. Persons who come to an area for noneconomic reasons but don't have a job will move again if employment does not develop. People who are repeat migrants (who move at least twice during a fixed period of time) include a high percentage who are returning to their original location. Families with working wives are as likely to move as those where the wife does not work. Moving destinations are selected that are compatible with both husbands' and wives' employment and interests.

Harbison (1981) has argued that the family is the context of migration decisions for most individuals. As Figure 7.2 shows, the individual's decision whether or not to move is conditioned by family as well as environmental and sociocultural factors at both points of origin and destination. A critical factor in this decision is the perception of how well the family is situated with regard to adequate housing, economic satisfaction, and meeting other needs of its members.

One must remember that a family goes through a life cycle in which different members change statuses as they reach older ages. The age profile of mobility reflects these status changes. When children are born, housing frequently becomes inadequate, requiring a move to a larger place. When children are in primary and secondary school, families opt to try to remain in their locations so that the children's education will not be interrupted. Local moves that do not require a change of school are more likely than those that separate children from their schools. When secondary school is completed, such status changes as going to college, getting married, and getting the first full-time job are apt to take the young person away from the parental home. (When economic conditions are strained, young persons who have left home are often candidates for returning to the parents' home.) As adults, persons will be heavily influenced in their decisions on mobility by work considerations, although local moves often provide an adjustment to other needs within the community. When individuals reach retirement or older ages, they are likely to remain settled unless they can manage to go to a more satisfactory environmental area or until a spouse has died.

Root and DeJong (1991) have shown that family factors weigh heavily in the moving decision of individuals in developing countries just as they do in developed nations. In a rural province in the Philippines, the movement of a family as a group is based on input from critical members of the extended kin who live nearby as well as from immediate family members. Such influences may relate to the prospects of future extended family communication and to the joint economic activities of the larger family. The family also serves as a potent force when individuals move. While changes in life-cycle stages are important for determining an individual's mobility, the responsibility to assist the family economically remains an obligation. The person who leaves a family to take work elsewhere typically sends back money (remittances) to the members left behind to sustain their level of living (Lauby and Stark, 1988). In developed countries, some form of remittance is often involved when young people leave families which are at a lower socioeconomic level.

FIGURE 7.2 The Family as the Context for the Decision to Migrate: Direct and Indirect Effects

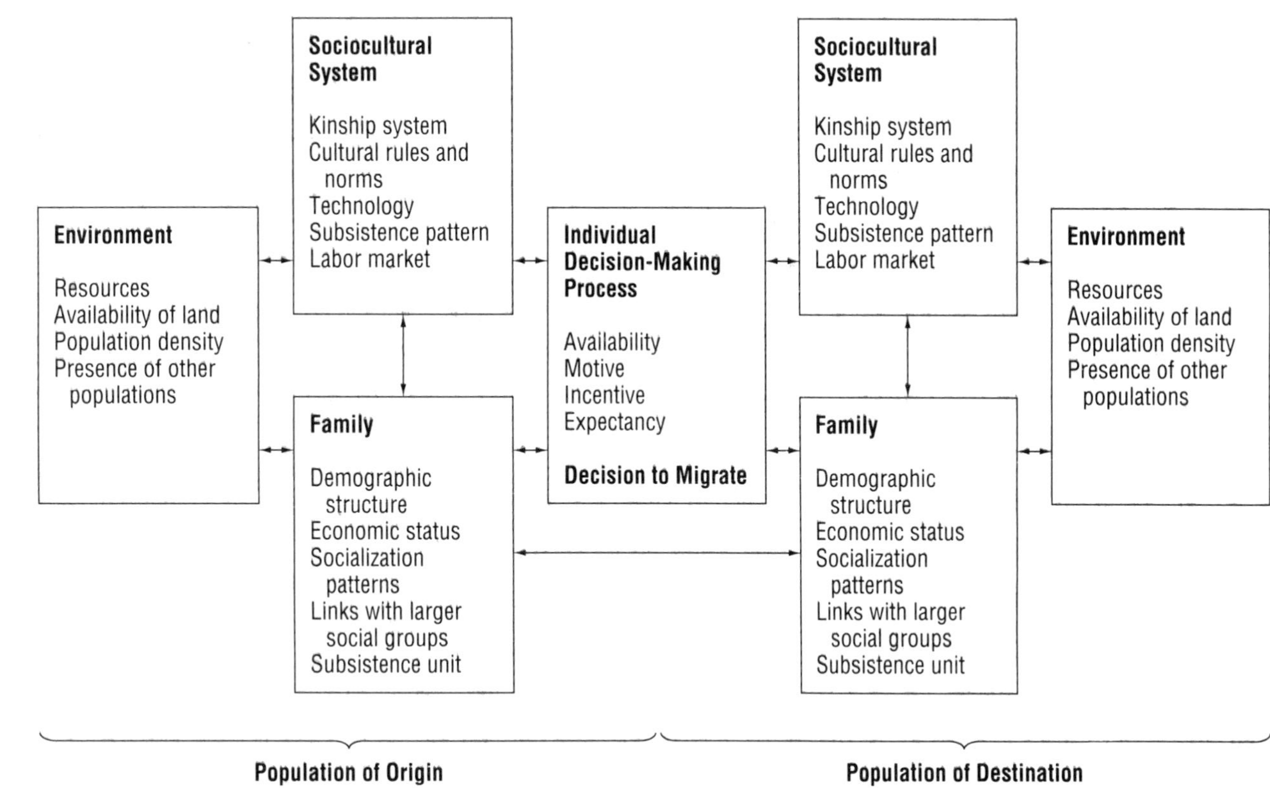

Source: Sarah F. Harbison, "Family Structure and Family Strategy in Migration Decision Making," in Gordon F. DeJong and Robert W. Gardner, eds., *Migration Decision Making*, pp. 225–251 (New York: Pergamon Press, 1981).

Although international movement may depend on some factors not found in internal mobility, by and large the ranges of explanatory factors are the same. The aim of individuals and families who want to adopt residences in other countries still is based on achieving maximum satisfaction of their needs and interests. The main difference between internal and international migration in understanding the moving patterns lies in the actions of governments, which have increasingly limited the opportunities for people from other countries to attain their satisfactions by moving across national boundaries.

An explanatory scheme is probably more demanding for mobility than for mortality or fertility both because mobility, as indicated, is a more general prospect for persons and because mobility is perhaps more generally embedded in the structure of society with more obvious links to all social institutions. As Zelinsky (1983) puts it, "[M]obility in all its permutations is no more than one phase of the even larger phenomenon of social change."

Goldscheider (1987) confirms this perspective by stating that studies of mobility must "fit solidly within a broader understanding of comparative development, community contexts, household and family analysis, stratification, and ethnic conflict...." To understand mobility, in other words, means understanding the societies and communities in which they take place as well as the people involved in the mobility process itself.

THE STAGES OF MOBILITY

Like mortality and fertility, mobility is a process that has been going on throughout all of history. It is very natural, therefore, to take a historical perspective of it and to identify the ways in which different kinds of mobility have changed in frequency and form.

We have already mentioned that this component of population change was belatedly included within the framework of the demographic transition. The architects of the transition idea were oriented mainly to the balance of births and deaths and how they affected population increase, much as Malthus was in his day. As decades of research showed mobility to be a powerful force in its influence on population change at all geographic levels across the Earth, developers of models of population change increasingly incorporated mobility, along with mortality and fertility, into their calculations. Several students of the field likewise added mobility to the framework of demographic transition.

Zelinsky (1971) is regarded as the first person to systematically include mobility in the transition. Although he recognized that the mobility types associated with each stage of the traditional demographic transition were more approximations to what took place at each stage, he knew too that mortality and fertility generalizations within the framework were also general and that departures from the types were often observed. His adoption of the notion of a *mobility transition* was an attempt to show that, at least in countries which were the basis of mortality and fertility transitions, there were some patterns in the different forms of mobility that were essentially repeated in country after country.

An essential point made by Zelinsky was that the mobility transition was intimately connected with the stages of modernization, much as were the mortality and fertility transitions. Acknowledging that the timing of the stages depended on the pace of social changes in the society, he stated that the historical process itself was irreversible.

Critics of the mobility transition presentation pointed to some of the same limitations earlier critics had expressed about the transitions of mortality and fertility. Questions of timing, specificity, irreversibility, and cultural relativity were raised (Pryor, 1982). Zelinsky himself later conceded that his formulation may have been too rigorous, even though he had offered it as only a very general integrating framework.

Those who echoed the criticism that the demographic transition was nothing more than an account of what took place in most now-developed countries revealed the unique aspects of mobility in now-developing nations. Hugo (1983), for example, surveyed the historical picture of mobility in West Java, Indonesia, and concluded that it does not conform to Zelinsky's hypothesized sequence largely because (a) colonialism, not modernization, dictated the economic and social changes of most less-developed nations, such as Indonesia, and (b) mobility is highly dependent on transportation technology, which was much more advanced when now-developing countries passed out of the first phase of the transition than when now-developed countries went through that stage. As a result, the nature of urbanization and of the importance of circulation mobility was quite different between the two types of areas.

Skeldon (1990) reviewed a wide range of mobility studies and considered the various criticisms made of Zelinsky's framework. He concluded that there was support for the idea of "definite patterned regularities in the growth of personal mobility" over time, but he amplified Zelinsky's transitional society phase and introduced two additions to the transition—changing urban destinations within the hierarchy and the changing sex composition within the population flows. He sees mobility changes as occurring less sporadically and more continually, but he maintains the core of the Zelinsky framework and just adapts it by making the necessary modifications. Skeldon's modified mobility transition is spelled out in Table 7.2.

Although the exact nature of the mobility transition may be in dispute, a consensus seems to have developed that there have been regularities in mobility patterns related to the historical stages of the demographic transition. Some of the disagreement among scholars may reflect different ways of viewing long-term transitional patterns versus shorter-term and less-predictable mobility cycles. Mobility is perhaps less fundamentally based in the normative structure than are mortality and fertility and, as a consequence, there may be relatively more cycles of mobility than of mortality or fertility.

In the following sections of this chapter, we will loosely tie examples of mobility throughout history to the transition framework, using the same transi-

TABLE 7.2 Skeldon's Modified Mobility Transition

PHASE I—PRETRANSITIONAL SOCIETY

1. Fluctuating levels of circulation, both long-distance (pilgrimages, warfare) and short-distance (to incorporate different ecological niches).
2. More permanent movement associated with slavery or the opening up of agricultural frontiers.

PHASE II—EARLY TRANSITIONAL SOCIETY

1. Growth of circulation as urban destinations, plantations or mines are incorporated as niches in rural-based circulation. Mobility is a support for rural communities.
2. Long-distance urban-to-urban movements up the hierarchy.
3. Stagnation of intermediate and smaller towns.
4. Increasing movement to frontier areas.
5. Increasing complexity of mobility fields.
6. All movement dominated by males.

PHASE III—INTERMEDIATE TRANSITIONAL SOCIETY

1. Long-term movement from areas close to the largest cities and the beginning of demographic stagnation in these areas.
2. Increasing lengths of stay at all urban destinations resulting in the rapid growth of intermediate and smaller towns. Rural-based mobility begins to undermine rural community economies and life.
3. Continued urban-to-urban movement mainly up the hierarchy.
4. Decreasing movement to rural destinations.
5. Great complexity in mobility fields.
6. Pronounced participation of women in no. 1 above.

tion categories applied to mortality and fertility in earlier chapters, but we will take into account both Zelinsky's and Skeldon's classifications of the typical mobility patterns that emerged in each stage.

Pretransition Stage

Societies go through long periods of time *before* they enter into the demographic transition. In the earliest period of history, people would have to forage for their food and shelter. As Petersen (1975) put it: "In a world relatively unpopulated by humans, presumably each small band of gatherers or hunters

continued

PHASE IV—LATE TRANSITIONAL SOCIETY

1. Massive rural-to-urban long-term movements with the largest cities the primary targets, the intermediate centers being short-circuited. The emergence of megacities.
2. Increasing urban-to-urban movement.
3. Emigration, if this option is available.
4. Decreasing rural-based circulation and stagnation; decline of the rural population.
5. Gradual simplification of mobility fields.
6. Movements nos. 1 and 2 are female-dominant, while no. 3 is male-dominant.

PHASE V—EARLY ADVANCED SOCIETY

1. Slackening rural-to-urban movement as urbanization levels exceed 50 percent.
2. Suburbanization and the beginnings of deconcentration of urban populations.
3. Increasing commuting.
4. Movements nos. 1 and 2 are sex-balanced while no. 3 is male-dominant.

PHASE VI—LATE ADVANCED SOCIETY

1. Continued deconcentration of urbanization.
2. Immigrant flows from countries in Phase IV, if this option is available.
3. Massive commuting.
4. Most flows are sex-balanced.

Source: Reproduced from Ronald Skeldon, *Population Mobility in Developing Countries*, © 1990, by permission of Belhaven Press (a division of Pinter Publishers Ltd.), London.

would follow wherever the available subsistence led, moving only a few miles a day but eventually perhaps covering considerable distances.... For ancient man, migration was not an occasional aberration from a settled life, but the norm...."

During the Agricultural Revolution, survival was dependent on access to arable land and water. Families and groups frequently headed off to find them. Some were successful and heralded others. Some were not successful and continued their mobility until they made a discovery. Often two or more groups converged on the same area and formed villages. Wandering was a common practice to fill the *ecological niches* as well as to escape from tyrants who held people in slavery, phenomena that are well documented in accounts of the Biblical period and for some centuries thereafter (Potok, 1978).

Pastoral nomadism (in terms of the maintenance of herds of animals all year round on free-ranging grazing areas), as distinct from hunters and gatherers (who moved more frequently), was also widespread in early times (Khasanov, 1984). These highly mobile nomads constituted a link between settled groups and often were communicators of the various cultures.

As the Agricultural Revolution proceeded, movement to the frontiers permitted the development of new lands. Even after cities and towns evolved, the rural populations continually looked for better land for their crops. One does not have to look far back in history to discover this phenomenon. In the pretransition societies of today, one can find many examples of agricultural resettlement. This is particularly true in areas hard hit by drought and other natural hazards or by the depletion or destruction of natural resources.

Ethiopia is a case in point. Wood (1982) has described the plight of the people of that country in the period 1950–74:

> ...spontaneous agricultural resettlement was a major phenomenon, examples of which could be found in all provinces. Although much of this resettlement took place within areas already settled, considerable tracts of land formerly unused or little used by cultivators were brought into cultivation....[A] conservative estimate could suggest that in the period considered the area settled and utilized by cultivators expanded by 25 percent and that more than one million people settled in these areas.

Mobility was also engendered by the development of cities that took place in colonial development. The colonized lands remained in the pretransition phase for all or most of the time during which they were governed by the ruling powers. While the fertility and mortality of the indigenous populations stayed high, the natives were recruited to work in urban areas (for an example see Box 7.3).

Prior to the European demographic transition, mobility was characterized by combinations of circulation, local mobility, and longer-distance movements, including international migration. Clark and Souden (1987) have described the prevailing situation in the England of that period as one in which the society was largely rural, marriage was typically late, and service jobs and apprenticeships were widespread. Given two villages, movement between them would include children from one area being hired as servants in the other, a newly married spouse arriving from the neighboring village, a son inheriting the property of a father, the hiring of new labor in commercial enterprises, and an elderly couple acquiring smaller quarters when their family is grown or when they want to move closer to their relatives. As additional villages and towns emerged, the growing complexity of agriculture and the rise of industry created new types of occupations for which people were sought in a wider area. Mobility was a central mechanism for these familial and economic changes.

In pre-Revolutionary America, the newly arrived immigrants did not remain in their initial locations. Many went toward the opening frontiers, but considerable numbers shifted their residence in their adjustment to the new

BOX 7.3 Migration to Batavia in the Seventeenth and Eighteenth Centuries

Spooner (1986) tells of the role of migration in the Dutch effort to build up the Indonesian city of Batavia (now Jakarta) during the late seventeenth and eighteenth centuries. Batavia was founded in 1619 when the governor-general of the United East India Company, a holding of the Dutch government, established a fortress at the site of an old Javan settlement at the northwest coast of the island. It was a strategic point in the seaward shipping lanes and an excellent vantage point for repelling enemy ships. Over the years, says Spooner, the city absorbed streams of migrants not only from other parts of Java (these individuals often circulating between their home areas and the city) and from the surrounding islands but also from other parts of Asia.

The Dutch designed the city as a copy of Amsterdam, with its canals, walls, commercial centers, churches, and floral gardens. But the infrastructure of Batavia was not that of Amsterdam, and the rapidly growing population of the city combined with the stagnant waters of the river and canals to produce disease epidemics (see the reference to Raffles in Chapter 5). Dredging of the canals and the river and extension of the shoreline provided some relief from excessive mortality, and the economic potential of the area attracted more migrants. All Europeans (including the Dutch) never constituted more than 3 percent of the population of Batavia, and that proportion declined after the seventeenth century. As the decades of the eighteenth century passed, the heaviest movements of people to the city were from other parts of Java, from Bali and the Spice Islands, from South India and Malaysia, and especially from China. This excludes a large number of slaves who were also brought in from some of these same areas. By 1790, there were almost as many Chinese in the area (28 percent) as there were Javanese and Balinese combined (33 percent). As was the case in all preindustrial cities, migration contributed substantially to the population and migrants were crucial to the city's development.

land. In his study of New England, Jones (1981) found that seventeenth-century settlers in the area moved away rather quickly from central areas of population near the seaports where they had first stopped. In two towns of Massachusetts to which many of these immigrants had moved, he discovered that slightly over half remained in them for ten years or more, whereas the rest headed for other places that satisfied their needs and interests better. The relative stability in these towns was reduced in the following periods as urbanization increased and mobility opportunities became more marked.

Early Transition Stage

The steady decline of mortality in countries undergoing the traditional demographic transition altered the dynamics of population change. Fertility first increased somewhat and then persisted at a high level for some time before it began a downward course. As a consequence, the rate of population growth rose and countries had to adapt to the greater numbers of people they had to accommodate. Davis (1963) related how countries that experienced a sustained mortality decline and a resulting rapid growth of population adopted a "multiphasic response" in dealing with the new demographic reality. Delayed marriage, more extensive use of contraception, abortion, and emigration were among the means used to soften the impact of population increase. Friedlander (1969) showed how this multiphasic response extended to various forms of internal migration that helped to redistribute people within a nation.

The most profound mobility of the early transition in Europe was the large emigration and the establishment of colonies in various parts of the world. England sent many people to populate the colonies it had founded, but significant numbers also came from the Netherlands, France, Scotland, Ireland, and Germany (Davie, 1936). While many came to America because of dissatisfaction with political, religious, and economic activities in their former lands, the rising tide of population in northern and western Europe was also a major factor.

Of course, not all movers out of Europe were emigrants. The shifts of people within each country were considerable and took many forms. Courgeau (1982) reports that the steady growth of the French population during the eighteenth century was accompanied by "changes in the routes and rhythms of the migratory flows during this period." Agricultural specialization led to a growing demand for farm workers, which occasioned increased seasonal and temporary mobility. After the harvest, workers would travel to towns and cities to take jobs in industry. As the early transition proceeded, the pace of urbanization quickened and circulatory mobility involving both movements from rural areas to towns and cities and from some cities to others provided labor in areas where the demand was greatest.

The great movements of the early transition period were not only of white Europeans to the Americas, Australia, Asia, and Africa and of the internal flows that allowed nations to adapt to a changing economy but also of slaves, mostly Africans, who were employed largely as field workers and household servants. The American colonies depended heavily on the African slave trade, and slavery continued for about eighty years after the American Revolution had created a new country (see Figure 7.3).

The bulk of the African slaves who came to the Americas did not come to the United States. They were mostly brought to South and Central America and the Caribbean islands, as shown in Figure 7.3. Some of them were later taken to the United States, and new waves of slaves imported directly from Africa came to the United States until such importation was banned in 1808.

FIGURE 7.3 The Transatlantic Slave Trade

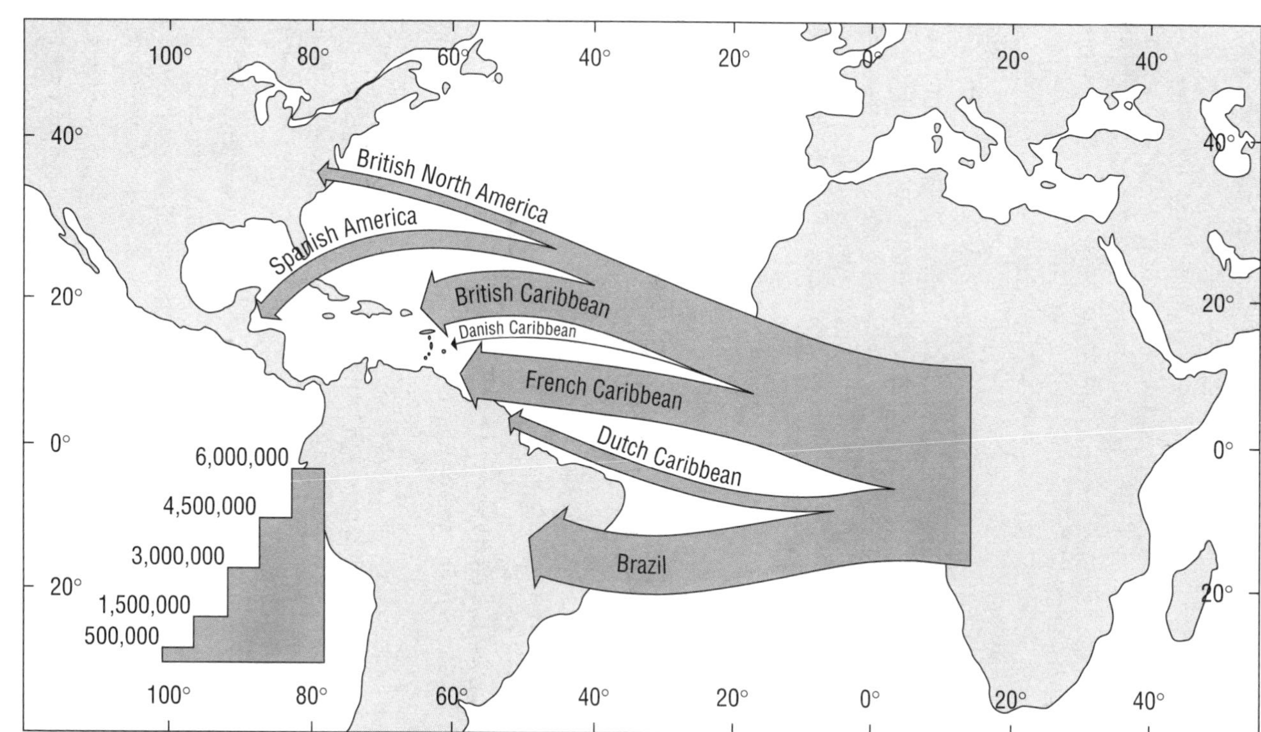

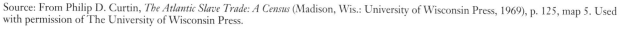

Source: From Philip D. Curtin, *The Atlantic Slave Trade: A Census* (Madison, Wis.: University of Wisconsin Press, 1969), p. 125, map 5. Used with permission of The University of Wisconsin Press.

But the mobility of slaves continued within the country for some time as part of an interstate slave trade (Finkelman, 1989).

While mortality declined significantly and fertility was steadily reduced from its previous high level in the United States during the nineteenth century, a declining volume of "old" immigration (from northern and western Europe) was compensated for by a rapidly increasing volume of "new" immigration (from southern and eastern Europe).

Among the eastern European arrivals during the intermediate demographic transitional period in the United States were Jews from the former Soviet Union (including Russia and the Baltic states) and Poland. The vast majority were victims of demographic growth and economic pressures, but anti-Semitism was also rampant. During the nineteenth century, the Jewish population of Czarist Russia increased from maybe 1½ million to over 5 million. Russia required the Jews to live within a confined area of the empire—the combined parts of Poland and Lithuania known as the Pale of Settlement. Because Jews were unable to seek work outside the area and were excluded from working in new factories, a high degree of poverty resulted (Stampfer, 1986). Through networks of relatives and others from their original towns and cities, they made their way to the United States via many transport routes.

Once in the United States, the Jews from eastern Europe were not likely to leave the country and certainly not to return to their homelands. Other immigrants of the period, however, did stay in the United States for short periods of time and then would go back to the places they came from. This was especially true of southern and eastern Europeans who left for purely economic reasons and subsequently earned enough money in the United States to reestablish themselves in the old country.

Some of these mobility experiences have been repeated in now-developing countries of the world as they go through the early demographic transition. In Latin America agricultural commercialization since the late nineteenth century brought about increased internal migration toward rural areas, largely seasonal in nature. Rapid industrialization beginning in the 1930s created internal migration that drew rural persons to cities and from small to large urban areas (Balan, 1983).

Circulatory migration is highly characteristic of areas in which the transition is definitely under way and urbanization is rapid. But circulation can take many different forms and recognition of this fact by local officials varies from country to country. In general, however, circulation is defined by Chapman and Prothero (1985) as follows:

> For the people who circulate, the basic principle involved is a territorial separation of obligations, activities, and goods. Throughout the Third World, this separateness manifests two major influences. On the one hand is the security associated with the home or natal place through access to land and other local resources for food, housing materials, and trading items; through kinship affiliation; through the presence of children and the elderly; and through common values and beliefs. There are, on the other hand, the locationally more

> widespread opportunities and associated risks involving local political and religious leaders; kinfolk; marriageable partners; items for exchange or trade, ceremonials and feasts; and the introduced goods and services of wage employment, commerce, medicine, education, religion, politics, and entertainment.

The tentativeness of residence in many developing country areas, owing to the need to travel to obtain paid work, makes distinctions between permanent mobility and circulatory mobility difficult to define. In Botswana, migrants tend to make short, temporary moves within the country for employment and visiting reasons. After an absence of varying periods of time, many return to their home villages. Others journey to South Africa to take jobs in the gold mines. According to Tarver and Miller (1990), "Miners enter into annual contracts to work in South Africa, then after eleven months return home for a month of vacation with their families. They sign new contracts and are given bonuses before returning to the mines. Many return to the mines repeatedly until they retire." Part of their earnings are remitted to their families for their upkeep. Strictly defined, these workers are international migrants; in a more general sense, they are circulatory mobile.

Many have argued that we can best see the various forms of circulation during the early transitional period as a facet of the urbanization process (Skeldon, 1985; Hugo, 1985). Rising cities first draw workers from the pool of nearby villages who do not sever their ties with their home areas but acquire second, short-term residences in the locations where they work. Later, as the boundaries of the expanding cities reach closer to those villages (which themselves are growing), circulation takes on the form of commuting on a weekly or daily basis. Eventually, a decision is made to settle in the city and forego the village, especially when the person's family networks and related social institutions in the village no longer have the same meaning.

The populations of societies in the early transitional period have large rural segments, and rural-urban migration continues to be a major form of mobility. Relocation from smaller to larger urban areas is also a predominant phenomenon. The desire to slow down the growth of large cities (discussed more fully in the next chapter) becomes a critical concern. Discouraging migration to the cities has often been a governmental policy in countries during this stage. Providing incentives for migration away from the cities has sometimes been another. The Indonesian government began in the early 1950s to give incentives to residents of the highly populated island of Java to resettle in other islands of the archipelago as a means of reducing the concentrations of people in that area. This planned resettlement (known as *transmigration*) has been included in each of the five-year plans of the government ever since (Hardjono, 1988). Although it has had some success (there are streams of transmigrants), the numbers involved have not been large enough to compensate for the population growth emanating from migrants who come to the large cities from rural areas and villages throughout the country and from the continuing excess of births over deaths in the region.

The countries of Asia now advancing from the early to the late stage of the transition have had an increasing scale of population mobility that extends beyond the types of circulation just described. Internally, areas peripheral to large cities have received movers as the metropolitan areas have expanded. These suburbs attract people from the rural areas as well. Where governments have opened up new frontier areas for development (agricultural or industrial), migrants from rural areas are apt to enter them. These movements are in addition to the continuing buildup of large cities with migration from rural and smaller urban places, and the growth of smaller cities which have become magnets for surrounding rural population. Internationally, there have been large forced migrations between Asian countries. In the twelve years following 1975, more than 1.7 million refugees left Vietnam, Kampuchea, and Laos for neighboring Asian countries. The Soviet intervention in Afghanistan in 1979 resulted in 2.7 million Afghans settling in Pakistan and 1.5 million in Iran. Camp cities were set up, many of them still in existence. Labor migration across national boundaries has also been extensive. By 1983 there were 3.6 million Asian migrants employed in the Middle East, most of them in oil-rich areas. The newest industrialized nations (Singapore, Hong Kong, and Taiwan) have received large numbers of other Asians for work purposes (Hugo, 1989).

Late Transition Stage

All now-developed nations and several newly developed areas (formerly part of the Third World) have advanced to a late stage of the demographic transition. What have been some of the dominant characteristics of mobility in those regions as they experienced significantly reduced fertility after achieving low mortality?

All these countries have undergone considerable economic and social development of some sort. All have urbanized greatly while reducing their rural populations. (Some, like China, still have a large segment of their population in rural areas, however.) All have seen both permanent mobility and circulation between urban areas, initially from smaller to larger places and later between larger places and, sometimes, from larger to smaller places. Most all have net immigration, and some have had to deal with substantial illegal or undocumented flows of immigrants as well as significant numbers of refugees, especially from countries in the less-developed Third World. Although social and cultural conditions in each area provide some unique patterns of mobility at the late transition stage, there are enough similarities in forms of mobility to mark the stage. The illustrations which follow are typical.

France is an example of a country which, like many of its European neighbors, completed the demographic transition by the middle of the twentieth century. In fact, the size of the French population remained fairly stable from before the beginning of the century until after World War II, and immigration was encouraged by the government in an effort to sustain population numbers. Then, a short-term baby boom coupled with continued immigration, mainly from North Africa, raised the population size (Courgeau, 1990).

Through the period of the country's industrialization, France experienced substantial rural-to-urban migration, in which Paris and other large cities gained large numbers from outlying regions. The rise of new urban areas in both the industrial and postindustrial eras provided economic incentives for people to move to other regions of the nation, and subsequently many escaped the old industrial areas of the north to establish themselves in the more environmentally attractive regions of the south. As with most countries in this transitional phase, smaller places became magnets for certain sectors of the population. As the new age produced improved transportation and telecommunications, the need for locating one's residence at the site of one's activities became less necessary. Numerous counterstreams of shorter-distance movers resulted in a low level of net migration.

A micro picture of mobility in France of those born during the late 1920s and early 1930s (Bonvalet and Lelièvre, 1990) reveals that the mobility of this cohort generally mirrored that of other cohorts in terms of life-cycle mobility determinants. However, because they were young adults in the postwar period, they first delayed leaving home because of a housing crisis and only later, when the housing market became more favorable, were they able to become home owners and leave their parents' home. As a consequence, their mobility was initially limited but then increased as they married and set up their own residences.

In the United States, the percentage of the population living outside their state of birth increased from 1900 to 1930. The subsequent economic depression, however, seems to have reduced the proportion as many young persons who had left farm areas for cities returned home when they lost their jobs. Following the Great Depression, the percentage of people moving away from their state of birth resumed its upward course, reaching almost 30 percent in 1980 (compared to 18 percent in 1900) (Long, 1988).

Two significant mobility cycles occurred in the United States in the early twentieth century. One was the westward migration of the economically depressed during the Great Depression of the late 1920s and early 1930s (referred to in Chapter 2). Another was the Great Migration of blacks from the South to the North. In response to a growing industrialization which was heightened during World War I and which created a demand for labor, the recruitment of blacks by employers was highly successful. As a result, in the period 1916–18, over 400,000 blacks migrated northward. In fact, between 1916 and 1930 over 1 million blacks made their way from the South to the North. The "pull" of prospective employment in the North was complemented by the "push" of conditions in the South. The cotton economy of the South, on which so many of the blacks depended for work, was depressed as a result of the infestation of cotton plants by boll weevils. Increasing "Jim Crow" legislation in southern states restricted the blacks' voting ability and reinforced separatism between the races. About this same time U.S. government limitations on immigration had caused the pool of new workers in the North to dry up (Marks, 1989). Compared to their plight in the South, the migrants were generally better off in the North, but the bulk of them never realized the expectations they had had for their families. Some succeeded in improving their status. Others, who became disenchanted by their failure to achieve economic success, returned to the South. (A later generation of blacks was to head back to the South in greater numbers.) Still others became residents of neighborhoods in the cities that were doomed to become economically deprived areas.

The pattern of residential changes in the United States has not changed much since mid-century. Between 1948 and 1984, the proportion making some type of residential move hovered around 20 percent. Roughly two-thirds of those who moved relocated within their own county; an additional 15 to 20 percent remained within their own state (Long, 1988). This relative constancy of mobility rates does not mean that people who moved followed the same mobility streams. For example, interstate migrants in the late 1930s were most likely to locate in adjacent states of the Northeast or Southwest; their counterparts in the 1950s were part of the Sunbelt movement, especially to Florida and California; and in the late 1970s interstate migrants were most likely to leave the Northeast, particularly New York, and head for the Sunbelt (although California was also beginning to lose residents to the Pacific Northwest).

Just as a substantial proportion of immigrants end up by being emigrants, so do many movers eventually return to their place of origin. In the 1975–80 period, 8 million Americans left their state of birth while over 3½ million returned to their birth state. Return migrants tend to be younger adults who have sought a better life elsewhere but either did not succeed economically or yearned to get back to the social and cultural setting in which they were reared.

By 1990, mobility in the United States assumed a profile that included both common historical features and some unique aspects. About 18 percent of Americans moved annually, down slightly from earlier years. Only 15 percent of those in families moved, as compared to 22 percent not in families. Migrants into metropolitan areas as a whole outnumbered migrants out of those areas, a reversal of trends in former periods. Cities were net losers through mobility while suburbs were gainers. Whereas the West and Midwest neither gained nor lost from interregional migration, the Northeast had a net out-migration during the 1980s and the South a net in-migration. Both black and white homeowners had a mobility rate of 7 to 8 percent annually, while 36 percent of white renters and 29 percent of black renters were mobile. Hispanics had a greater tendency for mobility overall (25 percent versus 20 percent for blacks and 17 percent for whites) largely because Hispanics included more renters than did non-Hispanics (DeAre, 1991).

The chief migration story in the United States in recent years has been the immigration of groups from Asia and Latin America. The typical international migration of people from less-developed to more-developed areas brought

Asians from many countries to the United States (Gardner, 1992). Some entered the country under the regular provisions of the immigration acts; others were admitted as refugees. They included Chinese, Japanese, Koreans, Vietnamese, Indians, Pakistani, Bangladeshi, and others.

The flow of people from the Philippines has been interesting to observe. Prior to 1934, Filipinos were recruited to work on sugar plantations in Hawaii and California. Their numbers reached 80,000 by 1929, supported by a U.S. law that treated them as U.S. nationals. When the Philippines received commonwealth status in 1935, their residents were subjected to the national origins quota system that limited their arrival to a maximum of 100 annually. After the Philippines gained independence from the United States in 1946, Filipino immigration increased but did not exceed 4,000 a year. Since the quota system was dropped, Filipino immigration has splurged (reaching an annual average of well over 40,000 during the early 1980s). For two decades now, at least one-fifth of all Asian immigrants have been Filipinos (Carino et al., 1990).

Much greater attention has been paid to the immigration of Mexicans to the United States primarily because it has involved a mixture of legal and illegal entries. Legal immigration of Mexicans first grew in the early 1900s while other immigration was declining. A second wave occurred after the Great Depression, stimulated by a U.S.–Mexican treaty providing for the admission of an unlimited number of temporary workers (*braceros*) in agriculture. A third phase of legal Mexican immigration began after the Immigration Reform Act of 1965 when, despite ceilings on arrivals from other Western Hemisphere countries, permanent Mexican legal immigration increased steadily. In recent years the number of legal Mexican immigrants has stabilized at a yearly average of 66,000 (Vernez and Ronfeldt, 1991).

Illegal immigration from Mexico has been a topic of considerable political and social concern in the United States since at least 1929. In recent years this concern has increased because illegal immigration has apparently been greater than legal immigration and has occurred during a time when U.S. officials have greatly strengthened efforts to control the number of persons entering the country. One difficulty in assessing the impact of such migration is that it is not documented; as a result, the numbers involved are subject to a wide range of estimates. A reasonable estimate placed the number of undocumented Mexican aliens in the United States in 1980 at less than 4 million (Bean et al., 1987). But this is only the net effect of illegal movements in and out of the United States. Recently as many as 200,000 Mexicans may have migrated to the United States illegally each year. These mobility streams have been circulatory, however, as many Mexicans move back and forth across the border, returning to their homes after periodic journeys in which they earn money in this country.

The flows and counterflows of illegal immigration from Mexico have been sustained by networks of the movers' relatives and friends on both sides of the border. Meanwhile, the U.S. Immigration and Naturalization Service (INS) has attempted to patrol the border and apprehend illegal movers through line watches, transportation checks, and checks of working establishments. When caught, the illegal alien is returned by the INS to the Mexican side of the border. The drama is likely to be repeated within a few days. This process has been referred to as a "cat and mouse game" (Koussoudji, 1992).

Although as many as 1 million persons may have been apprehended each year at the Mexican border in the 1970s, the number has undoubtedly been reduced by the Immigration Reform and Control Act of 1986 that prohibited employers from hiring undocumented workers, with fines for noncompliance. In addition, the act shored up border control across the 2,000-mile U.S.–Mexican boundary (Vernez and Ronfeldt, 1991). It also gave amnesty to over 2 million undocumented Mexican immigrants, allowing them the opportunity to apply for permanent legal status in the United States.

Little attention has been paid to the immigration of blacks to the United States in recent decades. Yet as many as 5,000 blacks migrated to the country in 1954, and the number swelled to 80,000 per year during the 1980s. Their countries of origin included Ethiopia, Nigeria, Ghana, Guyana, and Haiti. If immigration continues on this scale, the percentage of the U.S. black population consisting of recent foreign-born immigrants and their descendants will reach 8 percent by 2000 and 13 percent by 2030 (Reid, 1986).

Posttransition Stage

When Zelinsky (1971) formulated his typology of the mobility transition, he also speculated about what mobility patterns might be like in a "future superadvanced society." Based on what he saw as the logical extension of mobility trends in earlier transitional stages, he advanced the following conjectures:

1. We may see a decline in the level of residential migration as well a deceleration in some forms of circulation as a result of better communication and delivery systems.
2. Nearly all residential migration may be between cities or within cities.
3. Some further immigration of relatively unskilled labor from less developed areas is possible.
4. We may see a further acceleration in some current forms of circulation; new forms of circulation may begin to take shape.
5. Governments may impose a strict political control on internal as well as international movements.

Mobility forms do not occur in isolation. To talk about what to expect in the way of mobility after countries have gone through the demographic transition and beyond requires us to make reasonable assumptions about other aspects of the future society. Zelinsky assumed that fertility in a posttransitional stage would maintain its stability at a low level and would be highly controlled by the individual (and, in some cases, by sociopolitical forces). He further postulated that mortality would likewise stabilize, but at slightly lower levels than are observed at the end of the transition unless we are able to control organic diseases and/or extend the human life span. He made no assumptions about the nature of social institutions in a posttransition society.

The fact is that some countries have already moved into the early posttransition stage, and we can look to them to see what has already occurred in those areas. For example, what mobility patterns have emerged in Germany, Japan, and the United States? Further, what impact have social, economic, and political changes had on mobility trends in other posttransition countries? Finally, what mobility scenarios emanate from extreme assumptions about future conditions in the economically advanced regions of the world?

Germany is an interesting case of a European nation that has both completed demographic transition and gone through a division and later a reunification of its country. Zelinsky's forecast of mobility patterns in the superadvanced society ring true for Germany so far as normal population processes are considered. Fertility and mortality have remained low, creating a stable natural increase while the population ages. Some labor migration into the country and moderate amounts of interurban, intraurban, and circulatory movement have occurred. Apart from these, however, the creation of the separate countries of West Germany and East Germany after World War II and the recent unification of the two areas have added another dimension to the mobility patterns of greater Germany.

During the postwar period from 1950 to 1961 (when the Berlin Wall was erected), substantial movement from East to West Germany and a considerably smaller counterflow resulted in a net migration loss to East Germany of about 2 million people. From 1961 until 1988, movement between the two areas was greatly reduced but East German permission for residents to reunite with their families in the West led to about one-half million migrants between the countries. When the Berlin Wall was torn down in 1989, more than 2 percent of the total East German population (perhaps 350,000 persons) moved to West Germany during that year alone. A slightly larger number crossed the boundary of the two countries in 1990 before the two areas were reunited. From that point on, movement between the two geographic areas ceased to be an international migration and began to be an internal migration. These mobility cycles were superimposed on the more normal elements of the mobility transition.

Japan provides another interesting case of a posttransition country that generally follows Zelinsky's future model but retains some unique mobility features. In the period around 1980, only 1 in 10 Japanese was mobile at all, with half of these persons moving within their own community. Whereas the largest cities (especially Tokyo) had attracted many migrants in the earlier decades of this century, by 1980 the streams of movers between urban areas tended to offset each other to such an extent that net migration between prefectures (administrative areas) was very small (Otomo, 1990). In fact, many Japanese metropolitan areas have experienced in recent years *turnaround* (that is, more movement out of than into such areas). At the same time, a moderate amount of movement between cities and between one rural area and another has taken place. While economic reasons (especially job changes) motivated many Japanese to move, family factors (marriage, housing changes, and return to family homes) were also reasons expressed by residential movers. Temporary mobility, largely for purposes of visits and vacations, is widely practiced in Japan, which has developed first-rate means of transportation. The emerging picture is one of a high degree of residential stability in a country that is considerably urbanized. This picture comports well with the Zelinsky forecast for the future mobility transition phase.

Although economically advanced countries share the age pattern of mobility common at all transitional stages, with relatively low levels of mobility at the older ages (see Figure 7.1), it is also the case that the elderly who do move in the late and posttransitional stages do so generally for different reasons than do younger persons or older persons at earlier transitional stages.

One can say that the mobility habits of older persons, like those of persons at earlier ages in the life cycle, are also a response to life course events. According to Litwak and Longino (1987), older people are most apt to move at three points in their elderly life cycles—first, when they retire from full-time work or other activity; second, when they experience moderate forms of disability; and third, when they have major forms of chronic disability.

When people retire and are still in relatively good health, they can often realize their dreams of living in a new location that will maximize their leisure-time satisfactions. Yet in the United States, only 5 percent of those 60 and over will be mobile over a five-year period. Remaining near children and grandchildren sometimes outweighs striking out to new places that are some distance away from former residences. Economic limitations may also prevent people from achieving their retirement aspirations. In contrast with the comparison of wage rates that motivates many persons in the working ages to move, it is more likely to be the comparison of the cost of living that affects the decision of older persons, who are generally on fixed incomes, to become mobile (Fournier et al., 1988).

When an older couple or individual first experiences chronic disabilities, some of these persons will either return to their former locations or move on to still newer places (especially if they can reunite with children or other relatives). Even though older people may enjoy the friendly companionship of neighbors in retirement areas or at the old homesteads (which have become "empty nests"), they will not be able to find the personal support needed when chronic illness occurs. Such individuals may, therefore, return to their earlier places of residence. This development is even more likely to happen when a spouse who has been a faithful partner dies. When chronic illness becomes more severe, a third type of move among the elderly in many societies has to do with placement in a long-term care institution. Even devoted children or other relatives and friends are usually not in a position to provide the kind of care required by very sick people in their advanced years. To repeat, the incidence of old-age mobility is not very high, compared to the mobility at younger ages, but the reasons for older persons to move are linked to critical factors associated with reaching, and going through, older ages. Because the populations of countries that go beyond the demographic transition include high proportions of elderly people, we can expect that the mobility phenomena we have described will become quite familiar in the future of economically developed countries (Serow and Sly, 1991).

These patterns of elderly mobility are not just found in the United States and one or two other developed countries; they involve factors we can observe in all posttransition nations, including Australia, Belgium, Canada, Germany, Hungary, Japan, the Netherlands, and Poland (Serow, 1987). One would expect to see these patterns continue in all countries that reach or go through this stage of the mobility transition.

On the international migration front, the interacting dynamics of evolving political, social, and economic changes will strongly affect future prospects in all parts of the world. For example, the success of the most recent United States immigration law designed to control undocumented immigration, especially from Mexico and the Caribbean area, will depend on the ability of the several nations to achieve political and economic agreements as well as on the actual future course of the economies involved (Espenshade et al., 1991).

The political revolutions in Europe that have resulted in divisions of former countries into two or more new states serve to establish new national boundaries; this development increases the prospect of international migration (largely because of a tendency for ethnic groups in the former broad territory to gravitate toward the new state where those ethnic groups dominate).

The difficulty of determining patterns of migration of all sorts in the posttransition society is underscored if we examine the assumptions made by governmental officials in different developed countries. Wils (1991) points out that officials often base their assumptions on simple extrapolations of the past or on desirable targets to be reached rather than on reasoned calculations deriving from analytical perspectives (as we have increasingly seen in the case of fertility and mortality projections).

Uncertainties in mobility projections occur despite the normal procedure of basing them only on the traditional forces that trigger population movements. Makers of population projections usually provide the caveat that their projections assume no unusual occurrences in the area concerned. But what would be the impact on mobility trends if such occurrences did occur? While it is difficult to factor in the mobility consequences of wars, various types of conflicts do take place with regularity and their migratory impacts are often highly relevant.

Though we cannot easily predict environmental disasters, such as earthquakes, floods, and volcanoes, these events are frequent enough and are generally linked to residential and circulatory movements. Both wars and environmental disasters can lead to mobility cycles of long or short duration. But we can also envision more fundamental environmental changes creating mobility trends that may become a more regular element of the posttransition era. Likewise, we can imagine the real possibility that interplanetary travel will open up new travel vistas for many persons. Both expected and unexpected developments will together shape the kinds and levels of mobility that will characterize the later phases of the posttransition period.

Chapter Highlights

1. Mobility means movement, and in a demographic sense it means geographic relocation of people.
2. Mobility differs from mortality and fertility in that it is not biologically based; mobility both adds to and subtracts from different populations and is not an inevitable process.
3. Mobility can take the following forms: (a) temporary mobility (in which daily or other short-term movement does not result in changing one's primary residence); (b) circulatory mobility (in which a person does not give up a primary residence but maintains a secondary or other residence, and movement between the residences takes place at various time intervals); and (c) permanent mobility (in which a primary residence is changed).
4. We can classify permanent mobility according to the kind of geographic boundary crossed in changing residence. A local mover changes residence within the general community. A migrant moves beyond the community boundary in changing residence. Internal migrants migrate within their nation; they may cross county, provincial, state, or regional boundaries. Those who migrate across country borders are called international migrants.
5. Because mobility involves going from one place to another, movers are labeled according to whether they are leaving or entering an area. Thus a local mover is an out-mover from the area of origin and an in-mover to the area of destination. Similarly, persons moving within a country are outmigrants from the territories they leave and in-migrants to the territories in which they arrive. International migrants are emigrants from the country they depart and immigrants to the country of arrival.
6. We can obtain information about mobility from censuses, surveys, population registers, administrative records (such as those on immigration summarized by the Immigration and Naturalization Service in the United States), and indirect estimation.
7. There is a universal pattern of mobility by age that is observed in most parts of the world and for all types of mobility. Typically, movement is moderately high in infancy and early childhood, declines in later childhood and youth, and rises to a peak when people reach the normal ages for higher education, marriage, and employment. It then decreases progressively as people attain older ages.
8. Persons who migrate across national boundaries may be regular immigrants (who intend to settle permanently in the new country); refugees

(who fear persecution in their country of origin); or other nonimmigrants (including visitors, students, and temporary workers). National laws frequently identify those with indeterminant alien statuses as parolees or asylees. Also, persons who enter a country without permission are called illegal or undocumented immigrants.

9. Explanations of mobility encompass both involuntary reasons (those out of an individual's control) and voluntary reasons (those based on more-or-less conscious decision making). Variables weighing heavily in many such decisions are job prospects, changes in economic status, and housing improvements as well as life-cycle factors, such as college attendance, marriage, divorce, and retirement.
10. We can conceptualize mobility within a demographic transition framework. Examination of mobility patterns around the world and over time show that, while the mobility transition may be less regular than the mortality or fertility transitions, certain regularities do occur. Moreover, mobility cycles have frequently been observed.

Discussion Questions

1. Most demographers would agree that mobility has not received the amount of research and analytical attention given to mortality and fertility. What would you regard as the reasons for this relative neglect of the mobility topic?
2. Only in recent years have temporary and circulatory mobility been encompassed within the theories and analyses of mobility. Why do you think those mobility forms were so long absent from the demography of mobility?
3. Consider your own mobility history. How many moves have you made in your lifetime, and how would each of them be classified according to the definitions provided in this chapter? As a result of your analysis, what shortcomings in mobility definitions would you identify?
4. Movement between countries was once fairly free, but now it tends to be severely curtailed by immigration legislation in all parts of the world. Do you think that this change is a good or bad thing, and why?
5. Talk to a parent, grandparent, or neighbor about the last time they made a voluntary move. Have them reconstruct the decision-making process in terms of the pros and cons of moving that they considered and why they decided the way they did.
6. Review the discussion in this chapter about future mobility in the posttransition stage. Which factors seem to you most plausible and which least plausible? Can you think of other considerations not included in the discussion?

Suggested Readings

U.S. Bureau of the Census. *Current Population Reports*, Series P-20. Washington, D.C.: Government Printing Office. Issues of this governmental report periodically assess the current conditions of mobility in the United States.

Charles B. Nam, William J. Serow, and David F. Sly, eds. 1990. *International Handbook on Internal Migration.* Westport, Conn.: Greenwood Press. Chapters cover the mobility and migration processes within twenty-one countries of the world, including all parts of the globe. It provides a sense of the similarities and differences in internal migration cross-nationally.

William J. Serow, Charles B. Nam, David F. Sly, and Robert H. Weller, eds. 1990. *Handbook on International Migration.* Westport, Conn.: Greenwood Press. A companion volume to the previous one that focuses on international migration for nineteen countries, some the same and some different from those in the other volume.

International Migration: An Assessment for the 90's. 1989. *International Migration Review*, vol 23, no. 3. This special silver anniversary issue of the journal includes a range of articles which take stock of the various forms of migration across national boundaries and suggest what might be in store for the last decade of the twentieth century.

References

Balan, Jorge. 1983. "Agrarian Structures and Internal Migration in a Historical Perspective: Latin American Case Studies." In Peter Morrison, ed., *Population Movements: Their Forms and Functions in Urbanization and Development*, pp. 151–85. Liège: Ordina Editions.

Bean, Frank D., Edward E. Telles, and B. Lindsay Lowell. 1987. "Undocumented Migration to the United States: Perceptions and Evidence." *Population and Development Review* 13:4, 671–90.

———, Georges Vernez, and Charles B. Keely. 1989. *Opening and Closing the Doors: Evaluating Immigration Reform and Control.* Santa Monica, Calif.: Rand Corporation.

Bonvalet, Catherine, and Eva Lelièvre. 1990. "Residential Mobility in France and in Paris Since 1945: The History of a Cohort." *Population*, English Selection 2: 187–212.

Carino, Benjamin V., James T. Fawcett, Robert W. Gardner, and Fred Arnold. 1990. "The New Filipino Immigrants to the United States: Increasing Diversity and Change." *Papers of the East-West Population Institute*, no. 115 (Honolulu: East-West Center).

Chapman, Murray, and R. Mansell Prothero. 1985. "Themes on Circulation in the Third World." In R. Mansell Prothero and Murray Chapman, *Circulation in Third World Countries*, pp. 1–26. London: Routledge & Kegan Paul.

Clark, Peter, and David Souden. 1987. "Introduction." In *Migration and Society in Early Modern England*, pp. 11–48. London: Hutchinson.

Courgeau, Daniel. 1982. "Study on the Dynamics. Evolution and Consequences of Migrations—II: Three Centuries of Spatial Mobility in France." *Reports and Papers in the Social Sciences.* Paris: Unesco.

———. 1990. "France." In Charles B. Nam, William J. Serow, and David F. Sly, eds., *International Handbook on Internal Migration,* pp. 125–44. Westport, Conn.: Greenwood Press.

DaVanzo, Julie. 1976. *Why Families Move: A Model of the Geographic Mobility of Married Couples.* Santa Monica, Calif.: Rand Corporation.

Davie, Maurice R. 1936. *World Immigration.* New York: Macmillan.

Davis, Kingsley. 1963. "The Theory of Change and Response in Modern Demographic History." *Population Index* 29:4, 345–66.

DeAre, Diana. 1991. "Geographic Mobility: March 1987 to March 1990." *Current Population Reports,* U.S. Bureau of the Census, Series P-20, no. 456. Washington, D.C.: Government Printing Office.

Espenshade, Thomas, Michael White, and Frank Bean. 1991. "Patterns of Recent Illegal Migration to the United States." In Wolfgang Lutz, ed., *Future Demographic Trends in Europe and North America,* pp. 301–36. London: Academic Press.

Findley, Sally E. 1982. "Migration Survey Methodologies: A Review of Design Issues." *International Union for the Scientific Study of Population, IUSSP Papers,* no. 20.

Finkelman, Paul. 1989. "Introduction." In Paul Finkelman, ed., *Slave Trade and Migration,* pp. xi–xv. New York: Garland.

Fournier, Gary M., David W. Rasmussen, and William J. Serow. 1988. "Elderly Migration: For Sun and Money." *Population Research and Policy Review* 7: 189–99.

Friedlander, Dov. 1969. "Demographic Responses and Population Change." *Demography* 6:4, 359–81.

Gardner, Robert W. 1992. "Asian Immigration: The View from the United States." *Asian and Pacific Migration Journal* 1:1, 64–99.

Goldscheider, Calvin. 1971. *Population, Modernization, and Social Structure.* Boston: Little, Brown.

———. 1987. "Migration and Social Structure: Analytic Issues and Comparative Perspectives in Developing Nations." *Sociological Forum* 2: 674–96.

Goldstein, Sidney, and Alice Goldstein. 1981. "Surveys of Migration in Developing Countries: A Methodological Review." *Papers of the East-West Population Institute,* no. 71.

Harbison, Sarah F. 1981. "Family Structure and Family Strategy in Migration Decision Making." In Gordon F. DeJong and Robert W. Gardner, eds., *Migration Decision Making,* pp. 225–51. Elmsford, N.Y.: Pergamon Press.

Hardjono, Joan. 1988. "*Reorientations in the Indonesian Transmigration Program.*" Unpublished manuscript.

Hugo, Graeme J. 1983. "New Conceptual Approaches to Migration in the Context of Urbanization: A Discussion Based on the Indonesian Experience." In Peter Morrison, ed., *Population Movements: Their Forms and Functions in Urbanization and Development,* pp. 69–113. Liège: Ordina Editions.

———. 1985. "Circulation in West Java, Indonesia." In R. Mansell Prothero and Murray Chapman, eds., *Circulation in Third World Countries*, pp. 75–99. London: Routledge & Kegan Paul.

———. 1989. "Internal and International Migration Flows: Some Recent Developments in Asia." In *International Population Conference, New Delhi, 1989*, vol. 2, pp. 239–60. Liège: International Union for the Scientific Study of Population.

Jones, Douglas Lamar. 1981. *Village and Seaport*. Hanover, N.H.: University Press of New England.

Keely, Charles B. 1981. *Global Refugee Policy: The Case for A Development-Oriented Strategy*. New York: Population Council.

Khasanov, A.M. 1984. *Nomads and the Outside World*. Cambridge: Cambridge University Press.

Kols, Adrienne, and Dana Lewison. 1983. "Migration, Population Growth, and Development." *Population Reports*, Series M, no. 7 (Baltimore: Johns Hopkins University).

Koussoudji, Sherrie A. 1992. "Playing Cat and Mouse at the U.S.–Mexican Border." *Demography* 29:2, 159–80.

Lauby, Jennifer, and Oded Stark. 1988. "Individual Migration as a Family Strategy: Young Women in the Philippines." *Population Studies* 42:3, 473–86.

Lee, Everett S. 1966. "A Theory of Migration." *Demography* 3:1, 47–57.

Levine, Daniel L., Kenneth Hill, and Robert Warren, eds. 1985. *Immigration Statistics: A Story of Neglect*. Washington, D.C.: National Academy Press.

Linford, Lloyd. 1973. "America: An Immigrant Nation." *Equilibrium* 1:3, 6–15.

Litwak, Eugene, and Charles F. Longino. 1987. "Migration Patterns among the Elderly: A Developmental Perspective." *Gerontologist* 27: 266–72.

Long, Larry. 1988. *Migration and Residential Mobility in the United States*. New York: Russell Sage Foundation.

Marks, Carole. 1989. *Farewell—We're Good and Gone: The Great Black Migration*. Bloomington, Ind.: Indiana University Press.

Otomo, Atsushi. 1990. "Japan." In Charles B. Nam, William J. Serow, and David F. Sly, eds., *International Handbook on Internal Migration*, pp. 257–74. Westport, Conn.: Greenwood Press.

Petersen, William. 1975. "A Demographer's View of Prehistoric Demography." *Current Anthropology* 16:2, 227–37.

Potok, Chaim. 1978. *Wanderings*. New York: Alfred A. Knopf.

Pryor, Robin J. 1982. "Population Redistribution, the Demographic and Mobility Transitions." In John I. Clarke and Leszek A. Kosinski, eds., *Redistribution of Population in Africa*, pp. 25–30. London: Heinemann.

Ravenstein, E.G. 1885. "The Laws of Migration." *Journal of the Royal Statistical Society* 48: 167–235.

———. 1889. "The Laws of Migration." *Journal of the Royal Statistical Society* 52: 241–305.

Reid, John. 1986. "Immigration and the Future U.S. Black Population." *Population Today* (a publication of the Population Reference Bureau) 14:2, 6–8.

Root, Brenda Davis, and Gordon F. DeJong. 1991. "Family Migration in a Developing Country." *Population Studies* 45:2, 221–33.

Serow, William J. 1987. "Why the Elderly Move: Cross-National Comparisons." *Research on Aging* 9:4, 582–97.

Serow, William, and David Sly. 1991. "Geographic Mobility of the Elderly in Industrialized Societies." In Wolfgang Lutz, ed., *Future Demographic Trends in Europe and North America*, pp. 399–419. London: Academic Press.

Shaw, R. Paul. 1975. *Migration Theory and Fact: A Review and Bibliography of Current Literature*. Philadelphia: Regional Science Research Institute.

Shryock, Henry S., Jr. 1964. *Population Mobility within the United States*. Chicago: Community and Family Study Center, University of Chicago.

Sjaastad, Larry A. 1962. "The Costs and Returns of Human Migration." *Journal of Political Economy* 70: 80–93.

Skeldon, Ronald. 1985. "Circulation: A Transition in Mobility in Peru." In R. Mansell Prothero and Murray Chapman, eds., *Circulation in Third World Countries*, pp. 100–20. London: Routledge & Kegan Paul.

———. 1990. *Population Mobility in Developing Countries: A Reinterpretation*. London: Belhaven Press.

Spooner, Frank. 1986. "Batavia, 1673–1790: A City of Colonial Growth and Migration." In Ira A. Glazier and Luigi DeRosa, eds., *Migration across Time and Nations*, pp. 30–57. New York: Holmes & Meier.

Stampfer, Shaul. 1986. "The Geographic Background of East European Jewish Migration to the United States before World War I." In Ira A. Glazier and Luigi DeRosa, eds., *Migration across Times and Nations*, pp. 220–30. New York: Holmes & Meier.

Stouffer, Samuel A. 1960. "Intervening Opportunities and Competing Migrants." *Journal of Regional Science* 2: 1–26.

Tarver, James D., and H. Max Miller. 1990. "Botswana." In William J. Serow, Charles B. Nam, David F. Sly, and Robert H. Weller, eds., *Handbook on International Migration*, pp. 25–36. Westport, Conn.: Greenwood Press.

Thomas, Dorothy S. 1938. *Research Memorandum on Migration Differentials*. New York: Social Science Research Council.

Vernez, Georges, and David Ronfeldt. 1991. "The Current Situation in Mexican Immigration." *Science* 251: 1189–93.

Wils, Anne B. 1991. "Survey of Immigration Trends and Assumptions about Future Migration." In Wolfgang Lutz, ed., *Future Demographic Trends in Europe and North America*, pp. 28–99. London: Academic Press.

Wood, Adrian P. 1982. "Spontaneous Agricultural Resettlement in Ethiopia, 1950–1974." In John I. Clarke and Leszek A. Kosinski, eds., *Redistribution of Population in Africa*, pp. 157–64. London: Heinemann.

Zelinsky, Wilbur. 1971. "The Hypothesis of the Mobility Transition." *Geographical Review* 61: 219–49.

———. 1983. "The Impasse in Migration Theory: A Sketch Map for Potential Escapees." In Peter A. Morrison, ed., *Population Movements: Their Forms and Functions in Urbanization and Development*, pp. 19–46. Liège: Ordina Editions.

8. Population Distribution and Composition Dynamics

Our initial discussion (in Chapter 1) of the ways in which the basic components of population change—mortality, fertility, and mobility—produce the additions and subtractions (pluses and minuses) to overall population change also mentioned the contributions of the same basic components to the size of populations in different geographic areas, different age and sex groupings, different racial and ethnic groupings, and different groupings of population characteristics.

Populations are not just statistics of abstract people who are all alike. They constitute sets of humans who vary in their personal traits, some of which they share with others and some of which differentiate them from others. The point of this chapter is to develop an understanding of those population traits incorporated under two general headings—population distribution and population composition. *Population distribution* refers to the spread of population over land area and the geographic location of individuals. *Population composition* refers to the spread of population over categories of variables that help us comprehend the makeup of people, as well as to the biological and social traits of individuals.

The French sociologist Halbwachs (1960) conceived of this complex of traits and characteristics as defining the structure of the population. Drawing on a term elucidated by his mentor, Emile Durkheim, Halbwachs referred to the linkage of population and society as constituting a *social morphology*. The form and structure of societies, communities, and neighborhoods are based not only on their physical location but also on the social attachments of their members.

This chapter will create the basis for you to understand Part Three, which will deal with the impacts of population change. This is because we need to keep in mind that social change is not only influenced by the number of people involved and the ways in which that number is modified; it is also influenced by the dynamics of who those people are and where they are located at different points in time.

As in the last three chapters, we will first pay attention to basic concepts and measures as well as their relevance. Second, we will note examples of how these concepts and measures develop over the course of the demographic transition.

CRITICAL CONCEPTS AND MEASURES

If the concepts discussed in this chapter seem to cover a very wide range of topics, it is because our plan is to identify the most critical elements of *population structure* and to suggest how their interrelationships signify demographic subgroups that are the real human stuff of societies, communities, and neighborhoods.

The first set of concepts and associated measurement issues relate to population distribution generally and to its more specific manifestations—various geographically bounded areas and unbounded geographic constructs. Thus, along with such configurations as cities, states, and nations, we have such derived classifications as rural-urban and levels of urbanization and metropolitanization.

The second set of concepts and associated measurement issues relates to population composition, generally, and to its important structural elements—age and sex, race and ethnicity, and selected physical, social, and cultural traits of individuals.

Putting these two together creates a variety of significant population structures—a suburban college town dominated by young adults in the Netherlands; a black urban ghetto in the northeast of the United States; a city neighborhood in Argentina whose residents are of Italian extraction; a rural farm settlement of predominately white Lutherans in Sweden; a retirement area in the Swiss Alps composed largely of recent migrants from the surrounding nations of Europe; an Indian tribal reservation in the American West; an African pygmy village; and many, many more. Sometimes, however, we will not be very specific about the place dimension. We may be concerned with socioeconomically deprived infants from around the world; all Muslim women in the Middle East; or deaf persons at working ages in the United States.

Sometimes distribution and composition variables will become the bases for differentiating levels of mortality, fertility, and mobility in a population. At other times we will examine their role in helping to explain other phenomena we are studying. For example, what impact does rapid urbanization have on a country's fertility level, or what effect does an aging population have on morbidity and mortality patterns? Still further, how do these distribution and composition factors influence the educational, economic, and political structures of the society?

Population Distribution

When a census is taken in a country, whether it is based on a *de jure* or a *de facto* count, each of the people enumerated is identified with a particular location. Likewise, when a survey is conducted or a population register is compiled, those covered are linked to a given place. These geographic locations may initially be a person's usual residence address. But that address is a point within many sorts of geographic categories. When we speak of *population distribution*, we mean how people are spread across varied geographic categories.

As populations grew in size, they extended themselves outward in space or concentrated themselves inward in space to such a degree that the geographic configurations used to describe their whereabouts at earlier times were no longer adequate in indicating the distribution of population. As time went by, therefore, we have had to create many new geographic entities. What, then, is the geographic nomenclature used to measure population distribution?

Let us begin by referring to familiar geographic entities, that is, *administrative or political areas*. These areas have definite geographic boundaries (sometimes streets or roads and sometimes natural dividers, such as a river, ocean, or mountain); they are territories maintained by governments or political subdivisions for governmental use. Included here would be countries or nations, states or provinces, counties or equivalents (including parishes or independent cities), minor civil divisions (such as townships and incorporated municipalities), incorporated places (such as cities, villages, or boroughs), and political subdivisions (such as congressional districts, legislative districts, and election precincts). We can all locate ourselves in at least several of these classifications.

There are other kinds of geographic units which are also bounded but which are not administratively or politically recognized. We call these units *statistical areas* because their boundaries have meaning for various kinds of data compilations. (Some of them are also convenient as cultural designations.) Included in this group of areas are the world itself, continents, regions of countries, urban agglomerations (such as metropolitan areas and urbanized areas), unincorporated places, census tracts, neighborhoods, city blocks, and rural land divisions. All such places may or may not have a popular identity, but they do have geographic boundaries. Furthermore, they are units that may encompass administrative or political areas (e.g., the U.S. South includes a grouping of states) or be subunits of such areas (e.g., city blocks are elements of cities).

There is still a third set of geographic identifiers that we can call *nonbounded residential classifications*. People covered by these units have similar characteristics with regard to certain kinds of land-based features, but they do not necessarily live in proximity to each other (they may be scattered about a more general area). Some examples of these classifications are rural and urban residence, farm and nonfarm residence, suburban or exurban location (without reference to any particular communities), and the size of the geographic unit of residence.

In a sense, the last two broad types of geographic labels—statistical areas and nonbounded residential classifications—were invented (by various people) to describe important aspects of population distribution. In the remainder of this section and the two following ones, we will employ many of these units to illustrate the substantial variations in how people are spread over the land and how these distributions change.

TABLE 8.1 Percentage Distribution of the World's Population among Broad Areas: 1750–1992

AREA	1750	1800	1850	1900	1950	1992
WORLD	100.0%	100.0%	100.0%	100.0%	100.0%	100.0%
ASIA	63.0	64.4	63.5	56.1	54.9	59.2
China	25.2	33.0	34.1	26.4	22.3	21.5
India, Bangladesh, and Pakistan	24.0	19.9	18.5	17.3	17.3	20.6
Japan	3.8	3.1	2.5	2.7	3.3	2.3
Indonesia	1.5	1.3	1.8	2.5	3.1	3.3
Remainder of Asia	8.5	7.1	6.9	7.2	9.0	11.4
AFRICA	13.4	10.9	8.8	8.1	8.8	12.1
North Africa	1.3	1.1	1.2	1.6	2.1	2.7
Remainder of Africa	12.1	9.8	7.6	6.4	6.7	9.4
EUROPE (excluding the former U.S.S.R.)	15.8	15.5	16.5	17.9	15.6	9.4
Germany	—	—	—	3.5	2.6	1.5
FORMER U.S.S.R.	5.3	5.7	6.0	8.1	7.2	5.2
AMERICAS	2.3	3.2	5.1	9.5	13.0	13.6
North America	0.3	0.7	2.1	5.0	6.6	5.2
United States	0.2	0.5	1.8	4.6	6.0	4.7
Canada	0.1	0.2	0.3	0.4	0.6	0.5
Middle and South America	2.0	2.5	3.0	4.4	6.4	8.4
OCEANIA	0.3	0.2	0.2	0.4	0.5	0.5

Source: John Durand, "The Modern Expansion of World Population," *Proceedings of the American Philosophical Society* (Philadelphia, June 1967), p. 137; derived from *1992 World Population Data Sheet* (Washington, D.C.: Population Reference Bureau, 1992) and from independent estimates.

Let us start with how the allocation of the world's population by regions and certain countries has shifted over almost two and one-half centuries (see Table 8.1). At least since 1750, people on the Asian continent have made up between one-half and two-thirds of the Earth's population. Actually, the proportion of Asians in the world declined from 64 to 55 percent during the span from 1800 to 1950; it then increased to 59 percent by 1992. One might first think that much of this increase was due to the Chinese contribution, but, in fact, the Chinese pattern runs counter to the development of Asia as a whole.

Despite the large number of Chinese, their percentage of all persons has declined steadily since 1850 (except perhaps during some intermediate years). The South Asian populations of India, Bangladesh, and Pakistan follow more closely the Asian pattern over time. Japan's share of the global population increased during the early part of this century (as the Japanese went through their demographic transition) and then decreased (when the transition ended). Indonesia and the remainder of Asia have steadily accounted for more of total population since the nineteenth century.

The similarity in changing relative contributions of Europe, the former U.S.S.R., and North America to that of Japan (in pattern, not in level) reflects the course of the demographic transition in those areas as well. The data for Middle and South America and Africa, with their growing share of the world's population up to 1992, is a consequence of their earlier point in the transition. Yet another perspective on this information would highlight both the 80 percent of the world's people who reside in Third World areas and the rise in that percentage since 1950 (when it was 67 percent).

We can also be impressed by the fact that population is distributed unequally over all types of geographic units, and that the redistribution of population over time alters the levels of distributional inequality. Box 8.1 gives three examples of variations in population distribution.

What we have to keep in mind about these examples is that, as we saw in Chapter 1, the basic components of population change combine in different ways to affect the size of each geographic unit as time goes by; in addition, the patterns of distributional inequality undergo change to the extent that various units gain or lose at different rates. As a result, in order to understand why the four U.S. regions have changed their share of the U.S. population over time, we need to know the course of mortality, fertility, and mobility in each region as well as how the net effect of these factors produced differing population gains. The increasing share of the southern population in the country since 1970 is owed to both natural increase and in-migration. This has resulted in a greater net population gain in the South than in other regions.

Rural and Urban Location

It is common to hear about people coming from rural and urban parts of the country. Those terms convey a general meaning that combines an idea of the relative population density where these people live with a sense of the character of those areas. When we think of *rural*, we are apt to imagine a sparsely populated area in a farming section typified by a slow pace of life. When we think of *urban*, our thoughts are likely to turn to a densely populated area with a commercial and/or industrial center characterized by a quicker pace of life.

Demographers and statisticians have attempted to capture those descriptions in their definitions and measurement of rural and urban, but differing circumstances in different areas plus dynamic changes in the nature of rural and

BOX 8.1 Patterns of Population Distribution

Population densities in Germany in 1989 varied considerably over the country's several hundred administrative districts, with fewer than 70 persons in some districts, 3,000 to 4,000 persons in others, and varying numbers in between in still other districts (Heilig, Buttner, and Lutz, 1990). But these densities were not always at the 1989 levels. Some areas increased their population levels more or less rapidly than before, while other districts lost population from previous points in time.

The balance of people in the four broad regions of the United States (Northeast, North Central or Midwest, South, and West) has shifted with time. Only the Northeast and South existed in 1790, with each making up half of the new nation's population. The frontier movement that opened up areas that were to become part of the Midwest drew people away from the Northeast and South. By the middle of the nineteenth century when the western region emerged, perhaps one-fourth of the total national population lived in the Midwest, with proportional reductions in both the South and Northeast. Of course, the growing size of the country's population through these decades meant that all regions were increasing in numbers, but that the fractions in each region were changing. As the West's numbers continued to expand, the shares of U.S. population from other regions diminished. By 1970, all four regions were approaching parity. The 1990 Census showed that 20 percent of U.S. residents lived in the Northeast, 24 percent in the North Central region, 34 percent in the South, and 21 percent in the West. The West had gained steadily in numbers over time, and the south had experienced a resurgence of population since the 1960s. In contrast, both northern regions, although gaining in absolute numbers, had been steadily accounting for a smaller share of the national population.

Examining the state of Florida's sixty-seven counties, we find the largest number of people in Dade County (where Miami is located), and this number is almost twice that of adjacent Broward County (the site of Fort Lauderdale). Combined with Palm Beach County, this southeast coastal area is a population stronghold. Pinellas and Hillsborough counties (locales for St. Petersburg and Tampa on the west central coast) have the second largest concentrations of people, and Duval County (home of Jacksonville in the northeast) and Orange County (site of the Disneyworld complex) are also major population centers. Together, these seven counties account for more than half of Florida's 1990 population. However, the most rapid rates of growth have been occurring in other counties.

urban areas make that attempt very difficult. The United Nations Secretariat (1974) referred to the "bewildering variety of definitions of 'urban' and 'rural' population now used in censuses" around the world.

Rather than elaborating this "variety of definitions," let us examine what are the 1990 U.S. Census definitions of urban and rural. Urban is first used to describe territory, persons, and housing units in:

1. Places of 2,500 or more persons incorporated as cities, villages, boroughs (except in Alaska and New York), and towns (except in the six New England States, New York, and Wisconsin), but excluding the rural portions of "extended cities."
2. Census designated places of 2,500 or more persons.
3. Other territory, incorporated or unincorporated, included in urbanized areas (U.S. Bureau of the Census, 1991).

Confusing? Perhaps so, but the Census Bureau's aim was to create a definition that would permit it to classify all geographic units as urban which, in fact, had an urban character. The cutoff of 2,500 people as representing a rural-urban dividing line has existed for a long time in U.S. censuses. (Similar cutoffs in other countries' definitions are frequently not the same.) As population concentrations have grown, those places having 2,500 or more people have been differentiated by categorizing them by size levels (e.g., 2,500–4,999; 5,000–7,499, and so forth, up to very large units). Sometimes the boundary of a place is easily recognizable or can be drawn for statistical purposes with ease; at other times, defining a place as having 2,500 or more people (especially if it is not incorporated or has appeared as a new isolated residential community) can introduce measurement problems. The real complicating factor has been what happens at the fringes of these places, where populations have extended beyond the established place or where there are mixed patterns of population concentration. (In the next section, we will come back to this issue.)

What, then, is "rural"? According to the Census Bureau, whatever is not urban is rural. Populated places can exist in rural areas, but they will have fewer than 2,500 people in each of them. Rural areas also encompass a vast territory of sparsely populated, open land. There is a recognition that land on which farms exist needs to be differentiated from other rural land which is lightly populated but not qualified to be regarded as urban. As a result, a distinction is made between *rural farm* and *rural nonfarm* areas and population. To be classified as a farm, the households associated with them must have sold at least $1,000 of agricultural products during the previous year.

Allowing for variations in the urban definition, slightly less than half of the world's population lived in urban areas in 1992. As shown in Table 8.2, there were considerable differences in the percentage of national populations that were urban and in their population densities. For the broad range of examples given in the table, only the city-state of Singapore is entirely urban by definition. Many countries, such as Hong Kong, Israel, and the United Kingdom (composed of England, Scotland, Wales, and Northern Ireland), have at least 90 out of 100 residents in urban areas. Three-fourths of the U.S. population lives in urban places. At the other end of the spectrum, both Bangladesh

TABLE 8.2 Population Size, Percent Urban, and Population Density for Selected Countries of the World

COUNTRY	POPULATION 1993 (MILLIONS)	PERCENT URBAN 1993	PERSONS PER KILOMETER OF SURFACE AREA 1987
Argentina	33.5	86	11
Australia	17.8	85	2
Bahrain	0.5	81	633
Bangladesh	113.9	14	712
Brazil	152.0	76	17
Canada	28.1	77	3
China	1,178.5	26	113
Cuba	11.0	73	93
Egypt	58.3	44	51
France	57.7	73	101
Germany (combined)	81.1	85	222
Ghana	16.4	32	57
Hong Kong	5.8	93	5,372
Iceland	0.3	91	2
India	897.4	26	238
Indonesia	187.6	31	89
Iran	62.8	54	31
Iraq	19.2	70	39
Ireland	3.6	56	50
Israel	5.3	90	207
Italy	57.8	68	190
Japan	124.8	77	323
Kenya	27.7	24	40
Malta	0.4	85	1,089
Mexico	90.0	71	41
Netherlands	15.2	89	359
Nicaragua	4.1	57	27
Pakistan	122.4	28	128
Peru	22.9	72	16
Philippines	64.6	43	191
Saudi Arabia	17.5	77	6
Singapore	2.8	100	4,228
Thailand	57.2	19	104
United Kingdom	58.0	90	233
United States	258.3	75	26
Zaire	41.2	40	14

Sources: *1993 World Population Data Sheet* (Washington, D.C.: Population Reference Bureau, 1993); and United Nations, *1987 Demographic Yearbook* (New York: United Nations, 1989), Table 3.

and Thailand are highly rural, with fewer than 20 out of 100 people in urban areas.

Population size does not seem to be a good indicator of the proportion in urban areas. Although one-fourth of the largest populations in the world (those of China and India) reside in urban areas, roughly the same can be said of the much smaller populations in Kenya and Ghana. High urban proportions can be found not only in Iceland and Bahrain, with their limited population size, but also in Brazil and Japan, which have substantially larger populations.

The high urban percentages in Singapore, Hong Kong, and Malta, all of which are situated on small parcels of land, lead to population densities in those areas in the thousands. People in those areas are highly concentrated. On the other hand, in Iceland the 91 percent urban population is associated with a population density of only 2 persons per square kilometer of surface area; in Canada the 77 percent urban is linked to a population density of only 3; and in Saudi Arabia the 77 percent urban is matched by a population density of 6. The reason for these seeming inconsistencies is that these latter countries have vast expanses of surface area, and that their national populations are concentrated in few locations, most typically relatively large cities. The overall population densities reflect the broad areas that have little or no population. Some parts of these countries have frontiers not yet traversed, but much of the land that is not populated is not arable and thus not attractive to settlers.

We sometimes have the idea that increasing urban populations means that rural populations will decline. The reason that this is not necessarily true is that the population pie is expanding in most areas, so that both urban and rural populations can be increasing. Table 8.3 gives us a view of that possibility. Between 1970 and 1990 the world's rural population grew almost as much in size as the world's urban population. As recently as the 1985–90 period, the average annual rate of population growth was faster for urban than for rural population in the world. Yet the rural population was expanding at over 1 percent per year. Why was this so? Despite net migration from rural to urban areas, the excess of births over deaths in rural areas was enough to more than compensate for the migration loss. Most rural areas still have relatively high fertility, and rural population will grow in size if the number of babies born there exceeds the number of deaths and net out-migration.

The urban and rural population growth patterns vary among parts of the world. In Asia, especially in China, despite a more rapid rate of urban population, the increase in rural numbers has been much higher because such a great many Asians live in rural areas. A similar picture emerges with regard to Africa. In North America and Oceania, although recent rates of population increase have been about the same for urban and rural areas, urban populations have increased more numerically because a large proportion lives in urban areas. Almost all population increase in Latin America between 1970 and 1990 was in urban areas; rural areas there experienced a slightly declining rate of population change. In Europe and the former U.S.S.R., urban populations have grown while rural populations have declined in size. In these areas net rural out-migration

TABLE 8.3 Total, Urban, and Rural Absolute Population Change, 1970–1990, and Average Annual Percentage Growth Rates, 1985–1990, for Areas of the World

	ABSOLUTE POPULATION CHANGE, 1970–1990 (IN MILLIONS)			AVERAGE ANNUAL POPULATION GROWTH RATE, 1985–1990 (PERCENTAGE)		
AREA	TOTAL	URBAN	RURAL	TOTAL	URBAN	RURAL
WORLD	1,595	886	709	1.7	2.5	1.2
ASIA	1,007	428	579	1.9	3.2	1.3
China	304	76	228	1.4	2.2	1.2
AFRICA	285	141	703	3.0	5.2	2.0
EUROPE	37	58	-20	0.2	0.6	-0.8
FORMER U.S.S.R.	45	57	-12	0.8	1.4	-0.4
NORTH AMERICA	49	37	11	0.8	0.9	0.7
United States	45	34	10	0.8	0.9	0.7
LATIN AMERICA	163	161	2	2.1	3.0	-0.1
OCEANIA	7	5	2	1.5	1.4	1.6

Source: United Nations, *Prospects of World Urbanization 1988*. Population Studies no. 112. (New York: United Nations, 1989), Tables 2 and 3.

has been combined with some urban areas sweeping out to convert rural lands to urban designations, thereby reclassifying rural residents into urban residents.

Urbanization and Metropolitanization

If we analyze the percentages of populations residing in urban (or rural) areas, and how they might increase or decrease, this is one way of studying the process of population distribution and change. But it is necessary to think more broadly about the *urbanization* process, which can be defined as the ways by which areas both increase the relative number of urban residents and intensify the concentration of urban population. Indicators of the latter phenomenon are the increasing number and size of cities, the formation and growth of metropolitan areas, the spread of what are called *urbanized areas*, and the imploding population of inner cities. Along with such indicators as measures of the urbanization process, we must consider the tendencies in many countries toward counterurbanization.

The number of all incorporated places in the United States increased from 17,589 in 1960 to 19,093 in 1980. The most rapid gain was in smaller places (under 25,000 people) that emerged in the outskirts of metropolitan areas (Fuguitt et al., 1989). Urban places at all levels have been increasing the size of their populations. Again, the newer places have been the ones that have shown the greatest relative increases in population.

An urbanization phenomenon that developed strongly during the middle of the twentieth century in many countries was the formation and growth of *metropolitan areas.* The current U.S. definition of such an area is "a large population nucleus, together with adjacent communities that have a high degree of economic and social integration with that nucleus" (U.S. Bureau of the Census, 1992). Each metropolitan area (MA) must have a place with a minimum of 50,000 people and a total population of at least 100,000. (Some exceptions to these rules exist.) Most important, counties are the building blocks of MAs. Hence, a county that meets the above criteria qualifies as an MA. If, in addition, adjacent counties meet requirements of economic and social integration with that county, based on such indicators as population densities, commuting patterns, and the like, they join the central county as part of a unified MA. Each MA must have a central city but, because a whole county is included, generally some rural population is found at the edges of MAs. This plays havoc with the idea of an MA as an urban concentration. Counties, however, are units regularly used for data collection and are therefore convenient geographic population markers.

Metropolitan areas may stand alone and be surrounded by counties that are nonmetropolitan in character (such MAs are sometimes called *metropolitan statistical areas* or MSAs). Alternatively, they may be adjacent to other MAs. This situation typically occurs where there are large population concentrations in that section of the country. If an area has more than 1 million persons and encompasses what can be defined as two or more adjoining MAs, the combination of adjacent MAs is termed a *consolidated metropolitan statistical area* (or CMSA) and the constituent MAs are called *primary metropolitan statistical areas* (or PMSAs). It is significant to note that all MAs in the United States combined cover only a minor fraction of the nation's land area. Yet they comprised half of the country's 1990 Census population.

The 284 MAs in the United States in 1990 ranged greatly in size, from the 56,735 people in the Enid, Oklahoma, area to the more than 18 million in the New York–Northern New Jersey–Long Island consolidated metropolitan area. MAs with over a million residents have been increasing sharply in number, from 14 in 1950 to 39 in 1990. The 1950 group accounted for 30 percent of the national population, whereas the 1990 group totaled 50 percent of the country's people.

Urban agglomerations (the term for metropolitan area equivalents throughout the world) have likewise grown in number and size. As of 1985, the Tokyo-Yokohama agglomeration and that of Mexico City both exceeded the population size of the New York consolidated area. It has been estimated, based on subsequent trends, that the greater Mexico City area will be the largest urban agglomeration (24.4 million) by the year 2000, and that São Paulo, Brazil, will become the second largest (with 23.6 million). Seven of the top ten urban agglomerations in the year 2000 will be in Third World countries (United Nations, 1991, Table 6).

Because metropolitan areas are not entirely urban, analysts have sought other indicators of large completely urban concentrations to reflect the urbanization process. An *urbanized area* (UA) meets this requirement especially well. It "comprises one or more places ('central place') and the adjacent densely settled surrounding territory ('urban fringe') that together have a minimum of 50,000 persons" (U.S. Bureau of the Census, 1992). The density of adjacent territory should be at least 1,000 persons per square mile, but small enclaves of lesser density are included in the area to solidify it. (Census data detailed by small geographic units is necessary to map the UA boundaries.) But the result is a truer definition of an urban concentration. Also, as urbanization creeps outward from existing urban boundaries, the UA moves with it but the MA does not. Still, because both MAs and UAs tend to share the same central cities, they cover similar areas of the map. UA boundaries may dip inside MA boundaries, where rural segments exist, and dip outside MA boundaries, where urban densities overflow the latter.

Urbanization deals not only with outwardly expanding urban populations but also with inwardly expanding ones. Cities often have core areas with heavy population concentrations that may grow in size faster than the city as a whole. We refer to what are called *inner cities* or *ghettos.* These population points have become havens, in many parts of the world, for pockets of excessive poverty, poor living conditions, and crime (see Box 8.2).

It is reasonable to suppose that there are limits to urbanization in some of its forms. In the early 1970s, there was evidence that metropolitan counties in the United States were not growing as fast as nonmetropolitan areas, and that some were actually declining in size. This pattern seemed to derive from a combination of a slowing down of rural-urban migration and an attraction of former city and suburban residents to outlying areas. *Counterurbanization* or *rural population turnaround* continued through the 1970s and early 1980s and was seen in other developed countries as well. But in the 1980s the turnaround reversed itself again in the United States and some other countries while continuing its course in still other developed areas (Champion, 1989).

These trends serve to emphasize the complexity of population distribution and redistribution. Migratory currents of various sorts sometimes reinforce and sometimes counter each other, while the processes of mortality and fertility likewise vary. The net population effects on geographic areas are also related to the nature of the areas studied and the proper interpretation made of the way people are distributed across them. For example, what pattern of turnarounds would be observed if analysis was based on urbanized areas instead of metropolitan areas?

BOX 8.2 Crowding in the World's Large Cities

Urban concentration highlights the plight of Harlem in New York City. Compared with the population density of about 75 persons per square mile (26 per square kilometer) for the United States as a whole in 1990, the population density of New York City (made up of five boroughs or counties) stood at about 25,000 per square mile. New York County (the borough of Manhattan) had roughly 75,000 residents per square mile, much higher than that of the other counties within the city. The neighborhood of Harlem (within Manhattan) had a density equivalent to 150,000 people per square mile. While New York City's population has not changed much in size for the past few decades, the ghetto of Harlem has not become less populated.

Large cities of Third World countries include substantial numbers of poverty-stricken people. It has been determined that 70 percent of the population of Casablanca (in Morocco) lives in shantytowns or slums. Comparable figures are 67 percent in Calcutta (in India), 60 percent in Bogotá (Columbia), 60 percent in Kinshasa (Zaire), and 42 percent in Mexico City. Residents in these areas erect temporary housing, but do not own the land. Because they lack formal ownership, few city services are provided. Often there is no electricity, heat, plumbing, or water. Furthermore, people in such shantytowns and slums have been increasing at twice the rate of people in those cities as a whole.

Population Composition

Our understanding of population change depends on knowing the numbers and geographic distribution of people as well as the relative contributions that the basic components of population change make to trends and variations in those numbers and distributions; but it also depends on knowing the traits and characteristics of the people involved. When we refer to *population composition*, we mean division of a group of individuals into clusters of categories that specify critical identifying traits and statuses.

Delineating these traits and statuses becomes important when either they help us to explain basic population change (as in the case of differential fertility) or they have significance in themselves (such as measuring racial or ethnic discrimination or recognizing an ethnic category for its cultural contribution to the broader community or society).

The population compositional variables most basic to demographic analysis are age, sex, and race and ethnicity (where the latter is indicated by nationality, language, or religion). In a more general sense of the term *population composition*, variables often treated within the rubric of *population characteristics* are also included. These can encompass physical traits, such as height, weight, and physical abnormalities; social identifiers, such as marital status, and educational and economic variables; and cultural traits, such as style of life and distinguishing customs.

In each of the following sections, compositional variables will be discussed within three headings—age and sex; race and ethnicity; and physical, social, and cultural traits—in terms of concepts and measurement issues. We will give illustrations which draw on data from a variety of countries and geographic areas within them.

While geographic areas are difficult to define on the basis of boundaries and functions and changes in them, many variables we regard as compositional are even more challenging to categorize and describe. This is because, in the realm of compositional items, we are apt to attach social meanings to particular categories. Although a scientific approach can help us to decide on classifications of compositional variables, it is still necessary to agree on the social and cultural significance of those classifications. Thus we wrestle with how to label the elements of some variables (for instance, what we will call *racial categories*), and we sometimes employ limited perspectives to divide variables (for example, grouping occupations from a labor market perspective when specific occupations can be grouped according to style of life, welfare, or prestige perspectives).

Age and Sex

We have already indicated the crucial aspects of the age and sex distributions of populations as structures that reflect the proportions of an area or group in the different stages of the life cycle and that mark the human demand social institutions must meet.

In its guide to census taking, the United Nations (1980) spells out the definitions related to age and sex as demographic variables. *Sex* is the biological division of humans into the categories of male and female. This is in contrast to *gender*, which social scientists define with regard to the social meanings attached to being regarded as male or female, or to *sexual activity*, which usually denotes the frequency and form with which sexual intercourse is practiced, or to *sexual preference*, which has come to mean the relative physical or emotional attraction of a person of one sex for someone of the same or opposite sex.

There is ordinarily little difficulty in specifying the sex of individuals in a census or survey, although census or survey procedures that permit one member of a household to provide information for others in that household, or depend on interviewers making judgments about sex on the basis of first names, could lead to occasional misreporting of biological sex.

The sex composition of a population is usually measured by relating the number of males to each 100 females in the population or in a particular age group, and this is called the *sex ratio*. The sex ratio changes over the age span of a population. In the United States, the sex ratio stands at about 105 at birth (excess of males), starts to decline at age 11 or so, reaches parity at about age

22, and continues to decline progressively to older ages, reaching a ratio of 83 at age 65 and becoming as low as 36 by age 95 or so. This pattern reflects the higher mortality of males at all ages. Sex ratios by age vary, to a small degree, for racial and ethnic groups within the population.

It has been noted that, in some less-developed nations, there is an abnormally high sex ratio at the younger ages, indicating what has been referred to as the *missing girls* (Johansson and Nygren, 1991). Since the sex ratio at any age is a combined function of the sex ratio at birth, the sex differences in mortality, and the selectivity by sex in mobility, any or all of these factors could explain the apparent deficit of girls in some populations. Coale (1991) has determined that the major factor is mortality, as reflected through the differential treatment of the sexes. (See also the relevant discussion in Chapter 5.)

Age is defined as the interval of time between the date of birth and the date of the census (or other data collection means), expressed in complete years. In different parts of the world, age is reckoned in different ways. The form common in most areas is the number of full years as of the last birthday. A form used in some other areas is the number of full years as of the nearest birthday. That form is also used for some purposes in areas that employ the first basis (such as in actuarial calculations). Still a third form, unique to many areas of the Orient, is a bit more complicated. According to the traditional Chinese method of counting age, a person is considered to be one year old at birth and becomes a year older at every subsequent Chinese New Year. Some countries, such as Hong Kong, whose residents include people using both the first and third bases of age reckoning, provide enumerators with conversion tables.

A preferred way of calculating age is to ask for *date of birth* and have the data collectors compute the number of years of age (typically through a computer operation). The reason for this is that most people can better remember their date of birth than accurately recollect how many years old they are. The older we get, the more likely we are to overlook a birthday. However, older persons who were born when birth certificates were not available, or who never knew their date of birth, may guess incorrectly at what that date was.

For many different reasons, the ages of people are often not recorded accurately. *Misreporting of age* may be intentional or unintentional. Intentional misreporting can include preference or aversion for certain years of age because of the social meaning attached to them (for example, 18 might be preferred and 65 avoided). When this phenomenon occurs, adjacent ages are typically reported. Unintentional misreporting can result from such practices as forgetfulness or a tendency for many persons to approximate their reported ages by rounding them. It has been shown that this phenomenon results in "heaping" on ages that are used in a country's numerical system. In most countries where the decimal system is used, there is an overreporting of ages ending in 0; secondly, there is an overreporting of ages ending in 5; and thirdly, of even-numbered rather than odd-numbered ages (Stockwell and Wicks, 1974; Ewbank, 1981).

In some countries, such as Thailand, there is a frequent tendency to report age as of your next birthday even when it is not the closest birthday. A Thai term for this is translated as "going-to age" (Chamratrithirong et al., 1978). Research on age reporting in two Thai censuses revealed that this practice seemed to have distorted the tabulated age distribution in the census.

In countries that are not highly literate or where emphasis is not placed on remembering one's age, data collectors are provided with calendars of historical events that are relevant in the local community. Respondents are asked to recall such events and to describe their statuses at the time. Another approach is to establish relationships between family members and to estimate one person's age on the basis of known ages of others in the family (Omondi-Odhiambo, 1985).

An age phenomenon of particular fascination is the passing of the 100th year of age, a milestone especially valued because the decimal system 10×10 is reached. We attach the term *centenarian* to someone who is 100 years or older. It stands to reason that it is a matter of great pride when an individual can claim to have reached that mark. (In Chapter 5, we indicated that 115 or so is regarded as the maximum age one could expect to live to and that few could be expected to get that far.) The U.S. Census of 1980 showed that there were 32,194 centenarians in the country. A careful evaluation of the data for these cases showed that probably less than half of them were truly 100 or over (Spencer, 1986). The overreporting of centenarians seems to be greater in the United States than in other developed countries (Coale, 1991), for reasons which can be related to variations in cultural and political orientations to attaining old age.

There are many graphic devices for depicting the age and sex distribution of a population, but a popular one is called the *age-sex pyramid* because it normally takes on a triangular shape that resembles one side of a geometric pyramid. It is plotted by presenting bars whose length is based on either absolute numbers or percentages of a population, with males shown to the left and females to the right of a vertical center line; the bar for each older age group is stacked on top of the earlier ones. The ages can be single or grouped into broader intervals.

Figure 8.1 demonstrates how the age-sex pyramids appear for three kinds of societies. The "expansive" age structure is typical of countries with high levels of fertility and mortality. The "constrictive" age structure is one resulting from declines in fertility. The "near-stationary" age structure is what one would find when fertility and mortality have reached low levels (Kinsella, 1988). More specific descriptions of age-sex pyramids at transitional stages will be given later in this chapter.

An interesting aspect of age-sex pyramids is that they can give us a visible idea about the composition of very specific or atypical populations. Figure 8.2 shows pyramids for nine different census tract areas of Seattle in 1940 (Schmid, 1951). The distorted representation of some of the structures tells us about the selectivity of who lives in certain areas. For example, both the Skid Row area and the central business district were occupied disproportionately by middle-aged men.

FIGURE 8.1 Three General Profiles of Age Composition

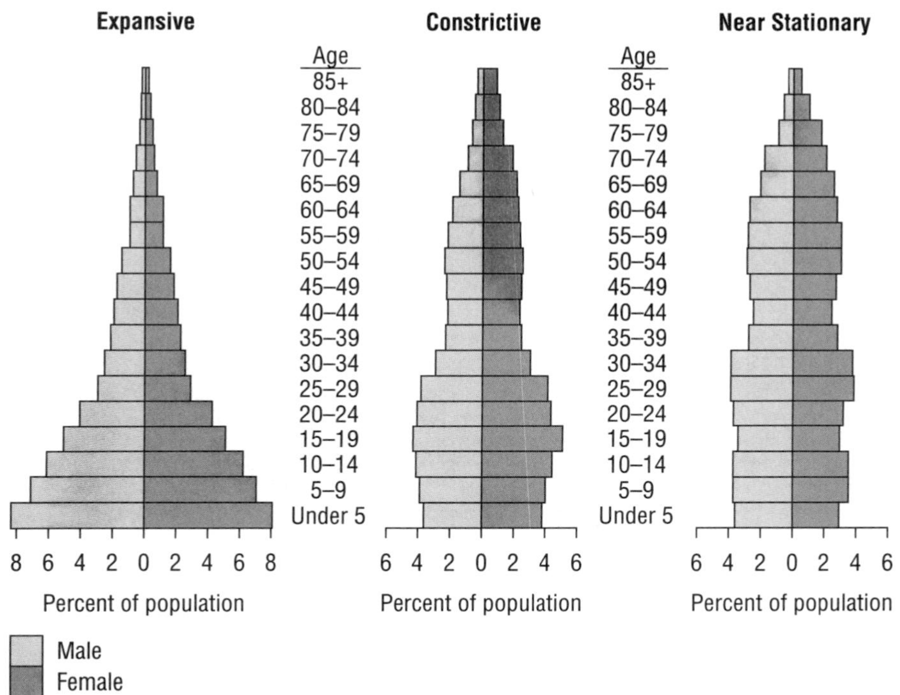

Source: Kevin Kinsella, "Aging in the Third World," U.S. Bureau of the Census , Series P-95, no. 79 (Washington, D.C.: Government Printing Office, 1988).

Since we have stressed the contributions of the basic components of population change to changes in all population structures, a couple of points about that process with regard to changing age structure are in order. First, during most of the demographic transition, the history of fertility in a country is the main explanation of the shifting proportion in each age category. That is both because reduced infant mortality acts like increased fertility in adding to the young population and because declining fertility reduces the size of a given population in an age group more than does declining adult mortality or, with some exceptions, net immigration (Coale, 1964). (When a fertility cycle like the baby boom occurs, however, it serves to increase the proportion of the population in the younger segment.) Second, as countries move into the late transition phase, and even more so into the posttransition phase, the stability of childbearing creates no "shocks" to the age distribution while improved mortality at the older ages adds disproportionately to the numbers at the top of the pyramid (Chesnais, 1990; Serow et al., 1990).

FIGURE 8.2 Age and Sex Composition for Certain Communities of Seattle: 1940

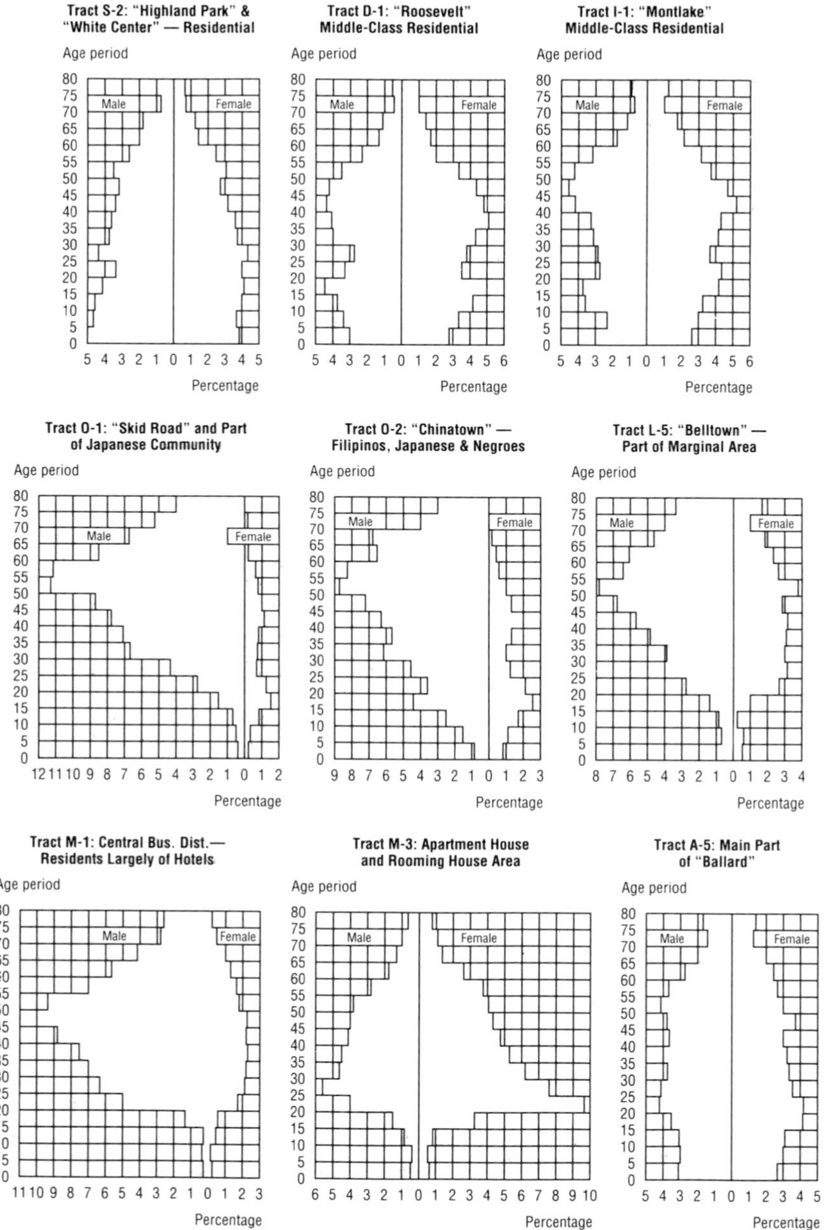

Source: Calvin F. Schmid, "Sex and Age Composition for Certain Typical Census Tracts." In Robert W. O'Brien, Clarence C. Schrag, and Walter T. Martin, eds., *Readings in General Sociology*, pp. 217–20. Boston: Houghton Mifflin.

Race and Ethnicity

Another dimension of population composition relates to the racial and ethnic traits of people. *Race* is a term coined by anthropologists to classify members of *Homo sapiens* by their dominant physical characteristics that differed because of centuries of location in given areas and hereditary persistence of certain physical traits. At first, three "great" races were delineated—Caucasoid, Mongoloid, and Negroid. Later, it was more common to recognize nine "major" races that were largely regionally based—African, American Indian, Asian, Australian, European, Asiatic Indian, Melanesian, Micronesian, and Polynesian. However, as science has become more proficient at analyzing the substantial variations in physical traits, such as skin color, facial features, blood type, and genetic makeup, it has become increasingly clear that such processes as natural selection, mutations, genetic drift, and interbreeding of peoples has produced extensive racial mixtures (Garn, 1972).

Yet we continue to refer to racial distinctions among people in demographic data collection and in public and private discourse because race has acquired a social meaning which goes beyond mere physical traits. The finding that infants categorized as black have twice as high infant mortality levels as those categorized as white in the United States helps us to direct programs for infant mortality reduction more concretely. While some choose to ingore their perceived racial identity, others choose to highlight it. When race ceases to have social meaning, the distinction will no longer be made.

In a number of countries, such as the United States, racial distinctions in official statistics are required by legislative or administrative acts. The classification of race in censuses usually follows the current conventions in referring to race in the society. Lee (1988) surveyed the history of race categories used in U.S. censuses since 1790 and discovered radical shifts from one census to another in how certain people were described racially. In the Census of 1890, for example, people with a black racial background were separated statistically into several categories based on how many of their parents and grandparents were black. Thus the census reports specify blacks ("three fourths or more black blood"), doubloons, quadroons, and octaroons. In some twentieth-century U.S. censuses, some data were published not only for specific racial categories but also for "whites" and "nonwhites." In the 1990 U.S. Census, the Census Bureau said that reports on race "reflected self-identification" because most people were counted by self-enumeration. It also recognized that the "race item" included "both racial and national origin or socio-cultural groups." Following federal guidelines, respondents could report themselves as white; black; American Indian, Eskimo, or Aleut; Asian or Pacific Islander, or other race. Write-in entries were accepted for specifying the last three categories.

Demarcations of *ethnicity* can be based on citizenship or nationality, language, religion, family name, or another ethnic grouping. The United Nations (1980) defines *citizenship* as the "legal nationality of each person." *Nationality* is often based on the country where someone was born (frequently called *national origin*) or the last country of citizenship or residence. Some demographic sources identify persons by their nationality background regardless of how many generations of their families have lived in the present country. This distinction is often complicated by the nationality mixtures of parents and grandparents, and by the difficulty of specifying countries whose boundaries have occasionally been changed. Sometimes, as in the case of the 1980 U.S. Census, people are asked about their *ancestry*, which is intended to be the nationality of earlier generations (other than the U.S.) with which they identify. Responses in such cases can include common mixtures (such as German-Irish).

There are at least three bases for identifying *language* as an ethnic trait—the language usually spoken in the person's home in early childhood (*mother tongue*), the language most often spoken by the person currently (*usual language*), or the relative ability to speak a specified language (usually the dominant language of the country where the inquiry is made).

Religion is normally defined according to belief in the tenets of a particular religious group, or identification with or affiliation with a religious organization. The Census of Canada and occasional U.S. Census surveys have used the simple question "What is your religion?" to determine religious identification. (The demography of religion is explored more fully in Chapter 13.)

Family name, as an indicator of ethnicity, has been used in demographic analysis. Persons were classified Hispanic in earlier U.S. censuses on the basis of the typicality of their Spanish surnames. The Census Bureau had a special problem in describing persons whose parents' nationality was Austrian or Hungarian. Because of boundary changes between Austria and Hungary in this century, the 1950 U.S. Census assessed the parents' ancestry on the basis of what it regarded as typical Austrian or Hungarian family names. Of course, intermarriage often leads to changes in surnames that can make such an approach inaccurate.

In some countries, other ethnic distinctions are made on the basis of "color," tribal affiliation, or caste identification. Tribes are recognized not only in parts of the Third World but also in some developed regions. In Canada and the United States, Indians are designated in the census according to their tribal identity. In India and some other South Asian countries, censuses until recently specified one's caste (a hereditary category of social organization).

The changing neighborhood distributions of white, black, Asian, and Hispanic populations (including mixtures of them) between 1970 and 1980 were studied by Denton and Massey (1991), using census tracts of sixty large metropolitan areas across the United States. They were able to describe the dynamic aspects of ethnicity and residence by showing that ethnic diversity within large metropolitan areas had increased during the 1970s, with all-white neighborhoods becoming less common. Multiple ethnic presence in some areas was highly evident, especially in tracts of residential transition (points where more solidly single-ethnic areas converged).

The breakup of several European nations in recent years has been related to the ethnic diversity of the former national population. The separation of the two parts of Czechoslovakia was largely due to the basic ethnic differences in the majority populations of the two areas of the nation and their alternative view of government policies. Likewise, the divisions within Yugoslavia resulted from ethnic cleavages that separated Serbs, Croats, and Bosnians. In the case of the former Soviet Union, Anderson and Silver (1989) point out that "the Soviet Union is a multi-ethnic country and that ethnic loyalties are an enduring aspect of Soviet society." According to these researchers, some of the most dramatic and violent instances of past intergroup conflict in that country foretold the imminent demise of the former Soviet empire. (Chapter 12 will elaborate on these and other political ramifications of demographic changes.)

We can attribute the distribution and redistribution of racial and ethnic categories of populations in different geographic areas to the mortality, fertility, and mobility history of each of the categories. The dynamic interplay of differential mortality, fertility, and mobility among racial and ethnic groups in U.S. metropolitan areas accounts for the rearrangement of these groups across census tracts of the areas. Similarly, the higher fertility of some minority republics in the former U.S.S.R. and the consequent more rapid population growth of their populations had changed the balance of power in the former Soviet legislature and disturbed the political balance that had existed, however tentatively, in the past.

Physical, Social, and Cultural Traits

Population structure involves age, sex, race, and ethnicity in fundamental ways. But still other features of people are important in considering the makeup of a population. Certain physical, social, and cultural traits are also relevant because they describe population subgroups who have unique needs and interests and who may participate in the community or society in different forms.

By *physical traits* we mean both the perceived and diagnosed attributes of a person's body that depart from the normal ones. Included under this rubric would be such information as height, weight, handedness, impairments of sight and hearing, and other physical handicaps resulting from disease or injury. Surveys dealing with health matters frequently incorporate questions relating to these kinds of items. Administrative records also provide information on these topics.

Height and weight are population characteristics that serve to portray body size and shape. Anthropometric data allow us to relate height and weight for persons of different ages in order to determine whether individuals are within a normal weight range for their height or are overweight or underweight. They can also be used to record the breadth and girth of body parts, such as length of limbs and waist circumference. The health implications of such measurements are obvious, but the same information is used by industry to specify space needs for school classrooms, seats in transportation vehicles, and other accommodations for people, as well as for determining size distributions in the manufacturing of clothing (Najjar and Kuczmarski, 1989).

Handedness, whether right-handed or left-handed, may not seem at first mention to be an important demographic characteristic but it has implications similar to those cited above. At one time in history, left-handed people were regarded as evil. (Our word *sinister* comes from a Latin word meaning "left" or "left-handed.") Today, we are aware that handedness is genetically determined and that people who are left-handed, right-handed, or ambidextrous can all function in all kinds of situations without being seen as unusual. Nevertheless, left-handers are a distinct minority in all societies and sometimes lack appropriate facilities (e.g., left-handed writing desks or golf clubs).

Blindness, deafness, and *speech defects* are physical limitations that can impair the daily activities of those who are so inflicted, especially for persons reaching advanced ages. In the mid-1980s in the United States, while only 2 out of 1,000 persons in the 45–69 age range were blind in both eyes, 95 others in 1,000 had cataracts, glaucoma, or other visual impairments. About 10 in 1,000 in that age range had speech impairments. As many as 13 in 1,000 were deaf in both ears, and 155 others in 1,000 of that age group had other hearing impairments. Although the incidence of these impairments was relatively less at younger ages, the numbers involved were sizable. At older ages, the risks of having these impairments were substantially greater (LaPlante, 1988).

Various chronic musculoskeletal conditions (e.g., arthritis) and other orthopedic impairments (e.g., loss of limbs, cerebral palsy, paralysis) affect a large number of people who require special assistance in travel, work, and home and leisure activities. The study of populations with these inflictions is called the *demography of disability* and has received increasing attention in recent years (Pope and Tarlov, 1991).

Social characteristics encompasses such statuses as educational attributes, employment and occupational positions, and other economic identifications of individuals, families, and households. These statuses are relevant bases for describing populations. At the same time, they reflect the workings of social institutions in the community and society that are influenced by basic demographic change. For the latter reason, we have chosen to defer discussion of these characteristics until later chapters in this book.

There has now even emerged a *cultural geography* (Zelinsky, 1992), which can be extended to a *demography of culture*. While there is an apparent overlap with other population compositional and population distributional factors, that fact only goes to point out the intricate complexity of societal demographic and social phenomena. Components of culture that can be analyzed demographically include what Zelinsky has called artifacts (such as human-made objects, types of clothing, medicines, and kinds of food and drink); sociofacts (such as social etiquette, family practices, types of social organizations, political behaviors); and mentifacts (such as language, arts, literature, and folklore). Zelinsky has attempted to show that the map of a country can be delineated by cultural regions that reflect the distinct cultural characteristics of areas.

We can identify the geographic strongholds of Appalachian hillbillies, Mormon devotees, Indian cultures of the West, New York's eastern European

Jews, remnants of the Old South, and many others. From a broader population point of view, the extent to which these groups are reproducing themselves demographically, maintaining their localities, and retaining their distinguishing cultural characteristics are all subjects for research and study.

THE STAGES OF DISTRIBUTION AND COMPOSITION

Just as mortality, fertility, and mobility typically go through the transition continuum and are modified by cycles and irregular deviations from the general trend, so are population distribution and population composition variables characterized by changes over time that we can tie to the developing stages of the demographic transition.

Relative differences in population growth (or decline) among geographic areas (countries, provinces, cities, neighborhoods, or any other type of unit) affect the way population is distributed over the land. At the time when demographic growth in an area is at its peak point in the transition, it will likely lead to a relatively larger share of the global population because other areas are growing less rapidly. Urbanization processes are apt to shift their course in fairly predictable ways as the transition unfolds. We can expect rural populations to experience a relative decline, although maintaining an absolute level of increase for a long while, when countries move from one phase of the transition to another.

In the same manner, elements of population composition are often seen to be transformed as demographic processes continue their course. Most obvious in this respect is the age structure of a population. Its shape assumes different forms as the basic transitions of mortality, fertility, and mobility unfold. Even racial and ethnic composition can change as a result of varying levels of demographic processes among categories of race and ethnicity. Higher or lower rates of birth and death, combined with selective internal mobility and international migration, can alter the composition of those categories in the population.

In the following pages we will give illustrations of many of these phenomena within the scope of transitional stages. Again, our aim is not to be encyclopedic but rather to use examples to spark the imagination to contemplate the intricacies of dynamic demographic change.

Pretransition Stage

Wherever humans have lived, they tended to congregate. Thus communities of people have existed from time immemorial. Although historical writings indicate that towns and cities in antiquity were the sites of kingdoms and marketplaces, by today's standards these places were sparsely populated. Even the cities of the Roman Empire were collections of people whose roots were not often firm, and the lack of institutional strength led to their decay.

As the medieval society of preindustrial Europe developed its economy, towns became the central places not only for markets but also for religious and educational functions. Yet by about 1330 only 9 out of more than 3,000 towns in northern Europe had over 25,000 people, with most of the places containing under 2,000 (not even urban by current definitions) (Hohenberg and Lees, 1985).

The growth of cities during the medieval period was stymied by hunger, war, and disease. As noted in Chapter 5, plagues and epidemics took heavy tolls of the population, especially of people living in proximity to each other in urban areas. Many cities declined in numbers. The Italian city of Florence is reported to have had its population at least halved during the fourteenth century. From perhaps 100,000 or so at the beginning of the century, there were only 37,000 residents by 1427. Population growth in the city was slow after that time, the number of people in 1552 being merely 59,000 (Hohenberg and Lees, 1985).

There is evidence that the European urban population continued to increase in the sixteenth and seventeenth centuries, especially in the larger cities which grew both from rural-urban migration and natural increase. But the countries of Europe were then dominated by rural areas. The percentage of people in places of 5,000 or more stood at 8 in the year 1500 and was still at 9 in 1600 (de Vries, 1981).

The colonization by Europeans of what is now the United States produced urban centers at Atlantic seaports that were valuable for commerce and trade. By 1690, the five largest places and their populations were Boston (7,000 inhabitants), Philadelphia (4,000), New York (3,900), Newport (2,600), and Charleston (1,100). Although small in comparison with European cities, they represented the beginnings of urban America. All increased their populations by 1742, with Boston still the largest (over 16,000) (Chudacoff and Smith, 1988).

The ancient regimes of Asia produced urban places that far predate those of Europe, but little reliable data exist that can enable us to describe those places in demographic terms. Many narrative reports suggest that people congregated in kingdoms and princely estates to service the royal houses and in small trading towns, but the vast majority of people were on farms and other outlying areas. Most Asian nations, however, did not enter into the demographic transition until well into the twentieth century so that a look at pretransition forms of population distribution among these nations can begin with the early 1900s.

The urban population of China may have constituted about 8 percent of the total before 1800; by 1900 it had actually fallen to 6 percent. An urban hierarchy, fairly common to most parts of the developing world even today, consisted of a *primate city* (one exceedingly larger than any other in the country), a number of regional cities of smaller size, still smaller local urban places, and numerous market towns of varying size (Schinz, 1989). Through contact with other nations and subsequent foreign influence in China, old cities expanded and new ones emerged.

There were similarities and differences in India's urban development in the pretransition phase. Mortality played a key role in the fortunes of urbanization as recently as the turn of the century. A great famine drove many from rural areas to towns and cities around 1900, but a plague in 1911 created an exodus from urban places of those who had survived. European intervention that fostered trade and industry spurred urban expansion. When the 1901 Census was taken, about 11 percent of the population was enumerated in urban areas. (However, the Indian definition of urban was not based on size of places but on the recognition of towns, villages, and cities, regardless of size.) India had been under British rule since 1858, and the development of New Delhi, Bombay, Calcutta, and Madras as cities was planned within the colonial framework that treated them as largely administrative centers (Bose, 1978).

The uneven population distribution and slow urbanization characteristic of much of Africa until the mid-twentieth century has been attributed to the following factors:

1. The vast array of deserts, semideserts, humid forests, savana woodlands, clay plains, and mangrove swamps, with occasional highlands and river valleys that provided varying opportunities for population settlements;
2. The less intensive economies based on hunting and collecting, pastoral nomadism, and shifting cultivation that did not require large population concentrations;
3. A plethora of small, sparsely located groups with distinct languages and social customs, causing internal schisms and political instability; and
4. Periodic mortality increases associated with conquest, destruction, disease, and slavery that limited population increase at some times (Kosinski and Clarke, 1982).

Pretransition societies, because of their high fertility and mortality and insignificant amount of mobility interchange, tend toward an age-sex structure whose pyramid reveals a broad base and rapidly narrowing peak. In the least developed societies, about 40 percent of the population would be under age 15 and less than 5 percent would be 65 or older. This is a consequence of the high level of childbearing followed by substantial infant and childhood mortality, with dim prospects of those reaching adulthood escaping the risks of death in an area that presents constant challenges to life.

People in such a society perceive age structure in a very different way from those in more developed areas. Very young boys and girls dominate the human landscape and have to perform tasks in the society not expected of their age counterparts in later transitional stages. The concept of *old* may not match the one shared in developed countries, or even early transitional nations. People who reach age 65 are exceptional, and those in their 50s and 40s are often seen as very senior people.

Racially and ethnically, the regions of a country are apt to be linked specifically to one group whose culture has restricted them from intermarrying or moving away from the area. In sub-Saharan Africa, a tribe is an indigenous ethnic group that speaks a common language and has a feeling of solidarity (Kaya, 1991). Although socioeconomic circumstances may force some residents of the area to seek food o· employment elsewhere, those who move for these reasons are almost invariably circulatory movers whose ties to the community of origin are strong. Hence, ethnic enclaves persist and constitute bounded population groups with high growth rates and their associated living conditions.

Early Transition Stage

The sustained mortality decline contributing to the demographic transition in sets of countries from time period to time period produced transformations in population distribution. In the early stage of the transition, the populations of cities and towns were no longer decimated by epidemics and plagues. In addition to the economic development that attracted people to jobs there, urban areas grew because they increasingly became magnets for rural dwellers.

What has been called *protoindustrialization* (forms of manufacturing that predate factory industrialization) first sprang up in the rural areas of Europe where textiles, metal products, and pottery ware were handmade by groups of people. The rising demand for such items, stimulated by population increase, required larger-scale operations. Technical, spatial, and organizational limits of rural villages or protoindustry led to the development of factories whose viability depended on links to outlying areas. The city, with its networks of transportation and communication, became the natural locus for such operations (Hohenberg and Lees, 1985). During the late eighteenth century, there was a sharp upturn in the number of protoindustrial towns and small cities in Europe.

Continuation of the mortality decline and a consequent rise in numbers of people, combined with the beginnings of a factory industry that used machinery for a range of products, ushered in further rural-urban migration and a sustained urbanization.

During the nineteenth century, the urban population of England and Wales grew steadily in size and as a percentage of total population. When the Census of 1801 was taken, 3 million urban residents made up 34 percent of all people. By 1831, over 6 million persons in urban areas constituted 44 percent of the total. When the 1861 Census count was completed, there were then 12 million urbanites, who were 59 percent of the nation's population (Lawton, 1989). As Weber (1899) indicated, growing urbanization in the area was accompanied by rural population declines arising from both migration to the cities and the conversion of what had been rural hamlets and villages into towns and small cities.

The early demographic transition in the New World resulted in similar changes in population distribution and redistribution. When the first U.S. census was taken in 1790, urban population overall was just 5 percent of the national population. There were only five cities with 10,000 or more inhabitants. The largest of them was Philadelphia, which had 44,000 people. But it was unlike today's cities of that size. Water supplies were inadequate, there were no sewers, and street cleaning was not practiced. Most people actually walked from place to place while the well-off used horses or carts. To travel between cities was a large undertaking. A trip from Philadelphia to Boston required overnight lodgings if one went by land or a cabin if by ship.

In the next few decades, immigration levels increased, peopling the cities and providing labor for farm areas as well. The advancing westward frontier spread the expanding population into new territories, and protoindustry and commercialization in established areas caused numbers in urban places to rise. By 1830, New York (with over 200,000 people) surpassed Philadelphia as the largest city. The percentage of the U.S. urban population rose to 9 percent. By 1860, nine U.S. cities had over 100,000 people, with New York approaching 1 million. About 20 percent of the nation's residents lived in urban areas. (Chudacoff and Smith, 1988).

While the early demographic transition in countries recently or now going through that phase has been determined by somewhat different sets of circumstances than those fueling the same phase in now-developed nations, shifts away from high mortality while fertility has declined much more slowly have resulted in rapid population gains in the developing world. What, then, has happened to population distribution during the early part of the population growth stage in these less-developed countries?

Generally speaking, rapid urbanization was associated with the early transition in every region of Asia, although the increase was differential among countries. Yeung (1989) put it this way:

> With the exception of China, all East Asian countries are urbanizing rapidly and have reached a level of urbanization markedly above the developing country norm. South Asian countries, at the other extreme, can be distinguished by their slower-growing economies and their lower than average level of urbanization. Southeast Asian countries may be placed in between these two extremes, with levels of urbanization and economic development intermediate between the other two subregions.

In countries throughout Asia, there has been a tendency for the primate cities to grow much more quickly than the rest of the urban population. Apart from Hong Kong, Singapore, Taiwan, and Japan, no country of Asia had more than a third of its population in urban areas in 1960, and most had urban percentages far below that. But, while Thailand's urban population is not large and its rate of urbanization has been very slow, almost three-fourths of urban dwellers have been concentrated in the capital city of Bangkok. Seoul (Korea), Manila (Philippines), and Kathmandu (Nepal) are examples of other Asian cities which have been dominant centers in their nation's urban population.

Indonesia's odd geographical configuration of a cluster of more than 13,000 islands, whose west to east span matches that of the United States mainland, makes it a somewhat unique setting for population distribution. As a consequence of its long history of invasions and successions, periods of colonization, and subsequent independence, resulting in a diverse population with tribal and linguistic distinctions tied to location, there are great disparities in population densities. The three islands of Java, Madura, and Bali, in 1980, had 64 percent of the country's population on 7 percent of its land. With natural increase being slower in these areas than in the rest of the country, and with transmigration compensating for much of the traditional migration to these islands, we can observe some slight change in overall distribution. The continued increase in rural population, despite a much higher increase in the rate of urbanization, kept the urban fraction below one-fourth. The capital city of Jakarta (in Java) is dominant, and includes more residents than are found in New York City. In addition, by 1980 Indonesia had three other cities with more than 1 million people and a vast array of cities with more than 100,000 residents that extend its urban network (Hugo et al., 1987; Wood, 1989).

The dynamics of population composition becomes evident as the demographic transition unfolds. With lower mortality, especially fewer infants and children dying, and continued high fertility, the base of the age pyramid remains broad while the somewhat older age groups become "filled in" as a result of greater survival to those age intervals. When fertility begins its downward turn, the proportions in the youngest age groups decline as well. In the city of Ghent, Belgium, in the late 1700s, slightly less than 30 percent of the people were under 15 and 7 percent were 65 or over. By the mid-nineteenth century in that area, the youth population was reduced even further as a percentage of the total, but the percent at ages 65 and over remained steady. This was an indication that improved mortality conditions were allowing young people to grow to middle-age categories, but that prospects for advancing to the older ages were not improved (Deprez and Vandenbroeke, 1989).

Indonesia's changing age composition over the time span from 1971 to 1990 was a response to the beginning of fertility decline accompanied by the mortality decline that had started earlier. By examining the panels at the left side and right side of Table 8.4, we can see that whether we view the compositional changes relatively (in percentages) or absolutely (in numbers) will affect interpretations considerably. The early decline in fertility overcame the greater survival of infants and children to such an extent that the percentages at younger ages dropped sharply in Indonesia between 1970 and 1990 (from nearly 18 percent to just below 13 percent at ages 0 to 4, and from nearly 45 percent to about 36 percent at ages under 15). In general, shifts in the percentage distribution of age were downward in the upper age range and upward in the lower age range; this is consistent with what we would expect for a country at this transitional stage. However, Indonesia's population was rising from 120 million to over 180 million during this time (a 50 percent increase). Consequently, the declining *percentages* of population at the younger ages was masking an increasing number of people in each age group. Between 1971 and 1990, the *number* at ages 0–4 had risen by 10 percent and the *number* at ages 10–14

TABLE 8.4 Changing Age Composition in Indonesia: 1971–1990

	PERCENT IN AGE GROUP		RELATIVE CHANGE IN NUMBERS (1971 = BASE YEAR)	
AGE GROUP	1971	1990	1971	1990
0–4	17.5	12.7	100	110
5–9	14.7	11.8	100	122
10–14	12.3	11.9	100	148
15–19	9.3	10.9	100	179
20–24	7.8	9.3	100	180
25–29	6.9	8.2	100	180
30–34	6.9	7.2	100	158
35–39	6.1	5.9	100	149
40–44	5.2	4.9	100	143
45–49	4.0	4.2	100	160
50–54	2.9	3.6	100	189
55–59	2.3	3.0	100	204
60–64	1.5	2.4	100	242
65–69	1.2	1.8	100	222
70–74	0.8	1.2	100	242
75 & over	0.6	1.0	100	227
TOTAL	100.0	100.0	100	152

Source: Derived from Charles B. Nam, Gouranga Lal Dasvarma, and Sri Pamoedjo Rahardjo, "The Changing Age Distribution in Indonesia and Some Consequences," *Bulletin of Indonesian Economic Studies* 27 (1991): 2, 121–36.

had increased by 48 percent. At the older ages, what appear as modest increases in the percentage of the population translate into substantial additional numbers at the later date. Those 70 to 74 went up from 0.8 to 1.2 percent of the population, but their numbers increased two and one-half times. At the same time that Indonesia's age structure has been shifting relatively, its population has been expanding at all ages.

What has been referred to as Indonesia's *ethnolinguistic mosaic* (Hugo et al., 1987) has undergone some change during the past few decades. Over 100 distinct ethnic groups and 300 or so different spoken languages were long tied to specified parts of the wide-ranging set of islands. Two factors produced appreciable alterations in the mosaic. First, after political independence following World War II, Indonesia focused on its national educational system and introduced Bahasa Indonesia, a national language, throughout the country. Traditional languages are still spoken locally, but the national language has become universal for education and business. Second, the transmigration process has shifted many Javanese to other islands, thereby redistributing the ethnic mix.

Indonesia is a country which has a high percentage of its population (88 percent) who are Moslems. In fact, as of 1988, the world had forty nations in which a majority of the population was Moslem and an additional seven countries in which 25 to 49 percent of the people were Moslem. In addition, there were nine countries in which the Moslem population was less than one-fourth of the population even though the number of Moslems was 2 million or more. All told, the Moslem population worldwide stood at close to 1 billion or nearly 20 percent of the world's total (Weeks, 1988). Largely because of their relatively high fertility levels, the Moslem population is expected to grow more rapidly than the rest of the world's population in the foreseeable future.

Early transition populations may fluctuate in their racial mix as differential mortality, fertility, and migration produce varying rates of population growth for different racial categories. As a result of the slave trade, the black population in the United States from 1790 to 1810 remained at about 19 percent. The white population actually had a higher reproductive rate throughout the nineteenth century and into the present century. Mortality declines for whites were steeper than for blacks; the fertility levels of blacks were hampered by various forms of infecundity; and the slave trade sloughed off. As a result, the percentage of total U.S. population that was black declined progressively, reaching 10 percent by 1920 (Farley, 1970). (In the late transition, the reproductive pattern was slightly higher for blacks than for whites, and by 1980 the black percentage had moved to 12 percent where it remained in 1990.)

Late Transition Stage

Where fertility declines have slowed the rate of population increase occasioned by the mortality revolution and in some cases by substantial net immigration, countries have moved into the late transition phase. Internal mobility shifts have combined with national population change to redistribute population in various ways. By and large, countries proceeding through the demographic transition into the later stage had experienced a continued urbanization, sometimes rapid and sometimes slower, and redistribution has occurred among various areal units.

France, which increased its population during the transition at a slower rate than its European neighbors, also urbanized more gradually during most of that time. After World War II, however, a rapid population increase was accompanied by urban growth. While all towns grew in size, the larger cities gained more than the smaller ones. Paris, in particular, reinforced its status as the primate city of France. By 1968, 70 percent of the country's people were located in urban areas (Winchester and Ogden, 1989).

Throughout the twentieth century, Denmark's urbanization exceeded its overall population increase as the transition proceeded. As in France, all urban areas grew in size but the population of Denmark's primate city, Copenhagen, expanded most rapidly. Moreover, growth in the larger cities spilled over into the outlying landscape, creating the suburban settlements that have become widespread in all developed countries (Court, 1989).

Multiplication of the number and size of metropolitan areas was the norm in Europe in the postwar era. As the rate of population growth slowed when fertility declines became sharper, metropolitan increase continued to characterize the demographic landscape. It was not until the transition had generally run its course (a drop in the rate of population change to near zero) that patterns of counterurbanization developed.

The late transition stage occurred somewhat later in the United States than in most of Europe, but the essential redistribution forms were replicated. Frey and Speare (1988) gave an overview of the metropolitan trend:

> The Twentieth Century has seen the rapid growth and spread of metropolitan areas throughout the United States. At the beginning of the century, less than one-third of the population lived in metropolitan areas and only five of these areas had populations over 1 million. By 1990 three-quarters of the population lived within metropolitan areas and there were 39 areas with populations over 1 million....

Although suburbs were created in the United States early in the twentieth century, their development was overshadowed by the sustained population increases in the central cities. After World War II, however, U.S. suburbanization became so substantial that the cities they surrounded became a smaller and smaller part of the metropolitan areas in most locations, first in the older, industrial regions of the North and later in the newer developing regions of the South and West.

In the post–World War II era, metropolitan area population increased both by the qualification of new areas as metropolitan and by a rise in the population of all metropolitan areas. Some of the greater population size was due to the inclusion of perimeter counties that had become socially and economically integrated with the central counties, while some was due to increase of population within existing metropolitan areas.

Although the *percentage* of the U.S. rural population has declined continuously until the present, the *number* of people living in *rural* areas has escalated through nearly all the time that the nation's population was increasing. In contrast, both the percentage and number of persons living on *farms* has been reduced. By 1990, merely 2 percent of Americans resided on farms, a reflection of both a reduction in farmland and the technical revolution in agriculture that required fewer persons to be productive. Even though half of the nation's farm population lived in the Midwest, farm residents constituted only 4 percent of that region's population in 1990 (Dahmann and Dacquel, 1992).

It has been pointed out that reaching the late stage of the traditional demographic transition can be accomplished in a variety of ways. The case of China is interesting because it achieved relatively low mortality and fertility in a manner not previously observed in any country. The transition, which took place more quickly than in any other nation, was effected by rigid governmental regulations relative to health practices and fertility control. Given the immense size of the Chinese population, is it distributed in ways similar to that of other countries in the late transition stage?

The facts are that China is still dominantly a rural nation, and that urbanization has taken place very slowly. The fraction of China's population that is urban, based on official statistics, rose from 11 percent in 1949 to 15 percent in 1983, far below the situation in developed nations. The rapid pace of population change was not matched by the substantial socioeconomic change generally a partner to urbanization. New towns and cities have emerged, but most of them have been scattered over the broad countryside. Small cities have developed into larger ones, but the greatest rate of urbanization has been in already existing metropolises (Ye, 1989).

According to Goldstein (1990), we can attribute China's slow urbanization to a public policy that has emphasized strict control over the growth of big cities, rational development of medium cities, and encouragement of the growth of small cities and towns. However, the government of China reported a sharp increase in urbanization during the late 1980s, in terms of both the number of cities and towns and the number of people living in them. Goldstein's analysis indicates that much of this more recent reported urbanization resulted from definitional changes. Some Chinese "float" between rural areas and cities as circular migrants. Some rural places have been reclassified as urban places even though their essential rural character has not changed. While it thus appears from official statistics that China's population redistribution is following the Western model, in actuality this is one more indication that China's demographic transition is unlike any other.

The population composition of areas that have experienced the late transition period has some common elements. The age-sex structure assumes a standard form for places that have reached relatively low mortality and fertility, and race and ethnicity tend to become more dispersed in the population. These developments are typified by what has occurred in Europe, North America, and Japan.

Sweden was the first country to bring fertility down to a low level and thus assume an age structure that had a narrowing base of young people and an expanding sector of adults; as a result, its age-sex pyramid approached a rectangular shape. The age pattern of countries of northern and western Europe and North America followed suit as their fertility declined to a level closer to that of their mortality.

While Japan completed its transition at a later date than the other developed nations, it did so more quickly and thereby acquired a typical late transition age structure. Furthermore, the aging process in Japan accelerated as mortality declined significantly for adults. In fact, improved life expectancy at the older ages pushed more and more people not only into what we commonly regard as the older years but even into the very old years. At the oldest years, however, the proportion of women was exceedingly high because of the increasing survival of females at older ages (Martin, 1989).

One should not assume that the age composition evolving during the late transition period resulted from an entirely smooth rate of change in age categories. Germany's age-sex pyramid in 1989 had the underlying form expected for a country in the late transition period, but its specific shape had bumps and dips that were the consequences of a history of mortality and fertility cycles. Fewer males than females at the older ages, beyond what would be expected in a late transition model, were due to military losses of men during World War II. An indentation in the pyramid for both males and females around age 70 could be attributed to a birth deficit during World War I, a time when the disruption of war served to restrict fertility among Germans excessively. A birth deficit during World War II led to indentations in the pyramid around age 40. Participation in the postwar baby boom was reflected in bulges in the pyramid of people in their twenties and early thirties in 1989. And the baby bust in subsequent years created another indentation in the pyramid among those in the teens and below (Heilig et al., 1990). Thus, critical events in Germany's twentieth-century history distorted the age structure, which otherwise would have headed toward a standard late transition form.

We can clearly see that the demographic cycles as well as the more continual processes of the demographic transition determine the age composition of a population by examining age-pyramids for the United States between 1930 and 1990 (see Figures 8.3, 8.4, 8.5, and 8.6). The basic data for the pyramids are presented in absolute numbers so that we can observe both the expanding population size and the changing shape of the age structure.

Prior to 1930, the age structure of the United States was evolving from its early to a late transitional form. By 1930, however, the greater-than-expected decline in fertility produced a disruption of the stepping-stone character of a "normal" pyramid; as a result, the numbers at the youngest ages were fewer than the numbers of survivors of the previous birth cohorts, who were now in their later childhood. By 1950, the resumption of a more normal course of fertility and the following baby boom led to increasingly larger numbers at the youngest ages. By that time the fertility reduction of the late 1920s and early 1930s revealed itself in the dent in the age structure at ages 15 to 24. The pyramid for 1970 shows the effect of the baby bust after the baby boom. The greater irregularity of the pyramid shape (or its ceasing to look like a pyramid) is a consequence of the ripple effects of the earlier fertility fluctuations into the later ages. Now the Depression period babies have survived to their thirties, and the peak of the baby boomers are reaching their teens. Noticeably, the older age segments are expanding as the improved survival of much earlier birth cohorts carries them into later ages. On top of that, the oldest segments are expanding greatly, and the bar for persons 75 and over no longer is adequate to contain what had been the smallest numbers in the pyramid. (Extension of the pyramid bars to age groups 75 to 79, 80 to 84, and 85 and over

FIGURE 8.3 Age-Sex Pyramid for the United States: 1930 (in Tens of Thousands)

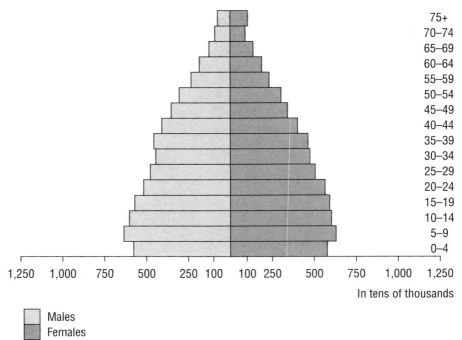

1930 United States

75+
70–74
65–69
60–64
55–59
50–54
45–49
40–44
35–39
30–34
25–29
20–24
15–19
10–14
5–9
0–4

1,250 1,000 750 500 250 100 100 250 500 750 1,000 1,250

In tens of thousands

would have enabled the structure to have retained its peak appearance.) The age composition emanating from the 1990 Census is a "snapshot" of the continuing aging process through which a stabilization of fertility levels has stopped the sharp fluctuations of numbers at the youngest ages. The "echoes" of the earlier fertility changes continue to be "heard" in the chamber of the age structure, and the rapidly increasing numbers at the oldest ages are disproportionately of women whose husbands have died. (Aging of a population is a phenomenon that has a substantial impact on several social institutions, as we will discuss in subsequent chapters of this book.)

The diversity of racial and ethnic categories, both in their variety and their geographical scatter, characterizes the late transition phase. The successive waves of immigrants who had come to such countries as Canada and the United States, their population redistribution over time, and their intermarriage among ethnic groups produced an ethnic mix described variously as a "melting pot," "cultural pluralism," a "mosaic," a "rainbow," and a tapestry resulting "from many strands" (Glazer and Moynihan, 1963; Nam, 1980; Lieberson and Waters, 1988; Halli et al., 1990).

FIGURE 8.4 Age-Sex Pyramid for the United States: 1950 (in Tens of Thousands)

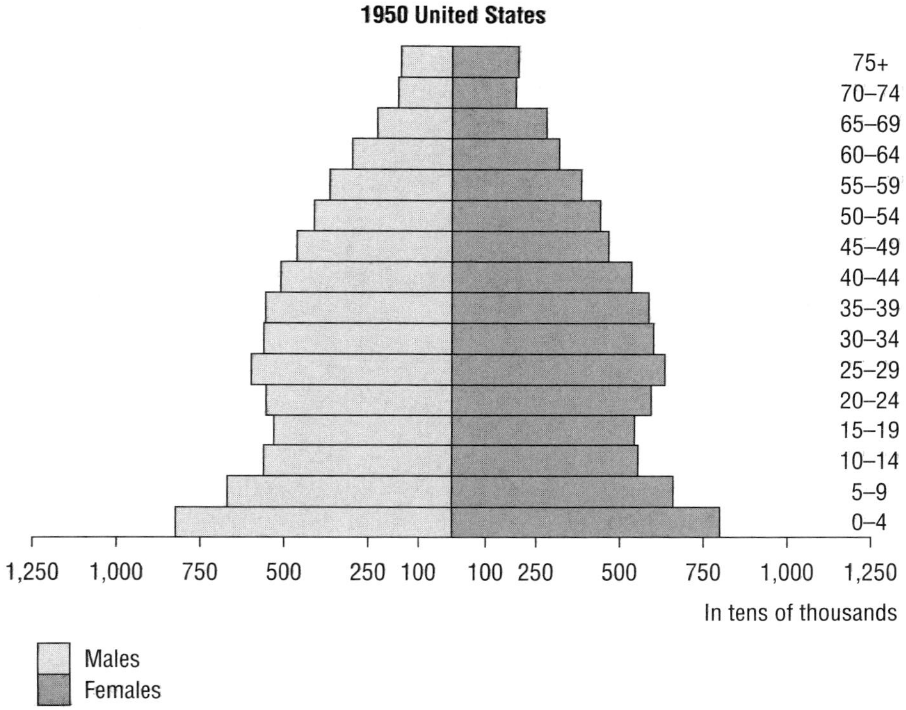

The differential mortality, fertility, mobility, and immigration processes for Native Americans, African-Americans, Hispanics, Asian-Americans, and other racial and ethnic groups in the United States, combined with their differing resulting age-sex structures, intermarrying tendencies, and self-identifying trends, have produced a continuing dynamic to this racial/ethnic configuration in the United States over the past several decades.

Posttransition Stage

What happens to population distribution and population composition after the demographic transition has run its course? As in the case of the basic components of population change, we have a relatively short period of experience in developed nations of such developments, and we can only speculate (it is hoped intelligently) about what alternatives there might be.

Frey and Speare (1988) point to the 1970s as a pivotal era in the population redistribution of the United States. Before 1970, the principal regional move-

FIGURE 8.5 Age-Sex Pyramid for the United States: 1970 (in Tens of Thousands)

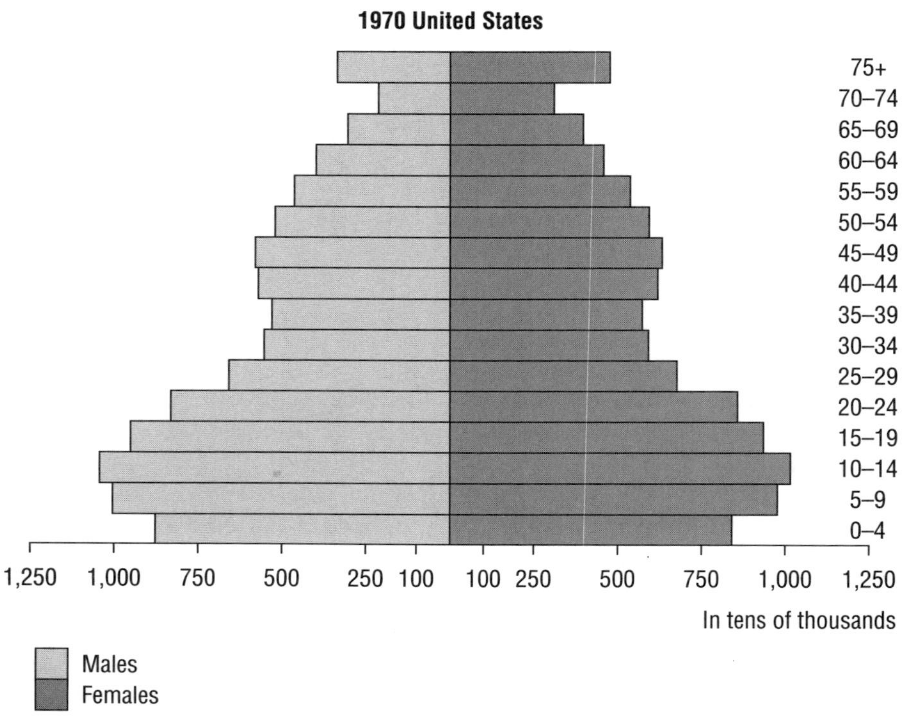

ment was westward; large metropolitan areas grew faster than smaller ones; overall metropolitan growth was greater than nonmetropolitan growth; and more metropolitan growth was occurring in suburbs than in cities. After 1970, these trends shifted. The South became a stronger magnet for population increase. Smaller metropolitan areas gained faster than larger ones. The larger metropolitan areas started to decline in size while nonmetropolitan areas had a resurgence of population increase. And the pace of overall suburbanization slowed down, with new suburban developments occurring more selectively.

If we allow for the fact that some reversals in pattern have occurred, such as renewed metropolitan growth in the 1980s at the expense of nonmetropolitan areas (a turnaround of the 1970s *metropolitan turnaround*), Frey and Speare attribute the general shifts that have taken place to broad economic and social changes that are likely to continue—worldwide markets leading to corporations with multiple locations; an extended technological revolution that broadens the service sector of the society and makes marketing of goods less tied to a single location; and changing work and leisure habits of the people that call for communities with specialized functions, such as retirement areas and resorts. Combined

FIGURE 8.6 Age-Sex Pyramid for the United States: 1990 (in Tens of Thousands)

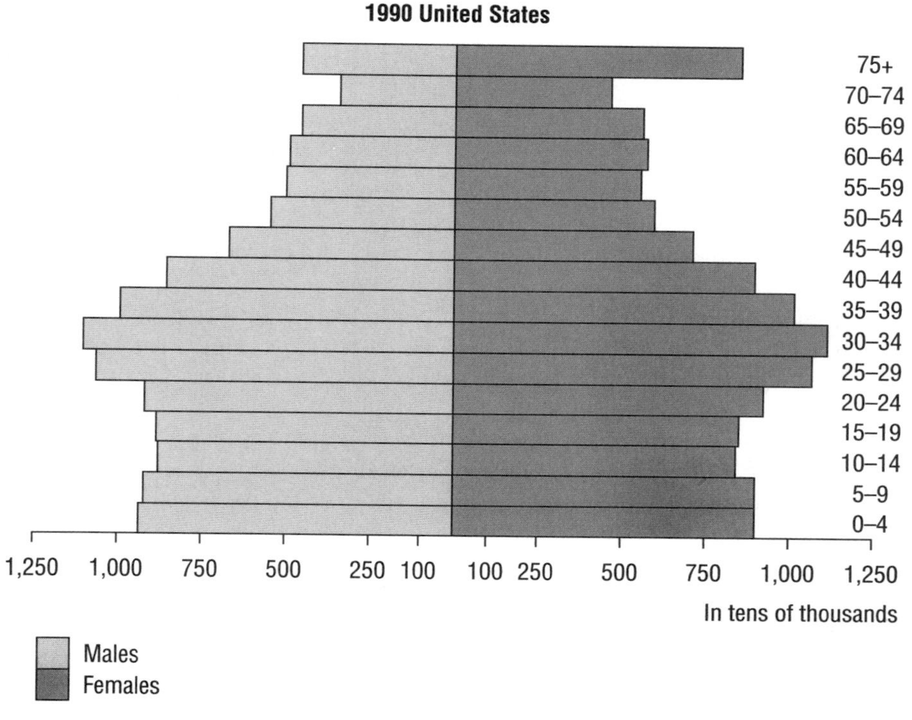

with increased opportunities for both short-distance and long-distance transportation, the types of residential location chosen by the public are in response to more particularistic kinds of needs and interests. As a consequence, redistribution processes have become, and probably will continue to be, more flexible.

Fuguitt et al. (1989) see the reversal of the metropolitan turnaround as an artifact of the way we define metropolitan areas. They point out that rapid growth is still occurring in the parts of metropolitan areas outside the cities (much of it rural to urban conversion). In addition, the preference of the majority of people for residence away from urban centers suggests that remaining open or sparsely populated spaces will be increasingly filled before urban areas become even more densely populated. This would be consistent with survey findings of the growing undesirability of large cities as places to live, but it assumes that cities will not be "revitalized" or that such a transformation of urban centers may lead to gentrification and force the large number of less-affluent current residents to seek residences elsewhere.

Champion (1989), after surveying counterurbanization trends in the 1970s and 1980s in a number of developed countries, reached conclusions about future population redistribution that mirrors aspects of the interpretations of both Frey and Speare and Fuguitt et al. He sees the general pattern of a continuing dispersal of population that relates to interdependent functions that can no longer be contained within one compact urban system. Urbanization becomes more understandable in a regional framework rather than in a more localized setting.

What redistributional tendencies occur in the future will, of course, depend not only on economic and social trends but also, and especially in a demographic context, on the ways in which mortality, fertility, and mobility interact in different locations. Further extensions of life expectancies, continuing low levels of reproduction and small family size, and persistent circulatory mobility and moderate amounts of international migration are the assumptions on which most forecasts of future population distribution are predicated. Should any of these trends be reversed, or should cycles of the components develop for significant periods of time, the demographic basis for population distribution could be altered considerably.

What about population composition in countries that have completed the demographic transition? What changes might we expect? In areas like the former Soviet Union, the compositional alterations will vary for the constituent new nations. Russia's population will age more rapidly than other nations in the area, whose reproductive rates have been significantly higher. In Europe at large, unless there is an unexpected turn in the basic components of population change, the proportion of oldsters in the countries should increase some but, in general, we do not anticipate any major shifts in the age composition (Lutz et al., 1991).

The number and percentage of senior citizens in the United States will undoubtedly increase for as much as three or more decades, especially rapidly in the latter period as baby boomers reach retirement age (Serow et al., 1990). (We will cover the consequences of this trend in Chapter 11.) Japan's population aged 65 and over is expected to exceed 23 percent by the year 2020, which would make it the "oldest" country in the world by that time. The average (mean) age of the population will exceed 40 then, a mark that will not have been reached by any country before. The ratio of persons 65 and over to those under 15, which in 1935 stood at 12 to 100 and in 1990 had risen to 64 to 100, will pass parity before the first decade of the new century is completed. By the year 2020, less than three decades from now, that ratio should reach 143 to 100 and strengthen the image of Japan as a "graying society" (Kono, 1989).

Racially and ethnically in the United States we would predict a faster growth among minority populations (especially Hispanics), even in the absence of further net immigration. The basic distribution by states should not change very much. Every racial/ethnic minority has its own pattern of uneven distribution in the country. About 53 percent of blacks nationally live in the South, with roughly 10 percent in New York and 7 percent each in California and Texas. American Indians are concentrated most heavily in Oklahoma (13 percent), California (12 percent), Arizona (10 percent), and New Mexico (7 percent), but they vary geographically by tribal affiliation. About 39 percent of Asians (of several national origins) are in California, 10 percent are in New York, and 9 percent are in Hawaii. Hispanics as a group are most heavily represented in California (34 percent—mostly of Mexican origin); in Texas (19 percent—also mainly of Mexican origin); in New York (10 percent—heavily Puerto Rican and Central American); and in Florida (7 percent—predominantly Cuban). No significant shifts in the national locations of these groups are projected.

Yet some intriguing questions remain about future race and ethnicity in countries that have gone beyond the transition. Some argue that the maintenance of residential segregation of these groups—a substantial part of it self-imposed in order to ensure cultural preservation—will continue as in the past. Others see increasing "leakage" from these racial and ethnic strongholds occurring for those who have weak ties to their racial and ethnic backgrounds and/or have ambitions for socioeconomic advancement that can only occur by leaving the area of their racial or ethnic concentration. A rising level of intermarriage and expressions of relative unimportance of ancestry to whites in many segments of the U.S. population suggest to others that we may be moving in the direction of an "era of optional ethnicity" for the majority of Americans (Farley, 1991). The importance of "roots" for some people (of all racial and ethnic backgrounds) and the lack of concern about origins by others may indicate that the population at large faces a dilemma of wanting to make race and ethnicity "invisible" while at the same time viewing them as both sources of pride and of stigma from which to escape. From a broader population perspective, these become issues only insofar as they lead to differential demographic behaviors affecting our understanding of population change.

A review of the topics in this chapter shows that assessing the posttransitional course of distribution and composition of population is related to all the phenomena we have studied earlier in this book. We can trace the dynamic aspects of population distribution and population composition, as they differ among groups of people and areas and as they are transformed over time, to the complex interaction of all demographic variables as changes in them take place.

Chapter Highlights

1. Population distribution refers to how people are spread across various geographic categories.
2. Geographic classifications that can be used to measure population distribution include administrative or political areas, statistical areas, and nonbounded residential classifications. We can indicate each of these classifications by a variety of specified measures.
3. An examination of long-term historical changes in world population distribution shows that the largest share of the world population held by an area occurs when that area is in the midst of its demographic transition (or has its greatest gap between births and deaths).

4. Redistribution of population can be observed for all areas over time as a result of the relative change in their mortality, fertility, and mobility, and through the reclassification of boundaries.
5. Urbanization is a process tending to increase over time as a result of the concentration of people in a given location and the intensification of that concentration due to rural-urban mobility and both the outward spread of urban boundaries and the inward increase in population densities.
6. Metropolitan areas and urbanized areas are geographic units often used to indicate urbanization; however, metropolitan areas, which are formed from whole counties, generally contain a rural as well as an urban population.
7. Population composition refers to the division of a group of individuals into categories that specify critical identifying traits and statuses.
8. We can separate compositional variables into age and sex; race and ethnicity; and physical, social, and cultural items. Each of these classifications can be indicated by a variety of measures.
9. Population composition can undergo change on the basis of variations in the basic components of population change.
10. Both population distribution and population composition typically pass through phases coincident with the stages of the demographic transition.
11. The changing patterns of distribution and composition from the pretransition to the posttransition periods can also be affected by mortality, fertility, and mobility cycles.
12. The dynamic aspects of population distribution and population composition, as they differ among groups of people and areas and as they are transformed over time, can be traced to the complex interaction of all demographic variables as changes in them take place.

Discussion Questions

1. Describe your own hometown in terms of items used to portray *population structure*. In what ways is your hometown's population structure similar to or different from that of other nearby places?
2. Using the perspective of an inner-city resident, how would you differentiate the demographic processes of your neighborhood from that of suburban residents?
3. Now using the perspective of a rural resident, how would you differentiate the demographic processes of your area from those of the nearest city?
4. Interview business leaders and governmental officers. Find out what it means to them to be part of (or not part of) a metropolitan area. Report to the class on your findings.

5. Construct an age-sex pyramid for your hometown or the nearest place for which data are available. Compare that pyramid with the one for your state as a whole. Which aspects are the same, which are different, and why?
6. What do you regard as the meaningfulness of race and ethnicity in demographic analysis? Are there better ways of measuring these variables than the conventional ones?
7. Demographers have not always been correct in forecasting future population trends. Do you see directions for population redistribution and population compositional changes in the future of your country that are at variance with those suggested in this chapter?

Suggested Readings

Frey, William H., and Alden Speare, Jr. 1988. *Regional and Metropolitan Growth and Decline in the United States.* New York: Russell Sage Foundation.

Fuguitt, Glenn V., David L. Brown, and Calvin L. Beale. 1989. *Rural and Small Town America.* New York: Russell Sage Foundation.

The above two books, part of a U.S. 1980 Census monograph series, are companions in the discussion of population distribution in America. Although they do not include material available since the mid-1980s, the analyses uncover a range of interesting phenomena about urban and rural processes.

Population Bulletin. An occasional publication of the Population Reference Bureau. Two issues are very relevant to elements of aging and race:

Martin, Linda. 1989. "The Graying of Japan." 44:2.

O'Hare, William P., Kelvin M. Pollard, Taynia L. Mann, and Mary M. Kent. 1991. "African Americans in the 1990s." 46:1.

Population Trends and Public Policy. Another series published by the Population Reference Bureau, two issues of which are especially pertinent with regard to ethnicity:

Valdivieso, Rafael, and Cary Davis. 1988. "U.S. Hispanics: Challenging Issues for the 1990s," no. 17.

O'Hare, William P., and Judy C. Felt. 1991. "Asian Americans: America's Fastest Growing Minority Group," no. 19.

Zelinsky, Wilbur. 1992. *The Cultural Geography of the United States.* Englewood Cliffs, N.J.: Prentice-Hall. A fascinating treatment of American culture from a variety of perspectives.

References

Anderson, Barbara A., and Brian D. Silver. 1989. "Demographic Sources of the Changing Ethnic Composition of the Soviet Union." *Population and Development Review* 15:4, 609–56.

Bose, Ashish. 1978. *India's Urbanization, 1901–2001*. New Delhi: Tata McGraw-Hill.

Champion, A. G. 1989. *Counterurbanization: The Changing Pace and Nature of Population Deconcentration*. London: Edward Arnold.

Chamratrithirong, Apichat, Nibhon Debavalya, and John Knodel. 1978. "Age Reporting in Thailand: Age at Last Birthday Versus Age at Next Birthday." *Institute of Population Studies*, Paper Series, no. 25. Bangkok: Chulalongkorn University.

Chesnais, Jean-Claude. 1990. "Demographic Transition Patterns and Their Impact on the Age Structure." *Population and Development Review* 16:2, 327–36.

Chudacoff, Howard P., and Judith E. Smith. 1988. *The Evolution of American Urban Society*. Englewood Cliffs, N.J.: Prentice-Hall.

Coale, Ansley. 1991. "People over Age 100: Fewer than We Think." *Population Today* 19:9, 6–8.

Coale, Ansley J. 1964. "How a Population Ages or Grows Younger." In Ronald Freedman, ed., *Population: The Vital Revolution*, pp. 47–58. Garden City, N.Y.: Doubleday.

———. 1991. "Excess Female Mortality and the Balance of the Sexes in the Population: An Estimate of the Number of 'Missing Females.'" *Population and Development Review* 17:3, 517–23.

Court, Yvonne. 1989. "Denmark: Towards a More Deconcentrated Settlement System." In A. G. Champion, ed., *Counterurbanization: The Changing Pace and Nature of Population Deconcentration*, pp. 121–40. London: Edward Arnold.

Dahmann, Donald C., and Laarni T. Dacquel. 1992. "Residents of Farms and Rural Areas: 1990." *Current Population Reports*, Series P-20, no. 457. (Washington, D.C.: Government Printing Office).

Denton, Nancy A., and Douglas S. Massey. 1991. "Patterns of Neighborhood Transition in a Multiethnic World: U.S. Metropolitan Areas, 1970–1980." *Demography* 28:1, 41–63.

Deprez, Paul, and Christian Vandenbroeke. 1989. "Population Growth and Distribution, and Urbanization in Belgium During the Demographic Transition." In Richard Lawton and Robert Lee, eds., *Urban Population Development in Western Europe from the Late-Eighteenth to the Early-Twentieth Century*, pp. 220–57. Liverpool: Liverpool University Press.

de Vries, J. 1981. "Patterns of Urbanization in Pre-Industrial Europe, 1500–1800." In H. Schmal, *Patterns of European Urbanization Since 1500*, pp. 77–109. London: Croom Helm.

Ewbank, Douglas C. 1981. *Age Misreporting and Age-Selective Underenumeration: Sources, Patterns, and Consequences for Demographic Analysis*. Committee on Population and Demography Report no. 4. Washington, D.C.: National Academy Press.

Farley, Reynolds. 1970. *Growth of the Black Population*. Skokie, Ill.: Rand McNally.

———. 1991. "The New Census Question about Ancestry: What Did It Tell Us?" *Demography* 28:3, 411–29.

Frey, William H., and Alden Speare, Jr. 1988. *Regional and Metropolitan Growth and Decline in the United States*. New York: Russell Sage Foundation.

Fuguitt, Glenn V., David L. Brown, and Calvin L. Beale. 1989. *Rural and Small Town America.* New York: Russell Sage Foundation.

Garn, Stanley M. 1972. "Races of Man." In *The World Book Encyclopedia*, vol. 16, pp. 50–58. Chicago: Field Enterprises Educational Corporation.

Glazer, Nathan, and Daniel Patrick Moynihan. 1963. *Beyond the Melting Pot.* Cambridge, Mass.: MIT Press.

Goldstein, Sidney. 1990. "Urbanization in China: Effects of Migration and Reclassification." *Population and Development Review* 16:4, 673–701.

Halbwachs, Maurice. 1960. *Population and Society; Introduction to Social Morphology.* Translated by Otis Dudley Duncan and Harold W. Pfautz. New York: Free Press.

Halli, Shiva S., Frank Trovato, and Leo Driedger, eds. 1990. *Ethnic Demography: Canadian Immigrant, Racial and Cultural Variations.* Ottawa: Carleton University Press.

Heilig, Gerhard, Thomas Buttner, and Wolfgang Lutz. 1990. "Germany's Population: Turbulent Past, Uncertain Future." *Population Bulletin* 45:4 (Washington, D.C.: Population Reference Bureau.)

Hohenberg, Paul M., and Lynn Hollen Lees. 1985. *The Making of Urban Europe, 1000–1950.* Cambridge, Mass.: Harvard University Press.

Hugo, Graeme J., Terence H. Hull, Valerie J. Hull, and Gavin W. Jones. 1987. *The Demographic Dimension in Indonesian Development.* Singapore: Oxford University Press.

Johansson, Sten, and Ola Nygren. 1991. "The Missing Girls of China: A New Demographic Account." *Population and Development Review* 17:1, 35–51.

Kaya, Hassan Omari. 1991. "Ethnicity and the Urban Setting in Africa." In Valentine James, ed., *Urban and Rural Development in Third World Countries: Problems of Population in Developing Nations*, pp. 149–55. Jefferson, N.C.: McFarland.

Kinsella, Kevin. 1988. *Aging in the Third World.* U.S. Bureau of the Census, International Population Reports, Series P-95, no. 79. Washington, D.C.: Government Printing Office.

Kono, Shigemi. 1989. "Population Structure." *Population Bulletin of the United Nations* 27, 108–24.

Kosinski, Leszek A., and John I. Clarke. 1982. "African Population Redistribution—Trends, Patterns, and Policies." In John I. Clarke and Leszek A. Kosinski, eds., *Redistribution of Population in Africa*, pp. 1–14. London: Heninemann.

LaPlante, Mitchell P. 1988. *Data on Disability from the National Health Interview Survey, 1983–85.* Washington, D.C.: U.S. National Institute on Disability and Rehabilitation Research.

Lawton, Richard. 1989. "Population Mobility and Urbanization: Nineteenth Century British Experience." In Richard Lawton and Robert Lee, eds., *Urban Population Development in Western Europe from the Late-Eighteenth to the Early-Twentieth Century*, pp. 149–77. Liverpool: Liverpool University Press.

Lee, Anne. 1988. "The Census and Definitions and Semantics of Race." Unpublished manuscript.

Lieberson, Stanley, and Mary C. Waters. 1988. *From Many Strands: Ethnic and Racial Groups in Contemporary America.* New York: Russell Sage Foundation.

Lutz, Wolfgang, Christopher Prinz, Anne B. Wils, Thomas Buttner, and Gerhard Heilig. 1991. "Alternative Demographic Scenarios for Europe and North America." In Wolfgang Lutz, ed., *Future Demographic Trends in Europe and North America: What Can We Assume Today?*, pp. 523–60. London: Academic Press.

Martin, Linda G. 1989. "The Graying of Japan." *Population Bulletin* 44:2 (Washington, D.C.: Population Reference Bureau).

Najjar, Matthew F., and Robert J. Kuczmarski. 1989. "Anthropometric Data and Prevalence of Overweight for Hispanics: 1982–84." *Vital and Health Statistics*, National Center for Health Statistics, Series 11, no. 239. Washington, D.C.: Government Printing Office.

Nam, Charles B. 1980. *Nationality Groups and Social Stratification.* New York: Arno Press.

———, Gouranga Lal Dasvarma, and Sri Pamoedjo Rahardjo. 1991. "The Changing Age Distribution in Indonesia and Some Consequences." *Bulletin of Indonesian Economic Studies* 27:2, 121–36.

Omondi-Odhiambo. 1985. "Age Estimation in Clinical and Public Health Research." *East African Medical Journal* 62:12, 861–76.

Pope, Andrew M., and Alvin R. Tarlov, eds. 1991. *Disability in America: Toward a National Agenda for Prevention.* Washington, D.C.: National Academy Press.

Schinz, Alfred. 1989. *Cities in China.* Berlin: Gebrüder Borntraeger.

Schmid, Calvin F. 1951. "Sex and Age Composition for Certain Typical Census Tracts." In Robert W. O'Brien, Clarence C. Schrag, and Walter T. Martin, eds., *Readings in Sociology*, pp. 217–20. Boston: Houghton Mifflin.

Serow, William J., David F. Sly, and J. Michael Wrigley. 1990. *Population Aging in the United States.* Westport, Conn.: Greenwood Press.

Spencer, Gregory. 1986. "The Quality of Centenarian Data in the 1980 Census." Paper presented at the annual meeting of the Population Association of America, San Francisco.

Stockwell, Edward G., and Jerry W. Wicks. 1974. "Age Heaping in Recent National Censuses." *Social Biology* 21:163–67.

United Nations. 1980. *Principles and Recommendations for Population and Housing Censuses.* Statistical Papers, Series M, no. 67. New York: United Nations.

———. 1991. *World Urbanization Prospects 1990: Estimates and Projections of Urban and Rural Populations and of Urban Agglomerations.* New York: United Nations.

United Nations Secretariat. 1974. "Statistical Definitions of Urban Population and Their Uses in Applied Demography." In Sidney Goldstein and David Sly, eds., *Basic Data Needed for the Study of Urbanization*, pp. 15–32. Dolhain, Belgium: Ordina Editions.

U.S. Bureau of the Census. 1992. *1990 Census of Population and Housing: Summary Population and Housing Characteristics, 1990 CPH-1.* Washington, D.C.: Government Printing Office.

Weber, Adna Ferrin. 1899. *The Growth of Cities in the Nineteenth Century.* Ithaca, N.Y.: Cornell University Press.

Weeks, John R. 1988. "The Demography of Islamic Nations." *Population Bulletin* 43:4 (Washington, D.C.: Population Reference Bureau).

Winchester, Hilary P.M., and Philip E. Ogden. 1989. "France: Decentralization and Deconcentration in the Wake of Late Urbanization." In A. G. Champion, ed., *Counterurbanization: The Changing Pace and Nature of Population Deconcentration*, pp. 162–86. London: Edward Arnold.

Wood, William B. 1989. "Intermediate Cities on the Resource Frontier: A Case Study from Indonesia." In Frank J. Costa, Ashok K. Dutt, Laurence J. C. Ma, and Allen G. Noble, eds., *Urbanization in Asia: Spatial Dimensions and Policy Issues*, pp. 191–206. Honolulu: University of Hawaii Press.

Ye, Shunzan. 1989. "Urban Development Trends in China." In Frank J. Costa, Ashok K. Dutt, Laurence J. C. Ma, and Allen G. Noble, eds., *Urbanization in Asia: Spatial Dimensions and Policy Issues*, pp. 75–92. Honolulu: University of Hawaii Press.

Yeung, Yue-man. 1989. "Bursting at the Seams: Strategies for Controlling Metropolitan Growth in Asia." In Frank J. Costa, Ashok K. Dutt, Laurence J. C. Ma, and Allen G. Noble, eds., *Urbanization in Asia: Spatial Dimensions and Policy Issues*, pp. 311–32. Honolulu: University of Hawaii Press.

Zelinsky, Wilbur. 1992. *The Cultural Geography of the United States*. Englewood Cliffs, N.J.: Prentice-Hall.

PART THREE

Social Consequences of Population Change

The first two parts of this book covered the fundamentals and dynamics of population change. If you learned your lesson well, you are now quite familiar with issues about population growth and decline and the demographic components of mortality, fertility, and mobility, as well as with the consequences of such variables as population distribution and population composition.

You have had impressed upon you the fundamental proposition that all elements in the foregoing set of variables are intertwined in complex, and sometimes complicated, ways, and that the net outcome of these relationships determines the demographic nature of a population at any point in time.

When we titled this book *Understanding Population Change*, we did not expect that the first eight chapters would tell the whole story. Rather, the first two parts of this book were to lay the foundation for understanding the rest of the story. Part Three will explain the communal and societal consequences of population change.

In thinking about population change generally, we need to remind ourselves that consequences are just as important as determinants. Population change is not just an abstract concept relating to people. It has to do with people, but not with just numbers of people. It is also concerned with their geographical locations and personal characteristics. Furthermore, it has to do with where these people fit into the social network; that is, we need to learn about the social consequences of population change. When we use the term *social consequences*, we treat it rather broadly. Each of the following chapters will deal with a social institution that reflects, we think, most of the social consequences linked to population change. Hence, the chapters will shift from families and households to educational and economic systems and then to religious, political, and environmental systems.

Each of the following chapters aims to acquaint you with the key concepts and measures describing that institutional area. In so doing, the chapters will indicate some of the ways that population factors covered in Parts One and Two are responsible for patterns in the institutional area. You can readily see that this is a two-way street. Social factors influence the variables of mortality, fertility, and mobility, as reflected both in the effects on those phenomena as processes and in differentials among social categories in basic population behaviors. But social factors are also influenced *by* basic population variables. In this part of the book, we will focus on the second set of influences, which are the impacts population changes have on communities and societies.

Sometimes a population effect on a social variable is very great; at other times it is quite small. The aim here is to explore the extent and nature of such population effects. Once we have done this, we will have broadened our understanding of population change and its many ramifications.

9. Families and Households

Much demographic behavior arises from the actions of individuals acting in concert as couples or small groups. Couples engaging in sexual behavior are the basis for potential fertility outcomes. Parents provide the environmental setting for their children and each other that influences their health and survival. Small kinship groups jointly make mobility decisions. If members of small groups are not directly involved in making demographic decisions, they can at least exert some influence on those decisions. Interests of the children can weigh heavily when parents contemplate making a residential move. Families and households, as small groups, have an effect on the basic components of population change. At the same time, families and households are critical population units that function as production and consumption entities at various stages of all societies.

The emphasis in this chapter will be on describing the different forms of families and households and on the demographic processes that create and modify them. Definitional issues are crucial because not all of us have the same thing in mind when we think of a family or a household. Differences in the way we conceptualize families and households may influence our notions about the viability of the family as a social institution and about whether "family values" are being upheld in certain societies (Bumpass, 1990).

The standard demographic definition of a *family* is "two or more persons related by birth, marriage, or adoption and residing together." Five conditions are specified. Two or more persons means that one person alone cannot constitute a family unit. Being related by "birth" signifies a genetic linkage present when one person is a natural parent or child of another person or a "blood" relative. Being related by "marriage" usually indicates that two persons have become associated through a legal or religious procedure. Relation by "adoption" is understood to mean that an infant or child has been legally treated as though she or he was a natural child of an older person. Residing in the same living quarters means that the persons involved share common housing.

Subject to the conditions given above, we have defined a family in a specified, traditional way. Within this definition, of course, there can be several types of families. A *conjugal family* involves a married couple but may also include other relatives (such as grandparents) living with the couple. A *nuclear family* is a form of conjugal family that includes a husband and wife and any children, natural or adopted, that they may have. When a family unit incorporates relatives in a broader range, we refer to it as an *extended family.* A family unit may also have embedded within it another family unit, such as the grandparents in the above example (who, if they obtained their own residence, would be established as a separate family). Family units nested within larger family units are referred to demographically as *subfamilies.* The traditional definition of a family also incorporates nonconjugal forms, such as two sisters living together, or a mother, son, and daughter in the same residence.

The traditional definition of a family is sometimes strained when specified conditions are not met precisely. For example, two persons of the opposite sex who cohabit without legal or religious sanctions can act as a de facto family unit with regard to fertility, mobility, and health preservation. On the other hand, we would exclude from a family unit the relatives who live next door or a short distance away but who interact frequently with their kin who live nearby.

The standard demographic definition of a *household* is "all of the persons who usually reside in a given housing unit, where housing units are distinguished by separate access (directly or through a common hall) and separate cooking facilities." The housing unit can be a house or apartment or any other living quarters (except group quarters, such as a dormitory, or a long-term institutional residence, such as a prison), and it can be constructed of any type of material. Units in residential hotels would be treated as apartments under this definition.

In contrast to a family, which must include at least two persons, a household can contain one or more persons. Someone living alone in a separate housing unit is regarded as a household. Households, therefore, can be made up of a sole person, two or more persons unrelated to each other, a family with no other persons present, a family plus nonfamily members, or two or more families not related to each other but who are residing together (sometimes distinguished as "primary" and "secondary" families, the first of these including the household head).

There are many ways in which families and households are created and become dissolved. Families are typically formed when two persons get married. There may never be any additions to the family, but there may be children added or other relatives may join the residential unit at some point. Keep in mind, however, that families can be formed without a marriage occurring (as when two sisters occupy an apartment together).

Families dissolve when there is some form of breakup of the family unit. This can happen when a husband and wife divorce or one of them dies, when children leave home, or when other relatives leave. The family unit ceases to exist only when fewer than two members of the unit are remaining in the residence. A nonconventional family, one that is not a conjugal or nuclear or extended type, likewise becomes dissolved when only one member or none is left in the residence. The concept of the *family life cycle* (discussed later in the chapter) is concerned with changes in family composition as the family unit proceeds through time.

Households are formed when any one or more persons (relatives or nonrelatives) jointly acquire a common residence. The household can be expanded by additional persons (babies, children, or adults) joining them. The household exists even when there is only one person left, so it ceases to exist when the last resident dies or moves on.

In principle, families retain their status when they move so long as they maintain at least the core of the family unit. That is, a mobile family is still the same family provided that it adheres to the conditions of the family definition. If a family becomes dissolved and then reforms (such as when a husband and wife without resident relatives go through a divorce and later remarry each other), a family unit disappears and a new family unit later appears. If a subfamily or secondary family leaves an intact larger family unit to establish its own residence, then the initial family unit remains and a new family unit is created (possibly in a different geographic area).

Households can also be subdivided in a variety of ways. In some cases, a household member may leave to set up a separate household. In other cases, that member may join an existing household, so that the number of households is not increased.

MARRIAGE AND COHABITATION

Getting married is still an expected event in almost all societies, and most people do eventually get married. Because societies frequently go through changes in patterns of age at marriage, it is often difficult to distinguish between marriage delays and never getting married. When a woman or man has not married by age 30, we do not know whether or not that person will subsequently marry even though the probabilities are reduced as a person ages beyond the peak years of marriage. Over 90 percent of people reaching marriageable ages in developed countries eventually get married. There are, of course, variations among people in different geographic areas and with specific characteristics.

Selection of marriage mates takes place in different forms among various groups. In very traditional societies, marriages are arranged, usually by the parents or community leaders, and the young man and woman may not even know each other before the marital ceremony. Societies undergoing social change may find their cultural practices altered. This does not necessarily mean, however, that persons getting married will be able to choose their own partners. Malhotra (1991) argues that totally arranged and completely self-chosen marriages represent two extremes of a continuum. In between are varying degrees of personal input, and the nature of choice for grooms may be quite different from that for brides. In central Java, for example, the typical marriage is moving away from parental arrangement but there is a mix of decision making with regard to the choice of a spouse that allows more input by males than females. In central Thailand, likewise, diversity in the form of mate selection exists, with a nonceremonial elopement being common along with parental involvement and self-choice. Which practice is followed depends on cultural and socioeconomic background as well as family predilection (Cherlin and Chamratrithirong, 1988).

In most societies *monogamy* (one male married to one female) is the accepted form of marriage, but in other places some form of *polygamy* (multiple spouses) is practiced. *Polygyny* (multiple wives for one husband) was a marital form for Mormons in the United States until the end of the nineteenth century and is still common in parts of Asia and Africa today.

In many societies persons of the opposite sex live together without having gone through legal or religious marriage rites. These have variously been termed *consensual unions*, *common-law marriages*, and *cohabitation*.

Consensual and common-law relationships of the sexes have been observed in many different societies over long periods of time. Unmarried cohabitation of the sexes, as an alternative way of forming a couple, was well established in Sweden early in the twentieth century, but the practice spread more quickly there during the late 1960s. Cohabitation has since become extensive in many countries of the world.

In Canada, while living together by a man and woman not legally married to each other was socially unacceptable and statistically rare before 1970, its incidence has increased. When the 1986 Census of Canada was taken, the results showed that one out of nine women aged 20 to 24 and a similar fraction of men 25 to 29 were cohabiting (Burch, 1990). Such relationships were most apt to occur in these age groups and represented first unions for women. At older ages, the incidence of cohabiting was much less, and typically formed after separation or divorce. Cohabitation rates varied by types of residence and population compositional traits. While cohabitants in early time periods were highly selective of the lower socioeconomic strata, by 1986 the socioeconomic difference was small (an indication that this practice had become more common among the better-educated).

Almost half of the women 25 to 34 in the United States in 1988 reported having cohabited at some time in their lives, most of them before marriage (including those who had not yet married). Of those cohabitations reported, more than half ended in marriage, one-third dissolved without marriage, and one-tenth were still in force. Black women were slightly more likely than white women to cohabit, but a slightly smaller proportion of cohabitations progressed to marriage for black women (London, 1991).

A study by Thornton (1988) of persons who had reached age 23 in 1985 in the Detroit metropolitan area revealed that one-third of men and women had experienced cohabitation by the middle of their 23rd year of life. He found that many cohabiting unions were dissolved fairly quickly, while numerous others were soon transformed into marriage. He concluded that most people will continue to spend substantially more time in marital unions than in cohabiting unions.

Bumpass and Sweet (1989) examined data from the 1987–88 National Sur-

BOX 9.1 Types of Cohabitation

Villeneuve-Gokalp (1991) points out that one could identify five different profiles of cohabitation in France. The first is when there was already a commitment to marriage, and cohabitation was a prelude to it. Marriage was likely to follow within one year. In the second, cohabitation was a form of trial marriage and lasted from one to three years. The third type was characterized as a temporary union without a commitment to marry and where the relationship lasted less than three years. The fourth also lacked commitment to marry, but the relationship was more stable and typically lasted three or more years without children. Lastly, what was termed a free union was one in which the couple lived together in a common-law situation, often with one or more children.

Of those French couples who entered into a cohabitation in the late 1960s and early 1970s (less than one-third of all first unions at that time), the first two types of cohabitation were most frequent. By the beginning of the 1980s (when two-thirds of first unions took place outside marriage), stable unions without commitment became increasingly popular. Thus the French experience supports the idea of cohabitation's tending toward an alternative to being single. But it also raises the question as to whether or not legal or religious sanctions, often challenged in other areas of social life, are seen by cohabitors as necessary for a union where children are not contemplated (and hence their legal status is not an issue).

vey of Families and Households and reported that almost one-half of the persons in their early thirties and half of the recently married have cohabited. They point out that much of the decline in marriage has been offset by increased living together without marriage. Most cohabitations end within a few years at the most, with 60 percent of them leading to marriage. Their data showed that higher rates of cohabitation were experienced by persons from lower socioeconomic strata. Still, more than one-fourth of married college graduates had cohabited before marriage.

While cohabitation has been typically viewed as either an alternative to marriage or as the last stage in the courtship process, Rindfuss and Vanden Heuvel (1990) argue that it might better be seen as an alternative to being single. Their analysis of the National Longitudinal Study of the High School Class of 1972 indicated that, in terms of characteristics and behaviors, cohabitors were substantially more similar to the single than to the married. These researchers suggest that cohabitation may be another step in the long-term rise of individualism relative to the decline of the institutions of marriage and the family. Yet not all cohabitations are of the same type (see Box 9.1).

The age at which first marriage (as well as first cohabitation) occurs differs with transitional stage and also varies cyclically. Least-developed societies tend to support early marriage, in part because it is consistent with a desired high fertility. In India, mean age at marriage for girls was as low as 12.5 in the 1920s (Srinivasan, 1989). Coincident with lower fertility orientations observed as the transition unfolds is a rising age at marriage. This is related to the structural changes in society that provide longer education for both men and women and introduce other role changes for women.

But marital patterns are not as solidly linked to the demographic transition as are the basic components of population. Fluctuations in marriage age can take place that are related to demographic as well as socioeconomic changes. The Irish age at marriage in the early transition period was quite low, in great part because living conditions were so poor and early marriage was seen as an opportunity for economic improvement and having children brought satisfactions that were seen as a compensation for poverty (Connell, 1950).

Age at marriage in Ireland increased with the developing transition, just as it did for other European countries. In fact, conditions such as the great famine and limiting land inheritance to one son led to an even greater postponement of marriage in Ireland than elsewhere in Europe (Kennedy, 1973).

Average age at marriage was never very low in the United States. It actually declined steadily from the late eighteenth century to the post–World II era and then climbed steadily back to where it is now, at the 1890 level. But this trend in average age at marriage masks some variations that occurred in the distribution of ages at marriage (here again, the dispersion around averages becomes important). As seen in Figure 9.1, white men and women in the period of the Great Economic Depression were less likely to get married and those who did so got married disproportionately at later ages. More married during World War II, including one group marrying later and one group marrying earlier, the first group continuing to defer marriage and the second group getting back on the normal schedule. In the postwar era, marriage rates were higher but there was a wide spread in ages at marriage (Carter and Glick, 1976), indicating that decisions about marriage age were quite variable in that period as well.

The older marriage ages for men than women in all of the periods is a reflection of the cultural practice in which men typically marry women younger than them, but here too the average pattern is surrounded by considerable variation and the ages of partners are a function of the marriage market as well as the preferences of individuals. During a period of rising fertility, females will outnumber males at somewhat older ages; during a period of declining fertility, there will be fewer females for the older male cohort. This inequality in the supply of mates with traditional male-female age differences can affect marriage rates at any particular time. However, prospective brides and grooms will then have to consider the importance of maintaining the normal age gap at marriage. They may choose to alter the age difference or accelerate or postpone marriage to take advantage of a more favorable supply situation. In actuality, we are talking about marriage opportunities at the margin. The choice of

FIGURE 9.1 First-Marriage Rates by Age at Marriage for Persons 30, 35, 40, and 50 Years Old in the United States: 1960

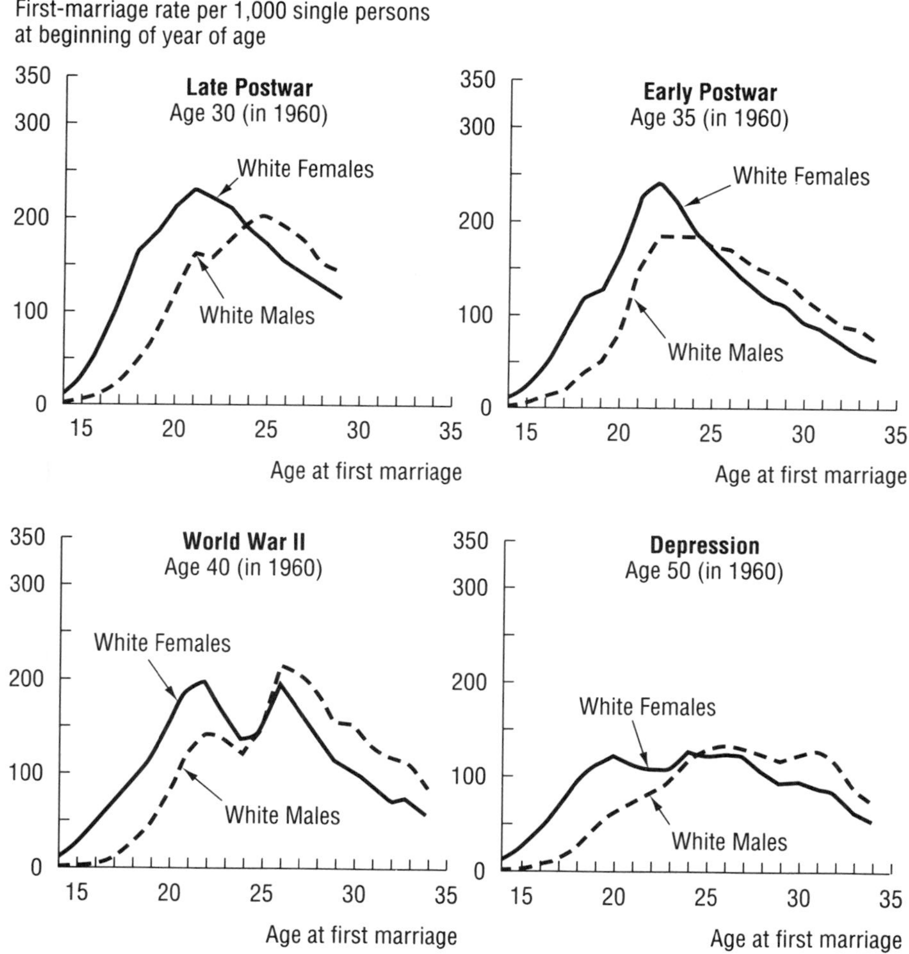

Source: Reprinted by permission of the publishers from MARRIAGE AND DIVORCE: A SOCIAL AND ECONOMIC STUDY by Hugh Carter and Paul C. Glick, Cambridge, Mass.: Harvard University Press, Copyright © 1970, 1976 by the President and Fellows of Harvard College.

marriage partners involves more than the appropriate age of a spouse; these other factors (such as socioeconomic standing, family background, physical features, and personality) usually will weigh more heavily than age in marital decisions. A study by Goldscheider and Waite (1991) found that the employment of men and women, and hence their economic status, were more important in their decision to marry than was the size of the eligible pool of the other sex.

MARITAL DISSOLUTION

Marriages can be disrupted by divorce, by other forms of marital separation, or by the death of one of the spouses. The grounds for legal divorce vary around the world and are heavily influenced by prevailing cultural practices. In more traditional societies, the male is the one who determines if a divorce takes place. In some countries, legal action is not required and the husband can just announce that he divorces himself from his wife.

Couples who do not want to go through a divorce for personal or religious reasons may separate themselves by living apart. One cannot assume, however, that couples who remain in a married state and live together are necessarily satisfied with their marriage. In earlier years, because of the great stigma attached to divorce or separation, unhappily married couples often continued to reside together although they may have reduced their social interaction. In recent years, much of the stigma of divorce and separation has been removed and couples who are not satisfied with their marriage are less reluctant to pursue a divorce or separate. Many marriage counselors and extended family members encourage divorce or separation when a marriage is regarded as no longer well suited for a couple. The presence of children in the family and the perceived impact of a divorce or separation on them often determines the decision to divorce or not.

The measurement of divorce has a considerable bearing on the levels that are calculated. The distinction between period and cohort measures are particularly relevant here. Period measures reflect what is happening in a specified time interval. Economic changes and wars and their aftermath often affect divorce rates in years when those events take place. Marriage rates tend to rise during wartime as men heading toward military assignment tend to accelerate rather than postpone marriage; many of these unions are ill conceived because the couple has not had enough time to get to know each other's faults as well as strengths. At the conclusion of the war, or before, the realization sets in for many of these people and a higher divorce rate ensues.

A cohort approach to studying divorce is based on tracing groups of people who married at about the same time and on examining the incidence and timing of divorce as the marital cycle continues. As in the case of period and cohort marriage measures, the two approaches address different questions. The period measures reflect what current conditions are, while the cohort measures indicate the lifetime continuity of marriage.

By either approach, the incidence of divorce has been increasing. The likelihood of a first marriage's ending in divorce was only 7 percent in 1880 but has reached 50 percent in recent years in the United States. Martin and Bumpass (1989) used a cohort approach in analyzing U.S. data from the 1985 Current Population Survey. They discovered that two-thirds of first marriages would be disrupted (mostly by divorce but some by separations without divorce) at some time during the marriage.

Some argue that divorce permits a necessary adjustment to family life in that a large proportion of divorced people tend to remarry and thus reinstate a family situation that, presumably, is better suited than the previous one. However, the remarriage rate has been declining in recent years (London, 1991). It is also the case that remarried persons have a higher divorce rate than first-married persons, possibly because persons who once divorced already regard divorce as an acceptable way of terminating an unsatisfactory marriage (Martin and Bumpass, 1989).

Chapter 5 reported that the longer life expectancy of women than men meant that more women than men would outlive their spouses. Thus, when death disrupts a marriage, it most often means that a woman either remarries or lives as a widow. The choice hinges on the age of the woman (or man) and the availability of appropriate marriage mates. It may also relate to the geographic location of extended family members and friends who can act as support for the person.

Espenshade (1987) used a cohort approach to estimate the forms of first marriage dissolution for white and black women in different birth cohorts in the United States. Table 9.1 presents his findings. Separation is seen to precede divorce for the vast majority of women who get divorced. Actually, immediate divorce is relatively rare and its incidence has not changed with time. On the other hand, the incidence of separation (usually followed by divorce) has increased tremendously with time for both white and black women. The length of separation (not shown in the table) averaged two to four years for white women and longer for black women, indicating that either the divorce took time to arrange or attempts at reconciliation intervened. Because of increasing life expectancy, the incidence of widowhood of the woman or her own death (when the husband survives) was sharply reduced with time. As a consequence of these trends, the proportion of all marital dissolutions resulting from separation or divorce increased from 12 percent for white women born from 1905 to 1909 to 47 percent for those born from 1940 to 1944. At the same time, the proportion due to widowhood or death decreased. For black women, the shifts were in the same direction but even more pronounced. More recent birth cohorts are still in the middle of their potential marital cycles, but expectations are that the trends noted for the older cohorts will continue for the younger ones.

What about marriages that follow cohabitation? Are they more likely to result in divorce? The answer is yes. According to Axinn and Thorton (1992), however, the reason is that people who cohabit are selective of those who are less committed to marriage and more accepting of divorce.

Marital dissolution is generally observed from the perspective of the couple who were married. It can also be examined from the perspective of children who may have been associated with that marriage. For example, Uhlenberg (1980) estimated that at the beginning of this century one-fourth of all children had lost at least one parent through death by the time they reached age 15. As the risks of parental death decreased, the risks of parental divorce increased. Yet Bumpass and Sweet (1989) estimated that 44 percent of children born be-

TABLE 9.1 Types of Marital Dissolution from First Marriage, by Race and Birth Cohort

	PROPORTION OF FIRST MARRIAGES TERMINATED BY:				PERCENT TERMINATED BY:	
	SEPARATION	DIVORCE*	WIDOWHOOD	DEATH	SEPARATION OR DIVORCE	WIDOWHOOD OR DEATH
POPULATION	(1)	(2)	(3)	(4)	(5)	(6)
WHITE FEMALES						
1940–1944	0.439	0.032	0.380	0.149	47.1	52.9
1935–1939	0.402	0.034	0.404	0.160	43.6	56.4
1930–1934	0.257	0.042	0.501	0.201	29.8	70.2
1925–1929	0.217	0.030	0.538	0.215	24.7	75.3
1920–1924	0.192	0.032	0.552	0.224	22.3	77.7
1915–1919	0.151	0.026	0.585	0.238	17.7	82.3
1910–1914	0.128	0.027	0.596	0.249	15.6	84.4
1905–1909	0.100	0.022	0.585	0.293	12.2	87.8
BLACK FEMALES						
1940–1944	0.608	0.029	0.264	0.099	63.7	36.3
1935–1939	0.571	0.024	0.269	0.136	59.5	40.5
1930–1934	0.465	0.027	0.338	0.169	49.2	50.8
1925–1929	0.363	0.062	0.357	0.218	42.5	57.5
1920–1924	0.314	0.037	0.396	0.254	35.0	65.0
1915–1919	0.251	0.062	0.398	0.289	31.3	68.7
1910–1914	0.237	0.050	0.406	0.307	28.7	71.3
1905–1909	0.201	0.071	0.438	0.289	27.2	72.8

*For this fraction of first marriages, the separation and divorce occurred in the same month, so there is assumed to be no intervening spell of separation.

Source: Thomas J. Espenshade, "Marital Careers of American Women: A Cohort Life Table Analysis," in John Bongaarts, Thomas K. Burch, and Kenneth W. Wachter, eds., *Family Demography: Methods and Their Application* (Oxford: Clarendon Press, 1987). Used by permission of Oxford University Press.

twen 1970 and 1984 will live in a single-parent family by age 16. These marital and family transformations are observed in most developed societies.

FAMILY AND HOUSEHOLD STRUCTURES

What emerges from these trends and patterns of family and household formation and dissolution is a variety of family and household structures. They tend to vary over time and differ among parts of the world. Because we often harbor idealistic notions of how families and households are structured, what we find in reality may not always accord with our impressions.

Wells (1982) points out that the family in eighteenth-century America was not the intact and stable unit that some imagine. In fact, it was in a constant state of flux as a result of demographic changes. High fertility levels meant that additions to the family were frequent, but high infant mortality as well as low life expectancy for those who survived infancy meant that there were also frequent subtractions from the family. Mobility often resulted in a breakup of the family unit as some members had reasons to stay whereas others chose to move elsewhere. From the perspectives of both parents and children, the family looked different each year, and the responsibility for caring for the family shifted from one member to another. Given the range of ages of children, older ones often became pseudoparents for the younger ones while the real parents who survived tried to make a living.

Watkins et al. (1987) view family changes in the United States since that time with a generally optimistic perspective. Despite overall declines in fertility and increases in divorce in the past century and one-half, members of the U.S. family in 1980 spent more years as children, more as parents, more as currently married spouses, and more in a conjugal family unit than its counterpart in 1800 or 1900. This is because greater survival more than compensated for the reduced fertility and growing marital instability effects in creating time during which the family remained intact. On the other hand, the percentage of one's life spent in family statuses declined.

An examination of family structure in the United States currently (Table 9.2) indicates the net result of demographic changes. Data are shown for all family units, separately for white, black, and Hispanic families, and distinctions are made by family type (married-couple families, those without a married couple and headed by a male, and those without a married couple and headed by a female).

Hispanic families average almost one more person than all white families (3.82 versus 3.12 persons), with black families in between (3.51 persons). These are small average family sizes, compared to those in earlier periods of the demographic transition. Only 13 percent of white families and 19 percent of black families include more than four persons, but over 28 percent of Hispanic families fall into that category.

The substantial difference in the race/ethnic categories is in the family types. As many as 83 percent of white families include married couples, whereas married couples are part of only 69 percent of Hispanic families and 48 percent of black families. Of those families without married couples, three times as many white and Hispanic families are headed by a woman, and almost eight times as many black families without spouses are headed by a woman, as by a man. There are almost as many female-headed families as married-couple families among blacks in the United States. The nuclear family is thus still a reality for most whites and a substantial majority of Hispanics, but for slightly less than half the blacks.

TABLE 9.2 Total, White, Black, and Hispanic Families in the United States, by Size and Type: 1991

FAMILY SIZE, RACE, AND ETHNICITY	ALL TYPES	MARRIED-COUPLE FAMILIES	OTHER FAMILIES MALE HOUSEHOLDER	OTHER FAMILIES FEMALE HOUSEHOLDER
ALL FAMILIES				
Total	100.0	100.0	100.0	100.0
2 persons	41.6	39.5	60.3	46.9
3 persons	23.1	21.7	23.9	29.1
4 persons	21.3	23.4	8.8	14.7
5 persons	9.0	10.0	4.1	5.5
6 persons	3.1	3.5	1.4	1.9
7+ persons	1.9	1.9	1.5	2.0
Number	66,322,000	52,147,000	2,907,000	11,268,000
Average size	3.18	3.24	2.78	3.00
WHITE FAMILIES				
Total	100.0	100.0	100.0	100.0
2 persons	43.2	40.8	61.8	52.4
3 persons	22.8	21.7	23.8	29.3
4 persons	21.0	23.1	8.6	12.1
5 persons	8.7	9.7	3.6	4.1
6 persons	2.8	3.2	1.1	1.2
7+ persons	1.5	1.6	1.1	0.9
Number	56,803,000	47,014,000	2,276,000	7,512,000
Average size	3.12	3.19	2.70	2.80

Over the past few decades, there has been a significant rise in the proportion of families headed by women, especially for blacks. What are the demographic sources of that change? Based on an analysis of a series of U.S. census returns, Wojtkiewicz et al. (1990) determined that for white women the major source of growth in female-headed families was an increase in the number of formerly married mothers who got divorced and did not remarry. For black women that same phenomenon explained the increase in female-headed families during the 1960s, but subsequently more of the change was accounted for by an increase in the number of never-married mothers who had children. Further explanation of these trends would depend on a better understanding of factors leading to the reduced chances of remarriage for divorced women and to the increasing incidence of nonmarriage and delayed marriage for women going through childbearing.

continued

FAMILY SIZE, RACE, AND ETHNICITY	ALL TYPES	MARRIED-COUPLE FAMILIES	OTHER FAMILIES MALE HOUSEHOLDER	OTHER FAMILIES FEMALE HOUSEHOLDER
BLACK FAMILIES				
Total	100.0	100.0	100.0	100.0
2 persons	33.4	28.8	55.9	35.1
3 persons	26.0	23.3	25.2	28.9
4 persons	21.4	24.4	9.3	19.9
5 persons	10.5	13.4	5.5	8.3
6 persons	4.4	5.7	2.3	3.3
7+ persons	4.3	4.4	1.7	4.5
Number	7,471,000	3,569,000	472,000	3,430,000
Average size	3.51	3.65	2.98	3.43
HISPANIC FAMILIES*				
Total	100.0	100.0	100.0	100.0
2 persons	24.7	19.8	44.4	33.2
3 persons	23.9	21.2	25.7	31.1
4 persons	23.0	25.1	15.2	19.1
5 persons	15.6	18.4	8.5	9.6
6 persons	6.9	8.4	2.0	3.7
7+ persons	6.0	7.2	3.8	3.2
Number	4,981,000	3,454,000	342,000	1,186,000
Average size	3.82	4.03	3.28	3.36

*All races.

Source: Derived from U.S. Bureau of the Census, Household and Family Characteristics, *Current Population Reports*, Series P-20, no. 458 (Washington, D.C.: Government Printing Office, 1991).

Although families constitute a large part of those living in households, the picture of the household structure includes some important nonfamily dimensions. First of all, counter to what might seem logical, the average size of households is smaller than the average family size. In the late 1980s, the average U.S. family size was over three persons but the average U.S. household size was between two and three persons. Despite the fact that some families live with nonfamily members, there is a large component of households without family units. Of all U.S. households in 1988, about 57 percent had married couples, half with children and half without, and an additional 8 percent were single-parent households. However, 24 percent were one-person households and another 11 percent were households where two or more unmarried persons lived together. Since about 1960, there has been a significant reduction in the percentage of households with married couples and children and a corresponding increase in the percentage of one-person and single-parent households. The same phenomenon has occurred in most developed countries of the world (Sorrentino, 1990).

Households in the past were often very large. Even allowing for high mortality, average household size during the American Revolutionary War period probably exceeded 6 or 7 persons, depending on whether or not slaves were counted. Perhaps two-thirds of the households at that time included 5 or more persons. Only 1 in 75 households would have been occupied by just 1 person. Throughout U.S. history, average household size had declined progressively.

The decline in household size and shift in household types is an outgrowth of the several demographic changes discussed previously. They include a decrease in the proportion marrying, delays in the timing of marriage, an increase in the divorce rate, a general decline in the number of children in marriages, an increase in the number of consensual unions, an increase in the number of women surviving their husbands (especially at the older ages), and a growing tendency for young people to leave their parental homes at an earlier time than in the past (Linke et al., 1990; Masnick and Bane, 1980).

Family households have become different structures, not only from the perspective of adults who may be spouses or parents or other relatives of the residents but also from the perspective of children and the elderly. The percentage of children under 18 in the U.S. living with two parents decreased from 85 to 72 percent between 1970 and 1991. For black children, the shift was from 59 to 36 percent. Those living with one parent (most often the mother) increased from 12 to 26 percent (32 to 58 percent for black children). Living without any parents present remained at a low level (3 percent for all households, 6 percent for black households with children under 18). However, a slight increase occurred in the proportion of children living in the homes of grandparents (Santi, 1988).

Figure 9.2 displays the living arrangements of older persons in the United States as of 1991. Of those who are 65 to 74 years of age, larger proportions of men than women live with a spouse (due to the longer life expectancy of women). As many as 34 percent of the women but only 13 percent of the men in this age category are living alone. Smaller proportions live with relatives or other persons. Among those who have reached their 75th birthday, two-thirds of the men still live with their spouses but only one-fourth of the women do so. A majority of these elderly women are living alone while a larger percentage have moved in with other relatives or nonrelatives. Excluded from these figures are those who entered nursing homes or other long-term institutions (Saluter, 1992). About 2 percent of persons 65 to 74 and 10 percent of those 75 and over were institutionalized in 1980, and like percentages still pertain today. A primary determinant of institutionalization in later life is the health condition of the person (Mutchler and Burr, 1991). Living alone at older ages is sometimes by choice but often occurs because a spouse has recently died and other family members are not able or willing to accommodate the elderly person.

FIGURE 9.2 Living Arrangements of the Elderly: 1991

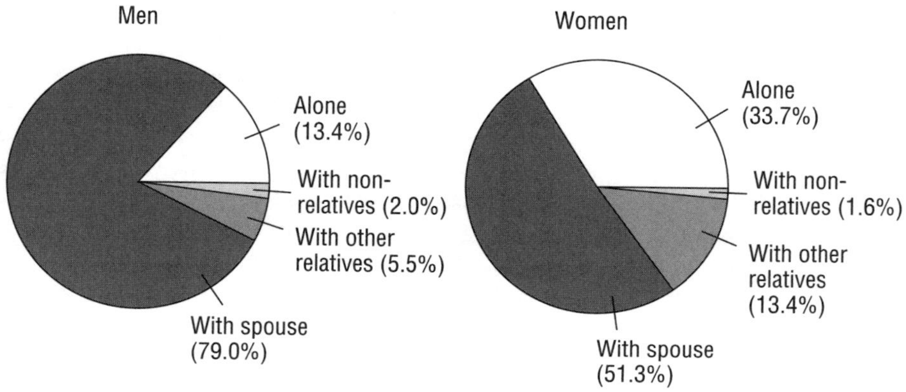

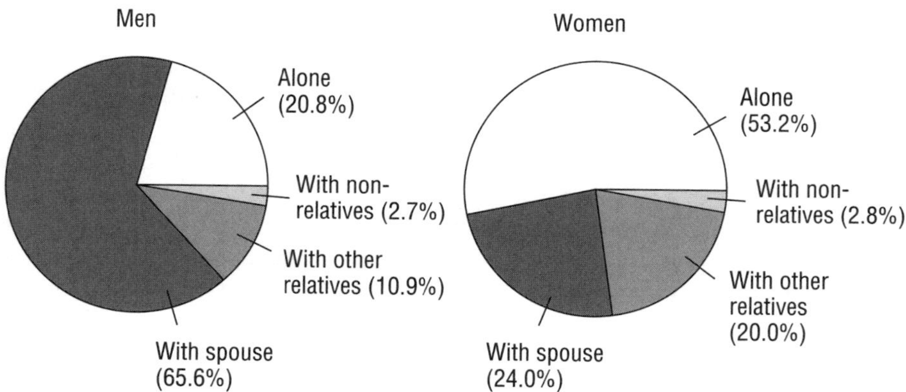

Source: Arlene F. Saluter, "Marital Status and Living Arrangements: March 1991," *Current Population Reports*, Series P-20, no. 461 (Washington, D.C.: Government Printing Office, 1992).

FAMILY LIFE CYCLE AND LIFE COURSE

These various changes in marriage, family, and household patterns have had significant impacts on the lives of individuals as well as on families and households as they progress over time. Some analysts have used a cohort or lifetime perspective to examine the net effect of the many demographic changes on the stages of family development.

Loomis (1936) introduced the concept of the life cycle of families, and Glick (1947) established a method for relating demographic changes to it. The *family life cycle* is considered in the context of the ages at which women experience critical family stages. Starting with the typical age of a woman at first marriage, the researchers also calculated the typical age of the woman when the first child is born, the last child is born, the last child gets married, and the spouse has died. Looking at these indicators for the period around 1900 and for recent times, we can see how reduced childbearing and increased longevity (especially of women) has shifted the typical ages of women at the time of these life-cycle events and thereby created different intervals of time between those events. In the United States, the age at first marriage did not change radically, but variations occurred in the start of family life. Having fewer children and narrowing birth intervals meant that the childbearing and child-raising part of family life was telescoped into a shorter space of time. It also meant that the last child to leave home did so at an earlier age of the mother today than in the past. Along with longer life, the surviving married couple now shared a longer time in the *empty nest stage* of family life. In fact, this was a stage known to no more than half the couples in 1900 since the spouse died before the last child left home in a near majority of cases. But this stage occurs to an overwhelming proportion of couples today. Furthermore, those who experienced the empty nest stage in 1900 would not have spent much time in it, whereas those who enjoy it today generally do so for a large span of years (Glick and Parke, 1965).

A major shortcoming of this traditional approach to looking at the family life cycle is that it assumes that all families are of the nuclear type and remain intact. This may have been more true several decades ago than today, but alternative family forms make the traditional conceptualization of the family life cycle applicable to a smaller proportion of families (Uhlenberg, 1989).

Norton and Miller (1990) revised the concept of the family life cycle to allow for some variation in family types. In particular, they took account of divorce and remarriage as events that reshaped families. Ages of women at the earlier life-cycle stages were then calculated separately for once-married, currently married mothers; once-married, currently divorced mothers; and twice-married, currently married mothers over periods of time (different birth cohorts of women).

For mothers still in their first marriage, age at first marriage decreased for those born between 1920 and 1939 and then increased for those born after 1939. A parallel shift took place in the ages of those women at the birth of their first child. Women in this category born since 1940 have had a later onset of childbearing, fewer children, and an earlier completion of childbearing.

Mothers born before 1940 who were divorced from their first marriage and had not remarried had older ages at first marriage than remarried mothers in those cohorts. The reverse was true for those cohorts born since 1940. Mothers who had divorced and then remarried had younger ages at divorce than those who did not remarry.

The facts of divorce and of remarriage are associated with different timing of life-cycle stages although there are many commonalities of family development experienced by all of the categories (for example, reduced childbearing). Moreover, there are still groups of women who got married but are not included in this typology. Some women remained childless, and these women typically married at a later-than-average age. If they divorced, they did so at a relatively early age. Other women had multiple divorces, and perhaps multiple remarriages. It is difficult to summarize their family experiences, but a result of the various family types is that it has led to compound family structures (often involving stepparents, stepchildren, stepsisters, stepbrothers, and duplicate sets of grandparents).

Because of difficulties in expressing family life-cycle processes in conventional ways, while allowing for the useful information that it generated, some analysts have adopted a *life-course* approach (Hohn, 1987; Day, 1989). By tracing the varying configurations of evolving families, one can discover the great complexity of family (and household) structures that exist (traditional as well as alternative), the emergence of three-generation family residential units, and the effects of ethnic and other cultural forces emphasizing families of one type or another.

Although family forms may vary to some degree among countries, the demographic changes associated with the demographic transition and some demographic cycles have produced common types of family life-cycle changes. In Japan, family and household sizes have decreased over time, single-person households have become more numerous, multigenerational families are now more prominent, and marital breakups have become more common (Long, 1987).

One of the immediate consequences of changes in the family cycle and in size and distribution of families and households is the altered nature of housing requirements (Sweet, 1990). Table 9.3 shows the variations existing in the types of housing related to different family types. Age of the householder, the presence of children of different ages, and the intactness of marriage are all significant factors in influencing the distribution of housing forms. The extent to which these housing patterns will change over time depends on the sorts of family changes that take place and the economic opportunities that permit housing choices. While the last part of the baby boom generation in the United States provided a potential boom for the home sales market, a long-term depressed economy made it difficult for most families to afford such housing. As a consequence, the rental market continued to prosper.

While demographic processes have modified the distribution of family and household types throughout the world, family and household units are still the principal forms of social units in all societies. Some have argued that nonconventional family and household forms represent adaptations to changing social settings in which the transitional and cyclical processes of mortality, fertility, and mobility have combined with evolving social roles of men and women and young and old to respond to new functional needs. Of the basic social functions once performed by families in societies and communities, many have been taken on by other social institutions. The functions that remain the main

TABLE 9.3 Percentage Distribution of Housing Types, by Life-Cycle Stage of Householder, 1980

FAMILY LIFE-CYCLE STAGE	OWNED HOUSING[a]	RENTED HOUSING SINGLE-FAMILY	2–4 UNITS	5–19 UNITS	20+ UNITS	MOBILE HOMES	TOTAL
NEVER MARRIED							
<30	11.6	16.6	20.4	25.8	21.1	4.4	100.0
30–44	30.1	12.6	15.5	19.3	19.4	3.2	100.0
45–59	44.7	10.3	11.8	12.8	16.5	3.8	100.0
MARRIED COUPLE WITH CHILDREN UNDER AGE 18							
Youngest child's age							
0-5	62.5	15.0	7.3	5.1	3.3	6.8	100.0
6–11	78.3	10.1	3.6	2.3	1.7	4.1	100.0
12–17	85.0	6.9	2.4	1.5	1.4	2.8	100.0
MARRIED COUPLE, NO CHILDREN UNDER AGE 18							
Husband's age							
<30	42.2	15.3	12.8	12.3	9.0	8.4	100.0
30–44	72.5	8.0	5.0	4.7	4.8	5.0	100.0
45–59	84.1	4.9	2.7	1.9	2.4	4.0	100.0
FORMERLY MARRIED WITH CHILDREN UNDER AGE 18							
Youngest child's age							
0–5	25.0	24.6	19.3	15.0	9.6	6.6	100.0
6–11	40.9	20.2	15.3	11.3	7.2	5.0	100.0
12–17	53.8	15.8	10.8	8.7	6.5	4.5	100.0
FORMERLY MARRIED, NO CHILDREN UNDER AGE 18							
<30	21.3	16.9	17.6	20.8	16.0	7.5	100.0
30–44	34.2	13.0	13.5	17.6	16.0	5.6	100.0
45–59	51.5	10.3	10.4	10.8	11.0	6.0	100.0
ELDERLY							
Never married	47.6	8.7	11.5	11.2	17.8	3.1	100.0
Married	79.8	5.1	3.3	2.6	4.1	5.0	100.0
Formerly married	57.5	9.0	8.8	7.5	12.3	4.9	100.0
TOTAL	60.9	10.7	8.1	7.7	7.6	5.0	100.0

[a]Excluding mobile homes.

Source: James A. Sweet, "Changes in the Life-Cycle Composition of the United States Population and the Demand for Housing," in Dowell Myers, ed., *Housing Demography: Linking Demographic Structure and Housing Markets*, Table 2.5, p. 49 (Madison, Wis.: University of Wisconsin Press, 1990). Used with permission of The University of Wisconsin Press.

province of families and households are sources of emotional support and the biological survival of the species. Even in these areas, other social institutions offer options that relieve families and households of these requirements. But the family and the household have not suddenly become social problem areas. As Wells (1982, p. 9) indicated:

> Families of the mid-twentieth century are in the process of adjusting to demographic realities unique in human history. It is much too soon to tell whether they will eventually meet the needs of their members and their society better, worse, or much the same as families of the past. Families of the past were far from perfect, and many arrangements that made sense in 1800 would be ill-suited to current needs. Thus, to perceive major alterations in the rhythms of family life is accurate; to interpret those changes as decline is not.

Chapter Highlights

1. A family is defined as two or more persons related by birth, marriage, or adoption and residing together.
2. Families assume different forms, the most familiar one being the conjugal family (a unit including a married couple with or without other relatives). A nuclear family is a conjugal unit restricted to a married couple and their children. But families do not have to include married persons.
3. An extended family is a unit that includes relatives beyond the immediate family. Often the extended family refers to a unit that encompasses kin who do not live with the resident family. Subfamilies are family units nested within larger family units (such as a couple living with the parents of either the husband or the wife).
4. Families undergo change over time by growing (such as through the addition of children to a married couple or the movement into a residence by a grandparent) or by declining (such as through divorce, the death of a member, or the movement of a member to another residence).
5. While marriages typically initiate a family unit, their dissolution (through divorce or the death of a spouse) may or may not lead to a breakup of the family (depending on whether or not two or more family members remain in the residence).
6. Cohabitation without marriage has been an increasing phenomenon in most Western countries and in some other parts of the world. In many instances cohabitation leads to marriage, but sometimes it is a residential accommodation that serves some family functions without eventuating in marriage.
7. A household is defined as all of the persons who usually reside in a given housing unit, where housing units have separate access and separate cooking facilities.

8. A household can include one or more persons, but it can also be made up of any combination of families and/or unrelated individuals. It can also increase or decrease in size and structure by adding or subtracting members (through the same processes that change families plus the movement in or out of the residence of persons not related to continuing household members).
9. Many societies have experienced an increasing incidence of divorce in recent decades. Although remarriage of divorced persons is common, there has also been an increase in the incidence of families and households with only mothers and children (usually called female-headed households).
10. There has also been an increase in developed societies of one-person households (especially of women at older ages who have survived their husbands).
11. Demand for housing of different types is related to the distribution, and changes in it, of different household types.
12. Changes in family stages over time are often described in terms of the family life cycle or life course. These stages are seen to evolve as a consequence of demographic changes, including births, deaths, marital dissolution, and mobility.
13. Perceptions of the strength and viability of the family as a social unit depend on one's definition of a family. If one accepts the demographic definition, then the family continues to be a viable institution, but the types of existing families have become more varied over time.

Discussion Questions

1. Is the "official" definition of a family consistent with the one you were accustomed to when you grew up? How would they differ, and what factors might explain the difference?
2. Why do you think there has been an increase in unmarried cohabitation in developed societies? What are the arguments for and against regarding a couple cohabiting without marriage as a form of family unit?
3. Discuss the social environment that relates to the increasing incidence of divorce in many societies. In light of the frequent remarriage of divorced persons, what are the arguments for and against regarding divorce as a termination of family life instead of a hiatus during family transitions?
4. Ages at first marriage differ among societies and over time in particular societies. Why do these variations occur?
5. What are the demographic determinants of increases in the trend of one-person households in many societies? How would you reconcile this trend with another one that has seen more three-generation households?
6. As a result of the changing family life cycle, varying intervals of time are created between critical events in the life course of families. Which intervals have changed the most, and what have been the social consequences?

Suggested Readings

Wells, Robert V. 1982. *Revolutions in Americans' Lives: A Demographic Perspective on the History of Americans, Their Families, and Their Society.* Westport, Conn.: Greenwood Press. A very readable account of American history that integrates population change and the family with other historical changes.

Goldscheider, Frances K., and Linda J. Waite. 1991. *New Families, No Families? The Transformation of the American Home.* Berkeley, Calif.: University of California Press. Examines new marriage, family, and household formations in the United States and assesses their consequences for the country in the future.

South, Scott J., and Stewart E. Tolnay, eds. *The Changing American Family: Their Sociological & Demographic Perspectives.* Boulder, Colo.: Westview Press. Reviews and summarizes changes in marriage patterns and living arrangements that have reshaped the family and the social situation of its members.

British Family Research Committee. 1982. *Families in Britain.* London: Routledge & Kegan Paul. A collection of essays on various types of traditional, alternative, and ethnic families in Britain that emphasizes their similarities and differences. The discussions are applicable to different family forms in other countries as well.

References

Axinn, William G., and Arland Thornton. 1992. "The Relationship between Cohabitation and Divorce: Selectivity or Causal Influence?" *Demography* 29:3, 357–74.

British Family Research Committee. 1982. *Families in Britain.* London: Routledge & Kegan Paul.

Bumpass, Larry L. 1990. "What's Happening to the Family? Interactions between Demographic and Institutional Change." *Demography* 27:4, 483–98.

———, and James A. Sweet. 1989. "National Estimates of Cohabitation." *Demography* 26:4, 615–25.

———. 1989. "Children's Experience in Single-Parent Families: Implications of Cohabitation and Marital Transitions." *Family Planning Perspectives* 21: 256–60.

Burch, Thomas K. 1990. "Families in Canada." *Focus on Canada.* Ottawa: Census Canada.

Carter, Hugh, and Paul C. Glick. 1976. *Marriage and Divorce: A Social and Economic Study.* Cambridge, Mass.: Harvard University Press.

Cherlin, Andrew, and Aphichat Chamratrithirong. 1988. "Variations in Marriage Patterns in Central Thailand." *Demography* 25:3, 337–53.

Connell, K. H. 1950. *The Population of Ireland, 1750–1845.* Oxford: Clarendon Press.

Day, Alice T. 1989. "Kinship Networks and Informal Support in the Later Years." In E. Grebenik, C. Hohn, and R. Mackensen, eds., *Later Phases of the Family Cycle: Demographic Aspects,* pp. 183–207. Oxford: Clarendon Press.

Espenshade, Thomas J. 1987. "Marital Careers of American Women: A Cohort Life Table Analysis." In John Bongaarts, Thomas K. Burch, and Kenneth Wachter, eds., *Family Demography: Methods and Their Applications*, pp. 150–67. Oxford: Clarendon Press.

Glick, Paul C. 1947. "The Family Cycle." *American Sociological Review* 12: 164–74.

———, and Robert Parke, Jr. 1965. "New Approaches in Studying the Life Cycle of the Family." *Demography* 2: 187–202.

Goldscheider, Frances K., and Linda J. Waite. 1991. *New Families, No Families? The Transformation of the American Home*. Berkeley, Calif.: University of California Press.

Hohn, Charlotte. 1987. "The Family Life Cycle: Needed Extensions of the Concept." In John Bongaarts, Thomas K. Burch, and Kenneth W. Wachter, eds., *Family Demography: Methods and Their Applications*, pp. 65–80. Oxford: Clarendon Press.

Kennedy, Robert E., Jr. 1973. *The Irish: Emigration, Marriage, and Fertility*. Berkeley, Calif.: University of California Press.

Linke, Wilfried, Michel de Saboulin, Gudni Baldursson, and Anton Kuijsten. 1990. *Household Structures in Europe*. Council of Europe, Population Studies no. 22. Strasbourg: Council of Europe.

London, Kathryn A. 1991. "Cohabitation, Marriage, Marital Dissolution, and Remarriage: United States, 1988." *Advance Data from Vital and Health Statistics of the National Center for Health Statistics*, no. 194.

Long, Susan Orpett. 1987. *Family Change and the Life Course in Japan*. Ithaca, N.Y.: Cornell University China-Japan Program.

Loomis, Charles P. 1936. "The Study of the Life Cycle of Families." *Rural Sociology* 1:180–99.

Malhotra, Anju. 1991. "Gender and Changing Generational Relations: Spouse Choice in Indonesia." *Demography* 28:4, 549–70.

Martin, Teresa Castro, and Larry L. Bumpass. 1989. "Recent Trends in Marital Disruption." *Demography* 26:1, 37–51.

Masnick, George, and Mary Jo Bane. 1980. *The Nation's Families: 1960–1990*. Dover, Mass.: Auburn House.

Mutchler, Jan, and Jeffrey Burr. 1991. "A Longitudinal Analysis of Household and Nonhousehold Living Arrangements in Later Life." *Demography* 28:3, 375–90.

Norton, Arthur J., and Louisa F. Miller. 1990. "The Family Life Cycle: 1985." *Current Population Reports*, Series P-23, no. 165. (Washington, D.C.: Government Printing Office).

Rindfuss, Ronald R., and Audrey Vanden Heuvel. 1990. "Cohabitation: Precursor to Marriage or an Alternative to Being Single?" *Population and Development Review* 16:4, 703–26.

Saluter, Arlene F. 1992. "Marital Status and Living Arrangements: March 1991." *Current Population Reports*, Series P-20, no. 461 (Washington, D.C.: Government Printing Office).

Santi, Lawrence L. 1988. "The Demographic Context of Recent Change in the Structure of American Households." *Demography* 25:4, 509–19.

Sorrentino, Constance. 1990. "The Changing Family in International Perspective." *Monthly Labor Review* 113: 45–49.

South, Scott J., and Stewart E. Tolnay, eds. 1992. *The Changing American Family*. Boulder, Colo.: Westview Press.

Srinivasan, K. 1989. "Natural Fertility and Nuptiality Patterns in India: Historical Levels and Recent Changes." In S.N. Singh, M.K. Premi, P.S. Bhatia, and Ashish Bose, eds., *Population Transition in India*, pp. 173–92. Delhi: B.R. Publishing.

Sweet, James A. 1990. "Changes in the Life-Cycle Composition of the United States Population and the Demand for Housing." In Dowell Myers, ed., *Housing Demography: Linking Demographic Structure and Housing Markets*, pp. 35–61. Madison, Wis.: University of Wisconsin Press.

Thornton, Arland. 1988. "Cohabitation and Marriage in the 1980's." *Demography* 25:4, 497–508.

Uhlenberg, Peter. 1980. "Death and the Family." *Journal of Family History* 5: 313–20.

———. 1989. "Remarriage: A Life-Cycle Perspective." In E. Grebenik, C. Hohn, and R. Mackensen, eds., *Later Phases of the Family Cycle: Demographic Aspects*, pp. 66–82. Oxford: Clarendon Press.

Villeneuve-Gokalp, Catherine. 1991. "From Marriage to Informal Union: Recent Changes in the Behaviour of French Couples." *Population: An English Selection* 3: 81–111.

Watkins, Susan Cott, Jane A. Menken, and John Bongaarts. 1987. "Demographic Foundations of Family Change." *American Sociological Review* 52:3, 346–58.

Wells, Robert V. 1982. *Revolutions in Americans' Lives: A Demographic Perspective on the History of Americans, Their Families, and Their Society*. Westport, Conn.: Greenwood Press.

Wojtkiewicz, Roger A., Sara S. McLanahan, and Irwin Garfinkel. 1990. "The Growth of Families Headed by Women: 1950–1980." *Demography* 27:1, 19–30.

10. Educational Systems

Education is regarded in every society as the acquisition of basic and specialized intellectual skills permitting those who receive it to function more effectively in their communities, families, and households, as well as in the work force and their personal lives. Population change in its many forms can have a significant impact on educational opportunities and on the population's educational characteristics; hence, it is important to understand the linkage between them.

A principal interest in this topic is the amount and kinds of education achieved by a population and its subcategories. We need to know what this "educational stock" of a population is, how it changes, and how it differs among various groups. Moreover, it is necessary for us to comprehend that the educational level of a population is the end point of a life-cycle process in which people are given knowledge they will need to become educated.

Clearly, we can obtain education in many ways, and what we think of as "education" fits only part of that set of ways. We learn through regular formal schooling (the most recognizable educational source), through irregular formal schooling (such as special courses, on-the-job instruction, or adult education), and through informal schooling (which provides us with knowledge by listening to our parents, our peers, and significant others, or by watching television programs or movies and reading books, magazines, and newspapers).

What knowledge we have at any point in time is undoubtedly due, to a considerable extent, to the informal processes of learning. Yet the indicators of education we typically use are based especially on the regular formal schooling we receive. There are no accepted measures of our informal education.

In the following pages we will divide a demographic analysis of education into three general parts:

1. First, we will look at the life-cycle patterns through which young people enter into and are moved through the various levels of formal schooling;
2. Next, we will examine the teacher force that is directly responsible for this schooling;
3. Finally, we will take stock of the formal educational attainments of various populations, including that of the United States.

As indicated earlier in this book, we can relate all aspects of population change to all facets of the world we live in. Girard (1975) has specified how changes in population size, mortality, fertility, mobility, age composition, and population distribution can all be linked to the educational composition of a population. Others have also discussed the strength of the ties between demographic forces and educational systems, and have pointed out that educational planners must take heed of population changes in making sound judgments about current and future schooling needs (Morrison, 1976; Hodgkinson, 1985).

Jones (1990) reminds us that countries at the earliest stage of the demographic transition, whose educational levels are most deficient, typically have demographic structures that are least favorable to educational development. High rates of population growth, fueled by high birth rates, result in an age composition heavily weighted at the youngest ages. In an economically deprived area where the ratio of people in the working force to those at school ages is relatively low, the demand for schooling will outstrip the supply of education that people can afford. The irony of this situation is that education (a characteristic of people most likely to propel its demographic evolution) is retarded by the very demographic forces a country wishes to change. This is often as true for economically disadvantaged categories within an economically rich country as it is for economically deprived countries as a whole.

SCHOOL ENROLLMENT

Educators and their administrative superiors use different terms to denote the placement of young people in school. Our use of the term *school enrollment* follows generally the traditional definition of registering a person in a school system and assigning her or him to a particular grade, level, or program. It is not the same as *school attendance*, which implies that the person is actually present in school on a given day. Still other terms, such as *full-time equivalents* and *average daily attendance*, which are aggregate concepts utilized in educational finance studies, are likewise different and outside the domain of our analysis of the relationships between population and education.

Formal school enrollment has tended to be sparse in nations not yet reaching the later stages of the demographic transition. In such nations most family and household functions are located in or close to the home. Young people in less-developed areas are needed in the fields in agricultural communities; as a result, most of the education they receive is of an informal nature. Since their parents (who are usually the children's main source of knowledge) did not receive much formal schooling, the education of these young people is rudimentary at best.

School enrollment statistics are lacking for most countries at early periods of time, and those which are available are not very reliable. Maynes (1985) reports that, as recently as the 1870s in Paris, France, only 76 percent of boys and 70 percent of girls at ages 6 to 9 were in school. By ages 10 to 12, the levels enrolled were 68 percent of boys and 58 percent of girls, and the percentages dropped further to 42 for boys and 34 for girls at ages 13 to 15. This was in France's major city; the proportions enrolled would have been far less in smaller towns and rural areas.

UNESCO (1989) has compiled comparative school enrollment data for areas around the world. Table 10.1 shows *enrollment ratios* (the percentage of persons in given age groups who are enrolled, regardless of the school level at which they are enrolled) for regions of the world in 1960 and 1987.

The contrasts for regions at different stages of the demographic transition and levels of economic development are striking. North America appeared to have complete enrollment at ages 6 to 11 by 1960 and at ages 12 to 17 by 1987. The levels for Oceania and Europe were not as high; they were higher for Europe than Oceania at the younger ages, and higher for Oceania than Europe at the teen ages. Enrollment levels for Latin America and Asia were still lower; those for Latin America were higher, however, than for Asia. The enrollment ratios were lowest for the African region. By 1987 fewer than six out of ten Africans at ages 6 to 11, and fewer than five out of ten at ages 12 to 17, were enrolled.

Two other features of the data in Table 10.1 are of special interest. First, there has been a significant amount of increase in enrollment ratios between 1960 and 1987 for all the regions, especially for the least-developed areas. Second, there are substantial differences between males and females in enrollment patterns, especially in the less-developed world, with girls at a disadvantage.

This information is important because it reflects the recent effort by countries to strengthen their educational systems. The age groups cited have the potential for extending their education beyond that of their parents, with a consequence of parlaying that schooling into facets of a better life. Gains in schooling in Africa, Asia, and Latin America have come about as Jones indicated, despite a burdensome demographic structure. Yet a gender gap in schooling continues in many areas.

Changes in *numbers* of students are a function of both changes in the size of school-age populations and changes in the *percentage* of those in school ages who actually enroll in school. In the United States in the late nineteenth century, when the country was experiencing sustained population growth, the numbers in school also grew significantly. It has been estimated that half of the growth in enrollments during that period was due to a growth in the population of school ages and half to a rising percentage of school going on the part of young people. In the twentieth century continued population growth was accompanied by a greater emphasis on the value of schooling. Between 1910 and 1950 increased enrollment rates played a somewhat more important part in enrollment increases than did the growth of population. After 1950, however, population increases at school ages (resulting from the baby boom) again became the driving force in the rise of school enrollments (Folger and Nam, 1967).

Table 10.2 provides more detailed data on school enrollment percentages for the United States in recent decades. Comparisons can be made by sex, race

TABLE 10.1 Enrollment Ratios by Age Group and Sex for Regions of the World: 1960 and 1987

	AGE GROUP AND SEX					
	6–11			12–17		
REGION AND YEAR	BOTH (%)	MALE (%)	FEMALE (%)	BOTH (%)	MALE (%)	FEMALE (%)
WORLD TOTAL						
1960	59.1	65.8	52.0	44.4	50.9	37.7
1987	78.8	83.6	73.8	52.2	57.2	46.8
AFRICA						
1960	31.6	39.6	23.7	17.0	23.1	11.0
1987	59.1	64.6	53.7	46.4	54.8	38.0
ASIA						
1960	52.2	62.2	41.7	40.7	49.2	31.7
1987	79.7	86.1	72.9	43.0	49.1	36.4
LATIN AMERICA						
1960	57.7	58.1	57.4	36.3	38.7	33.9
1987	86.3	86.9	85.7	68.2	69.2	67.2
EUROPE						
1960	86.8	86.8	86.8	60.1	62.5	57.7
1987	89.4	89.4	89.5	81.8	82.3	81.3
OCEANIA						
1960	88.9	89.2	88.7	60.6	63.1	58.1
1987	97.3	98.5	96.0	75.7	75.6	75.8
NORTH AMERICA						
1960	100.0	100.0	100.0	94.5	98.6	90.2
1987	100.0	100.0	100.0	100.0	100.0	100.0

Note: The enrollment ratios (reported as the percentage in an age group enrolled in school, regardless of the level of school) appear to overstate the percentages. In North America, a small percent at ages 6 to 11 would be mentally or physically incapable of being in school, and an even larger percent at ages 12 to 17 would have dropped out of school. Since there is probably a systematic overstatement of the ratios for all areas, relative comparisons are still valid.

Source: Derived from UNESCO, Table 2.11 in *Statistical Yearbook* (Paris: United Nations Educational, Scientific, and Cultural Organization, 1989).

and Hispanic origin, and age for the period from 1959 to 1989. At ages 10 to 13, which are in the compulsory attendance range in this country, virtually all persons were enrolled throughout the thirty-year period. At the beginning

TABLE 10.2 Percentage Enrolled in School at Selected Ages, by Sex, Race, and Hispanic Origin: United States, 1949–1989

SEX, RACE, AND HISPANIC ORIGIN	AGES 5–6 %	10–13 %	16–17 %	20–21 %	25–29 %
WHITE					
Males					
1989	95.4	99.2	92.6	39.3	9.0
1979	96.3	99.0	90.3	32.2	10.5
1969	88.5	98.9	92.2	48.9	12.2
1959	80.1	99.4	85.9	30.8	9.5
Females					
1989	94.9	99.6	92.1	39.7	9.6
1979	95.3	99.5	87.7	30.0	9.0
1969	89.8	99.5	88.2	25.8	4.5
1959	81.9	99.6	81.6	11.1	1.7
BLACK					
Males					
1989	92.9	98.8	95.6	23.2	5.5
1979	96.6	98.4	94.6	26.9	8.1
1969	83.1	98.9	87.4	28.4	2.8
1959	76.0	99.1	76.3	12.5	4.5
Females					
1989	97.1	99.9	91.7	37.3	7.1
1979	95.5	99.0	87.1	21.1	7.7
1969	85.0	99.2	84.3	19.6	5.5
1959	72.5	99.1	76.4	10.8	1.4
HISPANIC					
Male					
1989	92.5	98.6	88.7	17.1	7.3
1979	93.8	99.0	85.1	24.0	8.7
Females					
1989	93.3	100.0	83.7	20.8	5.8
1979	91.1	98.9	79.5	21.5	7.0

Source: Derived from Robert Kominski and Stephanie Roodman, 1991, Table A-2 of "School Enrollment—Social and Economic Characteristics of Students: October 1989" *Current Population Reports*, Series P-20, no. 452 (Washington, D.C.: Government Printing Office).

school ages of 5 and 6, percentages have tended to increase with time as a result of the spread of kindergartens within the school systems and earlier ages for starting school. Since ages 16 and 17 are outside the compulsory attendance range, we can expect a dropping out of school for some youths at those ages. Over the period covered, more and more students were retained in school in all subgroups. General parity in enrollment at these ages has been achieved for whites and blacks, with at least nine out of ten of both races still in school. Hispanic youths have been approaching that proportion. At ages 20 to 21, which are typical college ages, sharp gains for black females have put them on a par in enrollment with white males and females (almost four out of ten in the age category), but the proportion of black males enrolled at ages 20 to 21 was significantly less. Likewise, there were race/ethnic and sex differences among those enrolled at ages 25 to 29, reflecting the pursuit of advanced higher education for most who were enrolled at those ages.

We have placed great emphasis in recent years on having young people complete secondary school because it is often a minimum requirement for entrance into many jobs, and because it enables those persons to be considered for higher education. Measures of dropping out of school are, therefore, of particular interest. There are several ways to calculate the number of dropouts. Two of them that identify somewhat different views of noncontinuation of school are called the *event dropout rate* and the *status dropout rate.* The first is the proportion of students in grades 10 to 12 who leave school in a given year. The second is the proportion of the population at immediate postcompulsory school ages that has not completed high school and is not enrolled in school at a point in time.

As seen in Figure 10.1, the status dropout rate is higher than the event dropout rate because the former reflects the cumulative experience of dropping out at different grades and different periods of time. Both these rates have tended to remain fairly constant over time, despite targeted programs to reduce them. The dropout rate for blacks has declined the most.

Event dropout rates averaged about 3 percent at grade 10, 4 percent at grade 11, and 7 percent at grade 12 (Kominski and Roodman, 1991). Status dropout rates averaged about 15 percent for whites and blacks and about 35 percent for Hispanics (Frase, 1989). However, as many as half the dropouts later complete high school, either by returning to school after an adjustment period or by taking an equivalency examination.

Changing population size and age structure have strong effects on school and college enrollments in the United States at the present time. At ages when going to school is required, fluctuations in enrollment numbers are largely determined by fluctuations in population size at relevant ages. At college-going ages, population supply is a big factor but so also is the decision by eligible enrollees to go to college and persist there. In the United States, slightly more than one-third of high school graduates will go on to college, but one-half of those who start college will not finish. This is partly due to the popularity of the two-year community college, whose completion is a stopping point for

FIGURE 10.1a Average Event Dropout Rate from Grades 10–12, Ages 14–24, by Race/Ethnicity and by Sex: 1968–1987

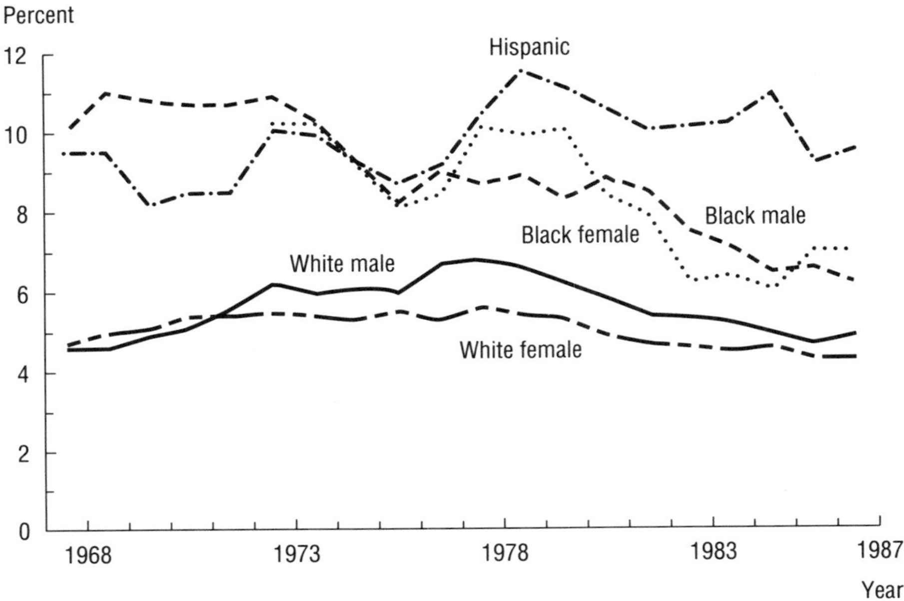

Definition: Event dropout rate is the proportion of students who drop out in a single year.

many students of higher education; it is also partly due to the inability of some students in four-year colleges to succeed in their academic work or to their inability to afford to continue in college until graduation.

In addition, as Hauser (1991) has pointed out, while going to college has become the critical point in advanced schooling, there are inequalities among population categories in the United States in college entry. He found that, relative to the college entrance chances of whites, those of blacks rose during the 1970s but declined from the late 1970s through the 1980s. In attempting to explain the recent divergency of racial differences in college entry, research showed that the following factors had no significant influence: changes in the income of black families; changing gender differentials in college entry; differential recruitment of the races into the armed forces; changes in academic performance or in the selectivity of high school graduation; and changes in plans to attend college. The factor that did explain the divergence, however, was change in the net cost of college attendance. During this period there was a shift in college financial aid from grants to loans as well as in the maximum size of the available grants and loans. Blacks suffered more than whites from these shifts.

FIGURE 10.1b Status Dropout Rate, Ages 16–24, by Race/Ethnicity and by Sex: October 1968 to 1988

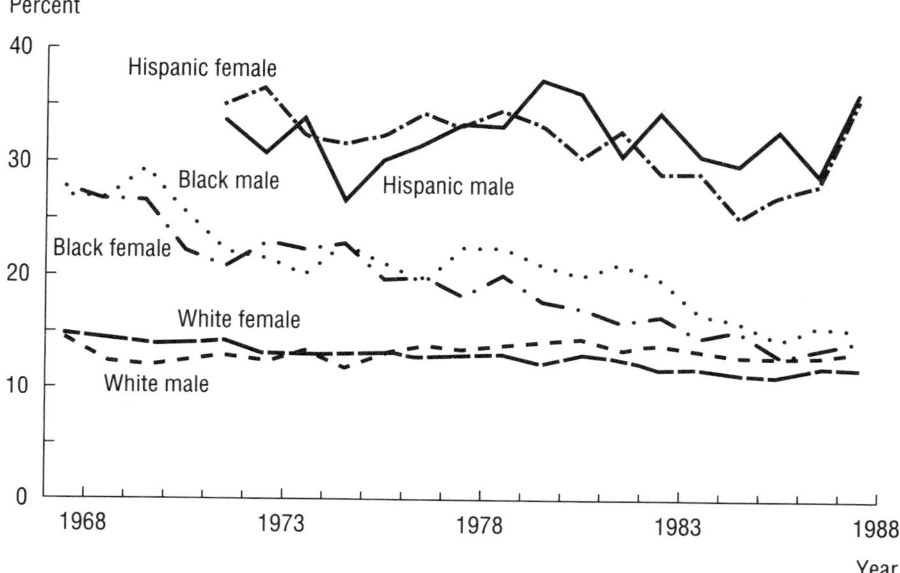

Definition: Status dropout rate is the proportion of the population who have not completed high school and are not enrolled at one point in time.

Note: Hispanics may be of any race.

Source: R. Kominski, "What is the National High School Dropout Rate?," unpublished paper, March 1989; U.S. Department of Commerce, Bureau of the Census, "School Enrollment—Social and Economic Characteristics of Students, October (various years)," *Current Population Reports*, Series P-20, and unpublished tabulations. Cited in Mary J. Frase, 1989, *Dropout Rates in the United States: 1988*. National Center for Education Statistics, Analysis Report 86–609.

Demographic factors affecting enrollments also loom large in other ways. For example, population redistribution accompanying population growth can have an impact on where new school buildings are located. When population declines (as in many rural areas), the decision to consolidate schools will probably also be related to where potential students live. In addition, we need to be aware of another dimension of demographic effects on enrollments: the narrowing of intervals between births. This will often lead to difficult family decisions about placing their children in college because two or more children in the same family may be candidates for going to college at the same time. Such a development may place an economic burden on those who have to support the college students. These and other links between population factors and schooling show how demographic changes can influence the educational system.

TEACHER SUPPLY AND DEMAND

Maintaining a school system is the responsibility of school boards and administrators, but teachers are the intellectual links between the knowledge to be passed along and the students who are to receive it. A proper balance between the number and kinds of teachers and the number and kinds of students is therefore essential.

The nexus between teacher supply and demand and student supply and demand is complex because it hinges on standards set by policymakers and on sociodemographic factors regulating the supply dimension. Floud (1975, p. 59) summarized the situation nicely when she wrote:

> The educational system (that is to say, the scale, distribution and organization of compulsory and voluntary schooling) is the immediate determinant of the demand for teachers, and the only source of their supply. But the nature of the system, and the flow of teachers through it, and their social and other characteristics, are the outcome of economic, political and social (including demographic) forces in complex interrelationship. These forces exert their influence through their effect on the public appetite for education, on the educational policies of government, on the educational decisions of children and young people in the age-groups for which schooling is publicly or privately provided, and on the occupational decisions of adults who are eligible, with or without further education or training, to take up teaching if they so wish or who, having trained for, or even embarked upon teaching, may abandon it for some other occupation.

In nations at the early stage of the demographic transition, the difficulty in expanding the school system is not only a matter of accommodating the rapidly increasing numbers of young people in school buildings but also of finding qualified persons who can teach them. In a society that has not previously valued education highly, there are likely to be very few adults who have been well educated and even fewer who were trained for instructional work. Consequently, teacher supply is apt to be both numerically and qualitatively deficient in these places. It is not uncommon to observe teachers in Third World countries who are very young and who lack strong credentials for their jobs. Moreover, it is typical to find extremely high student-teacher ratios in these areas.

The dilemma of matching teachers to students is aggravated in less-developed regions of the world, but is likewise a problem in more-developed areas. Demographic trends and fluctuations will create varying supply and demand factors for both students and teachers. As education progresses in a country, there will be a shift in the demand for teachers at given school levels. While declining fertility may lessen the number of children entering school, improved school continuation rates will carry them on to higher school grades and levels. Teacher demand will then shift from one level to another. A fertility cycle, such as the baby boom, can radically alter the number of children and youths reaching the several school levels and require sequential adjustments in the number of teachers needed at those levels over time. An areal redistribution of population that spreads the location of students differently means that teacher demand will also be needed in alternative locations.

The historical picture of teacher supply in the United States is a reflection of these many forces. In 1870 the country had about 6½ million public school students and 200,000 teachers below the college level, or roughly an average of 33 students per teacher. By 1900 public enrollments had risen to 15½ million and there were 423,000 teachers, or an average of almost 37 students per teacher. By 1950 enrollments had almost doubled and the number of teachers had more than doubled, thereby reducing the student-teacher ratio to just over 27. This view of the student-teacher relationship had become more complex, however, as more and more students were making it to secondary schools. In 1900 elementary teachers outnumbered secondary school teachers by 20 to 1, but the ratio declined to 6 to 1 by 1920, 3 to 1 by 1930, and 2 to 1 by 1950; this development reflected the persistence of young people to higher levels of schooling (Folger and Nam, 1967).

When there are sizable fluctuations in student enrollments, the demand for teachers varies. This has required adjustments in the preparation of teachers by colleges of education and reorientations by students who plan on becoming teachers. Edmonston and Knapp (1979) have shown that teacher demands occasioned by the baby boom and a higher proportion of students continuing through the educational system were met in several ways. First, the proportion of college students who went on to pursue degrees in educational fields increased during the post–World War II period; second, the probability of obtaining a teaching position became very high during the 1950s and 1960s; and third, a much higher proportion of experienced people, and even individuals with no explicit training in teaching, were recruited to the teaching force.

Once the birth rate declined, however, there was an overproduction of new teachers, although a need remained in some specialties (such as science and mathematics). But periodic fluctuations in school enrollments in recent times have necessitated a flexible approach to supplying the teachers to staff the schools. Furthermore, teacher demand is determined not only by changing enrollments at different school levels but also by state and local educational policies that can modify the priorities attached to programs of different kinds. Hence, teacher demand at any school level can be affected by changes in desired pupil-teacher ratios and in teacher turnover (resulting from retirements, deaths, disability, exits into nonteaching employment or homemaking, involuntary losses by firings or layoffs, and promotions) (Haggstrom et al., 1988).

EDUCATIONAL ATTAINMENT OF THE POPULATION

School and college enrollments and teacher supply indicate the educational inputs being made in a country or some segment of it. Because progression toward completion of given grades or levels of school is not always uniform, and because some students may stay in school for some time without meeting the requirements for graduation to another grade or level, input information is not an adequate indicator of educational outputs.

In determining the educational stock of a population, we can use several indicators. The ones we emphasize here are basic literacy, years of schooling eventually completed, and academic degrees earned.

Basic literacy is defined as the ability to read and write in some language. More specifically, as UNESCO (1988) indicates, a person is considered literate "who can with understanding both read and write a short simple statement on his everyday life." It is often difficult to make this determination from demographic inquiries, and there are certainly variations in the extent to which a person is literate. Nevertheless, this standard definition of basic literacy is widely accepted in international circles. Researchers who have studied literacy in earlier periods of history find a high correlation between the ability to write one's signature on records or registers and a census report of literacy (Maynes, 1985).

Basic literacy, in this sense, is to be differentiated from *functional literacy*, which has come to mean having enough ability to read, write, and calculate in order to function effectively in one's work or other community tasks. It has been established that basic literacy can be achieved with merely a few years of schooling or special training, whereas functional literacy usually requires more extended education.

Studies of England and France suggest that it took several centuries for illiteracy to be reduced from its near maximum level to near minimum level. In the year 1500, nearly all adult women and at least 90 percent of adult men in England lacked the ability to read and write. Illiteracy was brought down to less than 5 percent for both men and women in England by 1900, although near-universal literacy was attained earlier by men. A similar picture emerged for France (Maynes, 1985).

It is probable that one-third to one-half of adults in colonial America could not read and write. By 1840, when an inquiry on literacy was included in the census, adjusted data show that 22 percent of the population 20 and over was illiterate. The percent illiterate was gradually reduced over time, reaching under 11 percent by 1900, slightly over 4 percent by 1930, and around 2 percent by 1960. Of course, differences among population categories were observed. Possibly 81 percent of blacks were illiterate in the United States in 1870, and the percentage was lowered to only 45 by 1900 and remained nearly 8 percent by 1960 (Folger and Nam, 1967).

Although pockets of basic illiteracy can still be found in the United States, the vast majority of the population has acquired that level of language proficiency. Educational requirements in a modern society demand much higher levels of attainment, however. That is why there is continuing interest in helping everyone to become literate at the same time that greater stress is being put on at least advancing through secondary school, if not acquiring some college education.

In many parts of the world, illiteracy is still extensive despite the fact that

TABLE 10.3 Percentage of Population Which Is Illiterate, by Sex and Age: World Regions, 1970 and 1990

AGE AND REGIONS	BOTH SEXES		MALES		FEMALES	
	1970 %	1990 %	1970 %	1990 %	1970 %	1990 %
15 AND OVER						
World	38.5	26.5	30.4	19.4	46.5	33.6
Developing area	54.7	34.9	42.2	25.1	67.4	45.0
Sub-Saharan Africa	77.4	52.7	67.5	41.0	86.8	63.9
Arab states	73.5	48.7	60.5	35.7	86.3	62.0
Latin America/ Caribbean	26.2	15.3	22.5	13.6	29.9	17.0
Eastern Asia	46.8	23.8	32.7	14.3	61.3	33.6
Southern Asia	68.7	53.9	55.2	40.9	83.1	67.8
Developed area	6.2	3.3	5.0	2.6	7.3	3.9
AGES 15–19						
Developing area	33.9	19.1	23.7	13.9	44.5	24.7
Sub-Saharan Africa	61.8	35.9	49.9	28.5	73.5	43.3
Arab states	54.6	27.7	39.3	19.8	70.5	36.0
Latin America/ Caribbean	14.6	6.2	13.3	6.1	16.0	6.3
Eastern Asia	19.5	6.3	10.3	4.0	29.2	8.8
Southern Asia	56.7	37.7	42.7	26.8	72.0	49.5

Source: Derived from UNESCO. *Compendium of Statistics on Illiteracy–1990 edition* (Paris: UNESCO, 1990).

declines in the inability to read and write have taken place everywhere. Table 10.3 summarizes the situation for broad regions of the developing world in comparision with the developed world. By 1990 over one-fourth of persons 15 and over in the world were not able to read and write. Females were more handicapped by illiteracy, one-third of them falling into that category compared to one-fifth of males. Because literacy is now widespread in developed countries, the percentages of illiteracy worldwide are accounted for disproportionately by the developing world's people. In Latin America and the Caribbean, illiteracy rates are now as low as 14 percent for men and 17 percent for women, but that is still far above the rates for developed countries. In eastern Asia, while 14 percent of males are illiterate, the rate is as high as 34 percent for females. Such disparities by gender are even wider in sub-Saharan

Africa, the Arab states, and southern Asia. About two-thirds of women in those areas lacked literacy in 1990.

Because each younger age group typically improves its level of schooling, one would expect to find illiteracy reductions occurring more rapidly in the 15-to-19 age category. The table shows that this is indeed the case, but the relatively low levels of illiteracy for both men and women in the Latin American/Caribbean and eastern Asian regions are offset by the quite high levels in other part of the developing world. In sub-Saharan Africa, the Arab states, and southern Asia, illiteracy rates at ages 15 to 19 in 1990 were 20 to 30 percent for males and as much as 35 to 50 percent for females.

Social and economic development is likely to be retarded in areas where illiteracy remains a significant problem. That this problem exists in most of the developing world is indicated not only by persistent, though declining, illiteracy rates but also by *increasing numbers* of illiterates. For example, in sub-Saharan Africa, the Arab states, and southern Asia, where population growth rates are still quite high, reductions in illiteracy percentages between 1970 and 1990 were more than compensated for by rising population size in affecting the count of illiterates in the population.

Educational attainment is not measured effectively by levels of basic literacy, and more needs to be known about proportions of people who complete given educational levels. What percentages of a population have no schooling, or at least some primary, secondary, or postsecondary schooling?

When we compare the levels of education completed for Afghanistan and Hong Kong, two countries in Asia with widely disparate illiteracy rates, their distribution of years of schooling is found to vary as well. In 1985, 61 percent of males and 92 percent of females in Afghanistan could not read and write. Comparable percentages in Hong Kong in 1985 were 5 percent for males and 19 percent for females.

Virtually all Afghan women 45 and over had received no formal schooling by 1981. Even for the 20-to-24 age group of women, 90 percent lacked any schooling, and very few got beyond the primary level of education. When we consider the educational distribution of men, the situation is more favorable at the younger adult ages, indicating that males are more likely than females to have an opportunity for educational advancement in Afghanistan.

In Hong Kong, on the other hand, sharp improvements in education for the younger cohorts and relative equality of the sexes in educational achievement lead to the observation that the educational stock of the Hong Kong population will rise rapidly as the older cohorts, who had limited education, die off.

The U.S. population has had a long-time rise in the levels of education completed. In 1910 one-fourth of the population 25 years and over had not completed as many as five years of school, and only 14 percent were high school graduates. By 1940 the figures were reversed. Only 14 percent lacked five years of school and one-fourth were high school graduates (Folger and Nam, 1967).

As shown in Table 10.4, educational progress in terms of years of schooling attained was substantial in the fifty years from 1940 to 1990. For the total

TABLE 10.4 Percentage with Selected Levels of Education Completed by Persons 25 and Over, by Age and Sex: United States, 1940–1990

AGE, SEX, AND LEVEL OF EDUCATION	1940 %	1950 %	1960 %	1970 %	1980 %	1990 %
25 AND OVER						
Both sexes						
Less than 5 years	13.5	10.8	8.3	5.3	3.4	2.4
High school graduates	24.1	33.3	41.0	55.2	68.6	77.6
College graduates	4.6	6.0	7.7	11.0	17.0	21.3
Male						
Less than 5 years	14.8	11.9	9.4	5.9	3.6	2.7
High school graduates	22.3	31.5	39.4	55.0	69.2	77.7
College graduates	5.4	7.1	9.6	14.1	20.9	24.4
Female						
Less than 5 years	12.4	9.8	7.3	4.7	3.2	2.2
High school graduates	26.3	35.1	42.5	55.4	68.1	77.5
College graduates	3.8	5.0	5.8	8.2	13.6	18.4
25 TO 34 YEARS						
Both sexes						
Less than 5 years	6.5	4.9	3.1	1.3	1.0	1.2
High school graduates	35.4	47.0	58.0	73.8	85.4	86.2
College graduates	6.0	5.3	11.0	15.8	24.1	23.9
Male						
Less than 5 years	7.4	5.5	3.8	1.5	1.1	1.4
High school graduates	33.1	42.8	56.3	74.3	86.0	85.1
College graduates	7.1	4.7	14.5	19.7	27.5	24.3
Female						
Less than 5 years	5.5	4.2	2.5	1.1	0.9	1.0
High school graduates	37.5	51.0	59.6	73.3	84.8	87.4
College graduates	5.0	5.9	7.5	12.0	20.9	23.5

Source: Derived from Robert Kominski and Andrea Adams, "Educational Attainment in the United States: March 1991 and 1990," *Current Population Reports*, Series P-20, no. 462 (Washington, D.C.: Government Printing Office, 1992).

adult population (25 and over), a mere 2½ percent had not finished the 5th grade by 1990. On the other hand, whereas 24 percent had been high school graduates in 1940 the figure had risen to 78 percent by 1990. Only 5 out of 100 reported 4 or more years of college in 1940 and that proportion rose to 21 out of 100 by 1990. Women were as likely as men to exceed 4 years of school and to become high school graduates by 1990, but somewhat smaller proportions of women had completed 4 or more years of college.

Examining the same kind of data for persons 25 to 34 years of age gives a picture of educational attainments generated by more recent schooling experiences. In 1990 barely 1 percent of both young adult males and females lacked 5 years of school, over 85 percent were high school graduates, and roughly one-fourth had 4 or more years of college.

Comparing whites, blacks, and Hispanics in the 25-to-29 age range, both males and females among blacks show the greatest educational improvement in a recent two-decade span. As of 1990, 85 percent of white males and 88 percent of white females in this age category had completed high school or beyond, while 82 percent of black males and females had reached that level. For Hispanics, high school graduation was limited to 57 percent of the males and 60 percent of the females. Both male and female whites were more likely to have had at least 4 years of college than their black or Hispanic counterparts in 1990.

College enrollment has increased in the United States in recent decades as increasing proportions of people have continued on to college. At the same time, there has been a growth in advanced degree programs. Compared with the 20 percent of persons 25 and over who have received bachelor's degrees at some time, 7 percent have gone on to attain advanced degrees (master's, professional, or doctoral degrees) (Kominski, 1992).

The composition of the population by years or levels of schooling completed (and by graduation certificates and academic degrees) provides us with a general account of the educational stock of the population. It is not reasonable to think, however, that just years spent in school or certifications given are good indicators of learning.

A great deal of attention has been given in recent years to making assessments of knowledge and skills gained from various levels of schooling. Pendleton (1988) analyzed the results of the Young Adult Literacy Assessment conducted by the U.S. Department of Education in 1985. The data collected were used to estimate proficiency on three scales representing distinct aspects of literacy—prose literacy, document literacy, and quantitative literacy—as well as a reading scale. Young adults with different educational attainments were compared on these indicators.

It was found that the various literacy skills improved considerably with each additional level of schooling, even after controlling for the background characteristics of the persons studied. At the same time, literacy skills at each level of schooling were greatly limited for large proportions of the group. "While high school graduates scored substantially higher than dropouts on the literacy scales, many high school graduates, and even college graduates, did not have the basic literacy skills that might be expected of them" (Pendleton, 1988, p. 24). This research raises serious questions about the meaning of levels of school completed for the intellectual capabilities of the general population and for the assumed educational qualifications that people with given levels of schooling have for participation in the work force and in other personal and community activities.

Chapter Highlights

1. Education is the acquisition of basic and specialized mental skills that can be used to function in society. It is acquired in three ways: through regular formal schooling, through irregular formal schooling, and through informal learning. Although most of our basic, and part of our specialized, learning comes from informal education, we tend to measure education in terms of its formal components.
2. Countries at the earlier stages of the demographic transition generally have low levels of education, whereas those at the later stages have considerably higher levels. Demographic variables (especially population size and age composition) affect the capacity of nations to meet the demand for schooling.
3. School enrollment (registration in a school system and assignment to a grade, level, or program) is a key indicator of the placement and progression of young people in the formal educational system. Various studies indicate that enrollment levels are low in earlier transition stages, but are nearly universal at compulsory school ages in developed countries.
4. While all countries show improvements in percentages going to school, a gender gap in schooling is evident in Third World countries.
5. At postcompulsory educational ages, enrollments are a function of both population numbers in the relevant age groups and the percentage in those age groups which is enrolled. In the United States, the relative importance of those two factors has shifted over time. Race/ethnic and gender variations have also been observed.
6. Noncompletion of secondary school has been a concern in many countries. In the United States, event dropout rates now range from about 3 percent in grade 10 to 7 percent in grade 12. Status dropout rates (the proportion of the population at immediate postcompulsory school ages which has not completed high school and is not enrolled in school) average 15 percent for white and blacks and 35 percent for Hispanics.
7. Going to college has become more prevalent in the world, especially in developed countries. In the United States, variations among groups and over time seem to be affected greatly by economic factors (particularly financial assistance for college).
8. Teacher supply and demand is governed by the same demographic factors that regulate enrollment supply and demand; however, because teachers

are older than students, there is a time disparity in matching supply and demand for the two groups.

9. Educational attainment of the population can be indicated by measures of literacy, years of school completed, and degrees or other certifications.
10. Illiteracy (or the inability to read and write in some language) is widespread in less-developed parts of the world, and tends to be greater for females than males. Moreover, even as illiteracy *rates* decline in these areas, population growth leads to increasing *numbers* of illiterates. Countries reaching later stages of the demographic transition have very low illiteracy rates.
11. Years or levels of school completed by populations are correlated with their literacy levels, but the former levels indicate the extent of formal education received well beyond basic literacy.
12. Examination of years of schooling completed for the U.S. shows that there has been continued improvement over time, even though disparities continue to exist among categories of people. Among young adults who recently finished their education, 85 percent are high school graduates and one-fourth have had four or more years of college.
13. One should not assume that the attainment of given levels of formal schooling means that the persons involved have acquired high levels of competence in intellectual skills. Educational assessment studies reveal that many persons with high school completion, and even many with college degrees, lack levels of advanced literacy that we would expect to find in persons with their formal educational achievement.

Discussion Questions

1. Think about a country that has recently entered the early phase of the demographic transition. What are the conditions in both the country at large and in families generally that make formal education difficult to achieve?
2. Are the reasons that females tend to lag behind males in some countries the same as the reasons that certain racial or ethnic groups tend to lag behind others in educational attainments? Why?
3. Because demographic (as well as other) factors create imbalances in student and teacher supply and demand, what advice can you give to educational planners who have to determine the needs and training programs for teachers that might assist them in carrying out their mission?
4. If you were in a position to manage educational budgets for public and private comprehensive educational systems, which would you give higher priority to—reducing basic illiteracy or increasing the proportion of people with higher education? Why?
5. Many people are discouraged to find out that educational attainments are not necessarily related to the acquisition of skills that given levels of school-

ing are intended to achieve. What is your explanation for such a disparity, and what steps can be taken to bring educational attainments and intended skills into line?

Suggested Readings

Folger, John K., and Charles B. Nam. 1967. *Education of the American Population.* Washington, D.C.: Government Printing Office. A 1960 Census monograph report that provides a demographic perspective of the history of U.S. education up to 1960. It can be supplemented by more recent census and survey reports from the U.S. Bureau of the Census.

Muhsam, Helmut V., ed. 1975. *Education and Population: Mutual Impacts.* Dolhain, Belgium: Ordina Editions. Chapters written by international experts on the population aspects of education examine them as both determinants and consequences of demographic changes.

Hodgkinson, Harold L. 1985. *All One System: Demographics of Education—Kindergarten through Graduate School.* Washington, D.C.: Institute for Educational Leadership. A brief review of various population factors that influence educational trends and their past and expected future developments.

UNESCO. 1989. *Statistical Yearbook.* Paris: United Nations Educational, Scientific, and Cultural Organization. A useful international statistical reference book on education that complements other UNESCO publications in the education field.

References

Edmonston, Barry, and Thomas R. Knapp. 1979. "A Demographic Approach to Teacher Supply and Demand." *American Educational Research Journal* 16:4, 351–66.

Floud, Jean. 1975. "Determinants of Teacher Characteristics and Flow." In Helmut V. Muhsam, ed., *Education and Population: Mutual Impacts*, pp. 59–80. Dolhain, Belgium: Ordina Editions.

Folger, John K., and Charles B. Nam. 1967. *Education of the American Population.* Washington, D.C.: Government Printing Office.

Frase, Mary J. 1989. *Dropout Rates in the United States: 1988.* National Center for Education Statistics, Analysis Report no. 89–609 (Washington, D.C.: Government Printing Office).

Girard, Alain. 1975. "The Effect of Demographic Variables on Education." In Helmut V. Muhsam, ed., *Education and Population: Mutual Impacts*, pp. 25–42. Dolhain, Belgium: Ordina Editions.

Haggstrom, Gus W., Linda Darling-Hammond, and David W. Grissmer. 1988. *Assessing Teacher Supply and Demand.* Santa Monica, Calif.: Rand Corporation.

Hauser, Robert M. 1991. "Trends in College Entry among Whites, Blacks, and Hispanics, 1972–1988." *Institute for Research on Poverty Discussion Papers*, no. 958–91. Madison, Wis.: University of Wisconsin.

Hodgkinson, Harold L. 1985. *All One System: Demographics of Education—Kindergarten through Graduate School.* Washington, D.C.: Institute for Educational Leadership.

Jones, Gavin W. 1990. *Population Dynamics and Educational and Health Planning.* World Employment Programme Paper no. 8. Geneva: International Labour Office.

Kominski, Robert. 1992. "Educational Attainment in the United States: Results from the 1990 Census." Paper presented at the annual meeting of the American Sociological Association, Pittsburgh, Pennsylvania.

———, and Stephanie Roodman. 1991. "School Enrollment—Social and Economic Characteristics of Students: October 1989." *Current Population Reports,* Series P-20, no. 452 (Washington, D.C.: Government Printing Office).

———, and Andrea Adams. 1992. "Educational Attainment in the United States: March 1991 and 1990." *Current Population Reports,* Series P-20, no. 462. (Washington, D.C.: Government Printing Office).

Maynes, Mary Jo. 1985. *Schooling in Western Europe.* Albany, N.Y.: State University of New York Press.

Morrison, Peter A. 1976. "The Demographic Context of Educational Policy Planning." *Rand Papers,* P-5592. Santa Monica, Calif.: Rand Corporation.

Pendleton, Audrey. 1988. *Young Adult Literacy and Schooling.* National Center for Education Statistics, Analysis Report CS 88-604. Washington, D.C.: Government Printing Office.

UNESCO. 1988. *Compendium of Statistics on Illiteracy.* Paris: United Nations Educational, Scientific, and Cultural Organization.

———. 1989. *Statistical Yearbook.* Paris: United Nations Educational, Scientific, and Cultural Organization.

———. 1990. *Compendium of Statistics on Illiteracy—1990 Edition.* Paris: United Nations Educational, Scientific, and Cultural Organization.

11. Economic Systems

Economic change is a phenomenon that seems a constant aspect of societies. Stability of economic processes may occur over very short periods of time, but significant alterations in economic circumstances are typical in the long run. Moreover, economic conditions in one area or for one group are frequently different from those in other areas or for other groups.

Among the several sets of factors affecting these economic variations are population trends and makeup. As the population size increases or decreases, as each of the basic components of population change alters its trend or goes through a cycle, as population becomes redistributed, and as population composition takes on different forms, so does the economy of an area or group have the potential for being influenced by these demographic forces.

In the following pages our focus will be on population linkages to a number of dimensions of economic status and change. First, we will examine the attributes of the work force and associated conditions of employment and unemployment. Next, we will look at levels of living of people in terms of their incomes, wealth, and economic security. Then, we will turn to the macro concept of economic development, viewing it as it may be advanced or retarded by population factors. Lastly, we will pay attention to businesses and markets and how *demographics* has been a critical factor that determines the dynamics of those enterprises.

THE WORK FORCE

When governmental officials (national, state, and local) and private sector analysts try to monitor the state of the economy, one of the principal aspects they study is the nature of the work force. Is it growing or declining? Who makes up those who work, and how is that group changing? Which elements of the population are most at risk of not working? Are all of the dimensions of work status accurately captured by the conventional indicators used?

Throughout history, there was great sensitivity to the size of the work force and its impacts even though people did not have good mechanisms for measuring them. The mercantilists of the sixteenth and seventeenth centuries favored population growth because they saw it as expanding both the number of workers and the size of the markets to which trade was directed. During the Industrial Revolution, a revitalized work force was regarded as instrumental to the emerging economy. At times, however, caution was advanced about a work force growing too rapidly. Confucius, Ibn Khaldun, and Malthus, in their times, were all wary about the ability of an economy to absorb the total number of workers when it might relate to imbalances in other parts of the social system.

Ideas about how to *describe* a work force have not always been the same. When Karl Marx wrote about workers, he excluded the owners of enterprises even if they participated in its activities, and he treated differently the operators of small businesses. When Franklin D. Roosevelt started his presidency of the United States in the early 1930s by instituting economic reforms, he envisioned the work force as constituting all the people involved in any form of labor (including "captains of industry") as well as those who were not actually working but had the potential to do so.

Interestingly, society was concerned about the extent of those out of work, which prompted an overhaul of work force concepts and measurement in the Roosevelt era. Up to that time, the prevailing concept of the work force was that of *gainful workers* (those engaged in work for pay). Census and other economic statistics excluded from the concept those who did not work for pay, including unpaid family workers and persons out of work. It was not possible during the depth of the Great Depression to determine from available statistics just how many unemployed there actually were. It was also not possible to know who among the not-employed did or did not seek work and who among those not looking for work had work experience that could be utilized in an emergency situation.

New concepts and measurements were developed to remedy these shortcomings. Figure 11.1 outlines the dimensions of the work force classifications developed in that era and persisting to this day. It reveals the complexity of work and nonwork statuses in the population, and it shows why simple explanations of trends and variations in such concepts as employment and unemployment can be misleading.

Let's start with the total population of an area. Not everyone in that population is capable of being part of the work force. In order to encompass all the persons in the population who have the potential for working (under some set of circumstances), we have to exclude infants and children at prework ages (persons regarded by different countries as below work ages range from 10 to 15) as well as people too disabled to work (of course, most disabled persons can work) and the extremely aged (who may lack the physical capacity for work). The remaining persons constitute the potential labor force, which is often called *manpower*.

Under the current work concepts, the term *labor force* refers to those who would be at work if everyone who wanted to work could find a job. In some

FIGURE 11.1 Schematic Classification of the Working Status of the General Population

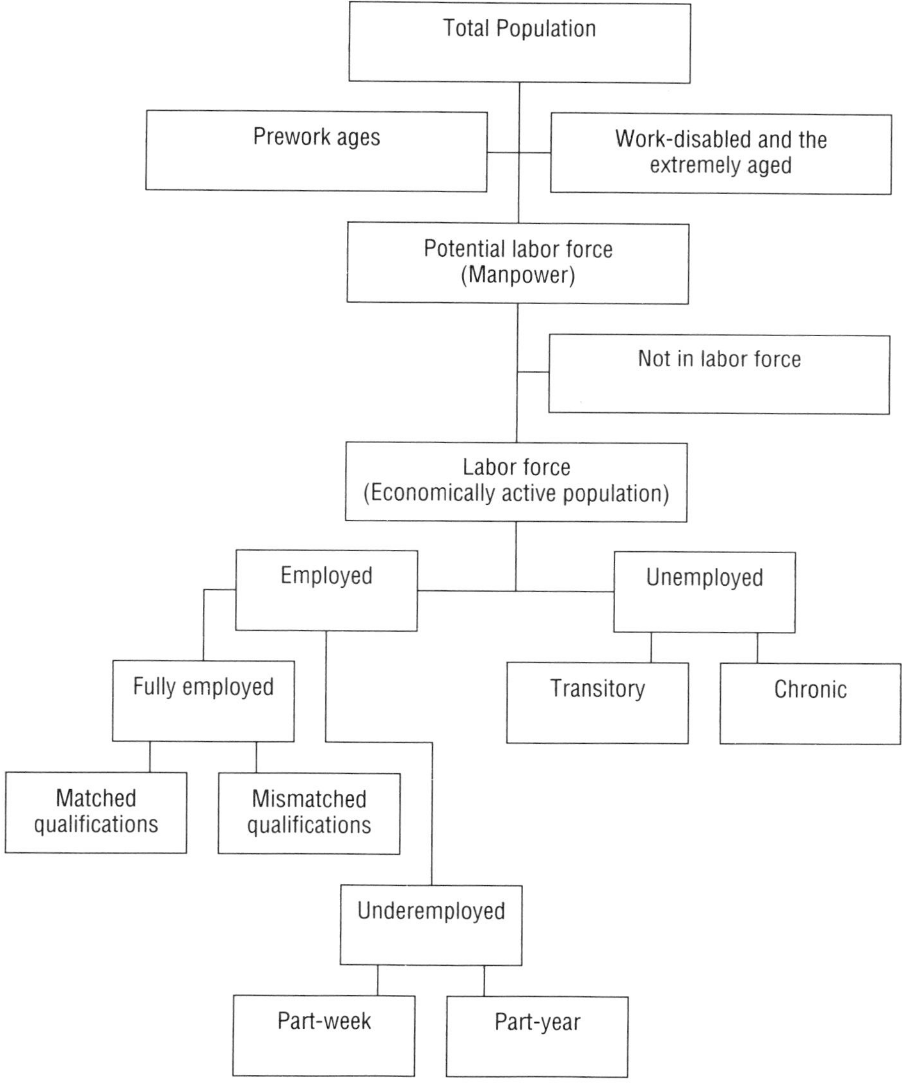

countries the labor force is called the *economically active population*, but the labor force is not to be equated with employed persons. In fact, both employed and unemployed persons are included within the labor force under the assumption that the *unemployed* are persons who have no employment but who are actively seeking it and who would be employed if jobs were plentiful. Also, the *transitory unemployed*, who are out of work for short periods of time, move out of and into the employed ranks without any appreciable effect on their employment. The *chronically unemployed*, on the other hand, are out of work for longer spells of time. It is this group which is apt to become discouraged about getting jobs and which might, therefore, stop looking for work. When its members do that, they cease to be in the labor force, as defined. This can have a significant impact on the *unemployment rate*, which is measured as the ratio of the unemployed to the total labor force (U.S. Bureau of Labor Statistics, 1992).

The *employed* category encompasses all of those who work for any amount of time and in any occupation (although household work is not considered as work in the standard definition). Even those who are "fully employed" (in terms of working full-time) may not be well suited to their jobs. In terms of their education and training, they may not be in the jobs they were prepared for. Such persons are treated as having *mismatched qualifications*. Those who are employed, but not full-time, are regarded as *underemployed* (meaning that they work fewer than thirty-five hours a week). Others may work a full week but only for part of the year (such as at seasonal jobs). It is true that, from a personal standpoint, some of the underemployed may only want part-time work; from the perspective of full employment in a society, however, they are underutilized.

What was the magnitude of these dimensions in the United States in 1992? In April of that year, there were roughly 254 million persons in the country. Excluding those under 16 (the U.S. cutoff for work statistics) and those institutionalized in some type of long-term facility, that left 192,745,000, an approximation to the potential labor force. The actual measured labor force was 128,407,000, so that about one-third of the potential labor force was not in the actual labor force. Of that labor force, 9,155,000 (or 7.1 percent) were unemployed in that month. Of the unemployed, 32 percent had been unemployed for less than 5 weeks but 40 percent had been unemployed for 15 or more weeks. In addition, the rate of unemployment varied considerably among categories classified by age, sex, and race. It was as high as 50.3 percent for black males at ages 16 and 17 (many of them high school dropouts who could not find work) and as low as 1.4 percent for white males at ages 75 and over (not many of whom sought work but most of whom were successful at finding it). Looking at ages 40 to 44 as among the peak working ages, we find that the unemployment rate in April 1992 was 4.6 for white men, 4.2 for white women, 12.8 for black men, and 8.9 for black women. Thus the unemployment risk varied substantially among population categories (U.S. Bureau of Labor Statistics, 1992).

Of those reported as employed (119,252,000), as many as 1,577,000 were in the armed forces. Among the remaining 117,675,000 civilian employees, roughly four-fifths worked full-time and one-fifth part-time. Three-fourths of part-time workers chose part-time work, whereas the other one-fourth worked part-time although they preferred full-time work. It is also the case that being fully employed does not mean that such workers are content with their jobs or suitably qualified for them. Having mismatched qualifications is extensive, more so in some types of occupations than in others, but many workers in that situation do adapt well to the needs of their jobs.

Brinkmann (1987) has indicated some of the key demographic determinants of the size of the labor force. These are the rise and fall of fertility levels that alter the size of cohorts entering and proceeding through the labor force ages; changes in life expectancy along with changes in retirement ages; the shifting family structure, leading to different orientations to entering the labor force; the internal movement of population that modifies the regional and local supply of workers; and international migration, which introduces an extraneous element to the work force. All these factors have affected the supply of workers in one or another European country during the past few decades.

Fullerton (1991) has shown how the baby boom has had a very profound effect on time trends of the labor force in the United States and will continue to do so. He notes that the baby boom cohort has already entered the peak ages of employment and is now advancing to the older working ages. The smaller cohort of children of baby boomers is now moving into the labor force. These people will slow down the pace of the labor force growth, although numbers in the labor force will continue to rise.

The size of the labor force depends on both the size of the population and the extent to which persons participate in the labor force. Women of the baby boom generation increased their participation in the labor force at the same time that their generation was entering ages of high labor force participation. As a consequence, they contributed disproportionately to the labor force increase. Shank (1988) describes the phenomenon, in which women in the age range 25 to 54, who had labor force participation rates of somewhat over 30 percent at the end of World War II, increased their participation rates to over 70 percent by 1987 (Figure 11.2). In the process, the age pattern of working women changed its form. In earlier years women's work participation was reduced while they were in childbearing and early childraising ages and increased only after that family life-cycle stage. Now, both the lesser fertility and the changed attitudes about working even when children are in the household means that the age curve of working is similar for women and men, both rising gradually to a maximum at ages 35 to 44 and then declining. Furthermore, women are now more likely to be full-time, year-round workers, in contrast with their earlier more part-time participation in the labor force.

This U.S. phenomenon has been duplicated in most of the developed countries of the world (Brinkmann, 1987). In less-developed countries women have also increased their labor force activity but have not yet reached the levels attained by women in developed regions. In addition, Third World women are less likely to enter the mainstream of the work force. They are increasingly drawn into informal-sector employment (typically self-employment and/or part-time work), which keeps them at an economic disadvantage relative to men (Greenhalgh, 1991).

Lumsdaine and Wise (1990) have analyzed the impact of an aging population on labor force participation. The growing number of elderly resulting

FIGURE 11.2 Civilian Labor Force Participation Rates for Women, by Age: United States, 1946–1987

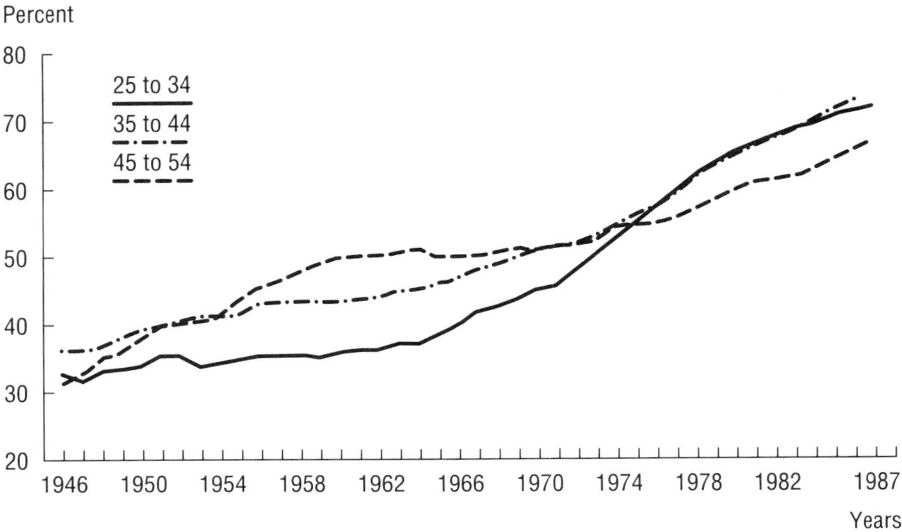

Source: Susan E. Shank, "Women and the Labor Market: The Link Grows Stronger," *Monthly Labor Review* (March 3–8, 1988), Chart 2.

from an extended life expectancy and the beneficial pension and Social Security provisions for them has led to a lowering over time in their retirement age, despite a changed public policy that now makes retirement voluntary at least until age 70. Consequently, the labor force participation rate of older persons has declined markedly, falling from 65 percent in 1930 to about 30 percent in 1980 for men over 60. Rates for women in that age category began to turn down after 1970.

Population dynamics also affects the components of the labor force. Younger workers are less attracted to agricultural jobs. Especially are those with higher education more attracted to the technological and professional jobs likely to be found in urban areas. As a result, when the age pattern of the labor force shifts toward a younger population, employment in the preferred areas will increase. As the population and labor force age, the relative pool of training and skills will change. That factor, in turn, will affect the labor force.

Flaim (1990) links the baby boom with unemployment in the United States. When baby boomers entered the work force in the late 1960s and 1970s, they swelled the group of young workers whose employment is more tentative and whose unemployment rate is higher. Even though relative unemployment had declined for other age groups in that time period, the inflated unemployment numbers represented by the baby boomers more than compensated for the opposite trend; this, in turn, led to a larger net unemployment rate for the whole labor force. When baby boomers entered the prime working ages during the 1980s, their employment was stable, as was typical for that age group. The smaller birth cohorts that followed them dampened the unemployment rate of younger workers and, consequently, of the total labor force. So the rise in the national unemployment rate during the 1970s was not due to a deteriorating economy but rather to a transformation in the age composition of the population that caused supply to exceed demand for labor in the affected age groups.

During the 1990s the baby boom effect should exert a downward pressure on the unemployment rate. Yet such an effect may be countered by a declining economy that limits employment and generates more unemployment. Even when the economy first takes a turn for the better, the unemployment rate may still rise for a while because unemployed persons who had stopped looking for work when they saw no prospect for a job will be drifting back into the job market; not all of them can be absorbed by an early economic improvement.

Mobility can influence work patterns. After World War II young couples seeking a better environment for their children than the city settings where many of them lived were attracted to the suburbs. Suburban residential development was a major force in reshaping business and service locations, and it brought to these areas many jobs that previously had been in the cities. We must recall, however, that population and economic variables are mutually influential. Part of the reason that suburban movement was possible for the young people of that time was that the economy was favorable enough for them to afford the move.

LEVEL OF LIVING

Work status is only one of several aspects of the economy that is affected by population changes. Others include variables that can be encompassed within the broad category of level of living. We refer here specifically to income, wealth, poverty, and social security.

Because societies tend to be socially stratified, income and wealth are unequally distributed in the population. We are accustomed to speaking about the rich and the poor and the middle class of a country, and a common phrase is that "the rich get richer and the poor get poorer." The fact of the matter is that substantial economic inequalities have always existed. Patterns of inequality, however, have shifted over time, sometimes in one direction and sometimes in another.

Soltow (1989) studied the *distribution of income* in the United States around 1798 and discovered that "the employed well-being of Americans is much more homogeneous today than it was two centuries ago." The Gini coefficient or ratio—an index of population inequality in money distribution that is 0 when there is perfect equality and 1 when there is complete inequality—is currently about .43 in the United States, whereas it was as great as .63 to .71 in 1798. Early American society was highly stratified.

In fact, U.S. society is still economically stratified to a high degree, and population inequality in income has increased since 1970, especially from 1980 to 1990. Table 11.1 shows aggregate income shares for each fifth of the households arrayed from low to high income. (*Household income* is defined as the income received jointly by household members from earnings in all jobs and from other cash benefits. It does not include noncash benefits or what is sometimes termed *income in kind.*) The lowest fifth (the 20 percent of households with the lowest incomes) had 4 percent of the aggregate income. Although the shares of the second and third fifths were higher, they were not so high as the 20 percent of the households each represented. The next-to-highest fifth had 24 percent of aggregate income, while the highest fifth (the 20 percent of the households with the highest incomes) had nearly 47 percent of aggregate income.

It is interesting to note that, allowing for the fact that average income disparities were great among the race/ethnic categories in 1990 (median household income being $31,231 for whites, $18,676 for blacks, and $22,330 for Hispanics), within each category the disparities were also great. Actually, the Gini ratio (for within-group inequality) was significantly higher for blacks (.464) than for whites (.419) or Hispanics (.425). Thus income inequality is appreciable both between and within race/ethnic categories.

Income status also varies according to other characteristics of households, such as age, educational level, type of household, and geographic location. However, even when the effects of these variables are controlled, substantial inequalities remain. For example, a broad distribution of income exists for households in which there is a white married couple in the age range 45 to 54 years which has completed high school and has no college experience. Gini ratios vary marginally across all subcategories of the population. Even when we modify the definition of income to take account of differential tax rates, employer contributions to health insurance, and government benefits, the Gini ratio fluctuates only between 3.8 and 4.9.

Demographic factors clearly have some influence on changes in income inequality. The altered composition of families and households has had an effect, mainly through an increase in the proportion of households that include broken families. The aging of the population has likewise had effects, particularly in the creation of more households of smaller size whose members have reduced incomes. As the baby boom generation passes through the life cycle, its impact is being felt as it moves in and out of the peak earning years.

The income phenomena described for the United States are not peculiar to this country. Population distributions of income are unequal in all countries, and recent increases in income inequality have been recorded in other developed nations. In less-developed parts of the world, income inequalities may be even greater than those observed in developed countries.

If one examines *wealth* instead of income, the pattern of population inequalities are similar. (*Household wealth* is defined as the estimated net worth of

TABLE 11.1 Share of Aggregate Income Received by Each Fifth of Households, by Race and Hispanic Origin: United States, 1970, 1980, and 1990

RACE/ETHNIC CATEGORY AND YEAR	TOTAL	PERCENT DISTRIBUTION OF AGGREGATE INCOME LOWEST FIFTH	SECOND FIFTH	THIRD FIFTH	FOURTH FIFTH	HIGHEST FIFTH	GINI RATIO
TOTAL							
1990	100.0	3.9	9.6	15.9	24.0	46.6	.428
1980	100.0	4.2	10.2	16.8	24.8	44.1	.403
1970	100.0	4.1	10.8	17.4	24.5	43.3	.394
WHITE							
1990	100.0	4.2	10.0	16.0	23.9	46.0	.419
1980	100.0	4.4	10.5	17.0	24.6	43.5	.394
1970	100.0	4.2	11.1	17.5	24.3	42.9	.387
BLACK							
1990	100.0	3.1	7.9	15.0	25.1	49.0	.464
1980	100.0	3.7	8.7	15.3	25.2	47.1	.439
1970	100.0	3.7	9.3	16.3	25.2	45.5	.422
HISPANIC*							
1990	100.0	4.0	9.5	15.9	24.3	46.3	.425
1980	100.0	4.3	10.1	16.4	24.8	44.5	.405
1972†	100.0	5.3	11.2	17.2	24.0	42.3	.373

* Persons of Hispanic origin may be of any race.

† Data for Hispanics not available prior to 1972.

Source: U.S. Bureau of the Census, "Money Income of Households, Families, and Persons in the United States: 1990." *Current Population Reports*, Series P-60, no. 174 (Washington, D.C.: Government Printing Office, 1991).

households based on the sum of the market value of assets owned by every member of the household minus secured or unsecured financial liabilities.)

Soltow (1989) determined that inequality of wealth in the United States was high in 1798 when only half of the male adults had any appreciable wealth and the Gini ratio was about .6 for those who did have wealth. Moreover, he finds that inequalities in wealth did not change significantly in the century prior to the Civil War.

In the United States in 1988, the distribution of net worth by income quintiles was very similar to the distribution of income by those same quintiles

(Eargle, 1990). One might have expected a greater disparity in the distribution of wealth because of the recognized holdings of persons with large incomes. Households in the lowest income quintile (which had about 4 percent of the aggregate income in 1990) were recorded as having about 7 percent of the aggregate wealth of households in the country. Households in the highest income quintile (which had about 47 percent of the aggregate income in 1990) had about 44 percent of the aggregate household wealth. The slightly lesser inequality of wealth than income is due to the fact that equity in one's home and motor vehicles were the biggest components of net worth, and the household disparity was not so great in those categories as it was for financial holdings.

Median net worth varied among race/ethnic categories to a considerable extent, and the differences were appreciable between younger and older ages. Both varied according to household types, as shown in Table 11.2. The largest median net worth was among households including a married couple whose head was at least 55 years old. Minority female-headed households were especially disadvantaged with regard to net worth, relative to both married couples in their race/ethnic category and whites of all household types. Hence, the other population compositional variables contribute greatly to overall race/ethnic differences in wealth. As population composition shifts over time, wealth disparities among population categories will also change.

Still another measure of level of living is the percent of the population regarded as in poverty. (*Poverty* is defined as having an income below a cutoff that varies by such factors as family size, sex of the family head, number of children under 18, and farm-nonfarm residence, and which has as its core an economy food plan.) In the United States as of 1991, about 14 percent of all persons were below the poverty line but there was considerable fluctuation by demographic categories, as shown in Table 11.3. The poverty rate was as low as 5.9 percent for white males 45 to 54 years of age and as high as 46.7 percent for black females under 18. Generally, the youngest and oldest persons in the population have poverty status. The chances of being in poverty also vary by family type; only 5.7 percent of married persons 35 to 54 years old with children under 18 are below the poverty line, while 33.0 percent of females living without a spouse and having children under 18 are so classified. Race/ethnic variations persist even for persons 35 to 44 with children under 18. Hispanic couples are twice as likely as black couples and almost four times as likely as white couples in that category to be in poverty. Among female-headed families with children under 18, almost half of such black and Hispanic women (but only one-quarter of white women) have poverty status.

Population change influences the national level of poverty. Shifts in age composition and family type will affect the overall risk of being below the poverty line. Since the chances of being in poverty are different for those living in inner cities, suburbs, and farm areas, population redistribution will affect the total poverty rate. Yet poverty is by no means confined to areas where poor people are highly concentrated. Sixty percent of persons in poverty live in central cities of metropolitan areas, whereas 27 percent are outside metropolitan

TABLE 11.2 Median Net Worth according to Type of Household, by Race and Hispanic Origin and by Age: United States, 1988

RACE/ETHNIC CATEGORY AND AGE	MARRIED-COUPLE HOUSEHOLDS	HOUSEHOLDS WITHOUT MARRIED COUPLES	
		MALE HEAD	FEMALE HEAD
TOTAL	$57,134	13,053	13,571
White	62,386	16,584	22,099
Black	17,635	1,457	757
Hispanic*	15,691	2,973	736
TOTAL	57,134	13,053	13,571
Under 35	12,041	4,959	1,378
35 to 54	60,611	17,055	10,945
55 to 64	120,158	34,722	40,796
65 and over	124,419	48,883	47,233

*Persons of Hispanic origin may be of any race.

Source: Judith Eargle, "Household Wealth and Asset Ownership: 1988," *Current Population Reports*, Series P-70, no. 22 (Washington, D.C.: Government Printing Office, 1990).

areas and over 13 percent live in suburbs. In fact, the proportion of the poor residing outside central cities has increased over time (Littman, 1991).

Still another set of economic conditions relates to one's *economic security* beyond having work and acquiring sufficient income and wealth. Because income and wealth are expendable and some persons spend them more completely than others, a critical issue is the extent to which the population is distributed with regard to savings, debt, insurance, social security, and other indicators of economic security throughout life. These factors are especially important during the later years when income is generally declining.

Since we are concerned here with population characteristics and demographic effects on the economic status of people rather than on economic analysis itself, we will not explore all of the dimensions of economic security. It is enough to say that increasing proportions of people over time in the United States have obtained life insurance (although the percentage is not high) and improved their life-style by increasing their debt (with the help of readily available credit mechanisms). Yet these practices vary considerably by population categories and are affected by the dynamics of changes in population phenomena.

With regard to savings, the population has experienced a significant decline in personal savings since the 1960s (quite apart from the decline in national savings and the increase in our national debt). Demographic factors do not appear to explain the drop in the savings rate during the 1980s; as a matter

TABLE 11.3 Percent of Persons in Poverty, by Age, Sex, and Race/Ethnic Status, and by Family Type for Persons 35 to 44 Years Old: United States, 1991

AGE, SEX, AND FAMILY TYPE	TOTAL	WHITE	BLACK	HISPANIC*
BOTH SEXES	14.2	11.3	32.7	28.7
Under 18	21.8	16.8	45.9	40.4
18 to 24	16.9	14.0	31.9	27.6
25 to 34	13.1	11.0	26.3	24.1
35 to 44	9.1	7.1	22.1	20.7
45 to 54	8.0	6.6	19.5	18.1
55 to 59	9.6	7.9	21.3	17.0
60 to 64	10.6	8.7	27.5	19.6
65 to 74	10.6	8.2	32.9	18.8
75 and over	15.0	13.3	35.3	24.3
MALE	12.3	9.8	28.5	26.2
Under 18	21.3	16.5	45.2	40.5
18 to 24	13.5	11.4	23.9	23.2
25 to 34	9.7	8.5	17.2	18.0
35 to 44	7.7	6.3	16.8	17.6
45 to 54	6.8	5.9	15.8	16.5
55 to 59	7.6	6.2	16.2	17.8
60 to 64	8.2	6.7	21.6	16.2
65 to 74	7.6	5.6	26.1	13.4
75 and over	8.5	7.0	24.6	19.3
FEMALE	16.0	12.7	36.5	31.2
Under 18	22.2	17.2	46.7	40.4
18 to 24	20.1	16.5	39.1	32.1
25 to 34	16.5	13.5	34.1	31.0
35 to 44	10.5	7.9	26.6	23.9
45 to 54	9.2	7.4	22.5	19.5
55 to 59	11.5	9.4	25.8	16.2
60 to 64	12.7	10.4	32.0	22.3
65 to 74	13.1	10.4	38.3	22.7
75 and over	18.9	17.0	40.8	27.4
35 TO 44 YEARS				
Married persons with children under 18	5.7	5.0	9.0	18.1
Female head with children under 18	33.0	25.7	48.1	48.1

*Persons of Hispanic origin may be of any race.

Source: U.S. Bureau of the Census, "Poverty in the United States: 1991." *Current Population Reports*, Series P-60, no. 181 (Washington, D.C.: Government Printing Office, 1992).

of fact, economists had mistakenly anticipated an increase in savings on the basis of our changing population patterns. Yet the future aging of the population should increase the savings rate appreciably over the next thirty years. The rate will then probably moderate for the following twenty years because of the succession of baby boomers and later smaller birth cohorts as they reach older ages (Auerbach and Kotlikoff, 1989).

The situation regarding *Social Security* is a concern to many people, partly because many have not understood how the system works and also because demographic change has played havoc with the system. The Social Security system in the United States, which was modeled after German pension systems in the earlier part of the century, is perhaps the most popular economic security system developed in the United States. In fact, the vast majority of the population depends on it for part of its old age security.

The U.S. Social Security system works through a payroll tax on workers providing proceeds for a trust fund that pays out Social Security pensions to qualified persons who reach retirement age. (There are also other elements in the system, such as medical and disability benefits, that we will not discuss here.) It is not an insurance program since you do not get back what you put in plus interest. Instead, people who are working provide the economic security for people who are retiring. It assumes that when the workers who are themselves paying will retire, younger workers will be paying into the system that will insure that the older workers can receive their benefits.

The system was first established in the 1930s and worked very effectively until recently because there were always more workers paying into the system than retirees looking to get benefits. Population dynamics has changed all that. The birth rate dropped, life expectancy increased, and the balance of workers and retirees started to get unfavorable. The size of the trust fund decreased for a while and the government had to modify the requirements of the system. Social Security payroll tax rates were raised, the age at which one can first expect benefits was scheduled to rise over time, and other adjustments were made to guarantee that the trust fund would be adequate for the expected number of retirees in the near future. (The inclusion of Medicare and Medicaid provisions in the Social Security law complicated the requirements; as a result, it has been necessary at times to negotiate shifts between the retirement trust fund and other funds set up for different provisions.) While baby boomers were in their prime working ages, the trust fund was able to expand, but that phenomenon will prove to be short-lived.

The longer-run solvency of the Social Security trust fund is still in question for two reasons: First, improvement in life expectancy at the older ages has exceeded what anyone had anticipated at an earlier time (producing more retirees); second, the baby boom cohort will soon reach retirement ages and greatly inflate the number of retirees at the same time as later smaller cohorts are asked to pay sufficient payroll taxes to maintain the trust fund. A further complication is that basic assumptions of the system about the state of the economy during the next few decades do not allow for economic recessions. Instead, they expect real wages to increase by a significant amount. Yet both of these assumptions have recently been violated and their recurrence cannot be considered certain. As a consequence of these developments, whereas people who worked and paid into the system in the 1940s and 1950s and retired have realized substantial benefits from the Social Security system relative to what was deducted from their earnings, the youngest working age groups today will probably get less in Social Security benefits than they are required to contribute through payroll taxes. What has seemed for a long time like a foolproof actuarial system seems to be coming apart in terms of its original design, principally because of unanticipated demographic changes (Longman, 1989).

ECONOMIC DEVELOPMENT

From a more global perspective, people often ask to what extent do population changes affect the economic development of a country. This issue is one that has persisted since Malthus' time, involving numerous scholars in a debate.

The generally accepted view of the 1950s and 1960s was that rapid population growth hindered economic development. This opinion was consistent with concepts about the early demographic transition that tied the two together. Since little empirical research had been done on the subject up to that time, scholars largely assumed this relationship on theoretical grounds.

Even after an increasing amount of research has been done on the topic, the conclusions of various studies are often in conflict. There are problems in defining economic development and deciding on its measurable indicators. Different studies have frequently employed alternative measures of the concept, including changes in per capita income and per capita gross national product. A question has also been raised about the measure of population change in the context of its relationship with economic development. Some have argued that the rate of population change is most appropriate, while others have opted for the rate of change based on natural increase or decrease, or on fertility alone. Furthermore, there is disagreement as to what other demographic or economic variables we need to include in the analysis.

In its 1984 annual report the World Bank indicated that it was still taking the traditional position that "population growth at the rapid rates common in most of the developing world slows development" and that "failure to address the problem will itself reduce the set of macroeconomic and sectoral policies that are possible, and permanently foreclose some long-run development options."

A report of the National Academy of Sciences (National Research Council, 1986) gave the findings of an expert panel on population and economic development. Panel members concluded that the impact of population growth on economic conditions has often been exaggerated, and that slower population growth was not likely to make much difference. At the same time the academy tempered its findings and underscored its uncertainty by stating: "On balance, we reach the qualitative conclusion that slower population growth would be beneficial to economic development for most developing countries."

Preston (1982) recognized the influence of population factors when joined with other factors, stating that "population growth is not so overwhelmingly negative a factor for economic advance as to swamp the impact of all other influences. That is a worthwhile lesson that bears repeating, but it is no argument for faster demographic growth." Kelley (1986) took a similar position, remarking that "prospects for development are not precluded by rapid population growth, but they are enhanced by slower growth rates. Neither alarmism nor total complacency about population growth can be supported by the current evidence."

Some analysts have not hedged on their view that population growth has a positive effect on economic development. Notable among these has been Simon (1981, 1992) who argued that technological progress was well served by population growth because more heads are better than fewer for generating new ideas, and because of economies of scale occurring when populations get larger. Boserup (1990) has also countered the Malthusian notion that population growth tends to outstrip the availability of food supply and hamper the economy by pointing out the contribution made by technological innovations (such as the one that led to rises in agricultural productivity like the so-called green revolution) and by infrastructural investments. Horlacher and MacKellar (1988), who acknowledge that "population growth may be an important, though not decisive, barrier to the economic progress of developing countries" also contend that it is "clear that population growth has not prevented the growth of per capita food production in the developing countries as a whole."

Bloom and Freeman (1987) make the point that "despite the unprecedented magnitude of population growth and the existence of imperfections in the labor markets, developing economies tended to shift between 1960 and 1980 from low-productivity agriculture to higher-productivity service and industrial sectors, and albeit with some exceptions, to raise real income per capita." But those researchers recognize that "the pessimists advance the view that rapid population growth hinders the growth of income per capita, thereby reducing rates of savings and investment, and resulting in mass underemployment, unemployment, and poverty. The optimists, on the other hand, stress the point that population growth can stimulate both technological change and the adoption of techniques that realize economies of scale, and therefore promote economic growth." Bloom and Freeman's reaction is that "these alternative views are overly simplistic."

According to Bloom and Freeman, each of the basic components of population change will affect economic conditions differently. With regard to labor supply, the effect of population growth will result after a time lag whose length depends on the reasons for the underlying growth. If the growth was due primarily to net in-migration, then the labor force will be affected immediately because a sizable part of the migration will be composed of people who are already of working ages. If acceleration of population growth results mainly from an increase in fertility, it will take ten to fifteen years before the births reach working ages and twenty to twenty-five years before they are of prime working ages. Age structure is a critical intervening factor in the population-development relationship. However, mortality decline and fertility decrease can influence the working force directly as well through "behavioral" effects, such as a rising level of women's participation in the labor force and the deferred entry of workers into the labor force because of rising educational expectations.

Population growth can also affect a variety of economic development components differently. For example, even if population growth can affect the growth of average income, its effect on income inequality and other welfare functions may not be the same (King et al., 1974). Moreover, population growth largely in rural areas will not lead to the development of industry or high-technology enterprises, whereas rapid urbanization may engender more economic diversification and spawn increases in the service sector of the economy.

Blanchet (1991) makes the point that optimists and pessimists support their respective interpretations of the population-development relationship by accepting only underlying assumptions consistent with their beliefs. In fact, he argues, the relationship is complicated by numerous interactions of factors—population change in its transitional, cyclical (he calls it *shocks*), and random variations; age compositional and other derivative demographic changes; economic development in its various forms; and all of them playing back and forth in their influences. As a result, whether there exists or does not exist a causal association between population change and economic development probably depends on what stage of the transition we are examining and the extent and nature of the feedbacks. If so, no simple generalization about the association is warranted.

Most of the controversy surrounding this topic has concerned itself with developing nations and the question about the need to see high rates of population growth slow down so that economic growth can take place. But the same debate goes on when we consider developed nations. Here the issue is whether a slow rate of population growth, common to posttransition countries, inhibits further economic development. A series of analyses addressing that issue has not reached a definitive position (e.g., Espenshade and Serow, 1978). One could, however, make an argument that applies equally to developing and developed countries, namely, that the *pace* of population change is crucial in its effects on economic change. If demographic changes are so gradual that economic institutions have sufficient time to respond to them and adjust their course, then improved economic circumstances might follow. If, on the other hand, demographic change is sharp (as in the case of some cycles or population "shocks" to the system, such as the baby boom or unanticipated heavy immigration flows), then the society may be ill prepared to alter the economy in ways that will maintain or improve the country's economic status. This perspective suggests that the linkage between population and economic changes are shaped as much by public and private economic interventions (such as job programs, better regulation of employment practices, and adjustments to Social

Security and welfare systems) as by the normal course of social institutional processes. (We will say more about this matter in Chapter 14.)

BUSINESSES AND MARKETS

Demographic information has become a vital aspect of the planning done by commercial enterprises to improve the climate for their products and services. This component of the economic system has increased efficiency in business activities by using demographic data (which business executives usually refer to as *demographics*) both to estimate and find the people they are trying to reach and to adapt their activities to the markets in which they operate. More specifically, demographic data and expertise are being applied to develop consumer profiles, determine site selection for business locations, identify market areas in ways helping to focus on the geographic distribution of clients, achieve more precision in making demand and sales forecasts, and approximate the share of the market that a given company has in relation to its competitors (Pol, 1987).

Publications oriented to commercial and industrial firms and professional business groups provide numerous examples of particular applications of population information to business planning. The population cycle of baby boomers have been called "a marketer's dream" because of their large numbers and their fairly homogeneous outlook that stresses "quality and value rather than indulgence and luxury" (Russell, 1991). However, businesses are cautioned that the baby boomers are moving through the life cycle and their household composition and outlook can change as they reach older ages.

Migration patterns are seen as restructuring population composition and characteristics and thereby altering the demand for hospital and physician services and supplies (Kinstler and Pol, 1990). Companies aware of these effects can better adapt their activities to meet the new demand. The health situation of the elderly, which becomes a greater concern as that segment of the population increases its relative size, can be specified more clearly through demographic information in order to better meet the needs of particular subgroups (Pol, May, and Hartranft, 1992). Distinguishing among the young-old and old-old as well as their marital, work, and health statuses helps to pinpoint the required products and services.

The movement of increasing numbers of blacks to suburban locations (that is, the movement of the group of blacks whose level of living has improved in recent years) is observed in metropolitan areas across the United States, especially in medium-sized southern areas (O'Hare and Frey, 1992). Because their taste profiles vary to some degree from those of other groups, commercial organizations have a new market target. Population change is also seen to have an impact on the stock market (Dunn, 1992). Financial analysts dealing with Wall Street now pay more attention to demographic dynamics, both because it aids them in anticipating turns in the economy itself and because it assists in predicting the relative attractiveness of different kinds of stocks.

Examining demographics is only part of the way that business demography has advanced the successes of many commercial enterprises. Broader understanding of population change and, in particular, the utilization of "dynamic models of population" have been heralded as necessary in market planning (Pol, 1986).

Additionally, the demographic perspective has become a tool for directing proactive campaigns to include more women and minorities in business organizations (Sekaran and Leong, 1992). Such a movement that recognizes the combination of population and social change, it is argued, benefits both women and minority groups on the one hand and businesses on the other.

Chapter Highlights

1. Population change can affect several aspects of the economy, including levels and trends of the work force, levels of living, national and regional economic development, and business activity.
2. The work force is now described universally in terms of the labor force or economically active population. The labor force is composed of the currently employed (regardless of the amount and kind of work) and the unemployed (those out of work but looking for work). Excluding some categories of people who are incapable of working, such as the very young and the very old, the remaining population is regarded as "not in the labor force."
3. The employed can be differentiated by such dimensions as part-week work and part-year work (that is, the underemployed) as well as the mismatch of work qualifications with the kind of work actually performed. We can also differentiate the unemployed by the length of their unemployment (e.g., transitory or chronic).
4. Populations tend to be socially stratified, as indicated by inequalities in various measures of level of living, such as income, wealth, poverty, and social security. Historical trends of these indicators in the United States reveal very small changes in these demographic inequalities over time.
5. Whether or not population change influences the economic development of a nation and how it does so is an issue complicated by the mutual interaction of the two conditions. The relationship may be different for developing and developed parts of the world as well. While population change may or may not be linked to economic development, gradual rather than sharp changes in population factors are probably more compatible with orderly economic change. Because so many variables can have an impact on the health of an economy, it is likely that economic change in developed countries is more responsive to nondemographic than to demographic factors.
6. The fact remains that trends and cycles in mortality, fertility, and mobility, as well as in population composition and distribution, can potentially alter economic conditions.

7. Businesses and markets are especially influenced by population factors because these economic phenomena are often keyed to particular segments of the population. Such population phenomena as the baby boom, the aging of the population, and the changing participation of women in the labor force have been seen as critical in reshaping the commercial world.

Discussion Questions

1. What criteria would you establish for determining whether or not certain work activities are included in the official definition of the labor force? In particular, should maintaining the home (e.g., cooking, cleaning, yardwork) and caring for children in one's own home be counted as labor force activity?
2. As you look at Figure 11.1, which elements, if any, of the schematic classification of working status would you regard as questionable? What changes would you make in the classification to better reflect what is important about working conditions in a society, and why?
3. Differentials in income and wealth and the existence of a poverty class seem to be persistent features of societies. Is there a population change scenario that you believe would alter these economic patterns in the population significantly? What would that be?
4. Countries in the high population growth stage of the demographic transition generally have difficulty in bringing about economic development. Yet economic development can also be absent or stymied in nations going through the low population growth stage of the transition. Does this mean that demographic change has no impact on economic development. If so, why?
5. If you were a demographic adviser to the president of a small business enterprise, what advice would you offer her or him with regard to how to improve the success of the business?

Suggested Readings

Crawford, Everett, and Carol J. Romero. 1991. *A Changing Nation—Its Changing Labor Force.* Research Report no. 91–04. Washington, D.C.: National Commission for Employment Policy. Examines the diversity of labor supply both among and within categories of the population.

Nuss, Shirley, Ettore Denti, and David Viry. 1989. *Women in the World of Work.* Women, Work, and Development Series no. 18. Geneva: International Labour Office. An analysis of the trends since 1950 in women's participation in the labor force worldwide, with separate attention to the different regions of the world.

Summers, Lawrence H. 1990. *Understanding Unemployment.* Cambridge, Mass.: MIT Press. An intensive exploration into the many facets of unemployment, including aspects of concepts and measurement as well as the factors associated with cyclical and structural forms of unemployment.

Simmons, Ozzie G. 1988. *Perspectives on Development and Population Growth in the Third World.* New York: Plenum Press. A good overview of the interrelationships between demographic change and the challenge to less-developed countries of advancing their nations economically and socially.

Osberg, Lars, ed. 1991. *Economic Inequality and Poverty: International Perspectives.* Armonk, N.Y.: M.E. Sharpe. Focuses on the measurement of economic phenomena and compares countries around the world in terms of income and wealth inequalities and poverty.

References

Auerbach, Alan J., and Laurence J. Kotlikoff. *Demographics, Fiscal Policy, and U.S. Saving in the 1980's and Beyond.* NBER Working Paper Series no. 3150. Cambridge, Mass.: National Bureau of Economic Research.

Blanchet, Didier. 1991. "On Interpreting Observed Relationships between Population Growth and Economic Growth: A Graphical Explanation." *Population and Developent Review* 17:1, 105–14.

Bloom, David E., and Richard B. Freeman. 1987. "Population Growth, Labor Supply, and Employment in Developing Countries." In D. Gale Johnson and Ronald D. Lee, eds., *Population Growth and Economic Development: Issues and Evidence*, pp. 105–47. Madison, Wis.: University of Wisconsin Press.

Boserup, Ester. 1990. *Economic and Demographic Relationships in Development.* Baltimore: Johns Hopkins University Press.

Brinkmann, Christian. 1987. *Demographic Aspects of the Labour Force and Employment.* Strasbourg: Council of Europe.

Dunn, William. 1992. "The Demographics of Wall Street." *American Demographics* 14:7, 42–46.

Eargle, Judith. 1990. "Household Wealth and Asset Ownership: 1988." *Current Population Reports*, Series P-70, no. 22 (Washington, D.C.: Government Printing Office).

Espenshade, Thomas J., and William J. Serow. 1978. *The Economic Consequences of Slowing Population Growth.* San Diego, Calif.: Academic Press.

Flaim, Paul O. 1990. "Population Changes, the Baby Boom, and the Unemployment Rate." *Monthly Labor Review* (August): 3–10.

Fullerton, Howard N., Jr. 1991. "Labor Force Projections: The Baby Boom Moves On." *Monthly Labor Review* (November): 31–44.

Greenhalgh, Susan. 1991. "Women in the Informal Enterprise: Empowerment or Exploitation?" *Population Council Working Papers*, no. 33.

Horlacher, David E., and F. Landis MacKellar. 1988. "Population Growth versus Economic Growth (?)." In Dominick Salvatore, ed., *World Population Trends and Their Impact on Economic Development*, pp. 25–44. Westport, Conn.: Greenwood Press.

Kelley, Allan C. 1986. "Review of National Research Council, Population Growth and Economic Development: Policy Questions." *Population and Development Review* 12: 563–68.

King, Timothy, Roberto Cuca, Ravi Gulhati, Monowar Hossain, Ernest Stern, Pravin Visaria, K.C. Zachariah, and Gregory Zafros. 1974. *Population Policies and Economic Development.* Baltimore: Johns Hopkins University Press.

Kinstler, Steven B., and Louis G. Pol. 1990. "The Marketing Implications of Migration on Hospital and Physician Supply and Demand in the United States." *Journal of Hospital Marketing* 4:1, 119–41.

Lamison-White, Leatha. 1992. "Income, Poverty, and Wealth in the United States: A Chart Book." *Current Population Reports*, Series P-60, no. 179 (Washington, D.C.: Government Printing Office).

Littman, Mark S. 1991. "Poverty Areas and the "Underclass": Untangling the Web." *Monthly Labor Review* 114:3, 19–32.

Longman, Phillip. 1989. "Social Security and the Baby Boom Generation." *Journal of Aging & Social Policy* 1:1, 2, 131–53.

Lumsdaine, Robin L., and David A. Wise. 1990. *NBER Working Paper Series*, no. 3420. Cambridge, Mass.: National Bureau of Economic Research.

National Research Council. 1986. *Population Growth and Economic Development: Policy Questions.* Washington, D.C.: National Academy Press.

O'Hare, William P., and William H. Frey. 1992. "Booming, Suburban, and Black." *American Demographics* 14:9, 30–38.

Pol, Louis G. 1986. "Marketing and the Demographic Perspective." *Journal of Consumer Marketing* 3:1, 57–65.

———. 1987. *Business Demography.* New York: Quorum Books.

———, Michael G. May, and Frank R. Hartranft. 1992. "Eight Stages of Aging." *American Demographics* 14:8, 54–60.

Preston, Samuel H. 1982. "Review of Julian Simon: The Ultimate Resource." *Population and Development Review* 8, 176–77.

Russell, Cheryl. 1991. "On the Baby-Boom Bandwagon." *American Demographics* 13:5, 24–31.

Salvatore, Dominick, ed. 1988. *World Population Trends and Their Impact on Economic Development.* Westport, Conn.: Greenwood Press.

Sekaran, Uma, and Frederick T. L. Leong. 1992. "Summary, Recommendations, and Conclusion." In Uma Sekaran and Frederick T. L. Leong, *Womanpower: Managing in Times of Demographic Turbulence*, pp. 252–59. Newbury Park, Calif.: Sage Publications.

Shank, Susan E. 1988. "Women and the Labor Market: The Link Grows Stronger." *Monthly Labor Review* (March): 3–8.

Simmons, Ozzie G. 1988. *Perspectives on Development and Population Growth in the Third World.* New York: Plenum Publishing.

Simon, Julian L. 1981. *The Ultimate Resource.* Princeton, N.J.: Princeton University Press.

———. 1992. *Population and Development in Poor Countries.* Princeton, N.J.: Princeton University Press.

Soltow, Lee. 1989. *Distribution of Wealth and Income in the United States in 1798*. Pittsburgh: University of Pittsburgh Press.

Srinivasan, T. N. 1987. "Population and Food." In D. Gale Johnson and Ronald D. Lee, eds., *Population Growth and Economic Development: Issues and Evidence*, pp. 3–26. Madison, Wis.: University of Wisconsin Press.

U.S. Bureau of Labor Statistics. 1992. *Employment and Earnings* 39:5 (Washington, D.C.: U.S. Government Printing Office).

U.S. Bureau of the Census. 1991. "Money Income of Households, Families, and Persons in the United States: 1990." *Current Population Reports*, Series P-60, no. 174. (Washington, D.C.: Government Printing Office).

World Bank. 1984. *World Development Report*. Washington, D.C.: World Bank.

12. Religious and Political Systems

In Chapters 9 through 11, we reviewed various ways in which three social institutional areas—families and households, education, and the economy—are influenced by changes in various aspects of population. It was made clear that all those areas are subject to modification by transitions, cycles, and irregular fluctuations in mortality, fertility, and mobility as well as by changes in population distribution and population composition.

We will now turn our attention to two more social institutional forms—religion and the polity. As in the case of families and households, education, and the economy, we can examine from two directions the relationships between religion and the polity, on the one hand, and population, on the other hand. Let me explain what I mean by the statement that these relationships involve influences that run in two directions. For example, it is obvious that social conditions and change have affected the dynamics of mortality, fertility, and mobility trends as well as population redistribution and the changing composition of population. But it is also true that population variables, in turn, have contributed to changes in social conditions.

First of all, we will focus on the effects of population variables on religious composition and dynamics. Next, we will take up the ways in which population variables affect political representation, electoral behavior, and the political world order.

RELIGIOUS DISTRIBUTION

Because religion is such a critical part of every society's social landscape, it is of interest to know the geographical distribution of religious groups as well as the extent to which these groups are represented in different populations.

Earlier in the book (in Chapter 8), we regarded religion as one aspect of ethnicity. In fact, religion and nationality are often intertwined because of the tendency of some religious groups to be located primarily within certain geographical areas. Thus the ethnic backgrounds of people are generally mixtures that reflect both their religious and geographical origins as well as the languages they speak and other cultural factors in their lives.

How we define religion in a demographic context is a debatable issue. Religion can be viewed in terms of membership in a religious body, personal identification with a religion, preference for a religious orientation, or degree of devoutness and belief in certain religious tenets. People may identify with a religion even though they are not members of the group or do not participate in its activities. Likewise, persons may state a preference for a religion that is not in their background or is not their present affiliation. People who are not formally members of a religious group may still identify with, or state a preference for, that religion, or they may indicate no identification with, or preference for, any religious group.

As in other areas of population analysis, our definitions of religion are governed to some extent by available data. Membership data are accessible for most religious categories, but are rarely combined with information about the demographic characteristics of individual members. Data on devoutness and belief are generally regarded as beyond the scope of demographic analysis. Although preference and identification are seen to be highly correlated, both are used in demographic research. A typical question to elicit responses on *religious identification* is "What is your (his or her) religion?" A question on *religious preference* usually takes the form of "What is your (his or her) religious preference?" The next question will often be "What specific denomination is that, if any?" The U.S. Bureau of the Census used the identification question in its current Population Survey in 1957, and the preference question has been used in regular General Social Surveys in the United States by the National Opinion Research Center. Membership data are collected by specific religious organizations and are reported periodically by the National Council of Churches of Christ of America, the Roman Catholic Church, and other religious organizations (Bogue, 1985). Data for the Jewish population in the United States are gathered at various times through a privately conducted national sample survey and through Jewish community studies.

Data on religion are collected in a majority of national population censuses around the world, including those of Canada. In years ending in 6 through 1936 the United States conducted a separate Census of Religious Bodies that focused on *aggregate institutional* data. Because of the principle of separation of church and state, the United States has never included a question about religion on its population censuses (Foster, 1961; Petersen, 1962).

It is difficult to assemble data on the world's religious composition and distribution because of the unevenness of reporting of such information. Carey (1792) estimated that 57 percent of the world's population in 1790 were "Pagans"; 24 percent were Christians (of whom 14 percent were Catholics, 6 percent Protestants, and 4 percent adherents to various Eastern Orthodox churches); 18 percent were Muslims; and 1 percent were Jews. Sopher (1967) estimated that the comparable numbers in 1963 were 47 percent for "Pagans" (down about 10 percent); 30 percent for Christians (up about 6 percent, more for Catholics than for Protestants); 14 percent for Muslims (down about 4 percent); 0.4 percent for Jews (down half of 1 percent), and over 8 percent for others (mostly persons of Christian origin). In the next section of this chapter, we will speculate about subsequent changes in world religious composition based on an examination of the demographic dynamics of the various groups.

The religious composition of the United States is quite different from that for the world as a whole, both because of more universal identification with some religious group and because of fewer religious groups with any great numbers. In 1980, over 64 percent of persons in the United States stated a Protestant religious preference, 25 percent a Roman Catholic preference, over 2 percent a Jewish preference, over 1 percent other religious preferences, and 7 percent no preference. (A question on identification results in very similar distributions.) Among the Protestants, a Baptist preference was mentioned by 22 percent, Methodist by 13 percent, Lutheran by 8 percent, Presbyterian by 5 percent, Episcopal-Anglican by nearly 3 percent, and other Protestant groups by 13 percent (Bogue, 1985).

There is a disparate geographic distribution of these religious categories in the country. Table 12.1 shows both the regional distribution of the religious groups and the religious composition of each region. (The regions are actually the standard geographic divisions outlined by the U.S. Bureau of the Census.) Looking first at the regional distributions of religious categories, Baptists are heavily concentrated in the South (especially the South Atlantic area). Lutherans (who often have Scandinavian roots) are most likely to be found in the North Central area. Methodists are most overrepresented in the South Atlantic division. Presbyterians are most apt to be located in the Mid-Atlantic area, as is the Episcopal-Anglican group, which is also overrepresented in the New England area. Other Protestants are distributed more like the total population than any other group. Catholics are most concentrated in the New England and Mid-Altantic divisions, Jews in the Mid-Atlantic area also, and other religious groups on both coasts (Mid-Atlantic and Pacific regions). While there are some overlaps in religious concentrations, it is also the case that each group has its unique distributional pattern.

Looking next at which religious categories most dominate each geographic region, we find that 55 percent of New Englanders are Catholics, 40 percent of those residing in the Mid-Atlantic division are Catholics as well, 52 percent of those living in the South Atlantic division are Baptists, and 38 percent of residents of the Mountain area are other Protestants (in this case, mostly Mormons). Bradley et al. (1992) did an extensive analysis of the religious composition of 2,973 counties or county equivalents in the United States. They found that Baptists predominated in 1,322 of them, Catholics in 959, Lutherans in 266, Methodists in 249, Latter-Day Saints (Mormons) in 83, and Christian Church adherents in 54. Presbyterians were dominant in only 5 counties, Jews in only 2, and Episcopalians in only 1.

The location of persons in various religious groups is mainly a consequence of where each group's forebears first settled in the United States. The heavy concentration of Roman Catholics and Jews on the East Coast reflects the streams of immigration from parts of Europe in the late nineteenth and

TABLE 12.1 Geography of Religious Preference in the United States: 1977

Religion	Total	New England Region	Middle Atlantic Region	E.-N. Central Region	W.-N. Central Region	South Atlantic Region	E.-S. Central Region	W.-S. Central Region	Mountain Region	Pacific Region
DISTRIBUTION OF RELIGIONS										
TOTAL	100.0%	4.5%	17.2%	21.2%	7.5%	18.5%	5.9%	8.4%	4.2%	12.7%
Protestant	100.0	2.2	11.9	20.5	8.0	24.0	8.4	9.4	4.3	11.3
Baptist	100.0	1.6	6.2	13.8	4.7	36.6	13.5	14.1	2.0	7.5
Lutheran	100.0	1.2	18.8	37.1	18.3	7.2	1.0	3.7	3.8	8.9
Methodist	100.0	1.5	10.1	22.7	8.7	28.9	7.8	8.0	3.9	8.5
Presbyterian	100.0	2.3	23.1	19.3	9.3	19.1	4.9	4.9	3.9	13.2
Episc.-Angl.	100.0	7.8	27.3	10.2	2.7	19.0	4.1	6.1	7.1	15.8
Other Prot.	100.0	3.3	12.4	20.7	7.9	14.8	8.3	9.3	7.6	15.8
Roman Cath.	100.0	10.0	27.2	24.4	6.8	7.2	1.0	7.7	3.6	12.1
Jewish	100.0	5.7	52.0	10.9	3.8	9.0	1.4	2.5	0.5	14.2
Other religions	100.0	5.7	23.9	21.5	1.9	11.0	0.5	3.3	5.7	26.4
No religion	100.0	5.9	16.8	19.0	6.8	12.7	3.7	4.4	6.2	24.5
COMPOSITION OF REGIONS										
TOTAL	100.0	100.0	100.0	100.0	100.0	100.0	100.0	100.0	100.0	100.0
Protestant	64.4	31.4	44.6	62.3	69.2	83.6	90.9	72.2	65.8	57.3
Baptist	34.8	25.8	17.7	23.7	20.1	51.6	54.5	51.6	17.1	25.1
Lutheran	13.0	7.2	20.3	23.8	29.0	3.8	1.5	5.0	12.0	11.1
Methodist	19.7	13.4	16.5	22.0	20.9	23.0	17.7	16.6	18.4	16.1
Presbyterian	7.5	7.7	14.3	7.1	8.5	5.8	4.3	3.9	7.1	9.6
Episc.-Angl.	4.3	15.3	9.8	2.2	1.4	3.3	2.1	2.8	7.4	6.6
Other Prot.	20.7	30.6	21.3	21.2	20.0	12.4	20.0	20.2	38.0	31.6
Roman Cath.	25.0	55.0	39.7	28.9	22.9	9.7	4.1	22.9	21.8	23.8
Jewish	2.4	3.0	7.2	1.2	1.2	1.1	0.5	0.7	0.3	2.6
Other religions	1.3	1.7	1.9	1.4	0.3	0.8	0.1	0.5	1.9	2.8
No religion	6.9	8.9	6.7	6.2	6.3	4.7	4.3	3.6	10.2	13.4

Source: Donald J. Bogue, *The Population of the United States* (New York: Free Press, 1985), Table 18.6 (based on data from the National Opinion Research Center General Social Survey).

early twentieth centuries. The density of Catholic population along the southwest border results largely from the Mexican-American immigration. Concentrations of other religious categories in coastal or border sections of the country can also be ascribed to previous mobility to the United States by earlier generations. The fact, however, that there is a substantial mix of religious categories in most parts of the country is due to a considerable amount of internal migration and mobility as well as to other demographic processes and both religious conversions and defections.

DEMOGRAPHY OF RELIGION

Put in a broader context, changes in the size of a religious group will depend on several factors, among which are (1) the marriage and fertility patterns of the group, (2) its mortality patterns, (3) net migration of adherents, (4) additions to the group through baptism or conversion, and (5) losses from the group through conversion or withdrawal (Nam, 1968). The relative size of any religious category is a consequence of the net effect of these factors for this group as compared to all other groups. Thus we have again the situation of the population balancing equation of pluses and minuses, with the added element of changes in religious adherence from one category to another.

Zelinsky (1992) asserts:

> Although information is scanty, it seems that differential fertility and mortality are of relatively minor consequence in accounting for the size or distribution of religious groups. It is their spatial movements and success in attracting new members and holding old ones that are most critical.

According to Sopher (1967),

> Christian population migrations have made dramatic changes on the map of world religions.... Mainly in this way, Christianity has become dominant in almost all of North America, Brazil, and extratropical South America, Australia, and New Zealand, in the South African areas settled by the Boers, and in the Siberian and Far Eastern lands settled by Russians of the Orthodox Church.

Redekop (1989) describes the migrations of Mennonite religious sects from different parts of Europe to the United States and their dispersion within the country after their arrival. Leaving European countries mainly to escape religious persecution, they expanded their numbers after coming to the United States through missionary work and subsequent conversions and through a high rate of reproduction. Some Mennonite groups have shunned attempts to convert others. The Hutterites and Old Order Amish have grown rapidly in size because of a large excess of births over deaths and a low defection rate. Other Mennonite groups have practised evangelism but have also lost substantial numbers of members through defections. Where these groups have increased their numbers appreciably, new colonies have been formed because of the determination to keep the size of colonies small so that their members can maintain an integrative style of life. The Hutterites have expanded their colonies in both the North Central United States and southwest Canada (Hostetler, 1974). Yet there are limits to growth that the Mennonites will have to face as their numbers continue to rise and available land becomes more scarce.

The fact that one-fourth of the U.S. population is Roman Catholic is due to the large immigrations of the mid- and late-nineteenth and early-twentieth centuries from European countries, to the subsequent movements into the country from Puerto Rico, Mexico, Cuba, and other Latin American areas, and to higher than average reproductive performance of these groups for many decades after their arrival.

In 1912, the most Reverend Regis Canevin, the Catholic bishop of Pittsburgh, was startled by "so many conflicting statements about the leakages and losses of the Catholic Church in this country that a careful inquiry into the historical facts and statistical proofs on which such statements are based ought to be made...." By employing a demographic perspective, Canevin (1912) deciphered the pattern of Catholic population changes and determined its extent. He recognized that some Catholic immigrants died within a short time of their arrival in the United States, and that some returned to their native lands after a period of time, but he also acknowledged the births (baptisms) that took place as well as conversions to the Catholic faith and set about to balance these factors in a demographic equation for the period from 1790 to 1910. He summed up his findings by illustrating that whatever losses to the church there may have been through death, emigration, and religious withdrawal were more than made up for by births, immigration, and religious conversion.

The *Official Catholic Directory* (1990) reports that the increase in Catholic population in the United States between 1980 and 1990 of over 7 million was due primarily to the immigration of Catholics, but it was also due, in part, to an excess of baptisms over deaths (of over half a million). Greeley (1989) indicates that the defection rate of Catholics (the percent of cohorts at age 16 who were no longer members of the church) was 16 percent in 1985, about the same as for Jews but higher than for Protestants. However, the net loss was only 2 percent because of conversions to the faith. The percent of Catholics who married non-Catholics in 1985 was about 21 percent, and that rate had not changed much since 1972. The various components of religious change for Catholics result in a substantial increase in absolute numbers but very little change in relative numbers in the U.S. population because non-Catholics are growing at comparable levels. Greeley finds this not surprising since there is a high percentage of individuals who are affiliated at present with the religious denomination in which they were raised.

While most religious groups sustain their numbers at a level that allows them to be viable, some groups that are declining numerically as well as relatively have expressed concern about their futures. A case in point is the Jewish population, whose worldwide numbers were diminished considerably by mortality during World War II. In 1990 there were 12.8 million Jews in the world, heavily concentrated in a few nations. Forty-three percent were in the United States and 31 percent in Israel (Schmelz and Della Pergola, 1992).

American Jewry has been said to be "progressively weakened demographically as a result of low fertility, high intermarriage, significant dispersion, and assimilatory losses" (Goldstein, 1992). Evidence from the National Jewish Population Survey of 1990 in the United States reveals that this is indeed true, and that the "demographic base of the Jewish population seems to have reached a plateau and may well decline in future years." But there is still a sizable number of Jews in the country, and the issue of who is a Jew and whether or not proselytizing should become a policy of the religion can affect the size of the Jewish population. Traditionally, a person is a Jew whose mother was Jewish or who became a Jew through conversion. The National Jewish Population Survey in 1990 identified as Jews those persons who were not Jews but lived in households with persons who were identified as Jews traditionally, since the former were likely to respect many Jewish religious and cultural practices. Some Jewish groups have considered active missionary work to recruit Jews.

While religion remains a critical characteristic of populations around the world, the relative size and growth patterns of each category vary as a result of the net effect of the several components of population change combined with switches in religious identification.

POLITICAL REPRESENTATION

Another social institution whose patterns can be linked to population change is the polity. Various aspects of political and governmental structures are influenced by the size, distribution, composition, and characteristics of population. In this section we will examine relationships between population factors and the size of governments, the representativeness of governments, and the ability of governments to function properly.

Weiner (1971) reminds us that, although the density of population of some European states in the late eighteenth and early nineteenth centuries was high, the size of the states by modern standards was quite small and thus governmentally manageable. In contrast, the populations of the most populous countries today approach or exceed 1 billion people, and many have at least 50 million or more. One consequence of population size, he points out, is that it creates special problems in the relationship between central and subordinate units of government. Plato and Aristotle wrestled with these problems in structuring their ideal city-states, but they only had to consider the political management of relatively small populations. Where countries have achieved large sizes, several layers of administrative hierarchy develop. Inevitably, there will be tensions among different governing units, in part because they represent different geographic areas which are often reflective of varying population characteristics and in part because the sheer number of governing units makes coordination of governments and their decision making difficult.

In all countries that have representative government, the determination of how the representatives are selected has been controversial. The U.S. Constitution provided for a population-based representative government in the same section that mandated a decennial census to provide a basis for determining the selection of representatives. The Constitution did not specify, however, how the apportionment was to be carried out (Poston, 1990). The controversial nature of the means to apportion is indicated by the fact that the first of the proposed amendments to the Constitution, prior to the ten amendments known as the Bill of Rights (which were subsequently passed), dealt with procedures for apportioning the Congress. Because a majority of state legislatures defeated that amendment in the ratification process, it did not appear as an adjunct to the Constitution. Instead, a series of methods for apportioning the House of Representatives have been tried during the history of the United States. There was considerable quibbling from the start about how many seats there should be in the House and how many people each Representative should represent; initial proposals by Jefferson and Hamilton about these points were turned down. Eventually, an alternative plan by Jefferson won favor. Called the *method of rejected fractions*, it divided each state's population by 33,000 and awarded each state a number of Representatives equal to the whole numbers in the quotient (the fractional balance being dropped or rejected). The Webster Plan (named after Daniel Webster) was instituted in 1832 but used only once. It responded to the concern that the existing plan discriminated against small states. Webster's adjustment gave a state an additional seat if the remaining fraction was at least a half. The Jefferson and Webster plans resulted in an enlarged House each decade as the population of the country increased. The Vinton Plan (named for an Ohio congressman) was used from 1850 through 1900. It fixed the number of House members, assigned quotas to each state on that basis, and devised a scheme for allocating the balance of population not represented in the quotas to the states with the largest fractions of a quota remaining. A more refined and complex version of the Vinton Plan, called the *major fractions method* (developed by Walter Willcox, a demographer) was used in 1910. This method overcame some of the arbitrariness of the Vinton Plan in allocating remaining seats, but it still did not sit well with persons who thought it did not conform to the intent of equality of population by Congressional districts.

In 1929, a committee appointed by the National Academy of Sciences devised a new plan, called the *method of equal proportions*, which was instituted in 1940 and is still in force today. It first assigns each state one seat and then allocates the remaining seats according to a formula that gives priority for each subsequent seat to the state with the greatest population claim to that seat. As with all the methods, there is controversy about assignment of the final seats, partly because different approaches to apportionment can alter the process of assigning those seats and partly because states whose populations are undercounted in the census more than others are disadvantaged when those last seats are awarded. In recent years a debate has ensued about whether or not to adjust the census counts for underenumeration and thereby correct population figures used in the apportionment as well as in revenue distributions to the states. The courts have not yet supported the use of census adjustments in order to determine apportionment populations.

Each state in the United States is entitled to two Senators, so there is no competition between states for these delegates, regardless of population size of each state. But there is now a fixed number of members of the House of Representatives (435) which the states must compete for under the apportionment procedures. Because states are changing in population size at different rates, they are relatively advantaged or disadvantaged in the competition. Just growing in size is not enough to maintain the number of Representatives, much less to increase that number. The states that have rapid growth stand to gain seats in the House at the expense of states that are growing more slowly.

In the period 1950 to 1990, while the U.S. population was increasing by almost 100 million people or about 65 percent, some states added or dropped a few seats in the House while other added or dropped larger numbers of seats. Montana, which had 2 of the 435 seats in 1950, was reduced to 1 seat in 1990. Alabama had 9 seats in 1950 but only 7 seats in 1990. Georgia picked up 1 seat (from 10 to 11) during the 1980–1990 period. The state of Massachusetts lost 4 seats (from 14 to 10). Pennsylvania dropped 8 seats (from 30 to 21), while New York had as many as 43 seats in 1950 but only 31 in 1990. The big gainers were Texas (up from 22 in 1950 to 30 in 1990), Florida (up from 8 to 23), and California (rising from 30 to 52 seats). In general, the states that lost in the competition were northern industrial areas whose populations were growing more slowly; the states that gained in the competition were in the Sun Belt area that had experienced greater population increases.

Apart from the issue of how many seats in the House of Representatives each state qualifies for, there is the matter of how many people each Representative serves and his or her ability to serve them well. Population growth has been crucial to this matter because the size of the House has been set at 435 since 1910 on the grounds that it would be unmanageable to organize and conduct a larger body of Representatives. As a consequence, we have the situation depicted in Table 12.2.

In 1790, with the national population about 4 million and with a House of 106 members and a Senate of 32 members, the average Representative served 37,100 people and the average Senator served 245,600 constituents. By 1990, the average Representative served almost a quarter of a million people and the average Senator served about 5 million. Of course, there have been some variations in representation among House members because district lines within states have not always been drawn in a fashion that led to equal numbers within the congressional districts, and the populations of the states have varied in size so that some Senators represented smaller numbers than did others. In fact, a Senator from California in 1990 served almost 30 million people while a Senator from Wyoming served less than a half million people.

The population dynamics of national political representation is further complicated by the changing characteristics of the constituents. As people relocate within governed areas and as the population composition of areas changes, Representatives and Senators are expected to serve mixes of people whose needs may be different than those of mixes at earlier times. Moreover, the more heterogeneous the populations served become (and more heterogeneity is a correlate of expanding populations), then the greater difficulty a Representative has in serving all of the constituents equally well.

The sheer growing size of populations served has also meant that congressional offices must cope with expanded operations. Although many citizens

TABLE 12.2 Populations Served by the U.S. House of Representatives and Senate: 1790–1990

YEAR	POPULATION (IN 000s)	HOUSE OF REPRESENTATIVES NO.	AVERAGE POPULATION PER REPRESENTATIVE (NEAREST 00s)	SENATE NO.	AVERAGE POPULATION PER SENATOR† (NEAREST 00s)
1790	3,929	106	37,100	32	245,600
1800	5,308	142	37,400	34	312,200
1810	7,240	186	38,900	46	314,800
1820	9,638	213	45,300	48	401,600
1830	12,866	242	53,200	52	494,800
1840	17,069	232	73,600	62	550,600
1850	23,192	237	97,900	66	702,800
1860	31,443	243	129,400	72	873,400
1870	39,818	293	135,900	76	1,047,800
1880	50,156	332	151,100	88	1,139,900
1890	62,948	357	176,300	90	1,398,800
1900	75,995	391	194,400	92	1,652,100
1910	91,972	435	211,400	96	1,916,100
1920	105,711	435	243,000	96	2,202,300
1930	122,775	435	282,200	96	2,557,800
1940	131,669	435	302,700	96	2,743,100
1950	151,326	437*	346,300	100	3,026,500
1960	179,323	435	412,200	100	3,586,500
1970	204,844	435	470,900	100	4,096,900
1980	226,546	435	520,800	100	4,530,900
1990	248,710	435	571,700	100	4,974,200

* Temporarily increased because of admission of Alaska and Hawaii to the United States.

† Each of the two Senators of a state represents the whole state.

Sources: Roger H. Davidson, "Population Change and Representative Government." In A.E. Keir Nash, ed., *Commission on Population Growth and the American Future: Research Reports*, pp. 59–82, vol. 4, *Governance and Population: The Governmental Implications of Population Change* (Washington, D.C.: Government Printing Office, 1972); and various census reports.

lament the bureaucracy that has formed around Representatives and Senators, the fact is that demands made upon them have increased greatly. Comparing the 1st Congress with the 91st Congress, the number of bills introduced went up from 268 to 24,631; the number of laws enacted from 118 to 909; the number of nominations confirmed from 211 to 133,797; the number of committee reports from 155 to 3,355; and the number of Executive Department communications received from 72 to 4,099 (Davidson, 1972).

Total population size is a determinant of district boundaries for congressional as well as state and local political areas. The 1965 Voting Rights Act, as amended in 1982, further required considerations of racial and ethnic equality in political representation. Hence, the issue of delineating electoral districts in a way that ensures political parity is difficult. After each decennial census in the United States, the job of drawing up the districts takes place in each state. There are numerous ways in which an area can be carved up to define district boundaries. Differences of opinion ensue when different population subgroups attempt to maximize their representation within the configuration of districts delineated (O'Hare, 1989). As a result of these varying political orientations, and taking account of the legal rules established for drawing up the districts, some states have ended up with districts that have very irregular shapes (see Box 12.1).

ELECTORAL BEHAVIOR

The terms *democratic* and *demographic* have common roots that refer to people (from the Greek *demos*), and the two are connected analytically. A democratic government is one elected by the people, and the demographic makeup of the voters has an influence on the election outcome because some categories of the population are more likely to register to vote and to cast their ballots than are others. Hence, the demographic composition of the voting population is crucial to determining election results.

There is also a fascination in several societies with trying to predict the outcome of elections in advance of their conduct through the use of surveys and polls. In the United States, a number of organizations conduct these inquiries; most of the pollsters tend to use somewhat different methodologies. Some interview people in person, and others do it by telephone or by mail. Some ask questions of all registered voters, and others limit their inquiries to those who are regarded as likely to vote. Who is likely to vote is hard to estimate because voting patterns of the past are not necessarily good predictors of who will do so in the future. The candidates, the issues, and the relative turnout of voters change from one election to another. Moreover, the pollsters have to hedge the statistics produced on the probable voting patterns because their surveys or polls are based on samples subject to chance variation. The small note on political poll results to the effect that the estimates are plus or minus 3 or 4 percent means that, if 100 similar samples were drawn and information gathered from each, in about 95 of the samples the results could be higher or lower by 3 or 4 percent. This is due to the statistical properties of randomly selected samples. The reliability of the sample data is even lower when we try to determine whether sample results at two different dates indicate a rise or fall of the estimated results. Additionally, if the sample is not drawn in

BOX 12.1 Odd-Shaped Congressional Districts

Drawing boundaries that separate congressional districts, as well as political districts within states and local areas, has become more complicated because the rule about "one person, one vote" was interpreted in the 1965 Voting Rights Act in the United States as requiring attention to equal opportunity for minorities to elect a representative for their area.

Even before attention had to be given to minority representation, election districts had to be designed to include equal numbers of all people among the several districts to which the political entity was entitled. A state or county with, say, seven Representatives could create many alternative patterns of seven districts, depending on where the boundary lines were set. It has been typical of the major political parties to come up with different sets of district boundaries, each party favoring a set that would maximize the percentage of probable voters who lean toward that party.

Consideration of minority representation as well means that some districts have to be designed to give a chance for the area's minorities to elect Representatives in relative proportion to their percentage of the state's or county's population. The number of permutations and combinations of district shapes expands greatly because not only the total population size but also the relative numbers of blacks and Hispanics are the criteria for drawing district lines.

Minorities do not all live in one consolidated area; typically, they live in some minority neighborhoods but many are also dispersed throughout the general area. To design a district that gives a minority group a reasonable chance to elect one of their own minority members to office sometimes requires that a district boundary be drawn in such a way as to encompass a majority of the minority group in the area. As a result, many states have come up with odd-shaped election districts. The map in Figure 12.1 shows the designed 12th Congressional District for North Carolina that follows Interstate Highway 85 through the state. Critics have challenged the design on the grounds that it introduces *reverse discrimination* by disenfranchising white persons in that district, and the issue has been placed before the Supreme Court of the United States. North Carolina, in fact, designed two odd-shaped districts to maximize the chances of minorities to be elected; as a result, two black House members were elected in those districts. But North Carolina is not the only state with odd-shaped congressional districts. Other states with similar ones include Alabama, Arizona, California, Florida, Georgia, Illinois, Louisiana, Maryland, New York, Pennsylvania, South Carolina, Texas, and Virginia (Yancey, 1993).

a completely random manner, not only are the statistical laws of chance in question but biases in the representation of certain categories of the population can distort the results. This is one of the reasons that pollsters are frequently

FIGURE 12.1 The 12th Congressional District for North Carolina

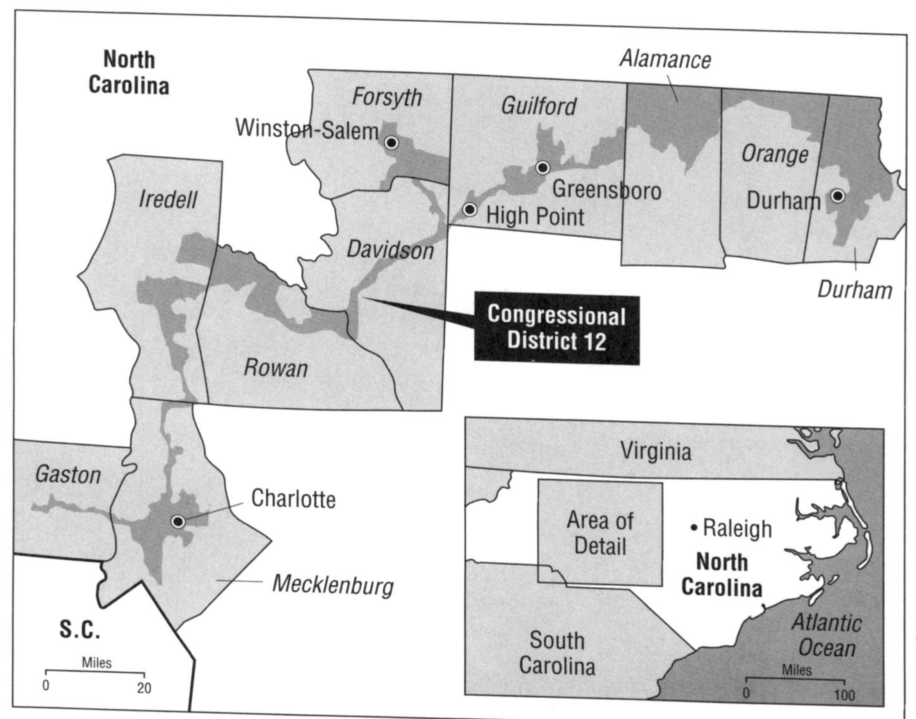

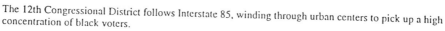

The 12th Congressional District follows Interstate 85, winding through urban centers to pick up a high concentration of black voters.

Source: *New York Times*, April 16, 1993, p. B9.

off the mark in predicting political outcomes. Another is that some voters may remain undecided or change their minds about candidates after the last poll is taken and before the ballots are cast.

Apart from these caveats, there is some predictability to election forecasting because the demographic patterns of voting are consistent to a high degree. This was called to the public's attention by the journalist Samuel Lubell (1956), who combined his insights into political trends with research on demographic changes and their import for the 1952 election. Lubell pointed out the following developments of the post–World War II period:

1. The children of the former immigrants from Europe to U.S. cities were moving to the suburbs and achieving upward social mobility;

2. The baby boom phenomenon was altering the patterns of U.S. family life; and
3. A great migration of blacks was taking place from the South to the North.

Lubell believed that these developments were leading to the formation of a new middle class that was reshaping the U.S. system of social stratification. He also predicted that such developments would give a new lease on political life to the Republican Party.

Other demographic trends since that time have modified the electoral balance in ways that puzzled the political pundits. A declining birth rate and longer life expectancy at the older ages led to an increasing percentage of the elderly in the population. Previously the concerns of this segment of the population had not been high on the political agenda. Because of increases in their numbers as well as a percentage of the population, Americans 65 and over have established a number of organizations to push for programs that sustain the elderly (such as Social Security, Medicare, and housing subsidies) (Fosler, 1990). In addition, the political parties have attempted to shape their party's platforms to appeal to these older Americans.

In like manner, newer ethnic groups (especially people of various Asian and Hispanic origins) have concentrated in certain parts of the country and solidifed their political power. As a consequence, they have been successful in getting their members elected to political offices and in influencing the electoral candidates who depend on votes from those areas.

Political campaigns have thus been designed to capitalize on knowledge about the electorate and to target appeals to win votes (Hill and Kent, 1988). Campaign directors have invested most of their campaign expenditures in areas and through various media in ways that pay attention to potential voters who are needed to tip the scales in favor of the campaign directors' candidates.

The association of population characteristics with the percentage of people registering to vote and actually voting is striking (see Table 12.3). About two-thirds of the people of voting age in the United States register to vote, but less than one-half of the voting-age population actually votes on election day. Equivalent percentages are much higher in most other Western countries. Both the percentage of registrants and the percentage of voters are slightly higher during presidential election years than in years when there is no presidential election. In the United States, there has been a downward trend until 1990 in the percentages for both registering and voting, but both these percentages increased for the 1992 presidential election.

Generally speaking, white persons are more likely to register and vote than blacks. Hispanics are least likely of the three categories to participate electorally. Females register and turn out to vote in slightly larger percentages than do males. Registration and voting increase with age, the percentages of those 65 and over being nearly twice those of persons 18 to 24. Persons are most apt to vote if they live in the Midwest. The greater the level of education, the more likely someone will vote. These findings show that certain categories of the

TABLE 12.3 Percent of Voting-Age Population Registering to Vote and Actually Voting in Presidential and Nonpresidential Elections, by Population Characteristics: United States, 1984–1990

	PERCENT REGISTERED				PERCENT VOTED			
CHARACTERISTICS	1990	1988*	1986	1984*	1990	1988*	1986	1984*
TOTAL, VOTING AGE	62.2	66.6	64.3	68.3	45.0	57.4	46.0	59.9
White	63.8	67.9	65.3	69.6	46.7	59.1	47.0	61.4
Black	58.8	64.5	64.0	66.3	39.2	51.5	43.2	55.8
Hispanic origin	32.3	35.5	35.9	40.1	21.0	28.8	24.2	32.6
Male	61.2	65.2	63.4	67.3	44.6	56.4	45.8	59.0
Female	63.1	67.8	65.0	69.3	45.4	58.3	46.1	60.8
18 to 24	39.9	48.2	42.0	51.3	20.4	36.2	21.9	40.8
25 to 44	58.4	63.0	61.1	66.6	40.7	54.0	41.4	58.4
45 to 64	71.4	75.5	74.8	76.6	55.8	67.9	58.7	69.8
65 and over	76.5	78.4	76.9	76.9	60.3	68.8	60.9	67.7
Northeast	61.0	64.8	62.0	66.6	45.2	57.4	44.4	59.7
Midwest	68.2	72.5	70.7	74.6	48.6	62.9	49.5	65.7
South	61.3	65.6	63.0	66.9	42.4	54.5	43.0	56.8
West	57.7	63.0	60.8	64.7	45.0	55.6	48.4	58.5
EDUCATION								
None/elementary school	44.0	47.5	50.5	53.4	27.7	36.7	32.7	42.9
Some high school	47.9	52.8	52.4	54.9	30.9	41.3	33.8	44.4
High school graduates	60.0	64.6	62.9	67.3	42.2	54.7	44.1	58.7
Some college	68.7	73.5	70.0	75.7	50.0	64.5	49.9	67.5
College graduates	77.3	83.1	77.8	83.8	62.5	77.6	62.5	79.1

* Presidential election years.

Sources: Jerry T. Jennings, "Voting and Registration in the Election of November 1988," *Current Population Reports* (1989), U.S. Bureau of the Census, Series P-20, no. 440; and Jerry T. Jennings, "Voting and Registration in the Election of November 1990," *Current Population Reports* (1991), U.S. Bureau of the Census, Series P-20, no. 453.

population are underrepresented in the election of candidates for public office because some of their numbers fail to utilize their right to vote. As a consequence, some population groups have a disproportionately high influence on elections, and candidates in their campaigns pay especial attention to these same categories because of their greater voting strength.

The 1992 elections in the United States seemed to take on a somewhat different tone from elections of the previous few decades. The following factors—

three major candidates for the presidential office; an unusually large number of female and minority-group candidates in congressional races; an economic recession; and a renewed interest in domestic-policy issues after years of national concentration on foreign-policy issues—all led to a heightened involvement in the electoral process. Although registration and voting increased, the disparities among population categories remained. Even so, the larger numbers of working-age people (mainly the baby boomers) and older-age people accentuated their importance in the overall voting patterns. The successful appeals of President Clinton to these segments of the population insured his margin of victory. Job creation and security as well as income growth were key issues for the baby boomers; health care costs were a vital issue for the elderly. These were the issues Clinton emphasized in his political campaign, especially when he addressed those segments of the population.

THE POLITICAL WORLD ORDER

At any point in history one can find political turmoil in some parts of the world. At present, political unrest exists in many different locations, and attempts to bring about peaceful settlements to conflicts have not been eminently successful. It is apparent that the political difficulties that do occur have their roots in economic and social inequalities among people and in the decisions of leaders of many factions not in control to change the imbalances by seeking to wrest political power form those who have it.

There are varying social theories about power politics that are not germane to our discussion here. But it is necessary to point out that demographic factors play some role—at times a great role and at other times a small one—in shaping circumstances that influence political problems and their solutions.

One can make a good argument that the effects of demographic conditions on the political world order are often understated. The United Nations Security Council, the most powerful UN policy-making body which is responsible for peace and security in the world, is composed of fifteen nations. Five of them have permanent seats; ten others represent, on a rotating basis, the remaining nations of the world. In 1992 the permanent seats were held by China, France, Russia (formerly the Soviet Union), the United Kingdom, and the United States, all of which had long occupied those positions. By 1993 a reassessment of which countries should be permanent members of the Security Council began to take place.

Population size was not a major factor in the selection of countries for the council. Table 12.4 shows the 21 countries of the world with the largest total populations (those with over 55 million people), arrayed by population size. The five permanent seats on the Security Council have been held by countries ranked 1st, 3rd, 6th, 17th, and 19th in total population. (Actually, the Soviet Union, of which Russia had been part, was ranked 3rd and the United States 4th prior to the breakup of the Soviet Union.) Why were the 17th- and 19th-

TABLE 12.4 Characteristics of World's Largest Populations: 1992 (Countries with over 55 Million People)

COUNTRY	POPULATION (IN MILLIONS)	RATE OF NATURAL INCREASE (% PER YEAR)	% UNDER 15	% URBAN	PER CAPITA GNP*
China	1,166	1.3	28	26	370
India	883	2.0	36	26	350
United States	256	0.8	22	75	21,700
Indonesia	185	1.7	37	31	560
Brazil	151	1.9	35	74	2,680
Russia	149	0.2	23	74	†
Japan	124	0.3	18	77	25,430
Pakistan	122	3.1	44	28	380
Bangladesh	111	2.4	44	14	200
Nigeria	90	3.0	45	16	370
Mexico	88	2.3	38	71	2,490
Germany	81	–0.1	16	90	†
Vietnam	69	2.2	39	20	†
Philippines	64	2.4	39	43	730
Iran	60	3.3	46	54	2,450
Turkey	59	2.2	35	59	1,630
United Kingdom	58	0.3	19	90	16,070
Italy	58	0.1	17	72	16,850
France	57	0.4	20	73	19,480
Thailand	56	1.4	34	18	1,420
Egypt	56	2.4	41	45	600

* In 1990 U.S. dollars.

† Not available.

Source: Population Reference Bureau, *1992 World Population Data Sheet* (Washington, D.C.: Population Reference Bureau, 1992).

largest nations permanent members of the Council, and why weren't the 2nd, 4th, and 5th in those positions? Moreover, what claim do Japan (ranked 7th) and Germany (ranked 12th) have to permanent seats on the council?

An examination of the several population indicators for each country in Table 12.4 tells at least part of the story. While the United Kingdom and France are not population giants, they have historically been political powers and formerly had vast colonial empires. In addition, they have traversed the demographic transition and have achieved demographic stability. Predominantly urban in character, their economies are highly competitive in world markets. It is interesting to note that Italy, which has a similar population size and structure, does not have a permanent council seat although it is a member of Group of Seven (the organization of the seven strongest industrial economies in the world).

Why aren't India, Indonesia, and Brazil with their large numbers of people in stronger world-political positions? They have rates of natural increase that approach 2 percent per year, and over one-third of their populations are under 15 years of age. It should be noted that the first two of these countries have substantial rural populations; as a result, their economies are not competitive in the world.

What about Japan and Germany, which are also beyond the demographic transition and have demographic stability with resulting economic strength? They logically should command permanent places on the Security Council. One might expect that further discussions of this matter could lead to an expansion in the number of permanent members, thus bringing in Japan, Germany, and possibly Italy.

We can also see demographic impacts on the international political process in cases of political unrest in different parts of the world. Let us examine two general areas in this regard. The Gulf War of 1991 involved several countries at early stages of the demographic transition which have had to cope with population problems. Countries with leading rates of natural increase in the area are Syria (3.8% per year), Iraq (3.7% per year), and Saudi Arabia (3.5% per year). Between 45 and 49 percent of their populations are under 15 years old. Iraq had recently fought a war with Iran for about ten years, suffering losses of its military-age population. By the time the conflict over Kuwait began, there was a deficit of military-age men (the culture did not accept women's fighting in combat). In order to marshal a military force, Saddam Hussein, the ruler of Iraq's 18 million people, had to draw on both older men and youths to replenish his forces. While the oil riches of the area contribute to a high average economic level, substantial economic inequality means that Iraq has a large percentage of its people in poor economic circumstances and in unhealthy condition. The demographic realities in Iraq did not bode well for a successful military encounter.

Both the Soviet Union and Yugoslavia have recently dissolved into a number of smaller nations. In both cases, ethnically heterogeneous populations with different demographic regimes may have contributed significantly to the conflicts that have ensued in these countries. Russia (as well as Belarus and Ukraine) are countries that have advanced into the later stage of the demographic transition and have fairly low and stable rates of natural increase. The other former republics of the Soviet Union, each with a predominant ethnic minority, are growing much more rapidly in size (the rates of natural increase being 3.2% per year for Tajikistan, 2.7% per year for Turkmenistan and Uzbekistan, and between 1.8% and 2.2% per year for Kyrgyzstan, Azerbaijan, and Armenia). Before the dissolution, Russia constituted a bare majority of the

Soviet Union's population, but controlled the national power. (Its capital, Moscow, was the site of the Kremlin.) In a short period of time, Russia would have had less than a majority of the U.S.S.R.'s population because of the population trends, and it would not have been able to dominate the Soviet legislature as it had done in the past. The separation of Russia from the other republics (some alliance with Belarus and Ukraine being maintained) means that Russia will not be threatened by the rising numbers of people in the ethnic republics.

In Yugoslavia, political demography was also affected strongly by ethnic diversity. Although all of the prior Yugoslav republics were demographically advanced, within each of them the resident ethnic minorities had higher rates of population growth and challenged the political dominance of the leaders of the various republics.

Demographic disparities have also been associated with regional and city-suburban political difficulties in many countries (Weiner, 1971). In addition, population experts have observed that international migration (both legal and illegal) has disturbed the political relationships of many nations (Fosler, 1990). Contemporary history is dotted with instances of countries whose imminent population declines have created concerns about the ability of those countries to maintain continental and world political power (Fosler, 1990).

Chapter Highlights

1. We can define the religion with which people are associated in terms of membership, preference, devoutness or belief, and identification or preference. While religious membership data are used in population analysis, the principal basis for determining religion as a demographic characteristic is the identification or preference of individuals.
2. Although data for describing the world pattern of religious affiliation or identification are unreliable, a 1963 estimate placed the distribution of the world's population as 47 percent "Pagans," 30 percent Christians, 14 percent Muslims, and 9 percent in other groups (including half of 1 percent who are Jews).
3. As of 1980, the religious composition of the United States was estimated as 35 percent Baptists, 25 percent Roman Catholics, 20 percent Methodists, 13 percent Lutherans, 8 percent Presbyterians, 4 percent Episcopalians or Anglicans, over 2 percent Jewish, 21 percent of other Protestant denominations, and over 8 percent in other religions or without a religious identification. The distribution varied considerably by geographic divisions of the country.
4. Religious categories of people change in relative size as a consequence of conversion to, or withdrawal from, the category as well as through the differential demographic processes of mortality, fertility, and mobility.
5. Political structures in societies are affected by population changes in various

ways. One way is through the pattern of legislative representation. In the United States, the slower growth in the size of the Congress, with fixed numbers in recent decades, has meant that each Representative has served larger and larger numbers of people over time. This has related both to problems in satisfying constituencies as well as to handling the volume of activities expected of legislators.

6. Because there is a patterned relationship between the demographic characteristics of people and whether or not they vote, electoral outcomes can sometimes be anticipated before the voting takes place. It is clear, however, that the size of the voter turnout is influenced by the relative success of candidates to attract voters with particular characteristics to their cause.
7. Changes in population composition and distribution can have an appreciable influence on election outcomes because of shifts toward, or away from, population categories and locations that generally have particular tendencies to vote.
8. The political world order can be affected by population conditions. While total population size is not highly related to the political power of countries or to the probability that political unrest may take place in an area at a certain time, such population phenomena as the age structure, rate of growth or natural increase, level of urbanization, and disparate ethnic composition often indicate political trouble spots.

Discussion Questions

1. What might account for the fact that religion is included as an item in the governmental censuses and surveys of Canada but not in those of the United States?
2. What legitimate uses do you think can be made of information on the religious characteristics of populations?
3. Analyze your own religious group in terms of how various population processes have changed the religion's population structure. Which population factors have produced the most change?
4. Realizing that large legislative bodies can become difficult to organize and operate but that most populations tend to increase over time, what would be your solution for improving the form of population representation in legislatures?
5. Examine election statistics for your hometown or a voting precinct within it for the last few elections. (Such information is available from the local supervisor of elections.) What can you discern about population characteristics that are related to political party preference and voting for particular candidates or issues to be decided?
6. Identify a political trouble spot in the world other than the ones mentioned

in the text. To what extent are demographic factors possibly linked to political problems?

Suggested Readings

Greeley, Andrew M. 1989. *Religious Change in America.* Cambridge, Mass.: Harvard University Press. An examination of shifts in religious composition and attitudes in the United States and of the variables that seem to be associated with them.

Nash, A. E. Keir, ed. 1972. *Governance and Population: The Governmental Implications of Population Change.* Vol. 4. *Reports of the Commission on Population Growth and the American Future.* Washington, D.C.: Government Printing Office. Although somewhat outdated, it provides a useful overview of many issues that tie population and the polity together.

Hill, David B., and Mary M. Kent. 1988. "Election Demographics." *Population Trends and Public Policy,* no. 14. A publication of the Population Reference Bureau, it introduces the reader to the ways that population factors relate to electoral behavior in the United States.

U.S. Bureau of the Census. *Current Population Reports,* Series P-20. Washington, D.C.: Government Printing Office. Reports in this series periodically cover election outcomes from the point of view of the extent of registration and voting in the most recent election and the characteristics of people associated with them.

References

Bogue, Donald J. 1985. *The Population of the United States.* New York: Free Press.

Bradley, Martin B., Norman M. Green, Jr., Dale E. Jones, Mac Lynn, and Lou McNeill. 1992. *Churches and Church Membership in the United States 1990.* Atlanta: Glenmary Research Center.

Canevin, Regis. 1912. *An Examination, Historical and Statistical, into Losses and Gains of the Catholic Church in the United States from 1790 to 1910.* Pittsburgh: no publisher cited.

Carey, William. 1792. *An Inquiry into the Obligations of Christians to Use Means for the Conversion of the Heathens. In Which the Religious State of the Different Nations of the World, the Success of Former Undertakings, and the Practicability of Further Undertakings Are Considered.* (Leicester: Ann Ireland, p. 62).

Davidson, Roger H. 1972. "Population Change and Representative Government." In A.E. Keir Nash, ed., *Governance and Population: The Governmental Implications of Population Change,* pp. 59–82. Vol. 4. *Reports of the Commission on Population Growth and the American Future.* Washington, D.C.: Government Printing Office.

Fosler, R. Scott. 1990. "Political and Institutional Implications of Demographic Change." In R. Scott Fosler, William Alonso, Jack A. Meyer, and Rosemary Kern, *Demographic Change and the American Future,* pp. 133–253. Pittsburgh: University of Pittsburgh Press.

Foster, Charles R. 1961. *A Question on Religion.* University, Ala.: University of Alabama Press.

Goldstein, Sidney. 1992. "Profile of American Jewry: Insights from the 1990 National Jewish Population Survey." In David Singer, ed., *American Jewish Year Book 1992*, pp. 77–173, vol. 92. New York and Philadelphia: American Jewish Committee and the Jewish Publication Society.

Greeley, Andrew M. 1989. *Religious Change in America*. Cambridge, Mass.: Harvard University Press.

Hill, David B., and Mary M. Kent. 1988. "Election Demographics." *Population Trends and Public Policy*, no. 14, 1–16.

Hostetler, John A. 1974. *Hutterite Society*. Baltimore: Johns Hopkins University Press.

Jennings, Jerry T. 1989. "Voting and Registration in the Election of November 1988." *Current Population Reports*, U.S. Bureau of the Census, Series P-20, no. 440 (Washington, D.C.: Government Printing Office).

———. 1991. "Voting and Registration in the Election of November 1990." *Current Population Reports*, U.S. Bureau of the Census, Series P-20, no. 453 (Washington, D.C.: Government Printing Office).

Kenedy, P.J., and Sons. 1990. *The Official Catholic Directory*. New York: P.J. Kenedy Sons.

Lubell, Samuel. 1956. *The Future of American Politics*, 2nd ed., rev. Garden City, N.Y.: Doubleday.

Nam, Charles B. 1968. *Population and Society*. Boston: Houghton Mifflin.

O'Hare, William P. 1989. *Redistricting in the 1990's: A Guide for Minority Groups*. Washington, D.C.: Population Reference Bureau.

Petersen, William. 1962. "Religious Statistics in the United States." *Journal of the Scientific Study of Religion* 1: 165–78.

Poston, Dudley L., Jr. 1990. "Apportioning U.S. Congress: A Primer." *Population Today* (July/August): 6–10.

Redekop, Calvin. 1989. *Mennonite Society*. Baltimore: Johns Hopkins University Press.

Schmelz, U.O., and Sergio Della Pergola. 1992. "World Jewish Population 1990." In David Singer, ed., *American Jewish Year Book 1992*, pp. 484–512, vol. 92, New York and Philadelphia: American Jewish Committee and the Jewish Publication Society.

Sopher, David E. 1967. *Geography of Religions*. Englewood Cliffs, N.J.: Prentice-Hall.

Weiner, Myron. 1971. "Political Demography: An Inquiry into the Political Consequences of Population Change." In Roger Revelle, ed., *Rapid Population Growth: Consequences and Policy Implications*, pp. 567–617. Baltimore: Johns Hopkins Press.

Yancey, Matt. 1993. "Court to Look at Racial Gerrymandering." *Tallahassee Democrat*, (April 21).

Zelinsky, Wilbur. 1992. *The Cultural Geography of the United States*. Englewood Cliffs, N.J.: Prentice-Hall.

13. Population, Resources, and the Environment

No public issue has captivated the interests of people in the contemporary world so much as concerns about our natural resources and the natural environment at present and in the future. Particular concerns may vary from area to area. For example, a livable habitat, drinking water, and food for a basic diet may be paramount matters for those in the least developed parts of the world, while the quality of air and water and the plentifulness of energy fuels may dominate the concerns of those in the most developed regions. In fact, the debate raging over the state of natural resources and the environment covers a wide array of specific items and engages population factors in different ways.

FRAMING THE ISSUES

Under the general rubric of *natural resources*, we can include the availability of *land and shelter;* renewable resources such as *water*, *agriculture*, and *food animals;* and nonrenewable resources, such as *fossil fuels*, *metals*, and *nonmetallic minerals*.

Included in the broad category of *environmental quality* are *air quality*, *water quality*, and *waste disposal*. The two general areas can be related to each other, as when large-scale removal of timber from land where it is grown can result in desertification of the land if the forests that are the source of timber are not replaced in an efficient manner.

From the point of view of this book, the critical question is "To what extent do population factors have an impact on resource depletion and environmental degradation?" We approach that question with a realization that, as in the case of other possible consequences of demographic change, the range of population variables can have an influence individually and jointly, and that population factors can be related to each element of natural resources and environmental pollution to different degrees and in different ways.

We come back again to the notion that pessimism and optimism characterize different groups of people in this regard as they do other areas involving population matters. There are advocates of the position that our resource and environmental problems are so severe that the Earth stands on the brink of a global natural disaster (for example, see the 1991 quotation from Brown in Chapter 3; or the position stated in Ehrlich and Ehrlich, 1979). There are others who believe that the ingenuity of the human race will probably provide solutions to all the resource and environmental problems that will ever present themselves, and that we need not fear them (for example, see the 1987 quotation from Repetto in Chapter 3). In between these more extreme positions, we can find an array of views that concedes some level of concern and also perceives at least partial solutions.

There is a growing recognition that understanding the linkage between population factors and the natural environment requires us also to include in our thinking the workings of other sets of conditions. Such conditions include the economic welfare of nations and individuals; the tendencies of each nation and individual to consume natural resources at a level that puts strains on resources and pollutes the environment; and the development of technologies that create environmental problems as well as those that can combat these problems. In other words, there is a complexity to the question asked above that must be unraveled, at least to some extent, in order to arrive at generally satisfactory answers.

In the three sections of this chapter, we will briefly examine the state of the resources people use and how it seems to be changing over time; the state of the natural environment in which people live and how that appears to be changing over time; and the relative contribution of population factors to each of these developments to the extent it is possible to do so.

THE STATE OF RESOURCES PEOPLE USE

Foremost among the resources on which people depend are the *land* on which to reside and the *shelter* that protects us from exposure to the harshness of climate and weather variations. On a finite Earth, increases of population will obviously result in rising population densities, as indicated in Chapter 1. Land for habitats competes with land for agriculture, commerce, industry, and entertainment, so that the relative availability of living space is conditioned on the priorities for the several forms of land use.

There are also great variations in population densities throughout the world. Crowding of populations is more common in some parts of the world than in others, mainly because people choose (or are impelled) to locate in urban areas. Sheer space does not seem to be a scarce resource if one considers that people do not only live on the surface of the Earth but can also reside in layers of space above the Earth (as witnessed by the splurge of high-rise residential structures in cities everywhere).

The nature of habitats in which people live depends on the allotment of space given to individuals and families and on the economic opportunity to purchase or build or occupy an appropriate form of shelter. But, while the rele-

TABLE 13.1 Housing Indicators for Selected Developing and Developed Countries: Circa 1975–1981

COUNTRY	AVERAGE NO. OF PERSONS PER HOUSEHOLD	PERSONS PER ROOM OF OCCUPIED HOUSING UNITS	PERCENT OF HOUSING UNITS: WITHOUT PIPED WATER	WITHOUT TOILETS	WITHOUT ELECTRIC LIGHTS
Cameroon	5.2	1.2	75.8	27.6	94.1
Pakistan	6.7	3.6	79.7	*	69.4
Thailand	5.2	*	85.8	49.3	76.0
Malaysia	5.2	*	35.0	16.5	35.6
El Salvador	5.0	3.3	*	37.6	*
Bolivia	4.3	*	60.7	78.2	65.7
Brazil	4.2	1.0	46.7	22.8	32.6
Japan	3.2	0.8	7.0	0.3	*
Belgium	2.7	0.6	2.0	0.2	*
Former Czechoslovakia	2.8	0.9	8.4	*	0.0
Ireland	3.7	*	5.0	6.9	5.3
Australia	3.0	*	0.4	1.5	0.5

* Not available.

Source: United Nations, *Compendium of Human Settlement Statistics* (New York: United Nations, 1985).

vant statistics are not routinely collected for very many nations, sharp disparities in housing indicators exist between developing and developed countries.

As can be noted in Table 13.1, the developing countries represented have more persons per household on the average, more persons per room on the average, and much higher percentages of housing units without piped water (either inside or outside the house); more households in developing countries are without a toilet and electric lighting. These indicators reflect partly the population growth rate of the countries and partly their economic conditions, which are related to their stage in the demographic transition and to heavily rural environments.

Other information about housing conditions in developing countries, however, indicates the deficient state of living conditions in both urban and rural areas. In the Sudan (Republic of the Sudan, 1991), 47 percent of urban residences and 89 percent of rural residences are made out of straw or mud, and 67 percent of urban residences and 96 percent of rural residences have earth or sand floors within the housing.

What about the supply of *renewable resources?* How adequate is the availability of water for drinking, cooking, and the irrigation of crops; of trees that will produce paper, lumber for housing construction, and fuel; of agricultural products and livestock?

On a global basis, fresh *water* is abundant; yet there are areas of the world where rain and melted snow are inadequate for the provision of water needs. It has been estimated that 22 nations already have renewable water resources of less than 1,000 cubic meters per capita (a level seen as severely constraining) and 18 other countries have less than 2,000 cubic meters per capita (an indication of substantial scarcity). The greatest water crises have taken place in the Middle East, North Africa, and sub-Saharan Africa, although northern China, west and south India, and Mexico are also experiencing shortages (World Bank, 1992).

This picture of the water supply is made more salient when we realize that 69 percent of the world's fresh water goes for the irrigation of crops, 23 percent for industrial uses, and only 8 percent for household use (Green, 1992). Moreover, there are seasonal patterns to the shortages. Countries with long dry seasons will fall short of their needs, especially during these spells. The technology that permits desalinization of salt water or allows for transport of water over long distances is expensive and thus not available to those parts of the world that would most profit from such developments.

Dependence of the world on *trees* not only for human needs but for climatic control as well has been eroded by an excessive amount of deforestation (more trees are cut down or burned than are seedlings planted for new trees). Myers (1991) estimates that about 10 thousand years ago there were 62 million square kilometers of forests. About two-thirds of that amount exist today. Of the 16 million square kilometers of *tropical* forests that existed just four decades ago, perhaps half as much is around today and most of those are projected to disappear within a few decades. This reduction came about because of the destruction of forests for cattle raising, fuelwood gathering, commercial logging, and the principal agents of deforestation—slash-and-burn cultivators, who are mainly landless peasants seeking farmland (and who frequently follow logging paths). Reforestation programs have been instituted in some parts of the world—in 10 percent of the forest areas lost annually in Africa and Latin America and in about 70 percent in Asia (principally in China, India, Indonesia, Japan, and North Korea) (Green, 1992).

The Malthusian question about sufficiency in *food production* in relation to population growth is still posed today. How successful has the world been in growing food to meet the needs of the people? On a worldwide basis, the generation of food has more than kept up with demand. The economically advanced countries have further developed their agricultural technologies and farm organization to produce even greater yields in crops than before. In developing countries as a whole, food production expanded by over 3 percent between 1961 and 1980. Per capita dietary energy (measured as energy equivalents of quantities of food items available for human consumption) rose from 2,340 to 2,630 calories during that time (Hendry, 1988). China and India became self-sufficient in grain/cereal production. Indonesia, once a net importer of rice, has become a net exporter. But not all areas of the world have had such successes. The Third World's per capita food production is not high enough to provide a level of nutrition that would prevent pockets of physical growth stunting, and the diets of many are insufficient in some of the necessary nutrients. In several countries, mostly in Africa, food production has grown only at the margin, and per capita diet energy either did not increase or declined during the 1970s and 1980s. Food shortages were common in arid territories of Africa, and hunger and malnutrition have been extreme in certain areas of that continent.

Because meat is an essential element of diets in most societies, trends in *livestock* production are important in the assessment of food sufficiency. According to Durning and Brough (1992):

> During the past 50 years, livestock industries have surged in one country after another as soaring grain yields made feeding animals on corn and barley relatively inexpensive and as intensive, specialized meat, egg, and dairy farms proliferated. In much of the world, meat consumption is climbing steadily; domesticated animals now outnumber humans three to one.

It has been shown that since 1950 there have been sharp increases in world meat production, with gains in pork, beef, buffalo, and poultry leading the way. But one must balance the potential gains of meat from these sources against other factors. First, there are significant regional and national differences in the livestock production trends. Only some of the developing nations, such as China, have shared those trends. Second, many societies of the developing world have religious prohibitions against eating some forms of meat (typically pork and beef) so that improvements in producing those animals does not affect their meat sources. Third, some of the animals that can be used for meat also are used for farm labor and for transportation. Therefore, killing them for their meat may compete with their uses in other respects. Fourth, 38 percent of the world's grain goes to feed livestock, and the greater production of animals for meat thus means that grain is drawn away from human consumption. Finally, medical reports reveal that the most prolifically produced meats (pork and beef) contain high levels of cholesterol and other negative dietary effects that should be minimized, so that some meats are not desirable components of human food consumption (Durning and Brough, 1992).

It is obvious that food shortages existing in some areas at the same time that food surpluses exist in others means that the world's food supply is not adequately shared. Even within the developing world, research has shown that 22 countries self-sufficient in food staples could have as much as 118 million tons of surplus production by the end of the century; however, as many as 83 developing countries will probably have a food deficit of 185 million tons by that time (Hendry, 1988). The surpluses of developed countries can more than make up for the remaining balance of food needs of the food-deficit nations.

Greater effort needs to be expended on improving the ability of food-deficit countries to grow their own food. This includes better techniques of increasing arable land, channeling water for irrigation, modernizing farm equipment, and raising the crop yields. This can be supplemented by increased transport of food from surplus to deficit areas and better methods for guaranteeing that the food reaches the people most in need. The challenges are both logistic and political.

Considerable attention has been devoted in recent years to the dwindling supply of *nonrenewable resources.* Fossil fuels, metals, and nonmetallic minerals, which are the foundation of modern industry, are nonrenewable in the sense that supplies are extracted mostly from deposits formed by extremely slow geologic processes and with existing technologies (Repetto, 1987). Some metals can be recycled, however, and substitutes for some nonrenewable resources have been found. Moreover, what we usually regard as *supplies* of these resources are really *reserves* (that is, sources known to be economically recoverable with our available technology and at specific prices). Materials present in the Earth's crust are far more plentiful and have the potential of more extensive extraction with improved technology and at probably higher prices.

Hence, the extraction of nonrenewable resources is based on control of the resource and what it costs to obtain it. That is why the oil-rich fields of the Middle East have generated several military conflicts, and why the Organization of Petroleum Exporting Countries (OPEC) can set the price on barrels of oil. Dependence on such commodities puts non–oil-producing nations at a disadvantage. It also spurs their search for alternative resources.

The price of oil has stabilized a great deal, and the costs of nuclear energy are maintained at a comparably low level with government subsidies. As a result, the project to make additional energy sources more readily available by harnassing the energy of the sun and the wind (renewable resources) has been stymied by the relative high price of those sources. As technologies for the development of these renewable resources proceed, we can expect such resources to become more cost-effective, thus permitting us to rely less on nonrenewable sources of energy.

It is also the case that great disparities exist in per capita energy *use* around the world. We can contrast the use of fuels by the average Canadian or resident of the United States (the equivalent of 40 barrels of oil in 1988) with the use of fuels by the average Nigerian or resident of India (the equivalent of 2 barrels or less) (Davis, 1990). Appeals have been made for those with high consumption levels to conserve their use of nonrenewable energy and other mineral resources. At the same time, it is probable that people in countries that today have lower consumption levels will want to raise their consumption per capita as they become more capable economically. It will be difficult to deny them.

THE STATE OF THE NATURAL ENVIRONMENT IN WHICH PEOPLE LIVE

It is clear that the deterioration of air and water quality, the erosion of shorelines, the degradation of plant life, and the rising levels of waste disposal result

FIGURE 13.1 Urban Air Pollution Levels and Trends: Concentrations of Sulfur Dioxide across Country Income Groups

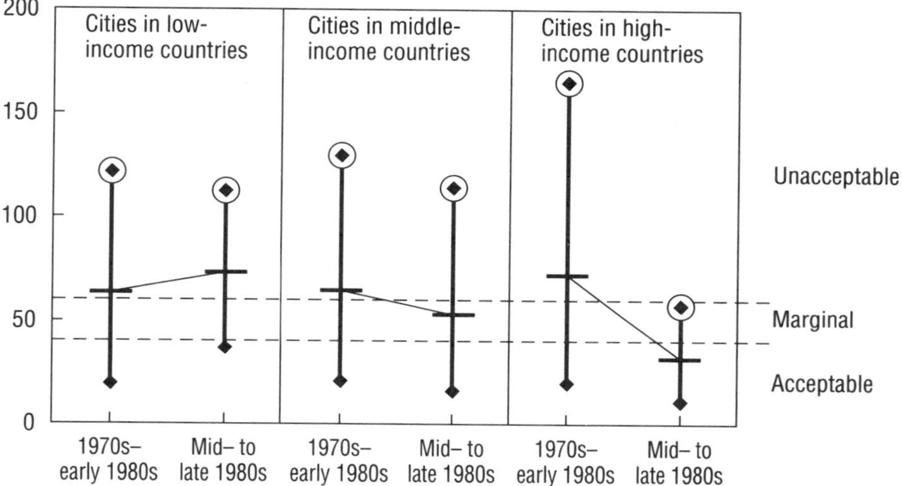

Note: Data are for seventeen urban sites in low-income countries, nineteen urban sites in middle-income countries, and forty-two urban sites in high-income countries. "Cleanest cities" and "dirtiest cities" are the first and last quartiles of sites when ranked by air quality. Periods of time series differ somewhat by site. World Health Organization guidelines for air quality are used as the criteria for acceptability.

Source: From *World Development Report 1992*. Copyright © 1992 by The International Bank for Reconstruction and Development/The World Bank. Reprinted by permission of Oxford University Press, Inc.

mainly from human actions. Natural catastrophes (such as hurricanes, tornadoes, earthquakes, volcanic eruptions, and floods) take their toll of nature, but much more of the environment is disturbed by the consequences of human resource use and our generation of environmental impurities.

Air quality has been of great concern in all parts of the world, especially in the largest cities. Figure 13.1 illustrates the level and trend of air pollution (in terms of sulfer dioxide concentrations) in three transitional stages at two time periods. Average amounts (in micrograms) of sulfer dioxide per cubic centimeter of air are shown, along with the range of extremes in each type of area and time span, and with designations of acceptable, marginal, and unacceptable pollution levels.

In the 1970s and early 1980s, cities in the most developed part of the world spanned the acceptable and unacceptable categories, the average city being in the unacceptable range. Because of improving technology and programs dealing with the problem, by the mid-to-late 1980s none of the cities in these high-income countries were in the unacceptable range. In cities in the middle-income category, some downward trend in sulfer dioxide levels was experienced; however, there were still cities with unacceptable levels of sulfer dioxide in the air. In the least-developed part of the world, the situation in the earlier period was about the same as in middle-income cities, but instead of a decline in average pollution levels there was an increase. This reflects the growing industrial base of some of these places and the lack of pollution controls. When other indicators of air pollution (such as suspended particulate matter) are used, the emerging picture is generally the same.

Another concern about air quality relates to what is called *greenhouse gases* and associated *global warming*. The energy absorbed from the sun must be balanced by outgoing radiation from the Earth and the atmosphere. Radiative atmospheric gases (called *greenhouse gases*) intercept part of the outgoing energy and consequently disturb the balance of the energy counterflows; this results in a warming effect.

The World Bank (1992) has estimated that the relative contribution of greenhouse gases to the change in heat trapping will be as great in the thirty-five years beginning with 1990 as it was for the two centuries from the preindustrial period to 1990. Chlorofluorocarbons, which are sources of global warming, have also led to *ozone depletion* over Antarctica and other areas; this results in greater biologically damaging ultraviolet radiation on Earth.

Apart from the availability of fresh water, there is the issue of *water quality* for both fresh and sea water. Because of inadequate sanitary waste facilities in developing countries and the dumping of waste products in rivers, lakes, and streams in all countries, water quality has been seriously affected (Green, 1992). More than half the people in Third World countries lack safe drinking water, and most of those, who do have access to potable water must pay for it. The practice of humans' washing themselves and their clothes in polluted waters in most developing nations leads to extreme health risks as well.

A further element of environmental deterioration has been the *erosion of water shorelines.* These shorelines and their beaches are the consequence of thousands of years of sand deposits from ocean waves. In the past few decades, in developed as well as developing areas, the building of sea walls, the digging of deep-sea inlets, and the construction of housing on beaches has contributed to an interruption of sand deposits from the ocean and has resulted in receding shorelines.

Soil erosion has increased inland, especially in Third World countries. Misuse of land, combined with natural phenomena, brings about *desertification* (advancing frontiers of sand that engulf pastures and agricultural land), deterioration of agricultural soils, and salinization and waterlogging based on irrigation (World Bank, 1992). Deforestation adds to these factors in affecting land use.

Not the least of the elements of environmental pollution has been the rising levels of *waste disposal* that affect air, water, and land resources. Such disposal includes nuclear waste; the everyday garbage and trash generated by households, businesses, and industries; and mercury poisoning associated with refuse generation.

Lenssen (1992) points out that we are yet to discover safe and permanent ways of disposing of radioactive waste from nuclear power. Options for dealing with irradiated fuel and its byproducts include the following possible solutions: burying the waste in Antarctic icecaps, in mined repositories hundreds of meters deep, and in deep ocean sediments; storing it indefinitely in specially constructed buildings; sending it into solar orbit beyond the Earth's gravity; chemically reprocessing it; and converting it to a form that will shorten its life. None of these approaches has yet proved satisfactory, and the cumulative output of irradiated fuel from nuclear plants in 1992 was twenty times what it was in 1970 and growing.

The more common dilemma of getting rid of everyday refuse is a considerable problem. Although it is difficult to determine the actual amount of garbage and waste generated today (much of it being converted through burning and reprocessing), estimates are that increasing production and consumption patterns have created rapidly multiplying waste levels. It is apparent that "nonbiodegradables probably accounted for a very large portion of the garbage that made it to ancient trash heaps ... [but today] potentially biodegradable materials have come to constitute a majority of everything that finds its way into a dumping ground" (Rathje and Murphy, 1992).

Since biodegradability takes place at a slower pace than many would think, the dumps and landfills that constitute the main locations of waste disposal can mount rapidly. Paper (especially newspapers) accounts for a high proportion of what goes into these sites. As a result, there are some enormous collections of waste in some locations. The Fresh Kills landfill on Staten Island in New York City, a principal garbage repository, now covers an area of 3,000 acres and rises at points to more than 155 feet above land level. It is planned that the landfill will be shut down in the year 2005, when it will have reached a height of 505 feet above sea level, making it the highest geographic feature along the Atlantic seaboard from Florida to Maine (Rathje and Murphy, 1992).

Like nuclear waste, the solutions for dealing with volumes of other wastes have not been forthcoming. Increased use of biodegrable products will have some impact on accumulation rates, as will reduced consumption levels. We can adopt a pessimistic or optimistic view about the ability of researchers to find technological answers to the problems.

Waste disposal has its multiplicative effects. It is not just its use of space that is troublesome but its chemical consequences that foul the environment as well. As an example, the release of toxic mercury in the atmosphere in the state of Florida was two-fifths due to mercury vapor escaping from soils and three-fifths due to other sources, of which a principal source was emissions from garbage incinerators and medical waste.

THE RELATIVE CONTRIBUTION OF POPULATION FACTORS

The foregoing discussion supports the notion that natural resource depletion and environmental degradation are severe problems throughout the world, but particularly in developing countries. In most respects, these problems are becoming more rather than less of a concern.

We get back to our fundamental question as to the extent to which population change can be implicated in these negative environmental consequences. Considering the several general factors that could be involved in accounting for resource and environmental changes, Commoner (1972) developed a simple algebraic formula that encompassed them:

$$\text{Pollutant (Depletion)} = \text{Population} \times \frac{\text{good}}{\text{population}} \times \frac{\text{pollution}}{\text{good}}$$

Population represents population size; *good/population* stands for the amount of goods or resources consumed per capita, or affluence; and *population/good* is the pollutant per unit of goods, or technology. By measuring the change in each component, Commoner was able to indicate the relative importance of population growth and the other two elements.

Commoner used this formula to estimate the effects of four pollutants—nitrogen oxides, phosphates, synthetic pesticides, and beer bottle trash—for the United States between 1950 and 1970. The results showed that the technology factor had the greatest impact and population the least. The population growth that took place ranged from 30 to 40 percent for the time period used, whereas the pollutants grew in much greater multiples (260 percent synthetic pesticides, 593 percent for beer bottles, 628 percent for nitrogen oxides, and 1,845 percent for phosphates!). In sum, population growth could be implicated to only a minor extent in each case. The pollutant per unit of goods produced was the main culprit.

In developing countries, the population factor would be relatively greater because of higher rates of population growth and the other two factors would be relatively smaller because consumption and technology levels are much lower. As time passes and the income levels of the developing countries rise, the relative level of the population effect will be diminished.

Davis (1990) examined world energy use from 1890 to 1990 and showed that, while the population increased by three and one-half times during that period, total energy use expanded almost fourteen times. Lenssen (1992) reports that rapid industrialization and urbanization have led to large increases in developing countries' use of oil, coal, and other sources of energy, with energy consumption nearly tripling since 1970—at a rate far faster than population and, in recent years, even faster than their economies (gross domestic product).

A study by Bongaarts (1992) of global warming determined that population increases determined about half of the increased emissions at present, but that the relative contribution of population growth would decline thereafter. Shaw

(1989) also found that population growth, mostly in developing countries, will account for slightly less than half of the increase in urban and industrial solid wastes in the world between 1985 and 2025.

Thus population growth represents no more than half of the increase in resource reductions and greater pollution, and for many indicators the relative contribution of population is much less. Thus, while population growth is definitely a factor in the generation of environmental ills, one cannot point to it as the principal factor.

We also need to reiterate the critical point that changing population size is only one of several demographic dimensions that should be examined in an analysis of environmental change. The nature of population distribution (especially urbanization) and population composition (particularly age structure) can introduce effects that outweigh changes in the size and growth of population alone.

To the extent that population factors cannot account for the level of, and increase in, resource depletion and environmental pollution, economic and technological factors make sizable contributions. These have been further specified as including property rights, trade relations, variations in technology types, variations in economic systems, and private as well as public decisions (Myers, 1991; Bernstam, 1991; Demeny, 1991).

The situation in developing countries is especially critical because some of the same efforts that must go into controlling environmental impacts (largely economic efforts) must also be expended in controlling population change. Thus, there are interactions among the several variables in the explanatory pattern; there are also tradeoffs to be made (Demeny, 1991; Repetto, 1987; Keyfitz, 1991). The future course of population, resources, and environmental linkages will depend on the degree to which the various factors and their separate and joint effects are managed to minimize the negative consequences for people and nature.

Chapter Highlights

1. Environmental issues of concern to the public fall under the broad categories of natural resources and environmental quality. Elements of the former are land and shelter, renewable resources (such as water, agriculture, and food animals), and nonrenewable resources (such as fossil fuels, metals, and nonmetallic minerals). Elements of the latter are air quality, water quality, and waste disposal.
2. The question of the extent to which population factors contribute to resource depletion and environmental degradation depends on an assessment of the levels and changes in each of the elements and the relative rates at which the changes take place.
3. Because land on Earth is finite, the extension of land for habitats will com-

pete with other uses of the land. However, we can provide shelter for people in structures that rise from the Earth and thereby accommodate some population increase. In the developing countries of the world, housing conditions are much less adequate than in developed nations and often are at a level that presents unacceptable living standards and risks to life.

4. Renewable natural resources have not always been available to everyone. There are vast expanses of the world where needed supplies of fresh water are lacking; deforestation has removed trees for human use; and food production is not sufficient to meet the nutritional requirements of the people.
5. Nonrenewable natural resources have become increasingly depleted in terms of their supply in the Earth's crust, although we have not nearly exhausted the supply because of the limits of technologies for extraction and because the economic costs for removal of fossil fuels, metals, and nonmetallic minerals from the Earth are relatively great. In addition, discoveries of renewable substitutes for some of the resources have lessened the need for removal of nonrenewable resources.
6. The actions of humans combine with those of nature to affect the natural environment in ways that often create reductions in air and water quality, erosion of shorelines, degradation of plant life, and rising levels of waste disposal.
7. Population factors can be implicated in all forms of resource depletion and environmental degradation, but the impact of population relative to other factors is relatively minor. The effect of population is quite small with regard to some environmental consequences and does not exceed half of the total effect in any instance. Population growth plays much more of a role in nations that are still in early stages of the demographic transition and have relatively high rates of population growth. Assuming that all countries will move through the demographic transition, population will have less and less of a relative effect on the environment in the future.
8. One must also view the contributions of population, technological changes, and economic changes as operating both separately and jointly as these factors are modified over time as the result of public and private actions.

Discussion Questions

1. How meaningful is the distinction between renewable and nonrenewable resources? What are some alternative terms that could be used to classify the various types of natural resources that exist in the world?
2. Identify one country in an early demographic transition stage and examine its sufficiency with regard to the several elements of natural resources. Com-

pare the situation with that of a country in a more advanced stage of the transition. What are the similarities and what are the differences?

3. Search recent issues of newspapers for examples of resource depletion and/or environmental degradation. To what extent are the accounts optimistic or pessimistic in their outlook?
4. Put yourself in the position of the leader of a country (developing or developed) who is faced with a particular environmental problem (one that you have read about). Outline the options that you think are available to deal with this problem. Define the tradeoffs involved.
5. Suppose that the world has reached a state when population size has stabilized (a zero rate of population change). Under such a circumstance, to what extent do you think resource depletion and environmental pollution would still exist, and why?

Suggested Readings

World Bank. 1992. *World Development Report 1992. Development and Environment.* New York: Oxford University Press. Explores the links between economic development and the environment throughout the world, including attention to various environmental elements and some alternative strategies for dealing with tradeoffs between development and environment.

Brown, Lester R., et al. 1992. *State of the World 1992.* New York: W. W. Norton. An annual review of environmental conditions in the world. This edition focuses on certain aspects of the environment and population that seem to be most critical areas of concern at present.

Davis, Kingsley, and Mikhail S. Bernstam, eds. 1991. *Resources, Environment, and Population: Present Knowledge, Future Options.* New York: Oxford University Press. (Originally published as a supplement to vol. 16 of *Population and Development Review.*) The proceedings of a conference on the title subject that encompasses statements on different aspects of the matter and includes reactions to these statements from the expert participants in the conference.

Rathje, William, and Cullen Murphy. 1992. *Rubbish! The Archaeology of Garbage.* New York: HarperCollins. Assesses the prospects for changing the pace at which we develop solid wastes and get rid of them, and in the process tells us what landfills and home garbage collections reveal about the kind of society we are and have been.

References

Bernstam, Mikhail S. 1991. "The Wealth of Nations and the Environment." In Kingsley Davis and Mikhail S. Bernstam, eds., *Resources, Environment, and Population: Present Knowledge, Future Opinions*, pp. 333–73. New York: Oxford University Press.

Bongaarts, John. 1992. "Population Growth and Global Warming." *The Population Council Working Papers*, no. 37.

Commoner, Barry. 1972. "The Environmental Costs of Economic Growth." *Chemsitry of Britain* 8: 52–65.

Davis, Ged R. 1990. "Energy for Planet Earth." *Scientific American* 263:3, 54–62.

Demeny, Paul. 1991. "Tradeoffs between Human Numbers and Material Standards of Living." In Kingsley Davis and Mikhail S. Bernstam, eds., *Resources, Environment, and Population: Present Knowledge, Future Options*, pp. 408–21. New York: Oxford University Press.

Durning, Alan Thein, and Holly B. Brough. 1992. "Reforming the Livestock Economy." In Lester R. Brown et al., *State of the World 1992*, pp. 66–82. New York: W. W. Norton.

Ehrlich, Paul R., and Anne H. Ehrlich. 1979. *Population, Resources, and Environment: Issues in Human Ecology*. San Francisco: W. H. Freeman.

Green, Cynthia P. 1992. "The Environment and Population Growth: Decade for Action." *Population Reports*, Series M, no. 10 (Baltimore: Johns Hopkins University).

Hendry, Peter. 1988. "Food and Population: Beyond Five Billion." *Population Bulletin* 43:2 (Washington, D.C.: Population Reference Bureau).

Keyfitz, Nathan. 1991. "Population and Development within the Ecosphere: One View of the Literature." *Population Index* 57:1, 5–22.

Lenssen, Nicholas. 1992. "Confronting Nuclear Waste." In Lester R. Brown et al., *State of the World 1992*, pp. 46–65. New York: W. W. Norton.

Myers, Norman. 1991. "The World's Forests and Human Populations: The Environmental Interconnections." In Kingsley Davis and Mikhail S. Bernstam, eds., *Resources, Environment, and Population: Present Knowledge, Future Options*, pp. 237–51. New York: Oxford University Press.

Rathje, William, and Cullen Murphy. 1992. *Rubbish! The Archaeology of Garbage*. New York: HarperCollins.

Repetto, Robert. 1987. "Population, Resources, Environment: An Uncertain Future." *Population Bulletin* 42:2.

Republic of the Sudan. 1991. *Sudan Demographic and Health Survey 1989/1990*. Columbia, Md.: Institute for Resource Development Macro International.

Shaw, R.P. 1989. "Rapid Population Growth and Environmental Degradation: Ultimate versus Population Factors." *Environmental Conservation* 16:3, 199–208.

United Nations. 1985. *Compendium of Human Settlement Statistics*. New York: United Nations.

World Bank. 1992. "Development and the Environment." *World Development Report 1992*. New York: Oxford University Press.

PART FOUR

Interventions Relating to Population Phenomena

This book has introduced a variety of perspectives and has covered a vast amount of information that should help you to understand the several aspects of population change. While you may not have become expert in this topical field, you very likely have greatly improved the range and depth of your knowledge about population phenomena. More important, you probably have acquired some insights about population determinants and consequences that will remain with you for a long time and serve you well as you face situations in your life in which aspects of population change play a significant role.

Our tale about population cannot end at this point, however, because we have not yet related population change to critical change agents. The early section of the book on philosophical/ideological and theoretical views about population acquainted us with general orientations to understanding demographic realities; discussions of population growth and decline, mortality, fertility, mobility, population distribution, and population composition, as well as consideration of the social consequences of these factors, identified those realities. But there was no systematic review of organizational and personal attempts to influence population change.

One might draw the conclusion from previous chapters that much of the course of demographic evolution was destined to take place, and that it wasn't necessary for humans to direct it. In fact, throughout the greatest part of history the predominant attitude of governments and the public toward population concerns was one of *laissez-faire* ("let it be," or benign neglect). The prevalent thinking was to attend to other matters of the society and population change would follow along in an appropriate manner. (There were, of course, some notable exceptions, as indicated in earlier chapters.)

Those people who saw the classic form of the demographic transition as inevitable assumed that intervention to keep it on course, or expedite it, was unnecessary. When it became clear that the demographic transition did not always follow the classic pattern, and that population cycles sometimes intervened to reform population history, then more persons and organizations became convinced that interventions were indeed required.

In the concluding chapter of this book, we will attempt to sketch some of the major processes and structures that can be placed under the heading of "interventions relating to population phenomena." Most of these became evident in a substantial way only after World War II. It was then that developed countries had essentially completed their transitions, and that those of developing nations were beginning to unfold. The relative rapidity of mortality declines, combined with the relative persistence of high fertility levels, led to rates of population growth in developing countries that alarmed some segments of the Western world. Later these developments brought leaders of Third World countries to the realization that laissez-faire was not the right strategy for having population change work for, instead of against, improvements in their people's lives. In this historical context, competition of ideas about regulating the demographic situation evolved.

14. Population Strategies, Structures, and Change Agents

Decisions to influence population change in a substantial way are part of a modern approach to dealing with demographic problems. They involve actions of governments at different levels as well as those of private organizations and individuals.

In this chapter, we have divided the relevant discussion into three sections concerning (a) the various strategies used to bring about population change, (b) the forms or structures employed, and (c) the several change agents that have been instrumental in effecting actions.

Each strategy, structure, and change agent differed from the others in terms of the time period when they were most effective, the strength of their effectiveness, and the extent to which they were publicly or privately supported. The sequence in which these interventions are discussed here does not imply any historical order. Moreover, while most are still quite active, some were more dominant in times gone by.

STRATEGIES FOR INFLUENCING POPULATION CHANGE

Although numerous strategies have probably been employed to influence population change, five general ones are identified here as symptomatic of the global efforts to alter the course of population change since the middle of the twentieth century. These strategies include the following: (1) general social and economic development; (2) the family planning movement; (3) modifying social structures; (4) educational programs; and (5) pluralistic approaches.

General Social and Economic Development

The common interpretation of the demographic transition that evolved in Western societies was that it was generated by the Industrial Revolution and sustained through urbanization and the economic progress provided by industrialization. Hence, if there was a lesson to be learned from that experience, it was that the demographic transition of any country depended on those processes and could be hastened if those processes were speeded up.

Where countries had begun to move through the transition but at a slow pace, and where the social and economic circumstances of the country were insufficient to foster further change, some type of external assistance was regarded as needed. The earliest forms of such assistance came in the form of aid to reduce the devastating mortality rates that plagued most developing nations. Here is where the transfer of materials and technology worked so well to reduce the incidence of deadly diseases (see Chapter 5). In country after country, declines in mortality were hastened by various forms of technical assistance from outside organizations. This aid was given to facilitate a goal for which there was a universal value—longer life. Aid intended to affect the welfare of people who would then lower their intended fertility and actual childbearing was much less effective because the values supporting high fertility were firmly planted in most of the recipient societies, and social and economic aid would have a modest effect on their level of living but hardly change their fertility orientations.

Ironically, as a result of social and economic assistance, mortality levels were brought down at the same time as fertility levels remained high and, consequently, population growth became accelerated. As a result, the assistance offered had the effect of "buying" another life. Instead of improving the per capita level of living, economic support only managed to subsidize the meagre economy of the recipient nations and thereby keep per capita income from falling.

This strategy of providing social and economic aid to nations that were not advancing sufficiently through the demographic transition had a humanitarian element but was also seen by donors as making an investment in economies that would later become self-sufficient and not be a burden to the rest of the world later on.

Simmons (1988) has described the cluster of activities that fall within this strategy as *official development assistance* or ODA, a term synonomous with foreign aid in some Western countries. The coverage of such assistance is "that part of the total flow of resources from rich to poor countries that consists of loans on concessional terms, grants, and technical assistance provided for the express purpose of social and economic development of the LDC's" (less-developed countries). Aid for military or strictly political purposes was not to be included, nor were flows of private sector funds which came through other channels.

Along with official development assistance came professional advisers and technicians as well as mechanisms for training citizens of the developing countries in needed areas. Consequently, there arose a new form of bureaucracy created by the "development assistance community" (Simmons, 1988). So broadly recognized and acceptable was this strategy for influencing population change that the United Nations designated the 1960s the "Development Decade."

Social and economic assistance continues today as a major form of attempt to influence population change. But recognition that the offer of such aid while populations were growing would not raise per capita economic welfare and hence not break the threshold of economic development led to searches for alternative strategies.

Family Planning Movement

The key to bringing down population growth rates in developing countries seemed to be reducing fertility. Social and economic assistance itself did have some effect on changing the values and motivations of some people to have fewer children, but in the main fertility levels remained high in LDCs.

During the 1960s, the introduction of the birth control pill and the IUD (intrauterine device) added to the range of fertility control measures available to women. Moreover, these contraceptive techniques had some distinct advantages over the less efficient techniques then used. Still, getting masses of people to accept and use birth control generally could not depend on announcements of these developments nor on the scattered agencies existing in some countries for making the techniques available and facilitating their use.

Organized efforts to promote family planning began after World War II and picked up speed in the ensuing decades. National governments of developing countries were seen to adopt family planning policies. India began its program in 1951, and other Third World countries followed shortly thereafter. The privately supported Population Council in the United States was established in 1952 to provide leadership in the area of population control, and much of its attention was on family planning. In the same year the International Planned Parenthood Federation (IPPF) was formed.

Donaldson and Tsui (1990) perceived the emerging international family planning movement as actually taking place in four phases. The first period extended from the late nineteenth century to the end of World War II and was highlighted by a woman's movement that advocated the doctrine of voluntary motherhood, the recognition of female sexuality, and the right of wives to use contraceptive techniques. Associated with the name of Margaret Sanger (1883–1966), who opened the first U.S. birth control clinic, this period gave rise to greater consideration about birth control generally and the formation of small agencies that advocated family planning.

During the second period, which lasted from the end of World War II until the late 1950s, family planning became a means of reducing population growth, and the formation of private family planning associations accelerated. IPPF extended its list of national affiliates. The Population Commission of the United Nations supplemented these efforts with studies of population trends and needs in member nations.

The third period of the international family planning movement began around 1960 and lasted until the mid-1980s. During this time family planning was incorporated as a central component of development assistance activities of both donor and recipient development programs. The United Nations elevated its involvement in the movement by establishing the United Nations Fund for

Population Activities (UNFPA). A number of private groups were formed to call attention to the dangers of rapid population growth and to urge family planning.

In the 1980s the movement was characterized by increasing commitment from Third World leaders to family planning, both to slow population growth and to improve the health of women and children. Freedman (1990) points out that most of the population of LDCs "now lives in countries with national family planning programs to reduce fertility and improve family welfare."

The family planning movement has been described by Back (1989) as a typical social movement "whose principal aims have been accomplished." The movement, he says, "clearly demonstrated two important features of social movements: the interplay of individual and social factors and the different steps of development."

While some have recognized the family planning movement as engineering a significant reduction of fertility in developing countries, others saw it as facilitating that reduction but not being sufficient to accomplish the broader goal of moving the demographic transition along in LDCs. The family planning movement has had its limitation, according to some, because it tried to work within the social and cultural constraints of the nations involved, and often this meant restricting birth control techniques to a few methods acceptable to the society. The movement also became embroiled in controversies surrounding the more sensitive topics of abortion and sterilization, positions on which sometimes divided family planning advocates. Furthermore, the movement has been accused of putting too much emphasis on birth control methods and not enough on factors that motivate people to want fewer children.

Modifying Societal Structures

In the context of the last set of criticisms of the family planning movement, increased attention was given to a strategy for getting people to change their values and motivations about family size. Davis (1967) was an early skeptic about the effectiveness of family planning programs and a proponent of alternative approaches. He agreed that family planning, by helping free women from the need to have more children than they wanted was "of great benefit to them and their children and to society at large." But he went on to say that his "argument is therefore directed not against family-planning programs as such but against the assumption that they are an effective means of controlling population growth."

What, then, are other approaches? In principal, he believed, it is necessary to modify the social structures of the society in such a way as to enhance motivations to lower fertility. These modifications might include encouraging the postponement of marriage, greater rewarding of nonfamilial than familial roles, opening up opportunities for women in the world of work, and extending education to women as well as men. In fact, all these suggested changes have come to pass, and they have served to enhance a modernization environment that motivates people to want to limit fertility and use family planning to do so.

Educational Programs

Acquiring more schooling can be viewed as the result of one aspect of the strategy of modifying social structures. Actually, advancing educational programs became an independent strategy for influencing population change as well. It took two forms: raising the general educational level of populations, and providing more specific population-oriented learning for people.

Many demographic studies have shown how important a woman's education was for determining her eventual fertility (Cochrane, 1979; Caldwell, 1980). In general, educational systems in developing countries were depressed, and women were less likely than men to receive formal education (see Chapter 10). Part of social and economic assistance programs was devoted to improving the school systems in such countries. Many family planning programs incorporated educational functions within their agendas. Building educational systems was a crucial element of modifying social structures. In each case, however, education was not getting primary attention and program leaders saw education as an adjunct of other activities.

Educational leaders became the focal point of a strategy to emphasize education as a force to deal with population control. Educational institution-building took root and led to illiteracy-reduction programs and a rise in secondary and higher educational establishments. General education had the effect of giving people a "window on the world" at the same time as it broadened perception of options with regard to how people lived and what could take place to change the pattern of living.

The United Nations and some individual countries led the movement to promote awareness and understanding of population issues through more concentrated "population information, education and communication" (IEC) programs (Sadik, 1991). The element of *population information* has been broadened through a network of informational sources that extends from the UN and national governments through universities and the mass media. In this way, the public has become more sensitized to the facts of population change. The element of *population communication* has engaged the mass media to become more outspoken reporters of the population scenarios that exist around the world. Every form of the mass media has participated in that activity, and population-related themes have been found in popular music as well as in books, magazines, newspapers, radio, and television.

The element of *population education* focuses on both the content of and methods for learning about the determinants and consequences of population processes and events. A field of "population education" sprang up that joined educational specialists with social scientists who tried to systemize the contents and methods of the new area. Population education was more succinctly summarized in a special report by UNESCO (1978), which identified its goals and objectives, sources, means, and implementation. It made clear that, while population education should be an integral part of formal public and private schooling, it should also be extended to out-of-school situations, such as the workplace, associations to which people belong, and adult education settings. In some countries, population education has acquired a tone of indoctrination, including the government's mandate that its citizens adopt a particular family size attitude or think positively about moving to or away from certain areas of the country. In a larger set of countries, however, population education is taught as a way for students to broaden their knowledge and make more informed decisions about population-related phenomena.

Pluralistic Approaches

While each strategy has had its advocates and each has made a contribution to the regulation of population change, no one of them would suffice to influence population change in a holistic manner. This has led to what we call *pluralistic approaches.* They involve not so much a single strategy but rather a recognition that the integration of several strategies increases the chances that given population goals can be achieved. It is also a recognition that most of the strategies outlined have had the fertility component of population change in focus, and that it is necessary, in order to have a more comprehensive population influential strategy, to take account of the other components of population change—mortality and mobility. It is most common today to observe governments adopting an integrated set of strategies for altering the population situation, although some governments have not been so forceful as others in moving in that direction.

STRUCTURES FOR DEALING WITH POPULATION CHANGE

Population strategies provide general orientations to how to deal with demographic issues that may arise. In the previous section, we alluded to several major strategies which have characterized the half of a century since World War II and which encompassed the main ideas for influencing population change in the world. It remained for individual countries (as well as groups of countries organized regionally or internationally) to implement the strategies in some fashion.

The process of implementation has assumed several forms that we have labeled *structures for dealing with population change.* Included are five broad categories called conferences and meetings, population law, population policy, population planning, and population programs. Each has its own scope, yet often they are intertwined in reality.

Conferences and Meetings

Like most areas of intellectual consideration, determination and implementation of population strategies often find their origins in gatherings of professionals concerned with the matters at hand. Major strategies and the means to implement them took shape in a few key conferences and meetings beginning in the 1960s and have continued to be discussed and modified in others since then.

Coming out of the International Conference on Human Rights in Teheran in 1968 was a statement that drew attention to the connection between population growth and human rights; it averred that moderation of the population growth rate and free and responsible decisions by couples on the number and spacing of their children would enhance human rights; and it urged member nations to act on the basis of these assumptions.

The World Food Conference in Rome in 1974 called on all governments and people to support rational population policies as part of development strategies. In the same year in Bucharest, a World Population Conference issued a World Population Plan of Action that reinforced the earlier proclamations and asked the nations of the world to follow the guidelines set down in the plan that would assist in moderating world population growth. This plan was originally advanced by Western countries with UN agency cooperation. By the close of the conference, it had been reshaped by Third World countries to put more emphasis on the need for social and economic assistance to complement family planning programs and further amended to permit acceptance by countries aligned with various interest groups (Finkle and Crane, 1975).

According to Andorka (1989), the Bucharest Conference produced the first international agreement on population matters (which most countries adhered to in subsequent years), and the International Conference on Population in Mexico City in 1984 reinforced and broadened the earlier plan to lay down recommendations in the areas of mortality and health, mobility and international migration, and fertility and family planning. Andorka asserts that such conferences "provide a reference basis when a sound, scientifically based population policy that does not infringe on human rights is required."

Conferences organized by the United Nations have the advantage of that organization's sanction, but other conferences and meetings (such as those held by the professionally based International Union for the Scientific Study of Population every four years and by the Population Association of America annually) have also had an impact on strategies for population change that have been adopted by various countries.

Elements of Population Law

Actions related to population matters can take place on an ad hoc basis, and often do, but actions that have significant impacts and lasting value are those rooted in some form of law. In the late 1960s, in recognition of the linkage between the two areas, a Law and Population Program was set up at Duke University and later transferred to Tufts University's Fletcher School of Law and Diplomacy (Lee, 1990). Although the area of *population law* has never become a substantial field of study, it has acquired a framework and topics of special interest (Isaacs, 1981; Barnett and Reed, 1985).

Broadly speaking, we can say that population law has come to mean "the body of knowledge that encompasses the various paths through which legal norms and practices have a bearing on population structures and processes and, in turn, the ways in which those structures and processes have served to create and modify legal structures and activities" (Nam, 1985).

This definition subsumes a vast array of specific topics. Population coverage includes all aspects of demographic concern: population growth and decline, fertility, mortality, mobility, and population composition and distribution. Legal forms encompass constitutions, treaties, statutes, executive orders, administrative regulations and ordinances, and jurisdictional systems, all of which can appear at international, national, or local levels.

Law can become the authority for population-related events, such as the U.S. constitutional mandate for taking a decennial census and the continuing congressional authorizations for funding of the censuses, a presidential order that forbids the inclusion of abortion services in foreign aid programs, and a Supreme Court decision that denies the right of a local government to keep people from moving into its community.

Like other forms of law, population law establishes the guidelines for appropriate behavior, in this case with regard to population issues. In this sense, it not only can serve as an authority for action but also can describe the boundaries of correct behavior and the sanctions that accompany deviations from it. The Supreme Court of the United States upheld a lower court ruling that found someone who refused to complete the mandated census forms was in violation of the law and subject to punishment. The U.S. Congress authorized the Food and Drug Administration to establish performance standards for various contraceptives that regulate their sale to the public.

Every country has some legal elements relating to population concerns, but in most countries these are scattered and do not appear collectively. Therefore, it usually seems that there is no body of law that affects population actions. In a few countries, however, a comprehensive set of population laws has been set up to govern population change in the nation. It is not the developed countries that have such comprehensive law but rather developing countries which saw the need for laying a legal foundation for population actions. A prime example is Mexico, which set up the General Population Law of 1974. Previous laws of the country had sought to encourage population growth by reducing mortality and encouraging births and immigration; the 1974 comprehensive law called for stabilization and regulation of population growth in order to improve the use of the nation's human and natural resources (United Nations, 1989a). The General Population Law of 1974 became Mexico's blueprint for additional population structures to influence population change.

The United Nations Population Fund (UNFPA) conducts an annual review of population law around the world and publishes its findings in a compendium (Boland, 1990). The report summarizes international resolutions and agreements, constitutional provisions, legislation, regulations, judicial decisions, and legal pronouncements covering a wide array of population topics. Later in this chapter we will discuss further UNFPA's work.

Dimensions of Population Policy

Governmental influences on population change typically are formulated in population policies that may or may not be grounded in population law. National leaders often give their opinions or express preferences about population matters, but these do not necessarily result in actions unless they are given the force of policy.

We can find many different definitions of *population policy*. Recently the United Nations (1987) referred to population policies as simply attempts by governments "to influence either directly or indirectly the demographic character of their population." A broader and more specific definition would indicate that a "population policy is an explicit statement of national goals regarding population size, rate of growth or transition to non-growth, distribution, and composition.... (and) should include specific measures and programs which will lead to the attainment of the goals" (Miller and Green, 1977).

The latter definition recognizes that there are numerous policies promulgated by a government; some of these policies that are intended principally to achieve other goals may also have an indirect impact on population phenomena, but it is more beneficial to express goals related to population explicitly, and hence directly. It also treats the scope of population policy as broad enough to deal with goals concerning all population events and processes.

There are several characteristics of population policy that describe its essential features:

1. To be forceful, it must be formulated by a national government through an authoritative political source.
2. Whatever population goals are enunciated, they msut go beyond platitudes (e.g., control of population growth) to specify elements of population change (size, fertility, mortality, mobility), targets (at least magnitudes of change), and general mechanisms for achieving the goals (at least types of programs).
3. Whatever population parameter is being considered, the policy can have a goal of increasing, decreasing, or maintaining it over some span of time.
4. A policy is a statement of present goals and is not fixed for all time; hence, a population policy can be changed over time in direction and/or magnitude.

The first characteristic of population policy is exemplified by the experience of Zambia, an African country with a rapidly growing population. Concerned about the ability to achieve its development goals, President Kenneth Kaunda instructed the National Commission for Development Planning to formulate a population policy. It did so by bringing together various interest groups that arrived at a consensus to lower the rate of population growth. The President was the authority who delegated some responsibility to an agency of his government for creating a policy (Goliber, 1989).

Indicative of the second characteristic of population policy was the Zambians' specification that population growth was to be reduced by lowering the fertility rate; this was to be done by designating child-spacing and family planning programs as the primary mechanisms.

In this case Zambia was exercising its prerogative to decrease simultaneously the population growth rate and the fertility rate, thereby indicating the direction of proposed change, the third characteristic of population policy.

Finally, Zambia had earlier taken positions on population change regarded as pronatalist or laissez-faire. The new population policy thus represented a reorientation of direction in influencing population change.

A different set of circumstances describes the population policy characteristics in the former East Germany in the 1970s. The East German (German Democratic Republic) government was dissatisfied with its below-replacement fertility level that followed previous liberalization of abortion laws in the country. A policy was formulated to increase the birth rate by providing incentives to couples to have more children. This was done by lengthening paid maternity leave from eighteen to twenty-six weeks, and by instituting a one-year-paid maternity leave for mothers with two or more children. Subsequently, the fertility level increased substantially (Heilig et al., 1990).

Still another example of population policy and its principal characteristics concerns immigration to the United States in the 1980s. We have already discussed (in Chapter 7) the history of U.S. immigration and changes in governmental policy in that regard. The Immigration Reform and Control Act of 1986 was directed to the national concern about undocumented/illegal immigration, principally from Mexico. This policy, put forth by the Congress of the United States, was specific to reducing undocumented immigration and included provisions that would sanction employers who hired such immigrants knowingly; it would give amnesty to those who had come into the country illegally during the previous five years; it would expand the seasonal agricultural worker programs under stricter supervision; and it would increase enforcement capabilities by adding to the policing functions along the borders of the country. Parts of the new policy simply reinforced earlier policies and "put more teeth" into their provisions, and parts of the policy involved new approaches to dealing with the problem (Espenshade et al., 1990).

A review of world population policies by the United Nations Secretariat (1990) showed that there was considerable variation in the positions of national governments about their population situations. In the late 1980s, out of a total of 170 countries, 79 viewed their rate of growth as satisfactory, 63 considered their rate as too high, and 28 perceived their rate as too low. Among those *satis-*

fied with their growth rates were Denmark, which had a near-zero rate of growth, and Democratic Yemen, where the growth rate was between 2 and 3 percent per year. Among those which thought their growth rates were *too high* were Botswana, where it was nearly 4 percent per year, and Jamaica, where it was 1.5 percent per year. Among those which thought their growth rates were *too low* were Kuwait, where it was over 5 percent per year, and Hungary, where the growth rate was nearly zero (United Nations, 1989). Similar variations also exist where positions about mortality and health, fertility and family planning, mobility and immigration, and population distribution are concerned.

The establishment of a comprehensive population policy or a set of discrete population policies relating to elements of demographic change regarded as crucial for a country has increasingly become a critical component of population influence in a nation's effort to deal with unsatisfactory demographic developments. While more and more countries are moving in the direction of policy formulation, some countries are still rather reluctant to take that step.

Planning for Population Change

Once a country has made a commitment to a population policy, the implementation phase can be more or less successful, depending on the extent to which carrying out the policy and relating it to policies in other areas (such as those dealing with social and economic development) are conducted in an orderly way.

Population planning constitutes the process by which that orderly implementation of policy can take place. It involves monitoring and directing population change in line with the views and policies of the government. It is sometimes thought that governmental planning is a function carried out only by countries with socialist forms of government. In fact, every form of government incorporates planning functions, and judicious planning is as valuable in the population sphere as it is in other areas of public policy.

India has had a development plan since 1950 that sets each five-year plan within a rolling fifteen-year horizon (United Nations, 1992). From the beginning, population planning was incorporated within the broader development planning. Background studies of demographic and socioeconomic trends and patterns were linked to targets in these areas, and estimates of where the country should stand at future time periods were assessed. The governmental agencies responsible for these activities could then monitor actual changes, both as a means of evaluating the effectiveness of current policies and as a basis for recommending needed modifications in those policies. In the case of India, a Planning Commission integrates the roles of a number of other agencies that have interests in population and socioeconomic development.

Similar planning functions are carried out in countries with such diverse cultures and economies as those of Turkey, Thailand, Tanzania, and Indonesia. In the last, five-year plans within a twenty-five-year framework include population dimensions; however, while the country has a central planning agency with a population section, population planning also takes place through the Ministry of Population and the National Family Planning Coordinating Board, which have direct lines to the presidential office (Hugo et al., 1987). Population planning thus receives relatively greater attention in Indonesia than in most other countries. Yet every country has its own political arrangements that are compatible with its overall governmental operations, and concerns about population are fitted into these.

Population planning is not restricted to developing areas. Although developed countries that have already completed the demographic transition are less likely to be engaged in that activity, those with a strong social service element are apt to include population planning in their broader governmental operations. The Netherlands is an example of the latter. The government is satisfied with a nongrowing population and thinks that population policy plays an important part in the attainment of socioeconomic goals. The Bureau for Population Affairs and the Interdepartmental Committee for Population Questions are responsible for population policy formulation and coordination, while the Social and Cultural Planning Office is charged with the responsibility of integrating population variables into general planning (United Nations, 1989b).

The United States has no specified population policy or planning units within the federal government, and policies related to population are limited to special areas of concern, such as immigration and health. Planning, as such, is not considered a prime function of the national government.

Population Programs

Population law, policy, and planning lay the groundwork for actions to influence population change. The actions themselves take place in the form of *population programs*, which entail projects that implement desired directions to various population phenomena.

Although population law, policy, and planning necessarily must be carried out by governments (particularly at the national level) because the authority exists there, population programs can be conducted by governments at all levels and by the private sector as well. In fact, it is generally the case that the range of needed population programs can only be implemented if governments and the private sector both contribute to them.

Population programs range over the full demographic agenda. They can concentrate on aspects of general health and mortality, reproductive health and fertility, temporary and permanent internal and international mobility, population distribution and redistribution, and many characteristics of the population. At times programs may be put into place that cover two or more of these phenomena.

Family planning programs provide assistance to women and men to regulate the birth of children. Such programs might be clinics or community-based distribution centers with medical or paramedical staff that advise persons and dispense materials for avoiding or delaying childbearing or facilitating it, or it may be in the form of circulated literature or media announcements about mothers' and children's health, contraceptive devices, abortion or sterilization procedures, prenatal care, and artificial insemination (Sadik, 1991).

Health and mortality-avoidance programs may focus on particular diseases or injuries and involve immunizations, preventive medical examinations, activities to lengthen life for those already ill, and behavioral modification (as in the case of eliminating smoking, drinking and driving, and other dangerous risk-taking behaviors).

An example of a program in the mobility area is the Indonesian Transmigration Program, which invites people from overcrowded locations (particularly the island of Java) to move to the outer islands where there is more space and a need for agricultural development (Hardjono, 1988). While specifically a mobility program, its aim is to redistribute population within the country and thereby reduce high population densities known to create social, economic, and political problems.

The number and kinds of population programs around the world are so great that it would be unmanageable to compile an inventory of them. Yet it is the task of planning agencies within national governments to be aware of the existence of these various programs and to assess the extent to which they are meeting the needs of the people and satisfying the policy goals of the government in the population realm.

THE ROLES OF POPULATION CHANGE AGENTS

Influences on population change do not operate in a vacuum nor do they take place naturally. Organizations and individuals are the forces that create population laws, policies, planning, and programs, and change behaviors. Who, then, are the influential groups and persons?

Those we identify below can be called *population change agents* because they are the instigators of new directions in demographic change. We have classified these change agents into three categories: international agencies, national governments and the private sector, and individuals. Which ones have been most influential would be difficult to determine, largely because contributions vary according to the time period, the geographic area, and the type of population phenomena examined. Without making judgments about their effectiveness, we will conduct a general review of the acknowledged agents and the nature of their activity.

International Agencies

Since World War II, population has become a major concern of international organizations, which have been called upon to participate in influencing population change (especially in Third World regions where population growth has been substantial while at the same time the economies of those countries have been struggling to expand). Among these international organizations have been the United Nations and its agencies, and the World Bank and regional banking groups.

Demographic concerns were expressed early in the work of the United Nations. A Population Commission set up in 1946 assumed responsibility for assisting in taking censuses in many parts of the world and in demonstrating the obstacles to social and economic progress of the then-rapid population growth. International population projections were produced that indicated the demographic direction in which the world's population was headed. The Population Branch of the Bureau of Social Affairs also undertook various studies of demographic phenomena and, in 1965, a World Population Conference was held in Belgrade to showcase the knowledge discovered about the world population situation (Sadik, 1990).

At the same time that these technical demographic activities were conducted, the UN became involved in the population debates of Asian nations and fostered discussions of politically sensitive problems, such as India's family planning program.

Throughout these activities, the UN expanded the roles of its agencies to encompass population matters. In the late 1960s, what is now the United Nations Population Fund (UNFPA) was formed for the purpose of providing technical assistance to countries in the population domain. To this day UNFPA has been at the center of international efforts to influence population change. Coordinately, the specialized agencies of the UN have been assigned the task of relating population issues to the main concerns of the agencies. These included the United Nations Educational, Scientific, and Cultural Organization (UNESCO), the World Health Organization (WHO), the Food and Agricultural Organization (FAO), the International Labor Organization (ILO), and the United Nations Childrens Fund (UNICEF).

Through these different mechanisms, the UN has played a significant role in arranging conferences to share information, in developing consensus among countries about population issues, and in funding worthy population-related projects. As such, it has perhaps been the major population change agent on the globe, not only being active itself but also setting a tone for other potential change agents to get involved in demographic areas.

The World Bank is an international development bank that provides assistance to Third World governments in securing economic and social development in the form of low-interest loans. Since it first lent money for a population project in 1970, the Bank has supported programs in numerous developing countries in amounts comparable to those of the UNFPA. It differs from the UNFPA in that it relies more heavily on expert groups to assess country situations, to engage in dialogues with country representatives about critical national problems, and to formulate development proposals. It also stresses programs that facilitate delivery of needed services and is willing to include construction projects when facilities (such as clinics or training centers) are lacking (Sai and Chester, 1990).

Because much of the attempt to influence population change now takes place in regional consortiums, banking programs similar to those of the World Bank have been organized in some regions of the world (the Asian Development Bank being a notable example). The lending approach permits a country to attack a problem while it recognizes the investment it is making in the future and its obligation to pay back the funds by some specified date. This is in contrast to grants (used by the UN and most other groups) that have no payback provisions. A consortium of developed nations, the Organization for Economic Cooperation and Development (OECD), while focusing on the economic status of member countries, also maintains a Development Centre that provides technical assistance (including on population) to developing countries.

National Governments and the Private Sector

International organizations are focal points for population influences based on multilateral arrangements. But a range of bilateral relationships in the population field has been undertaken by donors in the form of developed country governments and private agencies working with developing countries.

Most of the OECD members (countries of Western Europe, the United States, Canada, and Japan) have been active in providing bilateral assistance to Third World nations for population projects. Specialized agencies were formed in Great Britain, Sweden, Canada, France, Germany, and the United States for that purpose.

In the United States, governmental activities related to population are concentrated in two agencies. Domestic population projects are funneled through the National Institutes of Health, especially its National Institute on Child Health and Human Behavior (NICHD) and its National Institute on Aging (NIA). These largely involve competitive grant and contract research-and-development projects. Population-relevant activities are also funded through other agencies. In particular, demographic data collection is principally based in the Bureau of the Census (within the Department of Commerce) and the National Center for Health Statistics (within the Centers for Disease Control). These agencies (along with others that have more tangential connections to population matters) are very influential in domestic population matters.

On the international side, the main agency has been the Office of Population of the Agency for International Development (USAID) within the Department of State, which is responsible for foreign aid programs. USAID has been a controversial unit because of its political orientation (a logical outcome of its departmental base) and its almost exclusive attention to the fertility component of population change, which it has attempted to influence through advancing certain types of family planning efforts to the exclusion of others.

USAID's difficulties included controversy within the agency, as there were differences in population strategies and emphases between the Office of Population and other agency offices with regional and country responsibilities (Donaldson, 1990). The Office of Population owed its dominance within the agency to the rising importance of population concerns and to the charismatic leadership of its director. The controversies that took place engaged the participation of congressional committees and the White House as well as numerous other public and private organizations which took positions for or against the Office of Population.

The intrigue surrounding the activities of USAID in the population area may have drawn attention away from the fact that the United States was a major player in exerting population influence. It continues to be so today, both through bilateral arrangements with developing nations and through its substantial contributions to international agencies (some of which diminished during the 1980s when the U.S. Presidents were concerned about particular uses of the funds, including abortion programs).

The private sector has also played a substantial role in influencing population change. Although private organizations cannot establish population laws, formulate population policies, or engage in widespread population planning, they can and do take part in population programs. The Population Council (supported initially and primarily by Rockefeller Foundation and Ford Foundation funds) has been a major force in contraceptive research and development and in technical population assistance (Caldwell and Caldwell, 1986).

As indicated in an earlier part of this book (Chapter 3), judgments about population issues have been made by religious organizations which have had degrees of influence on the population-related behaviors of their members. Some, such as the Roman Catholic Church, have made it a point of emphasis to specify what the religion's teachings allow, and do not allow, in the way of such behaviors. In this way religious leaders have sometimes been strong population influentials.

Some private organizations have exerted influence largely through broadening communications outlets for population knowledge. Foremost among these are the Population Reference Bureau, the Alan Guttmacher Institute, and the Pathfinder Fund. Others have been most effective as lobbying groups in legislative settings. Examples are Zero Population Growth, Inc., the Population Crisis Committee, and Planned Parenthood federations.

Developing nations, themselves, have increasingly become important population influentials as they establish agencies with power to undertake programs of their own and to choose among those offered by multilateral and bilateral funding groups. The National Family Planning Coordinating Board in Indonesia has long been a major force, both because of its charismatic leader and the success of its programs that are now advertised in other developing countries as models of action.

Not everyone who observes these public and private efforts to influence population change see them as desirable or unbiased. Because there are optimistis and pessimists regarding population matters, and because the fortunes of politics result in changes in authority to determine the course of population influence, opinions about influences that have taken place often vary (Ehrlich et al., 1977; Finkle and Crane, 1975; Simon, 1990).

The Individual

The relative success of efforts to modify population change by governments and the private sector depends on a number of factors, including the efficiency of policy and planning, the specificity of programs and their costs, the facilitation or impediment of the cultural setting, and the acceptability of the activities by the families and individuals to whom they are directed.

Ultimately, it is the individual (singly and as part of a couple or family unit) who will eventually behave in a manner that affects the course of population. This is why individuals are sometimes referred to as *population actors* (Lyons et al., 1980). They are the ones who make decisions about whether or not to stay single, marry, or divorce; to have sexual intercourse, to use contraception, or to decide on a certain family size; to protect their health or to take mortal risks; to change their residential location and where to go, if they do make such a decision.

Generally speaking, every individual is unique (identical twins being the exception). But population-related behaviors such as those mentioned above do not take place in a social vacuum. Thus individual behavior is conditioned by cultural norms and social experiences. The notion of *population socialization* (see Chapter 3) captures those contexts by emphasizing how population behaviors, like other social behaviors, are learned. It also shows how the "significant others" in our lives—whether consciously or unconsciously—are our teachers in important aspects of our population-related behaviors (Philliber, 1980).

In a real sense, then, we must add to the various population change agents identified earlier both every individual and those who influence their population-related behaviors—parents, other family members, friends, acquaintances, other role models, and even those with whom we have no contact but who reach our minds through mass media or personal indirect communications.

In contemplating the total process by which interventions determine patterns of population change, we can see them in all their complexity as involving all sorts of people in every part of the world as time goes by. Truly understanding population change obliges us to see that big picture as well as the small pieces that make it up.

By way of conclusion, let's keep in mind an essential lesson from our study of population change. Not only does population change affect us, but all of us are also actors in the great drama of human existence. As William Shakespeare puts it in Jaques' soliloquy from Act 2, Scene 7, of *As You Like It:*

> All the world's a stage,
> And all the men and women merely players:
> They have their exits and their entrances;
> And one man in his time plays many parts....

Chapter Highlights

1. Intervening in population change involves the adoption of broad strategies, the organization of structures to carry out these strategies, and the emergence of population change agents.
2. Laissez-faire with regard to population change characterized most of history. Following World War II, however, population growth in many developing areas of the world made all nations more sensitive to the consequences of that growth and led to the introduction of different strategies to control population change. The principal strategies were social and economic assistance to developing areas, family planning programs, efforts to alter social institutions, educational programs, and various combinations of these strategies.
3. Country after country has instituted structures to facilitate population change. Some national governments have set up agencies to focus on population matters, and population policies; in addition, laws, planning, and programs have emerged. Conferences and meetings of governments and of professional groups have given some impetus to these efforts.
4. Various change agents have been involved in population dynamics. International agencies (especially the United Nations, the World Bank, and regional consortiums) have played vital roles in bringing about this heightened attention to population matters. Also, national governments have assumed greater responsibility for educating their citizens about the causes and consequences of population change. Not least of all has been the role of individuals, who make the crucial decisions related to population processes.
5. Understanding population change means comprehending all of these interventional forces as they relate to the many facets of population dynamics in history.

Discussion Questions

1. If you were asked to adopt a broad population strategy to guide a nation through the next ten years, which would you choose and for what reasons?
2. Is there an appropriate population strategy for an area like a city? What factors support such a strategy, and what factors militate against it?
3. Identify an element of population law that interests you. Trace the origins of the law and find out if it has always remained the same or has been modified at some point in time, and why.
4. The United States does not have a comprehensive population policy, as do some countries. Do you think that the country should have such a policy? What are the arguments for and against it?
5. Select one population program now being carried out in a country. Describe the history of the program. What evidence is there that the program is successful or not?

6. What experiences have you had in your lifetime so far that have identified you as a population actor? When you get to the age of retirement, will you still be a population actor and, if so, in what ways?

Suggested Readings

United Nations. Various publications dealing with population law, policy, planning, and programs. Consult with your librarian about what is available or contact the United Nations Publications Sales Section, 2 United Nations Plaza, Room DC2-853, Dept. 421, New York, NY 10017 for a catalogue listing publications related to population topics.

Barnett, Larry D., and Emily F. Reed. 1985. *Law, Society, and Population: Issues in a New Field.* Houston: Cap & Gown Press. If you have your sights set on becoming a lawyer or are just fascinated with legal issues, this book will introduce you to a range of population law topics you may not have even thought about.

Donaldson, Peter J. 1990. *Nature against Us: The United States and the World Population Crisis, 1965–1980.* Chapel Hill, N.C.: University of North Carolina Press. If your tastes tend toward foreign policy, you will find this volume an engaging account of how the United States dealt with population concerns during that period. You can do your own research on what has happened in this area since 1980.

Simmons, Ozzie G. 1988. *Perspectives on Development and Population Growth in the Third World.* Written by someone who served "in the field" as well as in academia in the United States, this is a full treatment of the linkages of population and development in countries beginning to move through the demographic transition.

References

Andorka, Rudolf. 1989. "Successes and Failures in the Field of Population Policies Since 1984." *Population Bulletin of the United Nations* 27: 30–41.

Back, Kurt W. 1989. *Family Planning and Population Control: The Challenges of a Successful Movement.* Boston: Twayne Publishers.

Barnett, Larry D., and Emily F. Reed. 1985. *Law, Society, and Population: Issues in a New Field.* Houston: Cap & Gown Press.

Boland, Reed. 1990. *Annual Review of Population Law.* Vol. 14. New York and Cambridge, Mass.: United Nations Population Fund and Harvard Law School Library.

Caldwell, John C. 1980. "Mass Education as a Determinant of the Timing of Fertility Decline." *Population and Development Review* 6: 225–56.

Caldwell, John, and Pat Caldwell. 1986. *Limiting Population Growth and the Ford Foundation Contribution.* London: Frances Pinter.

Cochrane, Susan H. 1979. *Fertility and Education: What Do We Really Know?* Baltimore: Johns Hopkins University Press.

Davis, Kingsley. 1967. "Population Policy: Will Current Programs Succeed?" *Science* 158: 730–39.

Donaldson, Peter J. 1990. *Nature against Us: The United States and the World Population Crisis, 1965–1980.* Chapel Hill, N.C.: University of North Carolina Press.

———, and Amy Ong Tsui. 1990. "The International Family Planning Movement." *Population Bulletin* 45:3 (a publication of the Population Reference Bureau).

Ehrlich, Paul R., Anne H. Ehrlich, and John P. Holdren. 1977. *Econscience: Population, Resources, Environment.* 2nd ed. San Francisco: W.H. Freeman.

Espenshade, Thomas J., Frank D. Bean, Tracy Ann Goodis, and Michael J. White. 1990. "Immigration Policy in the United States: Future Prospects for the Immigrant Reform and Control Act of 1986." In Godfrey Roberts, ed., *Population Policy: Contemporary Issues*, pp. 59–84. New York: Praeger Publishers.

Finkle, Jason, and Barbara Crane. 1975. "The Politics of Bucharest: Population, Development, and the New International Economic Order." *Population and Development Review* 1: 87–114.

Freedman, Ronald. 1990. "Family Planning Programs in the Third World." In Samuel H. Preston, ed., *World Population: Approaching the Year 2000*, pp. 33–43. *Annals of the American Academy of Political and Social Sciences*, 510.

Goliber, Thomas J. 1989. "Africa's Expanding Population: Old Problems, New Policies." *Population Bulletin* 44:3 (a publication of the Population Reference Bureau).

Hardjono, Joan. 1988. "Reorientations in the Indonesian Transmigration Program." Unpublished manuscript.

Heilig, Gerhard, Thomas Buttner, and Wolfgang Lutz. 1990. "Germany's Population: Turbulent Past, Uncertain Future." *Population Bulletin* 45:4 (a publication of the Population Reference Bureau).

Hugo, Graeme J., Terence H. Hull, Valerie J. Hull, and Gavin W. Jones. 1987. *The Demographic Dimension in Indonesian Development.* Singapore: Oxford University Press.

Isaacs, Stephen L. 1981. *Population Law and Policy: Source Materials and Issues.* New York: Human Sciences Press.

Lee, Luke T. 1990. "Law, Human Rights, and Population Policy." In Godfrey Roberts, ed., *Population Policy: Contemporary Issues*, pp. 1–20. New York: Praeger Publishers.

Lyons, Morgan, Charles B. Nam, and Kathleen A. Ockay. 1980. "Residential Mobility Orientations of Children and Youth." *Population and Environment* 3:1, 23–34.

Miller, Celia Evans, and Cynthia P. Green. 1977. *A U.S. Population Policy: ZPG's Recommendations.* Washington, D.C.: Zero Population Growth.

Nam, Charles B. 1985. "Foreword." In Larry D. Barnett and Emily F. Reed, *Law, Society, and Population: Issues in a New Field*, pp. ix–xi. Houston: Cap & Gown Press.

Philliber, Susan Gustavus. 1980. "A Conceptual Framework for Population Socialization." *Population and Environment* 3:1, 3–9.

Sadik, Nafis. 1990. "The Role of the United Nations—From Conflict to Consensus." In Godfrey Roberts, ed., *Population Policy: Contemporary Issues*, pp. 193–206. New York: Praeger Publishers.

———. 1991. *Population Policies and Programmes: Lessons Learned from Two Decades of Experience.* New York: New York University Press.

Sai, Fred T., and Lauren A. Chester. 1990. "The Role of the World Bank in Shaping Third World Population Policy." In Godfrey Roberts, ed., *Population Policy: Contemporary Issues*, pp. 179–91. New York: Praeger Publishers.

Simmons, Ozzie G. 1988. *Perspectives on Development and Population Growth in the Third World.* New York: Plenum Press.

Simon, Julian L. 1990. "The Population Establishment, Corruption, and Reform." In Godfrey Roberts, ed., *Population Policy: Contemporary Issues*, pp. 39–58. New York: Praeger Publishers.

UNESCO. 1978. *Population Education: A Contemporary Concern.* Paris: United Nations Educational, Scientific and Cultural Organization.

United Nations, 1987. *World Population Policies.* Vol. 1. Population Studies no. 102. New York: United Nations.

———. 1989a. *Case Studies in Population Policy: Mexico.* Population Policy Paper no. 21. New York: United Nations.

———. 1989b. World Population Policies. Vol. 2. Population Studies no. 102. New York: United Nations.

———. 1992. *Integrating Development and Population Planning in India.* New York: United Nations.

Appendix A Selected Techniques of Demographic Measurement

The main body of this book referred to various measures of population change and its components. The discussion of those measures was in terms of the concepts behind them and the general form in which they are calculated. The purpose of this appendix is to elaborate the techniques of calculation for a few of the measures cited. In this way we might satisfy those readers who have more extended quantitative interests or who are curious about some of the nuances of demographic measurement.

This appendix covers four general topics:

1. Measuring population change
2. Population estimates and projections
3. Demographic standardization
4. Life table construction

For each topic, there is a reference to the section of the book with which the discussion is correlated. At the end of this appendix are citations to several general readings on demographic techniques.

1. MEASURING POPULATION CHANGE

(See Chapter 1, page 10–12, and Tables 1.1 and 1.2).

Population change can be measured in several ways. We can calculate the *absolute amount of change* between two points in time by subtracting the number of people in a given area or group at the later time from the number at the earlier time. The change would be positive if the population were larger at the later time and negative if it were smaller at the later time. Depending on the detail wanted, the numerical difference can be calculated in terms of the full number or it can be rounded to the nearest hundred or thousand or some other approximate level.

If we are interested in the *percentage change*, we divide the absolute number (as calculated above) by the population size at the earlier date and multiply the result (being careful about where the decimal point belongs) by 100. The percentage will have either a positive or negative value, depending on the sign before the numerator. The percentage can also be carried out to one or more decimal places or rounded to the nearest whole percent.

Some population data users find the need for more refined indicators of population change, or they want to answer certain critical questions about such change. These questions might include the following:

1. What has been the *rate of population change* over time?
2. If a population continues to grow at a given rate over time, how long will it take for it to double or triple its size?
3. If a population changes by a given annual average amount, what will be its size in ten or twenty years or some other future point in time?

There are several formulas for measuring population change that incorporate the elements required to answer each of the questions asked above. Each of the alternative formulas makes a different assumption about the exact form of expected future growth, fitting data for past points in time into a particular mathematical expression—linear, other polynomial, exponential, or logistic. The exponential and logistic forms are analogous to the forms used to calculate compound interest on a bank account. If populations grow at a steady rate, the population base to which that rate applies is steadily expanding. We present one of those formulas below, along with an example of how the second question might be answered.

$$r = \frac{1}{n} \log_e \frac{p^{t+n}}{p^t}$$

where r = average annual rate of change
n = number of years in the time period
$\log_e$ = natural logarithm
p^{t+n} = population at the end of the period
p^t = population at the beginning of the period

If the two population numbers and the time period between them are known, one can derive the rate of change. If one knows the current population and assumes a given rate of change over a certain number of years, the resulting population can be estimated. If one accepts a given rate of change and sets the population at the later date to double the amount at the earlier date, then the doubling time (or value of n) can be estimated for that rate of change, as in the example below.

Continuing growth rate = 1.7 percent per year
Current (beginning) population = 5,500,000
Doubled (end) population = 11,000,000

Applying these to the formula, we get:

$$.017 = \frac{1}{n} \log_e \frac{11{,}000{,}000}{5{,}500{,}000}$$

or

$$n = \frac{1}{.017} \log 2.00 = \frac{.6932}{.017} = 40.78 \text{ or } 41 \text{ years}$$

In fact, as can be observed in the above example, that it takes 41 years for a population to double its size if it continues to grow at 1.7 percent per year is independent of the size level of the population. (More refined bases for making these calculations are suggested in the references at the end of this appendix.)

Since the link between a given growth rate and the number of years for a population to double its size is independent of the actual size of the population, it is possible to use a graphic approach, rather than a mathematical one, to estimate doubling time. Figure A.1 shows the graph for this purpose. One can locate a given rate of population change on the x axis of the graph and use a ruler to approximate the number of years it would take for a population to double its size on the assumption that the rate of change continues.

2. POPULATION ESTIMATES AND PROJECTIONS

(See Box 3.2 and Chapter 4, page 117.)

It was indicated, earlier in the book, that population estimates (including future estimates or projections) are needed when data for a particular time period or population category are required and available population data are not specific to that time or category.

Demographers can employ any of several methods to estimate or project populations. As in the case of refined techniques of measuring population change, all of these estimation approaches depend on assumptions about trends in population or its components that seem reasonable. Because these assumptions are usually difficult to make with a high degree of confidence that they are the best assumptions, population estimates are generally calculated using alternative assumptions and the varying results are presented as *series of estimates* (or *projections*) that follow from the basic data used and the assumptions made.

Among the most widely used methods of population estimation are the following:

Extrapolative techniques—where data for the past are fitted to a mathematical equation (as illustrated in Figure A.1 for the measurement of population change) and the values for the time of interest are "read off."

Symptomatic techniques—where independent information on variables that are associated with population change (e.g., school enrollments in an area), and which is known, is used as a basis for "prediction."

FIGURE A.1 Number of Years Necessary for the Population to Double at Given Annual Rates of Growth [Computed by use of the formula for continuous compounding $P_t = P_0e^{rt}$]

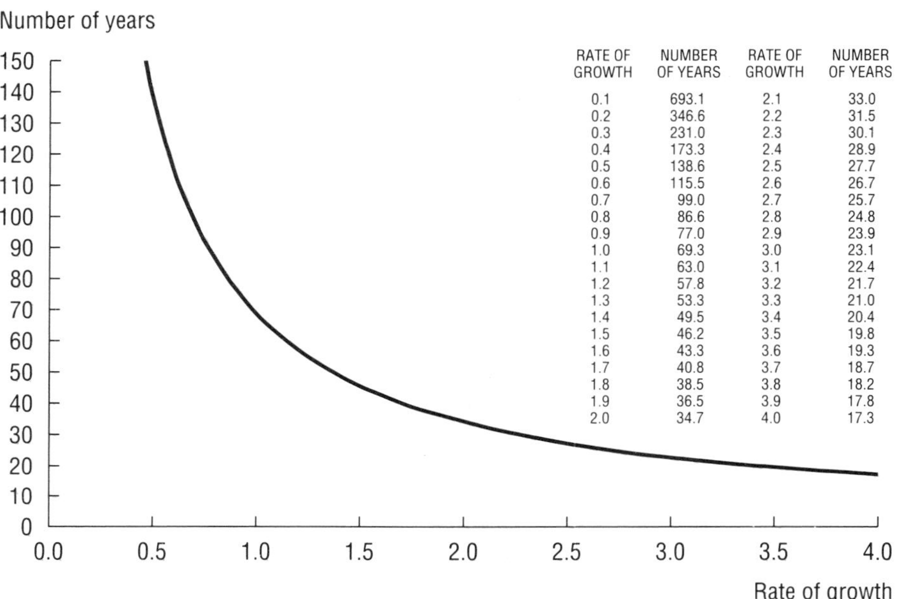

RATE OF GROWTH	NUMBER OF YEARS	RATE OF GROWTH	NUMBER OF YEARS
0.1	693.1	2.1	33.0
0.2	346.6	2.2	31.5
0.3	231.0	2.3	30.1
0.4	173.3	2.4	28.9
0.5	138.6	2.5	27.7
0.6	115.5	2.6	26.7
0.7	99.0	2.7	25.7
0.8	86.6	2.8	24.8
0.9	77.0	2.9	23.9
1.0	69.3	3.0	23.1
1.1	63.0	3.1	22.4
1.2	57.8	3.2	21.7
1.3	53.3	3.3	21.0
1.4	49.5	3.4	20.4
1.5	46.2	3.5	19.8
1.6	43.3	3.6	19.3
1.7	40.8	3.7	18.7
1.8	38.5	3.8	18.2
1.9	36.5	3.9	17.8
2.0	34.7	4.0	17.3

Source: Henry S. Shryock, Jacob S. Siegel, and Associates, *The Methods and Materials of Demography* (condensed edition by Edward G. Stockwell) (San Diego, Calif.: Academic Press, 1976).

Regression-based techniques—where a statistical regression formula incorporates several predictor variables with possible variation in the weight assigned to each in its relation to population level.

Component techniques—where population change is divided into its major components (mortality, fertility, and mobility), and one of the above approaches is applied to each component separately and the results then combined.

Variations of each of these methods exist, and it is up to the person making the population estimates or projections to decide on the most appropriate approach, given the kinds of data available and the degree of precision desired.

All the references at the end of this appendix discuss the various approaches in more detail. See especially Steve H. Murdock and David R. Ellis, *Applied Demography: An Introduction to Basic Concepts, Methods, and Data* (Boulder, Colo.: Westview Press, 1991).

3. DEMOGRAPHIC STANDARDIZATION

(See Chapter 4, page 120, and Chapter 5, page 134.)

In making comparisons of various population phenomena (e.g., fertility among various countries, or mortality as it is reported for different points in time, or mobility for different categories of education), we are often faced with the fact that the effect we are trying to focus on (the differences being analyzed) are confounded by the effects of one or more other factors that we are not focusing on. This confounding disturbs the comparisons being made, in that what appear to be genuine differences in the comparisons of focus may be due, partly or completely, to differences in the levels of the confounding factors.

Comparisons relating to various population phenomena are often confounded by different age compositions of populations being compared. In such instances, what appear to be underlying variations or trends in the population phenomena are reflective of a confounding factor (the age variations). The analyst faced with this situation will want to control for, or adjust for, the confounding factor. (In addition to age, the confounding factor might be sex, marital status, socioeconomic status, or any of a number of other variables, or combinations of these factors.)

You were told earlier in this book that such controls for confounding factors can be introduced by making comparisons within specific categories (of age, for instance) but that you then have to analyze a series of comparisons. It would be desirable to have a single measure of comparison that is free of the confounding factor.

The technique of *demographic standardization* permits us to develop a single measure of our subject of interest that is adjusted for the confounding factor. The principle of this technique is that one can assume that the populations being compared have the same distribution of the confounding factor, but that reported information on the variable of interest remains unchanged within categories of the confounding variable. By multiplying the values of the variable of interest within categories of the confounding variable by the assumed values of the categories of the confounding variable, one can derive adjusted measures for comparison that are free of the effects of the confounding variable. (An example below will clarify this technique.)

There are different approaches to performing the technique of standardization that depend on the nature of available data. The two principal distinctions in approach are referred to as the *direct method* and the *indirect method.* Examples of the two approaches are given below, comparing the death rates of two states with standardization for age (see Tables A.1a and A.1b). (A decision has to be made about the appropriate standard to use. Choices are generally relegated to using the broader population from which the populations are drawn, using the sum of the compared populations, or using one of the populations. In the first two cases, standardization answers the question: What if the populations being compared had the same age distribution as area A or consoli-

TABLE A.1a Work Sheet Showing Adjustment by the Direct Method of the Death Rates for Maine and South Carolina: 1930

		MAINE				SOUTH CAROLINA			
AGE (IN YEARS)	STANDARD MILLION FOR THE UNITED STATES IN 1940	POPULATION[1] IN 1930	DEATHS IN 1930	SPECIFIC RATES (PER 100,000 POPULATION)	EXPECTED DEATHS IN STANDARD MILLION	POPULATION[1] IN 1930	DEATHS IN 1930	SPECIFIC RATES (PER 100,000 POPULATION)	EXPECTED DEATHS IN STANDARD MILLION
	(1)	(2)	(3)	(4)= (3)/(2)	(5)= (4)×(1)	(6)	(7)	(8)= (7)/(6)	(9)= (8)×(1)
0–4	80,100	75,037	1,543	2,056	1,647	205,076	4,905	2,392	1,916
5–9	81,100	79,727	148	186	151	240,750	446	185	150
10–14	89,200	74,061	104	140	125	222,808	410	184	164
15–19	93,700	68,683	153	223	209	211,345	901	426	399
20–24	88,000	60,575	224	370	326	166,354	1,073	645	568
25–34	162,100	105,723	413	391	634	219,327	1,910	871	1,412
35–44	139,200	101,192	552	545	759	191,349	2,377	1,242	1,729
45–54	117,800	90,346	980	1,085	1,278	143,509	2,862	1,994	2,349
55–64	80,300	72,478	1,476	2,036	1,635	80,491	2,667	3,313	2,660
65–74	48,400	46,614	2,433	5,219	2,526	40,441	2,486	6,147	2,975
75+	20,100	22,396	3,056	13,645	2,743	16,723	2,364	14,136	2,841
TOTAL	1,000,000	796,832	11,082	...	12,033	1,738,173	22,401	...	17,163

$$M_{DM}\text{(Maine)} = \frac{12{,}033}{1{,}000{,}000} \times 1{,}000 = 12.03.$$

$$M_{DM}\text{(South Carolina)} = \frac{17{,}163}{1{,}000{,}000} \times 1{,}000 = 17.16.$$

$$\frac{M_{DM}\text{(South Carolina)}}{M_{DM}\text{(Maine)}} = \frac{17.16}{12.03} = 1.43$$

NOTE.—The formula is set up for rates per 1,000 population.

[1]Deaths and populations of unknown age excluded.

Source: Forrest E. Linder and Robert D. Grove, *Vital Statistics Rates in the United States 1900–1940* (Washington, D.C.: Government Printing Office, 1943), p. 67.

TABLE A.1b Work Sheet Showing Adjustments by the Indirect Method of the Death Rates for Maine and South Carolina: 1930

		MAINE		SOUTH CAROLINA	
AGE (IN YEARS)	STANDARD SPECIFIC RATES FOR THE UNITED STATES IN 1940 (PER 100,000 POPULATION)	POPULATION[1] IN 1930	EXPECTED DEATHS USING STANDARD SPECIFIC RATES	POPULATION[1] IN 1930	EXPECTED DEATHS USING STANDARD SPECIFIC RATES
	(1)	(2)	(3)=(2) × (1)	(4)	(5)=(4) × (1)
0–4	1,287	75,037	966	205,076	2,639
5–9	108	79,727	86	240,750	260
10–14	99	74,061	73	222,808	221
15–19	172	68,683	118	211,345	364
20–24	240	60,575	145	166,354	399
25–34	306	105,723	324	219,327	671
35–44	520	101,192	526	191,349	995
45–54	1,060	90,346	958	143,509	1,521
55–64	2,226	72,478	1,613	80,491	1,792
65–74	4,799	46,614	2,237	40,441	1,941
75+	12,910	22,396	2,891	16,723	2,159
TOTAL	1,075	796,832	9,937	1,738,173	12,962

$$M_{IM}\text{ (Maine)} = \frac{\text{United States 1940 crude rate}}{\dfrac{\text{Sum of (3)}}{\text{Sum of (2)}} \times 1{,}000} \times \text{Maine 1930 crude rate}$$

$$= \frac{10.75}{\dfrac{9{,}937}{796{,}832} \times 1{,}000} \times 13.91 = 11.99.$$

$$M_{IM}\text{ (South Carolina)} = \frac{\text{United States 1940 crude rate}}{\dfrac{\text{Sum of (5)}}{\text{Sum of (4)}} \times 1{,}000} \times \text{South Carolina 1930 crude rate}$$

$$= \frac{10.75}{\dfrac{12{,}962}{1{,}738{,}173} \times 1{,}000} \times 12.89 = 18.58.$$

$$\frac{M_{IM}\text{ (South Carolina)}}{M_{IM}\text{ (Maine)}} = \frac{18.58}{11.99} = 1.55.$$

NOTE.—The formula is set up for rates per 1,000 population.

[1]Populations of unknown age excluded.

Source: Forrest E. Linder and Robert D. Grove, *Vital Statistics Rates in the United States 1900–1940* (Washington, D.C.: Government Printing Office, 1943), pp. 70–71.

dated population B? In the third case, the question to be answered is: What if the other populations being compared had the same age distribution as category X?

In the examples, the direct approach is used when both age-specific death rates and the age distribution of the population are known, whereas the indirect approach is used when the age-specific death rates are not known. The indirect approach, in effect, makes an assumption about common age-specific death rates for the two populations, and "works backward" to determine the number of deaths that would be expected if the standard population age-specific death rates were the reality. The expected number of total deaths are then compared with the actual total number of deaths to obtain an adjustment factor for the unstandardized death rate.

In 1930 Maine had a crude death rate of 13.91 deaths per 1,000 population, as compared with South Carolina's crude death rate of 12.89 deaths per 1,000 population, a slight excess for Maine. After age adjustment by the direct method, South Carolina's death rate exceeds that of Maine by a substantial amount (17.16 versus 12.03). After age adjustment by the indirect method, the rate for South Carolina likewise exceeds that of Maine by a large amount (18.58 versus 11.99). Although the actual adjusted rates are different using the direct and indirect methods, both adjustment approaches result in similar comparisons of the death rates for the two states. While Maine has a lower crude death rate, South Carolina has a significantly higher adjusted death rate.

4. LIFE TABLE CONSTRUCTION

(See Chapter 5, page 136.)

If the questions we want to answer about mortality are posed in the context of risks over one's lifetime, then the appropriate form of data arrangement is the *life table.* Such a table is intended to represent the death and survival experience of a cohort of newly born babies as they age over time until the last one has died.

The types of questions a life table can answer include:

1. What are the prospects for survival to age 40 of those who are now age 20?
2. How many years, on the average, can a newborn baby (or a person reaching age 65) expect to live?

What we call *true cohort life tables* are rare, because it is difficult to locate the lifetime mortality records of a given set of babies. Even if such data were present for the past, that information might not be indicative of what mortality risks are at present, much less what they will be in the future.

Even though our questions about survival and life expectancy are usually directed to the future, reliable estimates of future mortality are not generally available. Therefore, we ordinarily construct *current or cross-sectional life tables* based on information about deaths that have occurred recently, and we regard the information derived from them as pertaining to the future as well. This assumption is valid in areas where mortality patterns are not likely to undergo very much change, such as most developed nations. For developing countries, which frequently do not have reliable mortality data, or whose mortality patterns are still changing appreciably, that assumption will not be valid. In such cases, in lieu of constructing life tables based on the country's own data, analysts will turn to *model life tables*, which are based on current mortality data for various sets of countries with differing characteristics and available data (see references at the end of this section).

Life tables are based on *age-specific death rates*, and all functions of a life table are derived from that information. What are the functions and, in simple terms, how are they derived? These questions can be answered by referring to the official life table for the population of the United States in 1989 (see Table A.2). (This example is of an *abridged life table*, so-called because the age detail has been abridged or shown in grouped-age categories. When a life table is presented in single-year-of-age detail, it is referred to as a *full life table.*) The life table is shown separately for males and females in the United States and refers to the year 1989. Explanations of life table columns given below use illustrative data from the table for males.

Column (1) shows the interval between two exact ages: for instance, 20–25 means the five-year interval between the 20th and the 25th birthdays.

Column (2) shows the proportion of the cohort who are alive at the beginning of the indicated age interval and who will die before reaching the end of that age interval ($_nq_x$). (This is somewhat different from the *age-specific death rate*, for which the age interval is from the midpoint of the beginning age to the midpoint of the ending age. Reported age-specific death rates are adjusted to shift the age reference for life table use, the reasons for which will become clearer as we proceed through the columns.)

Column (3) shows l_x values, which are the number of persons who survive to each exact beginning age in the distribution, on the assumption that the cohort begins with 100,000 newborn babies. The number of survivors is determined by multiplying the $_nq_x$ rate for an age interval by the number who survive to the beginning age of the interval. So, of the 86,502 male babies in the cohort who reached age 55, the proportion dying (.0598) before their 60th birthday means that 81,328 will still be alive by that later birthday.

Column (4) reveals the number in the cohort who died in each age interval, which is simply the difference in the numbers who survived to each beginning age of succeeding intervals. In the example, 5,174 deaths occurred in the 55–60 age interval.

Column (5) reports the number of *person-years lived* in each age interval. Those who live to the end of an age interval count once for each year that they lived in that interval. Those who died during the age interval are credited with living through part of that age interval, on the average half of it. The sum of the whole and part years lived by those who began the age interval (person-

TABLE A.2 Abridged Life Tables by Sex: United States, 1989

AGE INTERVAL: PERIOD OF LIFE BETWEEN TWO EXACT AGES STATED IN YEARS	PROPORTION DYING: PROPORTION OF PERSONS ALIVE AT BEGINNING OF AGE INTERVAL DYING DURING INTERVAL	OF 100,000 BORN ALIVE: NUMBER LIVING AT BEGINNING OF AGE INTERVAL	OF 100,000 BORN ALIVE: NUMBER DYING DURING AGE INTERVAL	STATIONARY POPULATION: IN THE AGE INTERVAL	STATIONARY POPULATION: IN THIS AND ALL SUBSEQUENT AGE INTERVALS	AVERAGE REMAINING LIFETIME: AVERAGE NUMBER OF YEARS OF LIFE REMAINING AT BEGINNING OF AGE INTERVAL
(1)	(2)	(3)	(4)	(5)	(6)	(7)
x to $x+n$	${}_nq_x$	l_x	${}_nd_x$	${}_nL_x$	T_x	$\mathring{e}_x$
MALE						
0–1	.0109	100,000	1,086	99,065	7,182,240	71.8
1–5	.0021	98,914	211	395,167	7,083,175	71.6
5–10	.0014	98,703	134	493,149	6,688,008	67.8
10–15	.0016	98,569	163	492,548	6,194,859	62.8
15–20	.0062	98,406	606	490,674	5,702,311	57.9
20–25	.0085	97,800	827	486,977	5,211,637	53.3
25–30	.0091	96,973	885	482,628	4,724,660	48.7
30–35	.0109	96,088	1,047	477,853	4,242,032	44.1
35–40	.0138	95,041	1,308	472,100	3,764,179	39.6
40–45	.0172	93,733	1,608	464,923	3,292,079	35.1
45–50	.0245	92,125	2,255	455,407	2,827,156	30.7
50–55	.0375	89,870	3,368	441,466	2,371,749	26.4
55–60	.0598	86,502	5,174	420,303	1,930,283	22.3
60–65	.0912	81,328	7,419	389,050	1,509,980	18.6
65–70	.1316	73,909	9,726	346,142	1,120,930	15.2
70–75	.1947	64,183	12,499	290,381	774,788	12.1
75–80	.2839	51,684	14,675	221,862	484,407	9.4
80–85	.4115	37,009	15,229	146,096	262,545	7.1
85 and over	1.0000	21,780	21,780	116,449	116,449	5.3

continued

AGE INTERVAL: PERIOD OF LIFE BETWEEN TWO EXACT AGES STATED IN YEARS	PROPORTION DYING: PROPORTION OF PERSONS ALIVE AT BEGINNING OF AGE INTERVAL DYING DURING INTERVAL	OF 100,000 BORN ALIVE: NUMBER LIVING AT BEGINNING OF AGE INTERVAL	OF 100,000 BORN ALIVE: NUMBER DYING DURING AGE INTERVAL	STATIONARY POPULATION: IN THE AGE INTERVAL	STATIONARY POPULATION: IN THIS AND ALL SUBSEQUENT AGE INTERVALS	AVERAGE REMAINING LIFETIME: AVERAGE NUMBER OF YEARS OF LIFE REMAINING AT BEGINNING OF AGE INTERVAL
(1)	(2)	(3)	(4)	(5)	(6)	(7)
x to $x+n$	${}_nq_x$	l_x	${}_nd_x$	${}_nL_x$	T_x	$\mathring{e}_x$
FEMALE						
0–1	.0088	100,000	882	99,247	7,860,815	78.6
1–5	.0017	99,118	171	396,063	7,761,568	78.3
5–10	.0010	98,947	101	494,460	7,365,505	74.4
10–15	.0010	98,846	100	494,014	6,871,045	69.5
15–20	.0025	98,746	243	493,161	6,377,031	64.6
20–25	.0027	98,503	264	491,867	5,883,870	59.7
25–30	.0032	98,239	317	490,419	5,392,003	54.9
30–35	.0043	97,922	416	488,618	4,901,584	50.1
35–40	.0056	97,506	551	486,250	4,412,966	45.3
40–45	.0084	96,955	817	482,884	3,926,716	40.5
45–50	.0130	96,138	1,251	477,790	3,443,832	35.8
50–55	.0213	94,887	2,022	469,694	2,966,042	31.3
55–60	.0338	92,865	3,141	456,935	2,496,348	26.9
60–65	.0523	89,724	4,694	437,568	2,039,413	22.7
65–70	.0778	85,030	6,613	409,483	1,601,845	18.8
70–75	.1183	78,417	9,280	370,076	1,192,362	15.2
75–80	.1815	69,137	12,547	315,798	822,286	11.9
80–85	.2898	56,590	16,402	243,090	506,488	9.0
85 and over	1.0000	40,188	40,188	263,398	263,398	6.6

Source: National Center for Health Statistics, *Vital Statistics of the United States, 1989*, vol. 2, sec 6, lifetables (Washington, D.C.: Public Health Service, 1992), Table 6.1.

years lived) is the cumulative years lived by the life table population up to the ending age of an interval. (When the life table is considered as a population closed to mobility but having the mortality and fertility patterns of the life table, it is known as a *stationary population*. These qualities enable the life table to be used in more sophisticated analyses of "intrinsic" population growth tendencies.)

Column (6) has the same kind of data as in column (5), except that the data are accumulated from the oldest to youngest age groups. Hence, the number 7,182,240 at the top of column (6) means that the 100,000 hypothetical male babies in the cohort, who died at the rates specified for each age interval, ended up living 7,182,240 person-years by the time that the last of the original babies died.

Column 7 shows the familiar *life expectancy*, or average remaining lifetime from the beginning of the age interval until expiration of all those who survived to the beginning of the age interval. It is derived by dividing the number in column (6) by the number in column (3) for the same age interval. The 51,684 male babies who reached age 75 lived a total of 484,407 more person-years. Dividing one into the other enables us to deduce that, on average, those 51,684 will live 9.4 more years.

As you can see, the life expectancies that come out at the end are a function of the age-specific mortality rates that are put in. Assuming a given number of babies born, all other statistics in a life table are products of that initial input.

Life tables can be calculated for any subgroup of the population for which age-specific mortality data are available. It is conventional to compute separate life tables in the United States by gender and racial categories because the distinctions are of general interest to users of the information.

General References on Demographic Techniques

Murdock, Steve H., and David R. Ellis. 1991. *Applied Demography: An Introduction to Basic Concepts, Methods, and Data*. Boulder, Colo.: Westview Press.

Palmore, James A., and Robert W. Gardner. 1983. *Measuring Mortality, Fertility, and Natural Increase: A Self-Teaching Guide to Elementary Measures*. Honolulu: East-West Center.

Saunders, John. 1988. *Basic Demographic Measures: A Practical Guide for Users*. New York: Lanham.

Shryock, Henry S., Jacob S. Siegel, and Associates. 1976. *The Methods and Materials of Demography* (condensed edition by Edward G. Stockwell). San Diego, Calif.: Academic Press.

Appendix B Glossary of Terms

The following terms used in the text are listed here with brief definitions and/or explanations as a ready reference for comprehending aspects of population change.

abortion Termination of conception, typically during early stage of pregnancy; usually refers to induced abortion but includes spontaneous abortion (or miscarriage).

administrative or political area Geographic areas with identifiable boundaries that are recognized for governmental administrative or political purposes.

age Interval of time between date of birth and present (or time of data collection), expressed in complete years.

age at marriage Age at which individual is legally or religiously married; normally refers to first marriage but may relate to later marriages.

age-sex pyramid A graphic device for depicting the age and sex distribution of a population, with relative size of each older age group represented by ascending order of bars (males to the left and females to the right of a center line).

age-specific rate A measure of a population phenomenon in which the ratio of the phenomenon to a population is shown for specific age categories (e.g., age-specific death rate).

age-standardized measure See *standardization.*

aging The increasing prevalence of older persons in a population; the increasing age of individuals.

apportionment Procedure for allocating governmental representatives to political units.

asylee Person in a country as a nonimmigrant unable or unwilling to return home because of fear of persecution.

average A measure of the central tendency in a distribution, indicated by such statistics as the median and arithmetic mean; the distribution around the average can be narrow or broad.

balancing equation Formula expressing population change as equal to the net effect of changes in population components.

basic components of population change Essential determinants of population change, including mortality, fertility, and mobility.

birth the complete expulsion or extraction from the mother of a product of conception, irrespective of duration of pregnancy, which, after such separation, breathes or shows any other evidence of life, such as beating of the heart, pulsation of the umbilical cord, or definite movement of voluntary muscles.

birth control See *contraception.*

birth interval See *child spacing.*

categorization specifying number and nature of categories as divisions of a variable used in analysis.

cause of death Condition certified by a physician as having contributed to a person's death; the most critical condition is regarded as the underlying cause.

celibacy Prolonged sexual abstention.

census Total process of collecting, compiling, evaluating, analyzing, and disseminating population data for all persons in a specified geographic area and at a specified time.

childhood mortality Aggregate deaths for persons from age 1 until age 5; deaths during second year of life are referred to as *toddler mortality.*

children ever born The number of live births to a woman up to the present, regardless of whether or not the baby survives.

child spacing Time intervals between union of a couple and their first child and between succeeding children they have.

child-woman ratio The ratio of children 0 to 4 in a population to the number of women in reproductive ages.

circulatory mobility Repeated movement between a primary residence and a secondary residence and back.

citizenship Legal nationality of a person.

civil registration See *registration.*

cohabitation Persons of the opposite sex living together without having gone through legal or religious marriage rites; sometimes termed *consensual union* or *common-law marriage.*

cohort A group of persons with a common starting time; a birth cohort has the same birth year; a marriage cohort has the same marriage year.

coitus interruptus Withdrawal of penis during sexual intercourse before ejaculation is reached; sometimes used as a birth control measure.

common-law marriage See *cohabitation.*

commuting patterns Temporary movement of persons to daily activity locations, such as school, work, and shopping centers.

conceptual framework Systematic interrelationship of variables used in data analysis.

conjugal family See *family.*

consensual union See *cohabitation.*

contraception Use of means to prevent conception when sexual intercourse takes place, and hence to control births.

crude rate A measure of the incidence of a population phenomenon that relates the incidence to the total population; for example, crude death rate or crude birth rate.

cumulative fertility Number of babies born to a group of women up to their present age; it becomes total fertility when reproductive ages are completed.

death Permanent disappearance of all evidence of life at any time after birth has taken place.

decision-making process Process through which individuals or groups decide on their population-related behaviors, such as how many children to have or when to change residence.

demand for children An aggregate perspective of the number and sex of children couples would choose, abstracted from all concern with the childbearing process required to attain that outcome.

demographic transition Long-term change in population conditions, as reflected in shifts of birth and death rates from high to low levels and related alterations in mobility patterns.

demographics Popular term for population factors, particularly as applied to business matters.

demography Scientific study of population.

descriptive analysis Reporting of data that simply describes the categorical distribution of variables.

desired fertility Number of children a person reports liking to have, without consideration of what might constrain that wish.

development Changes in institutions of a society from a more traditional to more modern form; greatest emphasis is usually placed on the economic institution.

differentials Differences in population phenomena between categories of a variable, such as persons with different educational levels.

disability Limitation on activities performed by a person because of a physical or mental handicap.

divorce Separation of a married couple through a legal procedure.

educational attainment The highest educational achievement of a person, as measured by years of schooling or academic degree received.

electoral behavior Registration and voting patterns of persons in a political election.

emigrants See *emigration.*

emigration Mobility of persons out of a country.

employment Working for any amount of time and in any occupation (excluding housework).

environment As used in this book, the natural atmosphere in which people live, including air, water, and land.

epidemiologic transition Shifts in health and disease patterns over a long period of time, typically coincident with the demographic transition.

ethnicity Identification of persons according to their citizenship, nationality, language, religion, or family name.

expected fertility The number of children a person expects to have, based on a realistic assessment of constraints that may operate in the future.

explanatory models Analytical approaches that attempt to explain the relationship among variables in a conceptual framework.

family Two or more persons related by birth, marriage, or adoption and residing together; a nuclear family includes the husband, wife, and children; an extended family includes other kin as well; a subfamily is a family unit nested within a larger family unit.

family life cycle The demographic history of a family as indicated by the stages through which it passes, including marriage, childbearing, childraising, and death of its members.

family planning Organized effort to achieve reductions in fertility in a population.

fecundity Biological capability to contribute to reproduction.

fertility Cumulative actual childbearing of a population.

fertility control Involves contraception (birth control), but also incorporates other means to regulate childbearing, such as deferred marriage.

fertility cycles See *population cycles.*

fertility orientations Modes of considering appropriate number of children to have, including ideal, intended, desired, expected, and wanted or unwanted fertility.

frailty Relative strength or weakness of the human body to resist disease and illness.

functional illiteracy Inability to read and write well enough to carry out basic functions in daily activities.

gainful workers Persons engaged in work for pay; the dominant work concept before the creation of the labor force concept.

gender The social significance attached to being male or female in a society.

general fertility rate Number of births related to number of women in reproductive ages, multiplied by a constant.

gross reproduction rate Average number of girls born to a group of women who complete their reproductive period after experiencing the prevailing age-specific fertility of the population.

household One or more persons residing in a separate housing unit.

ideal family size Number of children a person would consider most appropriate for couples to have.

ideological point of view Orientation based on a particular set of values held by an individual or group, stemming from a philosophy of life but tempered by associations and experiences.

illegal immigrants See *undocumented immigrants.*

immigrants See *immigration.*

immigration Movement of people into a country for purposes of settling, living, and, often, working in the new country.

incidence New cases of an event or characteristic in a time period; for example, reported cases of persons with AIDS during May 1993.

income Total money received from earnings for work and other money receipts, such as from Social Security, welfare, and rent payments.

infant mortality Cumulative number of deaths to babies, born alive, before they reach their first birthday.

infecundity Complete lack of ability of a woman to conceive a baby because of biological impairments.

infertility Failure to produce a child, regardless of the reasons for the failure.

in-migrant See *in-mover.*

in-mover Person who moves into an area; regarded as an in-migrant if movement into the area crosses a critical geographic boundary (such as a county or province).

institutional approach Approach to understanding population change that focuses on changes in one or more social institutions.

intermediate variables Factors in explanatory models that intervene between variables related to background of the persons studied and the event; often called *proximate variables.*

internal migrant Person who has moved across a critical boundary (such as a county or province) but has not left the country.

international migrant Person who has moved between countries; a person regarded as an immigrant from the perspective of the receiving country and as an emigrant from the perspective of the country of departure.

labor force Sum of employed (full-time or part-time) and unemployed (without any work and seeking work) at a point in time for ages 16 and over (14 or 15 and over in some countries).

level of living Economic welfare, as indicated by income, wealth, poverty, and social security.

life course Perspective that examines changes in the lives of individuals and families as they change over time.

life-cycle perspective See *cohort.*

life expectancy Average number of years of life remaining to a group of persons reaching a certain age, subject to specified death rates at each age.

life table A statistical table that includes, for each age group, measures of mortality, survival, and life expectancy.

life span Maximum number of years a person can be expected to live under ideal circumstances.

linked records See *merged records.*

literacy Ability to read and write at least a simple sentence in some language.

local mover A person who changes residence but remains within the same community (or county or province).

macro perspective Views population change in terms of general levels of concepts, measurement, and data to arrive at broad generalizations.

marital dissolution Disruption of marriage by divorce, marital separation, of death of a spouse.

marital status Classification of persons in census or survey according to their being single (never married), divorced, separated, or widowed.

marriage State of two persons joined in matrimony in a legal and/or religious ceremony; monogamy exists where one male is married to one female; polygamy exists where multiple spouses are involved;

polygyny is a form of polygamy where a man has multiple wives.

maternal mortality Deaths to women resulting from conditions associated with pregnancy and childbearing.

menarche Age at which menstruation begins for girls.

menopause Age at which a woman ceases to ovulate and menstruate.

merged records Joining of records from different data sources to create a broader set of analytical information.

metropolitan area County with large population nucleus, together with adjacent counties that have a high degree of economic and social integration with that nucleus; it is called an urban agglomeration in some countries.

micro perspective Views population change in terms of smaller levels of concepts, measurement, and data to reach more focused generalizations.

migrant Person who changes residence and, in the process, crosses a critical geographic boundary (such as a county or province).

mismatched qualifications Situation in which a worker's training and/or qualifications are not suited for work occupation.

mobility In population context, the movement of persons that results in their relocation.

mobility cycles See *population cycles.*

modernization Societal or community change that involves transformations of social institutions away from traditional forms; emphasizes division of labor and differentiation of functions.

monogamy See *marriage.*

morbidity Condition of limited health (for genetic or nongenetic reasons).

mortality Aggregate number of deaths occurring in a population at specified periods of time.

mortality cycles See *population cycles.*

multiple causes of death All the medical conditions associated with a recently deceased person, as indicated by a physician on the death certificate.

natural decrease Excess of mortality over fertility.

natural increase Excess of fertility over mortality.

natural resources Includes land; shelter; renewable resources such as water, agriculture, and food animals; and nonrenewable resources such as fossil fuels, metals, and nonmetallic minerals.

naturalization Process through which alien immigrants can acquire citizenship after five years of residence in the United States.

neonatal mortality Deaths to live-born babies during the first 28 days of life.

net reproduction rate Same as *gross reproduction rate,* but it further assumes that some women will die before the end of the reproductive period.

nonbounded residential classification Geographic identifiers that categorize people according to types of locations not necessarily in proximity to each other (e.g., rural areas, cities of 1 million or more residents).

normative perspective Views population change in terms of the ways that population-related actions of individuals are shaped by group guides to behavior.

nuclear family See *family.*

optimistic point of view Sees a large and growing population as the source of national strength and security and of power and wealth.

optimum population size Numbers of people that are consistent with the ability of social institutions to exist and develop.

out-migrant See *out-mover.*

out-mover Person who moves to another location, regardless of the distance or direction traveled.

parolees Persons allowed to enter a country temporarily under emergency conditions.

percentage A type of proportion, in which the ratio of numerator to denominator is multiplied by 100.

perinatal mortality Fetal deaths occurring during the last stage of pregnancy plus deaths in the first month of life; both types of deaths are heavily influenced by factors related to pregnancy and childbirth.

period measure Indicator of a population phenomenon that occurs in a specified point or period of time.

periodic sexual abstinence Form of birth control that includes the calender rhythm method and other "safe period" methods.

pessimistic point of view Sees a large population as outgrowing subsistence or otherwise being harmful to the quality of life.

philosophical point of view One rooted in the religious or ethical beliefs of a group of people.

political representation See *apportionment.*

polygamy See *marriage.*

polygyny See *marriage.*

population A collectivity of people in a particular area at a particular point in time.

population change The transformation of population over time, including its size, demographic components, distribution, and composition.

population change agents Instigators of new directions in demographic change, including international agencies, national governments and the private sector, and individuals.

population communication Transmission of population information through various media, especially the mass media.

population cycles Changes in population components (mortality, fertility, and mobility) that are of a shorter period than transitions but of such magnitude that they have a significant impact on population size or structure.

population density Relative concentration of population in specified geographic areas.

population distribution The spread of population over land area, and the geographic location of individuals.

population education Teaching about population phenomena in both in-school and out-of-school settings.

population estimates Information about population not directly available from known data sources and determined indirectly by using various approximation methods.

population law Body of knowledge encompassing ways that legal norms and practices bear on population structures and processes, and the converse.

population planning Monitoring and directing population change in line with the views and policies of government.

population policy Explicit statement of national goals regarding population size, rate of growth or transition to nongrowth, distribution, and composition, including measures and programs leading to the attainment of the goals.

population projections estimates of population phenomena that relate to future time periods and are based on assumptions about the direction of trends in critical factors.

population programs Projects designed to implement desired directions of population phenomena as specified in policies and plans.

population register A form of merged records maintained at a community level in some countries that integrates vital statistics with other information about resident families and individuals.

population socialization A process involving the shaping of population-related behaviors through learning about them from significant persons in one's life.

population strategies General orientations on how to intervene in producing population changes; historically, these strategies have included social and economic development, family planning, modifying social structures, educational programs, and pluralistic approaches.

population theory A rigorous, systematic approach to developing knowledge about some aspect of population.

postneonatal mortality Deaths in the second through the twelfth months of life.

poverty State of having income below a cutoff that varies by such factors as family size, sex of the family head, number of children under 18, and farm/nonfarm residence, which has as its core an economy food plan.

prenatal care Medical examination of a pregnant woman beginning within the first thirteen weeks of pregnancy and continuing regularly until delivery of the baby.

prevalence Total number of persons who have experienced an event or acquired a particular characteristic, regardless of when they had the experience or acquired the characteristic; for example, the prevalence of AIDS includes all persons with the condition, regardless of when in the past it was diagnosed.

proportion Type of ratio in which the denominator includes the numerator; for example, the ratio of females to the total population.

proximate variables See *intermediate variables.*

race Identification of a person according to dominant physical characteristics that are hereditarily transmissible; in censuses and surveys, formerly based on observation or inquiries by interviewers but now usually determined by respondent's self-identification.

rate A ratio in which events in the numerator are related to a population in the denominator and expressed in terms of a period of time; for example, annual birth rate.

ratio A statistic expressing the relative size of numbers in a numerator and a denominator, the two not necessarily related to each other.

refugees Persons who, owing to well-founded fear of being persecuted for reasons of race, religion, nationality, or membership of a particular social group or political opinion, are outside their country of nationality and unable or unwilling to seek protection of that country.

registration Process by which facts regarding individual civil or vital events, for example, birth and death, are recorded in official government records.

regulation costs In an aggregate perspective, the consequences of facilitating or impeding the fertility process.

religion A belief system with which an individual is associated through membership, identification, or preference.

replacement level Average number of children born to couples needed to replace current population.

residential mobility See *mobility.*

rhythm method See *periodic sexual abstinence.*

rural areas Land that is sparsely populated or having places with fewer than 2,500 residents.

school attendance See *school enrollment.*

school dropouts Persons who leave school before completing a critical level, usually secondary school.

school enrollment Persons registered in a school system and assigned to a particular grade or level of program; to be distinguished from *school attendance,* which indicates students actually present in school on a given day.

separation A category of marital status identifying a person who lives apart from the spouse.

sex Biological division of persons into categories of male and female.

sex ratio A measure relating the number of males to each 100 females in a population or age group.

socialization See *population socialization.*

sociocultural approach A macro approach to understanding population change in which an area's social and cultural systems are seen as shaping demographic processes.

standardization A demographic procedure to adjust population statistics to account for confounding variables that are not the topic of interest; for example, standardizing birth rates of two nations being compared to remove effects of different age structures.

statistical areas Geographic areas which are bounded but which do not have administrative or political boundaries; their creation is to serve statistical purposes.

sterilization Surgical method of contraception that makes the sexual organs of a person incapable of contributing to fertility.

subfamily see *family*.

subfecundity Diminished capability of a woman contributing to reproduction.

supply of children From an aggregate perspective, surviving children couples would have if they did not regulate their fertility.

survey A data collection mechanism through which information is gathered from a sample of a population.

teenage fertility Births to females under age 20.

temporary mobility Types of mobility that do not involve changes of residence, such as going to school and work.

toddler mortality See *childhood mortality*.

total fertility rate Average number of children a group of women completing the reproductive period would have if they had birth rates at each age as is true in the current population.

typologies Combinations or clusters of variables labeled so as to indicate an underlying concept broader than a single variable.

underemployed Persons who work fewer than the number of hours per week considered full time.

undocumented immigrants Persons who enter a country illegally or clandestinely, without official approval.

unemployment State of being without any job but actively seeking work.

urban agglomeration See *metropolitan area*.

urban areas Territory including places of 2,500 or more inhabitants plus densely populated areas just outside more populated places.

urbanization Process by which areas acquire urban character or intensify the concentration of urban population.

urbanized area Combined city of 50,000 or more people and the densely settled territory surrounding it; contrasts with a metropolitan area, which includes all residents of a county in which a city of 50,000 or more people are located.

vital registration See *registration*.

wealth Net worth of households based on the sum of the market value of assets owned by every member of the household minus secured or unsecured financial liabilities.

Geographic Index

Name Index

Subject Index

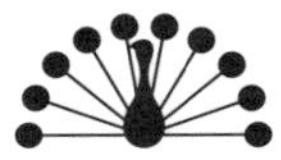

UNDERSTANDING POPULATION CHANGE
Edited by Robert J. Cunningham
Production supervision by Kim Vander Steen
Designed by Jeanne Calabrese
Composition by Point West, Inc., Carol Stream, Illinois
Paper, Finch Opaque
Printed and bound by Aracta Graphics, Kingsport, Tennessee